Capturing value increase in urban redevelopment

A study of how the economic value increase in urban redevelopment can be used to finance the necessary public infrastructure and other facilities

Sidestone Press

Capturing value increase in urban redevelopment

A study of how the economic value increase in urban redevelopment can be used to finance the necessary public infrastructure and other facilities

An Academic essay in Management Sciences

Doctoral Thesis

to obtain the degree of doctor
from Radboud University Nijmegen
on the authority of the Rector Magnificus prof. dr. S.C.J.J. Kortmann,
according to the decision of the council of deans
to be defended in public on Monday November 22, 2010
at 13.30 hours

by

Demetrio Muñoz Gielen
Born on May 20, 1970
in Málaga (Spain)

Supervisor:
Prof. dr. B. Needham

Doctoral Thesis Committee:
Prof. dr. ir. G.R.W. de Kam
Prof. dr. J. Roca (Politecnic University of Catalonia, Barcelona)
Prof. dr. M. Oxley (De Montfort University, Leicester)

A word of thanks is given here to the OTB Research Institute for the Built Environment (Delft University of Technology), which invested much in making possible this Doctoral Thesis. Also, thanks are due for financial assistance given by the Dutch government (Habiforum Program Innovative Land Use), and by the Delft Centre for Sustainable Urban Areas (Delft University of Technology).

Het verhalen van waardestijging in stedelijke herstructurering

Een studie over de manier waarop de economische waardestijging in stedelijke herstructurering gebruikt kan worden om de benodigde openbare infrastructuur en faciliteiten te betalen

Een wetenschappelijke proeve op het gebied van de Managementwetenschappen

Proefschrift

ter verkrijging van de graad van doctor
aan de Radboud Universiteit Nijmegen
op gezag van de rector magnificus prof. mr. S.C.J.J. Kortmann,
volgens besluit van het college van decanen
in het openbaar te verdedigen op maandag 22 november 2010,
om 13.30 uur precies

door

Demetrio Muñoz Gielen
geboren op 20 mei 1970
te Málaga, Spanje

Promotor: Prof. dr. B. Needham

Manuscriptcommissie:
Prof. dr. ir. G.R.W. de Kam
Prof. dr. J. Roca (Politechnische Universiteit van Catalonia, Barcelona)
Prof. dr. M. Oxley (De Montfort Universiteit, Leicester)

Dankwoord: het Onderzoeksinstituut OTB (Technische Universiteit Delft) wordt bedankt voor de materiele en menselijke inzet die dit proefschrift mogelijk hebben gemaakt. Tevens worden de Nederlandse overheid (Habiforum-programma Vernieuwend Ruimtegebruik) en het Delft Centre for Sustainable Urban Areas (Technische Universiteit Delft) bedankt voor hun financiële steun.

Published by Sidestone Press, Leiden
www.sidestone.com
Sidestone registration number: SSP56890001

ISBN 978-90-8890-059-4

Pictures: Demetrio Muñoz Gielen and Carles Gascó
Design: Corien Smit, Amsterdam
Illustrations: Felipe Fernández Córdoba, The Hague
Cover illustration: Tim Martin, Dreamstime.com
Cover design: Karsten Wentink, Sidestone Press
Printed and bound in Great Britain by
Marston Book Services Ltd, Oxfordshire

There are not enough words to thank to those that helped me to give birth to this research. This book is dedicated to my family, to all those that wisely advised me, and to those that had the patience to listen. It is dedicated also to Felipe Fernández Córdoba, Joost Zonneveld, Carles Gascó and Miles Roston for having me helped to 'make' this book. I thank Javier García-Bellido († 2006) for all his inspiration and friendship.

No hay palabras suficientes para agradecer a aquellos que me han ayudado a dar a luz a esta investigación. Este libro está dedicado a mi familia, a todos aquellos que me dieron sabios consejos, y a aquellos que tuvieron la paciencia de escucharme. Está dedicado también a Felipe Fernández Córdoba, Joost Zonneveld, Carles Gascó y Miles Roston por haberme ayudado a ´hacer´ este libro. A Javier García-Bellido († 2006) le agradezco toda su inspiración y amistad.

Table of Contents

CHAPTER 1

Introduction: problems in the financing of public goals in urban regeneration in the Netherlands

This research project is motivated by the experience nowadays with the regeneration of urban areas in many Dutch cities. On the one hand, regeneration can and often does create a significant value increase on some of the plots of land: on a particular plot, a new function comes which gives a much higher value to the land, and although significant costs might have to be made on that plot to realize that new function, there is nevertheless a net value increase. This is the case for example when developing free market housing or office space. On the other hand, there are other plots of land on which money has to be spent and which either give no returns or which give a return less than the expenditure: e.g. historic buildings might be renovated and integrated into the new buildings, inhabitants and firms might be compensated because they must move, some plots might have to keep a public function, there might be need for new roads and public space, drainage, public buildings and social housing, etc. In short, urban regeneration involves not only profitable parts but also unprofitable parts that are in the public interest either directly (like parks) or indirectly because they are necessary for the profitable parts (like sewerage). From now on, all these unprofitable parts, including all possible compensations, are called 'public infrastructure and facilities'.

When land is in public ownership, the public owner can choose to use the net value increase to cover (some of) the net costs of public infrastructure and facilities. When the land is not in public hands, public bodies can nevertheless sometimes require developers who own the land and benefit from the value increase to pay for the public infrastructure and facilities. Developers might be willing to contribute. However, there is often disagreement about the size and scope of their contribution. For example, often developers are willing to contribute only to local physical infrastructure situated within the development site, but not to other necessary compensations or infrastructure, such as off-site facilities (like access roads to the site, or public buildings located somewhere else). A major problem comes when some developers, the 'free riders', are not willing to contribute at all.

In order to understand this situation better, it is necessary to look first at the recent changes in Dutch land and housing policy.

1.1 Recent history in Dutch land & housing policies: towards more private involvement

The way urban regeneration is organized has changed in the last decennia more or less parallel to changes in urban development in general. Since the Second World War, and more or less until the 1980s, Dutch municipalities applied on a huge scale what was called an 'active land policy' (Greef, 1997: 9-17). An active land policy consists of buying that land that becomes zoned for development, providing the infrastructure, selling the serviced parcels and bearing the corresponding risks and eventual profits (Groetelaers, 2004: 20-23). This was applied to development for industrial areas, offices, and housing. For about four decennia, Dutch municipalities were the main parties in the market for urban land, which gave them a predominant position in urban development. This active public intervention was institutionalized through public land development companies, and almost all municipalities had one. Table 1 shows the extent to which municipalities were the predominant suppliers of serviced building plots, in this case for residential use. Housing associations and municipal housing companies bought many of these plots and developed social housing on them. Commercial developers also played an important role, not only buying some of the plots to build free market housing, but also to build some social housing, mostly owner-occupied. The central government played an important role by subsidizing and assuming the financial risks of both the active land policy of the municipalities and the building of social housing (Korthals Altes, 2007).

Table 1. Serviced building parcels sold for residential use, both in green field and urban regeneration schemes.

	Residential parcels sold by Municipalities (m^2)	%	Residential parcels sold by others (m^2)	%	Total
1965	8.645.000	67%	4.214.000	33%	12.859.000
1979	12.563.000	80%	3.177.000	20%	15.740.000
1980	12.011.000	81%	2.808.000	19%	14.819.000
1981	11.164.000	81%	2.567.000	19%	13.731.000
1982	11.086.000	80%	2.769.000	20%	13.855.000
1983	11.593.000	74%	4.140.000	26%	15.733.000

Source: own elaboration, based on CBS, Maandstatistiek Bouwnijverheid (in Needham, 1993: 92).

When regeneration became an important policy goal in the 1970s, this too was carried out in the same way, although with some delay. Municipalities became active not only on green field sites, but also in the existing city, buying, expropriating and redeveloping large deteriorated urban areas (Verhage & Sluis, 2003: 7-8). This led to a public predominance in urban regeneration instead of the previously common public-private partnership formulae (Kreukels & Spit, 1990: 388-389). Especially in large cities, municipalities bought much property, often deteriorated housing, and renovated it. For example, the Municipality of Rotterdam bought from 1974 to the middle of 1984 about 40,000 dwellings, drastically changing the property situation in certain neighborhoods from predominantly private to predominantly public ownership (Rotterdam, 1985: 18, 26).

At the end of the 1980s this way of working changed, both for greenfield development and for urban regeneration. Various changes coincided at that time. First, the economic recession in the 1980s led to an important rise in public expenditures on housing. This rise led to the need for budgetary cuts. Central government subsidies for public land development were reduced and those for the development of social housing abolished (Van der Schaar & Hereijgers, 1991: 183-189; Verhage & Sluis, 2003: 9; Priemus & Louw, 2003: 371-372; Groetelaers, 2004: 29, 32; Muñoz & Hoekstra, 2008: 202-203). Second, important changes in housing policy took place at that time, when the central government introduced in 1989 the housing policy called *Volkshuisvesting in de jaren '90* [Housing policy in the 1990s]. Moving from a policy very much oriented to the building of social housing, the new housing policy gave market parties a more prominent role in house building. This translated into a diminishing share of social housing and a rise of free market housing in new urban development. In 1993 housing associations became financially autonomous from the central government, consolidating a more general policy that was meant to situate public bodies in a new role of 'director at a distance'. Figure 1 illustrates the changes in house building by showing that since the 1980s social rented housing has diminished significantly its share in new building.

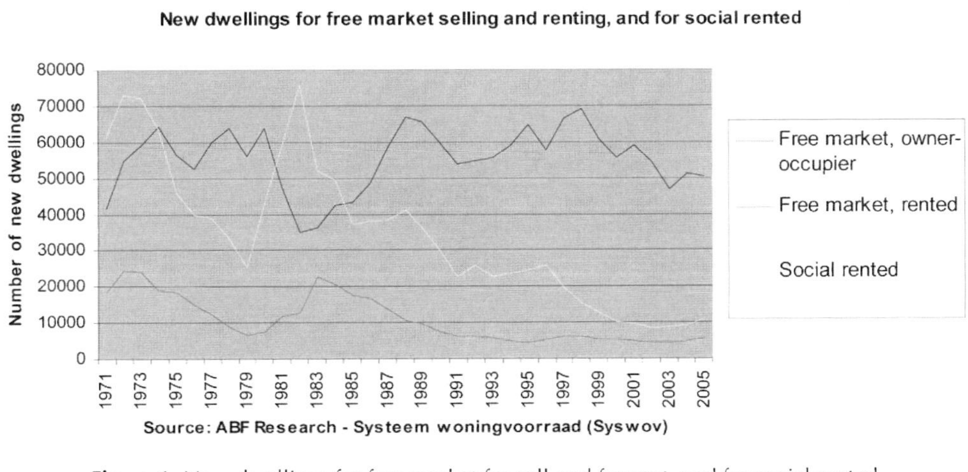

Figure 1. New dwellings for free market for sell and for rent, and for social rented.

As a consequence of these changes, the role of municipalities and market parties in urban development changed significantly. Municipalities changed the way they operate on the land market, and now they seek to share the risks with market parties in public-private partnerships. Also, many municipalities now play a more passive role, which is called a 'facilitating' land policy and which relies mainly on public law instruments such as the land use plan and building permits[1]. Most of the municipal land development companies have disappeared. Market parties, on the other hand, have increasingly taken over the former role of municipalities on the land market. Since the rise of free market housing and the increase in housing prices in the 1990s, the profitability of urban development has increased significantly. The increased profit margins, together with the strong position that the control of land gives in the development of a site, have attracted commercial developers to buy land (Groetelaers, 2004: 31-32; Priemus & Louw, 2003: 372). The introduction of the Fourth Memorandum on Spatial Planning Extra (*Vinex*) at the beginning of the 1990s roughly indicated the locations for major urban extension. This created the expectation of development on many greenfield locations, which stimulated developers to buy land there. In addition, public bodies stopped attempting to buy all the land and made the way open for developers to do so. Not only commercial developers became interested in land, the same could be said of housing associations. Corporations traditionally own much land in urban regeneration sites, especially in social housing districts, but they became also interested in acquiring land on green-field sites (Needham & De Kam, 2004: 2069-2070). Some describe the transition as a shift from a public monopoly on the land market towards private monopolies (Priemus & Louw, 2003: 369-370).

Municipalities still play an important role in urban development, and there are many examples of them applying an 'active' land policy. What is the situation with urban regeneration? Probably, active land policy is nowadays more common on greenfield sites than in urban regeneration, because in the latter land is more expensive and more difficult to buy. As a consequence, municipalities are less keen to buy land on regeneration sites than on greenfield sites (Buitelaar et al., 2008: 82, 100), although there are still many examples of municipalities buying land on regeneration sites. In any case, active intervention both on greenfield and on regeneration sites has changed in nature, as municipalities seek private parties with whom to share the risks. There is an increasing number of municipalities seeking new formulae in which private parties assume the financial risks and the responsibility for the implementation. As municipalities lose the powers they had as landowners, or at least must share their power with the developers that also control part of the land, they are increasingly relying on public law instruments such as land use plans and building

1 There is a distinction in European continental law systems between 'public law' or 'administrative law' and 'private law' or 'civil law'. The first ones regulate the actions of public bodies by which they impose their actions on others, e.g. expropriation law and planning legislation. Private law rules regulate obligations between equal actors, no matter whether they are public or private, e.g. the Civil Code, that sets the rules by which disputes between the actors will be resolved (Verhage, 2002: 160-161; Needham, 2006: 24-25).

permits, although they often combine these with private law agreements with these developers. In this way, municipalities are not intervening directly in the urban land markets, as they did until the 1980s. That is, they are not anymore buying all the land, providing the infrastructure and assuming all corresponding risks (Korthals Altes & Groetelaers, 2000). Increasingly, it is the market parties that buy the land, or most of it, and develop the site.

1.2 Problems with financing public goals in urban regeneration

Dutch municipalities have had high ambitions for their public regeneration schemes, and it was often possible to realize those when they owned most of the land and had the financial support of the central government. That is now different. If municipalities want to maintain their ambitions, they experience nowadays several problems. These concern a wide range of aspects: property rights, economic interests of users and owners, the expert knowledge available to municipalities, procedures, the cooperation among municipalities, commercial developers and housing associations, lack of a clear legal framework for negotiations, etc (Kolpron, 2000: 31-53; Verhage & Sluis, 2003: 11; Verhage & Needham, 2003: 20-21; Louw, 2008: 69-71; Van der Putten et al., 2004; Vrom et al., 2008: 19). Among those problems, the financing of public infrastructure and facilities, i.e. of the unprofitable parts, is an important obstacle to good urban regeneration: this was emphasized in a recent report of an advisory council of the central government (Vrom-raad, 2009: 5). Because of the transition from the traditional public dominancy in land development to more private involvement, the financing of public infrastructure and facilities has changed. When municipalities own the land and provide the infrastructure, public goals can be paid out of the profits from selling the plots, possibly complemented with public subsidies. However, when land is in private hands, municipalities have to work out other ways of financing, if they do not want to rely (or want to rely as little as possible) on public subsidies. The practice shows that it is difficult, in urban regeneration, to agree with landowners/developers the contributions, whether in money or in kind, that they should pay.

As a consequence, a common situation in urban regeneration on privately owned land is that agreements between municipalities and the landowners are achieved only with great difficulty. Long negotiations hamper development processes, so that targets for the regeneration of deteriorated Dutch neighborhoods have had to be lowered (Verhage & Sluis, 2003: 11). Another consequence is that public bodies, through subsidizing and/or direct realization, must pay an important share of the unprofitable parts. For an overview of the involvement of Dutch public bodies in the financing of public infrastructure and facilities in urban regeneration, see chapter 7.5. In short, Dutch public bodies are increasingly confronted with the need for large public subsidies.

On greenfield sites also the financial problems were increasing (Neprom, 2007; Buitelaar et al., 2008: 18-19; ABF-research, 2008; Rigo, 2008; Vrom-raad, 2008: 11-13). This situation has led to an important legislative modification. In 2008, a chapter dedicated to land development (from now on: Land Development Act) was introduced into the new Physical Planning Act with the goal of improving both the public steering of development processes and the financing of public infrastructure and facilities (Vrom et al., 2008: 20). This research studies how this recent legislative modification could be used to improve the situation.

1.3 Could legally binding land use rules help to improve the financing of public goals?

The Dutch Land use Plan (*bestemmingsplan*), together with the departure from it (*projectbesluit*, former *vrijstelling ex* art. 19.1 WRO) and the Development contributions Plan (*Exploitatieplan*) introduced in 2008 make it possible to impose a set of legally binding rules that regulate the use of land and real estate (from now on: binding rules). The owner or user of land is bound to use his land or property in the way prescribed by the binding rules (unless there are transitional provisions when new rules come into force). Binding rules delimit development rights or user rights, fulfilling a regulatory function. At the same time, binding rules allocate and guarantee certain rights to the property owner.

In the Netherlands, urban regeneration often involves building something new or refurbishing something old on a wide variety of sites, e.g. central areas in cities and towns, monofunctional residential districts, and brownfield sites. This usually requires a modification of the binding rules, whether this is for intensifying the actual use (e.g. more building volume), changing it for another use (e.g. housing instead of industry), maintaining the existing use (e.g. refurbishing historic buildings), or replacing the existing use with public infrastructure and *vice versa* (e.g. a park instead of buildings and *vice versa*).

Such a modification of the binding rules can affect the economic value of the property rights. For example, the value of land in the free market is lower when the site can be used for industry, than if it can be used for offices. Another example, very common in the Netherlands, is the difference in market value of land when it can be used for social housing, than if it can be used for free market housing. The basic idea that inspires this research, is that the increase in property values that follows the modification of binding rules could be used to finance all or at least part of the unprofitable parts, a sort of cross-subsidizing. The necessary modification of binding rules could be used in an operational way to achieve this. In short, this research focuses on how binding rules could be used in a strategic way to improve the financing of public infrastructure and facilities in Dutch urban regeneration on privately owned land.

In addition to binding rules under public planning law, we have to consider several formal rules that rule property rights in land. Furthermore, during data gathering it became clear that also not-legally binding zoning plans and other policy documents interact closely with binding rules and are also very relevant for capturing value increase. So this research considers all those formal rules that rule both binding rules (included the implications for property rights in land) and not-legally binding policy documents. We call all those formal rules 'formal rules relevant to zoning'.

1.4 Legitimacy of capturing value increase

The concept 'capturing value increase' includes several similar but not identical concepts. Before analysing them, it is important to distinguish among different causes of value increase. Value increase can be caused first by specific investments, e.g. in infrastructure that improves the accessibility of a specific site. Secondly, value increase can be caused by public decisions about land use planning regulations that do not necessarily cost money, e.g. a modification of the land use plan that allows more lucrative building. And third, value increase can be caused, only and independently from the first and second causes, by the general growth of society, i.e. by the accumulation of multiple decisions and choices of a multitude of anonymous actors in society (George, 1879: 89-94). For example the value of a house can increase very fast just because the area becomes fashionable.

But coming back to the meaning of 'capturing value increase'. In the literature there are multitude of terms, often meaning similar concepts, often overlapping each other (Alterman, 2009). Here we define three concepts that are relevant for this research: 'cost recovery', 'value capturing' and 'creaming off plus value'. 'Cost recovery' refers to the recovery, through contributions from private developers, of those costs that are directly related to the realization of public infrastructure and facilities that benefit the development. Developers might contribute either by providing infrastructure and facilities directly, or by paying public bodies for doing so. It is not relevant whether it is the developer or the municipality that realizes the public infrastructure and facilities, but whether those who benefit actually pay (in kind or in money) or not. 'Value capturing' or 'value capture' is the capturing by public bodies that have invested in, for instance, infrastructure, of the increased property values that are a result of that investment. Although private parties also might invest in public infrastructure, this term is generally meant for public investments. It is important to distinguish between the costs of the public investments, and the increase in value that results from them. For the costs might be greater, or less, than that value increase. If the costs are less than the value increase, full cost recovery can take place, leaving some of the value increase with the private developers. If the costs are greater than the value increase, there is no possibility of recouping all the costs. That is, 'value capturing' is limited to recouping the value increase that is the result only of public investments, and this value increase might be higher or lower than the investments. 'Value capturing' excludes thus the recouping of value increase caused by public decisions about land use planning regulations or by the accumulation of decisions of all the anonymous community members. 'Creaming off plus value' refers to a public body capturing the increase in value that is a result of any of the three causes: investments in infrastructure, decisions of public bodies, or just the general increase in the demand for land. 'Creaming off plus value' embraces thus the largest possible capturing and is irrespective of any costs that might have been made (Alterman, 2009: 5-6; Krabben & Needham, 2008: 4; Needham, 2007: 175-178; Smith & Gihring, 2006: 752; Kruijt, Needham, Spit, 1990: 32-4; Kruijt & Needham, 1980: 112-3).

A fundamental question is who should receive the value increase that accrues from any investment, public decision or general economic growth. This relates to the broader discussion about the contents of the right of land ownership. There are no social systems in which landowners have an absolute freedom to use their property, as norms and regulations limit property rights. Because norms and regulations are created by society, they reflect the prevailing powers and interests (Adams et al., 2001; Louw, 2008: 71). Translated to the capturing question, two conflicting theses exist. On one side is the thesis of full or conservative liberal ownership, where any value increase, no matter who or what caused it, belongs to the landowner. An alternative thesis, to be found also in liberal thinkers, advocates that the value increase belongs to the community because it is the community after all that is responsible for it. There is a distinction, based on an analysis of the historic evolution of ownership rights on land, between the 'use value' and the 'exchange value' of land. Full/conservative liberal ownership considers that ownership includes both the right to use and the right to benefit from property (should it be exchanged), which must include the benefit from the value increase caused by any factor. This definition of land ownership rights might be the result of the reinterpretation of the old Roman Quirinian law concept of property rights, made by the new liberal regimes in the 18th and 19th Centuries (*cfr.* García-Bellido, 1993, 1994). The alternative thesis considers that the use value can be indeed considered as fundamental to individual and social well-being, but that the exchange value does not (MacIntyre, 1984: 251; Christman, 1994; Krueckeberg, 1995). As Krueckeberg put it, the exchange value of land, "…has always been subjected to reasonable constraints for the benefit of the entire community and the society" (1995: 307). These constraints might have been inspired by the concept of the social function of property (García-Bellido, 1993, 1994; see also chapter 2.3.1). A common topic in the neo-classical theory of economic rent is the idea of taxing the value increase of land, which is considered as not being earned by the landowners because it arises from the general growth of society. The value increase is considered to be a surplus which, when removed, will not affect output or the price of the product. There is a long tradition of economists proposing such a tax for the benefit of the community. Variants of this argument have been advanced by Adam Smith, David Ricardo, J.S. Mill, Alfred Marshall, A. Pigou and, specially, Henry George (George, 1879: 89-94, 219-241; Prest, 1981: 7-21; Oxley, 2006: 103; Alterman, 2009: 4-5).

In short, there is much normative discussion about which sorts of capturing value increase are legitimate, and this discussion has crystallized differently in the planning system of different countries. For example these normative differences have led to different rationales behind instruments for capturing value increase. First there are those instruments that aim for a direct or 'pure' value capturing through direct taxation. The rationale of this first group of instruments is based on the argument that landowners do not earn the value increase, and that it is the community that deserves it. In other words, this rationale advocates creaming off the plus value. Other instruments do not use the 'unearned value increase rationale' but are based on the necessity of internalizing the negative impact of urban development, i.e. the need to compensate the costs that the community must make in order to implement or improve the necessary public infrastructure. This comes more in the neighbourhood of 'cost recovery' and 'value capturing'. This second rationale might choose for direct taxation of the value increase (e.g. property taxes, to be taxed periodically or at the moment of development) or for indirect instruments (e.g. land banking, land readjustment and developer obligations, Alterman, 2009: 3-5, 8-15, 23-24).

This research studies how the use of formal rules relevant to zoning influences any of the possible forms of capturing value increase, i.e. not only cost recovery, but also creaming off plus value. However, when formulating recommendations for the Dutch practice in chapter 9, the legal limits for capturing value increase in the Netherlands have served as a departing point. In the Netherlands, cost recovery only is permitted, excluding any additional capturing of value increase. The rationale here is the second mentioned: the necessity of internalizing the negative impacts of urban development. It must be said however that it is not always easy to clearly define cost recovery because it is not always clear what a negative impact is. Depending on the criteria used to define the negative impacts of urban development, cost recovery can include a narrow or a wide set of contributions. For the legal limits to capturing value increase in the Netherlands see chapter 7.2, in England see chapter 6.2 and in the Spanish region of Valencia see chapter 5.3.

1.5 Formulation of the problem

The problem to which this research wants to find a solution is formulated as follows:

How could formal rules relevant to zoning be used in the development phase of comprehensive urban regeneration developments on privately owned land in the Netherlands in order that the profitable parts finance the unprofitable parts?

How could formal rules relevant to zoning be used… means that this research wants to make recommendations for how Dutch public bodies, mainly municipalities, could use the relevant binding rules (those that might be relevant for the purpose of this research, which are in The Netherlands the Land use Plan, the departures from it and the new Development contributions Plan, including its implications for property rights in land) and other not-binding documents. The recommendations are of two sorts: the first fits within the existing Dutch legal framework, including the new Physical Planning Act and Land Development Act. The second sort of recommendations implies a modification of the legal framework.

… in the development phase of comprehensive urban regeneration developments on privately owned land in the Netherlands … means that this research looks for recommendations valid only for the development phase of comprehensive urban regeneration developments that are situated on privately owned land. The 'development phase' starts from the original situation and ends at the delivery and the beginning of the exploitation of the final real estate products. 'Comprehensive urban regeneration developments' mean physical interventions in the existing city with dimensions that cause a notable value increase. They always involve the construction or refurbishing, not only of profitable buildings but also of public infrastructure and facilities. This definition excludes other sorts of intervention in the existing city that might also fall under the category 'urban regeneration'. For example, those interventions are excluded that are only meant for the refurbishing of public infrastructure, without involving at the same time construction or refurbishing of commercial buildings. 'Situated on private owned land' means that the land, all or a majority of it, is owned by non-public bodies, e.g. commercial developers or housing associations and other non-profit developers. Those comprehensive developments in which land, all or a majority of it, was already in public hands (i.e. any public development company), before development started, are not included in this research.

… in order that the profitable parts finance the unprofitable parts means that this research focuses on getting those parties that benefit from development to finance (all or at least some of) the unprofitable parts, i.e. the public infrastructure and facilities. A wide range of unprofitable elements falls under 'public infrastructure and facilities': not only what Ennis (2003: 6-9) understands as 'physical infrastructure' (highways, footpaths, water, sewerage, electricity, parking, public transport infrastructure) and 'environmental infrastructure' (landscaping, open space, street furniture, green space). Other public facilities such as public buildings (schools, health centres, police, etc), social/affordable housing, etc. also fall under 'public infrastructure and facilities'. Public infrastructure and facilities can be both on-site (i.e. located within the development site) and off-site (located outside the development site, or located on-site but clearly serving a much wider area that the development site only). Also, any form of compensation that might have to be paid to realize the regeneration falls under this term. It is clear that with this problem definition, this research aims to improve in the Netherlands only a specific form of capturing value increase: cost

recovery. This research excludes thus in its final recommendations any measure that might be used in the Netherlands for other forms of capturing value increase that go beyond cost recovery.

1.6 Research Questions

In order to find an answer to the problem as formulated above, three preparatory research questions need first to be answered:

- Preparatory research question 1: *How can those formal rules relevant to zoning be used in comprehensive urban regeneration developments on privately owned land?*
  This question focuses on the variable 'formal rules relevant to zoning': how can they be used, following planning law and in practice? Here we do not try to make any connection with capturing value increase: that is the subject of preparatory research question 3.

- Preparatory research question 2: *What is the extent of capturing value increase in comprehensive urban regeneration developments on privately owned land?*
  This question focuses on the variable 'capturing value increase': which public infrastructure and facilities are paid or realized thanks to the profitable parts of the development in question? And, are the developments implemented on time, without delay and following previously established deadlines?

- Preparatory research question 3: *How does the way in which formal rules relevant to zoning are used influences capturing value increase?*
  Here we link the answer to question 1 (use of formal rules relevant to zoning) with the answer to question 2 (degree of capturing value increase). We want to know if certain ways of using formal rules result in this or that degree of capturing value increase. Is there a way of using the formal rules that results in market parties paying all or at least some of the unprofitable parts? And to do so without delay?

The main research question uses the findings of the preparatory questions to work out recommendations for the Dutch situation:

- *How could formal rules relevant to zoning be used in the Netherlands in order that the profitable parts finance as much as possible the unprofitable parts?*
  We want to know if certain ways of using formal rules relevant to zoning could help in the Netherlands to improve cost recovery in urban regeneration on privately owned land. This includes mechanisms for a more efficient plan process to lower development costs and to leave a larger part of the increased property values for cost recovery. And how could Dutch public bodies do that without at the same time delaying the implementation?

1.7 The structure of this report

In this **Chapter 1** I have introduced the motive, context, concepts and goals of this research. In **Chapter 2** I will introduce the relevant debates and conceptual frameworks that rule this research. They helped me first to position the goal of this research in the academic debate in such a way that the findings were relevant not only for the Dutch regeneration practice but also for science. In the second place they helped me to define and operationalize the research questions, for example, elaborating a causal model in which I positioned all the variables and the relations between them. In sum, chapter 2, together with chapter 3, sets out which data I will gather, where I am going to do it and how I will analyse the findings. In **Chapter 3** I needed to prescribe how to successfully gather the data and produce valid findings. Therefore I first explain the general principles of how I will produce findings with the necessary degree of internal and external validity. This has led to several choices: to focus on case research, to compare the planning systems of different countries, to a careful selection of cases and to systematically check the generalizability of the findings. Second I operationalize the data gathering by defining the independent and dependent variables, by distinguishing different, specific, sub-variables and by prescribing which data is used to answer which research question.

Chapters 4-7 present the gathered data. In **Chapter 4** I carry out an exploratory study of nine Western European countries: besides the Netherlands, also England, Spain/Valencia, Germany, France, Italy, Flanders, Denmark and Sweden. The goal is to select those countries that could provide the most interesting findings for the Netherlands. To select them I first offer insight into de use of formal rules relevant to zoning in these countries, second I position the Dutch rules into this international context, and finally I select those countries that will be the subject of in-depth research. In **Chapters 5 to 7** I present the gathered data from the in-depth research in the Spanish region of Valencia, England and the Netherlands. First I give an introduction of these countries and their planning systems, including the value capturing legal mechanisms and their limits. Second I present the studied cases. Third I answer research questions 1 to 3, including an evaluation of how the legal mechanisms affect the capturing of value increase. These answers form the basis for chapters 8 and 9.

In **Chapter 8** I draw conclusions for the academic debate and the theoretical framework set out in chapter 2. Here I use the answers to research questions 1 to 3 to test the hypotheses. I use all those answers and the results of the hypothesis testing, but incorporating also specific knowledge of the Dutch situation (legislation, political and cultural considerations), to answer in **Chapter 9** the main research question: how could the Dutch government (central and municipal public bodies) use the formal rules relevant to zoning to improve the capturing of value increase, but at the same time not delaying urban regeneration.

1.8 The practical value of this research

Different actors involved in urban regeneration in the Netherlands can use the findings of this research. This is, all those parties who might bear the responsibility for redeveloping urban areas, and therefore for finding financial sources to cover the unprofitable parts. These are mainly the municipalities, but also private parties: housing associations and commercial developers, or associations of property owners with commercial developers, which are in charge of the development.

The findings are also relevant to the introduction of the new Physical Planning Act and Land Development Act in the Netherlands. This law (the second is actually a new chapter included in the first) introduced in 2008 the Development contributions plan and modified substantially the legal framework for cost recovery. The findings include recommendations both for how this new legislation could be used to improve the financing of public infrastructure and facilities, and recommendations for further legislative modifications.

CHAPTER 2

Theoretical framework: capturing value increase within policy networks

In this chapter we set out the theoretical framework that we use for investigating the practical possibilities for improving the capturing of value increase in urban regeneration projects. We do this as follows.

First we look at the role of public bodies in general, and see them as acting in policy networks. More specifically, an urban regeneration project can be analyzed as a policy network in which public bodies try to achieve their goals by interacting with other parties. Second, we look at one of the most important power resources that are deployed in the interactions in the urban regeneration policy networks, namely property rights in land. It is in the nature of urban regeneration projects that this power resource is always present and cannot be ignored. We investigate the power that owning a property right in land can give, and how formal rules can affect that. Third, we look at one aspect in particular of the formal rules which affect how people in urban regeneration projects exercise their property rights in land. This is the degree of certainty about future development possibilities that is created by binding rules and other policy documents, and how this can influence the behavior of the property owner and the developer.

Finally, we apply those three sets of insights to the specific circumstances under which urban regeneration projects take place. This enables us to work out a causal model of the factors (including the use of the formal rules relevant to zoning) that affect the capturing of value increase. The chapter concludes with two hypotheses derived from this causal model. These are about two specific changes to the formal rules relevant to zoning which, it is hypothesized, will improve the capturing of value increase.

2.1 Power and the role of public bodies in policy networks

Capturing value increase in practice, in any of its forms (cost recovery, value capturing or creaming off plus value, see chapter 1.4) can be considered as an outcome of the interaction, in a network, of those parties involved in the implementation of public planning policies. All of them occupy a certain position within the network, and each of them pursues its own goals and interacts with the others in order to achieve them. This interaction is determined by aspects such as the power they might have to impose on, or to stimulate, others, in order to pursue their own goals. In short, in the networks that prepare and implement planning policies, different sorts of interactions might result in different outcomes of captured value increase. Taking into account the goal of this research, the crucial question is how public bodies could use the formal rules relevant to zoning to modify these interactions in order to improve the capturing of value increase.

Literature on policy networks provides some tools to understand how the parties involved in policy implementation (public bodies, property developers and landowners) interact with each other (Scharpf, 1978; Benson, 1982; Ostrom, 1986; Healey, 1992; Kickert et al., 1997; Klijn, 1997; Klijn and Koppenjan, 2000). The initial allocation of resources influences the position of public bodies within these networks, and public bodies have different techniques for intervening that might help to improve the capturing of value increase.

In the last decennia of the 20th Century, the role of public bodies changed significantly. From a situation in which public bodies were supposed to play a dominant role in policy making and implementation, the practice arose by which private parties began to gain a more prominent role. In the 1960s and 1970s, the limits became clear of what is called the Rational Central Rule Model for policy making and implementation processes, according to which the government was supposed to play a dominant role above the rest of involved parties. At the end of the 1970s, the academic debate about governmental steering changed in Europe and the United States (Kickert et al., 1997: 1-8). The critics argued that, under the welfare state, where the Rational Central Rule Model ruled the relationships of the government with the market, '...a substantial number of governmental policies (...) failed to meet their original targets. Despite the fact that large-scale policy programmes consumed enormous sums of money, they often failed to meet expectations, and the results were disappointing.' Sometimes policies were too ambitious, other times 'The implementation of policy seemed to recognize its own dynamics whereupon numerous policy plans broke down (...). At the end of the 1970s and in the 1980s this led to a pessimistic view of the government's abilities to achieve its goals and to influence social development' (op. cit.: 4). The decline and collapse of the centrally steered countries in Eastern Europe at the end of the 1980s reinforced the perceptions of the failures of central governmental steering. In the resulting debate about the changing relationship between public bodies and market parties, some critics advocated a total withdrawal of government steering and a reliance on the market.

2.1.1 The Policy network approach to power relationships

The 'policy network approach' can be seen as one of the results of that debate (Kickert et al., 1997: 3). The advocates of this approach position it as an alternative to the Rational Central Rule Model and to the market orientation approach, a sort of *third way* between both (op. cit: 7-8). In their overview of the foundations of the network approach to governance, Klijn and Koppenjan (2000: 136-139) found the first signs of the use of the network concept in policy science in the early 1970s. At that time, they argue, the network concept was used in the *bottom-up approach* (Hjern and Porter, 1981) and the intergovernmental relations literature (Friend et al., 1974; Scharpf et al., 1978) '...to map relation patterns between organisations and to assess the influence of these patterns for policy processes.' These two early proto-network approaches were influenced by the interactive policy approach (Allison, 1971; Cohen et al., 1972; Lindblom, 1965; Lindblom and Cohen, 1979) and the interorganizational approach (Levine and White, 1961; Negandhi, 1975; Aldrich, 1979). Kenis and Schenider (1991: 27-28) place the first signs of the use of the network concept in the 60s and 70s, seeing many aspects of the concept as an input from pluralist theories of policy making (see e.g. Bentley, 1967; and Truman, 1971; both quoted in Kenis and Scheinder, 1991: 27). Jordan places the first signs even earlier, in the 1950s and 1960s (1990; quoted in Rhodes & Marsh, 1992: 4-5). We could consider the policy network concept as meso-level, in the sense that it provides a link between the analysis of the relationship between interest groups and governments regarding specific policy decisions (the micro-level of analysis), and the analysis of the distributions of power within contemporary society (the macro-level of analysis, Rhodes & Marsh, op. cit.: 1). For an overview of literature on policy networks in the United States and Europe, see Klijn and Koppenjan (op. cit.: 136-139) and Rhodes & Marsh (op. cit.: 5-10). For an overview of literature in the Netherlands, see Spaans (2002: 34-36). For an extensive review of the literature and a discussion of the theoretical roots see Klijn (1996 and 1997). Besides being a different way of looking at government and markets, the policy network approach is also a different way of looking at public management.

In the traditional intra-organizational approach '...management consists of three main activities: setting the goals of the organization (planning), structuring and designing the organization (organizing) and "getting the job done" (leading). Management is a top-down activity based on a clear authority structure (...)' (Kickert et al., 1997: 11). The policy network approach advocates an alternative to this hierarchy. 'In a network situation a single central authority, a hierarchical ordering and a single organizational goal do not exist' (*ibidem*). Table 2 shows the main characteristics of the traditional intra-organizational and of the policy network approaches regarding the style of management.

Table 2. Two perspectives on management (op. cit: 12).

	Traditional intra-organizational approach	Policy network approach
Organizational setting	Single authority structure	Divided authority structure
Goal structure	Activities are guided by clear goals and well-defined problems	Various and changing definitions of problems and goals
Role of manager	System controller	Mediator, process manager, network builder
Management tasks	Planning and guiding organizational processes	Guiding interactions and providing opportunities
Management activities	Planning, design and leading	Selecting actors and resources, influencing network conditions, and handling strategic complexity

In the policy network approach, the power relationship between the actors is related to their interaction in the networks. The idea is that there are some factors that can explain the characteristics of this power relationship. Scharpf (1978: 353, 366) suggests a *structuralist* approach as a viable research method for studying inter-organizational policy making and policy implementation processes. It consists of focussing on the more stable (structural) factors that facilitate or impede certain types of power relationship between the involved actors. Of course, these structural factors do not fully determine those interactions, there are also other non-structural factors that may do so (e.g. consolidated game patterns and the contingent behaviour of individual actors). But the structural factors will at least explain the impossibility or improbability of certain forms of power relationships, and the feasibility and probability of others. The 'structures' facilitate or hamper certain types of power relationships. This research follows Scharpf's recommendation (1978: 354) to focus on resource dependence as a method to discover the structural factors. From this point of view, there are several important characteristics of policy networks (Spaans, 2002: 36; Klijn, 1997: 30-33).

2.1.1.1 First characteristic of policy networks: Actors pursue their own goals and are dependent on each other for realising those goals

Policy networks consist of different actors each of them pursuing its own goals, each of them following its own strategy. This carries the potentiality of a conflict, because these goals and strategies might diverge. In addition, actors in a network are mutually dependent. Dependence is the reason for the existence of a network. It is very unlikely that the implementation of public policy of any significance can rely on a single actor (Scharpf, 1978: 347, 350; Benson, 1982: 141, 148; Klijn, 1997: 30;

Kickert *et alii*, 1997: 2). As Klijn states, 'Networks develop and exist because of the interdependency between actors' (op. cit.: 31).

The concepts of power, dependence, rules and resources are central here. Following Giddens (1984: 14-16, 258; see also Verhage, 2002: 158), an agent exercises power if he or she can '...*make a difference* to a pre-existing state of affairs or course of events' (Giddens, 1984: 14). It is possible to categorise the following sorts of power: economic, politic, affective, and cognitive (Korthals Altes, 1995: 25). Almost all sorts of power (except maybe affective power, the capability to make others emotionally dependent) are generated thanks to what Giddens calls 'resources'. By means of the control of resources, an actor can influence the behaviour of others, and by doing so he 'makes a difference to a pre-existing state of affairs or course of events', he exercises power. Thus, power exists thanks to the control of resources. Elias (1971: 84-85; see also Verhage, 2002: 157) describes dependence relations between persons as the inverse of power relations. Actor A can exercise power on actor B when B needs one or more resources controlled by A. If so, A can exercise power on B because B depends on A. Summarized, the unequal allocation of resources can create dependence, and dependence allows the exercising of power.

The strength of this dependence depends on the importance of the resources, and on the 'substitutability' of the resource, i.e. the ease with which the resources can be replaced by other resources (Scharpf, 1978: 354-355; see also Klijn, 1997: 31; Spaans, 2002: 36). Scharpf distinguished different degrees of dependence, related to the importance and substitutability of the resources (*ibidem*):

- High dependence: high importance and low substitutability of the resources;
- Low dependence: low importance and low substitutability, or high importance and high substitutability;
- Independence: low importance and high substitutability.

Further, Scharpf distinguished three types of dependence (op. cit.: 356-358):

- Unilateral dependence: the interest of A in the maintenance of the relationship is greater that the interest of B. A is the more dependent party, B the dominant one. B might use this against the weaker party, A, and oblige him to accept interactions that are unattractive for him.
- Mutual dependence or interdependency: both A and B depend on the resources of the other, and they do not have easily available alternative sources of supply.
- Mutual independence: neither A nor B depends on the resources of the other. There is no dependency.

Giddens (1984: 258) distinguished two kinds of resources: allocative and authoritative. Allocative resources are the material features of the environment, the means of material production (technology) and the produced goods. Authoritative resources refer to the arrangements that create the time-space consuming patterns of societies, the arrangements that organize the interaction of people in societies, and the arrangements that create people's chances of self-development and self-expression, e.g. to be able to read and write. Healey (1992: 35; see also Verhage, 2002: 159) elaborates further on this distinction. She speaks of Giddens' 'allocative resources' and 'authoritative resources' as 'resources' respectively 'rules', and introduces a new sort of resource, 'ideas'. Using these concepts Healey develops a model to analyse the power-relationships in urban development processes.

Ostrom (1986: 466-467; see also Verhage, 2002: 160) made a distinction between 'working rules' and 'formal rules'. Working rules are more than formal rules: they are partly based on the formal rules but also on cultural or social ways of behaviour. Examples of working rules are policy paradigms, the unwritten rules about how people handle situations, etc. These informal rules can be partly based on formal rules but, as Verhage states, '(...) the rules that govern behaviour of actors are broader than only the legal regulation.' (op. cit.: 160). Formal rules are formalised in laws and administrative arrangements, and regulate the interactions between actors by defining rights and obligations and stating to whom they belong. For example, the Dutch Civil Code defines the scope of property rights (how the landowner may use his land) and the Physical Planning Act and the Housing Act limit these rights (he can only build if the Land use Plan allows it, and provided he obtains a building permit). Formal rules also create 'new' resources that become necessary, and allocate them to certain actors. Following the example above, the Physical Planning Act and the Housing Act create the new resources 'land use plan' and 'building permits', which can exclusively be approved by the municipality.

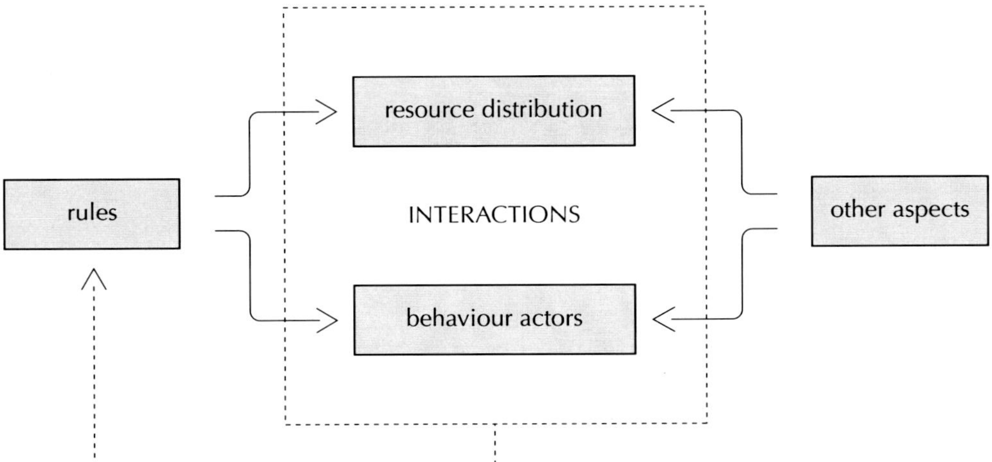

Figure 2. Relation between rules, resources, dependence and power in policy networks.

Thus, the relation between rules, resources, dependency and power is clear: rules regulate the behaviour of actors and the resource distribution in the network, and this shapes dependence among the actors. And finally, dependence shapes the power interactions between actors. However, this process is more complex, as the interactions within the framework often shape, consolidating or altering, the rules (Klijn & Koppenjan, 2000: 139; Klijn 1997: 33; Benson, 1982: 150-151). Summarized, rules shape the power interactions, but power interactions also shape the rules. See Figure 2.

2.1.1.2 Second characteristic of policy networks: There is no dominant actor, and governments are *primus inter pares*

Giddens said also that '...all forms of dependence offer some resources whereby those who are subordinate can influence the activities of their superiors.' He calls this the 'dialectic of control' in social systems (1984: 16). This means that each actor has at his disposal some resources/rules needed by other actors to achieve their goals, so that he can influence their behaviour (Verhage, 2002: 158). If each actor has resources/rules needed by others, there is no actor who has all the resources/rules at his disposal. There is no actor who can exercise power over all the other actors, because there is always at least one other actor who has some necessary resources/rules. That is, there is no actor who can exercise an absolute power over all the other actors. In fact, the policy network approach applies to the policy field the principles of Giddens' 'dialectic of control', when it assumes that various actors have a veto power. The need to cooperate is central in the policy network approach; policies can only develop or be implemented when each actor makes his resources available (Scharpf, 1978: 347, 350; Benson, 1982: 141, 148; Klijn and Koppenjan, 2000: 142-144). Kickert et al. emphasize this: 'Interdependency is the key word in the network approach. Actors in networks are interdependent because they cannot attain their goals by themselves, but need the resources of other actors to do so' (1997: 6).

Public actors occupy a special position, a position that is based on the unique resources that they have and on the democratic legitimization they enjoy. But a clear starting point in this approach is that '...public actors do not play the dominant role they often are ascribed in other public administration perspectives.' (Klijn & Koppenjan, 2000: 151). 'It is (...) clear that government cannot reclaim its post-war welfare state position as the central governing authority in society. The experiences of the 1960s and 1970s have shown that the steering potentials of government are limited and that it must deal with many other important actors in the policy fields in which it operates.' (Kickert *et alii*, 1997: 1). Klijn and Koppenjan speak of an '... apparently broad consensus that has developed around the idea that government is actually not the cockpit from which society is governed and that policy making processes rather are generally an interplay among various actors...' (op. cit.: 136). In short, though the policy network approach recognizes that the government is a special party, a kind of *primus inter pares*, the government is not any more the central actor that characterizes the Rational Central Rule Model, typical in the welfare state of the 1960s and 1970s.

2.1.1.3 Criticisms of the policy network approach

There are criticisms of the policy network approach, namely that it is said to devalue the status of the public sector (De Bruijn and Ringeling, 1997: 151-157; Rhodes

1997, quoted in Klijn & Koppenjan 2000: 151-154; Kickert et al., 1997: 170-171; Marsh & Rhodes, 1992: 263-268; Lowi, 1969: 85-97, 287-297: quoted in Marsh & Rhodes, op. cit.: 265; Ripley and Franklin 1987, Marin and Mayntz 1991 and Nelissen 1993: quoted in Kickert et al., *ibidem*). Compared to the dominant role that government has in other public administration perspectives, the policy network approach describes the public sector as being just another of the actors in the network, putting it on the same level as the non-governmental actors and denying it the possibility of playing an old fashioned dominant role. Thus, the network approach proposes that government bodies engage in the networks as the only way of successfully elaborating and implementing policies. The criticisms focus on the problems of democratic legitimacy or accountability that arise when governments cannot play a dominant role and have to engage in networks. They should not enter into interactions and partnerships with other parties in society because this hinders the fulfilment of the common interest. A government getting involved in networks is not able to fulfil the common interest it should pursue, because the decision making in networks is non-transparent and uncontrolled.

In a reaction to this criticism, Klijn and Koppenjan warn "...against mixing up the real world and the theoretical framework that is used to analyse, evaluate and improve it." (2000: 151). They argue that it is a fact that the government depends upon other actors, and that the policy network approach just tries to develop instruments, which - given that fact - enable the public sector to defend in the actual network context the public interest and the primacy of politics. As sections 2.1.1.1 and 2.1.1.2 show, the idea of interdependence in the policy network approach is based on an analysis of the distribution of resources. It is clear that the policy network approach takes the starting point that there is always more that one actor who has a 'veto power', because the needed resources are distributed between several actors and there is no actor who controls all them. Governments depend on other actors because they do not have all the needed resources, the missing resources belong to other actors, and these missing resources are not replaceable or if replaceable, this is too costly and time consuming. Therefore, the collaboration of all the actors who control the needed resources is indispensable for policy-implementation.

The idea that governments are inevitably dependent can be the subject of criticism, as e.g. Koffijberg did in a recent study on housing policy networks in the Netherlands. He argued to have discovered effective ways for public bodies to play a dominant role (2005: 322-323). Following this line, my research can be seen as a fundamental criticism of the basic assumption in the Policy network approach, that public bodies *always* have to be heavily dependent on other bodies in land development projects. The conclusions in chapter 8 provide instruments for making public bodies less dependent and allowing them to play a more dominant role, precisely in order to improve the capturing of value increase.

2.1.2 How to intervene in policy networks: Network management

Steering the interactions between the actors in policy networks may be necessary. One of the reasons is that these interactions are complex and there is always a potential conflict, since each actor pursues his own goals. Furthermore, because there are usually actors who have some veto power, the collaboration of all the necessary actors is necessary to obtain outcomes that satisfy all the actors. As Klijn and Koppenjan put it: 'Since co-operation and collaboration of goals and interests does not happen of its own accord, steering of complex games in networks is necessary.' (Klijn & Koppenjan, 2000: 140). The special position of public bodies makes them very suitable for the role of network manager. They can be a facilitator.

Obviously, the reason why a public body might want to intervene in policy networks is not only to guarantee that the outcome of policy processes satisfy other actors, but also to realise its own goals better. In this research we investigate whether the formal rules relevant to zoning could be used in an operational way to improve cost recovery, i.e. to finance the unprofitable parts with the value increase of land. Translated into policy network terms, we investigate the possibility of influencing, through Network management measures, the interactions within the networks and thereby the outcomes in capturing value increase.

It is possible to distinguish two types of network management: 'process management' or 'game management', and 'network constitution' or 'network structuring' (Klijn & Koppenjan, 2000: 140-142; Klijn 1997: 46-53; O'Toole, 1988: 426-433). Process management tries to influence the interactions between actors, with the existing rules and resource distribution as the starting point. This management method is appropriate for influencing interactions that are already underway. The second network management method, Network constitution, seeks institutional change. Network constitution is focused on making structural changes, and one of the ways of doing this is by changing the rules. This is based on the principle that rules can modify the distribution of resources and the behaviour of the actors.

In the rest of this chapter, two specific methods of Network management will be worked out, both of them involving the rules that public bodies might be able to modify. Both methods are inspired by two ongoing debates in the planning academic and professional world. The first measure (section 2.2) is inspired by the debate in the UK, but specially in Spain and the Netherlands, concerning the steering powers of public bodies in urban development, related to the contents of property rights in land. It is a clear Network constitution measure: modifying the contents of property rights that govern the transactions in infrastructure provision. The second measure (section 2.3) is inspired by the academic debate about the desired level of flexibility in planning. It also consists of a Network constitution measure that requires however almost no modification of formal rules and is thus feasible in a shorter term: it concerns the moment in the course of the development process at which public bodies approve land use prescriptions. Both measures have been analysed in a model that includes also all other factors that influence the capturing of increased value (section 2.4). Finally, both measures have been translated into two hypothetical assumptions (section 2.5).

2.2 The formal rules governing property rights in land

Introduction

The owners of property rights in land[1] have a very powerful position in urban regeneration projects, and they can – and do – use that power in the pursuit of their own goals in such projects. However, the contents of those powers are determined by formal rules, under both public and private law. In section 2.2.1 we first discuss those rules in general terms. Then in sections 2.2.2-4 we illustrate this with an exposition of the practice and political debate in three countries – England and Wales, the Netherlands, and Spain – which concern the relationship between formal rules governing property rights in land and the possibilities for capturing value increase. The British nationalization of development rights in 1947 forms a clear reference point in the debate. The discussion in the Netherlands and Spain is certainly relevant to local academic and professional debate, and the similarities between the debate in both countries are obvious, e.g. in both countries controversial proposals have been made to separate development rights from property rights. In 1994 the Spanish region of Valencia devised an alternative to separation that in fact separated infrastructure provision from property rights. Today, this innovation has been introduced in almost all of the remaining 17 Spanish regions.

2.2.1 Restrictions on the exercise of property rights in land

One might think, and actually there are many with a libertarian perspective who do, that property rights in land give the owner total freedom to decide how to use his land. The Roman Law concept of 'dominium' might best define what are the contents of such an absolute concept of property. 'Dominium' includes all the possible rights over a thing (thus also land) that one person can own: the right to use it (*usus*), the right to the fruits (*fructus*) and the right to disposal (*abusus*). However, the reality is that all countries, and certainly any country with a mature legal system, have issued in the course of history, and still issue, formal rules that restrict the exercise of property rights in land (Needham, 2006: 1-3, 36-38, 39). Before entering into the

1 Of the variety of possible property rights in land, it is the right of ownership that is at the centre of attention in this research. There are other possible rights, for example that another person is authorized to walk on the land, even if he is not the owner of the land, or that another person can as a tenant use the property to live or work in/on it (*cfr.* Needham, 2006: 34-36).

debate in England and Wales, the Netherlands and Spain, let us see first how private and public law can restrict the exercise of property rights in land and how this has evolved in the history.

The restrictions on the exercise of rights in land can come both from private and from public law. Private law rules are necessary to regulate how persons deal with each other with their property rights, i.e. *how* and *what* they can sell or buy or limit their rights. For example, if law (e.g. nuisance law in England and the United States) says so, one owner cannot use his property in such a way that he could harm a neighbouring owner. Another example is that private law rules whether an owner can or cannot split off from his freehold property right the right of a building lease and transfer it to another person. In addition, the owner of the freehold may not enter onto the land without permission of the owner of the building lease. Thus, restrictions under private law regulate the normal traffic between persons (Needham, 2006: 43-45).

Restrictions under public law allow state agencies to impose one-sidely restrictions to the exercise of property rights in land. First, a state agency can impose restrictions on the *use* of the right, e.g. if you want to build on your land, you must follow the building regulations. This first sort of restriction attenuates the exercise of rights, but does not take them away, although if it is permanent that amounts in fact to destroying part of the right. Second, a state agency may compulsorily *take away* rights, e.g. expropriating freehold rights of land, or the right to develop it. In this second sort of restriction, the right is transferred to someone else, usually a state agency (Needham, 2006: 46).

Generally speaking, since the liberal revolutions of the 18th and 19th Centuries we could summarise the evolution of the restrictions under public law as follows. At that time, the victorious bourgeoisie of the new liberal regimes rehabilitated (and reinterpreted) the old Roman Quirinian law's concept of property rights. The goal was to guarantee the economic position of the new dominant social class. Up to that time, the absolute control of land by the bourgeoisie was hindered by medieval attachments and rules. In the liberal reinterpretation, property rights included, as part of their *essential contents*, the faculty of doing *whatever* the owner wants *on, under* or *above* his land. *Essential content* means that it belongs to the *structural* or *genuine* elements of the property right[2]. If the essential contents become hollowed out, property becomes seriously harmed. *Whatever* means that the owner can decide, for the owned object, the *an* (whether to do or not to do), the *quomodo* (how, in which way, what for), the *quantum* (how much) and the *quando* (when). *On, under* or *above* means that the owner can do whatever he wants with the space situated above his plot (up to the sky), directly on his plot, and under his plot (down to the hell). The

2 The 'essential contents' of property rights in land could be identified, *grosso modo*, with what in the Anglo-Saxon legal tradition is called the minimal 'bundle of rights' that someone has to own in order to be regarded as the owner (*cfr.* Needham, 2006; 34-35, 38-40).

concept evolved with time showing some parallels with the historic transition of the Liberal State to the Social and Democratic State. First, the space above and under the land became public domain. In a second step, rivers, seas, coastal areas, etc. became also part of the public domain. The owner still controlled the space situated immediately above and under his plot, but not for long. With the transition to the 20th Century the *social function* of property appeared. Sanitary (fire and building hygiene) and social considerations further limited the contents of property rights. The broad competences of the owner became gradually limited and the exercising of his rights subjected to obligations. These limits and obligations, which derive from the interests of other individuals, and from public and collective interests, now prevail over the interests of the owner and have become *part of* the essential content of property rights. The owner can enjoy his property only if he/she does so within the legal rules and prescriptions, and after receiving a public authorization or concession. In other words, the public administration fixes now the *an*, the *quantum* and the *quomodo* (*cfr.* García-Bellido, 1991b: §1; 1993: 176, 179-180, 182; 1994: 130 and following; Mazzoni, 1990: 32, 34, 99-101, 104-121, 253-257, quoted in García-Bellido, 1993: 179; 1994: 136; Bassols, 1985a: 111-124; and 1985b: 11-24, 115-116: last edition quoted in García-Bellido, 1993: 179-180).

2.2.2 The nationalization of development rights in England and Wales

Already in 1909 and 1932, British planning law introduced the rationale of capturing the unearned value increase of land, without however effectively operationalizing it. Later on, the 1947 Town and Country Planning Act, following the conclusions of the 1942 Uthwatt Report, introduced what is called the 'nationalization of the development rights' (Booth, 2003: 89-92, 100-101, 105, 109; Cullingworth & Nadin, 2006: 195-197; Alterman, 2009: 4-5, 7, 15-17). The right of ownership was stripped of one of its partial rights – the right to develop, or the right to change the use of the land – and this partial right was compulsorily acquired by the state. This meant that development rights were vested in the state, not in the landowner. No development could take place without permission of the local planning authority, and then only on payment of a betterment charge to the Central Land Board (for the right to develop was owned by the state, and the developer had to pay to use that right). From this it followed that, if permission was refused, landowners had no right to compensation, and that if permission was granted, betterment (any increase in the value of land) was subject to a betterment charge. Landowners owned only the existing use rights of their land. In case of compulsory acquisition of land, the price to be paid as compensation would be equal to the existing use value, that is, its value excluding any allowance for future development. The act introduced a scheme of £300 million fund for payments (intentionally called 'payments', and not 'compensations') to landowners who could successful claim that their land had some development value before the introduction of the 1947's provisions. Some decades later, in 1974 and 1975, the

Labour government of the time proposed an initiative to nationalise land ownership (i.e. going a step further and nationalising all rights in land); however, this measure failed to materialise (Clusa & Mur, 2007: 122-136).

The 1947 Act had significant consequences for capturing value increase, as betterment (any increase in the value of land) became the subject of a betterment charge. From that time onwards, land value taxation has been short-lived and it was finally scrapped in 1985 (see chapter 6.2.1). Another important consequence of the 1947 provision is that development plans are not legally binding: someone who wants to develop does not have the right to do that simply because the application conforms with the development plan. In other words, the state can impose conditions on the right to develop, irrespective of the development plan. However, the 1947 Act did not alter the principle that landowners are the only ones who can develop their land. Landowners remain, in case planning authorities grant planning permission, the exclusive owner of the right to develop their land. They can exclude others from doing so. Before being entitled to develop, developers will have to acquire the land or to agree the availability of land with its owner.

2.2.3 The Netherlands: the debate about splitting development rights from land ownership

As mentioned in section 1.1, important changes took place in Dutch land and housing policies at the end of the 1980s and beginning of the 1990s. The effects of these changes have been already discussed there: private parties have assumed a more important role in land development and in housing production, and a shift took place from predominantly social housing to predominantly free market housing. Another change was the interest of private parties in buying land long before development takes place, which was relatively new in the recent history or Dutch urban development. These changes have consequences for the capturing of value increase in urban regeneration: the financing of the public infrastructure and facilities has come under pressure and development has been delayed significantly.

These changes, and their consequences, have been the subject of controversy and debate. The question has been discussed whether planning law and property rights offer enough instruments to public bodies to achieve their public goals. Often mentioned public goals concern the delivery of serviced land and the subsequent realisation of building quotas, and the financing of public infrastructure and facilities. Other debated issues, directly related to this discussion, concern the most desirable relationship between public and private actors, and whether municipalities need new statutory powers to regulate land markets. Probably, the most controversial issue has been the proposal for a separation of land ownership from development rights (CPB 1999; BCR, 1999; Canoy and Van Ewijk, 1999; Overwater, 1999; Priemus & Louw, 2000, 2003; Vrom-Raad, 2000; Korthals Altes and Groetelaers, 2000).

2.2.3.1 The debate

There is a certain consensus about the analysis that is briefly set out in sections 1.1 and 1.2. It is clear that the recent changes in land and housing policies do not allow municipalities to steer urban development *in the way they used to do*. The discussion however focuses on the question whether or not planning law offers, in the new context, enough instruments for municipalities to *satisfactorily* control urban development and its outcomes. Can municipalities *sufficiently* meet their public goals without performing an old-fashioned active land policy and dominating the land markets? In other words, without buying the land, providing the infrastructure and assuming all the corresponding risks?

Priemus and Louw (2003) are sceptical about the effectiveness of public law instruments. For example, they argue that pre-emption powers cannot always prevent developers from buying the land. Also, expropriation is not an easy instrument to use, for it is expensive, politically sensitive, and not always applicable if the landowners are willing to develop. The authors carried out a study of the functioning of Dutch land markets, and found that municipalities complained that the recent changes make it difficult to implement public planning policies. The most important bottlenecks mentioned by the municipalities are the assembling of land, the overrun of public legal procedures, and the recovery of costs. Municipalities said that they experienced in practice difficulties in achieving a comprehensive and integral development (Priemus and Louw, 2000: 6-10). The authors argue that, because land ensures a strong position in urban development, the chances for developers of surviving in the building market are based not on their abilities to offer a better and cheaper product, but on their position in the land market. Land is a necessary condition for urban regeneration, and the one who controls it has a monopoly on the supply of buildings in that particular location. As there are always in a particular urban market a limited number of suitable sites for building, actually we could talk of an oligopolistic market: in one urban market, the distribution and use of suitable building sites is controlled by a limited number of providers, the landowners. Because of the importance of land as the 'key' to urban development, developers tend to pay high prices for acquiring the land. This leads to high land development costs, costs that have to be recovered in the public infrastructure and the constructed buildings. The consequence is a diminishing and impoverishment of the public infrastructure and social housing, and of the quality of the development (Priemus and Louw, 2003). In a recent study of urban regeneration, Buitelaar et al. conclude that high development costs adversely affect the quality of public infrastructure. In addition, they conclude that high development costs stimulate maximisation of the building volume, which ultimately leads to massive buildings and scarce public space (2008: 17-18, 20).

A study conducted by Korthals Altes and Groetelaers (2000) put into perspective the claim that municipalities have lost their steering powers. In most of the 72 schemes they studied, the municipality exercised influence through buying land and/or through reaching contractual agreements with the developers. From this it is clear that the municipalities still retain, through buying land and/or contractual agreements, ways of influencing urban development and its outcomes. However, the question remains unresolved whether this is enough to *sufficiently meet* the public planning goals. Korthals Altes and Groetelaers take a step further by arguing that the available instruments are indeed *sufficient means* for preserving the public interest and influencing urban development (op. cit.: 43-45). However, Priemus and Louw disagree and are more pessimistic about the effectiveness of public steering powers (2003: 373-375).

2.2.3.2 The proposal for separating development rights

Some authors argue the need to introduce more competition in the building market (Priemus and Louw 2000, 2003; CPB, 1999: 11, 21, 39-40; BCR, 1999; Canoy and Van Ewijk, 1999). In the current situation, they argue, the chances of private actors are based on their position in the land market, not on their creativity and efficiency in producing good and cheap real state products. Increasingly, private actors are acquiring land in early stages of development processes. The authors argue that this limits the competition between property developers and harms the public interest in urban development, including the capturing of value increase.

To introduce more competition between developers, the authors argue that the contents of property rights should be modified. Currently, property gives to the owner the right to develop the building prescribed in the binding rules, in the Netherlands most of the time a land-use plan. If the landowner is able and willing to implement the land-use plan, expropriation might be difficult. This is called the 'self-realisation right': the owner of the land has the right to develop it in accordance with the land-use plan. This development right spans the whole development process, from infrastructure provision to the building. In other words, property gives to the owner the exclusive right to develop and build on the respective plot. The authors argue that separating the development and building rights from the right of land ownership would stimulate free competition.

Several, similar proposals have been made for separating landownership from development and building rights. Canoy and Van Ewijk (1999: 25) propose an obligatory public tender for the development of a site. In their proposal, the landowner must tender the development and building rights on his land. Similarly, Priemus (1996: 32) and Priemus and Louw (2003: 376-377) propose a modification of the Expropriation Act (*Onteigeningswet*) to allow expropriation when the landowner does not develop and build his plot in a 'competitive manner'. Landowners should be obliged to organize a public tender, and if they do not do so, the municipality would have the right to expropriate the plot and organize the public tender. From that time onwards, other reports have included in one or other way the topic of separating development rights from landownership, for example by analyzing the effects of a possible separation and expropriation of development rights (Needham & Geuting, 2006: 18-19; Vrom, 2006: 4-5). The topic remains in the spotlights, as shown by the fact that a governmental advisory commission has recently proposed limiting in some strategic areas the self-realization right of landowners by e.g. facilitating expropriation or introducing new forms of compulsory purchase of the land (Vrom-raad, 2009: 41-42).

2.2.4 The separation of infrastructure provision from property rights in the Spanish region of Valencia

In Spain, the course of the discussion is roughly as follows (Bassols Coma, 1996a, 1996b; Bidagor Lasarte, 1996; García-Bellido, 1991a, 1996; Menéndez Rexach, 1996; Parejo Alfonso, 1996; Perales Madueño, 1996; interview with García-Bellido in 2005; Muñoz & Korthals Altes, 2007). Since the 19th Century, the difficulties faced by public bodies in financing public infrastructure and facilities inspired proposals and measures that affected the scope of the contents of property rights. Public bodies had neither an efficient legislative framework (expropriation, taxes), nor enough financial resources for the realization of public infrastructure and facilities. As a consequence, buying the land and providing the infrastructure became a considerable challenge for public bodies.

Ildefonso Cerdá (1815-1876) was a consistent critic of the legislative framework for urban development. As an alternative, he proposed a formula for distributing between all the involved owners the costs that arise from urban development. Landowners should share the costs through a form of land readjustment. In 1861 a proposal for a town planning act which included Cerda's approach was submitted before Parliament in Madrid. However, this proposal did not succeed, and the 1864 Town Extension Act, which relied on the existing inefficient expropriation legislation, was passed instead. Cerda's revolutionary ideas had to wait a century for another chance. It is not clear whether Cerda's ideas and proposals influenced directly the 1956 Act, but anyway this act included a similar approach. From 1956 onwards, subsequent planning acts fine-tuned the 1956's approach in order to facilitate a private financing and implementation of public infrastructure and facilities. From the 70's onwards, more fundamental criticism led to more radical proposals and to more audacious experiments in the deployment of available instruments and in developing new instruments. The Valencian 1994 Act could be considered as one of the most relevant of these experiments.

In 1956, the Land and Urban Planning Regulatory Act and in 1976 its modification succeeded in introducing a totally new approach: a land readjustment regulation geared at changing property rights. The regulation makes profiting from betterment conditional on taking responsibility for infrastructure provision. Landowners were, since then, obliged to provide the infrastructure, organized in joint development organizations and sharing the costs. As compensation, they could also share the serviced building plots, i.e. the development profits. To create certainty about the development profits, municipalities were obliged to approve a legally binding General Land use Plan for the whole municipal territory. This plan delimitated the future developable sites, and those to be redeveloped. The detailed character of this general land use plan, and its strong legal binding status has made Spain a singular case in the international context (see chapter 4). The land readjustment regulation was in principle based on voluntary participation, but it also included the possibility of compulsory readjustment and expropriation. However, the regulation failed to assure good and enough public infrastructure and facilities. Since the 1980s, critics such as García-Bellido (1989; 1991b; 1993, 1994) and Parejo Alfonso (1993) advocated reform, arguing that landowners usually had no background as developers and were not well equipped to organize development processes. For more details about the working of the 1956's land readjustment regulation, see section 5.2.1.

2.2.4.1 The proposal for separating development rights from land-ownership

In García-Bellido's view, the shortcomings of the 1956's system were due to a lack of real and effective liberalization in the production of urban land. He made a proposal for re-shaping the system, giving the development rights to the public bodies and aiming at improving the functionality of the land markets. García-Bellido's ideas were based on a criticism of the historic fundaments of the contemporary concept of property rights (1989; 1993; 1994). The British 1947 Act, and legal reforms of the Labour government in 1974 and 1975, which reintroduced the taxation of land values and proposed the nationalization of land, influenced García-Bellido´s proposals (Clusa & Mur, 2007: 122-136).

Incomplete evolution of the concept of property rights

We have seen above in section 2.2.1 that thanks to the social function of property, and to sanitary considerations, the broad competences of the owner have been gradually restricted, and that the public administration nowadays fixes the *an*, the *quantum* and the *quomodo*. However, García-Bellido argues that the problem is that the *quando* (when to use or build upon the property) remained under the control of the landowner. The realization of the public goals is still dependent on the decision of the owner to develop his land. Consequently, undesired phenomena, such as speculative retention of land, cannot be avoided. As a reaction to this, since the 1956 Act, in Spanish planning law the social function has incorporated a new dimension, of an economic character: owners have also to comply with the obligation to implement the public infrastructure and facilities within prescribed deadlines. If they do not fulfill their duties properly, the municipality can apply compulsory land readjustment or expropriate the land. However, in practice it was under the 1956's legislation very difficult for public bodies to effectively control the *quando*. Public control instruments were not always effective: for example, expropriation is a very controversial and politically troublesome instrument. Usually, landowners/developers can wait, while the public administrations have the goal of delivering large building quotas. Confronted with the choice between (1) maintaining the requirements but then not obtaining the collaboration of the private actors, and (2) lowering the requirements in order to achieve an agreement, many public bodies choose the second alternative (*cfr.* García-Bellido, 1993 and 1994).

The captive market

Together with this analysis that the historic evolution of the concept of property rights was incomplete, the idea of a *captive market* is central to García-Bellido's thought. Due to restrictive zoning and the natural features of land (each location is unique as land is not reproducible), land is not a normal production factor or merchandise. Its reproduction, distribution and use are not subjected to free competition. Property rights give powers to the owner to use his land and exclude others from doing so. Others cannot find an alternative provider of the land, except of course if they move to another location, where they will meet the same situation (again an owner who can exclude them from access to land). In other words, landowners do not need to compete with others, because they control the most important production factor: land. They form a monopoly (there is only one supplier) or an oligopoly (there are only few suppliers) in the land market, the virtual place where the producers of urban land are supposed to acquire undeveloped land. Competition arises to acquire land, not to develop it. The strength and survival chances of the supplier in the urban markets are based on his monopolistic or oligopolistic privileges, not on the quality or other advantages of his buildings. He can wait, without needing to make any investment or effort, and ask the maximal price for his land, absorbing all the residual profit margins from the building. The legal certainty about future development possibilities, provided by the obligatory General Land use Plan introduced with the 1956 Act, reinforces the position of landowners. Suppliers in housing and land markets show a common strategic behavior: they wait until the various segments of the demanders (price/quality ratio) are willing to pay the maximum price possible. Even when prices rise, an important part of the potential supply waits until prices reach even higher levels (García-Bellido, 1994: 114-115/578-579; Mangada, 1990: 179-180; Martín Mateo, 1980: 13-18; Roca Cladera, 1992: 13: quoted in García-Bellido, 1993: 191).

Proposal for a real liberalization

García-Bellido proposed an alternative to the above-mentioned liberal interpretation of property rights (Roca, 2007). He proposed the 'desaggregated' or 'separated property' (1993, 1994). To improve the functionality of the land markets, it is necessary that at the same selling point at least two suppliers compete with each other, thus lowering the price and/or bettering the quality in order to sell more goods. Suppliers can move to other selling points where more scarcity could provide higher profit rates, provided that there also at least a second supplier can compete with them. Only the actor who offers the best quality for the lowest price should develop each location. The community should control the quality of the different proposals and decide who earns the right to develop.

To formulate his alternative paradigm, García-Bellido uses the 'dualistic theory', which divides property rights in two, separated rights (García-Bellido, 1993: 186-187):

a) The right to the non-urban use of land, which belongs to the landowner and allows him/her to use the land for the non-urban functions, e.g. agriculture. In case the land becomes rezoned into urban land, the landowner has the obligation to give freedom to the owner of ...

b) The right to the urban use of land. This right can belong to a different person and gives this individual the development rights, i.e. the right to provide the infrastructure, to build on the serviced parcels and to use the buildings.

García-Bellido positions his proposal as a logical and inevitable continuation of the above mentioned historic process of limitation of property rights. He places the dualistic theory as a continuation of the thesis of *ius publicista*, which is opposed to that of *ius privatista*. In the thesis of *ius publicista*, (b) belongs to the public domain, and not to the landowner (García-Bellido, 1993: 182; Parejo, 1991: 19-20). Both sorts of property, (a) and (b), become completely separated. The first belongs to the owner and his successors; the second belongs to the public bodies, which may use it or transfer it to a market party. After the building is finished, both rights come together again and are transmitted together to the successors of the owners. Later, should the building be demolished and ready for redevelopment, both property rights are again separated, and the right to the urban use comes again in public hands, which can decide whether or not to rebuild it, and who can do it. The economic rent generated in each redevelopment ends thus in public hands (García-Bellido, 1993: 186-188). It is clear that this proposal is very similar to the nationalization of development rights, introduced in England and Wales in 1947.

2.2.4.2 The Valencian model: separation of development rights from landownership?

In the early 1990s, the Ministry of Planning of the social-democratic regional government of Valencia – one of the 17 Spanish regions – was willing to tackle stagnation and speculation in development processes, and to improve the capturing of value increase. The aforementioned criticisms influenced this aim, and García-Bellido became directly involved in the preparations for a new planning act. Each Spanish region (or 'autonomous community') has its own planning legislation (Roca Cladera and Burns, 2000). The 1978 Spanish Constitution however reserves to the national government the competence of guaranteeing all Spaniards, regardless of the region in which they live, an equal level of protection of their property rights. Thanks to this constitutional principle, the *essential* contents of property rights became a central government competence. According to the central planning law, building rights belong to these essential contents of property rights. Regional legislation is therefore unable to remove building rights from the landowner, as García-Bellido's first proposal aimed to do. The makers of the 1994 Valencian Planning Act (*Ley Reguladora de la Actividad Urbanística*, LRAU), therefore, did not change the ownership of building rights, but devised an alternative. The alternative consisted of introducing important changes in the land readjustment regulation. The most important change was the revival of the figure of *urbanizing agent*, already introduced in the 1975-6 Planning Act. Public bodies could choose a developer to provide the infrastructure, without this developer necessarily owning the land. However, the 1975-6's novelty did not work, because this agent had no security, either about the acquisition of land for the public infrastructure and facilities, or about the financing of it. The Valencian 1994 Act introduced some changes that made this way of development feasible (for more details about the 1975-76's and 1994's innovations, see section 5.2.2).

An important question must be answered: does the Valencia system separate development rights from landownership? Infrastructure provision is a public task in Spain. Until the passage of the 1956 Land Act, public bodies were active in the implementation of this public task, buying the land and constructing the public infrastructure. In an attempt to make implementation feasible, the 1956 Land Act assigned the duty of infrastructure provision to landowners, with legal certainty about building rights as compensation, but without altering the rule that the ultimate responsibility is public. Consequently, if landowners do not fulfill their duties properly, the municipality can recover its original power of implementing directly, through compulsory land readjustment or through expropriation. According to the 1956 legislation, therefore, failing to fulfill the duty to provide infrastructure could eventually lead to loss of property rights. The Valencian model did not introduce this possibility; it merely made it practically feasible. The model made compulsory land readjustment the default procedure for urban development and reinforced the possibility, which had been introduced in the 1975-6 Act, of appointing an *urbanising agent* – a third party, besides the municipality and the landowners – as the executor.

2.3 Binding rules which influence certainty and flexibility in planning

Introduction

When thinking about the use of binding rules in policy preparation and implementation, one has to think about two important functions. First, binding rules commit the public body that approves them. This public body might become committed to the implementation, e.g. promising the needed investments in public infrastructure and facilities or committing itself to fulfil the needed procedures. Second, binding rules have consequences for the expectations of others about the future development possibilities of land. After all, binding rules regulate the use of land and real estate. The owner or user of land is bound to use the property in the way prescribed by the binding rules. Binding rules delimit development rights or use rights, and once approved they also guarantee these rights.

Additionally to those two functions, we need to distinguish between three characteristics of binding rules that affect the certainty that these rules create about urban development. First, the contents of binding rules, i.e. which commitments and which use possibilities and obligations do they exactly prescribe. Second, the moment of approval of the binding rules, i.e. at what moment in a development process do they create certainty about the commitments and the future development possibilities and obligations. The third characteristic is the possibility of modifying the binding rules, i.e. whether and how the contents of binding rules can be modified. All three characteristics (contents, moment of approval and possibilities of modification) are more or less regulated in planning law. In some countries binding rules can include a wider range of obligations than in others, prescribe an earlier approval than in others, and in the course of the development process public bodies are allowed to modify the binding rules (or the interpretation of them) more easily than in others. When binding rules include much content and are approved early in the process and cannot be easily modified, the certainty is higher than if binding rules include little content and are approved late in the process and can be easily modified.

Not all the parties want certainty at all stages in the project. The public body might want to guarantee beforehand some public goals, but it is also reasonable that a public body might want to keep some flexibility about how it will commit itself, and also about how it will handle a planning application. And commercial actors might prefer that development requirements are known with certainty beforehand, but they might also want to be able to influence the content of a plan during the development process, and to react to changes that arise in the course of time. There are so many uncertainties in the circumstances surrounding a development process that parties might want to be able to react to them flexibly.

We make here a link with a lively debate in planning profession about the needed degree of flexibility in planning: must planning create certainty at early stages of development processes (fix the future) or be flexible (adapt to circumstances)? Here we define flexibility as the room for changes and alterations in the binding rules during the development process. Flexibility was seen as a negative feature in the 1960s planning practice, whereas the planning profession, at least in the Netherlands and the UK today, perceives flexibility as a positive way of coping with the challenges of growing complexity, opportunism, and diversity in cities. The discussion about flexibility contrasts two approaches. On the one hand, planning should be flexible to facilitate a non-linear and multi-layered decision making system. On the other hand, when implementation is too flexible, the public sector loses the controlling power and the private sector influences the urban development in an incremental (i.e. not planned) way. But before entering into this discussion, we first explain the differences in planning traditions regarding flexibility.

2.3.1 Plan-led versus development-led planning systems

There are different traditions in planning related to the moment at which, in development processes, binding rules come legally into force. This difference causes different degrees of certainty. *Grosso modo* there is a distinction between the 'plan-led' tradition, where legally binding land use plans are made before there is contact between public bodies, developers and land owners, and the 'development-led' tradition, in which the negotiations with developers and land owners precede the making of legally binding land use rules. If we define flexibility in planning as the room for changes and alterations in the binding rules during the development process, then the former tradition gives less flexibility than the latter.

The planning literature makes various categorizations of planning systems. Here we use a categorization based on the legal and administrative systems in which planning systems operate, for the distinction between plan-led and development-led planning systems is related to the distinction between the continental and the British system[3] (Nadin & Stead, 2008: 38-40). We complement this with Faludi's analytical distinction between theory A and B (1987), because this distinction connects better to the data gathering possibilities.

'Plan-led' systems are similar to what Faludi defines as proto-planning theory B. 'Development-led' systems, on the other hand, can be compared with Faludi's proto-planning theory A (1987: 185-192; see Figure 3). Development-led systems characterize the British situation, and plan-led, supposedly, planning in most of the other countries. In development-led systems, the public authority decides cases on their merits. The land use plan merely gives an idea of the intentions of the local authority. As Faludi expresses it for theory A, 'Zoning then merely expresses guidelines which the environmental authority gives to itself – for its own convenience so to speak - and from which it is at liberty to depart' (p. 186). Faludi calls this the *indicative theory of zoning*. In plan-led systems, the land use plan is more important. The local authority fixes the desired environmental outcomes in the land-use plan, which becomes legally binding. This statutory fixation of the land-uses occurs at the *plan production moment* (this is the moment in which the first projections are made for development, and it is indicated with the star on the left in Figure 3), while in development-led systems this occurs at, or shortly before, the *development moment* (this is the moment in which local authorities and developers face a specific proposal for development, the star on the right in Figure 3). In other words, in plan-led systems the regulations about the future use possibilities are supposed to become legally binding before intending developers find out whether their intentions conform to the conditions imposed. Once the developer submits a building application, the local authorities check whether it fits into the legally binding land-use plan. If it does not, the application should be rejected. Faludi calls this the *imperative theory of zoning*.

Summarizing, plan-led systems differ from development-led systems in two aspects: (1) there is in plan-led systems always a legally binding land use plan, and (2) this plan acquires legal status at an early stage, at the plan production moment.

---

3 In another approach, planning systems are classified using a wide set of criteria, such as the distribution of powers relevant to planning among levels of government, or the maturity of the system.

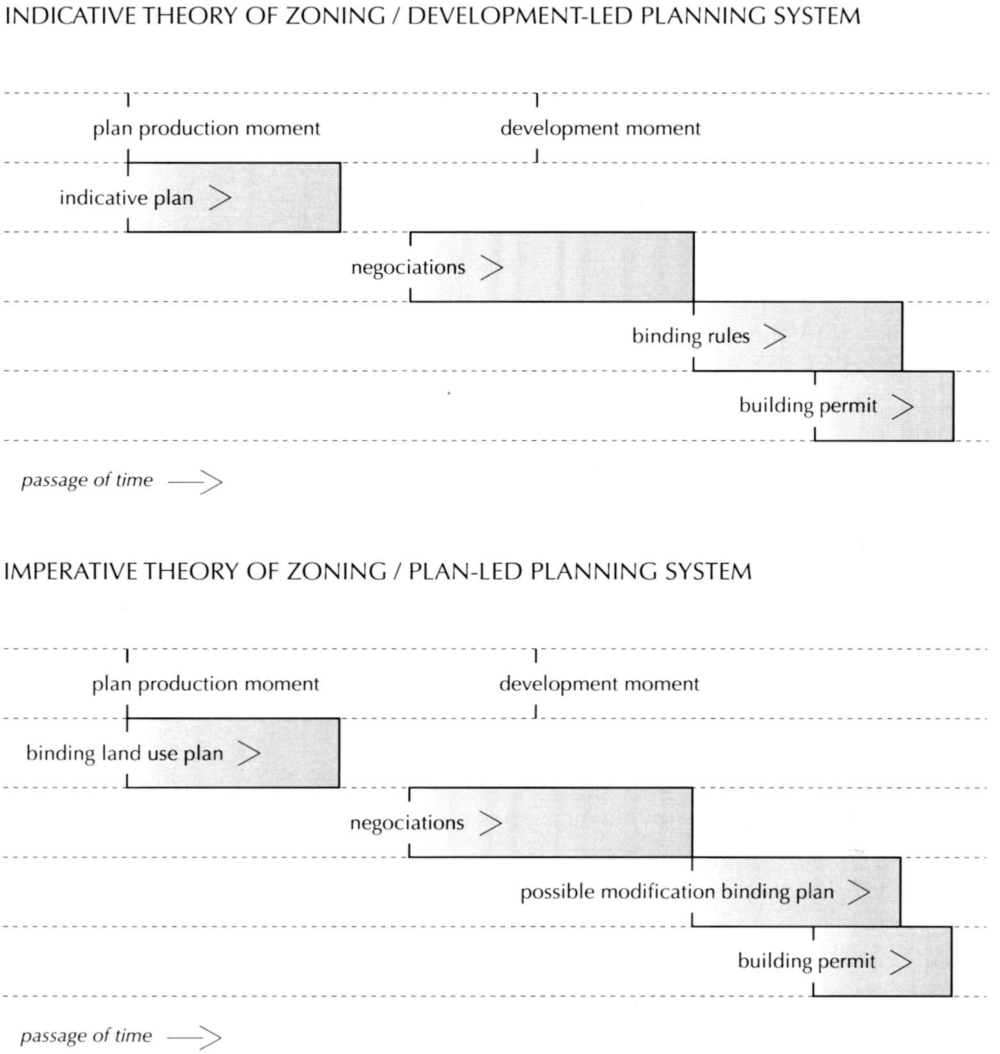

Figure 3. Categorization between Development-led and Plan-led planning systems.

These differences between the British (development-led) and the plan-led system seem to be the consequence of historic differences in the juridical systems. Two long-standing legislative traditions are important for understanding this British peculiarity (Booth, 2003: 4). The first is the heavy reliance on judge-made law in the common law system, where the UK belongs. In common law systems, the judgements of the courts on individual cases have a more central role than in other law systems (Waldron, 1990: quoted in Booth, 2003: 4). The second legislative tradition that underlies the discretionary powers of public bodies in British planning is that of procedural fairness. As Booth states it, 'The power to decide is legitimated, not by reference to regulation carrying the force of law, but by the way in which the decision is taken' (op. cit.: 4).

The rule of law, central in the plan-led planning system, is held in high regard by liberal thinkers. Its origins can be found in the struggle of the bourgeoisie against the arbitrary powers of the king and the administration. In the Middle Ages, law was found, not made, and authority was fragmented. There was no central legislator that could guarantee security and certainty. After the Middle Ages, new states with a centralized and professionalized administration worked gradually towards unification and streamlining of the fragmented law. In the 19th Century, the proponents of the *Rechtstaat* (literally a 'state of rights', but often linked to 'rule of law') pleaded for a state with a constitution, separation of powers, and with individual basic human rights. The notion of 'vertical legal certainty' came to its full development. In this notion, certainty can be found primarily or exclusively in the text of the enacted law. This led to a central role for legislation, administrative authority based exclusively on enacted law, and judicial review of administrative action by independent courts. The translation into the planning system of the principles of the *Rechtstaat* had major consequences. The land-use plans acquired a statutory character, as a piece of legislation that regulates the land-uses at the local level. When considering building applications, the public administration should just check whether or not the application conforms to the zoning map. There should not be any room for discretional considerations (*cfr.* Van Gunsteren, 1976: 81-83; Faludi, 1987: 187).

In short, plan-led systems (like the Dutch one) are supposed to provide at early stages certainty about the future development possibilities. On the other hand, development-led systems (like the British planning system), although there might be some indicative zoning plans in early stages, are supposed to give less certainty about the definite development possibilities.

2.3.2 The arguments for and against certainty and flexibility in planning

There are various reasons why planning practices move between more or less flexibility (Tasan-Kok, 2008). The planning profession has changed, in line with the changes already mentioned in section 2.1 about the role of public bodies in policy networks, from a dominant role to that of *primus inter pares*. Already in the 1970s, John Friedmann drew the attention of scholars by saying that direct control cannot be the role of the planner. However, although he emphasized that planning intervention should be filtered through a series of complex structures and processes (Friedmann, 1973), he still defined the role of the planner as a guiding/controlling one. Precisely 30 years later, he emphasized the shift in planning from an instrument of control to an instrument of innovation and action (Friedmann, 2003). This illustrates the shift in the planning literature, which has implications for flexibility in planning practice as well. What might have happened during those 30 years is that planning practice incorporated greater flexibility and the loosening of rigid rules (Healey and Williams, 1993). This requires however some nuance: the trend in professional and academic debate has not necessarily resulted in practice in more countries extending development-led practices, and it seems to coincide with a contradictory trend in which some development-led countries assume some plan-led practices[4].

There are various arguments for and against more or less flexibility in planning practice. Moroni (2007: 146-7, 153), being critical of the current support for flexibility, claims that continental European planning systems are usually able to guarantee the certainty of the law due to the strict nature of master plan and zoning ordinances, and he suggests that flexible planning systems (such as the British development-led system) are unpredictable and unstable as each case is judged on its merits and cannot be predicted in advance. In the same publication however he advocates that more flexible (abstract, general and end-independent) rules and actions are needed to deal with the complexity of the contemporary urban systems (op. cit.: 156). Needham (2006: quoted in Moroni, 2007) also gives the British system as a case of being too open to the state administration's discretion and not meeting the Rule of Law. On the other hand, he puts certainty in the framework of *predictability* when he emphasizes that public authorities do not want to be bound to the principle of predictability. Instead they want to be able to examine plans informally and if necessary change land-use plans to accommodate to unpredictable planning applications. In such circumstances, certainty can be provided to citizens only if strict rules are followed when the plan is being changed (Needham, 2007b: 186). Thus, plan-makers, especially local governments using public-private partnership instruments, do not want to provide this kind of strict certainty, for they want to leave some room for negotiation or for contingencies that might occur during the process of implementation (Buitelaar et al, 2007). Faludi (1986: 185-192) argues that the assumptions underlying the plan-led system (i.e. planners can predict the nature and quantities of a community's needs and convert this quantification into an allocation and designation of land uses) are invalid. Moreover, the idea that economic and political forces in a community will respond compliantly with these designations and for prescribed uses might be incorrect. At the development moment, the developer may propose something better than what is already in the land-use plan. Or he/she may offer something that the local authority really wants, on condition that the municipality change the land-use plan. Departures from plans are inevitable, all-out commitment to environmental plans (legally binding land-use plans) is unreasonable, and as a consequence, departures from the land-use plan in order to adapt it to the circumstances of each development project are the rule, and not the exception.

4 In a comparative study, the European Commission found a double trend in planning practice: countries operating in rigid plan-led systems tend indeed to incorporate flexibility, but those operating in development-led systems seek to provide greater certainty (1997: 45).

2.3.3 Some financial aspects of certainty in planning

During the data gathering, some additional aspects of the arguments for and against certainty became apparent.

The first aspect derives from the Ricardian rent theory, in which land price is a result of the disposal price of the final real estate products (Ricardo, 1821). Provided that a minimum developer's profit and the development costs are covered, any residual determines the maximum market value of the land. In other words, the price of land in a free market is the residual value. From this it follows: (1) that certainty about building possibilities (i.e. the strong expectation that it is possible to build) affects the residual price of land; and (2) that variations in capturing value increase (i.e. the amount of obligations to be paid in kind or in money to the public bodies) also affect the residual price of the land, but not the final price of the real estate[5]. A second aspect is that certainty or uncertainty might affect the negotiating position of the municipality. If there is much certainty about future building possibilities, municipalities have less discretion and therefore less room to negotiate. On the contrary, if there is much uncertainty about what may be developed, the municipality might be able to ask for more contributions in exchange for creating certainty about building possibilities.

These considerations lead us to the assumption that, when developers have no expectation, or a low expectation, of being able to build, land prices will not rise above the level of existing use value. The book value will remain low, and even if the land is transacted this will be at that low price. When initiating a project, the developer will bring in the land at a value near the market price in the existing use. Or, if the developer must buy the land, he will offer to the landowner a price near to the market price in the existing use. On the contrary, if there is a strong expectation of development, the developer will bring his land in at a higher book value, or will pay a price for the land that reflects the expected profits. In other words, certainty that building will be possible will have an inflationary effect on the price of land. This is relevant for capturing value increase, because high initial land prices narrow the financial room of the developer when asked to contribute to public infrastructure and facilities. Also, certainty about future building possibilities gives the municipality a weaker position in negotiations, which might also be negative for capturing value increase. The municipality cannot negotiate by allowing building possibilities (i.e. modifying the binding rules to allow more profitable building possibilities) in exchange for contributions.

The analysis of the financial aspects of certainty leads us to a second assumption. Namely that when developers are aware in early stages that they are likely to face obligations, they will incorporate them into the finances of the operation. For example,

5 This theory of land rent contravenes the argument that planning requirements of public bodies might be responsible for the raising of the price of land (Ball, 1983; quoted in White, 1986: 104-107).

if the developer already owns the land, he will - when determining the book value of land, other development costs and his profit margin - consider the obligations to be paid. If the developer has not yet bought the land, he can agree with the landowner that the agreed price will be subjected to a deduction for the obligations to be paid. If there is (at the moment at which developers calculate book price, development costs and profit margins, and at the moment when developers agree the price with the landowners) no certainty about the obligations to be paid, developers might make financial calculations that assume maximal profit margins and low obligations. In other words, if local authorities introduce new obligations too late in the process, there might be no financial room anymore in the developer's budget (*confero* Rowan-Robinson & Lloyd, 1988: 128-130; Campbell et al., 2000: 769-771).

Based on these two assumptions, made during data gathering, we differentiate between two sorts of certainty: certainty about the *building possibilities* (how much and what the landowner will be able to build), and certainty about *future contributions* (how much the landowner will have to contribute, in kind or in money).

2.4 Model of the causal relationship between formal rules relevant to zoning and capturing value increase in urban regeneration

Introduction

In section 2.1 we discussed urban regeneration projects and the outcomes concerning the degree of captured value increase as being the result of the interaction between different actors, each of them with different goals and different means to achieve them. We also discussed the basic functioning of these policy networks and the ways of possibly modifying this functioning in order to improve the capturing of value increase. In Sections 2.2 and 2.3 we presented two topical discussions in England and Wales, the Netherlands and Spain about the possibly role of formal rules in improving the capturing of value increase.

Based on these discussions it is possible to develop a model of the inferred causal relationship between certain ways of using the formal rules relevant to zoning and the capturing of value increase in urban regeneration projects. The model not only includes the formal rules relevant to zoning as causality of the degree of captured value increase, but analyses also the wider complex of causalities. It is the intention that this model be applicable not just to urban regeneration in England, Spain and the Netherlands, but also to other countries too. Let us see first which activities and which actors are involved in urban regeneration.

2.4.1 The activities and the actors in urban regeneration

2.4.1.1 The activities

As already explained in section 1.5, this research focuses on comprehensive urban regeneration projects located on privately owned land. We mean here physical interventions in the existing city that have the following characteristics:

- They produce a notable value increase due to the rezoning of the land and to the dimensions of the development area. The value increase derives from the returns that will accrue from selling the final real estate.
- They require the making of important costs for public infrastructure and facilities, costs that cannot be recovered by selling or managing that infrastructure or those facilities.
- We study only those comprehensive urban regeneration projects that are situated on privately owned land.

Within these projects, we focus on the development phase. The 'development phase' starts from the original situation and ends at the delivery and the beginning of the exploitation of the final real estate products. Within this phase, this research focuses on a specific phenomenon: the interaction between public bodies making use of their competences regarding the formal rules relevant to zoning, and the developers/landowners who redevelop the site. The capturing of value increase is one of the results of this interaction.

2.4.1.2 The actors

To identify the involved actors, we use a combination of two techniques. First is the 'imperative' approach, which asks who has an interest in or feels the consequences of the problem. The second is the 'positional' approach, which identifies those actors who have a formal position in actual policy making (Mitroff, 1983: 33-34). Table 3 summarizes the interests and formal position of the involved actors. This research assumes that actors pursue their interests rationally within the context of their interactions.

Starting with the imperative approach, we identify first the problem-owner (the actor that has a direct interest and that serves as starting point of this research). The problem-owner is that public body (possibly more than one) that wants to implement its planning policies (see section 1.2). In order to do that, it might have to subsidize urban regeneration in order to achieve the desired quality of the regenerated areas. Although not a problem-owner in that sense, property developers and landowners also have a direct interest: they have a financial interest in the regeneration of the site, namely profit maximization in the short or long term. However, when considering that profit maximization is also related to the quality of the regenerated areas, they could also be considered as problem-owners similar to the public body because problems with the financing of public infrastructure and facilities can affect the quality in a negative way. Other directly interested actors are the actual users and inhabitants of the deteriorated areas that are the subject of regeneration: they are mostly interested in receiving high compensation for any loss suffered. The future inhabitants, i.e. people who stay in the regenerated area, or new ones, also have a direct interest because they will use the regenerated urban areas. The interest of the future inhabitants is similar to that of civic organizations, who are mainly committed to the physical, social and/or environmental quality of urban regeneration.

Within the public bodies it is possible to distinguish municipalities on the one side and the ministry of planning of the central government on the other. In Spain and the Netherlands there are in addition regional, respectively provincial, public bodies that play a relevant role. Besides having a direct interest (always related to the implementation of their planning policies, and in the Netherlands also because often they subsidize), these public bodies have also a regulatory role (they are empowered to elaborate the formal regulations that rule the regeneration). There might be other national public bodies with some financial or political involvement, for example the ministries of Infrastructure, Finance and Economic Affairs, but usually they have few or no regulatory responsibilities.

Table 3. Involved actors, their interests and status in decision-making in urban regeneration

Actor	Interest
Public bodies	
- Municipalities	Fewer subsidies; High quality regenerated areas (enough public infrastructure and facilities)
- Possibly Provincial/Regional government	
- Ministry of Planning	
- Other ministries, e.g. Infrastructure, Finance and Economic Affairs	idem
Civic society	
- Current users/inhabitants	High compensations
- Future users/inhabitants	High quality regenerated areas
- Civic organizations	High quality regenerated areas
Developers	
- Without land	Profit maximizing
- With land	Profit maximizing
Landowners	
- Large companies (see also developers with land)	Profit maximizing
- Small owners	Profit maximizing

Hatched: actors that have a final formal responsibility
Transparent: actors without a final formal responsibility.

Within the developers it is possible to distinguish between those that have not yet bought land within the development site and those that have already bought part or all the land. Within the original landowners there are two sorts: large companies owning land in regeneration sites (e.g. old firms, energy and railway companies), and individual owners-users. Large companies with land can sometimes be regarded as developers with land, because such companies often have a development department (e.g. public utility companies such as electricity and railway companies often have such a department). Housing associations and other social housing landlords are often involved in urban regeneration because they often own land in those locations: they can also be considered as developers if they have a development department.

Of all these actors, the only ones with a final formal responsibility (the positional approach) are:
- Public bodies at the central level: the ministry or department of planning (responsible for policy, planning law and for circulars and directives);
- Public bodies at the regional level: the Dutch provinces (responsible for regional policy and the application of planning law), and in Spain the regional ministry of planning (responsible for policy, planning law and for circulars and directives);
- Public bodies at the local level: the municipalities or 'local planning authorities' in England (responsible for the local policy and the application of planning law);
- The property developers (they have knowledge and financial means);
- The landowners (they control the land).

The other parties have an advisory role (see table 3).

2.4.2 Causalities of the amount of value increase finally captured

It is a necessary condition of being able to capture value increase that there is some value to be captured, that is, that there is an initial profit (or the potential profit) from the urban regeneration project. 'Initial profit' means that the economic value of the site clearly increases due to the regeneration. If there is, then some of this can – in principle – be captured by public bodies. However, whether this initial profit translates into a 'final profit' for the developer that allows him to contribute depends on the interaction of several variables. We need thus to make a distinction between the variables that influence the *size* of the initial profit, and variables that influence the *distribution* of that initial profit and result in the final profit. If for example an initial positive profit finally ends in excessive high prices paid for the development land, or ends in inflated development costs, the final profit for the developer might be negative. For both sort of variables, some of them are determined outside the urban regeneration project (they are context variables) and some are determined inside the project, either by the physical conditions within the site or by the actions of the various actors in interaction with each other.

We can identify thus four sets of variables:

A. Context variables that influence the size of the initial profit;
B. Context variables that influence the distribution of the initial profit, i.e. **the formal rules relevant to zoning**;
C. Actions of those directly involved in the project, **including those with formal powers**, which influence the size of the initial profit;
D. Actions of those directly involved in the project, **including those with formal powers,** which influence the distribution of the initial profit.

Together, those variables determine the value increase that is finally captured for the benefit of the public infrastructure and facilities in the regeneration project.

Some of the variables under B, C, and D – namely those in bold print – can be deliberately manipulated by public bodies in order to influence the captured value increase. But all variables need to be taken into account when explaining a particular case. Some variables influence the final degree of captured value increase more directly than others. When the causal link goes through other variables, we speak here of 'intermediary variables'. We will now discuss each of those sets of variables separately. Figure 4 gives an overview of all variables, and section 2.4.3 illustrates them with one of the studied cases.

2.4.2.1 Context variables that influence the size of the initial profit (variables A)

A1) Real estate markets

The price of real estate is fundamental for determining the returns and costs:

- Returns: the prices of the final offices, dwellings and other commercial real estate are one of the, if not the most, relevant factor.
- Costs: high prices for the finished product (the buildings) stimulate higher prices for acquiring the land and existing properties, as owners tend to ask for their property the residual value of the land after redevelopment, which is the final value of the real estate minus the costs of capital, workforce, building materials and knowledge. The price of the land and existing properties can thus be much higher than the minimum land price, which is the residual value of the land taking into account *only the previous use possibilities*. Thus the accounted cost of the land, i.e. the price of the land that is regarded as one of the costs of the development (*inbrengwaarde* in Dutch), can be much higher than the minimum land cost. The accounted land costs are often one of the largest costs of redeveloping a site. This is one of the main ways in which the initial profit 'leaks out', i.e. in which the initial profit is not available anymore to pay the public infrastructure and facilities. However, this difference between the 'minimum' and the 'accounted' land costs is actually not only caused by the context variable 'Real estate markets', but also by the context variables A2, B1 and B2 and the actions of those involved in the project (variables D1.1, D2.1, and probably also D4 and D5) that influence the distribution of the initial profit (see under).

A2) Plan and site features

Another relevant variable is the type, quality and quantity of the land and the previous public infrastructure and buildings that must be removed or refurbished in the regeneration site. This will have a direct effect on costs of the project (the minimum costs of acquisition of the properties, demolition of the previous buildings). The presence and type of soil contamination has a direct effect too on the costs of the project. The location of the site within the urban fabric will affect the development potential of the site (e.g. offices with a high or low rental value) and thus the possible returns from the development.

A3) Markets of workforce and building materials, and fiscal regimes

The price of hiring skilled people to draft plans, studies, buildings and infrastructure, and to build them, is fundamental for the costs. Labour costs can differ from year to year, from region to region, from country to country. Also, the price of building materials might change with time and differ between regions and countries. Finally, differences in fiscal regimes can augment or diminish these costs, or the amount of taxes to be paid, e.g. profit tax, land transfer tax, etc.

2.4.2.2 Context variables that influence the distribution of the initial profit, i.e. the formal rules relevant to zoning (variables B)

These are the more stable (structural) factors that facilitate or impede certain types of power relationships between the involved actors and thus their ability to take possession of a share of the initial profit. They form the independent variable 'formal rules relevant to zoning', on which this research focuses (see chapter 3). In section 2.1.1 and Figure 2 we already introduced these structural factors: they are the rules that influence the resource distribution and the behaviour of the actors involved in urban regeneration projects. In other words, these structural factors, together with the context variables A, influence the actions of those directly involved in the project (variables C and D).

B1) Formal rules about property rights

We have seen earlier in section 2.2 how property rights in land have become weaker, from the almost unrestrained interpretation of the new liberal regimes in the 18th and the 19th Centuries to the increasing limitations based on the concept of the social function of property and other (e.g. sanitary) considerations. However, the landowner still retains the control over the *quando*, i.e. when to use or build on his property. Since the landowner can exclude others not only from deciding when to use or build on his property, but also from actually using or building on it, he acquires a privileged position in the urban markets: he is the only one who can provide land, and the only one who decides when. This power has major consequences for the capturing of value increase because it influences decisively the behaviour of the involved actors (see variable D2). This variable 'property rights' embraces formal rules under public law that might limit property rights, as e.g. the possibility of expropriating land or of obliging landowners to participate in land readjustment.

B2) Formal rules about certainty and flexibility in the development terms
We have seen earlier in section 2.3 that certainty or the lack of certainty beforehand about the definitive development terms can have major consequences for capturing value increase. This is because certainty influences greatly the behaviour of the involved actors (see variable D1). The variable 'certainty' embraces e.g. those regulations under public law that limit the costs that can be recovered from the property developers and landowners, because these legal limits determine the possible contents of binding rules and other plan documents. Also included in this variable is whether local public bodies can prescribe not only the physical zoning, but also aspects related to the financing and implementation of public infrastructure and facilities. Do binding rules regulate only a desired final picture without stating who is responsible for its implementation, or also the obligations that must be fulfilled by the developer? How far can binding rules go in enumerating obligations? Can they include off-site infrastructure? Social housing? Also, the variable 'certainty' embraces those regulations under public law concerning whether public bodies can condition the approval of legally binding plans to the developer securing his contributions to the public infrastructure and facilities. The approval of binding rules containing financing and implementation schedules about developers' contributions does not automatically mean that developers are committed to implement them. Additionally, there is the need of a contractual commitment of the developer.

B3) Formal rules about the procedure of making land-use plans and granting planning permissions
Planning law might include some guarantees for the handling of development applications, and there are differences between countries in the sort of guarantees and how hard they might be in practice. Also, there are differences in how long and easy the procedures are for modifying binding rules. And finally, there are also differences in the possibility of approving binding rules gradually, plot by plot. We include these variables because they might influence the behaviour of the involved actors (see variable D3) and thus be of importance for the capturing of value increase.

2.4.2.3 Actions of those directly involved in the project, including those with formal powers, which influence the size of the initial profit (variable C)

C1) Definition of the contents and geographical scope of the plan
At the start of a project, the involved actors must define the contents of the plan and the boundaries of the development site. The contents of the plan can be relevant for the possibility of capturing value increase. For example, depending on how many buildings the plan includes, the returns can be higher or lower. Also, it is relevant for the costs how much quality and quantity public bodies pursue for the public infrastructure and facilities, or for the architecture etc., and how high are the contributions that public bodies expect from landowners and developers. More quantity and quality might imply higher costs. The cases show a struggle here between at one side

the public bodies, which pursue a large contribution from landowners and developers, and at the other side the landowners and developers, which pursue large public subsidization. Large contributions might lower the accounted price of the land and/ or narrow the final profit of the developer. But at the same time large contributions relieve the municipality's budget and/or allow more quality and quantity of public infrastructure and facilities. And *vice versa*. Also, the boundary chosen for the plan area (or geographical scope) of the development site might be relevant, for example whether it excludes or includes the most profitable or unprofitable parts. The definition of the plan contents and geographical scope is thus one of the most important steps in urban development because it influences both the returns and the costs.

2.4.2.4 Actions by those directly involved in the project, including those with formal powers, which influence the distribution of the initial profit (variables D)

D1) How the local public bodies use their formal powers about certainty in the development terms

The actions of local public bodies making use of their formal powers about certainty on development terms can influence the capturing of value increase. These actions do not influence the capturing of value increase in a direct way, but through other variables, or 'intermediary variables'. That is, the use of these formal powers influences intermediary variables, which in turn influence the final degree of captured value increase.

D1.1) Accounted price of land and regular profit margins

On the one hand, if the local public body creates certainty beforehand about *future building possibilities*, this has an influence on the accounted land costs because the landowner, thanks to his monopolistic-oligopolistic position, is able to successfully ask a price for his land that internalizes the maximal possible price in the future. Thus he anticipates the future building possibilities by asking the price that would be economically reasonable in that future. On the other hand, if the local public body creates certainty beforehand *about which contributions the developer has to deliver*, this can also influence the accounted land costs, but inversely. When the developer knows how much these contributions will cost him, he will internalize them into the price of land in different ways. In case the developer has not yet bought the land, he will internalize the contributions into the price to be paid to the landowner. In case the developer has already bought the land, he will internalize the contributions into the accounted land cost or into the regular profit margin[6] he will aim for in the operation. Accounted land costs and regular profit margins are often not defined at the start of development processes. At that time, developers can often set them higher

6 We are talking here about the 'normal' or regular profit margin, i.e. the profit margin that the developer charges as a kind of normal fee to each operation. This is different than the 'final profit', which is additional to this regular profit margin.

or lower. For example, developers often enter all the land for different development sites in a common account. Losses and profits are compensated with each other. A developer confronted with a high contributions package will tend to account the land for a lower price and accept that this development site will not contribute much to the losses in other sites. Conversely, a developer confronted with a low contributions package will tend to account the land for a higher price. Regarding regular profit margins, developers can consider at the beginning of development processes the size of the profit, which may vary[7]. Once the accounted land costs and the regular profit margin have been established, lowering them is usually complicated. Both are important 'channels' through which the initial profit can leak out, leaving less money over to contribute to the public infrastructure and facilities.

D1.2) Negotiation position

If before the start of the negotiations the local public body has already created certainty *about future building possibilities*, this public body has lost a powerful negotiation tool. It cannot offer anymore the building possibilities (i.e. to approve new binding rules or modify the existing ones to allow more building possibilities) as a medium of exchange. On the other hand, if the local public body has already created certainty about which contributions the developer has to deliver, his negotiation position will be better as these requirements become the starting point of discussion. Finally, if the public body openly makes the approval of legally binding plans conditional on the developer securing his contributions to the public infrastructure and facilities, its position will be stronger than if it does not.

D2) How owners use their property rights

The actions of private bodies using their property rights can influence the capturing of value increase. This influence takes place through other variables, or 'intermediary variables'. Property rights influence these intermediary variables, which in turn influence the final degree of captured value increase.

D2.1) Accounted price of land and inflated development costs

Since the control of land gives a monopolistic-oligopolistic position, there arises competition to acquire the right to control the land. The stimulant for actors to compete for the land is that once acquired, there is no more need to compete. The initial landowners make a profitable use of this situation. They are in a privileged position compared with the providers of the other production factors (capital, workforce, building materials and knowledge), thus they are in an ideal negotiating position that allows them to ask the maximum possible price for their right to control the land. The consequence is that the price of land in a free market tends to absorb all the profit: it tends to be the residual value of the land after redevelopment, which is the final value of the real estate minus the costs of capital, workforce, building materials and knowledge. In sum, the privileged position of landowners stimulates the inflation of land

7 E.g. in the Netherlands the regular profit margin can differ from roughly 20% to 5%.

prices from their minimum to their maximum value. This causes high accounted land costs (i.e. the price at which the land is 'bought in' to the accounts of the project), which reduce the initial profit.

Those owning land can also use their property rights to delay regeneration, which in turn can have an inflationary effect on development costs. Delay might be larger when ownership is very dispersed because it might be more difficult to assemble all the needed land. However, it can also be that land is in hands of just one powerful actor, who can afford to delay more than a multitude of small landowners can. See below for how owners using their property rights can cause delay. Delay inflates development costs in different ways: first because delay might imply more studies, negotiations, reports, meetings, of public officers but also of developers; second because delay implies uncertainties and risks, which can translate into higher reserves for unforeseen expenses; third, delay might imply higher costs to finance investments that cannot be delayed, while the selling of the final real estate products might last longer. High development costs, together with high accounted land costs, jeopardize the initial profit and leave less money over to pay the public infrastructure and facilities. This leads to higher public subsidizing and/or to lower quality and quantity of the public infrastructure and facilities.

D2.2) Negotiation position and delay

Since landowners do not feel threatened by other providers of land, they have a powerful negotiation tool. They can wait, without this necessarily damaging their future negotiation position, as they will retain their monopolistic-oligopolistic position. The consequence is that delaying development processes becomes a real alternative in the negotiation strategy of landowners. But why would landowners delay? Because waiting to develop can be more profitable, as land also has an option value (Turnbull, 2005). If the landowner expects that the price of land could increase in the future, and he is not in a hurry, it is economically rational to wait. For example, he might expect that the local public body will finally lower the requirements, or that with time the price of land will increase. It is very common that landowners profit from delay, as land prices often increase (at least during the period of data gathering in this research). Waiting might be therefore a favourable option (Quigg, 1993; Capozza and Li, 2002; Ball, 2003: 909).

Note that in this discussion about how landowners might use their property rights in a particular regeneration project, we are assuming that it is private bodies that own the land, or at least that the landowners seek economic profit when using their property rights. Public bodies owning land might choose to act in the same way as private landowners do, or not. We are ignoring the possibility of a public body owning land, so the possibility that a public body acts as private landowners is not relevant here.

D3) How the local public bodies use their formal powers for the procedure of approval of land use plans and planning permissions

We might expect that differences in the flexibility of the procedures can have an effect on regeneration projects. For example, if the local public body can approve the binding rules gradually, in case negotiations with the developers/landowners of a plan area do not finish all at the same time and there are still disagreements with some of them, the local public body would be able to approve first the binding rules for the plots where the agreements were already concluded, and wait until the other owners/developers agree. However, the relation between this variable with the final degree of captured value increase is not clear.

D4) How local public and private bodies interact informally

Informal rules, or what Ostrom called 'working rules' (1986: 466-467; see also Verhage, 2002: 160), might govern the behaviour of actors, and thus influence many of the variables, and thereby influence in a direct way the capturing of value increase. For example, the special relationship between housing associations and municipalities in the Netherlands largely influences the willingness of the associations to assume the costs of public facilities. The same could be said about a possibly special relationship between a specific developer and a specific municipality. Another example in the Netherlands is that local public bodies prefer to reach consensus about urban development with all the relevant involved parties. This might be partially a cultural factor, i.e. the importance of consensus in Dutch local decision-making. However, this might be also the consequence of the above-mentioned limited possibilities of local public bodies to oblige landowners to cooperate. In other words, the preference of local public to achieve an agreement with the landowners might be the consequence of how landowners use their property rights, and not (or not exclusively) an ideological preference.

D5) Specific circumstances

There might be specific circumstances of the persons involved, or of any other kind, that can directly influence the final degree of captured value increase. For example the negotiation abilities of the involved public officers or developers, or specific unforeseen technical problems. Another example, possibly relevant for the tempo of implementation of realising the public goals, is whether or not public bodies use their powers to force developers to provide on time the public infrastructure and facilities. Nothing can be said in general about these specific circumstances, but when analysing a specific case we should be aware that they might be present.

2.4.2.4 How the intermediary variables influence capturing value increase

The discussion above has been summarised in Figure 4. We have distinguished between four sets of variables (A, B, C, D) which in one way or another can affect the capturing of value increase. However, they do not usually do that directly but by influencing certain intermediary variables.

Variables *real estate markets* (A1), *plan and site features* (A2), *markets of workforce and building materials, and fiscal regimes* (A3) and *definition contents and geographical scope plan* (C1) shape together the intermediary variable *initial profit*. Variables *public bodies using power certainty* (D1) and *owners using property rights* (D2) shape together intermediary variables *accounted land costs, regular profit margins, inflated development costs, negotiation position* and *delay*. The intermediary variable *initial profit*, together with intermediary variables *accounted land costs, regular profit margins* and *inflated development costs* (which in their turn are influenced by intermediary variable *delay*) shape together the intermediary variable *final profit*. The final profit is crucial for the final degree of captured value increase because it determines the financial room that the developer has for contributing to public infrastructure and facilities. For example, if the developer who is negotiating with the municipality has paid too much for the land and existing properties, or has already internalized a high land price or regular profit margin into the accounts of the operation, or has already made too high development costs, whereby the returns are not large enough, he will not be able and/or willing to contribute much, and *vice versa*.

Regarding the intermediary variables *negotiation position* and *delay*, those are relevant for intermediary variables *accounted land costs* and *regular profit margins*. If landowners do not face disadvantages from waiting, they might use this as a negotiation tool and wait until the municipality lowers the requirements. If municipalities prescribe the building possibilities before negotiations start, landowners are already sure about the potential residual value of land and developers about the potential profit margins. Assuming that the residual value is indeed higher than the previous value, landowners can thus sell their land for a price higher than its minimum value, and/or developers can enlarge their regular profit margin, without necessarily having to agree with the municipality. In short, the municipality has less to offer to the landowners and developers, and is thus in a weak position to require contributions. Regarding the intermediary variable *delay*, this is also relevant for intermediary variable *inflated development costs*, as delay can have an inflationary effect on the costs of developing the site. In addition, *delay* is indirectly negative for capturing value increase because it implies delay in the realisation of the public infrastructure and facilities. That is the reason that in the formulation of the research questions of this research (see section 1.5) it was decided to include delay as one of the aspects to be taken into account when measuring de degree of captured value increase.

In sum, there are different ways that can lead to the size of the initial profit, to some or all of this profit leaking away, and thus to the size of the final profit. The consequence of the initial profit leaking away is that public bodies might be forced to subsidise more, or to accept fewer and worse public infrastructure and facilities.

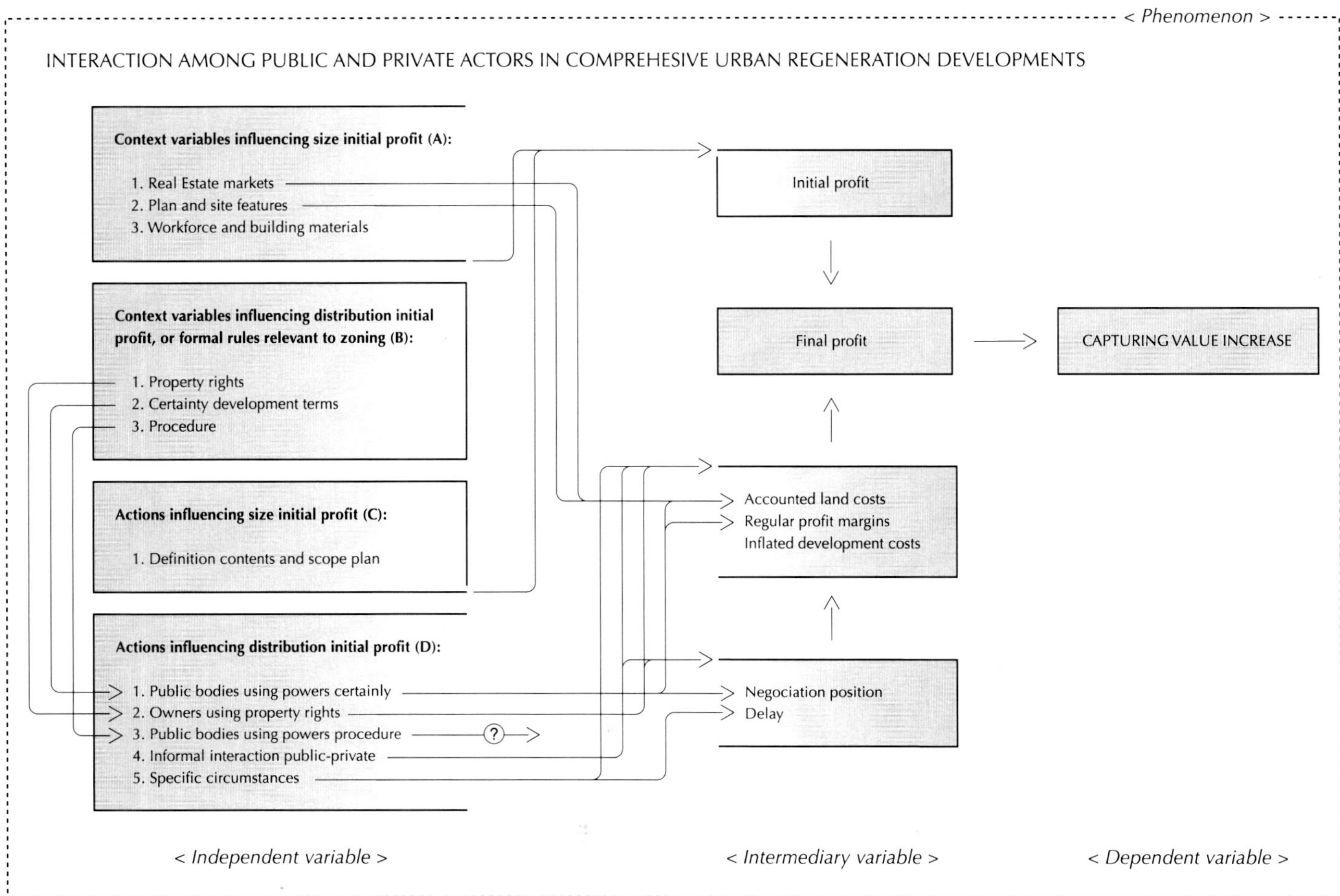

Figure 4. Illustration of the modelled causalities that explain the influence of third variables and formal rules relevant to zoning on capturing value increase directly but mostly through several intermediary variables.

2.4.3 Financial analysis of the cases

In the previous section 2.4.2 it has been made clear that although there might be an initial profit that would allow contributing to public infrastructure and facilities, in the course of development processes this initial profit might be distributed in such a way that finally there is no money left. The money might have 'leaked out' to inflated land prices or just to high regular and/or final profit margins of the developer. It might also be that the initial profit disappeared before the developer could gain from it, so he cannot contribute. As De Greef put it, in this way the whole development process can be regarded as a struggle between the various actors to gain more of the increased value (1997). In addition, we have also seen that as a result of this struggle, land development costs might increase more than is necessary, diminishing even more the initial profit from which public infrastructure and facilities can be paid.

In sections 5.5, 6.4 and 7.4 it is explained, for respectively the region of Valencia, England and the Netherlands, how all the mentioned variables shape the final degree of captured value increase. The financial information about the studied cases, as far as available, has been analyzed. This financial analysis uses partially the model developed by Verhage & Needham (2003: 25-28). The following sections give an example of a financial analysis of how the initial profit has leaked away to the involved actors in the Dutch case *Kop van Oost*[8]. For a financial analysis of the other cases, see Annexes 3, 4 and 7.

2.4.3.1 Definition of costs and returns

First we distinguish the following costs and returns:

LAND COSTS

1. **1a. Minimum land costs:** the market value of the land in its current use; **1b. Accounted land costs:** the land price that the developer includes into the calculations[9].

DEVELOPMENT COSTS

2. **On-site infrastructure provision costs:** this includes not only the on-site infrastructure provision works, but also reserved amounts for unexpected expenses, the overhead costs, possible 'hidden' profit margins of the developer, etc. In the

8 The site in the Dutch case 'Kop van Oost' (5 ha, Groningen) was no longer in use, and 60% of the land was owned by the former user, a wood-processing company. In 2000 intermediary Hollestelle bought the land. After general development terms with the municipality had been negotiated, the land has been re-sold twice to commercial developers: in 2001 to IBC and in 2002 to Heijmans. Negotiations with Heijmans crystallised in 2005 in a Development Agreement. The plan was definitively approved in 2006, including 430 dwellings, most of them apartments, and about 4,000 m^2 commercial space. In October 2007 infrastructure provision was ongoing. For more detailed information see sections 7.3.3 and 7.4.

9 This is similar to the accounting term 'book value'.

Netherlands they comprise: *Slopen, bouw en woonrijp maken, risico en onvoorzien*. It should also include the financing costs (interest payments etc.).

3. **Plan preparation costs:** the costs of the preparation of plans, studies, etc (*Plankosten*, or *Voorbereiding, toezicht en planontwikkeling*).
4. **Soil decontamination costs.**
5. **Compensation costs:** this includes compensation to existing owners and inhabitants, for removal of activities and residence, demolition of constructions and buildings, etc.
6. **Additional contributions of the developer:** contributions of the developer, in cash (payments) or in kind (construction or building of public infrastructure and facilities) to public goals **additional** to his contributions to the on-site infrastructure provision costs (even if these might serve a wider area than the development in question), which are already included in (2).
7. **Real Estate development costs:** this includes the whole development of the real estate, thus not only the building costs, but also the preparation of plans (not for providing the infrastructure but for the building), overhead costs, possible 'hidden' profit margins of the developer, etc.

DEVELOPMENT RETURNS

8. **Total returns:** the total returns accruing from the selling of the real estate (offices, dwellings, etc).

2.4.3.2 Definition of the Initial and the Final profits

INITIAL PROFIT

The value increase that accrued from the regeneration of the site and could have been initially available to pay public infrastructure and facilities:
$8 - [\ (1a + 2 + 3 + 4 + 5 + 6 + 7)^{\text{not-inflated}}$ – (those costs of 2-7 subsidised by public bodies)]

Here we assume costs 1 till 7 are not inflated.

FINAL PROFIT

The profits of the final developer:
$8 - [\ (1b + 2 + 3 + 4 + 5 + 6 + 7)$ – (those costs of 2-7 subsidised by public bodies)]

To this final profit must be added the regular profit margin in case the final developer had included such in posting 7.

2.4.3.3 Financial analysis in case Kop van Oost

Let us first see in Table 4 the costs and returns in this case:

Table 4. Costs and returns of Dutch case Kop van Oost

LAND COSTS	
1) Land costs	**1a. Minimum land costs: € 3.6m** At the time of data gathering (2008), the market price for the actual land use before regeneration (industrial land) in this part of the city was about € 60-70/ m^2, and the best locations had a price of about € 80-90/m^2. The developer had to buy about 4 ha. Thus, the market value of this industrial land in current use, i.e. the minimum land cost, could not be more than: 40,000 m^2 X € 90 = € 3,600,000. **1b. Accounted land costs: at least € 12m** € 12m is the price paid by developer IBC to intermediary Hollestelle in 2001. Because the last developer Heijmans bought the land in 2002 (as part of IBC), the price paid by Heijmans was probably higher.
DEVELOPMENT COSTS	
2) Infrastructure provision costs	**Ca. € 7m (€ 1.9 m if not inflated, paid by the developer) + public subsidies for infrastructure surrounding the new building (an unknown amount to us)** This € 7m is €368/m^2 new public space[10] (19,000 m^2, 24% total plan area of the Land use Plan); or €148/m^2 total redeveloped land (47,200 m^2, 59% total plan area of the Land use Plan). Most probably, these costs include the financial costs of the investments. € 7m is much larger than the equivalent costs in the region of Valencia, which are of about €100/m^2 new public space and would have resulted in € 1.9 million if translated to *Kop van Oost*, that is € 5.1 million lower. The contrast with the region of Valencia is even larger taking into account that the figures in Valencia include the costs of the infrastructure between and in the wide surroundings of the new buildings. On the contrary, in *Kop van Oost* this € 7m includes almost only that public infrastructure situated between the new buildings, or in the inmediate surrounding (the footpaths). The municipality had to subsidise heavily the wider infrastructure surrounding the new buildings, that is the refurbishing of the Sontweg and the Europaweg, the reparation of the quay along the canal (about € 0.6m), and about 4,000 m^2 of new public space. Most of these works (except the Sontweg) benefit exclusively, or mostly, the new buildings. The works on the Sontweg also benefit other areas.
3) Plan preparation costs	
4) Soil decontamination costs	**€ 0.375 m paid by the developer, and € 0.125 m public subsidy of the central Dutch government.**
5) Compensation costs	**€ 162,500,- paid by the developer** Removal petrol station.
6) Additional contributions of the developer	**None**
7) Real estate development costs	**Ca. € 90m, paid by the developer** €90m is an estimation given by the final developer, Heijmans.
DEVELOPMENT RETURNS	
8) Total returns	**Ca. € 112m or ca. € 139m** The developer Heijmans estimated the total revenues for the selling of the real estate to be € 112m, inclusive VAT. Own estimations, based on the actual selling prices of real estate, produce higher figures, between € 139m and € 189m. Consulted about this, experts assessed the first estimation (€ 139m) as more realistic (Stauttener & Van Bladel, interview 2008).

10 New public space is the surface that becomes redeveloped and will be used for public uses. Most of land development costs relate to the construction of public infrastructure and facilities above or under this surface.

How large was the Initial profit?

The initial profit in *Kop van Oost* was, according to the above formula 8 – [(1a + 2 + 3 + 4 + 5 + 6 + 7)$^{\text{not-inflated}}$ – (those costs of 2-7 subsidised by public bodies)]:

- With the minimum returns (€ 112m) and assuming that costs 1 to 5 *are not* inflated and follow the average costs in Valencia, this is 112 – [(3,6 + 1.9 + subsidies municipality for infrastructure surrounding new buildings and of central + 0.5 + 0.1625 + 0 + 90) – (subsidies municipality + 0.125)] = 112 – [(96.1625 + subsidies municipality) – (subsidies municipality + 0.125)] = € 15.9625 million.
- With the maximum returns (€ 139) and assuming that costs 1 to 5 *are not* inflated and follow the average in Valencia, this is 139 – [(3,6 + 1.9 + subsidies municipality for infrastructure surrounding new buildings + 0.5 + 0.1625 + 0 + 90) –(subsidies municipality + 0.125)] = 139 – [(96.1625 + subsidies municipality) – (subsidies municipality + 0.125)] = € 42.9625 million.

In this calculation, the Initial profit excludes those necessary investments made by the developer in public infrastructure and facilities. This was most of costs 2-3 (€ 1.9m), of cost 4 (€ 0.375m) and of cost 5 (€ 162,500,-), in total € 2.4375m. Most of these € 2.4375m could be considered as necessary for the realisation of what this research defines as public infrastructure and facilities (see section 1). If the calculations were to include these investments in public infrastructure and facilities, the Initial profit would have been:

- € 15.9625m + € 2.4375m = € 18.5 million;
- € 42.9625m + € 2.4375m = € 45.4 million.

In other words, of this larger Initial profit, the developer has spent (assuming that costs 1 to 5 *are not* inflated) € 2.4375m in necessary investments in public infrastructure and facilities. The rest of the Initial Profit has not been spent on public infrastructure and facilities, at least not on necessary investments.

What has leaked out of the Initial profit?

We conclude that in case *Kop van Oost* the Initial profit was large but most of it has leaked away. This leaked money (i.e. € 15.9625 to € 42.9625 million) has not been spent on investments necessary for the public infrastructure and facilities. Clearly, the subsidies of the municipality (an unknown amount for us) and the central government (€ 0.125 million) would have not been necessary if a larger part of the Initial profit had not leaked away.

Where has the leaked Initial profit gone?

The leaked Initial profit has been consecutively been collected by the following private parties:

- Inflated land costs: Accounted land costs – Minimum land costs = € 8.4 million + extra paid by Heijmans to IBC for land (price last land transaction - € 12 m). The land was subjected to several resellings for a much higher price than the price of the use possibilities before regeneration, so the first owner, the intermediary Hollestelle and first developer IBC have collected each a share of this leaked Initial profit. Let us see this more in detail:

- The wood-processing company who initially owned the land: it appropriated a sum equal to the amount paid by intermediary Hollestelle (unknown to us) minus the minimum land costs (€ 3.6m), minus its development costs (its capital costs, probably not existing, as the company owned the land for a while, plus the costs of selling the land);
- Intermediary Hollestelle who bought the land in 2000: he appropriated a sum equal to the amount paid to him in 2001 by developer IBC (€ 12m), minus the price he paid to the wood-processing company (unknown to us), minus his development costs (his capital costs, probably small as he had an option to buy the land that allowed him to delay the payment of at least most of the price, plus the costs of negotiating with the municipality, plus the costs of selling the land);
- Developer IBC, who bought the land in 2001: it appropriated a sum equal to the amount paid in 2002 by developer Heijmans (unknown to us), minus the price it paid to Hollestelle (€ 12m), minus its development costs (its capital costs, plus the costs it could have made in preparing plans and negotiating with the municipality, plus the costs of selling the land);

- Inflated land development costs: € 5.1 million
  Development costs 2 and 3 might be inflated because of the delay in the development process and the risks involved. This money has gone to all those four private parties involved in the regeneration process. This money went to costs that might have been avoided in the Spanish region of Valencia. It could also be that developer Heijmans has hidden here high regular profit margins.

- Final profit of the last developer:
  The Final profit of the last developer (Heijmans) is, according to the above formula 8 – [(1b + 2 + 3 + 4 + 5 + 6 + 7) – (those costs of 2-7 subsidised by public bodies)]:
  - With the minimum returns (€ 112m) and assuming that costs 1 to 5 *are* inflated, this is:
    112 – [(12 + extra + 7 + subsidies municipality + 0.5 + 0.1625 + 0 + 90) – (subsidies municipality + 0.125)]
    = 112 - [(109.6625 + extra + subsidies municipality) – (subsidies municipality + 0.125)]
    = € 2.4625 million – extra paid to IBC for land (price last land transaction - € 12 m).
  - With the maximum returns (€ 139) and assuming that costs 1 to 5 *are* inflated, this is:
    139 – [(12 + extra + 7 + subsidies municipality + 0.5 + 0.1625 + 0 + 90) – (subsidies municipality + 0.125)]

= 139 - [(109.6625 + extra + subsidies municipality) – (subsidies municipality + 0.125)]
= € 29.4625 million – extra paid to IBC for land (price last land transaction - € 12 m)

2.5 The hypotheses

In section 2.1 we considered the power-relationship between public and private bodies in urban regeneration, and said that public bodies need to work with private bodies in policy networks in order to achieve their goals (including capturing value increase). We saw also that public bodies might be able to gain a more powerful role in these policy networks in order to influence the other actors in the network and so to improve the capturing of value increase. This can happen through two network constitutions measures, which are formulated in this research as two hypotheses (informed speculations; Bryman, 2004: 540) about how public bodies can use their formal powers on rules relevant to zoning for better capturing of value increase. Whether these hypothesised causalities are found in practice depends, however, not only on the correctness or otherwise of the hypotheses but also on the strength of all the other variables that affect the capturing of value increase and which are included in the model set out above.

2.5.1 The first network constitution measure: modifying the contents of property rights

The inspiration for the first network constitution measure is explained in section 2.2 and concerns the formal contents of the right of property ownership. Splitting development rights from land ownership is assumed to be relevant for capturing value increase. In an exploratory study in chapter 4 of nine Western European countries (besides the Netherlands, also England, Spain/Valencia, Germany, France, Italy, Flanders, Denmark and Sweden), no country showed a full splitting, so it was not possible to do empirical research on such a splitting. However, the study also showed the singularity of the modifications in 1994 in the Valencian land readjustment, which could be considered as a light or indirect form of splitting: in Valencia, infrastructure provision is in practice separated from the property rights. The generalized application of the model made it possible to collect abundant empirical data about the practical consequences for capturing value increase.

The speculation is that a modification of formal rules regarding land ownership could modify the distribution of resources and the behaviour of actors within policy networks, in such a way that this could shape the sort of dependence, and hence the power interactions between actors. In other words, temporarily taking over some property rights during a land readjustment procedure could improve capturing value increase. Within the model set out above, the hypothesis is that a modification of one of the context variables (formal rules on property rights, variable B1) could modify the actions of the involved actors (how private parties use their property rights, variable D2). The first hypothesis speculates therefore that:

A specific form of splitting the property rights on land (separating infrastructure provision from property rights) can modify the power-relationships in the network of actors involved in urban regeneration, and this can improve capturing value increase.

2.5.2 The second network constitution measure: modifying the level of certainty about future development terms

The inspiration for the second network constitution measure is explained above in section 2.3 and concerns whether public bodies create certainty about the future development terms before the regeneration project starts. Should certainty be created *before* or *after* negotiations take place? The degree of certainty depends on the moment at which it is created, but also on the contents of the plan documents that create certainty. Are they legally binding or only indicative? Do they regulate only the physical zoning, or also other socio-economic requirements as for example whether housing has to be social or free market? During data gathering an additional aspect became apparent: do binding rules regulate only a desired final physical picture without stating who is responsible for its implementation, or also the obligations and contributions that must be fulfilled by the developer?

Within the model set out above, the hypothesis is that a modification of one of the context variables (formal rules about certainty on development terms, variable B2) could modify the actions of the involved actors (how the local public bodies use their formal powers about certainty on development terms, variable D1). The second hypothesis speculates therefore that:

Creating uncertainty in early stages of development processes about future building possibilities, and certainty about future contributions, can influence capturing value increase in a positive way.

CHAPTER 3 Method

This research studies a 'phenomenon': the interaction between municipalities making use of their competences regarding formal rules relevant to zoning[1] and the developers/landowners regenerating a site. This is the same phenomenon in all the studied countries, although there are differences in the features of the phenomenon in each of the countries, and even in each case[2].

We focus on several variables of our phenomenon, meaning by 'variable' an attribute on which our phenomenon varies (Bryman, 2004: 29). Our goal is to know whether the application of particular sorts of formal rules relevant to zoning (the independent variable, which includes the variables B of the causal model in section 2.4.2) could contribute to more effective capturing of value increase (the dependent variable). We also take account of side effects (or side dependent variables), to one of which special attention has been paid: the tempo of implementation. The reason for this is that there might be a conflict between on the one hand improving the capturing of value increase, and on the other a delay in the project (e.g. developers might not be willing to agree to more contributions). The goal is thus to find out which measures might be positive for capturing value increase without at the same time delaying the implementation. The final goal is to produce knowledge that supports the formulation of recommendations for how Dutch practice could improve the recovery of costs made for public infrastructure and facilities.

---

1 'Formal rules relevant to zoning' are all those formal rules that rule both binding rules (included the implications for property rights in land) and not-legally binding policy documents (see section 1.3).

2 Swanborn makes a distinction between the 'phenomenon' and the 'carrier' who carries the phenomenon. In this research we use the term 'case' meaning what Swanborn actually names 'carrier' of the phenomenon. Thus, the carrier or case in this research is a specific network of people and institutions that interact with each other in a specific site, and doing so *produce* or *bear* the phenomenon (1996: 17, 28-29).

Taking into account these goals, and also the limitations of data gathering, we made several choices:

1. First, this research is mainly based on several cases, as it was not possible to gather data from a large enough sample of cases that would allow a statistical analysis that would isolate the relationship between the independent and the dependent variables (see section 3.1).
2. Second, this research needs to produce findings with a high validity and to avoid the risk, inherent to case-based research, of producing knowledge, so specific that it could not lead to general conclusions and recommendations (see section 3.2). This meant introducing three groups of measures to increase both the internal and the external validity of the findings:
   a) Using the hypothetical-deductive method to empirically test the hypotheses introduced in chapter 2 in such a way that, if they are found to be valid, they can be applied to the Netherlands (see section 3.2.1.1);
   b) Using variants of the 'method of difference' to tackle the risk of third variables, a risk that, following the model in section 2.4, is very high: this meant for example choosing an international comparison of planning systems and selecting cases very carefully (see section 3.2.1.2);
   c) Using some techniques specifically to strengthen the external validity of the findings, for example using data sources additional to the cases (see section 3.2.2).

Once the method and data gathering have been explained, section 3.3 will focus on how each research question has been answered.

3.1 Why case research?

The findings in this research are based on the following sources of data: available literature, eleven project cases (three/four in each country) and many interviews with involved persons and relevant experts. Is was however not possible to study sufficient cases for a statistical analysis of the causal relationship between the independent variable 'formal rules relevant to zoning' and the dependent variable 'capturing value increase'. There are two main reasons for this:

1. Urban (re)development projects are not so easy to reproduce in a laboratory as for example physical, biological or even psychological phenomena. Our phenomenon is an open social system and thus too complex to be ´modulated´ in an experiment (Swanborn, 1996: 22-24, 38-45);
2. The needed data are usually not fully available nor operational: there is not a list of all the urban (re)development projects in the country (total population) which would make possible a random selection of representative projects (sample). And even if this random selection was possible, there are not enough data available for all these projects and/or the data are not available in the needed form, be-

cause the data are not quantifiable, because the projects are too old, or because very relevant information is not available to the public (this is specially the case in the Netherlands, and to a lesser extent, in England[3]), or because there are no good archives, etcetera. But even if that information had been available, we did not have the time to study a representative sample (Swanborn 1996, p. 59).

3.1.1 Multiple case design

Therefore, although available literature has been extensively used, this research can be considered as a case-based one. We applied what the literature calls a 'multiple case design' (N > 1), in Dutch *'meervoudige case-study's'* (Yin, 1989; Van Hoesel, 1985: 239; both quoted in Swanborn, 1996: 23), or a 'cross case display' design (Miles en Huberman, 1994: 172-177). Such a research design consists of studying several cases (four in Valencia, three in England and four in the Netherlands) and comparing them with each other.

We chose case research not only because of the data gathering limitations. Also, the case-study method was an appropriate complement to the available literature, which often does not include up-to-date information about the studied phenomenon. In particular, the answer to Preparatory Research Question 2 in the Netherlands has rested heavily on cases, as there is not much available data about the degree of captured value increase in Dutch practice. Also, the case-study method was necessary to get the detailed information about the studied phenomenon, for this required using different sources, paying attention to many aspects and measuring them at different moments. This is not possible with a one moment-survey, there was need to be involved more deeply in the phenomenon by studying some 'carriers' of it, i.e. some cases. We studied the development phase, which starts from the original situation and ends at the delivery and the beginning of the exploitation of the final real estate products. This went from the first plan documents up to at least the signing of the development agreement, using a variety of data sources (documents, interviews, visits to the site, etc). Finally, the case-study method was necessary because there was need to study the cases in their *system*, in their *natural environment*. It is not only that, as already mentioned, it is not possible to isolate the phenomenon from the context and reproduce it in the laboratory experiment. In addition, it is not desirable to do so for then we would have missed the interactions with the context (Swanborn, 1996: 22-24, 38-45).

However, cases have not been studied in a 'holistic' way. This research was not interested in the whole phenomenon, i.e. in a description of *all* the characteristics

3 An important part of data gathering was collected from the agreements between the involved public and private parties. While in the Netherlands these agreements are not fully available for the public, in England and Spain they are. In England the available agreements regard the contributions made by the developers to the public. In Spain the available agreements have broader contents: besides the contributions, they also include a detailed calculation of all land development costs.

of the phenomenon, but rather in isolating the relevant variables of the phenomenon from the rest of the infinite other aspects or variables that could characterize the phenomenon (Swanborn, 1996: 11-18, 22-24, 26-28). The relevant variables are the above-mentioned independent and dependent variables, which are subdivided into several sub-variables in sections 3.3.1 and 3.3.2. Except for the Dutch case *De Funen*, all the cases have been studied following the same check lists that were used in the literature research (see Annex 1). So both literature research and case research have focussed on the same variables and sub-variables, complementing each other. *De Funen* diverges somewhat because it served as pilot study. The definitive approach and check-lists are based on the results of this pilot study (Swanborn, 1996: 100).

Cases have been selected as to strengthen the validity of the findings (see sections 3.2.1.2 and 3.2.2.2). In addition, some other, more practical selection criteria have been used: those projects have been selected that were available in terms of availability of archives, willingness of the involved persons to collaborate, visibility of the results, etc. The American literature speaks here of 'convenience sample' (Swanborn, 1996: 59).

3.1.2 Interviews

Interviews have been an important data source. There were of two different sorts: (1) Specific interviews, each one being different from the others, meant for finding specific knowledge to fill in the holes in literature and cases; (2) Generic interviews, meant for obtaining knowledge about the possible causal relationship between the independent variable and the dependent variable: this sort of interview was used for answering Preparatory research question 3. The construction of the questionnaire for the generic interviews has followed a meticulous method (Emans, 2002: 114-160). All those interviews have the same semi-structured form: all the relevant sub-variables of 'formal rules relevant to zoning' were listed that might influence any of the sub-variables of 'capturing value increase'.

3.1.3 Moment of data gathering

The data gathering took place before the international financial and economic crisis, which started in Summer/Autumn of 2008. For Spain, the data gathering took place before the start at the end of 2007 of the crisis in the Spanish real estate market. This means that one of the context variables that influence the size of the initial profit in urban regenerations projects (real estate markets, variable A1 in the causal model, see section 2.4.2.1) might be different nowadays (projects are nowadays confronted with substantially lower returns). For each country, data gathering took place at the following times (see, for more details, section 'Sources'):

- Exploratory study of the Netherlands, England, Spain, Germany, France, Italy, Flanders, Denmark and Sweden: desk research and most of the interviews in the

Spring of 2006, rest of interviews during 2006, 2007 and beginning 2008.

- Region of Valencia: desk research in Summer and Autumn 2006, *in situ* research (the cases and most of the interviews) in November and December 2006, and several interviews during 2007 and 2008;
- England: desk research in Winter and Spring 2007, *in situ* research (the cases and some interviews) in June 2007, and most of the interviews during 2006 and 2007;
- The Netherlands: desk research in 2005, in Summer and Autumn 2007, and most recent literature in Autumn 2009 and winter 2009-2010; *in situ* research beginning of 2005 for case and interviews *De Funen*, and Winter of 2007-2008 for the rest of cases including the interviews. Some additional interviews have been made in Autumn 2007 and the Spring and Summer of 2008.
- Last uptodate: for important data we have made a last round of data gathering at the end of 2009 and during 2010.

3.2 The validity of the findings

A fundamental question in case-based research is whether the findings are valid. How trustworthy are they? Central to this question are the concepts of 'internal validity', i.e. can the findings explain the studied cases?; and of 'external validity', i.e. are the findings generalizable to other cases? (Miles & Huberman, 1994: 278; León y Montero, 1997: 71-75, 122-124, 136-138; Polit et al., 2001: 192-195; Campbell & Stanley 1963: quoted in León & Montero: 122 and in Polit et alia: 193). There is neither a unanimous opinion about how to reach this trustworthiness, nor whether it is necessary or not to achieve it, and to which degree (Miles and Huberman, 1994; Myers, 2000; León & Montero, 1997; Swanborn, 1987: 82-83).

It has already been mentioned that the limitations of data gathering made it impossible to produce findings with the validity that characterizes experimental and statistical research, i.e. that kind of research that has the possibility of totally isolating, through experiments or through statistical analysis, the studied variables (Swanborn, 1996: 59). In spite of these limitations, this research needs to achieve a certain level of validity in order to produce good recommendations for the Dutch practice, i.e. to avoid recommendations that are too case specific. In this we agree with Miles and Huberman when they say, referring to this dilemma, that "Although we may acknowledge that 'getting it all right' is an unworkable aim, we should (...) try to 'not get it all wrong'" (1994: 277).

3.2.1 Internal validity

Internal validity means that the findings can explain the case projects studied in this research. We need a reasonable level of internal validity in order to be able to claim, when answering Preparatory Research Question 3 (see section 3.3.3), that we can infer in the studied cases the causal nature of the relationship between the variable 'formal rules relevant to zoning' and the variable 'capturing value increase'. Only by obtaining true knowledge about how the former does actually influence (or not) the latter *in the studied cases* is it possible to claim that the findings are internally valid. In order to increase the internal validity of the findings, two methodological strategies have been applied that reinforce each other: the hypotheses-deductive method and the method of difference.

3.2.1.1 The hypothetical-deductive method

The first methodological strategy is the hypothetical-deductive method (León & Montero, 1997: 8-21). Both the causal model set out in section 2.4 and the two hypotheses included in section 2.5 speculate about the possible relationship between variables 'formal rules relevant to zoning' and 'capturing value increase'. We checked empirically whether these speculations match the real world or not. That is, this research is an empirical testing of the speculations. See chapter 8 for the confrontation between speculations and findings.

3.2.1.2 The method of difference

The second methodological strategy is a more classical method: see if differences in the variable 'formal rules relevant to zoning' correspond or not with differences in the variable 'capturing value increase' (León & Montero, 1997: 106-117). This is actually based on what Mill called in the XIX Century the 'method of difference': if a specific value of a first variable happens in one situation, but not in the other, and both situations are exactly the same except for a second variable, than the second variable is the cause or the consequence of the differences in the value of the first variable (Mill, 1846: quoted in Swanborn, 1994: 239; 1996: 132).

a) The risk of third variables

The main problem to be dealt with when applying the method of difference is the possibility of third variables, also called 'alternative independent', 'confounding' or 'extraneous' variables. The methodological risk is that the changes in the variable 'capturing value increase' are not caused by changes in the variable 'formal rules relevant to zoning', but by another variable, for example any specificity of the context of the cases (variables A in causal model, see section 2.4.2), or by the contingent behavior of those involved in the cases (variables C and D). It might look as if changes in the variable 'formal rules relevant to zoning' cause changes in the variable 'capturing value increase', but actually both changes are caused by that third variable. In other words, the correlation between the variables 'formal rules relevant to zoning' and 'capturing value increase' is spurious, and the findings might not be relevant for elaborating recommendations.

b) Measure to assess the role of third variables: list of possibly third variables

To avoid the problem of a 'spurious' correlation, this research should check every possible third variable, and assess if that can explain *all* the correlation between our variables. This project has pursued this by elaborating a list of possible third variables and assessing their role in each country and case. These possible third variables were: personal circumstances of the involved persons and political circumstances (variables D4 and D5), market price of housing (variable A1), and any other possible third variable named (at our invitation) by the interviewed persons (D5). This has led to substantial expansion of the initial conclusions about the inferred causal relations. For example, the cases in England and especially in the Netherlands showed that a third variable, the financial feasibility of the projects, influences very much the capturing of value increase, which modified substantially our causal analysis. In addition this led us to research more deeply into the returns and costs of all the cases, and thus to include in the analysis the features of the site and the plan (variable A2), the situation in the markets for workforce and building materials, the fiscal regimes (A3), and the definition of the contents and boundaries of the plan (C1).

c) Measures to control third variables: limiting the total population of cases and applying cross-country comparative method

Other measures have been introduced to 'control' *all* or at least *as many as possible* alternative third variables (León & Montero, 1997: 110-117; Polit *et alia*, 2001: 188-192). The general principle underlying these measures is to hold the context as constant as possible, introducing changes only in the variable 'formal rules relevant to zoning', and seeing what happens with the variable 'capturing value increase'. So several measures have been introduced to isolate both variables from possible third variables. These measures are of two sorts: a first group aims at holding the context as similar as possible, and a second group aims at selecting countries that show the broadest variance in the variable 'formal rules relevant to zoning'. This combination is a methodological strategy referred to as 'most similar systems design' and is appropriate to uncover causal relationships between two variables (Pierre, 2005: 454-455).

i) Maintaining the context as similar as possible

- Limiting the total population of cases: to minimize the potential variance of third variables, the total population of possibly cases is limited to those that fit within the formulation of the problem of this research (see section 1.5). Besides helping to keep the context constant, this assures also that the cases bear enough information. This is what Swanborn calls 'information-rich' cases (1996: 61), and Miles and Huberman the 'intensity' of cases (1994: 28). We have studied those cases that fit the following criteria:

- Urban regeneration schemes;
- Land is mostly in private hands, i.e. mostly not owned by public bodies;
- There are public infrastructure and facilities that cost money;
- Comprehensive development areas of a certain size that involve a notable value increase;
- Projects are finished or quite advanced (at least, the development agreement is already sealed), and results on captured value increase can already be measured.

- Cross-country comparative method among relatively similar countries: to further minimize the potential variance of third variables, those countries have been studied in which the general political, economical and social context was somewhat similar. This led first to an explorative research of several countries that are likely to have a similar context to the Dutch. They are, besides the Netherlands, eight other West European countries, all of them EU-members: England, Spain, Germany, France, Italy, Flanders, Denmark and Sweden. We are aware of the large differences between these countries, but we are at the same time convinced that these differences are less than if having chosen countries in other regions or continents.

ii) Cross-country comparative method among countries with broadest variance in independent variable

Of all these eight countries, those were selected for in-depth research that show the broadest variation in the variable 'formal rules relevant to zoning': these are England and the Spanish region of Valencia. Both countries could be considered in some relevant aspects as examples of opposite models (see chapter 4). This choice corresponds with the strategy 'heterogeneity in the independent variable' (Swanborn, 1996: 62-64), which consists of maximizing the variation in the variable 'formal rules relevant to zoning'. This increased the chances that a possible causal relationship with the variable 'capturing value increase' becomes visible. This makes this research an international, comparative study that seeks inspiration in other countries in order to elaborate recommendations for the Dutch government.

d) Measures to control the third variables: selecting innovative cases

The strategy of 'heterogeneity in the independent variable', which led to a cross-country comparative method (see above), has been continued by selecting cases that might include innovative practices in the way municipalities used the formal rules relevant to zoning. To find out which these cases were, local experts and directly involved persons have been asked. The innovative practices have been grouped following the same grouping of sub-variables as in Preparatory Research Question 3 (see section 3.3.3).

i) Certainty beforehand about future development possibilities and contributions (sub-independent variables Where & When)

Cases were selected in which municipalities have used this aspect, whether it was creating flexibility about the future *building possibilities* (Valencia: *Periodista, Camino* and, to a lesser extent, *Benalúa*; England: *Megabowl* and part of *Temple Quay*; The Netherlands: all cases); or creating certainty about the future *contributions* (Valencia: all cases; England: *Megabowl, Harbourside* and part of *Temple Quay*; The Netherlands: *Kruidenbuurt* and *Stationskwartier*).

ii) Possibly contents of the relevant binding rules (sub-independent variable What)

There are two possibilities: *i)* In Valencia and England, binding rules can include affordable housing, and this actually happened in the Valencian cases *Guillem* and

Periodista and in all the three English cases. In the Netherlands, in principle, binding rules, under the Physical Planning Act before 1 July 2008, cannot require affordable housing. However, in practice municipalities might try to find a way of doing this. In case *De Funen* the municipality included affordable housing in the Development Agreement, and in *Kruidenbuurt* affordable housing was included not only in the agreement, but also in the Explanation (*Toelichting*) of the Land use Plan. *ii)* In Valencia and England, binding rules may include a wide range of contributions, including payments, implementation of public facilities, etc., and this is what happened in all studied cases. In the Netherlands, the possibilities to include contributions in the relevant binding rules were limited under the Physical Planning Act in force till 1 July 2008. Two cases have been selected in which the municipality tried to include a wide range of contributions in the development agreement: *Kruidenbuurt* and *Stationskwartier*. The Development contributions Plan, new since 1 July 2008, has introduced the possibility of including contributions in the binding rules (the Development contributions Plan) also, but this came too late for the data gathering.

iii) Making the Land use Plan conditional on capturing value increase (sub-independent variables When and What)

In Valencia and England, municipalities can make the approval of the binding rules conditional on a development agreement that secures the capturing of value increase, which is what actually happened in all the studied cases. Formally, Dutch municipalities cannot condition the Land use plans to a contractual commitment in a direct and open way. However, in practice this happens often, as was the case in all the four studied cases.

iv) Using the land readjustment regulation to oblige developers to compete with other developers (sub-independent variable Who)

Of the three countries, only in Valencia is there a land readjustment regulation. Almost all urban development there follows this regulation, and this was so in all four cases. The regulation makes it possible for developers not owning land to be selected as urbanizing agent. Municipalities can organize a public tender in which more than one proposal is evaluated. In all the cases there was such a tender, and in *Guillem, Camino* and *Benalúa,* more than one developer competed to be selected as urbanizing agent.

v) Procedural guarantees for the initiative-holders (sub-independent variable How)

These are of three sorts: *i)* Those cases have been selected in which developers used legal guarantees to force the procedure of approval (Valencia: *Periodista*) or they did not but these guarantees might have been indirectly relevant by limiting the freedom of action of municipalities (Valencia: all the cases; England: *Temple Quay* and *Harbourside*). *ii)* Binding rules in all three countries can include global land use regulations that can be detailed afterwards. This could allow an operational use in the negotiations with landowners. Cases have been selected that included this provision (Valencia: all cases; England: *Temple Quay* and *Harbourside*; the Netherlands:

Kruidenbuurt and part of *Stationskwartier*). *iii)* Ease of modifying the binding rules: binding rules in all the three countries can be modified. Cases have been selected where the binding rules were modified (Valencia: *Periodista, Camino* and *Benalúa*; England: *Temple Quay* and *Harbourside*; the Netherlands: *Kruidenbuurt, Kop van Oost* and *Stationskwartier*).

e) Measures to control third variables: repeated measurement
Another technique to control possible third variables is to study the phenomenon before and after a modification of only the independent variable 'formal rules relevant to zoning', and see what happens with the dependent variable 'capturing value increase'. The phenomenon is thus measured at two different moments: before and after the modification of the independent variable, while the rest of the context (the potential third variables) remain the same, or almost the same. In the Spanish region of Valencia it was possible to apply this technique: here, in 1994 a new law introduced very important changes in the land readjustment regulations (sub-independent variable *Who*), while possible third variables like culture, public policies, financial situation of the municipalities (variables D4 and D5 in causal model) and developments in the real estate markets (variable A1) remained the same. Because there were no dossiers available of suitable cases in the period before 1995, this research had to limit the data gathering for Spain for that period to literature and interviews. For the period after 1995, case-research also was used. In England also it has been possible to apply this technique: in cases *Megabowl* and part of *Temple Quay*, the Development Agreement was negotiated after the Bristol Local Council approved in 2005 the policy document SPD4. This document created certainty about the future contributions (sub-independent variables *Where* and *When*). The introduction in the Netherlands of a new Physical Planning Act in 2008 offers in principle similar opportunities, but came too late, as the data gathering finished before the new Act has had consequences in practice.

f) Inferring causal relationships
Thanks to all mentioned measures it was possible for us to achieve valid knowledge about the studied cases. When formulating our conclusions about the causal relationship between the independent and the dependent variables however, we are however cautious. Instead of claiming that we *prove* a causal relationship, we claim that we *infer* the possibly causal nature of the relationship, i.e. we argue why it seems reasonable to us that there might be causality in a certain direction (Bryman, 2004: 76, 230-1).

3.2.2 External validity

The other important aspect of the validity of the findings is the external validity. This refers to the generalizability of the research findings to other cases.

3.2.2.1 How much external validity do we need in case-research?

There is much discussion about the minimum needed level of external validity in case-research. Is internal validity alone enough to understand how the real world works? Some authors consider that internal validity is good enough because it proves that something can happen (León & Montero, 1997: 123-124). Miles and Huberman talk here about 'analytic induction' (1994: 146), and Yin about 'analytic' or 'theoretical generalization' (1989: 21, 44): instead of generalizing to populations or universes, it is possible to generalize to theoretical propositions, i.e. lending greater confidence to the hypothesis by testing it against the findings in the cases. Therefore, the goal is not to demonstrate the validity of a finding for the samples not studied, but to demonstrate that the theoretical assumptions/hypotheses actually work in the studied cases and are thus reasonably generalizable to the rest of the population of similar cases. Or, as Niederkofler stated it:

> *'The case-study investigator's goal is not to demonstrate the validity of an argument for statistical populations or universes. Rather, he aims to create and expand rich theoretical frameworks that should be useful in analysing similar cases'* (Niederkofler, 1991: quoted in Swanborn, 1996: 67).

Actually, as Swanborn observes (*ibidem*), what Yin does is consider the studied case to be the same as a causal experiment in a laboratory. In experiments, the context of the studied variables (all possibly third variables) is perfectly controlled, so that there is no doubt that the findings are absolutely internally valid. Such findings allow theoretical statements: the theory is true or not true because the results of the experiment confirm or deny it, even if only one or several cases were involved. In other words, in experiments it is possible to control all the differences in the context of all the cases of the total population, and therefore it is possible to reject any possibly alternative explanation to the findings. There is thus no need for any 'representative' sample of cases because the studied cases are representative enough. The findings are thus externally valid, and are also transferable to all the cases in the total population.

We share the opinion of Swanborn (1996: 67) that cases in social science research in general, and thus also in this research, are not fully comparable to a laboratory experiment as Yin implicitly postulates. The application of the above-mentioned hypothetical-deductive method and the measures for controlling all possible alternative third variables might offer some external validity: we can reasonably expect that other similar cases also would produce the same or similar results. However, this is not enough, as we still must face the risk of basing the findings upon too specific cases. What if the studied cases are rarities, extremes within the total population of cases? Too specific findings impede a *ceteribus paribus* reasoning, because there are not other similar cases, i.e. cases with comparable circumstances in which the conclusions would be valid. The findings would be interesting only for the studied cases, but neither for the rest of the population nor for the recommendations for the

Dutch practice. In our opinion this research must be able to claim that what happens in the studied cases is not exceptional and is valid for other cases. Or, if our cases are exceptional, at least we need to identify the specific features that make them exceptional. Anyway, whether or not we want our findings to stand for other cases, or at least to explain why they are an exception, we need some knowledge about the other cases in the population, i.e. some knowledge of the context. In other words, there is need to strengthen the validity of the findings by means additional to those explained up to now. The goal is to be able to claim that it is reasonable to expect, or plausible, that the recommendations would be applicable in other cases.

Table 5. Selection of cases according to the main sorts of urban regeneration projects.

	Valencia	England	The Netherlands
Multifunctional central areas	*Guillem de Anglesola* and *Periodista Gil Sumbiela*	*Temple Quay*	*Stationskwartier*
Monofunctional residential areas	*Guillem de Anglesola* and part of *Benalúa Sur*	(*)	*Kruidenbuurt*
Old Brownfield sites	*Periodista Gil Sumbiela*, *Camino Hondo* and part of *Benalúa Sur*	*Megabowl* and *Harbourside*	*De Funen* and *Kop van Oost*

- Multifunctional central areas consist of city/town central areas and sites around railway stations.
- Monofunctional residential areas consist of districts with a predominant residential use.
- Old brownfield sites are derelict sites: business and other sorts of economic-industrial activities; gas and electricity factories; harbor areas; railway infrastructure; and hospitals, government buildings and military sites.

(*) It was not possible to find a case in England that would fit within this category.

3.2.2.2 How to strengthen the external validity of the findings

a) Representative cases

A first attempt has been made to achieve some general knowledge by selecting cases that somehow stand for the main sorts of urban regeneration projects in that country. This leads to a selection of cases that span the range of sorts of urban regeneration projects that are common in the Netherlands (Kolpron, 2000: 8-31). See chapter 7.1 for an extensive explanation of this categorization, and table 5 for how the studied cases fit within the categorization. Doing so we avoided the risk of focusing only on a specific sort of cases and ignoring other relevant sorts of regeneration schemes.

b) Supplementary sources

To further increase the external validity of the findings, other sources of more or less general knowledge have been analyzed:

- Data has been sought about other cases. Sometimes there was quite generalizable data available, specially in Valencia and England;
- Interviews with experts, who gave information about other cases they know.

The case-based findings have been positioned within this more general knowledge. This has allowed assessing the external validity of the findings from the cases. This was particularly relevant for the findings about the third variable 'development costs' (initially a third variable that became part of the focus of this research and has been renamed an 'intermediary variable', see figure 4 in section 2.4.2.4). The first findings for the Netherlands (that suggested that development costs are much higher there than in England and, specially, in Valencia) were based on just three cases, as there were no other available relevant sources. In order to check the validity of these findings, we approached two Dutch experts. They validated our initial findings by making a study of the equivalent development costs in three current Dutch cases and comparing their findings with the findings of our three cases.

3.2.2.3 Some examples

By applying these measures, it was possible to assess the specificity of the findings, and whether they could serve or not for the final conclusions. Here are several examples:

- In the Valencian cases *Guillem* and *Periodista,* the municipality had introduced social housing in the binding zoning plan, and we concluded that this was an important cause of the developer finally realizing social houses. However, after studying statistics about social housing production and interviewing several experts, it became clear that these cases are more an exception than the rule (see section 5.5.2.2). Valencian municipalities seem, until recently, not have included much social housing in the binding zoning plans. Does this mean that the finding (including social housing in binding zoning plans leads to more realized social housing) was not useful? Not at all, as the findings were clear that *if* municipalities include social housing in binding zoning plan (what is more and more the case the last couple of years), *then* this leads to mores social housing being built.
- In the English case *Megabowl* the local development plan (a non-legally binding zoning plan) foresaw no redevelopment of this former bowling alley (see section 6.4.1.1). We concluded that this has had a positive effect for the captured value increase: due to the complete absence of any building prospective, developers were not interested in buying the site, which discouraged any price increase of the land, which in turn left more financial room for the owner to contribute more generously to public infrastructure and facilities, as he indeed did. However, during the interviews it became clear that this case was certainly special, as another variable was also relevant, of the sort A1 in causal model (see section 2.4.2): the last years other bowling alleys were opened in the city, which damaged the profitability of the bowling alley in our site and thus lowered its market value. This played a role in the willingness of the owner to contribute so

generously. Does this mean that the finding (low certainty about future building possibilities leads to high capturing value increase) is not valid? We concluded that the finding was valid because: 1) the low market value of the bowling alley might have influenced the willingness of the owner, but not the lack of interest of developers in buying the land; and 2) the financial outcomes of other urban regeneration cases (e.g. case *Harbourside* in England, but also other cases in Valencia and the Netherlands) also are affected by the fact that the former use in the site has a low market value (old deteriorated industrial areas, etc).

- In the Dutch cases *Kruidenbuurt* and *Stationskwartier,* the developer and the public administration agreed the contributions in early stages of the development process, while in the cases *De Funen* and *Kop van Oost* they did not (see section 7.4.1.1). After consulting additional sources and interviewing several experts, we concluded that the first two cases are the exception, and the last two the rule. It became clear that both in *Kruidenbuurt* and *Stationskwartier* there was a specificity that explained why contributions were agreed in early stages: in *Kruidenbuurt* a special relation between the developer (a housing association) and the municipality, and in *Stationskwartier* the specificity of the project (a semi-public railway company wanting a new railway station), both variables of the sort D4. Is the finding (early certainty about contributions is good for capturing value increase) valid? Yes, because it is clear that *if* there is certainty, whatever the reason might be for this, *then* it results in better capturing. Also, this led to additional data gathering that led us to conclude that in the Netherlands, housing associations contribute more to public infrastructure and facilities than commercial developers because associations always have a special relation with public bodies and the achievement of public goals, specially in the field of social housing.
- Supplementary sources have been very relevant for answering the Preparatory research question 2. In sections 5.6, 6.5 and 7.5 we explain the degree to which developers contribute to public infrastructure and facilities. In those sections the case-based data have been systematically placed against other available studies (abundant in Spain and England) and against the interviews with many experts that assessed whether the case-based findings were representative or not. For example, in the Netherlands the interviews and a small survey confirmed that commercial developers do not contribute at all to off-site public infrastructure and facilities. However, some experts pointed out that, sometimes, there are some contributions to local funds for off-site infrastructure (see section 7.5).

3.3 Answering the Research Questions

In chapters 5 to 7 (chapter 5 for Valencia, 6 for England and 7 for the Netherlands) first a general introduction is given to the studied countries and cases. This general introduction describes the allocation of competences on planning law and on the making and implementation of planning policy, and describes the different actors involved in urban development, the policies for urban regeneration, and the legal framework for capturing value increase. For each case there is given a separate introduction to the development site, to the history of the development and to the current situation. Additionally, we studied for each case the amount of development costs and profits, distinguishing between land development costs (land price, infrastructure provision costs, soil decontamination and compensation costs), real estate development costs and the final profits.

Then, we answer three Preparatory Research Questions for each country and case. These questions are:

- Preparatory research question 1: *How can those formal rules relevant to zoning be used in comprehensive urban regeneration developments on privately owned land?* This focuses on the independent variable 'formal rules relevant to zoning'.
- Preparatory research question 2: *What is the extent of capturing value increase in comprehensive urban regeneration developments on privately owned land?* This focuses on the dependent variable 'capturing value increase'.
- Preparatory research question 3: *How does the way in which formal rules relevant to zoning are used influence capturing value increase?* This focuses on the causal relationship among the independent and the dependent variables.

We answered the research questions as follows. The theoretical framework served to formulate a causal model (see section 2.4.2) and, central to this causal model, two hypotheses (section 2.5):

1. Hypothesis 1: *A specific form of splitting the property rights on land (separating infrastructure provision from property rights) can modify the power-relationships in the network of actors involved in urban regeneration, and this can improve capturing value increase.*
2. Hypothesis 2: *Creating uncertainty in early stages of development processes about future building possibilities, and certainty about future contributions can influence capturing value increase in a positive way.*

Preparatory research question I

Using variables B2 and D1 of the causal model and the second hypothesis we saw that in order to answer Preparatory Research Question 1 we needed information about three sub-variables (Where, When, What). In addition, using variables B1 and D2 of the causal model and the first hypothesis we saw that we needed a model of dependence analysis and information about a fourth sub-variable (Who). Finally, based on variables B3 and D3 of the causal model we realized that we needed information about a fifth sub-variable (How).

Preparatory research question 2

We used a criterion of conformance (i.e. whether the actual spatial development is according to plan) to answer Preparatory research question 2. We needed information about: 1) what are the goals for capturing value increase?; 2) who pays to achieve those goals?; and 3) is the implementation on time? Using this we defined all the sub-variables (sorts of capturing value increase).

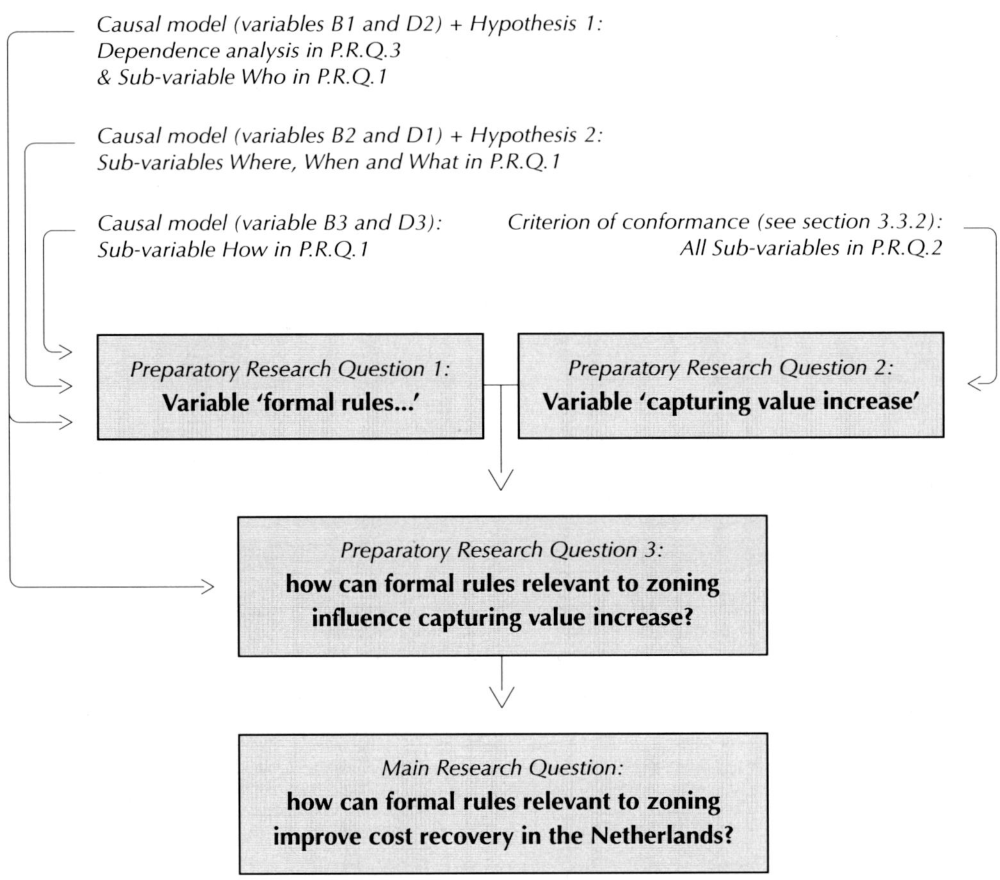

Figure 5. Inputs in the detailing and answering of the research questions.

Preparatory research question 3

In order to answer this question we needed to infer the sort of causal relationship between the independent and the dependent variables. We did so using the model of dependence analysis (that presupposes the possible causal relationship on the basis of the allocation of resources) and the method of difference.

Main Research Question

After each preparatory question had been answered for each country in chapters 5 to 7, those answers were used to answer in chapter 9 the Main Research Question:

- Main research question: *How could formal rules relevant to zoning be used in the Netherlands in order that the profitable parts finance as much as possible the unprofitable parts?* This focus on elaborating recommendations for the Dutch practice.

See Figure 5 for an overview of how the different inputs have been used to operationalize the research questions.

3.3.1 Answering Preparatory Research Question 1

Preparatory Research Question 1 is:

> *How can those formal rules relevant to zoning be used in comprehensive urban regeneration developments on privately owned land?*

To make this question operational for data gathering, the variable 'formal rules relevant to zoning' has been divided into five sub-variables. Four of them are taken from the causal model (variables B1, B2, D1 and D2), two hypotheses and a model of dependence analysis. The fifth sub-variable is taken from the causal model alone (variables B3 and D3).

Causal model (variables B2, D1) + Hypotheses 2 → sub-variables Where, When and What
The second hypothesis is: *Creating uncertainty in early stages of development processes about future building possibilities, and certainty about future contributions can influence capturing value increase in a positive way.*

This assumption has been translated into several researchable sub-variables of the independent variable. Based on these sub-variables it was possible to elucidate whether there is, or is not, certainty, which type of certainty (about building possibilities or about contributions), and when (early or later in development processes):

- *Where (in which planning documents) are the relevant zoning regulations brought into force?*
- *When (in relation to the negotiations) are the relevant zoning regulations approved?*
- *What are the possibly contents of the relevant zoning regulations?*

Causal model (variables B1, D2) + Hypothesis 1 → sub-variable Who
The first hypothesis is: *A specific form of splitting the property rights on land (separating infrastructure provision from property rights) can modify the power-relationships in the network of actors involved in urban regeneration, and this can improve capturing value increase.*

This assumption has been translated into one researchable sub-variable of the independent variable. This sub-variable is meant to elucidate whether development rights belong to the landowner or to the public:

- *Who has the right to develop whatever the binding rules (excluding the not-legally binding zoning regulations) prescribe?*

However, this sub-variable was not specific enough to allow data gathering. Therefore, we made it more specific by investigating who controls the resources that are needed in each of the transactions in development processes. These transactions are (Alexander, 2001a; 2001b):

1. Land purchase and assembling;
2. Financing;
3. Land preparation and development;
4. Land disposition;
5. Construction;
6. Property transfer.

Steps 1-4 belong to the infrastructure provision, steps 5 and 6 to the building. Each of these steps implies transactions of some kind (land, money, property, etc). Urban regeneration, i.e. developing whatever is prescribed in the binding rules, can only happen after completing each of these transactions. By analysing who has the control over each of these transactions, it was possible to discern who has which development right, and whether public law regulations (formal rules such as expropriation and the Valencian land readjustment regulation) might have restricted the use of property rights in land. The sub-variable becomes more specific:

- *Who has the control over each of the six transactions in development processes?*

Model of dependence analysis → sub-variable Who

However, we needed an analytical model that allowed us to discover who has the control over each of the six transactions. We therefore developed a dependence analysis model based on the concepts (explained in section 2.1.1.1) of power, rules, resources and dependence, and based on the ideas of Healey (1992: 35-38; see also Verhage 2002: 159) and, specially, Verhage (2002: 161). The model allowed us to analyse the influence of public law regulations on the control of resources and how this influences power-relationships within policy networks. These are the characteristics of the model:

1. Resources are not only material resources (land and investment capacity), but also regulatory resources (Land use plan, building permits, etc);
2. Rules are what Ostrom (1986: 466-467) understood under 'formal rules': those formalised in laws and administrative arrangements;
3. Ideas and informal rules have not been included in this model as it was quite difficult to measure them in an objective way. However they were taken into account in an analysis made of the possible third variables D4 and D5, an analysis that complements the conclusions of this dependence model (see section 2.4.2).
4. To analyse the strength of the dependence, this research adds the concept of 'avoidability' of the dependence. This idea is partly based on Scharpf's concept of 'substitutability' of the resource that causes the dependence. To us, depend-

ence is avoidable when it is possible and feasible for the dependent actor to achieve his goals without being dependent on a particular actor. A dependence is not avoidable when it is not possible or, if possible, too costly or politically too risky to avoid it.

5. After analysing in each case the distribution of resources and the resulting dependence patterns, the formal rules are analysed that explain why the resources are distributed as they are.

We used this model to further specify sub-variable Who into several sub-sub-variables:

- *Which are the resources (material and regulatory resources) needed for each of the transactions?*
- *How are these resources distributed between the involved parties?*
- *What are the dependence patterns that result from the allocation of resources?*
- *Are these dependence patterns avoidable?*

Causal model (variables B3 and D3) → sub-variable How

Several practical considerations, related to the flexibility of the procedure for preparing and approving binding rules, have helped to make operational the last sub-variable in PRQ1:

- *How flexible is the procedure of preparing and approving the binding rules (excluded the not-legally binding zoning regulations)?*

This has been made more specific:

- Which guarantees have initiative-holders (the developers who wants to regenerate a site) that the municipality will seriously assess their application?
- How easy or difficult is it to modify the binding rules? Three sub-sub-variables have been researched: (1) what are the procedural requirements for modifying (*wijziging* in Dutch), (2) departing from (*vrijstelling*) and (3) detailing (*uitwerking*) the existing binding rules?
- Can the geographical scope of binding zoning plans be varied according to the negotiations with different landowners/developers? Three sub-variables have been researched: (1) the rules for the delimitation of geographical scope of the plans; (2) whether there is a maximum number of different binding zoning plans per area; (3) whether municipalities are free to approve as many binding zoning documents as they wish.

Description problem

Preparatory research question 1 has been answered as a description problem (Swanborn, 1987: 68-70): introducing first each country and case, and describing then what each country and case look like in each of the mentioned sub-variables, i.e. measuring each sub-variable (see Table 6). For the detailed check-lists that were used in the data gathering, see Annex 1. The answer consists of statements describing how formal rules relevant to zoning in the different countries could be used following planning law, and how they are used in practice.

Table 6. Structure of the answer to P.R.Q.1

Country/sub-variable	Introduction to country	Introduction to cases	Where	When	What	Who	How
England							
Valencia							
The Netherlands							

3.3.2 Answering Preparatory Research Question 2

Preparatory research question 2 is:

What is the extent of capturing value increase in comprehensive urban regeneration developments on privately owned land?

To make this question operational, the dependent variable 'capturing value increase' has been divided into several sub-variables. They are based on the criterion of conformance, which refers to whether spatial development is according to plan (Korthals Altes, 2006: 97-99). If the goals for capturing value increase included in the zoning regulations are secured in terms of their financing and their realization within the established deadlines, we could consider that the conformance has been high, and vice versa. A list of possible goals for capturing value increase has been designed that covers all possible forms of contributions from developers and takes into account possible side effects, to one of which special attention has been paid: the tempo of implementation. That is, Preparatory research question 2 focuses not only on whether the goals for capturing value increase have been achieved, but also whether this happened on schedule. The sub-variables are:

- *Who pays the following capturing value increase goals?* [a list of possible contributions from the developer to public infrastructure and facilities]
- Are the capturing value increase goals implemented on time?

However, during data gathering it became clear that it was very difficult to fully apply the criterion of conformance. The reason is that it was not always possible to discern what the goals for capturing value increase were, as during the development process, especially in the Netherlands, these goals changed. It was also not always possible to discern whether the goals were genuinely set at the beginning of the process, or were the result of self-censure of public bodies aware of the low chances of obtaining contributions from developers. Nevertheless, when possible we have applied the criterion of conformance, comparing the results with the initial goals, and in addition we always measured the degree of captured value increase, following the same list for all cases and countries. So the measured degree of captured value increase was sometimes related to the specific goals of the public bodies, and was always related to the same list for all cases and countries. The differences of measured degree of captured value increase between cases and countries were large enough for suggesting in Preparatory research question 3 a causal relationship with the independent variable.

Preparatory research question 2 is also answered as a description problem (Swanborn, 1987: 68-70): describing what each country and case looks like in each of the mentioned sub-variables, i.e. measuring them (see Table 7). For the detailed checklist, see Annex 1. The answer consists of statements describing which capturing value increase goals are paid or not by the market parties, and whether this happened on schedule.

Table 7. Structure of the answer to P.R.Q.2

Country/sub-variable	Capturing value increase goals				Implementation within schedule?
England					
Valencia					
The Netherlands					

3.3.3 Answering Preparatory Research Question 3

Preparatory research question 3 is:

How does the way in which formal rules relevant to zoning are used influence capturing value increase?

This question links the answer to P.R.Q.1 (use of formal rules relevant to zoning) with the answer to P.R.Q.2 (degree of capturing value increase). The goal is to know if certain ways of using formal rules relevant to zoning in the studied countries could influence capturing value increase. Because the goal of this research is to elaborate recommendations for the Dutch practice, knowledge about this relationship must include knowledge about a possible causality. In other words, this research is interested in the possibly causal relationship between both variables (see Figure 6).

Figure 6. This research is interested in nature of the relationship among variables 'formal rules relevant to zoning' and 'capturing value increase'.

Because P.R.Q.3 works with the answers given to P.R.Q.1 and P.R.Q.2, there is no need of specific data gathering, except for the generic interviews in which involved persons were asked about the possible causal relationship (see section 3.1.2). The answer to P.R.Q.3 argues why the sub-variables of P.R.Q.1 can or cannot influence the sub-variables of P.R.Q.2. The sub-variables have been grouped, due to narrative purposes, into the following:

a) Certainty beforehand about future building possibilities and contributions (Where and When)
Zoning regulations can create certainty about future use possibilities and contributions before, during or after negotiations with developers take place. Certainty can be very hard, when it consists of binding rules; less hard, when consisting of non-legally binding zoning regulations; or not even existing if there is no kind of policy document.

b) Possibly contents of the relevant binding rules (What)
Binding rules (excluding the not-legally binding zoning regulations) might be useful in negotiations if local public bodies can include there not only the physical zoning, but also aspects related to the financing and implementation of public infrastructure and facilities. Do binding rules regulate only a desired final picture without stating who is responsible for its implementation, or also the obligations that must be fulfilled by the developer? How far can binding rules go in enumerating obligations? Can they include off-site infrastructure? Social housing?

c) Making the relevant binding rules conditional on the developer securing the capturing of value increase (When and What)
Binding rules (excluding the not-legally binding zoning regulations) might be useful in negotiations if local public bodies can make them conditional on the developer financing and implementing the public infrastructure and facilities. The approval of binding rules containing these schedules does not automatically mean that developers are committed to develop whatever is foreseen in them. Additionally, the commitment of the developer to secure them is needed.

d) Modulating property rights in land (Who)
The negotiation position of local public bodies may depend on the contents of property rights, more specifically on the degree to which landowners control all transactions in development processes, and the degree to which public bodies may restrict the exercise of property rights through public law regulations.

e) Procedure for the preparation and approval of relevant binding rules (How)
Three aspects related to the procedure of binding rules (excluding not-legally binding zoning regulations) might be relevant for capturing value increase:

- Guarantees to the initiative-holders: when developers undertake the initiative, there are many uncertainties about the decision of the local public body. Is it going to assess seriously the application, or not even consider it? This might affect the negotiation position of developers and local public bodies, and therefore influence the capturing of value increase. Also, this might affect the risks and costs that market parties have to deal with, which might also affect the keenness of market parties to undertake the initiative and contribute to the unprofitable parts.

- Flexibility to modify existing binding rules: easy and short procedures for modifying the existing binding rules could improve the usability of binding rules in the negotiations.
- Flexibility to determine the plan area of the binding rules accordingly to negotiations with landowners: another important aspect could be whether the size or geographical scope to which the binding rules apply (i.e. the plan area) could be adapted in a way that favours negotiating with each individual landowner, without delaying the rest of the process. Can the local public body first approve the binding rules for the plots where the agreements have already been concluded, and wait until the other owners/developers agree?

The answers to this Preparatory research question 3 are in fact the tested hypotheses, for example: "if municipalities establish in early stages of development processes which contributions developers will have to pay/realize, capturing value increase will improve". These tested hypotheses (see chapter 8) are the fundaments for answering the Main Research Question in chapter 9.

3.3.4 Answering the Main Research Question

The Main research question is:

> *How could formal rules relevant to zoning be used in the Netherlands in order that the profitable parts finance as much as possible the unprofitable parts?*

The answer will follow the same grouping of sub-variables as in Preparatory research question 3 (groups of sub-variables a-e). Based on the findings of Preparatory research question 3, the Main research question designs specific recommendations for the Dutch situation. These recommendations are based on the tested hypotheses, but incorporating specific knowledge of the Dutch situation, e.g. legislation, political and cultural considerations. This results in statements of the type: "if Dutch municipalities want to increase cost recovery in similar urban projects, they should in early stages specify in Structure Visions (*Structuurvisie*) their requirements on cost recovery". Recommendations are divided between those that fit within the actual legal framework, and those that require a legislative modification.

CHAPTER 4

Quick scan: formal rules relevant to zoning in Western European countries

As argued in chapter 3.2.1.2, methodological considerations require that this research investigates the situation in several countries. The first step is exploratory research in countries that have a similar context to the Netherlands, because studying countries with a similar context reduces the influence of third variables. The second step is to select for in-depth research those countries that show the broadest variation in the independent variable 'formal rules relevant to zoning'. The reason is that this increases the possibilities of producing significant findings.

The exploratory research is of the situation in the Netherlands and eight other Western European countries: Germany, England (part of the UK), Flanders (part of Belgium), France, Sweden, Denmark, Italy, and Spain (focusing mainly on the region of Valencia). Special attention has been paid to a limited number of variables namely the five sub-variables of the independent variable 'formal rules relevant to zoning': Where, When, What, Who and How (see section 3.3.1). The difference between the exploratory research and the in-depth research lies in the sources (in the exploratory research only literature and interviews, in the in-depth research also cases), the time spent, the level of detail, and the number of interviews[1].

1 The sources in the exploratory research have been literature (Acosta & Renard, 1993; Ave, 1996; Bassols, 2002, Betancor & García-Bellido, 2001; Booth, 2003; De Wolff, 2000; Dieterich et al., 1993; Stig, 2002; European commission, 1997 and 1999; García-Bellido, 1993 and 1994; Kalbro & Mattsson, 1995; Kalbro, 2002; MiljØministeriet, 2002, Moore, 2005; Muñoz & Korthals Altes, 2007, Needham et al., 1993; ODPM, 2004b, Oliva, 2006; Ratcliffe et al., 2002; Rodríguez, 2001; Ruiz de Lobera, 1996; Williams & Wood, 1994) and interviews with relevant experts of each country (Crow, Davy, Renard, Oliva, Kalbro, De Wolff, Wouters and Enemark, interviews in 2006, 2007 and 2008).

Sections 4.1-4 present the results of the exploratory research: a cross-national survey of the main aspects of the formal rules relevant to zoning, summarized in table 8. Based on the findings of this exploratory research, in section 4.5 two countries have been selected that show the broadest variation in the ways formal rules relevant to zoning are used: these are England and the Spanish region of Valencia. These two countries and the Netherlands are the subject of in-depth research in chapters 5-7.

4.1 Zoning regulations in the negotiation processes

The position of municipalities in the negotiations with landowners and developers may vary depending on whether there already exist binding rules or indicative zoning regulations concerning the development in question.

4.1.1 Are zoning regulations (binding and not-binding) approved in early stages of development processes?

In several countries, before negotiations start, there are already binding rules concerning the intended development. In Spain and France for example, as a rule, municipalities are obliged to approve binding land-use plans that have to cover the whole municipal territory (*Plan General de Ordenación Urbana* respectively *Plan Local d'Urbanisme. PLU*). However, in France, most of the municipalities have not yet (January 2007) approved PLUs. Although the old *Plan d'Occupation des Sols* (POS) still applies in these cases, there seems to be flexibility regarding projects that do not fit into it. In Italy also, until recently, municipalities were obliged to approve such a binding land use plan for the whole municipal territory (*Piano regolatore generale comunale*), but this plan is becoming gradually replaced by a new sort of plan, the *Piano Operativo,* which usually covers only part of the developable land. In Flanders, based on legislation of the 60's, Regional Plans (*Gewestplannen*) were enacted that cover most of the territory of Flanders, both built and not-built areas.

These already approved outline land-use plans include land-use regulations with statutory consequences for the use of the land: they zone land into different uses, and often also define the building density (not very common however in the Flemish *Gewestplannen*). As a rule, these plans do not take account of specific projects, they are approved only occasionally, every many so years (except Italy, where the *Piano Operativo* is approved more or less each five years), and they constitute the existing planning frame before development processes start. Although these plans are supposed to create legal certainty about the future building possibilities, in practice, this certainty is often not so strong, at least in France, Italy and Flanders. The reason is that, when development is near, (1) in France the planning framework might not always be clear; (2) in Italy the new *Piano Operativo* no longer covers the whole

municipal territory, and (3) in those four countries, these plans very often need to be detailed, complemented or modified.
In the other countries, the only planning documents that might say, in the early stages, something about the possible future developments are non-binding zoning plans. The English *Structure/Local/Development plans* or the new *Local Planning Frameworks*, and the Dutch *Structuurplan* or the new *Structuurvisie* are good examples of this. Because these regulations are only indicative, they give no legal certainty about the future use and building possibilities. Other countries also have similar indicative plans: the German *Flächennutzungsplan*, the Swedish *översiktsplan* and the Danish *Kommuneplan*.

4.1.2 Approval of detailed binding rules at the development moment

When negotiations have been successfully converted into development agreements, binding land-use plans for specific areas and in detail are approved. It is possible to differentiate between the countries according to whether this happens at one time or in different steps.

In several countries, municipalities approve the detailed legally binding rules in one step, in one planning document (English *Planning Permission*, Dutch *Bestemmingsplan* and Danish *Lokalplan*). However, in those countries it is possible to approve first an outline version (*Outline Planning Permission, Globaal Bestemmingsplan* and 'framework' *Lokalplan*), and afterwards approve a detailed version (*Full Planning Permission, uitwerking* and detailed *Lokalplan*). Sweden is a case in-between: in the case of private developments which do not fall within any joint development statutory formula (see under), municipalities usually approve the detailed binding rules in one step, the *omra°desbestämmelser* or the *detaljplan*. However, in case of joint development formula, binding rules are approved in two steps.

In other countries, binding rules are usually approved in two steps and in two different sorts of planning documents: (1) a binding land-use plan, and (2) a detailed and/or implementation-oriented planning documents, i.e. a document including not only the physical zoning, but also or exclusively the arrangements that are necessary for the implementation. They are the German (1) *Bebauungsplan* and (2) *Umlegungplan* (in case of land readjustment); and the Swedish (1) *omra°desbestämmelser/detaljplan*, and (2) *anläggningsbesluit/exploateringsbeslut* (in case of a joint development statutory formula). Though formally both sorts of documents have to be approved at different moments, in practice it is not infrequent that the approval takes place simultaneously or close after each other. In this sense, they are similar to the English, Dutch and Danish binding rules, which are usually approved in just one step. The Netherlands introduced in 2008 the *Exploitatieplan*, an implementation-oriented document that in some cases must be approved together with the *Bestemmingsplan*.

Finally, in those countries where there are binding rules before negotiations start (Valencia and all other Spanish regions, France, Italy and Flanders), the phasing seems to be clearer: the general binding land use plans are already approved in an early stage, and when the development moment nears it remains only to detail or modify the general plans for specific areas, and/or to approve implementation-oriented plans (the Valencian *Programa para el desarrollo de una Actuación Integrada* and *Proyecto de Reparcelación*, the Italian *Piani attuativi/Programma Complesso*; the French *Plan d'Lotissement*; the Flemish *Ruimtelijk Uitvoeringsplan* and *Verkavelingsplan/vergunning*).

4.1.3 Conclusions regarding the place of binding rules in the negotiation process: Plan-led versus Development-led

In section 2.3.1, a distinction was made, based on Faludi's categorization of proto-planning theories A and B (Faludi, 1987: 185-192), between plan-led and development-led planning systems. The plan-led system is supposed to characterize planning systems in most of the countries, and the development-led system the British system. Summarizing, plan-led systems differ from development-led systems in two aspects: (1) there is in plan-led systems a legally binding land use plan and (2) this plan acquires legal status at an early stage, at the 'plan production moment'.

This research supports that categorization in one respect: among the studied countries, only England and all other British constituent countries have no kind of legally binding land use plan, and in the other countries this is usual. In the UK there is only one binding land-use document, the *Planning Permission*. However, regarding whether the land use plan is approved at an early stage or not (i.e. previous to the development moment) the results of this study diverge from the categorization. Of the studied countries, only Spain, France, Italy, and Flanders could be called plan-led, for only in these countries are there general binding land-use rules approved in early stages, at the 'plan production moment' (this is the moment in which the first projections are made for development, and it is indicated with the star on the left side in Figure 7), before the 'development moment' nears (this is the moment in which local authorities and developers face a specific proposal for development, star on the right side in Figure 7). However, as mentioned above, the legal certainty that might be created by these early zoning plans is in practice not as strong as could be expected, especially in France, Italy and Flanders.

In the other countries that might appear to have a 'plan-led' system, the actual use of binding land-use plans seems to differ from how it should be according to the plan-led principle. As a rule, in the Netherlands, Germany, Sweden, and Denmark, binding land-use rules (whether this is a new land-use plan or a modification of it to include the new building possibilities) are approved only and for the first time when negotiations with developers/landowners have already taken place or, at least, when

ENGLAND

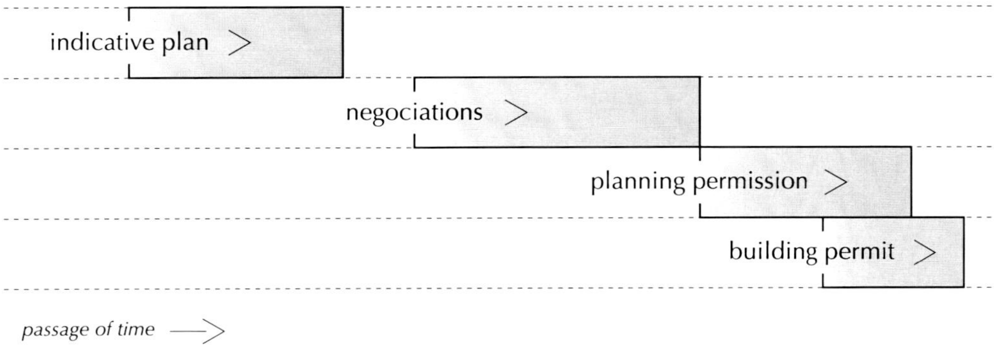

THE NETHERLANDS / GERMANY / SWEDEN / DENMARK

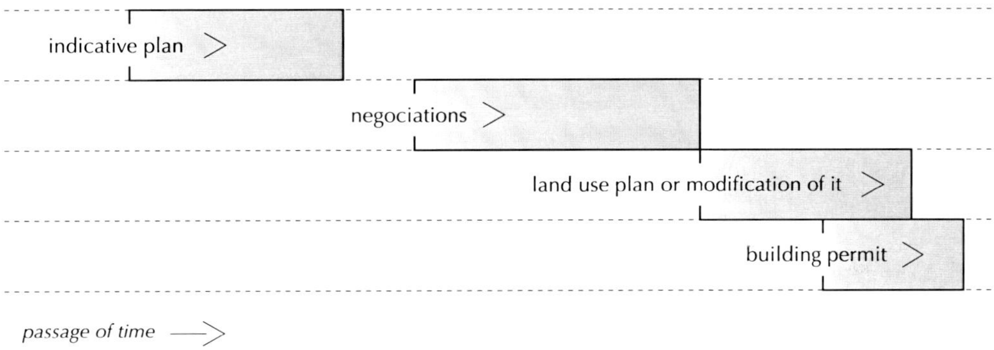

SPAIN / ITALY? / FRANCE? / FLANDERS?

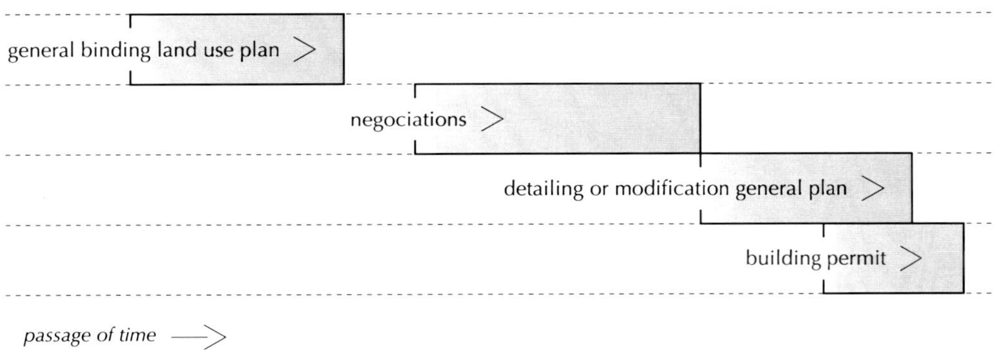

Figure 7. Actual place of zoning regulations (binding and not-binding) in development processes in several Western European countries.

there is enough certainty about the successful conclusion of those negotiations. In the Netherlands, the studied cases and several other studies confirm this, and it seems that this has been the case for a long time. At the beginning of the 1980s, departures from land use plans were very common, and since then things have not changed much (Thomas et al., 1983: quoted in Faludi 1987: 116, 185; Bröcking & Geest, 1982; Bosch & Hanemaayer, 1992: both quoted in Buitelaar et al., 2007: 54). So the binding land-use rules that make new developments possible are approved only after intending developers have negotiated a content that the municipality wants to approve. In other words, binding land-use rules are in practice approved at, or shortly before, the 'development moment', the same as in the UK. A comparative study of the European Commission agrees with these findings. In the 1990's, when this study was carried out, most of the countries belonging to the plan-led system showed in practice similar deviations as in our nine countries (European Commission, 1997: 45-46)

4.2 Contents of binding rules

The utility of binding rules in negotiations might depend on whether they can formally prescribe implemented-oriented requirements, e.g. obligations and deadlines for the implementation. Further, it might be important whether they can formally prescribe unprofitable uses, e.g. social/affordable housing. Finally, it might be also important whether municipalities, formally and directly, can make the approval of the binding plan conditional on a contractual commitment that secures the implementation. Regarding these three aspects, it is possible to make the following distinctions.

4.2.1 Zoning plans vs. implementation-oriented plans, both binding

Almost all the countries have legally binding planning documents that are intended to apply to the implementation. That is, documents that prescribe aspects directly related with the practical development of an area: temporal regulations (when to start/finish development), financial regulation or other kind of regulations (who pays what, who does what). These binding planning documents are the English *Planning permission*, the Valencian *Programa*, the German *Umlegungplan*, the French *Plan d'Lotissement*, the Italian *Piani attuativi/Programma Complesso*, the Flemish *Verkavelingsplan/vergunning* and the Swedish *anläggningsbeslut* and *exploateringsbeslut*. The English *Planning Permission* includes, besides the implementation-oriented regulations, also the legally binding physical zoning. In Valencia, Germany, France, Italy, Flanders and Sweden, there is a distinction between these implementation-oriented planning documents and the land-use plans.

In contrast, the Netherlands (until 2008) and Denmark have almost no implementation-oriented binding planning documents. The exception is the building permit, which can include temporal regulations (it expires if the landowner/developer does not build on time). This means that up to the granting of the building permit, implementation-oriented aspects are as a rule not included in any public law binding planning document; if they are included anywhere, it is only in indicative zoning plans or in private contracts. In the Netherlands, a legal modification in 2008 has changed this situation, introducing a legally binding implementation-oriented plan, the Development contributions plan (*Exploitatieplan*).

In summary, most of the countries have not only binding plans that include the physical zoning, but also implementation-oriented binding documents. The Netherlands (up to 2008) and Denmark could be considered as an exception to this.

4.2.2 Limited vs. broad contents binding rules

Concerning the scope of the possible contents of binding plans, in England the equivalent of the land use plan prescribes the broadest. The *Planning Permission* includes, besides the physical zoning, also temporal deadlines, financial contributions or other kind of contributions. The rest of the countries have binding land use plans with a more limited scope. Land-use plans can include only delimitations of zoning categories, of building envelopes, of social housing as a zoning category, and they can state, within certain limits, temporal deadlines. In short, in those other countries, land use plans can include not much more than the physical zoning. The most restricted seem to be the Dutch *Bestemmingsplan* (up to 2008) and the Danish *Lokalplan*: both include binding regulations concerning zoning categories and the building envelope, but exclude all other aspects (e.g. deadlines). In the other countries (and in the Netherlands from 2008 onwards) there are, besides the land use plan, other implementation-oriented binding planning documents that 'catch' the missing aspects, such as obligations, deadlines, etc. In conclusion, England has binding rules with the broadest contents, and the Netherlands (up to 2008) and Denmark with the narrowest contents.

4.2.3 Conditioning the approval of binding rules to securing implementation

Another important difference between the studied countries is that in some of them it is possible to condition, in a formal, open and direct way, the approval of the binding rules (the binding document that includes the physical zoning) to a development agreement between the municipality and the developer/landowner. That is, the binding plan sets out the requirements that must be afterwards agreed, and the definite approval of this binding plan is conditional on such an agreement; i.e. the binding plan only becomes legally valid after this agreement is signed. This is meant to guarantee the implementation of the binding rules. Such formal and direct conditioning exists at least in England and Valencia, and Italy shows similar features. In the other countries this seems not to be possible, formally speaking, although this does not mean that conditioning does not happen, indirectly and/or informally.

In England and Valencia, a first version of the binding rules (*Planning permission* respectively *Programa*) includes the requirements (*planning obligations* in England, *cargas urbanísticas* in Valencia) that must be secured with a Development Agreement (*Planning Agreement* respectively *Convenio Urbanístico*). Only when this agreement is signed do the binding rules become legally valid. In Italy, a Development Agreement (*convenzione*) must be signed before the *Piano di lottizzazione* and the new *Programma Complesso* become valid. At least in England and Valencia, the agreements are accessible for the public. Recently, English cities started to allow direct on-line access to those documents.

In the rest of the countries, it seems not to be possible, formally, to condition planning consent (the approval of binding rules) in a direct and formal way to a contractual commitment to implement the binding rules. Some of them (France, Sweden, Flanders, and, since 2008, the Netherlands) might be allowed to condition the granting of the building permit or similar to free cession of (some) land or to a contribution to (some of) the costs. This means that the obligation comes into play only after the landowner applies for a building permit and accepts the obligations attached to it. However, this does not imply a contractual obligation to do so, so not fulfilling this obligation can result in the building permit being annulled, but nothing more.

In sum, in England, Valencia and Italy the legally binding land use plan is directly and formally made conditional on the formalization of a development agreement. This contract commits the developer to provide the infrastructure, to cede land for free, to contribute to the infrastructure provision costs, etc. In the other countries, this conditioning is not possible, at least not in a direct and open way.

4.3 Procedure for the approval of binding rules

The utility of binding rules in negotiations might depend on whether municipalities are allowed to modify existing binding plans, and whether this requires a simple or a heavy procedure.

In several countries, when the development moment nears, instead of making a new land-use plan, it is also possible to follow, for minor modifications of/departures from the land-use plans, a much simplified procedure. A good example of this was the Dutch *vrijstelling* under the Physical Planning Act previous to 2008. The German

Baudispens, the French *Modification*, minor deviations in Sweden, the *afwijking/anticipatie* in Flanders and departures in Denmark are also similar. In all the studied countries, if the modifications of the land-use plan are major, they follow procedures that are simpler (but still heavy) than the procedure for the approval of a new land use plan.

In England, a modification, however small, of the *Planning Permission* itself (the binding physical zoning regulations) always needs a new permission. However, the procedure for the modification or removal of *planning conditions* is slightly simpler, and a modification of the *planning obligations* (implementation terms and contributions), if voluntarily agreed with the developer, does not require an extensive procedure at all. In Valencia and in Italy, a modification of the General Land use Plan (*Plan General de Ordenación Urbana* respectively *Piano regolatore generale comunale/Piano Operativo*), however small, can only be through processing and approving a detailed land use plan (*Programa* respectively *piani attuativi/Programma Complessi*). A modification of these detailed land use plans, however small, can only take place through processing and approving a new plan, which requires the same procedure.

In many countries, major modifications of the land use plan, whether this happens through the simplified procedure or not, seem to be very common. This is certainly the case in the Netherlands and France. Spain might form an exception to this. Here, major modifications (of the General Land use Plan through detailed land use plans), such as rezoning non-urban land into urban, do certainly take place but seem not to be as common in practice as in other countries.

To conclude, minor modifications through a very simple procedure are possible in almost all the studied countries. The exceptions are Valencia and in Italy, where even a minor modification of the binding rules requires a heavy procedure: the processing of a new planning document equivalent to the one that has to be modified. Regarding major modifications, in all countries, except in England, such a modification of the binding rules is possible only through a simpler (simpler than the making of a new Land use Plan), but still heavy, procedure. In England, major modification of planning obligations (realization terms and financial regulations), if there is agreement between the developer and the municipality, does not require a heavy procedure at all.

4.4 Binding rules in relation to property rights

The utility of binding rules in the negotiations might depend on the contents of property rights. More specifically, the degree of control that landowners have over the transactions in development processes might influence their negotiating position, and therefore the feasibility of the municipalities' value capturing goals.

4.4.1 Is infrastructure provision separated from development rights?

In all the studied countries, ownership rights include the right to build. There is no case where property rights are fully separated from the right to develop the land. That is, landowners are the only ones entitled to build on their land, and they can exclude others from doing so. However, this right acquires a concrete form only after the law and the binding land-use rules allow the possibility of building on the plot in question. In other words, binding rules limit the building rights and landowners have no right to a ´minimum´ amount of building rights. For example, the owner of land that is zoned as agricultural has no right to transform his land into an urban area. He acquires the right to do so only if the legally binding land-use regulations state it, and he is also obliged to exercise his right according to the law and after applying and obtaining the needed permits. An example of the wide scope that governments in Europe have for limiting the owner's right to develop his land is the fact that there is no room in legal systems for a generous (with respect to the landowner) concept of 'regulatory takings', at least as generous as in the United States of America. 'Regulatory takings' is the American legal concept that limits governmental regulation on private property that is deemed to be too onerous (Jacobs, 2008: 52, 67-68, 71-72; Needham, 2006: 47).

Although it became clear to us that building rights (more or less limited by binding rules) belong to the landowner in all the studied countries, it became also clear that there are important differences regarding infrastructure provision. These differences made us conclude that in some countries we could speak of a splitting of infrastructure provision from property rights. We look first at the differences in the formal responsibility for infrastructure provision, i.e. at the question who is formally responsible for it. In some countries, the law explicitly refers to the infrastructure provision as something differentiated from the rest of development rights, and labels it as a ´responsibility´ or a ´task´ of the public bodies, but not of the landowner or the developer. This happens in Valencia, Germany, France and Sweden. It could be said that in these countries, the right to provide infrastructure formally belongs to the municipality. In the other countries, there is neither an explicit mention in the law of infrastructure provision being a particular component of development rights, nor of any kind of public priority in this.

4.4.2 Control of transactions in infrastructure provision

Besides the formal responsibility for infrastructure provision, there is the question of the actual powers of public bodies for the provision of infrastructure. Here also there are important differences between the studied countries that led us to conclude that in some of them infrastructure provision is actually split off from property rights. More specifically, the question is: who has the development rights in each of the different steps in development processes? We applied here the model described in section 3.3.1 to analyse the power/dependency relationships between the involved actors (municipality, developer, landowners) in each step of the development process. The steps are grouped into those related to infrastructure provision, and those related to building on the serviced plots namely: (1) land purchase and assembling, (2) financing, (3) land preparation and development, (4) land disposition, (5) construction, and (6) property transfer. Steps 1-3 belong to the infrastructure provision, steps 5 and 6 to the building. Each of these steps implies transactions of some kind (land, money, property, etc). Developing whatever the binding rules prescribe can only happen after the first five transactions have been completed. By analysing who has the control over each of these transactions, it was possible to discern who has which development right. There are no relevant differences between the studied countries in the building (steps 4 to 6). However, regarding the position of the actors in the transactions involved in infrastructure provision, it is possible to distinguish two groups of countries:

Dependence on agreement with landowner

In some countries, transactions 1-3 are quite dependent on agreement between the municipality and the landowners. This seems to be the case in the Netherlands, England, France, Italy, Sweden (for the larger schemes), Flanders and Denmark. As a rule, if there is no agreement about the purchase and assembly of land and about the financing of the infrastructure provision, municipalities that want things to happen, have to apply pre-emption, expropriation and/or an *a posteriori* special tax formula. In other words, the only way of avoiding dependence on the landowner in steps 1-3 is public land development, or at least public infrastructure provision for private development. By doing this, municipalities get financially involved in the development: they have to lead the process, advance the money to purchase the land and provide the infrastructure, bear the risks of eventual delay, and possibly not recover all the costs made. Neither expropriation, nor special taxes are commonly used instruments.

Compulsory land readjustment as alternative to agreement

Besides voluntary agreement (or, in case of disagreement, pre-emption, expropriation and/or special taxes), Valencian and German municipalities have an alternative that allows them to obtain all or part of the land and the money needed for the infrastructure provision, namely land readjustment. In this way, and possibly a compulsory variant of it, Valencian and German municipalities can provide the infrastructure without depending on the passive or active collaboration of the landowner.

Sweden is an in-between case: Swedish land readjustment is dependent on the collaboration of at least a majority of the landowners, and can be compulsory for a minority of non-collaborating landowners. Also, land readjustment is meant only for local and minor facilities in minor greenfield residential schemes. In Flanders a land readjustment instrument is available, but it is not used at all. France also has a land readjustment regulation, but although it is quoted as being applied very often (Karki, 2003:

69; Turk, 2008: 234), a consulted expert considered it as not really relevant in practice (Renard, interviews 2006 and 2007). In Italy there is a land readjustment formula based on civil law that is used very often. In the winter of 2007 a draft of the new Italian national planning act included a statutory, public law version. However, it is based on the agreement of all the landowners. It is noteworthy that those countries, where planning law refers to infrastructure provision as a public responsibility or task (Spain, Germany, Sweden, France), also have a public law land readjustment regulation. It seems that only in the first three of them is the regulation also relevant in practice.

There are important differences between the Valencian, German and Swedish land readjustment:

1. Public involvement: in the Valencian *Reparcelación* and the Swedish joint development/land readjustment, the municipality can place on others the task of providing the infrastructure. In Valencia, municipalities can place this task on the landowners or on a commercial developer without land, or with only a little land. In practice these developers, called urbanizing agents, usually own a part of the land, or act on behalf of landowners, but it is not rare to find urbanizing agents with just a little or even no land. In Sweden, the municipality can place this task only on the landowners. On the contrary, in the German *Umlegung* it is the municipality that provides the infrastructure, advancing the finance. Only afterwards do landowners contribute to the costs. Therefore, German municipalities bear the financial risks, also of delay;
2. Cost recovery: in the Valencian *Reparcelación* all the involved costs and needed land are paid/ceded by the landowners, including money and land for off-site infrastructure. The German and Swedish municipalities can demand land and contributions only for the local facilities within the plan, but not for facilities that serve a wider area. In Germany, the compulsory variant implies that the municipality becomes more involved in the management and can recover a smaller part of the infrastructure provision costs. German municipalities often do not recover all the costs made. Swedish municipalities usually recover all the costs of local facilities.
3. Application: the Valencian readjustment is applied in practically all developments, whether they are greenfield, brownfield, redevelopment, low/high density, small/large areas, etc. The German *Umlegung* is a widely used (but not predominant) instrument, especially in city extensions, but also in regeneration projects in the existing built up areas (Larsson, 1997: 143; Karki, 2003: 69; Turk, 2008: 234). Of the two ways of Swedish joint development/land readjustment, only the 1973 Joint Facilities Act is applied in practice, and then only in minor residential schemes in greenfield areas. The 1987 Land Readjustment formula has not been used very much.

Conclusions

To conclude, there are clear differences in the position of public and private actors in the transactions that relate to infrastructure provision. As a rule, in the Netherlands,

England, France, Italy, Sweden (for the larger schemes), Flanders and Denmark, the transactions that are needed for infrastructure provision are dependent on agreement between the municipality and the landowners. To avoid this dependence, municipalities have in practice the alternative of pre-emption, expropriation and special *a posteriori* tax formulae. Thus, they have to get directly involved in the infrastructure provision, in financial and organizational terms. In Valencia and Germany, besides pre-emption and expropriation, municipalities can choose land readjustment, eventually compulsory readjustment. In Valencia, municipalities do not need to get directly involved in the development, can place the task on the landowners or on a commercial developer without land, and do not need to subsidise. In Germany, municipalities have to get directly involved in the development. In Sweden, in small residential schemes in greenfield areas, municipalities can apply joint development/readjustment and place the task on the landowners, but they need agreement with at least the majority of the landowners.

4.5 Selection of countries

The zoning regulations (binding and not-binding) in nine Western European countries have been compared in order to select those countries which, between themselves and in comparison with the Netherlands, show the broadest variation in the independent variable 'formal rules relevant to zoning' (for the methodological reason, see section 3.2.1.2).

The selected countries are the Spanish region of Valencia and England, countries that stand somewhat for opposite models. On each sub-variable of the independent variable 'formal rules relevant to zoning', the differences were remarkable. (1) Regarding the place of binding rules in the negotiation processes (Where and When), England represents the 'development-led' planning system model, and Valencia (together with France, Italy and Flanders) the 'plan-led'. The Netherlands fall in the middle, for it is in theory plan-led but does not work as such in practice. (2) Regarding the contents of binding rules (What), the Netherlands (up to 2008), together with Denmark, have almost no development-oriented binding rules, while England and Valencia do. Further, the Dutch binding rules, together with the Danish, have the narrowest contents, while England has the broadest. Finally, the approval of the Dutch binding rules (planning consent) cannot be made, formally and openly, conditional on securing the implementation, while in England and Valencia this is possible and constitutes the standard procedure. (3) Regarding the procedure for approval of the binding rules, in England certain major modifications are possible with a very simple procedure, while in the Netherlands and Valencia a heavy procedure is needed. (4) Regarding the relation between binding rules and property rights, in Valencia the infrastructure provision is in the planning law explicitly identified as a public task, while in the Netherlands and England it is not. Further, in Valencia infrastructure provision can

Table 8. Summary of main aspects of formal rules relevant to zoning.

	NL	England	Valencia (Spain)	Germany	France	Italy	Sweden	Flanders	Denmark
Formal rules relevant to zoning in the negotiation processes									
Early stages in development process, before negotiations	No binding Land use plan	No binding Land use plan	General binding land use plan	No binding Land use plan	General binding land use plan, but in transition to new sort of plan	General binding land use plan, but in transition to indicative structure plans	No binding Land use plan	Regional binding Plan	No binding Land use plan
Development moment, after negotiations	Binding rules approved for the first time, and in one document/ step	Binding rules approved for the first time, and in one document/ step	General binding plan becomes detailed in another plan document.	Binding rules approved for the first time, but in more than one document, although often simultaneously	General binding plan becomes detailed in another plan document.	General binding plan becomes detailed in another plan document.	Binding rules approved for the first time, but in more than one document, although often simultaneously	Regional binding Plan becomes detailed/ modified in another plan document.	Binding rules approved for the first time, and in one document/ step
Plan-led or Development-led?	Not really plan-led	Development-led	Plan-led	Not really plan-led	Plan-led	Plan-led, in transition	Not really plan-led	Plan-led	Not really plan-led
Contents binding rules									
Implementation-oriented binding plans?	No until 2008, yes after, in separate document	Yes, together with binding land use document	Yes, together with detailed land-use plan	Yes, in separate document.	Yes, in separate document	Yes, in separate document	Yes, in separate document	Yes, in separate document	No
Limited vs. broad contents binding Land-use plan	Limited	Broad	Broad	Limited, somewhat	Limited, somewhat	Limited, somewhat	In-between	Limited, somewhat	Limited

	NL	England	Valencia (Spain)	Germany	France	Italy	Sweden	Flanders	Denmark
Planning consent conditioned to contractual obligation?	No	Yes	Yes	No	No	Yes	No	No	No
Procedure approval binding rules									
Heavy/light procedure for major modification binding rules?	Heavy procedure	Light procedure for certain major aspects	Heavy procedure	Heavy procedure	Heavy procedure	Heavy procedure	Heavy procedure	Heavy procedure	Heavy procedure
Heavy/light procedure for minor modification?	Light procedure	Light procedure	Heavy procedure	Light procedure	Light procedure	Heavy procedure	Light procedure	Light procedure	Light procedure
Binding rules in relation to property rights									
Who has the responsibility to provide infrastructure?	It is not made explicit in law	It is not made explicit in law	To the public bodies	To the public bodies	To the public bodies	???	To the public bodies	It is not made explicit in law	It is not made explicit in law
Dependence on agreement with landowner to obtain land and contributions for infrastructure provision	Only avoidable through land acquisition or through a posteriori special tax	Only avoidable through land acquisition.	Avoidable through land acquisition and Land Readjustment.	Avoidable through land acqui, Land Readjustment and a posteriori special tax.	Only avoidable through land acquisition.	Only avoidable through land acquisition.	Only avoidable through land acqui, land readjustment if agreement majority landowners and special tax.	Only avoidable through land acquisition.	Only avoidable through land acquisition.

be implemented without need of agreement with the landowner, as there is the possibility of compulsory land readjustment. On the contrary, in the Netherlands and England, infrastructure provision in mainly dependent on agreement with the landowners, and this dependence can only be avoided through major public involvement (pre-emption, expropriation or *a posteriori* special tax formulae).

Valencia and England, together with the Netherlands, have become thus the focus of this research. They will be the subjects of in-depth research in chapters 5-7.

CHAPTER 5 The Spanish region of Valencia

Traditionally, public bodies have aimed in Valencia to finance the unprofitable parts in urban regeneration with the profitable parts. This aim has been central in the evolution of the Spanish planning system, and has led to conscious efforts to give responsibility to private parties for financing and implementing the public infrastructure and facilities. The first successful effort led to the introduction in 1956 by the central government in Madrid of a land readjustment regulation, meant to oblige landowners to do that. In 1994 the Valencian regional government introduced important innovations to resolve the serious shortcomings of the 1956 regulation.

Frame 5a

The institutional context: Spain, the region of Valencia, provinces and municipalities

Spain is a decentralized state, with a system of constitutional parliamentary monarchy. Since the Constitution (Constitución Española) of 1978, seventeen Autonomous Communities (Comunidades Autónomas, from now on 'regions') came into being, each of them with its own parliament and executive power. The decentralization of competences to the regions is such that Spain became de facto a federal state.

The Autonomous Community of Valencia (*Comunidad Autónoma de Valencia, CAM*, from now on 'region of Valencia') became in 1982 one of the seventeen regions. It occupies an area of 23,255 Km^2 (5% of Spain) and had in 2005 4.7m inhabitants (11% of the Spanish population, at an average density of 200 inhab/Km^2). In economic terms is nowadays one of the most dynamic Spanish regions. In the last years, the tourism industry has experienced a big rise. The region includes three provinces (*Castellón*, *Valencia* and *Alicante*) and 541 municipalities. The governmental layers (regional government – *Generalitat*, provincial government – *Diputación Provincial*, and municipality–*Ayuntamiento*) are organized hierarchically: the planning policies and plans of provinces and municipalities are subordinated to the law, policies and plans of the regional government. Of these three governmental levels, provinces have the least competence and weight.

The distribution of competences between Madrid and each of the regions is based on the principle of symmetrical division of competences. Both the central and the regional governments produce 'formal legislation' (laws) and 'legislation in a material sense' (decrees and regulations). There are exhaustive lists of competences, some of them reserved exclusively for the central government, some of them exclusively for the regional government. But there are also policy fields in which the central government has the competence for making 'basic' legislation, and the regional government that for developing and detailing this basic legislation. In complex policy fields such as planning, central and regional competences are intimately related to each other. Within the planning field, Madrid has the exclusive competence for property law, and the competence to issue basic legislation on common administrative proceedings and environmental protection. Regions can, within limits, detail and develop this basic legislation. As a result, Madrid has, for example, important competences for national infrastructure and the exclusive competence for expropriation law. The region of Valencia has exclusive competences for practically the rest of planning law (Betancor & García-Bellido, 2001: 88, 90, 92). For a list of legislation, relative to planning, see Annex 2.

Sections 5.1 to 5.3 introduce the context of how public bodies capture the value increase in urban regeneration in the region of Valencia. Section 5.4 introduces the studied cases. Section 5.5 describes the working of the formal rules relevant to zoning within the value capturing mechanisms. This is the answer to Preparatory research question 3: how can formal rules relevant to zoning influence the capturing of value increase in Valencia? The question has been divided into several sub-questions that correspond to the sub-variables a-e (for more details about these sub-variables, see section 3.3.3). Each of the answers to the sub-questions consists of an assessment of whether the sub-variable can influence the capturing of value increase. There is therefore not one single conclusion, but as many conclusions as sub-questions. All these conclusions have provided the ingredients for the final conclusions in chapter 8 and the recommendations for the Dutch practice in chapter 9. Section 5.6 assesses the degree of actually captured value increase, taking account of the side effects on the tempo of implementation. Finally, section 5.7 summarizes and makes some statements about the inferred causalities between formal rules and capturing value increase. This includes an assessment of the role of third variables.

5.1 Urban regeneration in the region of Valencia

It is possible to differentiate two different urban regeneration policies, or groups of policies, in the region of Valencia. First there are those policies designed at the regional/national level, oriented basically to the revitalization of historic areas and some other deteriorated neighborhoods. In the second place, there are those policies designed at the local level that focus on facilitating the redevelopment of old industrial and office sites into residential areas (Blanc, interview in 2005; Sanchis, interview in 2008).

5.1.1 Revitalization of historic centers and deteriorated neighborhoods

What characterizes these urban regeneration areas is that landownership is usually fragmented. Regeneration often has to deal with many landowners, who usually stay in the regenerated area. Since 1992, the Ministry of Housing of the central government in Madrid, together with the regional Valencian government and the cities of Valencia and Alicante, have set up in total three revitalization programmes for historic neighborhoods (*Áreas de rehabilitación integrada y concertada*): one for the historic center of the City of Valencia (since 1992), the second for the XIXth Century's Cabanyal district (since 2004), also in the City of Valencia, and the third for the historic center of the City of Alicante (since 1993). At the middle of 2008, a fourth programme was being set up for the XIXth Century's Ruzafa district in the City of Valencia. These programmes include two sorts of public investment. The central and the regional governments give subsidies to the owners for the rehabilitation of their properties. Alongside these subsidies, the regional government and the municipality intervene directly through refurbishing public infrastructure and facilities. These programmes could be considered as the most intensive and complete direct public interventions in urban regeneration in the region of Valencia.

Alongside these, other more modest and numerous programmes have been set up in the last years (*Áreas de rehabilitación*). They are meant for the regeneration of other historic neighborhoods and also of peripheral 1960's and 1970's social housing districts. These programmes (about 200 of them) include a combined subsidization: national and regional subsidies to landowners, and a modest direct municipal public intervention in refurbishing public infrastructure. Finally, the central and the regional governments are nowadays setting up new programmes for the demolition and rebuilding of several seriously deteriorated districts.

5.1.2 Rezoning old industrial and office sites into residential

Some municipalities, generally at their own initiative, have developed since the end of the 1990s local policies to facilitate the rezoning (*recalificación*) of old industrial and offices sites located within the existing urban areas. Due to urban growth and economic changes, these sites have often become surrounded by residential and office functions. Rezoning seems a logical step and attracts the interest of property investors because these sites are located at the heart of large and active markets for multi-family housing and office space. Confronted with numerous proposals from market parties, some municipalities decided to allow rezoning and regulate it with *ad hoc* policy. An important difference between these schemes and those mentioned in 5.1.1, is that these rest exclusively on private initiatives and do not imply any public expenditure. Here, profits have to pay *all* the unprofitable parts. This research focuses on this sort of projects, thus the studied cases belong to this sort. For an introduction to the cases see section 5.4

It seems that at least in larger cities, rezoning has become common in the last years (Rubio, Montiel, Sanchis, interviews 2006 and 2008). For example, in the city of Valencia, more than 90% of all locations zoned in the 1988 General land use plan as industry have been re-zoned into housing and office (see Figures 8). And between 50 and 80% of all locations zoned as commercial and recreational (offices) have been re-zoned too (Raga, Rubio, interviews in 2006). Three of the four studied cases correspond to this sort of rezoning: *Camino, Periodista* and *Benalúa*[1]. Regeneration in these sorts of sites has to deal with many landowners, who tend afterwards to sell their land to private developers. Municipalities do not usually buy land. However, landowners do not usually sell immediately, but choose most of the time to participate in the land readjustment (Modrego, 2000).

Frame 5b
General Land Use Plans and Detailed Plans
Municipalities have the competence for making the binding rules at their level. There are two sorts of relevant binding rules documents at this level: General Municipal Planning (*Planeamiento General Municipal*) and Detailed Planning (*Planeamiento de desarrollo*) (Parejo & Blanc, 1999: 111-113, 264-286, 317). The General Land-use Plan (*Plan General de Ordenación Urbana, PGOU*) belongs to the first sort and covers the whole municipal territory. Each municipality must approve one of these plans, which to be (re-)approved each 5-20 years. The small municipalities have a simpler form (*Normas Subsidiarias*). The region approves them definitively. Detailed Planning documents are meant for detailing afterwards the approved General Plans for specific sites, and they can modify their contents (Betancor & García-Bellido, 2001: 108).

General Plans have a legally binding character, i.e. they have statutory consequences for the use possibilities of land. Planning law prescribes the contents of General Plans.

1 The fourth case, *Guillem*, consists of rezoning old deteriorated housing.

For the whole municipal territory, they must set out the most important zoning rules, labelled 'structural binding rules' (*ordenación structural*, Parejo & Blanc, 1999: 274-277, 287-305):

- Strategic choices: possible building typologies, maximal number of dwellings and sometimes a maximum floor space index;
- The 'classification' or zoning (*clasificación*) of the entire territory into: (i) Existing Urban land (*suelo urbano*); (ii) Land to be developed in the future, soon or in the longer term (*suelo urbanizable*); and (iii) Non-developable land or rural area (*suelo no urbanizable*);
- The logical phasing of development;
- Land use designations for the Non-developable land;
- Zoning of land into Building regulation zones (e.g. historic city, urban extension, area of scattered buildings, etc). The 1999 Standard Building Regulation Order defines these zones, although municipalities are allowed to modify them or even to adopt a completely different version;
- Delimitation of sectors (*sectores*), development sites that have to be detailed afterwards;
- Main public infrastructure and facilities: important leisure centres and the 'Primary Network of public facilities' (*Red Primaria de dotaciones públicas*: road network, public facilities and green areas);
- Delimitation of the 'Redistribution Areas' (*Áreas de reparto*) and for each area a 'Reference Development Allowance' (*Aprovechamiento tipo*), a kind of floor space index, which forms the basis for the calculation of the building rights of each landowner, see under;
- Regulations regarding public infrastructure and facilities not belonging to the municipality (e.g. highways, railways).

Planning law also prescribes that for Existing Urban land and for Land to be developed soon, General Plans must also state the complementary zoning rules, labelled 'detailed binding rules' (*ordenación pormenorizada*, Parejo & Blanc, 1999: 287; Romero, 2002: 234-239, 353-354):

- The alignment of the buildings;
- The ground level of the street (*rasante*);
- Local public infrastructure and facilities: delimitation of the 'Secondary Network of public facilities' (*Red Secundaria de dotaciones públicas*);
- What is called the 'qualification' of land (*calificación*), the zoning of the land into different land use categories: free market housing, affordable/social housing, commercial space (office, shops,...), industrial, etc;
- The building volumes;
- Delimitation of the 'Development Units' (*Unidades de Ejecución*), the sites to be developed in an integrated way.

For all the studied cases, the General Plan had prescribed not only structural, but also detailed binding rules: the 1988 General Land use Plan of the City of Valencia for cases *Guillem, Periodista* and *Camino*, and the 1987 General Land use Plan of the City of Alicante for case *Benalúa.*

Detailed Plans (Special Plans –*Plan Especial,* Partial Plans –*Plan Parcial,* and Urban Renewal Plans –*Plan de Reforma Interior*) are meant for specific sites, and can modify and must anyway detail, if they are not detailed already, the structural binding rules contained in the General Planning. The contents of the Urban Renewal Plan are very similar to those of a Partial Plan. It is not only public agencies who can submit a Partial Plan and an Urban Renewal Plan, commercial developers can do so also (Betancor & García-Bellido, 2001: 108).

Municipalities and other public bodies with competences for policy fields with planning implications (e.g. regional agencies for industry and social housing) can make and approve provisionally a Special Plan. However, whatever public agency approves the Special Plan, the region must approve it definitively. These plans can cover small areas, all the municipal territory or more than one municipality. They tackle a specific field: landscape, nature and cultural protection, protection of infrastructure, public facilities, industrial areas, and affordable and social housing.

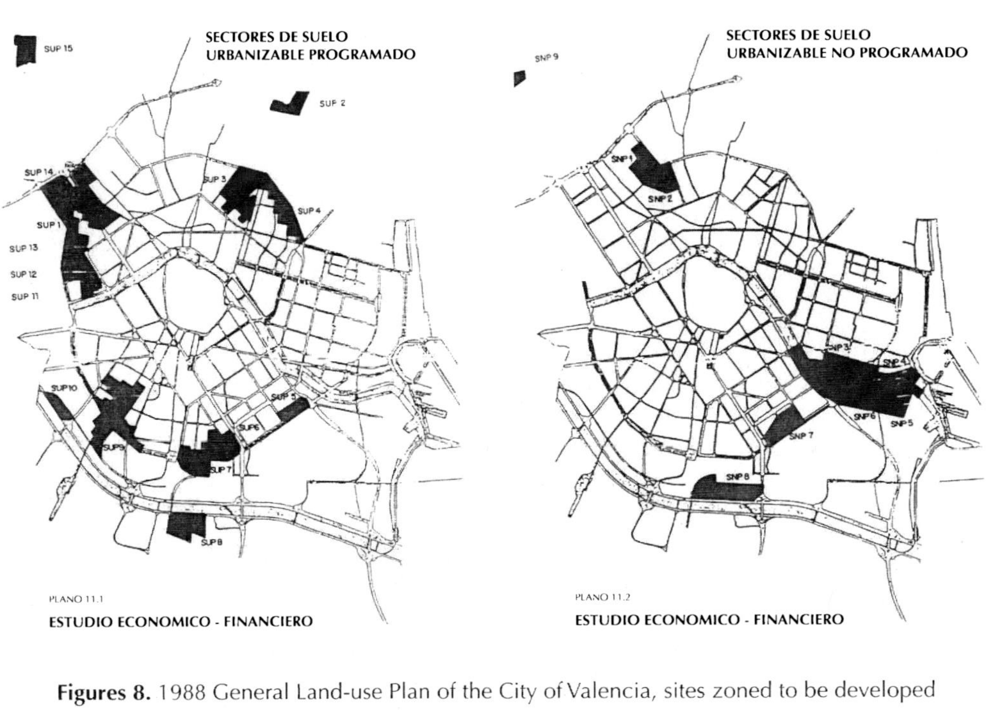

Figures 8. 1988 General Land-use Plan of the City of Valencia, sites zoned to be developed in the future (soon left, in the longer term right).

5.2 Capturing value increase through the land readjustment regulation

Urban regeneration is implemented almost always through the Land readjustment regulation (*Reparcelación*), which organizes not only the property readjustment, but also the allocation of costs and profits between the landowners. All the studied projects apply the readjustment regulation. All the profitable *and* unprofitable parts are distributed between the landowners. As mentioned, the regulation was introduced in 1956, and in 1994 the region of Valencia introduced some important modifications.

5.2.1 Landowners lead land readjustment: 1956-1994

Together with the Planning Acts of 1975-6, 1990-92, 1998 and 2007, the planning act of 1956, issued by the Franco regime, articulates the foundations of the present Spanish planning system, including that of Valencia nowadays. This system reinforces the certainty which landowners have about the development possibilities of their land, through the legally binding General Land Use Plan. This plan zones the entire municipal territory into urban, developable and non-developable land. Also, this plan and, in some cases, the Detailed Plan, establishes the exact amount of building rights that belong to each landowner, giving a very high certainty about the future building possibilities. Banks accept these building rights as collateral for loans and mortgages. In market transactions, the price of land tends to incorporate the residual value of these building rights.

Frame 5c
Calculation of building rights of landowners
The building rights of the landowners are established as follows: the General Plan delimitates the Redistribution Areas (*Áreas de Reparto*). Landowners included in a Redistribution Area share the building rights. Also, the General Land Use Plan and, in some cases, the Detailed Plan, establish a Reference Development Allowance (*Aprovechamiento tipo*) for each Redistribution Area. This Allowance is a kind of weighted floor space index. 'Weighted' means that the economic value of land is weighted, depending on its use (affordable housing, free-market housing, office space, shops, etc) and on its location (along the main road or in a more tranquil and isolated area). Therefore, the Reference Development Allowance is expressed in units of 'modal use' (*unidad de aprovechamiento*). The weighting is made in two steps: first the differences in value are weighted due to differences in use. Second, in the Land Readjustment Project (see under), the differences due to the location are weighted.

The Reference Development Allowance is calculated as follows (Parejo & Blanc, 1999: 296-304; Romero, 2002: 206-219): the total units of modal use (in m² floor space modal use) are divided by the total area of the Redistribution Area *minus* the area of existing public infrastructure and facilities that public bodies obtained in the past through free cession (but not through buying or expropriation). Therefore, the Reference Development Allowance is calculated as follows:

- *Building volume expressed in units of 'modal use' : (area Redistribution Area - area of existing public facilities that public bodies obtained previously through free cession) = x m² floor space modal use / m² land*

Example of calculation of the Reference Development Allowance in a Redistribution Area of 1,000 m² of land of which 100 m² public infrastructure were previously obtained through free cession, and where the General Plan and/or Detailed Plan foresee a total building volume of 2,000 m² floor space modal use:

- *Reference Development Allowance: 2,000 : (1,000 – 100) = 2.2 m² floor space modal use/m² land.*
- *Example of calculation of building rights of an owner of a parcel of 100 m²: 100 x 2.2 = he has right to 220 m² floor space modal use.*

The Reference Development Allowance was in case *Guillem* 1.367, in *Periodista* 1.87, in *Camino* 1.6537 and in *Benalúa* 0.6.

Although the infrastructure provision, also called 'urbanization' (*urbanización*) in Spain, is still considered a public task, its implementation has become since 1956 both a duty and a right of landowners through the principle of 'equitable redistribution of benefits, costs and duties' (*redistribución equitativa de beneficios y cargas*) of urban development. Value increase and costs of development are proportionally distributed between all landowners according to the area of their original property. Value increase thus serves to compensate landowners for taking responsibility for the unprofitable parts of urban development, i.e. for providing the public infrastructure and facilities and ceding the needed land.

The planning system specified several instruments for operationalising this system of redistributing betterment and costs. The underlying idea was that the readjustment of the property boundaries and the infrastructure provision had to be organised by all the landowners themselves, not necessarily giving primacy to an intermediary agent (e.g. one public or commercial developer owning part/most of the land). The Land readjustment regulation made this transformation possible without depriving landowners of their ownership. Landowners were obliged to form a joint development organisation (*Junta de Compensación*), which organised and financed the infrastructure provision through voluntary land readjustment (*Sistema de Compensación*). After municipal approval was obtained, the *Junta* arranged the engineering works, provided the site with the needed public infrastructure, redistributed the resulting parcels and infrastructure and, finally, dissolved itself. The planning system included in addition two major instruments with which municipalities could intervene directly. First, the municipality could overrule the landowners and take the lead by providing the infrastructure and applying compulsory land readjustment (*Sistema de Cooperación*). In this case, the landowners were obliged to pay the total costs six months in advance to the municipality. The second instrument was expropriation and implementation of the plan (*Sistema de Expropiación*).

Another important component of the system was the introduction in the 1978 Planning Regulation of a set of legal minimal standards for public infrastructure and facilities (*Estándares urbanísticos*). These legal standards, together with the prescriptions included in the General Land Use Plan, created certainty about the public infrastructure and facilities to be paid/realized by the landowners. The 1990-92 Act raised these standards considerably.

The results of the planning system were ambiguous. On the one hand, it succeeded in one of the main goals of the 1956 Act, which was to organise and finance the private implementation of public infrastructure and facilities. On the other hand, the system clearly failed to assure an efficient (quantitative and qualitative) implementation. As a rule, landowners did not proceed quickly and processes were slow. The transaction costs associated with organising landowners and developing a plan could be high (see intermediary variable *inflated development costs* in causal model section 2.4.2). In addition, buying land and waiting was very common, and speculation in the land market was said to have achieved critical levels. Some have argued that this is clearly related to the high certainty about future building possibilities that arises after the approval of the General Plans. High accounted land costs (see intermediary variable *accounted land costs*) and the costs of organising landowners and infrastructure provision made development feasible only when high housing prices allowed high final profits or when the quantity and the quality of infrastructure and public facilities (variable A.2) were low. It is argued that this delayed development processes (intermediary variable *delay*) and resulted in poorly serviced building sites, with inferior public infrastructure and facilities and huge building volumes. Confronted with this failure, public bodies had not used their legal instruments adequately to intervene directly through compulsory land readjustment or through expropriation. Compulsory land readjustment entails more involvement of the municipalities, which had to prepare the plans, organize the land readjustment, possibly expropriate some owners, and advance some financing, bear some financial risks, etc. In case of expropriation, compensation includes part of the market value of the use possibilities of the new land-use plan: this makes expropriation expensive. Also, compulsory land readjustment and expropriation remains a politically sensitive matter, especially at the local level (Parejo & Blanc, 1999: 479-480).

5.2.2 The urbanizing agent leads the land readjustment: 1994 - onwards

Since the 1980s, critics such as García-Bellido (1989; 1991b; 1993, 1994) and Parejo Alfonso (1993) advocated reform of the 1956's land readjustment regulation. In 1994, the social-democratic regional government of Valencia, influenced by this criticism, approved the Valencian Planning Act (*Ley Reguladora de la Actividad Urbanística*, LRAU). The 1994 Act made feasible some novelties previously introduced in 1976. The 1975-6 Land use and Urban Planning Act introduced an innovation that was derived from the idea of *urbanisme concerté* in the French legal reform of 1973. The innovation consisted of introducing a third party, in addition to the municipality and the landowner/developer: the urbanising agent (*agente urbanizador*). This third party is not required to own land and can be directly appointed by the municipality (public land development company) or be chosen in a public tender (commercial builder or developer). After being assigned as concession holder, the urbanising agent assumes responsibility for the infrastructure provision and for the proportional redistribution of betterments and costs between the landowners. In theory, therefore, this innovation assigned the task of redistribution and infrastructure provision to the urbanising agent alone; it was no longer a right and duty of landowners, as had been specified in the 1956 Act.

The innovation in the 1975-6 Act did not work. After being appointed by the municipality, urbanising agents needed the voluntary consent of the landowners and had no guarantee that the municipality would apply compulsory land readjustment if the landowners did not collaborate. In such cases, urbanising agents would be obliged to ask the municipality to expropriate, and they would be required to pay the full market value of the landowner's building rights. In short, urbanising agents had to commit themselves to the implementation of a plan without knowing for sure whether possible difficulties with landowners could be resolved within the schedule. Furthermore, agents were likely to be faced with paying high compensation to landowners. This situation impeded the success of the innovation of 1975-6 (García-Bellido, 1993; 1994). Moreover, the possibility of appointing an urbanisation agent was limited to that part of the land classified as developable in the future and to those cases in which the municipality explicitly had decided to follow this formula. It did open a door, however, by introducing the possibility of public bodies deciding in a public tender where to place development rights and the possibility of involving a third party (who is, in principle, not linked at all with landownership) to be responsible for infrastructure provision.

The Valencian 1994 Act made the 1975-6's innovation feasible. First, the 1994 Act specified land readjustment and, if necessary, compulsory land readjustment, as the default procedure. Urbanising agents therefore knew beforehand that the possible resistance of landowners could be overruled after proper proceedings. Second, the Act subjected all developable land (both regeneration in urban land and greenfield sites) to this new formula for development. What the 1994 Act actually did was to generalize the compulsory land readjustment formula, adding the possibility of appointing a third party as implementor. A third important novelty of the 1994 Act is that it gave guarantees to the initiating parties about the handling of their proposals. This was meant to prevent municipalities from being too discretionary in their decisions. These three modifications allowed initiating parties to have a reasonable idea of their risks and costs, before entering into a public tender. A fourth novelty was to link the legally binding physical zoning (the Detailed Plan) to the scheduling of its implementation: Detailed Plans are now accompanied by a new sort of plan, the Joint Development Programme, which includes all the development-oriented aspects: calculation of costs, obligations of all parties, and a Development Agreement to secure the financing and implementation of the public infrastructure and facilities.

The 1994 Act was originally an initiative of the social democratic PSOE (*Partido Socialista Obrero Español*), and the conservative *Partido Popular* voted against it at the time of the parliamentary approval in 1994. However, the *Partido Popular*, after winning the regional elections in 1995, decided to maintain the law. Since then, most of the other seventeen Spanish regions, although parties with a variety of political opinions administer them, have introduced the Valencian innovation into their own planning legislation (Burriel, 2008). In December 2005, the regional government of Valencia approved, in reaction to criticisms of the 1994 Act, the 2005 Planning Act (*Ley Urbanística Valenciana*, LUV)[2]. This revision modifies some important aspects of the 1994 Act, which can be summarized in two aspects. First, it reinforces the procedural guarantees and relieves the obligations on owners in semi-consolidated areas. Second, it introduces a double-tender procedure: the first public tender is for choosing the urbanising agent. Once selected, the urbanising agent is obliged to organise a second tender for the public works. The first tender follows part of the European public procurement regulation[3]; the second follows the entire regulation. The European Commission did however not agree and has submitted in the summer of 2008 an appeal to the Court of Justice of the European Union[4]. In September 2010 the Advocate General of the EU advised to dismiss the Commission's case (Advocate General of the European Union, 2010). It is expected that the Court of Justice will pass judgement at the end of 2010.

2 The European Parliament has played a central role in this criticism by criticizing the urban policy of the regional Valencian government (Burriel, 2009).

3 Directive 93/37/EC and Directive 2004/18/EC, concerning the coordination of procedures for the award of public works contracts.

4 Action brought on 9 July 2008 - Commission of the European Communities v Kingdom of Spain, (Case C-306/08), (2008/C 223/58).

Frame 5d
Joint Development Programmes
Under the 1994 Act, where the implementation of a Detailed Plan implies the need to construct new public infrastructure and facilities, or to refurbish the existing ones, the plan *must* be accompanied by a Joint Development Programme (*Programa para el desarrollo de una Actuación Integrada,* PAI, also translated sometimes as 'Integrated Action Programmes'). The initiating party that submits the Detailed Plan (whether this is a public or a private party), must also submit the Programme. Municipalities can choose whether to approve first the Detailed Plan and, afterwards, the Programme, or to approve both documents at the same time. In practice they proceed and approve both documents at the same time, as part of the same development initiative that has to be evaluated as a whole. This was the case with all the studied cases, except for a small part of the plan area in *Benalúa*. A Programme has also, the same as a Detailed Plan, a legally binding character. Planning law prescribes its contents, which are divided in two groups of documents (Parejo & Blanc, 1999: 329-333):

1) Technical Alternative (*Alternativa Técnica*), that includes the documents with the physical zoning: (1a) The Detailed Plan that modifies, completes or details the General Plan; it can also include a Land Readjustment Project (*Proyecto de Reparcelación*, see under); (1b) A Provisional or Definitive Infrastructure Provision Project (*Anteproyecto/ Proyecto de Urbanización*), which includes a scheme for the public infrastructure, with a description of those elements that determine the total costs, such as the quality of the public space, a scheme of the sewerage network, a scheme of the road network and the other facilities, a description of existing networks (sewerage, water, roads, electricity, cables), and the feasibility and the costs of connection to the new development (Merlo & Ribes, 2004: 53-54).

2) Juridical-economic Proposal (*Proposición Jurídico-Económica*), which includes the documents with the financing and implementation schedules: (2a) The Economic-financial Proposal (*Proposición Económico-Financiera*); (2b) A proposal of Development Agreement (*Convenio Urbanístico*). Financing and implementation schedules consist of the following:

- Infrastructure provision costs: a provisional estimation of these costs, and the allocation of these costs to each landowner, as well the form of payment (in money or in kind, in building rights);
- Land to be ceded freely;
- Additional contributions: e.g. extra financial contributions, building of public facilities, extra contributions for social/affordable housing;
- Deadlines for the submission of the Land Readjustment Project: in the studied cases within 3 to 5 months after the definitive approval of the Programme;
- Deadlines for the commencement and completion of the infrastructure provision: within the legal maximum of 5 years for the completion of the works (three cases),

or 3 years in case the landowners, organized in an association, become selected as urbanizing agent (case *Camino*);
- Deadlines for the building works: of the four studied cases, only one, *Camino*, included a deadline for the building, in this case for the commencement of the building.

The municipality approves both documents, Alternative and Proposal, and the regional government intervenes only to approve definitively the Detailed Plan in case it modifies the structural binding rules of the General Plan. In practice, the regional government uses this competence very often, and it is not exceptional that it rejects or requires the modifications of the plans. In exceptional situations, the regional government can also suspend the municipal plan and approve a new plan in its place. Such a measure has always a temporary character (Parejo & Blanc, 1999: 111-112, 256, 311), and is not very common in practice.

Anyone can submit a Programme, including a Detailed Plan, to the municipality, as landownership is not required. The proposal usually follows the provisions of the General Land Use Plan. If the General Plan is not yet detailed, the Detailed Plan details it. However, for Existing Urban land, the General Plan is always detailed: i.e. the General Plan establishes already whether land is meant for residential, industry or offices, the maximal building volume, which sites should be redeveloped, building alignments, etc. So in these cases there is no need for Detailed Plans, unless it is necessary to modify the General Plan.

The municipality can reject the Programme, including the Detailed Plan, or initiate a formal public tender procedure. After a Programme has been published, anyone can submit objections or alternative programmes. Candidates negotiate with landowners to obtain support; they may publish their offers in newspapers and invite landowners to join them. After evaluation and negotiations with the candidates, the Local Council decides on a definitive Programme and selects the urbanising agent. Selection criteria are the total infrastructure provision costs, the quality of the plan and the public infrastructure and facilities, the advantages offered to the municipality, the price offered to the landowners for their building rights, the support of landowners, the implementation schedules, and the amount of the bank guarantees. The tender can be declared void if none of the proposals satisfies the municipality, but such decisions must be justified (Blanc, 2003; Muñoz et al., 2004). Municipalities can grant concessions to public agencies without public tender. About 30% of all schemes in the region are developed by public companies, which are dependent on national, regional or municipal public bodies (figures from 1994 till 1998, Modrego, 2000). However, most (from 1994 until 1998: 72%) of the urbanisation projects have been the result of private initiatives (Modrego, 2000).

After the approval of the Programme, landowners can decide whether they want to be expropriated or to continue in the development process. If they choose for expropriation, the municipality is responsible for the expropriation, and the urbanising agent is obliged to pay the compensation. The urbanising agent (a public agency, or a private developer selected in the public tender) makes and submits to the municipality an Infrastructure Provision Project and a Land Readjustment Project. These documents must fit within whatever is prescribed in the General Plan, Detailed Plan and Programme. After the period of public consultation, the municipality may reject, amend or approve the documents.

Frame 5e
Procedure for the compulsory land readjustment
Planning law prescribes the following procedure for compulsory land readjustment (Parejo & Blanc 1999: 454-460):

- Public consultation of the Land Readjustment Project: it is announced generally in newspapers, and announced individually only to the registered titleholders, that is those owners that are registered in the Property Register (*Registro de la Propiedad*).
- Application to the Property Register of a note that certifies who are the titleholders and which charges exist on the property (*certificado de dominio y cargas*). At the same time, the Register notes the initiation of the readjustment procedure.
- Additional hearing of 10 days in case there turn out to be titleholders that have not been formally addressed because they were not inscribed in the Property Register. Also, an additional hearing of 10 days for the affected persons in case of modification of the Project.
- During the Public consultation, affected persons can claim compensation from each other. The owner of the freehold of the land has to compensate the titleholders of other rights on his property that have to disappear. This may delay the procedure.
- During the Public consultation, owners can also offer to, or demand from, each other shortages and surpluses of building rights (*defectos y excesos de aprovechamiento adjudicado*). It is not always possible to allocate all the building rights of each landowner onto a particular building plot. When there are shortages or surpluses, and it is not possible to divide the new plot between several owners (*pro indiviso*), owners have to buy or to sell the remaining rights. The Project proposes a unitary price for the building rights. If the owners and urbanizing agent do not agree with this price, the landowners can propose another price.
- Definitive approval: the Local Council (*Pleno del Ayuntamiento*) approves definitively the Land Readjustment Project. Other public authorities also can approve it definitively, should they have the competence for expropriating land on the site in question.
- Publication, individual announcement to the affected persons and registration of the approved Project in the Property Register.

Procedure for the voluntary land readjustment
The procedure for voluntary land readjustment is simpler. The proposal of readjustment has to be endorsed by all the affected persons (landowners and other titleholders).

Once the proposal has been submitted, the municipality decides right away: there is no period of public consultation (Parejo & Blanc, 1999: 461). Most of landowners usually prefer the voluntary way.

The approval of the Land Readjustment Project and its registration in the Property Register has important consequences:

- Allocation to each new plot, in accordance with the Detailed Plan, of the building possibilities (volume and use typology) and of the public facilities and infrastructure;
- Automatic modification of the property boundaries, with: i) assignment (*subrogación*) of the old private plots into the new private serviced building plots, proportionally to the area of the former property and if possible on or nearby the former property; ii) and transfer to the public domain of the public infrastructure and facilities and possibly of some serviced building plots. The urbanizing agent, as concessionaire for the public task of urbanisation, is allowed to occupy the plots (also the new private plots) to provide the infrastructure.
- The new serviced building plots are charged with the obligation of paying the corresponding contribution to the infrastructure provision costs, according to the share in the building rights. Landowners usually pay in instalments during infrastructure provision. In 2000, more than half of all landowners paid their contributions in cash (*Generalitat Valenciana* 2000), although landowners may also pay in kind (i.e. in building rights). If the landowner does not cooperate, a part of the building plot, equivalent to the building rights that are necessary to pay the contribution, is transferred to the urbanizing agent. The remaining building plot goes, free of charge, to the landowner.
- Old rights and charges on the old plots are transferred to the new plots provided that they are compatible with the new plan. However, when the new plot is transferred to the urbanizing agent as payment in kind (*finca de garantía*), the land has to be transferred free of old rights and charges. Old rights and charges that have to disappear have to be compensated by the former landowner.

Finally, the owners of the serviced building plots submit building applications and the municipality issues as-of-right building permits, according to the General and Detailed Plans and the building regulations.

5.3 The legal limits for capturing value increase in the region of Valencia

How far can the required contributions of landowners and developers go? The legal principles that delimit the scope of the contributions that can be obtained through land readjustment are described below.

5.3.1 Public share of value increase

Following the Spanish Constitution of 1978, 'The community shall have a share in the benefits accruing from the town-planning policies of public bodies' (section 47). This constitutional principle authorizes municipalities to capture part of the betterment, on top of the development costs and other charges mentioned below. In developable areas (e.g. case *Benalúa*), municipalities had until 2007 the right to 10% of the building rights, and from 2007 onwards between 5 and 15%. Landowners are obliged to cede without any charge to the municipality the serviced building parcels that are needed to make up this percentage. Note that they are ceding land, but not building rights, because following planning law these building rights never belonged to the landowners, but to the municipality. It is also important to note that the ceded plots do not necessary turn out to be the same percentage, as building rights refer to the economic value of the new buildings, and not to their land area. The ceded land may become part of the Municipal Patrimony of Land (*Patrimonio Municipal de Suelo*), which is intended for affordable housing and other social purposes.

5.3.2 Value increase as compensation for taking responsibility for public infrastructure and facilities

As mentioned, the principle of 'equitable redistribution of benefits, costs and duties' rules that landowners, in exchange for the building rights, are obliged to pay the infrastructure provision costs and to provide the needed land to the urbanizing agent. The infrastructure provision costs are called 'urbanization charges' (Parejo & Blanc, 1999: 329-333, 409-415, 474-475).

Frame 5f
Infrastructure provision costs, i.e. Urbanization charges (*cargas de urbanización*) consist of:

- 'Urbanization costs' (*costes de urbanización*), the costs of preparing plans and technical projects, of damage compensation, and of the civil works for streets, pathways, electricity, public light, planted trees on path and gardens, water and sewage, gas, telephone, cables, etc;
- 'Urbanization canon' (*canon de urbanización*), a contribution to the costs of off-site public infrastructure that serves the scheme in question, but has been previously realized in other schemes;
- Profit margin of the urbanizing agent, which usually charges around 10% of the 'urbanization costs';
- Overhead costs, the organizational costs made by the urbanizing agent.

Besides a contribution to the Urbanization charges, landowners have also to cede free of charge the land that is needed for public infrastructure and facilities. This includes not only the civil works, but also other public facilities (such as public schools, sport installations, kindergartens, parks, municipal offices, police station) the building and exploitation costs of which must in principle be paid by the respective public body. Additionally, on developable land it is also possible to oblige landowners to cede land situated elsewhere that is needed for off-site infrastructure. In case *Benalúa* (plan area 8.2 ha), the landowners had to cede 5.4 ha of land located off-site and meant for a highway. The building rights of the Redistribution Area of the development site have to be shared with the 'off-site' owners of the land on which this road is located. These owners receive the same (proportional) share of the building rights as the on-site landowners.

Municipalities are free to agree additional obligations with the urbanizing agent, as for example the building and exploitation of public facilities, additional contributions to the municipality, or additional compensation for damages. However, the urbanizing agent cannot charge landowners for this, but must pay from his own resources. Usually urbanizing agents own an important part of the land, so they are able to pay these extras from the profits from the development of the real estate. Municipalities can also agree additional contributions for social housing: this can be in addition, or not, to the land zoned for social/affordable housing, see under.

5.3.3 Social/affordable housing

Spanish municipalities can, since the 1990 Land Use and Urban Planning Act and its Refunded Text (definitive version, after integrating its determinations with other still ruling regulations) of 1992, zone land for social/affordable housing. The possibility of zoning land for this was, at that time, a very important novelty in Spanish planning law, and became the subject of discussion. The Supreme Court of Spain and the jurisprudence considered it very disputable to zone land for affordable housing without compensating the landowners. Since 1997, the regions have taken over the competences on this matter, by-passing the discussion at the national level. Valencia and other regions have included this 1992's novelty in their regional planning legislation (Burón, 2006: 87). Social/affordable housing is called in Valencia by different names, depending on whether it is based on the national or the regional social housing legislation: *Vivienda con Protección Pública* respectively *Vivienda Protegida* (Fernández *et al*, 2003: 91).

Frame 5g
The amount of social/affordable housing built
The building of affordable housing in Spain and Valencia has decreased in the last years

In 1996, 30% of all new housing in Spain was affordable housing. During the government of the right-wing Partido Popular in the national government (1996-2004), this figure dropped significantly, to less than 10%. Since 2004, the new social democratic government of Zapatero and most of the regions have declared affordable housing as a priority of their planning policy. The Regional Government of Valencia introduced recently the obligation to build a minimum percentage of 25% affordable housing in urban land, and 40% in urbanizable areas. Including a legal quota is a recent general trend in Spain, with almost all the regions fixing such minimum percentages. The Basque Country was the first region to do so. In 1994, it included, in municipalities with more than 7,000 inhabitants, the legal minimum of 20% of affordable housing in urbanized land and 65% in extension areas. In 2006, it lowered the criterion to municipalities of more than 2,000 inhabitants and increased the quota to 40% respectively 75% (*Burón, 2006*: 85). In 2007 the government in Madrid approved a new Land Act, which established a minimum of 20% for the whole country.

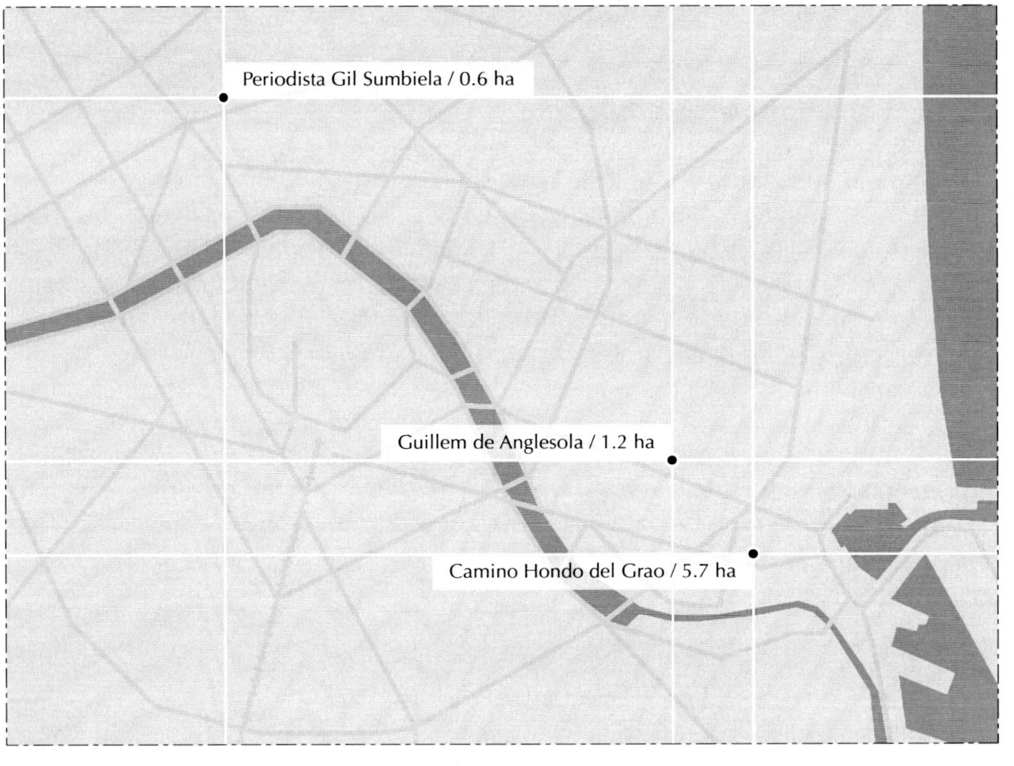

Figure 9. Location of the cases in the city of Valencia.

The effect of zoning land for affordable housing in the zoning plan is that, later on, once land readjustment takes place, the serviced building plots are inscribed in the Property Register as affordable housing. As a consequence, the actual and the future owners can only develop affordable housing on it. Affordable housing in Spain and in Valencia receives a subject subsidy from central and regional government in the form of a subsidy to the mortgage interest and sometimes of a lump-sum subsidy to the buyer. The price of land for affordable housing is regulated (about € 100-150/m^2 floor space in 2006), much lower than for free-market housing (€ 300-1,100/m^2 floor space, depending on the location). This difference in land price between affordable and free-market housing is shared between all the landowners through the land re-adjustment.

Thanks to the regulated low price of land, developing social/affordable housing is a profitable activity. Profit rates from developing social/affordable might be not large, but it is a very safe product, for the demand is guaranteed since selling prices of affordable housing are at least 50% and lower than prices for free-market housing. Both commercial developers and housing cooperatives develop social/affordable housing. Housing cooperatives (*Cooperativas de vivienda*) arose as cooperatives of individual citizens meant for commissioning their own dwelling. In time they became more professionalized and independent from the future occupiers of the affordable dwellings.

5.4 Introduction to the studied cases in the region of Valencia

In all cases, there was a General Land-use Plan that included binding rules that prescribed the future development possibilities (see figures 9 and 10). Before being allowed to redevelop the site, a Detailed Plan had to be approved. In cases *Camino* and *Benalúa,* the Detailed Plan modified the structural binding rules in the General Plan, thus it also had to be approved by the regional government. In *Guillem* and in *Periodista,* the Detailed Plan only detailed and modified the detailed binding rules of the General Plan, so in principle there was no need for regional approval. However, because the General Plans were made before the 1994 Planning Act, regional approval was in any case necessary.

In all the studied cases, new public infrastructure and facilities were needed, so a Joint Development Programme had to accompany the Detailed Plan and an urbanizing agent had to be selected. In all the cases, the urbanizing agent is a private party selected in a public tender. Urbanizing agents are most of the time professional developers, as in *Guillem* and *Periodista*. However, sometimes landowners join together and become the urbanizing agent, as in *Camino* and *Benalúa*.

Since the introduction in 1994 of the urbanizing agent, the number of urbanizing agents without land has increased. They can charge around 10% of the infrastructure provision costs as profit margin. However, as the cases show, most of the time urbanizing agents not only develop serviced building parcels, but also buy some land and become developer of the buildings. In *Periodista,* most landowners sold their property relatively quickly to the urbanizing agent, before the approval of the Joint Development Programme. In *Guillem,* they waited a while and most of them sold at the time of the land readjustment procedure. In *Camino* and *Benalúa,* the land was already the property of the urbanizing agent (as landowners themselves became the urbanizing agent).

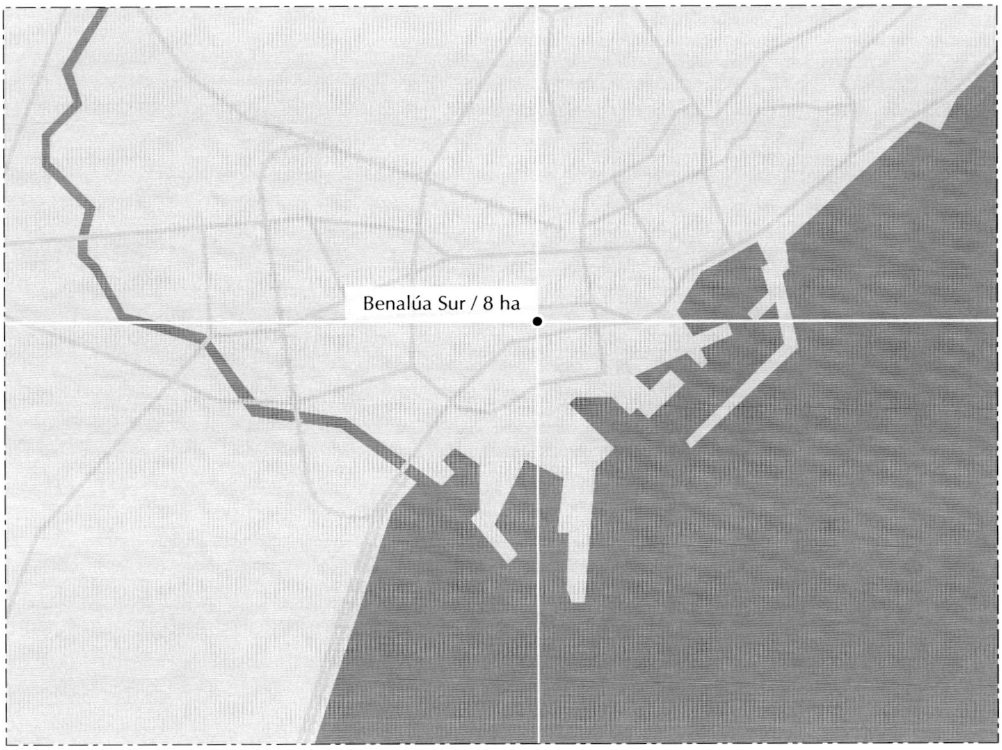

Figure 10. Location of case 'Benalúa Sur' (8 ha) in the city of Alicante.

Here follows a brief introduction to the cases. The rest of the case-based information has been included in the rest of the chapter.

5.4.1 *Guillem de Anglesola,* City of Valencia

Urban Regeneration project 'Guillem de Anglesola' (1.2 ha, about 125 apartments, 104 units/ha, plus some retail, see figure 11) is located in the east of the city of Valencia. It concerns the demolishing of about 50 old and deteriorated housing buildings. The 1988 General Plan foresaw the redevelopment of this old residential area, located in a densely built up area. The General Plan proposed the construction of a main road through the site and multi store buildings along that road, with a total building volume of 15,706 m² floor space (1, 6 and 7 floors). In 1999 a commercial developer (*Proara Promotores Aragoneses SA*) submitted a Joint Development Programme, including an Urban Renewal Plan. After a public tender in which other three developers submitted an alternative plan, Proara's proposal was provisionally approved in 2003. In 2005, after the signing of the Development Agreement, Proara was definitely selected as the urbanizing agent. The Urban Renewal Plan included in the Programme detailed outline provisions and modified marginally the already detailed provisions of the 1988 General Plan. The procedure for land readjustment began in 2006. In May 2008 works had yet not started. It was expected that the infrastructure provision would be ready no later than 2010.

Figure 11. 2005 Joint Development Program.

There are 49 small parcels in the plan area. Almost all these parcels are owned *pro indiviso* by several owners, each of them owner of a flat, so the total number of owners was much higher than 49. The smallest parcel has 26 m², the largest 548 m², and the average size is 100-200 m². Alongside the plan process, the urbanizing agent negotiated with the individual owners and acquired land. When the urbanizing agent submitted the Land Readjustment Project in March 2006, he already owned about 30% of the land.

5.4.2 *Periodista Gil Sumbiela*, City of Valencia

Urban Regeneration project 'Periodista Gil Sumbiela' (0.6 ha, about 100 apartments, 166 units/ha, plus some retail, see figure 12) is located in the north of the City of

Valencia. It is located in a densely built up area, and was previously occupied by a warehouse, some office space, some industry and an empty plot. The 1988 General Plan foresaw redevelopment into some residential use, some commercial/recreational, in total 5,556 m² floor space (1-2 floors), and some public infrastructure. In 2005, a commercial developer, *Prodaemi S.L.*, with the support of a majority of the landowners, submitted a Joint Development Programme, including an Urban Renewal Plan. This plan proposed an increase of the building possibilities (from 5,556 to 11,000 m² floor space; 1-2 to 6 floors) and rezoning to residential, of which the majority should be affordable housing. After evaluation and several modifications, *Prodaemi's* proposal were approved provisionally in 2006, and definitely in 2007. In November 2006 it was expected that the infrastructure provision would be finished not later than 1012.

Figure 12. 2007 Joint Development Programme.

Property was originally divided among several landowners. The owners of 65% of the land supported the proposal of *Prodaemi*. Once the Programme became provisionally approved in July 2006, *Prodaemi* bought all the land.

5.4.3 *Camino Hondo del Grao*, City of Valencia

Urban Regeneration project 'Camino Hondo del Grao' (5.7 ha, about 465 apartments, 82 units/ha, plus a considerable amount of building space for offices and retail, see figure 13) is located in the east of the City of Valencia. Before redevelopment, the site was used for industry. It includes several old industrial buildings with a historic-monumental value. The 1988 General Plan foresaw the continuation of these uses. In 2000, a commercial developer submitted a Joint Development Programme proposing the redevelopment of the location into a residential area. Some other parties, among them the owners of the majority of the land, organized into an

Association of Urbanistic Interest (*Agrupación de Interés Urbanistico, AIU*), and submitted alternative Programmes. Finally, the municipality rejected all the proposals. In 2003 another commercial developer tried again, and two others (among them, again, the landowners), submitted alternatives. Finally, in 2004, the municipality decided to choose the Programme of the owners, which became the urbanizing agent. The Urban Renewal Plan included in the Programme rezones the existing industrial use into residential and public facilities, and increases the building volume. The regional government approved it definitely in 2005, and the Development Contract was formally signed in 2006.

Figure 13. 2005 Joint Development Programme.

The property was initially divided into 18 parcels, owned by seven private landowners, most of them (81% plan area) members of the Association that won the public tender. The rest of the land belongs to an electric company (0,08%), the railway company (8%), and the Municipality of Valencia (5%). The municipality owned also the existing roads and the land that is reserved for the school. *Inmuebles Barrera S.A.* was the private landowner with the largest ownership: 32% of the plan area. In 2005 *Vallehermoso*, one of the national leading commercial developers, bought 59% of the urbanizing agent (almost 50% of the plan area). In April 2008 another developer, *Coperfil Inmobiliaria*, has bought most of the land and is in charge of the infrastructure provision, for which the demolition phase had already started at that time.

5.4.4 *Benalúa Sur*, City of Alicante

Urban Regeneration project 'Benalúa Sur' (8 ha, about 600 apartments, 75 units/ha, plus a considerable amount of building space for offices and retail, see figure 14) is located in the southwest of the City of Alicante. Before redevelopment, the site included some undeveloped plots, some old and deteriorated housing and several industrial firms, of which some were still active. The 1987 General Plan foresaw the redevelopment of the site into a new residential area for 735 dwellings, some commercial space and public facilities. In addition, a piece of land located at the outskirts of the city (5.4 ha) was ascribed to the site. This land is necessary for a new highway surrounding the city, and its landowners participate in the land readjustment together with the rest of the landowners. In 1997, the municipality modified slightly the regulations of the 1987 General plan for this site, reducing the plan area and the number of dwellings.

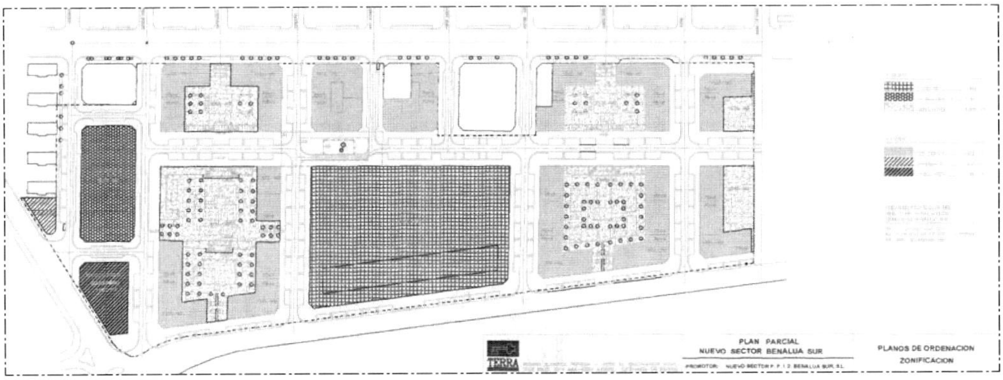

Figure 14. 2003 Joint Development Program.

In 1998, *Nuevo Sector P.P. 1.2 Benalúa Sur S.L.* submitted a Joint Development Programme for the redevelopment of the site that included a Partial Plan. *Nuevo Sector* was a development company founded by the owners of about 60% of the land. These owners founded an Association of Urbanistic Interest also. The initiative and the lead was taken by one of the owners, *Urban Programas Urbanos*, a consultancy that had bought about 15% of the land (situated in the ascribed piece of off-site land). In 2002 *Urban Programa Urbanos* sold its land and its participation in *Nuevo Sector* to a developer, *Grupo P.R.A.S.A.*, who became the leading party. After a public tender in which three other proposals were evaluated, in 2003 the Programme was provisionally and then definitely approved. The Development Contract was formally signed in 2004. The municipality approved the Land Readjustment Project in 2006. The infrastructure provision works started in 2007.

5.5 How formal rules relevant to zoning in Valencia can be used

This section describes the working of formal rules relevant to zoning within the value capturing mechanisms. There are different ways (or sub-variables) in which these rules

in Valencia can be used in an operational way to improve capturing value increase:
- Creating certainty or uncertainty beforehand about future building possibilities and contributions;
- Choosing the contents of the relevant binding rules;
- Conditioning the relevant binding rules to securing the capturing of value increase;
- Modulating property rights;
- Using the procedure for the preparation and approval of the relevant binding rules.

Here follows an assessment of whether each of these sub-variables can affect the capturing of value increase.

5.5.1 Creating certainty beforehand about future building possibilities and contributions

Summary of the findings

It is remarkable about the Valencian planning system that it provides beforehand a relatively high degree of legal certainty, certainly when compared with England, The Netherlands and other Western European countries (see section 4.1 for an international comparison). This is mainly due first to a wide set of legal minimal standards for public infrastructure and facilities, established in planning law; second to the legal duty for municipalities to approve a legally binding General Land-use Plan that must cover the whole municipal territory; and third to local policy for the modification of the General Plan.

Because of these three measures, the main determinants of the economic value of land are already fixed when the development initiatives take place. There is a very high level of certainty about both building possibilities and the contributions. Nevertheless, there is some room for flexibility that municipalities can use purposefully, mainly related to capturing value increase. This flexibility does not diminish the certainty about the *minimal* building possibilities and contributions, which are already stated in the legal standards and the General Plan, and which cannot be relaxed. What happens is that there is some flexibility to *augment* the building possibilities, that is, there is some uncertainty about the maximum possibilities. If municipalities augment the building possibilities, they create at the same time certainty about the additional contributions. In other words: (1) there is legal certainty about a minimum, both of building possibilities and of contributions; (2) there is some uncertainty about the possibility of augmenting building possibilities; (3) there is certainty about additional contributions, in case of augmenting. Table 9 summarizes the level of certainty, before definitive negotiations take place, about building possibilities and contributions.

Table 9. Level of certainty in the Valencian cases

	Certainty about future building possibilities	Certainty about future contributions
Guillem, City Valencia	Very high	Very high
Periodista, City Valencia	Very high about min, less about max	Very high
Camino, City Valencia	Very high about min, less about max	Very high
Benalúa, City Alicante	Very high about min, less about max	Very high

The findings from the studied cases and other sources strongly suggest that uncertainty about the future building possibilities, together with certainty about the future contributions, might be positive for capturing value increase. Let us now see in detail whether municipalities create certainty or uncertainty and about what, in what sort of documents: then we infer the consequences for capturing value increase. Here a distinction is made between certainty through legal minimal standards and the General Land Use Plan, and certainty through indicative local policy documents meant for the case that the General Plans are modified.

5.5.1.1 Creating certainty through the minimal legal standards and the General Plan

Since 1978, planning law prescribes a wide set of legal minimal standard contributions (*Estándares urbanísticos*). The 1998 Planning Regulation, which was in force for the studied cases, differentiates between *standards* and *prescriptive determinations* for residential, commercial/recreational and industrial developments. Also, it differentiates between standards that must be included in the General Land use Plan and those that must be included in the Detailed Plans, whether in the form of structural or detailed binding rules.

Frame 5h

Examples of legal minimal standards for residential schemes in the 1998 Regulation

- Minimal public space: depending on the floor space index of the scheme, different percentages of minimal public space are given for roads, green areas and public facilities. E.g. with an f.s.i. of 1 m^2 floor space per m^2 land, at least 63% of the plan area must be used for public space: 15% for green areas, 20% for public facilities and 28% for roads. Also, the area for public facilities must be at least 35 m^2 per 100 m^2 floor space.
- Minimal number of plots for public facilities: schemes with more than 8,000 m^2 floor space of residential use must provide at least one plot for public facilities, which must be situated in the most appropriate location and within an urban context that fits with its function.

- Minimal parking places: per dwelling, at least one parking place must be provided, and in case of schemes of more than 10 dwellings, per 10 dwellings an additional parking place must be provided. At least 50% of these parking places must be situated in or under the buildings, not in the public space.

Example of prescriptive determination for residential schemes in the 1998 Regulation
Municipalities must establish in their General Land use Plan a minimal amount of commercial/recreational uses in residential developments.

When a development initiative takes place, there is almost always an approved General Land Use Plan. This was also the situation in all the studied cases: the 1987 Plan in the city of Alicante (case *Benalúa*) and the 1988 Plan in the city of Valencia (the other three cases). A General plan sets out for the whole municipal territory the structural binding rules and, in urban development areas, usually the detailed binding rules also. That is, the General Plan establishes whether land is meant for residential, industry or offices, the maximal building volume, which sites should be redeveloped, building alignments, and also details of the public infrastructure and facilities which must be realized, etc. This was also the case in the four studied cases. The 1988 General Plan of the city of Valencia prescribed detailed regulations for the three studied cases in that city. In *Guillem* and *Periodista,* the 1988 document prescribed for example the alignments of the public streets and the apartment buildings (including the height), and the maximal building volume, 15,468 respectively 5,556 m² floor space. In *Camino,* it prescribed the continuation of the industrial use, added some commercial use, prescribed a maximal building volume of 72,663 m² floor space and delimitated the buildings and public infrastructure. The 1987 General Plan of the city of Alicante, and its later modification in 1997, prescribed detailed regulations for the case *Benalúa,* such as the detailed alignments of public infrastructure and the apartment buildings, and a maximal building volume of 103,670 m² floor space, maximal 742 dwellings.

What is the effect of this certainty on capturing value increase? It has not been possible to measure in our cases those effects, because this was the situation in all the cases and there was no example of the contrary to compare with. However, it seems reasonable to conclude that municipalities might lose some negotiation room when creating absolute certainty about the future building possibilities. Also, certainty about building possibilities might inflate the accounted land costs and the regular and final profit margins of the developer (see causal model in section 2.4.2). On the contrary, uncertainty about future building possibilities might be positive for capturing value increase. This conclusion is based on the fact that the captured value increase improved in those cases in which municipalities made use of their statutory potential to deviate from the General Land-use Plan, that is, in cases where municipalities created some uncertainty about additional building possibilities (see below). After all, the General Plans had already 'given away' their treasure (the allocation of building possibilities), so landowners and developers were already secure and able to internalize part of the value increase in the accounted land costs and profit margins. The municipalities had less to offer, unless *additional* building was possible.

5.5.1.2 Effects of modifying the General Plan on capturing value increase

The legal framework in Valencia offers the possibility to modify the General Plan. Detailed Plans can modify the General Plan in different ways: they can rezone one urban use into another (industrial to housing, industrial to office, office to housing, etc - called *recalificación*); increase the building volume (*aumento de edificación*); or rezone land from non-developable to developable (agricultural to housing, agricultural to industrial, etc – *reclasificación*).

In green-field sites municipalities usually follow the provisions of the General Plan strictly. Re-zoning land from agricultural into an urban use (*reclasificación*) was not a common practice. Up to 1998, statistics show that Detailed Plans re-zoned almost no agricultural land into land to be developed (Modrego, 2000). That is, whether land may be developed or not is mainly and firmly established in the General plans. From 1998 onwards, there are neither published nor other available figures. Based on interviews with several relevant experts, it seems that the situation has not changed significantly (Rubio, Munoz & Canellas, Blanc, Escribano, interviews in 2006 and 2007), although other sources do not agree (Burriel, 2008). The general picture that arises from the mentioned interviews is that, since 2004, there have been many proposals to re-zone agricultural land into golf courses *annex* residential schemes, but most of them seem to have been rejected or are still being processed. This picture might be compatible with the existence of some well-known examples of approved re-zonings (Blanc, Escribano, interviews in 2006 and 2007), and the political and social repercussion of these re-zonings might be anyway much higher than the figures could justify (*cfr.* Burriel, 2008). None of the studied cases included such a re-zoning. In the city of Valencia there seems to be only one case of *reclasificación*, in *Barrio de la Torre*. Anyway, cases of *reclasificación*, if they exist, are irrelevant for urban regeneration because they almost always concern green-field developments.

On the contrary, in urban regeneration it seems clear that municipalities often use this possibility to re-zone one urban use into another and/or to increase the building volume (*recalificación* and *aumento*, Rubio, Montiel, interviews in 2006). In exchange, they ask for more contributions, additional to the legal minimum standards mentioned above. Modifications mostly involve the re-zoning of industrial and commercial/recreational space (offices, shops, etc) into housing. For example, in the city of Valencia, more than 90% of all locations zoned in the 1988 General plan as industry have been re-zoned into housing and office space. Between 50% and 80% of all locations zoned as commercial/recreational areas have been re-zoned too (Raga, Rubio, interviews in 2006). In three of the four cases – *Periodista, Camino* and *Benalúa* - the Detailed Plan indeed increased the building volume and/or re-zoned the use of land from one urban use into a more profitable one.

The uncertainty that this regulatory power to modify the General plan might create has however been limited: Valencian municipalities usually specify which sorts of modifications are possible, and approve criteria about additional contributions, in case of modification. This happens in indicative documents, approved by the Local Council. The example of the Municipality of Valencia could be representative. At the end of the 90s, more and more market actors took the initiative to ask for re-zoning. However, up to 2000 the Municipality of Valencia did not accept them (Raga, interview 2006). In 2000, the municipality decided to make it possible to modify the General Plan so as to rezone land from one urban use to another. In addition, it elaborated several criteria, most of them related to capturing value increase (see Frame 5i).

Frame 5i
Criteria for the modification of the General Plan in the Municipality of Valencia
The Municipal Council of Valencia approved on 28 July 2000 several criteria for the rezoning of one urban use into another (*recalificación*), and modified these criteria in new resolutions on 22 May 2002 and 30 April 2004:

- Rezoning is only possible in case of old industrial areas or office buildings to be redeveloped into residential areas.
- The rezoning has to improve the urban quality: reducing the total building volume; or the new residential use must fit better in the neighbourhood; or introducing any other objective improvement.
- 20% of the total building volume has to be used for commercial/recreational uses, or for affordable housing.
- Compensation: for each new m^2 floor space, landowners have to cede 1 m^2 land for public facilities (additional to the minimal obligations already established in the legal standards and in the General Plan), or 0.5 if the urbanizing agent uses at least 20% of the building volume for affordable housing (before the municipal resolution of 22 May 2002, this was 50%). These m^2 of land may also be ceded outside the plan area, or paid in money. Therefore, appraisal of the value of the new floor space is based on cadastral values. In *Periodista* and *Camino*, the municipality introduced instead an independent appraisal made by the Polytechnic University of Valencia. The University increased in both cases the value of the new floor space, when compared with the cadastral values. As a consequence, the compensation sum increased notably.
- The resulting housing density in the plan area cannot exceed 75 dwellings/ha.
- If the new dwellings add more than 1,000 inhabitants to the area, landowners have to cede at least 5,000 m^2 land for a park (additional to the legal minimal cessions).

In *Benalúa*, in the City of Alicante, the municipality did something similar. The 1987 General Plan established structural binding rules for this site. However, in 1997 the Local Council, after a legal judgement against the 1987 Plan, approved the Municipal Criteria, a document that detailed how exactly a future Detailed Plan should modify the 1987 General Plan: for example, the exact amount of building volume and the detailed binding rules. So in fact, although the latter Detailed Plan modified the 1987 Plan, actually there was already in 1997 certainty about the modification possibilities.

Neither the 2000 resolution of the Municipality of Valencia, nor the 1997 Municipal Criteria of Alicante were legally binding for the use of land (the municipality retained fully discretional powers to decide). However, in both cases the municipality decided publicly to handle those rules very strictly as evaluation criteria. The cases confirm this.

Besides those sorts of modifications that are foreseen in local policy documents, there are other sorts of modifications that are less regulated. For example, in the City of Valencia the second possibility of modification (increasing the building volume) is not covered by formal policy. Asked about this, a public officer (Raga, interview 2006) confirmed that there are 'informal' criteria for this. 'Informal' because they are not formulated explicitly by the Local Council. In very specific cases, the public officer states, it is possible to increase the building volume.

Frame 5j
The 'informal' criteria for increasing the building volume laid down in the General Plan in the Municipality of Valencia, handled in case *Periodista*, were these:
- The same as for *recalificación* (see frame 5i).
- The urbanizing agent proposed to use 80% of the building volume for affordable housing;
- The urbanizing agent proposed a building envelope that fits within the surrounding buildings.

What are the effects on capturing the value increase? The cases confirm the idea that the possibility of modifying the General Plan (rezoning the land and augmenting the building volume) may increase the negotiation strength of the municipality. In addition, it is plausible to conclude that the certainty created about the additional contributions in case of modification influences the accounted land costs and profit margins, similar to the effect of the certainty mentioned in the previous section (the certainty created by the General Plan and the minimal legal standards). In *Periodista,* both (possibility of modification + certainty about additional contributions) led to a share of 80% affordable housing in the building, an enlargement of public space from 1,805 up to 2,597 m², and the payment of a substantial amount to the municipality. In *Camino* it led to an enlargement of public space and facilities from 16,186 to 38,720 m², the rehabilitation and free cession to the municipality of four old industrial buildings, and the payment of an important amount to the municipality. All these contributions were additional to the contributions prescribed initially in the

General Plan and in the legal minimal standards (for a comparison of contributions in all four cases see section 5.6). It is very plausible that similar effects took place in other modifications of the 1988 General Plan of the city of Valencia.

5.5.2 Possible contents of the binding rules

The Spanish 1978 Constitution gives a broad definition of the goals of public activities in planning: to pursue an adequate environment for the development of the individual, to protect historical and cultural heritage, to fight against speculation in order to guarantee decent and adequate housing for each Spaniard, and to share a part of the benefits accruing from public planning. Planning law operationalizes these broad constitutional goals by allocating many competences to public authorities (Parejo & Blanc, 1999: 133-138). This might be the reason for the broad range of prescriptions that can be included in the Valencian binding rules, both prescriptions related to the physical zoning (*Planeamiento Físico*), and prescriptions related to the organization of the implementation (*Planeamiento Programático*).

Summary of the findings

There are two sorts of physical zoning prescriptions that seem clearly to have, or potentially to have, a positive effect on capturing value increase: (1) Planning law defines much broader obligations for landowners under the category 'Land to be developed' than under the category 'Existing Urban Land'. In Land to be developed, binding rules can include the broadest range of obligations: such as more public facilities, off-site infrastructure, and a public share of 10% in the building rights. It seems clear that this leads to higher captured value increase. (2) Planning law opens the possibility of including in the binding rules prescriptions regarding social/affordable housing. These are of two sorts: first, since 1992 municipalities can zone land for social/affordable housing; second, municipalities and developers can reach agreements about additional social/affordable housing. For the present, these measures seem not to have been systematically applied. However, the findings suggest that they are potentially useful for getting more social/affordable housing built.

Regarding the organization of the implementation, there are three sorts of prescriptions that seem also clearly to have a positive effect on the capturing of value increase: (3) Planning law defines the possibility of ascribing off-site infrastructure to the development site in question. Landowners of the off-site land share the building rights with the owners of the development site, and cede their land freely. Thanks to this measure, Valencian municipalities have obtained in the last years a very important part of the land needed for main public infrastructure and facilities. (4) Planning law allows municipalities to agree contributions additional to the minimal legal package. This has clearly provided a significant benefit for the public, also for social/affordable housing. (5) The 1994 Act rearranged the contents of the General and Detailed Plans. The Act included the financing and implementation schedules (included previously in the General and Detailed Plans), and the agreed additional contributions (included previously in external agreements) into a new sort of document, the Joint Development Programme. The positive effects of this 1994's reorganization on capturing value increase are however unclear, because there seems to be a more relevant independent sub-variable: this is that the 1994 Act introduced the obligation of *always* achieving a Development Agreement to secure the investments and schedules. This was previously an option, not an obligation (see under in section 5.5.3).

The following sections include a detailed assessment of these five sorts of prescriptions, and how they work within the value capturing mechanisms.

5.5.2.1 Prescriptions related to physical zoning: Zoning land into the class 'Land to be developed'

Probably the most important function of the General and Detailed Plans is to categorize land into three sorts or 'classes': 'Existing Urban land', 'Land to be developed in the future', and 'Non-developable land or rural area'. It seems that municipalities sometimes categorize as much land as possible into Land to be developed, with the intention of improving capturing value increase. Owners of Land to be developed are obliged to pay/realize higher contributions than owners of Existing Urban land: for example more public facilities, off-site infrastructure and a public share of 10% in the building rights. The legal criteria for categorizing land are very strict: land that is already provided with the needed public infrastructure *must* be classified as Existing Urban Land; land that is not yet provided with such infrastructure, and is meant to be, *must* be classified as Land to be developed. However, although these criteria seem clear, in practice there is some room to draw the line some meters to the right or to the left. For example, the 1988 General Plan of the city of Valencia classified as much land as possible as Land to be developed. This led often, in the periphery of the city, to drawing the border between Existing Urban land and Land to be developed along the party walls of existing buildings. The same happened in the 1987 General Plan of the city of Alicante, for example in case *Benalúa*.

What was the effect of zoning as much land as possible as Land to be developed? That there is certainty about *more contributions*, thus plausibly a lowering influence on the accounted land costs and the profit margins of the developer, and a strengthening of the negotiation position of municipalities. In general, developments on Land to be developed provide higher captured value increase than on Existing Urban land. That was clearly the case in *Benalúa*, the only case where land was classified as Land to be developed. In *Benalúa* the municipality receive 17% of all building rights and a large piece of land for off-site infrastructure. Both advantages are the direct result of the fact that the site falls under the class Land to be developed.

The strategy of delimiting very strictly the line between Existing Urban land and Land to be developed might have been more successful in the City of Valencia than in Alicante. In the City of Valencia, this strategy has been systematically applied in the 1988 General Plan, and this has resulted in an improvement of the public space situated in the urban periphery. All around the city, the new schemes on Land to be developed of the 1988 General Plan have paid, in the urban periphery existing at that time, for the green space and other public space in-between the existing buildings (Blanc, interview in 2006, see also figures 15). However, in the City of Alicante, where the 1987 General Plan had also drawn the line very strictly, the municipality seems to have made legally risky delimitations, which has led to delay. For example, in *Benalúa* the municipality zoned several parcels as Land to be developed that could also be considered as Existing Urban land. Landowners took the 1987 municipal delimitation to the courts, both in case *Benalúa* and in *Playa de San Juan*, another scheme in the city of Alicante. The courts have granted some of the appeals, e.g. in *Benalúa* part of the land became an own development site subjected to the lower contributions regime of Existing Urban land, reducing the area of our development site from 98,000 to 82,451 m^2.

5.5.2.2 Prescriptions related to physical zoning: Zoning land for Social/affordable housing

Before 1992, planning legislation did not allow the zoning of land for social/affordable housing. This changed with the 1992 Refunded Act. Since then, General and Detailed Plans can establish a minimum percentage of social/affordable housing, of the total number of dwellings in the plan area. Also, they can establish on which parcels that housing to be built.

In practice, many General Plans did not zone land for social/affordable housing, because most of them were made before 1992. This is the case in the cities of Valencia (1988 General Plan) and Alicante (1987). From 1992 onwards, there are no data available about whether General and Detailed Plans include affordable housing or not, but following some experts, municipalities, in general, have not done this. This lack of political will has led to discussion. A widely shared opinion among experts is that municipalities are not reliable in fulfilling the function of guaranteeing enough social/affordable housing. The only solution, they argue, is to introduce minimal quota in regional planning legislation. This discussion has had consequences in practice. It seems that in the last years, when housing prices have risen spectacularly and when the affordability of houses has become a main political issue, municipalities have begun to zone land for affordable housing. For example, the General Plan of the city of Castellón de la Plana (2000) has done so (Roger, Blanc, Rubio, Montiel, Muñoz & Cañellas, Escribano, interviews 2006). One of the four studied projects (*Periodista*) included affordable housing in the Detailed Plan (80% of the scheme).

Municipalities can also require contributions for social/affordable housing and include them in the Programmes, contributions that are additional and complementary to the mentioned legal minimal package and specially zoned land. Additional contributions might include extra cession of land, or a minimum percentage, or the obligation for the landowners to pay their contribution to the infrastructure provision costs in building rights, and the obligation for the urbanizing agent to use these building rights for affordable housing. It seems that municipalities have only recently begun to do so. Case *Guillem* included affordable housing in the Programme but not in the Detailed Plan, and *Periodista* both in the Programme and in the Detailed Plan.

Figures 15. (1-2) Nou Campanar/Jorge Comín; (3) San Pau; (4-6) Beniferri. These are examples of older buildings in the former northern urban periphery of the City of Valencia. The green space has been paid by the new developments on Land to be developed (Copyright Demetrio Muñoz, nov 2006).

What are the effects for the building of social/affordable housing? Two measures are evaluated here: (1) the fact that, since 1992, binding rules can zone land for social/ affordable housing; (2) and the fact that municipalities can agree additional contributions regarding social/affordable housing and include them in the Programmes. The conclusion is that both measures *can* have a positive effect on the actual realization of social/affordable houses because they *can* create certainty about *more contributions*. Up to recently, municipalities did not use these measures, thus building rates were influenced mainly by the housing market: in times of low housing prices, developers seek safer products such as affordable housing. Because from 1998 till circa 2007, housing prices rose spectacularly, the building of social/affordable housing dropped very significantly (see Table 10).

Table 10. Percentage affordable housing of total new houses.

	Valencia city	Alicante city	Region Valencia
1992	6%	12%	18%
1993	22%	28%	32%
1994	27%	45%	43%
1995	35%	65%	52%
1996			
1997	45%	47%	50%
1998	33%	38%	
1999	22%	16%	37%
2000	7%	11%	22%
2001	3%	8%	14%
2002	4%	2%	
2003	0%	0%	

Sources:
- Cities of Valencia and Alicante: Generalitat Valenciana, Informe de oferta de vivienda nueva en la Comunidad Valenciana, on-line site Generalitat Valenciana, visited on 9 Febr 2007, http://www.cth.gva.es/ovv/ovv.htm (Estadísticas:.../Estadísticas../BD Municipal/Valencia 1991-2006 and Alacant 1991-2006).
- Region Valencia: Generalitat Valenciana, Informe de oferta de vivienda nueva en la Comunidad Valenciana, on-line, visited on 10 Febr 2007, http://www.cth.gva.es/ovv/ovv.htm/(Estadísticas:.../Estadísticas../Coyuntura/Gráficos: Precio medio del metro cuadrado de la vivienda/Informe de oferta de vivienda nueva...: Participación de la vivienda protegida: Evolución anual).

As mentioned, municipalities have now changed their policies and are including more affordable housing in the binding rules: both by zoning land as affordable housing, and by agreeing additional contributions and including them in the Programmes. Whether this has been a success is not possible to evaluate here. There are no available statistics about building rates from 2003 onwards. Based on the interviews and the studied cases, it is possible to conclude however that building of affordable housing is indeed rising. Of the studied cases, only those that included affordable housing in the binding rules (*Guillem* and *Periodista*) will indeed provide affordable housing. It seems plausible thus that including affordable housing in binding rules could indeed lead to more being built (Roger, Blanc, Rubio, Montiel, Escribano, interviews 2006).

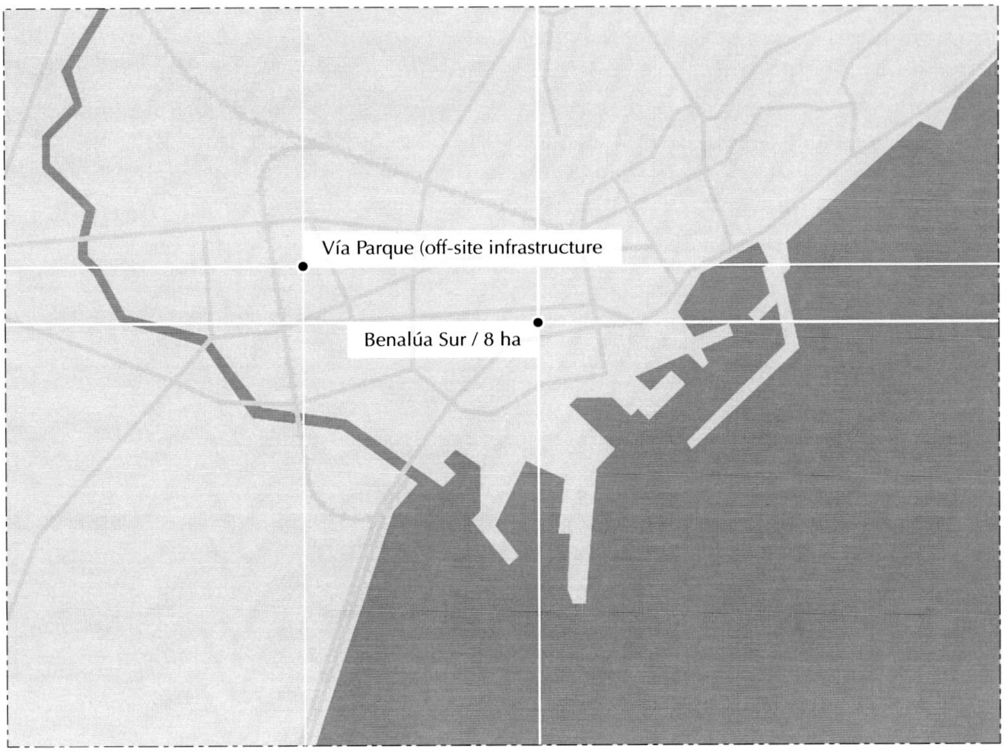

Figure 16. Piece of off-site infrastructure ascribed to the Redistribution Area of Benalúa Sur. The General Land use Plan of 1987 allocated the building rights as follows (the Program modified these figures slightly, e.g. reduced the area of the development site from 98,000 to 82,451 m² of land):

- Area development site: 98,000 m² of land
- Area off-site infrastructure to be included: 54,398 m² of land
- Total Redistribution Area: 98,000 + 54,398 = 152,398 m² of land
- Building volume Redistribution Area/site: 103,950 m² floor space modal use
- Reference Development Allowance: 103,950 : 152,398 = 0,6 m² floor space modal use/m² land
- Building right of owner parcel of 100 m² land, whether situated in development site or under the off-site infrastructure: (100 x 0,6) x 0,9 [10% belongs to the Municipality] = 54 m² floor space modal use.

5.5.2.3 Prescriptions related to the organization of the implementation: Ascribing off-site infrastructure to development sites

In Land to be developed, General Plans can charge infrastructure and facilities with an off-site function into the development site (sector) in which they are located. Also, the General Plan can ascribe a piece of land situated off-site to a particular development site. The owners of the land under the infrastructure or facility (whether situated or not on the development site) belong to the same Redistribution Area, i.e. they share the building rights of the development site and, in exchange, cede their land freely. This seems to be a very common practice. Benalúa, the only case situated on Land to be developed, does so. The 1987 General Plan of Alicante attached 5.4 ha of off-site infrastructure (Via Parque) to the Redistribution Area/sector of Benalúa (8.3 ha, see figure 16). This was part of a wide strategy of ascribing off-site infrastructure all around the city to those sites to be developed. The 1987 General Plan foresaw an urban extension area of about 200 ha, and ascribed 37 off-site ha to the land to be developed in the period 1987-1991 (Benalúa was part of it). For the period 1991-1994, the General Plan ascribed 15 ha. Similarly, the 1988 General Plan of the city of Valencia, that foresaw an urban extension of about 700 ha, ascribed to it about 2/3 of all new off-site infrastructure in the city (230 of 350 ha). This led to an average of about 0.3 m^2 of off-site land per m^2 of urban extension area (Roger, Blanc, Escribano, interviews 2006). When ascribing off-site infrastructure, municipalities take account of the profitability of the development site (i.e. of the residual value of each scheme). The goal was that each scheme should bear a proportional part of the off-site infrastructure without compromising its economic feasibility.

What has been the effect of ascribing off-site infrastructure? Probably positive because it creates certainty about *more contributions*. It seems that Valencian municipalities manage in this way to obtain free most of the land needed for new main public infrastructure and facilities. In general, the interviewed experts and public officers consider that this works well. Case *Benalúa* and general information about the cities of Alicante and Valencia confirm this. In case *Benalúa,* the municipality will receive for free 5.4 ha of off-site infrastructure. In the city of Valencia, about 230 ha have been obtained for free since the approval of the 1988 General Plan, for example the land under the new *Cortes Valencianas* Avenue and under the new Football stadium of C.F. Valencia (Roger, Blanc, Escribano, Muñoz & Cañellas, Baño, Raga, interviews 2006).

5.5.2.4 Prescriptions related to the organization of the implementation: Agreeing additional contributions

Planning law, both before and after the 1994 Act, prescribes the formal possibility of negotiating additional contributions in a Development Agreement: e.g. extra financial contributions, building of public facilities. They are additional to the legal minimal package of contributions. Extra contributions can include, besides those just mentioned, contributions for social/affordable housing (see above).

Has the possibility of agreeing additional contributions improved capturing value increase? It is common that municipalities manage to obtain additional contributions in this way. Additional contributions are in practice the following (Blanc, Muñoz & Cañellas, interviews 2006):

- Building of public facilities (swimming pools, public buildings, etc): this happens, following one expert (Blanc, interview 2006), almost only in the larger schemes, where these costs do not exceed 8%-12% of the total infrastructure provision costs. It seems that urbanizing agents often manage to make landowners pay for it. A main difficulty with this sort of contribution is that it is not regulated properly and might therefore disturb the necessary conditions for free competition (Blanc, Escribano, Baño, interviews 2006). Municipalities often reject additional contributions if it seems difficult to objectively compare different proposals, and this happens often with the building of public facilities, because the characteristics of the public buildings to be constructed are not specified previously. An example is *Camino,* where the winning urbanizing agent proposed the rehabilitation and free cession of several historic industrial buildings, but the municipality had not established *a priori* any specification about this. Another aspect that might disturb free competition is that urbanizing agents in principle cannot charge these costs to the landowners. Thus, only those agents that also own much land, or can manage to charge the landowners anyway, can afford to make such proposals, and the others cannot compete.
- Developing less profitable products: more frequent seems to be that the urbanizing agent commits itself to develop on its land less profitable products with a high social profitability. For example, a hotel or recreational building, instead of residential, in a tourist residential scheme.
- Financial payments to the municipality, or other kind of extras: this seems also to happen, e.g. in cases *Periodista* (€ 1.6m) and *Camino* (€ 4m).
- Additional contributions for social/affordable housing: see above.

In the studied cases, additional contributions were very frequent. In *Camino*, the urbanizing agent undertook important additional investments for the removal of existing industries, and for the rehabilitation and free cession of several historic industrial buildings. Also, the municipality will receive almost € 4 million, which is included in the infrastructure provision costs and will therefore be paid by the landowners. In *Guillem,* the urbanizing agent assumed an important part of the infrastructure provision costs, costs that, following planning law, should be paid by the landowners. Also, the urbanizing agent will pay additional compensation to the existing house owners. In *Periodista,* the urbanizing agent will provide some infrastructure outside the plan area and will pay € 1.6m to the municipality.

This sub-variable (Municipalities can negotiate additional contributions) is a direct consequence of planning law: planning law prescribed, before and after the 1994 Act, the formal possibility of negotiating such contributions in a Development Agreement. Before 1994 these agreements were common, but there were also many zoning plans approved without an agreement backing them. The 1994 Act has reinforced this sub-variable by introducing another sub-variable: Programmes *must* now include a Development Agreement (see section 5.5.3), which has generalized the use of development agreements, and increased the total number and amount of additional contributions.

5.5.2.5 Prescriptions related to the organization of the implementation: Investment and implementation schedules (before 1994 in General and Detailed Plans, after 1994 in Joint Development Programme) and Development Agreements (before 1994 in extern documents, after 1994 in Programme)

Before the 1994 Act, General Plans included schedules for the public investments. This occurred in an 'Action Programme' (Programa de Actuación) and an 'Economic-Financial Study' (Estudio Económico-Financiero). These documents were exhaustive studies that foresaw the investments of public bodies (local, provincial, regional and national public bodies) in the public infrastructure and facilities needed for the implementation of the General plans. For example, the 1988 General Plan of Valencia foresaw € 1,160m of public investments for the period 1989-1996[5]. The municipality of Valencia would pay € 364m and the other public administrations the rest. The Economic-Financial Study foresaw a public investment of € 925,558 in case Guillem to construct a broad road, and € 135,227 in Periodista to build a public facility. In addition to the public investments, General Plans included the schedules within which landowners were obliged to implement the public infrastructure and facilities following the voluntary land readjustment procedure.

The 1994 Act introduced some modifications to this. Since 1994, General Plans can only contain the *ex lege* prescription that General Plans foresee the urban expansion of the municipality for approximately 10 years, and a brief description of the needed public facilities and infrastructure for a longer period. However, this includes neither compulsory implementation schedules, nor does it result in concrete deadlines, although the validity of the General Plan is indefinite (Parejo & Blanc, 1999: 265-266; Romero, 2002: 340). There might be one exception: in some areas, General Plans can include rules regarding the logical order of developments (*condiciones objetivas de urbanización*): detailed objective and technical criteria that have to be fulfilled before each site can be developed. These criteria may result in a logical order of developments, and are compulsory for the subsequent Joint Development Programmes (Parejo & Blanc, 1999: 267). Regarding financial aspects, General Plans no longer include the exhaustive public investment schemes. Only municipalities of more than 50,000 inhabitants are obliged to include a brief and very general socio-economic assessment of the plan. Also, General Plans no longer include the implementation schedules for landowners.

Something similar has happened with the Detailed Plans. Before the 1994 Act, Detailed Plans included a 'Plan of Phases' (*Plan de Etapas*) and a 'Economic-Financial Study', which included deadlines for the implementation of the Plan and an assessment of the needed investments and financial resources, including the obligatory schedules for the landowners. Since 1994, Detailed Plans no longer include deadlines or time schedules for their implementation, nor any calculation of investments or similar items (Romero, 2002: 341-342).

5 Change rate: 166.386 pesetas = 1 euro.

The 1994 Act created a new sort of plan, the Joint Development Programme, which includes more or less the same investment and implementation schedules as in the old General and Detailed plans. This means that since 1994 detailed investment and implementation schedules appear only after a Programme has been approved, not before. Another novelty of the 1994 Act is that the Programmes also include, in the Juridical-economic Proposal, a Development Agreement. Agreements were common before the 1994 Act, but they were external documents, formally speaking not included in the binding rules. Has the fact that the Programme now includes the schedules and the agreements had any effect on capturing value increase? All available data, including the cases, suggest that the financing and implementation schedules of the old General and Detailed plans suffered much delay, and that after 1994 this speeded up greatly. The question, however, is whether the creation of a new sort of plan document, the Programme, could in it self be the cause of these improvements. It seems plausible that not the creation of this document as such might be the relevant variable. Other sub-variables could be relevant here: this is that the 1994 Act introduced the obligation of *always* achieving a Development Agreement to secure the investments and schedules (see next section).

5.5.3 Conditioning binding rules on securing capturing value increase

Summary of the findings

Before 1994 municipalities could not make the approval of binding rules conditional on securing the minimal legal package of obligations, but only on securing additional contributions. Since 1994, municipalities *can* and *must* condition the approval of binding rules on securing *all* the contributions, both the minimal legal package and possible additional contributions. This novelty has improved the capturing of value increase and the tempo of implementation of the public infrastructure and facilities (*cfr.* Blanc, interviews in 2008). However, another novelty too has played an important role in this improvement: the introduction of the land readjustment procedure with the urbanizing agent as leading party (see section 5.5.4).

5.5.3.1 No obligatory Development Agreement before the 1994 Act

Before the 1994 Act, Valencian public bodies were not allowed to openly condition planning consent on a commitment of the developer/landowner to effectively implement and pay that part of the public infrastructure and facilities that, following planning law, *must* be charged to developers/landowners, i.e. the 'minimal' legal package of obligations. Planning consent refers to the approval of a new General Plan that modifies the previous one, or the approval of a Detailed Plan that modifies the General Plan, or the approval of a Detailed Plan that just details the General Plan. However, public bodies were allowed to openly condition planning consent on the effective implementation and payment of *other additional contributions*, additional to the minimal legal package. For example, the legal minimal package included the obligation to cede land for primary schools, so agreements could include the obligation to cede land for high schools and universities also. Another common example was the free cession of historic buildings for their conversion into public facilities. In practice, Development Agreements were very common, especially in the 1980s, when many municipalities made General Plans. Alongside the preparation of and procedures for, for example, the 1987 Plan of Alicante and the 1988 Plan of Valencia, municipalities required many developers owning land to sign these agreements. Usually, the agreements concerned small plan areas, owned by one developer. After the approval of these General Plans, the number of these agreements diminished.

5.5.3.2 Obligatory Development Agreement after the 1994 Act

The 1994 Act introduced some important modifications. First, municipalities were allowed to condition planning consent not only on securing additional contributions, but also on securing the minimal legal package of obligations. Second, this was not an option, but a *must*: municipalities were obliged to ask for a Development Agreement; otherwise the binding rules are not valid. All the cases illustrate this: the Development Agreement secured indeed all the public infrastructure and facilities in all the cases, both the minimal legal package and the additional contributions. Third, municipalities can now ask for a Development Agreement not only when planning consent is necessary, but also in those cases in which the binding rules are already detailed and approved, and provided there is need of investments in public infrastructure and facilities. For example, in case *Guillem* the 1988 General Plan already included all the detailed binding rules, and there was in principle no need to approve new binding rules. However, investment in public infrastructure was necessary, so a Joint Development Programme *annex* a Development Agreement were *sine qua non* condition before development could start.

In other words, after the 1994 *all* the public infrastructure and facilities (minimal legal package *and* additional contributions) of *all* developments (those that require planning consent, and those that do not) *must be secured* through a Development Agreement. The procedure is as follows: the submitted Programme includes a proposed Development Agreement; once the local council has possibly introduced modifications and approves the Programme, the municipality asks the selected party to sign the Agreement. If the local council introduced modifications (either additional contributions or the result of detailing the provisionally approved Programme), and if as result of these modifications the selected Programme becomes substantially modified (which in theory cannot happen but is not rare in practice), the winning party can refuse to sign the Development Agreement and withdraw from the development. However, refusing is not frequent in practice. In case *Camino*, the Development Agreement doubled the initial infrastructure provision costs from € 5 million to € 10 million, and in *Periodista* it diminished the building volume from 15,757 m2 floor space to 11,000, without in either case the developer refusing to sign. The rise of housing prices in the meantime (variable A1 in causal model section 2.4.2) might explain why developers agreed to the extra requirements. Once the Agreement is signed, the municipality publicises the approval of the Programme, which becomes at that moment, and not before, legally into force.

These modifications in 1994 have had important consequences for capturing value increase. This might have not happen in a direct way, but by influencing sub-variables b. The idea is that, not the fact of being able to include contributions in binding rules seems to be effective, but the fact of being obliged by law to condition planning consent to securing *all* contributions. In other words, *i)* being obliged to condition binding rules to securing all the contributions reinforces *ii)* the positive effect of being able to include certain contributions in binding rules on *iii)* the negotiation position of municipalities, the accounted land costs and the profit margins of the developer; *i)* might also have a direct positive effect on the speed of the implementation. Before 1995, not all the binding rules were accompanied by a development agreement. If they existed, such agreements secured only the additional contributions, obligations that came into force once the developer/landowners had implemented the minimal legal package. It seems that such agreements augmented the additional contributions, such as providing land for secondary schools and university and historic buildings (Blanc, interviews in 2008). However, what seems clear is that the minimal legal package of public infrastructure and facilities was not implemented on time: after all, there was no agreement that secured their financing and implementation. This is the reason that in general the financing and implementation schedules made before the 1994 Planning Act were not effective in practice. In other words, scheduling investments in the General and Detailed Plans without a real engagement of the investing party may have disadvantages for the speed of implementation of the public infrastructure and facilities (Romero, 2002: 336, 339; Muñoz & Korthals Altes, 2007). Since the 1994 Act, there is always an agreement that secures all the public infrastructure and facilities, both the minimal package and the additional obligations. This may explain the improved effectiveness of the schedules.

This sub-variable (there is since 1994 always a Development Agreement that secures *all* the public infrastructure and facilities) is a direct consequence of the 1994 Act. The act prescribes the formal obligation of adding an Agreement to the Programme, and broadens the coverage of this agreement to include also the minimal legal package. However, this sub-variable operates together with another sub-variable: the 1994 Act also introduced a new form of land readjustment, with a third party, the urbanizing agent, as provider of the public infrastructure and facilities (see next section). This modified substantially the power relationships because municipalities have now the power of obliging landowners to cooperate. In sum, both sub-variables ('formal obligation to secure public infrastructure and facilities' and 'modulating property rights') are likely together to have caused the generalization of the use of Development Agreements for all schemes and for all public infrastructure and facilities.

5.5.4 Modulating Property rights

Summary of the findings

Building rights belong to the landowner, in the region of Valencia and in the rest of Spain. It has already been explained that infrastructure provision (*urbanización*) is considered a public task, and that landowners are obliged since 1956 to implement it, assuming all the unprofitable parts. The 1956 Land Readjustment regulation helped in this, but there was a strong interdependency: local authorities and developers/landowners were mutually dependent because of the distribution of resources. Authorities have the statutory powers for planning permissions, and developers/landowners have the financial means and the land. Looking it from the point of view of capturing value increase, this interdependency was disadvantageous. It gave to the developers/landowners the option to wait, and as waiting might bear advantages, the negotiation space of municipalities deteriorated. The result was that often municipalities lowered the public requirements for infrastructure and facilities, or that often development processes were delayed, or both. The introduction of the 1994 Act has had important consequences here. The Act introduced some important modifications in the land readjustment regulation that divested landowners from the possibility of using the option to wait. The modifications gave Valencian municipalities relatively large powers for infrastructure provision, compared with England, The Netherlands and other Western European Countries (for an international comparison, see chapter 4.4). Municipalities are no longer dependent on the landowners to provide the infrastructure, and the consequence has been that municipalities have increased their requirements. Another consequence has been a significant increase of private investments and an acceleration of urban development. Let us see this in more detail.

5.5.4.1 Who owns development rights in Valencia?

There is a distinction between infrastructure provision and the building. As mentioned, the infrastructure provision is a public task. The landowner (before the 1994 Planning Act), or the urbanizing agent (after the 1994 Act), bears as concessionaire the responsibility to provide the public infrastructure and facilities, and to redistribute betterment and costs between the landowners. Following national planning law for the whole of Spain, the right to build belongs to the 'essence' of the contents of property rights, and thus belongs to the landowner (see section 2.2.4.2). But this is not an unlimited right. The law and the binding rules limit these building rights. Landowners have no right to any kind of 'minimum', and they are obliged to apply and obtain the needed permits. Also, other legislation might even lead to the removal of the building rights (e.g. expropriation). Once the landowner is authorized to develop on his plot, and provided that the land has not been expropriated, he is the only one entitled to build on that plot and he can exclude others from doing so. So we must differentiate between the right to provide the infrastructure, which belongs to the public, and the right to build, which remains under the *dominium* of the landowner.

Nevertheless, the fact that infrastructure provision is defined as a public task does not automatically mean that public bodies have all the powers to exercise it. Neither does it automatically mean that landowners have lost some of the powers over their property. By analysing who has the control over each of the transactions in infrastructure provision, it has been possible to discern who has which development right in the infrastructure provision. The steps are: 1) land purchase and assembling, 2) financing and 3) land preparation and development.

5.5.4.2 Mutual dependence of municipalities and landowners before 1994

To analyse the consequences of steps 1-3 in the power-relationship between municipalities and landowners, this research developed and applied a model of dependence analysis (see table 11; for more details of the model, see chapter 3.1.1). Before the 1994 Act, municipalities depended heavily on the passive consent or active collaboration of the developer/landowner to gather the land (step 1), gather the financial resources (step 2) and develop the land to produce serviced plots (step 3). The dependence was because the landowner/developer controlled two important resources: land and investment capacity. Moreover, this dependence was not easily avoidable. The land readjustment regulation relied on the support and active collaboration of a majority of the landowners: land readjustment took place only when the owners of at least 60% of the land constituted a joint development organisation, responsible for the infrastructure provision and redistributing betterment and costs. If a minority of landowners did not want to collaborate, the joint organisation was allowed to apply, after municipal approval, compulsory land readjustment. If the owners of 60% of the land were not even willing to take the initiative, municipalities could overrule all the landowners and take the lead, applying compulsory land readjustment. Municipalities had the option also to acquire the land, through amicable agreement, through applying the pre-emption right (*derecho de tanteo y retracto*), or through expropriation. Public authorities are allowed in Spain and also in Valencia to expropriate land not only for the public infrastructure and facilities, but also for private uses, i.e. for housing, office space, etc. There is no kind of 'self-realisation' right of the landowner[6], who can prevent public authorities from expropriating the land. In Spain, municipalities are free to choose between land readjustment and expropriation; there is in planning and expropriation law no hierarchy that privileges one formula before the other. Expropriation was and still is a common way for sectorial regional and national public bodies to implement their policies (e.g. social housing, industrial areas). In theory thus, municipalities could avoid the dependence. However, in practice municipalities usually applied neither compulsory land readjustment nor expropriation, because both meant a direct public involvement, including the corresponding risks, and were a sensitive matter politically.

On the other hand, the landowner depended on the municipality because of its regulatory powers of approving the binding rules and granting the building permit. This

6 'Self-realisation' is a common term in the Netherlands, see section 7.4.4.

dependence also can be labelled as strong because it is not avoidable, as public bodies are the only actors who can exercise these regulatory powers.

Table 11. Dependence analysis Valencia before 1994 Planning Act.

	Dependence because of land	**Dependence because of investment capacity**	**Dependence because of regulatory resources**
Municipality depends on the landowner/ developer	**Dependence.** Developers/landowners own most of the land. Dependence is only avoidable through public leading in land readjustment or expropriation. However, both options were not easy for municipalities.	**Dependence.** Municipalities had in general not much financial resources to invest in public development, so the landowners/developers were the only ones who could invest.	
Landowner/developer depends on municipality			**Dependence.** The municipality approves the binding rules. Dependence is not avoidable.

The consequences in practice of this strong mutual dependency were significant. Landowners had the option of not agreeing with the contributions package or other requirements of the municipality. Since waiting can bear advantages, it was a favourable option to wait (see variable D2.2 in causal model section 2.4.2). As developers may not control all the land, and thus depend on other landowners, it took some time to reach an agreement with all the landowners about the desirable price of land. Land readjustment was an option only when the owners of more than sixty percent of the land support the plan. In practice, this was a high threshold**.** Success depended on the expectation that, by delaying negotiations, development profits would increase in the future. Municipalities were confronted with developers that were not willing, and maybe not able, to agree to the required financing and implementation schedules. This affected the negotiating position of the local authorities and thus capturing value increase, as municipalities were forced to lower the contributions package if they wanted to reach an agreement. And anyway, this affected the speed of implementation, as under those circumstances landowners did not proceed quickly and the development was delayed.

Regarding the effects on the quality of the public infrastructure and facilities, consulted about this, all the interviewed experts, public officers, developers and representatives agreed that the 'old' land readjustment indeed did not function properly (Blanc, Roger, Rubio, Montiel, Muñoz, Cañellas, Escribano and Baño, interviews in 2006 and 2007):

- Small development sites: sites were too narrow and small, just large enough to provide infrastructure for a few plots;
- Deficient public infrastructure and facilities: schemes included very minimal packages of public infrastructure; just the least needed to service the plots;
- Not real readjustment: most of the time, readjustment followed very much the will of landowners to receive building plots on their former property. Instead of following the most suitable parceling, readjustment adapted very much to the landowners' interests.

The result, all interviewed agreed, was an irregular, unordered, neither systematic nor logical urban growth of low quality and with scarce public infrastructure and facilities. For example, in the city of Valencia, it resulted in the 1980's in an urban periphery of low urban quality. It received the name 'buildings in the onion field' (*edificios en campos de cebolla*, see figures 17): buildings in the middle of deteriorated agricultural land, without proper public infrastructure.

Figures 17. Examples of the periphery of the City of Valencia in the 80s: (1) Nou Benicalap; (2) Beniferri; (3-4) Orriols; (5) Torrefiel (Copyright Demetrio Munoz, Nov 2006).

The consequences for the speed of implementation seem also to have been significant. In the 1980's, with the first democratically chosen local governments after Franco's dictatorship, many municipalities made General Plans that included high standards of public facilities and infrastructure. The goal was to reduce the scarcity of public facilities and infrastructure that was the inheritance of the previous, pre-democratic political regime and the inefficient application of the land readjustment regulation. The General Plans included large contributions from the landowners of those areas to be developed, and ambitious deadlines for the implementation. However, the implementation of these ambitious plans stagnated. It is clear that the reason for stagnation was the lack of will of a big enough majority of landowners to develop their land under the high level of contributions prescribed in the General Plans, regardless of the quality of the plans. A consulted expert considered that these plans, although ambitious, were financially feasible, and that the attitude of the landowners could not be excused by the fact that contributions were impossibly high (Blanc, interview 2006).

5.5.4.3 No mutual dependence of municipalities and landowners after 1994

After the introduction of the 1994 Act, there is no longer a mutual dependency, as the possibilities to take the steps 1-3 do not depend anymore on the landowner's passive consent or active collaboration, nor do municipalities need anymore to take the lead in land readjustment or to expropriate the land (see table 12). The landowner still controls two important resources: land and investment capacity. However, the municipalities now have the possibility of appointing a third party as urbanizing agent, and do not need to get financially involved in order to oblige landowners to collaborate with land readjustment. Neither are municipalities dependent on the urbanizing agent, as they can select him in a public tender, or select another one, or a public company. What remains is that landowners still depend on the municipality, because of its regulatory powers of approving the binding rules and granting the building permit.

All the studied cases demonstrated in this. The only exception seemed to be case *Benalúa,* where the municipality seemed to depend very much on the collaboration of the owners of two flour-mill factories for the development of a small part of the site. This dependence seems to be of political nature, i.e. the Municipality of Alicante had in theory legal instruments to override these owners, but this seemed to be politically not feasible.

The consequences in practice of the modifications to the land readjustment regulation have strengthened the negotiation position of the municipality, lowered the price of the land and the profit margins of landowners and developers, and quickened the tempo of implementation. Positive thus for the capturing of value increase: the available data provide generalizable knowledge about this (Blanc, 1997, 2003; Modrego 2000; Muñoz & Korthals Altes, 2007: 69-73). The Valencian 1994 Act breaks through the previous pattern of landowners having the option of not sharing in the infrastructure provision and of speculating on better market conditions, by divesting landowners of the option of waiting. Landowners can no longer service the plots whenever they consider it best. When a developer submits a proposal and the municipality approves it, the landowners must follow. The consequence was an extraordinary

Table 12. Dependence analysis Valencia after 1994 Planning Act.

	Dependence because of land	Dependence because of investment and management capacity	Dependence because of regulatory resources
Municipality depends on the landowners	**Dependence, avoidable.** Landowners have most of the land. However, dependence is avoidable without much difficulty because of the possibility of applying compulsory land readjustment, if necessary.	**No dependence.** There is no municipal dependence on the landowners in this matter. The municipality can appoint a third party, the urbanizing agent, as the one who invest and provides the infrastructure.	
Landowner depends on municipality			**Dependence, not avoidable.** Landowners cannot develop without being selected as urbanizing agent or without the Municipality selecting a third party as urb. agent. Also, the municipality approves the binding rules. Dependence is not avoidable.
Municipality depends on urbanizing agent		**No dependence.** There is no municipal dependence on the urbanizing agent in this matter. The municipality can appoint in a public tender another party as urbanizing agent, or select right away a public company as urbanizing agent.	
Urbanizing agent depends on municipality	**Dependence, not avoidable** Urbanizing agents depend on the municipality to apply compulsory land readjustment, if necessary.		**Dependence, not avoidable.** Urbanizing agents cannot provide the infrastructure without being selected as urbanizing agent. Also, the municipality approves the relevant binding rules. Dependence is not avoidable.
Landowner depends on Urbanizing agent		**Dependence, avoidable.** Landowners cannot invest and develop without the urbanizing agent first providing the infrastructure. Dependence is avoidable since landowners may submit an own plan and became them selves urbanizing agent.	
Urbanizing agent depends on landowner	**Dependence, avoidable.** Landowners control the land. However, dependence is avoidable because of the possibility of applying compulsory land readjustment, if necessary	**No dependence.** There is no dependence on the landowners in this matter. If the municipality selects him as urbanizing agent, he will be able to invest and provide the infrastructure, while the landowner is obliged to pay the costs.	

increase of public and especially private initiatives, and an acceleration of urban development. The improvement has not only been quantitative, but affected also the quality of the public infrastructure and facilities: the hitherto common subdivisions with a poor quality of infrastructure ceased.

Each of the four studied cases was the result of a private initiative, and the selected urbanizing agent was also a private party. In three cases a public tender took place between different proposals (four in *Guillem*, three in *Camino* and four in *Benalúa*). In three cases (*Guillem*, *Benalúa* and *Periodista*), the private party who first took the initiative (who submitted the first Programme) became the selected urbanizing agent. In all the cases the initiating party had no land or just part of the land, but once selected, often bought land progressively.

The cases confirm that the possibility of selecting as urbanizing agent an 'external' developer, not linked to the landownership in the area, was a crucial factor. In *Guillem* the plan area was owned by hundreds of persons. Also, many of these owners were residents, or rented their property to tenants. It seems impossible that all these actors would have agreed a voluntary land readjustment. As one interviewed public officer states, the 'local' actors were not interested at all in redeveloping the area (Raga, interview 2006). It seems thus plausible to conclude that the possibility of 'by-passing' the landowners has been crucial for this project. Proara bought land once it had been selected, and when this developer submitted the Land Readjustment Project to the municipality it owned already 30% of the land. Competition seems also to have stimulated the payment of additional contributions: during the tender procedure Proara assumed an important part of the infrastructure provision costs, while following planning law these costs are for the landowners. Also, Proara will pay additional compensation to the existing house owners.

In *Periodista* the situation was similar. It seems clear that here also the selection of an 'external' developer (Prodaemi), initially not linked to the landownership in the area, has been a crucial factor. Several private persons and companies owned the site, with economic activity in some of the buildings (a printing office). Landowners seem not to have been interested in redeveloping the area themselves, but only in selling their plots. The whole project came into being only after Prodaemi took the initiative. Asked about this, the developer stated that before the 1994 Act, developers in the same position as Prodaemi were regularly confronted with landowners asking very high prices, higher than the residual value of their plot. Their position was strong because the developer needed a voluntary agreement with all the owners. The 1994 Act gave developers such as Prodaemi the possibility of avoiding such situations. Competition seems also here to have stimulated additional contributions: Prodaemi will provide some infrastructure outside the plan area and will pay € 1.6m to the municipality.

In *Camino* the landowners of a majority of the land (about 10 landowners) became themselves urbanizing agent. However, the first initiative was from an external developer, not linked to the landownership in the area, who submitted the first Programme. Then, other parties, among them the owners, submitted alternative Programmes. Finally, the municipality, after considering in total four proposals, selected the Programme of the landowners. It seems clear that the possibility of appointing an external developer, with no land in the area, has been a crucial factor: landowners would never have undertaken such an initiative, or at least this would have been delayed, if the external developer had not taken the initiative. Competition seems here also to have stimulated additional contributions: the urbanizing agent assumed important additional investments in the removal of existing industries, and the rehabilitation and free cession of several historic industrial buildings. Also, the municipality will receive almost € 4 million.

In *Benalúa* the situation is less clear. On the one hand, the owners of about 60% of the land joined together and submitted the first initiative, and were finally selected as urbanizing agent. Thus, in theory the old voluntary land readjustment regulation would have been enough. On the other hand, the fact is that the development process started only after a small consultancy company, which had only about 15% of the land, undertook the initiative in early stages. The fact that it could do so without formally having the support of the other owners may have stimulated these other owners to join the initiative. The owners might have supported the initiative of the small consultancy company once they realized that the municipality could 'by-pass' them and appoint this small company as urbanizing agent.

5.5.5 Procedure for the preparation and approval of the binding rules

Summary of the findings

Municipalities must since 1994 make careful decisions about the development proposals of market parties, and this seems to have stimulated private initiatives and accelerated urban development. However, the consequences for capturing value increase might have been less favorable. Regarding the 'procedural' flexibility of the binding rules, i.e. the possibilities to modify the binding rules, and to freely determine the geographical scope (the plan area) of the binding rules, the findings are less conclusive. The relative difficulty in Valencia to modify and determine the geographical scope of the binding rules seems not to be relevant for the degree of private contributions to the unprofitable parts. That is, there seems not to be a clear causality between this sort of flexibility of the procedures and capturing value increase.

5.5.5.1 Guarantees for the initiative takers

Before the 1994 Act, developers were allowed to submit proposals of Detailed Plans, and municipalities could in theory not ignore that. To reject the proposal, the local council had to take a formal decision, otherwise the initiating party could appeal to the courts. However, it seems that in practice municipalities systematically did not fulfil these legal prescriptions, and developers went regularly to the judge. Judges often sentenced against municipalities, but the inconvenience for the developers to initiate long judicial processes did not compensate the benefits of doing so.

The 1994 Act has given to developers the possibility of initiating the procedure themselves, without having to wait for municipal consent: the developer submits the Programme to the municipality and to an office of notary, publishes it, announces it, and deposits the Programme in that office. Anyone can submit objections or alternatives, but to the office of notary and not to the municipality. The procedure is fully organized and paid for by the private initiator. When the public consultation finishes, the developer submits the Programme and all the submitted objections and alternatives to the municipality, which further organizes the procedure and finally decides about the proposals. This possibility of 'private' public consultation through an office of notary has become a relatively frequent phenomenon: from 1995 until 1998, 25% of the Programmes followed this procedure (Modrego, 2000: 18, 22). Consulted about this, a relevant expert considered that, from 1998 onwards, this percentage may have increased very much (Blanc, interview 2007). 'Private' public consultation takes place more often in large cities than in small ones. Of the four studied cases, only in *Periodista* did the developer do this.

How has this novelty of the 1994 Act affected capturing value increase? The interviewed expert considers that the possibility of 'private' public consultation has stimulated private parties to undertake initiatives. The reason, the expert insisted, is that the discretional room of municipalities in the situation previous to the 1994 Planning Act created many uncertainties that developers had to deal with. Being able to force a formal procedure has allowed developers to reduce some uncertainties. Municipalities are now obliged to evaluate formally and with publicity whether proposals are good or not, and to give elaborated arguments. This has increased the transparency of the municipal decisions and has reduced municipal discretion (Blanc, interview 2007). This might have reduced the development costs, as uncertainty can translate into higher risks and risks into costs. Also it might have accelerated development processes, stimulating private parties to submit proposals, and avoiding municipal hesitation. However, it can have also a negative effect for capturing value increase: municipalities have now less elbowroom in the negotiations, and this might reduce contributions additional to the minimal legal package.

5.5.5.2 Inflexibility in modifying the existing binding rules

The only way of modifying, departing from or detailing existing binding rules in Valencia is by approving new ones to replace them. There is no simplified procedure for this. Departing from the General Land use Plan, no matter how small the departure, requires the preparation of a new Detailed Plan. For example, in *Guillem* the General Plan zoned a small plot for one floor, while this was technically speaking impossible. An Urban Renewal Plan covering the whole plan area was necessary to rezone that small plot into five floors. One might argue that this inflexibility can worsen the negotiation position of municipalities. However, there are no indications that the relative inflexibility in modifying binding rules in Valencia has worsened public value capturing.

5.5.5.3 Inflexibility in determining, according to negotiations with landowners, the geographical scope (the plan area) of the binding rules

There are in Valencia rigid legal criteria for the delimitation of plan areas, and these make it very difficult to negotiate separately with each owner about the conditions for rezoning. As a result, plan areas have to be of certain dimensions, covering at least several plots. It is not impossible for a binding plan to cover just one plot. However, then we are talking about plots of at least 2,000-3,000 m^2, which fulfil detailed legal criteria. In practice, it seems that municipalities follow the legal criteria very strictly. There is clearly not much room to negotiate individually with each landowner, although we do not deny that this happens for very specific cases (although this was not the case in any of the studied cases). The smallest of the studied cases was *Periodista*, with a plan area of 0.6 ha and more than ten initial parcels.

This remarkable inflexibility of the Valencian binding rules, when compared with England and The Netherlands, seems however not to have weakened the negotiation position of the municipality. There is no indication that this sub-variable has influenced capturing value increase. The reason is that another sub-variable, the modifications in 1994 to the land readjustment regulation, actually eliminates the need for an agreement with each individual landowner (see chapter 5.5.4). In other words, due to the modifications in 1994 of the land readjustment regulation, this sub-variable (inflexibility to size the plan area) has apparently become irrelevant.

5.6 The actual degree of captured value increase in Valencia

This section focuses on whether the goals for capturing value increase are achieved. Also, it looks at the actual distribution of costs between the involved parties: who has paid which public infrastructure and facilities, and possibly some extras? We look also at whether the capturing value increase goals have been achieved on time. The main sources of information are the four cases, complemented with other written sources and interviews with relevant experts. The conclusions are set out in Table 13.

On-site infrastructure provision costs

A basic principle of the Spanish planning system is that urban development can take place only if the landowners (whether or not they are also the urbanizing agent) assume *all* the on-site infrastructure provision costs. Also, the full ownership of the resulting infrastructure must be ceded free of charge to the municipality. Based on the

Table 13. Comparison table results on captured value increase in Valencia.

	On-site land development costs		Land for on-site public infrastructure		Land for on-site public buildings		On-site public buildings		Affordable housing		Contributions off-site public infrastructure and facilities	Cream off value added
	Landowners	Public body	Landowners	Public body	Landowners	Public body	Urbanizing agent	Public body	Landowners	Public body		
General knowledge region Valencia	All or almost all these costs	No (only if receiving building rights)	Almost all the land	That land that was already public infrastructure	Almost all the land	That land that was already public infra	Sometimes	Almost always	Almost all	Subject subsidies	Landowners cede significant quantities of land, and sometimes pay construction.	10% building volume in Developable land, often money
Guillem de Anglesola (total value building plots €9.4m)[6]	€2.7m (30% total value building plots)	No.	45%	29% was already public infra	No	No	No	No	30% total housing units	Subject subsidies	Landowners cede much land for main road and pay construction together with developer (incl in On-site land dev costs)	Nothing
Periodista Gil (total value building plots €3m)	€4m (125% total value building plots)	No.	44%	No.	No	No	No	No	80% total housing units	Subject subsidies	Nothing	€ 1.6m (53% total value building plots)
Camino Hondo (total value building plots €95m)	€10.6m (11% total value building plots)	€0.6m (1% total value building plots)	About 70%	A small part was already public infra	No	No	Rehabilitation/ free cession buildings, ca. € 15m.	Extension existing school	No	No	Landowners pay € 168.010 for construction road alongside dev site	€ 4m (4% total value building plots)
Benalúa Sur (total value building plots €92.5m)	€7.7m (8.3% total value building plots)	€0.25 (0.2% total value building plots)	About 79%	No.	20% (including a school)	No	No	New school	No	No	Landowners cede 54.398 m² of land and pay about € 400,000 for pipelines and other under. infra.	17% total building volume

Grey: case in which the developer/landowner contributes the most of the four cases.
Light Grey: case in which the developer/landowner contributes the second/third of the four cases.
White: case in which the developer/landowner contributes the less of the four cases.

7 'Total value building plots' are the total returns accruing from selling serviced building plots (thus excludes the posterior selling of the new buildings).

studied cases and on the interviews with experts, it is possible to conclude that this is also the case in practice. Only when the municipalities receive building rights they do contribute to these costs, as any other landowner would. If municipalities must contribute, they do not usually pay in money but in building rights. In *Guillem* and in *Periodista,* the municipality will not receive building rights, so it does not contribute. In *Camino,* the municipality owns about 5% of the land (excl. public infrastructure), so will contribute 5% of the costs. In *Benalúa* the municipality does not own land but receives some of the building rights thanks to legal prerogatives, and thus pays a contribution. These findings are generalizable to all comprehensive urban regeneration and greenfield projects on private owned land in the region of Valencia, but not to projects where public bodies intervene directly (through expropriation, a minority) nor to very specific strategic interventions (airports, motorways, railways, etc).

Land needed for on-site public infrastructure and facilities
The mentioned basic principle prescribes also that urban development can take place only if the landowners provide freely *all* the land needed for on-site public infrastructure and facilities. The exception is land that was already on-site public infrastructure (i.e., if the land is already public, landowners do not have to buy it and cede it freely). Landowners must cede land not only for roads and public space, but also for other public facilities, such as schools, sport installations, kindergartens, parks, municipal offices, police station, although the building costs of these are, in principle, paid by the respective public body (see below). The full ownership of the land is ceded freely to the municipality. Public infrastructure and facilities are standardized in planning law, and between fifty and eighty-five percent of the total plan area is used for public infrastructure and facilities. In general these figures are higher in greenfield developments than in urban regeneration. In the cases studied this was between 44% and 79%. These conclusions have the same external validity (generalizability) as the above-mentioned infrastructure provision costs.

On-site public facilities (the buildings)
As mentioned, landowners cede freely the land needed for public facilities, also for public buildings. The development of these public buildings has, in principle, to be paid by the respective public body. However, based on the interviews, it seems that in practice sometimes private parties also pay for the public buildings. All the interviewed experts and representatives of interest groups agree in this. However, precise figures are not available. It is also not clear whether the costs are borne mainly by the landowners or by the urbanizing agent/landowner. Of the cases we studies, only in *Camino* will private parties pay for public buildings: the urbanizing agent will cede freely and rehabilitate several historic industrial buildings which will be used for public functions.

Land and money for on-site and off-site social/affordable housing
The costs of developing social/affordable housing are mostly borne by the landowners. These landowners bear the costs by providing cheap land, for a regulated price

of about € 120-150/m² floor space (figures of 2006). Because the market price of serviced building plots for free-market housing is much higher (€ 300-1,100/m² floor space, depending on the location) we could speak of a form of subsidizing the land price, borne by all landowners together. Thanks to this cheap price, commercial or non-profit developers can develop affordable housing and profit from it. The central and regional governments also finance a little, through a subject subsidy (to the buyer) in the form of a subsidy to the mortgage interest and sometimes a lump sum.

In two cases there was affordable housing: in *Guillem* about 1/3 of the dwellings, in *Periodista* most of them. The following figures show that developing social/affordable housing actually involves a financial charge for the landowners. In *Guillem* the infrastructure provision costs of the affordable units amount to about € 0.97 million, and the regulated value of the plots € 0.69 million. The balance of the project will thus not only bear the difference between the regulated value and the free-market value, but also a shortage of about € 0.28 million (this is the regulated value minus the costs). In *Periodista* infrastructure provision costs amount to about € 3.2 million, and the regulated price of the plots € 1 million (shortage of about € 2.2 million). The landowners must in both cases bear these costs, plus their land costs (the price they paid for the land plus the financial costs).

It seems that cases *Guillem* and *Periodista* are not representative for practice in the last decennium. It is clear that since the end of the 90's, the building of affordable housing has decreased in Valencia and in the rest of Spain also. In the first years of the 21th Century, less than 10% of all new dwellings were affordable housing (see section 5.5.2.2). However, in the last years, there is a tendency for this to increase. Cases *Guillem* and *Periodista* could be representative of this tendency.

Land and money for off-site public infrastructure and facilities
Regarding public infrastructure and facilities situated *outside* the plan area, these are the findings. All development sites situated on land classified as 'Land to be developed' have, since the end of the 80's, been ascribed a piece of off-site public infrastructure and facilities situated somewhere else in the municipal territory. The owners of the land thus ascribed shared the building rights of the development sites and, in exchange, ceded freely their land. In general, the respective public body (municipality, provincial, regional or national government) pays the construction of these off-site public infrastructure and facilities. In case *Benalúa,* the municipality obtained thanks to this measure 5.5 ha of land situated far away from the development site. Although there are not available figures for the whole region, interviews and some specific figures seem to support the generalizability of the findings in *Benalúa*. In the cities of Valencia and Alicante, since the end of the 80's, almost all the land needed for new main public infrastructure and facilities has been ceded freely. In Valencia, in total about 230 ha have been ceded freely to the municipality. For example, the land for the extension of the cemetery and a part of the land for the new University of Valencia. In the city of Alicante, about 52 ha of land have been

ceded freely to the municipality through the same system. The examples of these cities seem to be representative (Roger, Blanc, Raga, Escribano, Muñoz & Cañellas, Baño, interviews 2006).

There are also cases of public infrastructure and facilities situated *within* the development site but serving a wider area. Case *Guillem* includes within the development site a main road that we consider off-site infrastructure because it serves a much wider area than the development site itself. The landowners will cede freely the land for this main road. Also, the landowners and the urbanizing agent will pay the construction costs of this road (these costs are included above in the on-site land development costs). In *Camino,* landowners contribute to the costs of a road situated alongside the development site that serves a wider area. Another developer constructed this road several years ago and claimed a contribution from our development site. In *Benalúa* landowners will pay most of the costs of several new pipelines and underground infrastructure that belong to the general system of the city.

Consulted about this, interviewed experts considered that these cases are not unusual: land for main infrastructure serving an area wider but situated within the development site is often ceded freely, and landowners/urbanizing agents often pay the construction costs also (Roger, Blanc, Rubio, Escribano, interviews 2006). It is however not clear whether the landowners or the urbanizing agent pay most of the construction costs in general.

Creaming off plus value

The constitutional principle, that allows municipalities to capture part of the surplus that arises in urban development (for more details about this principle, see section 5.3.1), materializes in two ways:

First, where there is 'Land to be developed', municipalities have the right to 10% of the building rights. Landowners are obliged to cede freely to the municipality the serviced building parcels that are needed to build 10% of the total building rights. Urban regeneration usually takes place on 'Existing Urban Land', rather than on 'Land to be developed', which means that in urban regeneration municipalities do not usually profit from this provision. The cases seem to confirm this general picture: of the four cases, only *Benalúa* includes 'Land to be developed'. In general, on 'Land to be developed', it seems that municipalities receive indeed about 10% of the total building rights. However, although 10% of building rights can in theory turn out to be more than 10% of the real building *volume,* this does not seem to happen often. Case *Benalúa,* where the municipality has right to the 17% of the building rights, seems to be an exception. In general, it seems that municipalities often use these building rights to pay for public infrastructure and public buildings, instead of depositing the building rights in the Municipal Patrimony of Land, as they in theory should. Case *Benalúa* confirms this; here the municipality will use at least an important part of its 17% to pay its share of the infrastructure provision costs.

Second, sometimes landowners/urbanizing agents pay extra financial contributions to the municipality. There are no available figures about how often this happens. In cases *Camino* and *Periodista,* the municipality received important contributions in money.

Tempo of implementation of the capturing value increase goals
Sections 5.5 and 5.6 (so far) have analyzed the working of binding rules and the results on capturing value increase. What are the possible side effects, in particular the tempo of implementation of the capturing value increase goals? A certain measure might be good to increase the contribution of developers to public infrastructure and facilities, but might also delay negotiations. Or *vice versa*: a certain measure might not directly increase contributions, but accelerate negotiations and thus help to realize sooner the public infrastructure and facilities. A distinction has been made between the situation before and after the introduction of the 1994 Planning Act.

In general, it seems that before the 1994 Act the goals for capturing value increase aimed at in the binding rules (the public infrastructure and facilities and some creaming off added value) were indeed implemented, but with considerable delay. For example, the deadlines included in General Plans turned out to be systematically neglected in practice (Romero, 2002: 336, 339; Muñoz & Korthals Altes, 2007). The 1988 General Plan of the city of Valencia foresaw a total expansion area of 700 ha, all to be developed within the period 1989-1996. However, in practice, only one site (*Avenida de Francia*) was actually developed before 1995. In the city of Alicante, the 1987 General Plan foresaw a total expansion area of almost 200 ha, all to be developed within the period 1988-1995. However, in practice, only few sites were actually developed before 1995 (Gascó, 2006). The same happened with the financial schedules prescribed in the General Plan for all the cases, and with the deadlines prescribed, also in the General Plan, for case *Benalúa*.

The 1994 Act has had important consequences in practice. General figures show that development processes have accelerated very much, both in greenfield and urban regeneration. For example, the process of approving the Detailed Plan (from submitting the first proposal up to the municipal decision) decreased from between three to five years before 1994, to between three and seven months in the period between 1994 and 1998. The process from municipal approval to the delivery of serviced building parcels took an average of 33 months in 1998 (Modrego Caballero, 2000), which was much longer before. Unfortunately, the regional government stopped collecting data in 1998. All the indications, however, suggest that development processes between 1998 and 2006 have continued to be very fast (see Gascó 2006 for recent figures in the municipality of Alicante).

It seems that the investment and implementation schedules are implemented on time. These schedules are no longer included in the General Plans, but in the Joint Development Programmes, and they are now always secured in a Development Agreement. General figures up to 1998 suggest that the schedules contained in the Programmes are most of the time achieved, without delay (Modrego Caballero, 2000). These general figures refer to the definitive approval of Programmes, not to their actual implementation. However, it is very plausible that approval of Programmes implies also their actual implementation. This is because Programmes *must* include a Development Agreement that secures the financing and investment schedules. Also, the Agreement *must* include economic sanctions in case of not fulfilling the schedules.

Investments also have increased very much since 1994. A combined effect of acceleration and increase of investments has been an increase in the number of development sites: from an average of forty each year between 1990 and 1994, to 59 in 1995, 135 in 1996, 221 in 1997, and 242 in 1998[8] (Modrego, 2000; Muñoz & Korthals Altes, 2007). Although the figures show an increase in public initiatives (i.e. public bodies acting as urbanizing agents), most of this increase has been due to private investments (i.e. private parties acting as urbanizing agents). There is no indication that the trend has changed between 1998 and 2006 (see Gascó 2006 for recent figures in the municipality of Alicante). The stagnation of urban development that followed the approval of the ambitious General Plans of the 1980's has disappeared. The cities of Valencia and Alicante are good examples: the General Plans of 1988 respectively 1987 have almost all been implemented with high standards of public facilities and infrastructure. Based on interviews (Raga, Rubio, interviews in 2006), it is also possible to conclude for at least the city of Valencia that there has been a significant increase of private initiatives and an acceleration also in urban regeneration, mainly concentrated on rezoning former industrial sites into housing.

However, the information collected in January 2010 suggests that, since about 2008, implementation schedules might be suffering delay:

- In *Benalúa* infrastructure provision commenced on time, and in January 2010 it was not yet finished. The deadline for completion is the summer of 2010. It is uncertain whether a small part of the plan area, which includes two active industries, will be finally redeveloped.
- *Camino* has commenced the infrastructure provision on time: the demolition of existing buildings started in 2007 and in January 2010 the historic industrial buildings are being refurbished. However, it is uncertain whether infrastructure will be finished before the deadline of Augustus 2011 because the urbanizing agent (a commercial developer who bought most of the land after the plan was definitively approved and the Development Agreement already sealed) went bankrupt and a bank has taken over the property.
- In *Guillem* and *Periodista,* although the urbanizing agents initiated the land readjustment procedure, there are serious delays in the definitive approval of the

8 The figure for 1998 is an extrapolation based on real figures for the 1st trimester, so possible increases in the 2nd, 3rd and 4th trimesters have not been considered.

land readjustment. This makes uncertain the achievement of the deadlines for the completion of infrastructure provision (November 2010 respectively May 2013), especially for *Guillem*.

These case-base findings (that since 2008 in some of the cases the infrastructure provision is being delayed) might be generalizable to other schemes in the region of Valencia (*cfr.* Interview with Raga, 2010).

5.7 Causal relationships between formal rules relevant to zoning and capturing value increase in Valencia

Section 5.5 answered Preparatory research question 3: it inferred the possible causal relations between the independent variable 'formal rules relevant to zoning' and the dependent variable 'capturing value increase'. This section summarizes the inferred causalities. Then it assesses the influence of possible third variables.

5.7.1 The inferred causalities

The findings suggest that the following sub-variables can influence positively or negatively the degree of capturing value increase (see also the causal model in section 2.4.2 and figure 18):

- Sub-variable a, Uncertainty about the future building possibilities, together with Certainty about the future contributions: this seems to lower intermediary variables *accounted land costs, regular profit margins* (of the developer) and strengthen the *negotiation position* (of the municipality), i.e. positive for capturing value increase;
- Sub-variable b, Contents of the binding rules: (1) Zoning land as Land to be developed-class; (2) Zoning land for social/affordable housing; (3) Ascribing off-site infrastructure to the development site; all three seem to have been positive for capturing value increase, probably because they have lowered intermediary variables *accounted land costs, regular profit margins* (of the developer) and strengthened *negotiation position* (of the municipality);
- Sub-variable b, Contents of the binding rules: (4) Agreeing additional contributions; it seems to be positive for intermediary variable *negotiation position* (of the municipality);
- Sub-variable c, Conditioning binding rules to agreement: the 1994's novelty of introducing a formal obligation to make the approval of binding rules conditional on securing the public infrastructure and facilities and other possible contributions: this seems to have been positive for capturing value increase, plausibly

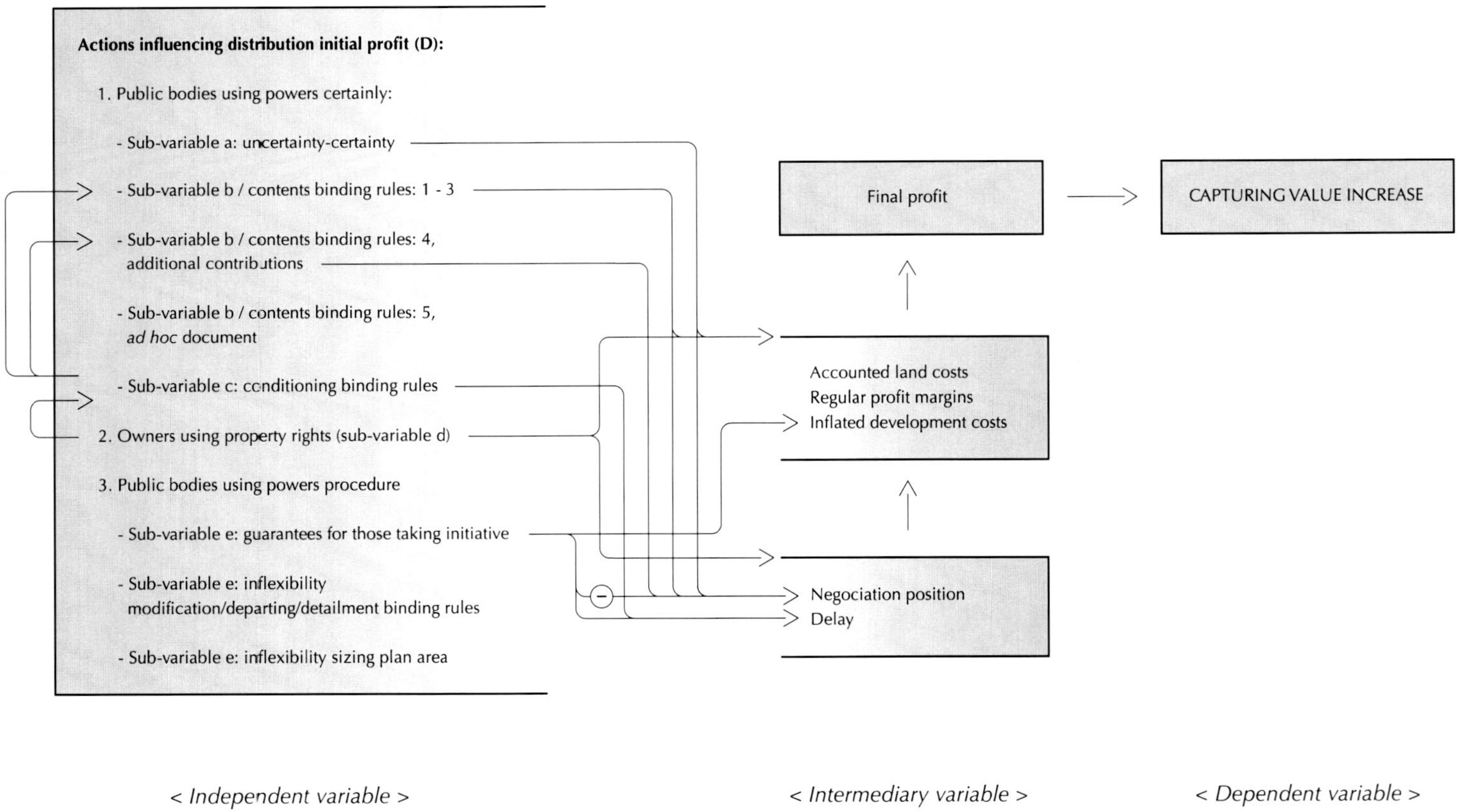

Figure 18. Scheme of the inferred causal relations in Valencia between independent variable 'formal rules relevant to zoning', the intermediary variables and the dependent variable 'capturing value increase'.

through reinforcing the positive effects of sub-variables b on intermediary variables *accounted land costs, regular profit margins* (of the developer) and *negotiation position* (of the municipality); and a direct positive effect on intermediary variable *delay*;
- Sub-variable d, Property rights: the 1994's modifications of the land readjustment regulation: this seems to have been positive for both capturing value increase and the tempo of implementation. The causal links works plausibly by being positive for intermediary variables *delay, negotiation position* (of the municipality), *accounted land costs* and *regular profit margins* (of the developer);
- Sub-variable e, Guarantees for those taking initiative: the 1994's novelty of allowing initiating parties to initiate the procedure: this seems to have been positive for intermediary variables *delay* and *inflated development costs,* but negative for intermediary variable *negotiation position* (of the municipality).

The findings also suggest that the following sub-variables might *not* affect the degree of capturing value increase:
- Sub-variable b/Contents of the binding rules: (5) the 1994's novelty of including the financing and implementation schedules of public infrastructure and facilities in an *ad hoc* plan document: this seems not to be relevant;
- Sub-variable e, Inflexibility in the modification/departure/detailing of binding rules: this seems not to be relevant;
- Sub-variable e, Inflexibility in adapting the size of the plan area of the binding rules according to negotiations with each landowner: this seems not to be relevant.

Sub-variables b/1-4 (contents binding rules), c (Conditioning binding rules to agreement) and d (Property rights) are intimately related to each other. It seems that they are consecutively and causally related to each other, in an inverse order. The modifications to property rights introduced in the 1994 Act (sub-variable d) have generalized the use of development agreements (sub-variable c). And this seems to have stimulated the effectiveness of the contributions included in the binding rules (sub-variable b/1-4). See the respective sections for more detail.

5.7.2 Possible third variables

Here the effect of other, possible third, variables is assessed, related first to the specific circumstances in the studied cases (variables D4 and D5 of the causal model in section 2.4.2), and second to market circumstances (variable A1). The goal is to examine the possibility that the inferred causal relationships turn out to be spurious correlations (see section 3.2.1.2 for more detail about this methodological approach).

Specific circumstances in the studied cases

In *Periodista* the developer considers that the quality of the plan has accelerated implementation because nobody has submitted objections, but this does not seem to be a strong argument. Also, the developer says that since the municipality added extra requirements to the original Programme, he will have to fill the gap with his own resources. This third variable (having access to own resources to cover an eventual financial deficit) might explain part of the success of this project. In *Camino* the interviewed developer mentioned a third variable that can delay development. In the southern part of the plan area, railway wires have to be dismantled. The railway company belongs to the central government in Madrid, so it could take a long time to get the needed permits. In *Benalúa* the developers consider that the slow functioning of the Municipality of Alicante has delayed the process greatly. The interviewed public officer agreed with some of these criticisms, but stated that some delay has been caused by the developers themselves. It seems also that in *Benalúa,* appeals to the courts against the Land Readjustment Project might delay the infrastructure provision. In *Guillem* the large number of owners, tenants and inhabitants of the houses to be demolished has delayed the public participation processes of both the Programme and later on of the Land readjustment Project.

In short, except maybe in *Periodista,* in none of the cases did the interviewed persons or our analysis of the facts support the idea that specific aspects (regarding the involved local politicians, public officers or developers, or regarding any other aspect) might have influenced *significantly* the positive outcomes on the actual degree of captured value increase. On the other hand, specific circumstances might have delayed three of the cases.

Market circumstances

In section 5.5 several causalities have been inferred between some modifications in the 1994 Act and the improvement of capturing value increase and the acceleration of development that has been experienced from 1995 onwards. Some argue that the changes after 1995 might be more related to the rise in housing prices than to the 1994 Act itself. This third variable, housing prices (variable A1 in causal model section 2.4.2), can affect capturing value increase (because it influences intermediary variable 'Initial profits' and might thus influence also 'Final profit', in other words, it creates financial room for more contributions) and the speed of implementation (more profits attract more investments, and remove obstacles). This research concludes however that the influence of housing prices has not been so significant as to make the inferred causal relationships spurious. In other words, housing prices might have been relevant third variables, but have not caused all the changes after 1995. Let us see first the available general knowledge and second the case-based findings.

In the whole region of Valencia, prices of all housing (new & existing stock) and of new housing decreased in real terms between 1990 and 1997. Only in 1999 did prices begin to increase significantly. These figures are similar in the cities of Alicante and Valencia (see figure 19). This recession in housing markets (1990-99) coincided with the increase in urban development. So, at least between 1995 and 1998, development processes accelerated and investments grew while real housing prices decreased or increased very modestly, i.e. when the expectations of land value increases were modest. It is possible to conclude that there is not a *direct* causal relationship between changing housing prices and the general acceleration of development processes and growth of investments, at least in the first years after the introduction of the 1994 Act (Blanc, 1997: 265).

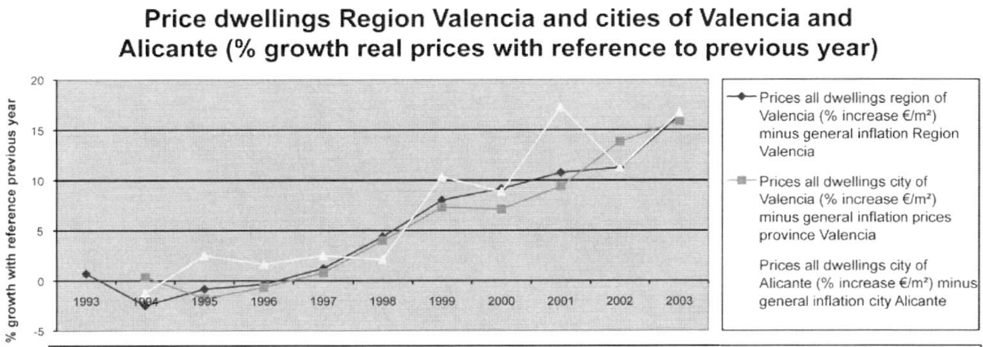

Own elaboration, based on following sources:
- Prices all dwellings Region of Valencia and Spain: Ministerio de Fomento, on-line site Generalitat Valenciana, visited on 9 Febr 2007, http://www.cth.gva.es/ovv/ovv.htm/(Estadisticas:.../Estadisticas../Coyuntura/Gráficos: Precio medio del metro cuadrado de la vivienda/Evolución: Series históricas 1988-2001: Comunidad Valenciana y España)
- Prices all dwellings city of Valencia: Ministerio de Fomento, on-line site Generalitat Valenciana, visited on 9 Febr 2007, http://www.cth.gva.es/ovv/ovv.htm/(Estadísticas:.../Estadísticas../BD Municipal/Alacant 1991-2006)
- Prices all dwellings city of Alicante: Ministerio de Fomento, on-line site Generalitat Valenciana, visited on 9 Febr 2007. http://www.cth.gva.es/ovv/ovv.htm (Estadísticas:.../Estadísticas../BD Municipal/Alacant 1991-2006)
- Inflation province of Valencia: Instituto Nacional de Estadística, on-line, visited on 9 Febr 2007, http://www.ine.es/cgi-bin/certi. Data refer to variation from December to December.

Figure 19. Growth real prices (minus general monetary inflation) dwellings Region of Valencia and cities of Valencia and Alicante.

The findings of the cases fit within this general conclusion. The procedure (submission Programme) of *Camino* started in 2003, and of *Periodista* in 2005, when housing markets in the city of Valencia were already expanding (7% price rise all housing, above general monetary inflation in 1999 and 2000, 9% in 2001, 14% in 2002 and 16% in 2003). However, the procedures for the other two cases started under less positive expectations. The procedure of *Guillem* started in May 1999, the first year of significant price rise of new housing (7%). The preparation of the Programme started earlier, in times of a 'bad' housing market (1% rise in 1997 and 4% in 1998), and it is not clear whether the developer in *Guillem* was aware of the promising future. In the city of Alicante, *Benalúa* started the procedure in 1998, when prices of new housing decreased in real terms by 0.4% and prices of all housing increased in real terms by only 2%. Programmes include detailed and quasi-definitive investment and implementation schedules, also a draft of Development Contract, so financial feasibility must be clear before submission. The interviewed developers insisted that profits at that time were large enough to cover infrastructure provision costs[9].

In all four cases, both the interviewed developer and public officer agreed that the projects would have been financially feasible also in times of decreasing or modestly rising housing prices. Moreover, development seems less sensitive to market circumstances since the modification in 1994 of the Valencian land readjustment. For the new regulation has lowered the risks for developers:

- No need to own land: the Valencian formula allows developers to develop without the need of buying (all) the land. Indeed, the initiating developers owned initially (before municipal approval of the Programme) no land in *Periodista* and none in *Camino*. In *Guillem* the developer had just a little land, and in *Benalúa* the developer consisted of several existing firms that had owned the land for a long time and a consultancy company that had bought some land for a low price. In *Camino* the selected developer consisted of several existing firms that had owned the land for a long time. Thus, initially, the initiating parties had almost no need to invest in acquiring land, only in preparing the Programme.
- Landowners are obliged to contribute to the infrastructure provision costs: thus, in case of poor market conditions, developers were assured of the financing of the infrastructure provision. Payment of contributions in building rights seems to follow prudent market appraisals, and in case of expropriation the compensation is based on the former use of the land, not of the future one: thus, if landowners chose for payment in kind or for expropriation, developers were assured of building rights for a relatively low price. In case of good market conditions, as actually happened since 1999 onwards, developers were in a privileged position to buy land and building rights in the area. This is what actually happened, and in Nov 2006 the four urbanizing agents owned already almost all the land/building rights.
- The initiating developer commits himself to provide the infrastructure within the estimated budget, and the landowners pay for it. So he bears the risks only of exceeding the budget. The costs of plans preparation and of infrastructure provision are quite predictable, and price rises are around the general monetary inflation.
- In *Guillem* and *Periodista* the Programme included 50% respectively 80% affordable housing. Affordable housing is a profitable product and the risk is low, provided that the developer can acquire the land for an affordable housing-price

9 At the time of data gathering, end of 2006, the prices of new housing in the free market in the City of Valencia varied from about € 2,000 to 3,000 per m² floor space, depending on the location. The average price per m² floor space in the city of Valencia was in the last trimester of 2006 for new housing € 2,561 and for second hand housing € 1,932, and the average price for both new and second hand € 2,058 (Ministerio Vivienda, Base general, consulted at on line site Generalitat Valenciana, visited on 24 January 2010, http://www.cma.gva.es/ovv_estadisticas). In another source the average price new and second hand is € 2,003 (Source Colegio de Registradores, in Observatorio Valenciano de la Vivienda, *Informe annual de coyuntura del sistema de indicadores 2008*, Informe nr. 5, April 2009, p. 22).

(about € 125-150/m² floor space), which was guaranteed here through the land readjustment.

In almost all the cases, developers assumed contributions in the course of the planning process, additional to those additional contributions already included in the Programme as initially submitted. It is likely that this third variable (rising housing prices) has stimulated the negotiation of these extra contributions after the submission of the Programme and before the sealing of the Development Agreement. For example, in *Benalúa* the municipality and the regional government made several important extra requirements during the long process of approving the Programme. First the regional government demanded the conservation and rehabilitation of two old industrial chimneys, which required extra costs and the modification of the plan. Second, the municipality demanded a contribution towards the plan preparation and off-site infrastructure costs, which initially it was going to pay itself. In *Guillem* the municipality introduced after the initial approval of the Programme an extra requirement: the developer had to pay part of the infrastructure provision costs, costs that following planning law should be paid by the landowners. In *Periodista* the municipality reduced the building volume and in *Camino* the municipality doubled the infrastructure provision costs.

In sum, the increase in housing prices cannot explain on its own why the developers submitted the Programmes. It might have been an important stimulant, especially in *Periodista* and *Camino*, but the financial feasibility of the proposals did not depend on expanding market circumstances. Furthermore, the increase in housing prices can explain on their own *part* of the additional contributions: those extra contributions not included in the submitted versions of the Programmes and agreed afterwards, during the procedure and before the sealing of the Development Agreements. Also, the increase in housing prices explains why in *Periodista* and *Camino* the developer decided not to refuse to sign the Development Agreement, despite the fact that the municipality introduced costly modifications long after the initial approval of the Programme.

Last developments since 2008

It seems however that the bad circumstances in the housing markets since the end of 2007 are stimulating and often forcing developers to delay many urban development schemes. Many developers have gone into bankruptcy or had no choice other than to pass over the property to the banks, as case *Camino* shows. This is a third variable of the type A1 in causal model section 2.4.2. It seems that many urbanizing agents, confronted with the bad market circumstances, are trying to delay the implementation (i.e. the achievement of the deadlines included in the Development Agreements) through delaying the administrative procedure of land readjustment. Although municipalities have powers to force implementation (including a bank guarantee of at least 7% of the infrastructure provision costs, a guarantee that following planning law must be included in the Development Agreement), it seems that municipalities are not fully using them (*cfr.* interview Raga, 2010). This is third variable D5.

INER·OF·BRISTOL.

CHAPTER 6

England

In the last decennia, public bodies in England have been seeking a larger involvement from commercial developers in the financing of the unprofitable parts of comprehensive urban regeneration schemes. An old statutory provision gives, since 1932, local planning authorities the power to require private contributions towards public infrastructure and facilities. Since the 1970's, this provision has been enlarged and can include nowadays a wide variety of private contributions. Stimulated by the central government, local authorities are developing systematic policy for these contributions.

Frame 6a
The institutional context: United Kingdom, England, the regions and the local public bodies
The United Kingdom of Great Britain and Northern Ireland (from now on UK) is a country made up of four constituent countries: England (50.7m inhabitants), Scotland (5m), Wales (3m) –the three of which form together Great Britain- and Northern Ireland (1.7m). The UK is a unitary state with a system of constitutional parliamentary monarchy. Scotland, Wales and Northern Ireland each has its own parliament or assembly. England does not, and is ruled directly by the UK government.

England is subdivided into nine regions. Regions are subdivided into metropolitan counties (including Greater London), and non-metropolitan counties. Counties are often subdivided into districts or boroughs. This leads sometimes to a double tier of local government, with a County Council and a District Council (Cullingworth & Nadin, 2006: 64-65). In this case, both the county and the district are Local Planning Authorities (LPA). Other 'sectoral' or *ad hoc* organizations can be Local Planning Authorities also, such as National Park authorities, Urban Development Corporations and the Urban Regeneration Agency. The City of Bristol, where the studied cases come from, is a unitary authority, a county with a single-tier governmental structure (a district council), and therefore only one LPA (Moore, 2005: 26-27, 31-32).

The *planning policies* of regional and local governmental bodies are subordinated to the law and policies of the UK government. Subordination of *planning legislation* is guaranteed through the 'parent acts': the laws of the UK Parliament that delegate legislative powers to other bodies and set out the principles, rules and procedures under which delegated legislative powers can be exercised. Almost all the UK legislation on any field is made under delegated powers: regulations, orders, directions, rules and by-laws, all collectively known as 'Statutory Instruments' (Williams & Wood, 1994: 67-68).

Subordination of *planning policies* is guaranteed by the obligation of local and regional authorities to comply with policy guidance of the UK government. Policy guidance consists of policy statements that cannot be considered as legislation: they have no statutory consequences. However, they are very important in defining and detailing the way in which planning legislation has to be applied. They reflect how the UK government considers that planning legislation should be interpreted and implemented. Since the UK government plays a quasi-judicial role of arbitration in conflicts between local planning authorities and developers, national policy guidance has a quasi-legislative function. It plays a very important role in practice, and may be referred to in any judicial review. Also, the policy guidance documents include the results of judicial scrutiny. There are two sorts of policy guidance documents (Williams & Wood, 1994: 68; Evans & Davoudi, 2005: 25): 'Circulars' or 'Policy Guidance notes', related to planning control decisions; and 'Planning Policy Guidance notes' (PPGs) and 'Minerals Policy Guidance notes' (MPGs), related to the preparation and contents of zoning plans. Since 2004, PPGs are being gradually replaced by Planning Policy Statements (PPS).

For a list of relevant legislation and policy guidance, related to planning, see Annex 3.

Sections 6.1 and 6.2 introduce the context in which value increase is captured in urban regeneration. Section 6.3 introduces the studied cases. Section 6.4 describes the working of formal rules relevant to zoning within the value capturing mechanisms. This is the answer to Preparatory research question 3: how can formal rules relevant to zoning influence the capturing of value increase in England? The question has been divided into several sub-questions that correspond to the sub-variables a-e (for more details about these sub-variables, see section 3.3.3). Each of the answers to these sub-questions consists of an assessment of whether the sub-variable can influence capturing value increase. There is therefore not a unique conclusion, but as many conclusions as sub-questions. All these conclusions have provided the evidence for the final conclusions in chapter 8 and the recommendations for the Dutch practice in chapter 9. Section 6.5 assesses the degree of value increase actually captured, taking account of the side effects on the tempo of implementation. Finally, section 6.6 summarizes the inferred causalities between formal rules relevant to zoning and capturing value increase: this includes an assessment of the role of third variables.

6.1 Urban Regeneration in England

There is not a single urban regeneration policy or a set of policies, but different policy initiatives that have not been designed and implemented in a coherent and connected way. Instead, the field can be characterized as an "...endless experimentation with new and often disconnected initiatives" (Cullingworth & Nadin, 2006: 350). These initiatives are the result of the interaction between central, regional and local public bodies (op. cit.: 350-392), and can be subdivided into regeneration policies meant for inadequate housing, and those focusing on the regeneration of the inner cities.

There is a long tradition of regeneration policies for inadequate housing. The low quality of a large stock of old housing has been the subject of public intervention since the nineteenth century, an intervention that has not ceased since then. In the first instance, before and after the 2nd WW it led to clearance (demolishing) and redevelopment of old housing areas. Soon clearance gave way to 'renewal', a move that was characterized by: (1) a gradual shift from individual house improvements to the improvement of wider areas; and (2) a redefinition of the problem, from building-technical considerations to a broader set of socio-economic and environmental considerations. In the 1970s these comprehensive area-based and socio-economic strategies of renewal were reinforced. In the 1980s, while the comprehensive area-based approach was retained, a shift took place to economic considerations, in the sense of seeking more involvement of private investment (including e.g. the selling of some affordable housing to its tenants) and bringing implementation considerations to the fore such as enhancing the role of private parties in investing in regeneration. Since the end of the 1990s, more attention is being given to improving the building-technical quality of 'non-decent' dwellings.

While policy specifically oriented to improvement of inadequate housing has a long tradition, specific policy for inner cities appeared for the first time in the 1970s. At that time, 'Urban programmes' funded regeneration interventions. In the 1990s the 'City Challenge' and the 'English Partnerships' programmes also funded regeneration interventions. For example, in one of the studied cases in this research, case *Harbourside*, English Partnership supports the infrastructure provision and soil decontamination works through a cheap loan. Since 1995, Urban and City Challenge programmes have been taken over by the 'Single Regeneration Budget' (SRB), which brought together twenty previously separate funding programmes and has been far more widely applied than previous ones (Booth, 2005: 262).

During the Conservative Government in the 1980s and 1990s, emphasis was given to the stimulation of private investment, instead of relying exclusively on public funding (Booth, 2005: 259; Verhage, 2005: 220-221). Since the 1990s, emphasis on sustainability considerations is growing. The 1980s saw the introduction of the Urban Development Corporations (UDC), UK Government agencies with large powers for plan implementation (through land acquisition) that usurped the local authority's development control functions (granting of planning permissions). These corporations have spent most of the public resources available for urban regeneration and have restructured many degraded old industrial sites in the inner cities. At the end of the 80s criticism arose about these corporations (Booth, 2005: 261), in spite of which the Labour government has continued them with no structural modifications but fewer in number. For example, in case *Temple Quay*, an UDC and its successor, a regional regeneration public agency, bought part of the land and played a role in stimulating the regeneration of this derelict site. Labour created Urban Regeneration Companies (URC), which operate at the local level but are still dependent on the UK Government. An important difference with the UDCs is that local authorities are heavily involved in the URCs. The Labour Government that came to power in 1997 brought forward a raft of new initiatives to attack social exclusion, improve the quality of the public housing stock and redirect funding through local authorities. One important novelty in Labour's approach was the emphasis on more community involvement. The Single Regeneration Budget (SRB), already existing, and the New Deal for Communities (NDC) programme, created in 1998, became the main instruments for this enhanced regeneration policy (op. cit.: 262-3; Verhage, 2005: 224).

Urban regeneration in city centres is often confronted with many small private owners, while in brownfield sites, land is often owned by public or private institutions (Ministry of Defence, health authorities, ex-public companies, private developers, property investors, etc). Land ownership in Britain is usually freehold ownership, where the rights in land are held in perpetuity (Williams & Wood, 1994: 122). Private landowners, if present at early stages, are not often directly involved in the rest of the development. They do not usually share risks nor participate in the whole operation. Most of the time they disappear before the start of the project, and their role is limited to that of provider of the land. Urban regeneration is in general an institutionalized phenomenon, being the task of public bodies, housing associations and commercial developers rather than private landowners. Regeneration initiatives usually take place within the framework of the specific local urban regeneration policy. Local authorities prescribe their regeneration policies in indicative zoning plans. Once a planning application has been evaluated within that framework, local authorities issue planning permissions.

Frame 6b

Indicative and binding plans

At the local level, Local Planning Authorities (LPA) have the competences to prepare and approve zoning documents, both of an indicative character and with legally binding consequences (Cullingworth & Nadin, 2006: 47, 49, 134, 113-124, 150-151).

Regarding the indicative plans, these can be *ad hoc* documents, site-specific, not regulated in planning law. Or they can cover wider areas and be regulated in planning law: before the 2004 Planning and Compulsory Purchase Act there were 'Structure plans', 'Local plans' and 'Unitary development plans', depending on the sort of LPA. Bristol, as a unitary authority, approved in 1997 the Bristol Local Plan. Since 2004, these plans are being gradually replaced by 'Local development frameworks', which are made by the LPA of the lowest tier, i.e. the District Council only instead of both the District and the County councils. Therefore, counties with a two-tier governmental structure no longer have two plans, but just one. Local development framework is a non-statutory term that comprises different documents (Moore, 2005: 31-32): (1) Development plan documents: Local development scheme, Statement of community involvement, and Annual monitoring report; (2) Supplementary documents. None of these documents is legally binding, in the sense that it has direct statutory consequences for the use of land and real estate. This does not mean, however, that they cannot play an important role in development control. The Planning Inspectorate, a central public body, approves definitively the local development frameworks.

The LPA of the lowest tier has the competences of preparing and approving 'Planning Permissions'. Planning permissions include the legally binding land use rules for a specific site. They are the only relevant binding rules, following the definition used in this research. A planning permission can be detailed or outline. An outline permission leaves several matters open (mostly design and external appearance aspects) and reserves approval to a later moment.

After a developer submits an application for a planning permission, LPAs have to decide on it within eight weeks (Moore, 2005: 199-213). Applicant and LPA can also agree another term. LPAs decide whether to grant a planning permission, to impose planning conditions on it, or to refuse it. In practice, most of the applications are determined within the statutory eight-week period (percentages vary from 65% to 80% of all applications, Moore, 2005: 201, Williams & Wood, 1994: 73-78).

However, instead of determining a planning application within this period of eight weeks, LPAs can also decide to negotiate with the developer what the law calls 'planning obligations' (and in the literature is also called 'planning gains', or 'planning contributions'). It is also possible that the developer assumes unilaterally an obligation (an undertaking) (Ratcliffe *et alia*, 2002: 154). Planning obligations may include a broader scope of contributions than planning conditions and are therefore more relevant for capturing value increase (see, for the possibly scope nowadays, and the differences between planning conditions and obligations, Frame 6c). In case of negotiations, the granting of planning permissions is made conditional on the signing of a Planning Agreement that secures the planning obligations. These are the section 106-agreements, so called because the 1990 Town and Country Planning Act included this statutory provision in section 106: in the 1991 Planning and Compensation Act, which rules nowadays, this is the new sections 106, 106A and 106B.

The procedure is as follows: the Council approves the permission provisionally including the contributions that it expects from the developer. The approval is made conditional on achieving a Planning Agreement, which secures the planning obligations included in the provisionally approved document. Then, LPA and developer enter into negotiations, for which there is no legal maximum time period because we are speaking here of a voluntary negotiation. In a survey of a sample of local authorities taken between 1987 and 1990, in 80% of such applications it took around one year to seal the legal agreement (DoE 1992, in Ratcliffe *et alia*, 2002: 155). Of our cases, *Megabowl*, the smallest, fell within this average, while in *Harbourside* and *Temple Quay*, the largest cases, the procedure took about two years.

The Secretary of State (SoS) of the central government sanctions planning permissions definitively in case they should depart from Development Plans (part of Local Development Framework). The Planning Inspectorate resolves appeals against the decision of the LPA's to refuse or impose conditions on planning permissions.

6.2 The legal limits to capturing value increase in England

In England, the financing of the unprofitable parts in comprehensive urban regeneration schemes is largely by contributions from developers. These contributions might be in kind or in money, and they are included in planning permissions as planning conditions and obligations. This was the case in all the studied projects. How far can the contributions from landowners and developers go? Here we give the legal principles that rule and delimit those contributions.

6.2.1 Taxing betterment

We already saw in section 2.2.2 that the nationalization of development rights introduced in the 1947 Town and Country Planning Act did not actually affect to the right of the landowner to develop his land. In other words, the landowner remained the only one entitled to develop his land, after of course having obtained all the needed permits. However, the nationalization had important consequences for capturing value increase. The landowner lost the right to the increase in value caused by that development. That right belonged to the state. Therefore, any landowner developing his land had to pay the state for the use of that right. The consequence was that betterment (any increase in the value of land) was the subject of a betterment charge, and no development could take place without the payment of a betterment charge to the Central Land Board. The 1947 Act foresaw in a 100% tax on the betterment. From that time onwards, taxing development gains has been short-lived because of a lack of political consensus and because it was often seen as over-complex and not yielding enough revenue. In 1953, a new Conservative government abolished the 1947´s tax. Similarly, a 40% levy introduced by Labour in 1967 was abandoned by a Conservative government in 1971. The last major attempt to tax development gains was the Development Land Tax Act 1976, introduced by a Labour government, a betterment tax to be levied on increases in land values due to the granting of planning permission. It would apply where land in private ownership was sold to private development companies. The betterment tax was severely modified by a Conservative administration that came into power in 1979 and eventually scrapped in 1985 (García-Bellido, 1975; Spaans *et alia*, 1996: 302-304; Oxley, 2006: 104; Clusa & Mur, 2007: 124-127; Alterman, 2009: 8, 15-17).

Nowadays there is no betterment tax in the UK. The Barker Review recommended in 2004 the introduction of a 'Planning-gain Supplement'. The recommendation was that the two roles fulfilled by planning obligations (mitigating the direct impact of development, and sharing part of the windfall gain that accrues from development) should be separated. The first part, planning obligations should be scaled back and restricted to dealing with the direct impacts of developments. The second part, Planning-gain Supplement, would be used to extract some of the windfall gain to help local authorities to finance the facilities currently funded by developers (see Oxley, 2006). The supplement consists of adding to the existing negotiated obligations a charge calculated in accordance with previously set criteria, whether these criteria are in a development plan or some other document. The 2004 Planning and Compulsory Purchase Act foresaw the introduction of the Planning-gain Supplement, when its provisions are fully implemented. This had however not happened yet in the winter of 2009-2010.

6.2.2 Capturing value increase through section 106-agreements

Capturing value increase in practice takes place through negotiation of planning obligations and conditions (for the contents nowadays of planning obligations and conditions, and the differences between both, see under Frame 6c). It was the 1932 Town and Country Planning Act that for the first time gave to LPAs the power to enter into planning agreements with landowners for regulating the development or use of their land. Initially, this provision was not used very much. As Moore stated, "...in the 25 years up until 1968, no more than 500 agreements were made. In the 1970s the situation began to change dramatically, when LPAs saw the statutory provision as an opportunity for obtaining a 'planning gain' for their community (...). In return for the grant of planning permission, the developer would be expected to enter into an agreement to provide some public benefit,.." (Moore 2005: 346). The use of section 106-agreements has continued to grow in the last years. The proportion of planning permissions accompanied by planning agreements, including unilateral undertakings, has risen from 1,5% of all permissions and 26% for major developments in 1997/98, to 6,9% respectively 40% in 2003/04. Major developments are residential schemes of more than 10 units or carried out on a site having an area of 0.5 ha or more; or commercial schemes with more than 1,000 m^2 floor space or carried out on a site having an area of one ha or more. Major developments, and the southern areas of England, usually collect more obligations than minor developments and the northern part of the country. The proportion of contributions in money has grown in relation to contributions in kind (Campbell et al., 2001; Department for Communities and Local Government, 2006: 3-4, 17, 41-42).

Over time, the scope of planning conditions and obligations has increased to include, besides physical infrastructure provision, also environmental, community and social infrastructure. The use of obligations has evolved from removing physical constraints on development and mitigating direct impacts, to the ameliorating of more diffuse social, economic and environmental impacts, the provision of community benefits, and the support of wider policy objectives. In short, there has been a shift from 'hard' to 'soft' infrastructure provision: from on-site infrastructure and connections with off-site infrastructure, towards contributions to affordable housing, to off-site public infrastructure and to off-site facilities and other public policy programmes (Ennis, 1997: 1935-6). This increase is said to be related to the austere financial environment within which local authorities must operate (Campbell et al., 2000: 767). It is expected that in the next years, the planning obligations mechanisms will play an important role in capturing some of the development profit and using it for investing back into essential infrastructure (Gallent & Tewdwr-Jones, 2007: 211-213, 257).

Controversy has risen the last years because agreements seem to have enabled local authorities to agree significant contributions from developers that go beyond matters strictly related to the development in question. This is for example the position of the Home Building Federation, the representative of the British housing developers (Whithaker, interview in 2007). Other institutions and experts seem to share this view to some extent, and much literature and even relevant governmental studies and reports are influenced by it (Department for Communities and Local Government, 2006: 6; Barker, 2004: 66; Corkindale, 2004: 13-14). Because of some legally doubtful use, the statutory provision raised both moral and legal issues. A small number of judgments have been very important in constraining the discretionary freedom of local planning authorities. In turn, this case law has been 'repatriated' into the planning system through new policy guidance, which focused on preventing abuse.

Conditions and obligations will be legitimate and lawful only if they are correctly applied (Booth, 2003: 113-115; Ratcliffe *et alia*, 2002: 140-159). As Booth states it, 'the apparently unfettered freedoms contained in sections of the Town and Country Planning Act have in practice been subject to judicial scrutiny and the limits to discretionary behaviour have been set' (2003: 4).

Limits to planning conditions

Case law (House of Lords, *Newbury DC versus Secretary of State for the Environment*, 1981) developed criteria to which planning conditions must comply (Moore, 2005: 286-287):

- They must be imposed for a planning purpose and not for an ulterior one;
- They must fairly and reasonably relate to the development permitted;
- They must not be so unreasonable that no reasonable authority could have imposed them.

Circular 11/95 amplified and slightly reordered these criteria. Following this Circular, conditions should be:

- Necessary;
- Relevant to planning;
- Relevant to the development to be permitted;
- Enforceable;
- Precise and reasonable in all other respects

Limits to planning obligations

The 1991 Planning and Compensation Act (Section 106.1) states that obligations can be agreed:

a) Restricting the development or use of the land in any specified way;
b) Requiring specified operations or activities to be carried out in, on, under or over the land;
c) Requiring the land to be used in any specified way; or
d) Requiring a sum or sums to be paid to the authority on a specified date or dates or periodically.

Circular 05/2005 (Annex B.5) states that Planning Obligations must be:

1. Relevant to planning;
2. Necessary to make the proposed development acceptable in planning terms;
3. Directly related to the proposed development;
4. Fairly and reasonably related in scale and kind to the proposed development; and
5. Reasonable in all other aspects.

There is discrepancy in the jurisprudence about prerequisites 2 and 3, prerequisites that were first introduced in 1991 (Circular 16/91), and continued in Circulars 1/97 and 05/2005. Several important judgments in the 1980s and 1990s have considered it acceptable to lay down obligations that are not necessary to make the proposed development acceptable in planning terms (prerequisite 2), and obligations that are not directly related to the development in question (prerequisite 3), as long as prerequisites 1, 4 and 5 are satisfied (Moore, 2005: 345-349, 354-357). This leaves the door open for a wider range of contributions, often located off-site. These contributions could be classified under the following: training and recruitment initiatives in the construction sector and possibly other sectors, town centre improvement, public art, countryside management, community forests, contributions to cultural plans, theatres, museums, etc. (ODPM, 2004b: 16). It is clear that these obligations (neither necessary to make the development acceptable, nor directly related to the development in question) may be sought or offered. However, the question remains whether LPAs may *impose* them.

There are other limits to the scope of obligations. Circular 05/2005 clearly disapproves the use of planning obligations so far as they are only used for collecting the betterment that results from development: "...planning obligations should never be used purely as a means of securing for the local community a share in the profits of development, i.e. as a means of securing a 'betterment levy'." (Circular 05/2005, Planning Obligations, Annex B.7). It is important, however, to remember that governmental Circulars and other policy guidance are not directly legally binding. Their importance derives from the fact that they incorporate previous case law and that they serve as evaluation criteria when government resolves appeals against decisions of LPAs. This means that practice might deviate from the criteria set out here, without this deviation been necessarily considered as illegal (Moore, 2005: 357). This happens often, as the mentioned example with prerequisites 2 and 3 shows.

6.2.3 Social/affordable housing

Traditionally, social/affordable housing was provided directly by local authorities and housing associations, and funded by the tenants (through rents) and public subsidies. Encouraged by the central government, with for examples its Circulars 1991/7 and 1998/6, since the end of the 1980s a shift has taken place. Nowadays developers are being asked to provide affordable housing within private housing schemes. This means that developers are being asked to subsidize social/affordable housing with the profits accruing from the free market housing in the schemes in question (Crook &Whitehead, 2002: 1259-60). Planning obligations can establish a minimum percentage of affordable housing, or a specific number of affordable units. Also, planning obligations can determine on which parcels affordable housing has to be built. It is also possible to include the obligation to make payments for off-site affordable housing, to be developed elsewhere by somebody else; or to include the obligation for the developer to provide off-site land; or to himself provide off-site social/affordable housing (Circular 05/2005).

Frame 6c
Contents of Planning obligations and Planning conditions

As mentioned before, planning obligations go further than planning conditions, and are the result of negotiations. If a LPA wishes to obtain contributions that go further than what planning conditions can be, it must enter voluntary negotiations with the developer. The then agreed contributions are called planning obligations. Planning conditions and obligations can thus overlap and coexist. Planning *obligations* can include a broad range of contributions:

1. Contributions in kind, i.e. the obligation for the developer to transfer land free and to undertake a broad range of investments: provision of services, building of public buildings, social/affordable housing, bus or railway stations, provision of infrastructure above (roads, surfacing materials, furniture, lighting, etc) and below ground (sewerage, drainage, cables, pipelines, etc), decontamination of soil, construction of play areas, demolishing of buildings and constructions, management and maintenance of public open space after its delivery, etc (Moore, 2005: 289, 346, 351-2, 359-360; Circular 11/95: Appendix A.23-25, 31, 32, 38-40, 58, 59; Circular 05/2005: Annex B.18).
2. Planning obligations can also include payments in cash to the LPA: e.g. contributions to educational and healthcare facilities, for public transport, for affordable housing, for training and recruitment programmes, for town centre improvements, for library facilities, for social and community facilities and payments of compensations (Moore, 2005: 349, 351, 359-360; Circular 05/2005; ODPM, 2004b: Appendices, p. 16, 19).
3. Planning obligations can also include meeting deadlines for the completion of development and the realization/payment of the obligations.

The contents of planning *conditions* are narrower than planning obligations. Planning conditions may include the requirement to undertake also investments/contributions in kind, provided that these actions are not considered as a public function. The construction of sewerage under the site to connect it to the public sewerage system, for example, is not considered as a public function and may therefore be included in a planning permission as a planning condition (Moore, 2005: 290-291, 294). Conditions cannot include payments in cash, but can include deadlines for the completion and for the commencement of development.

6.3 Introduction to the studied cases in England

The 1997 Bristol Local Plan gave, for all the studied cases, indicative prescriptions. However, before redevelopment is allowed, one or more planning permissions have to be granted, and these include the legally binding land use regulations. The planning permission has a physical zoning function but can also include implementation and aspects for capturing value increase. Because in all the cases there was a need for new or refurbished public infrastructure and facilities, the City of Bristol included planning conditions in the planning permission and decided in addition to negotiate planning obligations with the developers. Here follows a brief introduction to the cases (see figure 20 for an overview of the cases). The rest of the case-based information has been included in the rest of the sections.

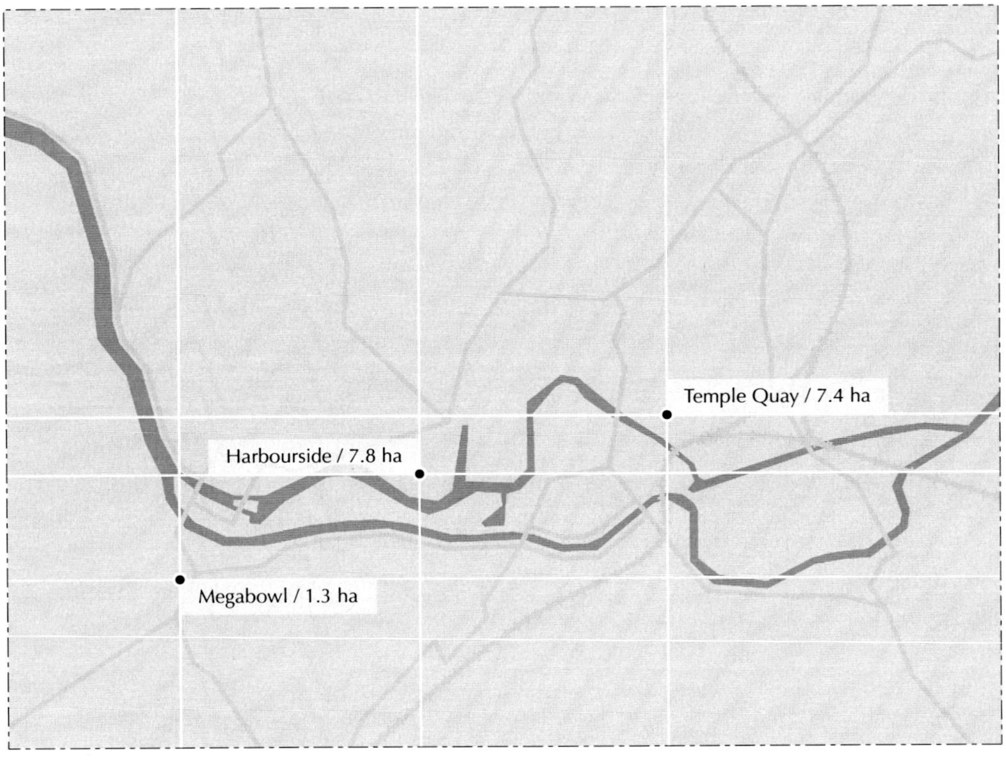

Figure 20. Location of the cases in the city of Bristol.

6.3.1 *Harbourside (Canon's Marsh)*, City of Bristol

Urban regeneration project 'Harbourside/Canon's Marsh' (7.8 ha, 45,000 m² apartments, 700 units, 44,000 m² office, 30,000 m² leisure and facilities, see figure 21) is located in the city centre of Bristol. It forms the last and largest part of the redevelopment of a wider area, also called 'Harbourside', which comprises 27 ha of former dockland and industrial areas. Before redevelopment, the site was largely flat and contained a number of almost disused industrial installations. The site is one of the Council's main priorities for regeneration, and plan preparation has a long history

(Askew, 1996; Buitelaar, 2007: 89-92). The 1997 Bristol Local Plan and the 1998 Planning Brief Implementation Phase for the Harbourside regeneration (a supplementary document to the Local Plan) foresaw the redevelopment of the site into a mixed used area with office space, housing and retail. In 1999 a developer (Crest Nicholson PLC) submitted a first application. Both this application and a second one were rejected. Finally, in 2001, a third application for outline planning permission succeeded. The permission came definitively into force in 2003, after negotiations under section 106 ended with the sealing of a Development Agreement. Afterwards, the developer and the Council negotiated some minor modifications to the outline planning permission. The central government regeneration agency English Partnerships supports the redevelopment of the site through cheap loans for the infrastructure.

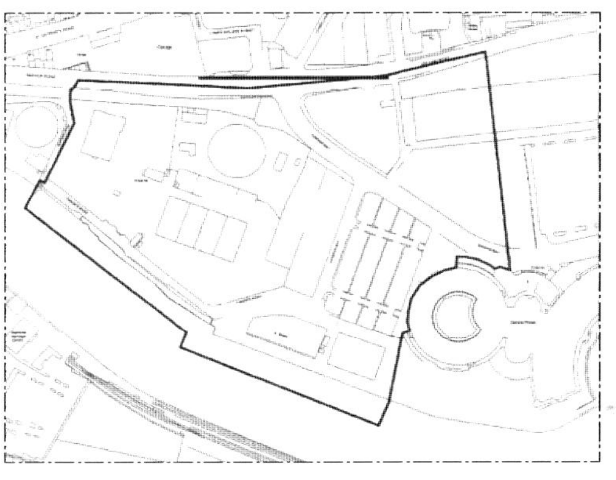

Figure 21. Plan area development site 'Harbourside/Canon's Marsh' (source: Report Head Bristol Planning Services to Bristol Local Council Committee 17 October 2001).

At the moment of the signing of the Planning Agreement in 2003, the land was owned by Secondsite LTD (39% of the site), Transco PLX (9%), Lloyds TSB Bank PLC (9%), and the City Council of Bristol (several plots and the existing streets, in total 43% of the site). The infrastructure works commenced in 2004. In June 2007 more than the half of the development was already completed or under construction, and the first dwellings, office space, a hotel and a casino were already occupied and in use. At that time, Crest Nicholson, the developer, had already bought all the land.

6.3.2 *Temple Quay North*, City of Bristol

Urban regeneration project 'Temple Quay' (7.4 ha, 45,000 m^2 apartments, 495 units, 61,000 m^2 office, and 7,000 m^2 leisure and facilities, see figure 22) is located to the east of the city centre of Bristol. This area had been for the last years the subject of redevelopment, most of the time to develop office buildings. The site covers former railway sidings and industry, and is largely flattened and vacant at the moment of redevelopment. Only a couple of small buildings and a school remained at that time. The school has been integrated into the regeneration. The site is one of the Council's main priorities for regeneration. The 1997 Bristol Local Plan and the City Centre Strategy (a supplementary document to the Local Plan) foresaw the redevelopment of most of the site into a mixed used area with office space, housing and retail. During the 1990s, various planning applications have been granted for redevelopment of the site. However, at least four of these permissions have expired without having been implemented. The central UK government appointed an Urban Development Corporation (UDC) for this area. This UDC took over the local competences and bought part of the land. After the UDC wound down in 1996, The South West of England Regional Development Agency (SWRDA), a regional public body, took over that land. In 2001, the SWRDA, together with the developer (Castlemore Securities Ltd), submitted a planning application to redevelop the site. The planning permission came definitively into force in 2003, after negotiations under section 106 ended with the sealing of a Development Agreement. The infrastructure works commenced in 2004. In June 2007 about one quarter of all building was completed, other plots were under construction and the infrastructure works for the rest of the site were going on.

At the moment of the submission of the planning application, the land was owned by Castlemore (47% of the site), another developer (Verclutt, 8%), the SWRDA (25%), and the City Council of Bristol (the existing school, that has been maintained, 12%; and the existing streets, 8%).

Figure 22. Plan area development site 'Temple Quay' (source: Report Head Bristol Planning Services to Bristol Local Council Committee 5 June 2002).

6.3.3 *Megabowl*, City of Bristol

Urban regeneration 'Megabowl' (1.3 ha, 13,500 m^2 apartments, 184 units, 142 units/ha, see figure 23) is located in the west of the City of Bristol. The site is within the city, but is relatively isolated from it by a busy highway. It has been used in the past as a tram terminus, military barracks, cold store, and for light industrial purposes. Since the 1990s up to the start of the redevelopment, it was used as a bowling alley. The 1997 Bristol Local Plan and the 2003 Proposed Alterations to the Bristol Local Plan (a supplementary document to the Local Plan) foresaw no redevelopment of the site. In 2006, the owner (Tenpin Limited) submitted an application for planning permission to redevelop the site. The Council granted provisionally the permission at the end of the same year. Then, Tenpin Limited sold the site to George Wimpey, a commercial developer. The planning permission came definitively into force in 2007, after negotiations under section 106 between the Council and George Wimpey ended with the sealing of a Development Agreement. The demolition works started in June 2007. At that time the infrastructure provision was expected to start at the end of 2007, and the building to be completed one year later. The infrastructure provision started indeed in that year but the works have delayed largely, and in April 2010 the building was still not completed.

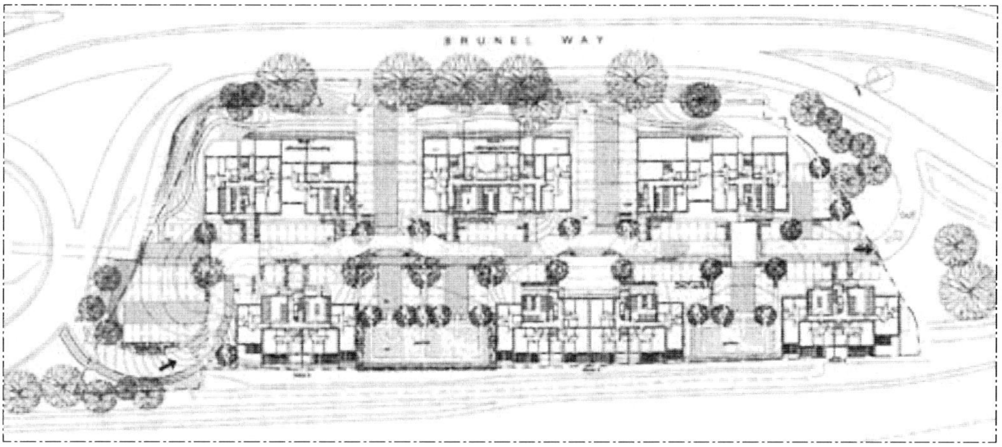

Figure 23. Plan area development site 'Megabowl' (source: Report Head Bristol Planning Services to Bristol Local Council Committee 27 September 2006).

6.4 How formal rules relevant to zoning in England can be used

This chapter describes the working of formal rules relevant to zoning within the value capturing mechanisms. There are different ways (or sub-variables) in which these rules in England can be used in an operational way to improve the capturing of value increase:

- Creating certainty or uncertainty beforehand about future building possibilities and contributions;
- Choosing the contents of the relevant binding rules (the planning permission);

- Conditioning the relevant binding rules (the planning permission) to securing the capturing of value increase;
- Modulating property rights;
- Using the procedure for the preparation and approval of the relevant binding rules (the planning permission).

Here follows an assessment of whether each of these sub-variables can affect the capturing of value increase.

6.4.1 Creating certainty beforehand about future building possibilities and contributions

Summary of the findings

The British planning system is not designed to provide certainty beforehand, neither about future building possibilities, nor about future contributions. However, zoning plans and supplementary planning guidance often create some certainty, although this is limited: those two instruments are usually vague, not detailed, and anyway LPAs can and usually do depart from them, as they are not legally binding.

The general trend is that LPAs are increasing the certainty about future building possibilities given by indicative zoning plans and site-specific supplementary policy guidance. In the studied cases, there was some certainty. In cases *Harbourside* and about half of *Temple Quay,* the 1997 Bristol Local Plan created a strong expectation of being able to redevelop these sites. In the rest of *Temple Quay* and in the whole of *Megabowl* there was no such expectation. Of the three, only in *Harbourside* did a site-specific supplementary planning guidance (the 1998 Planning Brief) create some detailed certainty about the development possibilities.

Table 14. Level of certainty in the English cases.

	Certainty about future building possibilities	Certainty about future contributions
Harbourside	some	high
Temple Quay	low	Low for 2/3 site, high for renegotiation 1/3 site
Megabowl	none	high

Regarding the obligations to be met, the trend to give more certainty seems clearer. LPAs are increasingly elaborating obligations policy that acquires the status of supplementary guidance. This was the case in Bristol after the approval in 2005 of SPD4, a generic policy document about capturing value increase. Thanks to this document, certainty was high in part of case *Temple* (the renegotiation in 2007 of the modification of the planning permission for about one third of the site) and in case *Megabowl.* The 1998 Planning Brief, a site-specific document, created certainty for *Harbourside.*

The uncertainty was the largest in the first planning permission for *Temple Quay*, which was processed and negotiated in 2001-2003, before the introduction of SPD4. Table 14 summarizes the level of certainty, before definitive negotiations took place, about building possibilities and contributions.

The findings suggest that uncertainty about the future building possibilities and certainty about future contributions might both be positive for capturing value increase. This is because they reinforced the negotiating position of the municipality, and because they might have lowered the land price. Let us see in detail what it is that local authorities create certainty or uncertainty about, in which sort of documents, and what are the inferred consequences for the captured value increase.

6.4.1.1 Intrinsic uncertainty of the British system, and the recent trend of creating some certainty through indicative zoning plans and supplementary policy guidance

Before development initiatives appear, there are usually in England non-site specific zoning plans with various names: 'Structure plans', 'Local plans', 'Unitary development plans' and, since 2004, 'Local development frameworks'. In addition, local authorities can make *ad hoc*, often site-specific planning documents that might not be defined in planning legislation, but receive the status of supplementary policy guidance. Local authorities have tended in the last years to develop many informal and formal policy documents and zoning plans that make clearer to themselves and to applicants how the LPA's intend to act (Booth, 2003: 12-13).

When considering applications for a planning permission, the 1990 Town and Country Planning Act gives the local authorities broad competences to evaluate them. When considering applications, authorities 'shall have regard to the provisions of the zoning plan (and supplementary planning guidance, red.), so far as material to the application, and to any other material considerations' (section 70.2). The courts have held that the expression 'shall have regard to the provisions of the zoning plan' does not require that the plan should be slavishly adhered to (Moore, 2005: 223, §12.32). The possibility of considering the zoning plan and the supplementary planning guidance as not determining, and the possibility of having regard to 'any other material considerations', give LPAs much discretion to decide about applications. LPAs have a certain amount of room to decide each case on its own merits. By refusing applications or by submitting them to planning conditions and obligations, municipalities may refer to broad principles and ambiguous concepts like 'amenity'. It is this that distinguisheds the British planning system from other Western European countries: it is the genuine representative of the 'development-led' planning system, which is not required to approve beforehand legally binding zoning plans (see, for an international comparison, section 4.1).

LPAs often use this provision to depart from the zoning plans and supplementary planning guidance (Whitaker, interview 2007). The cases confirm this general statement. Bristol made use in all three cases of the possibility of departing, although this happened in different degrees: in *Harbourside* and *Temple* the departure was large, and in *Megabowl* the departure was the largest. In addition, the cases show that zoning plans and supplementary planning guidance are not always detailed. The 1997 Bristol Local Plan is not a detailed plan: it includes neither the maximal building volume, nor the amount of each land use, nor the building envelope and alignments, etc. In *Harbourside* the 1998 Planning Brief provided additional certainty by specifying the development possibilities and the obligations to be paid; however, this did not result in detailed prescriptions. It might be that this case-based finding (zoning plans and site-specific supplementary planning guidance are often not detailed) is not an exception in England. It is clear anyway that planning law does not prescribe that indicative zoning plans should be detailed.

Thus, there is in the British planning system an intrinsic uncertainty, but local authorities usually create some certainty through indicative zoning plans. Additionally, there is a clear trend of local authorities increasing the certainty about the future contributions. It seems that, at least since the late 1990s, English local authorities are increasingly elaborating policies on planning obligations, policy that has the status of complementary planning guidance. These policies have clarified the likely obligations that developments have to face, and are in two different forms:

1. Generic non-site specific policy for all the territory or parts of it, e.g. Bristol's Supplementary Planning Document Number 4, SPD4 ('Achieving Positive Planning through the use of Planning Obligations'), adopted in 2005. This document was important in case *Megabowl* and part of *Temple Quay*.
2. Site-specific documents for important development sites, e.g. Bristol's 1998 Planning Brief. This document was important in case *Harbourside*.

Central government advice has encouraged this trend, and it seems that these moves are, in part, a response to criticism. The development sector has objected strongly to the delays associated with negotiating planning agreements, and there is a wide concern about the lack of accountability of the negotiation process. Nowadays, a majority of local authorities have enacted, in different ways, formal policy about planning obligations (Campbell *et alii*, 2000: 760, 763-764; Department..., 2006: 19-20).

In the studied cases, the situation was varied. In *Harbourside* there was some certainty at the time of the application procedure and negotiations (March 2001-February 2003). The 1997 Bristol Local Plan zoned the whole site as 'Major regeneration area', with offices (no specific building volume), leisure/tourist activities, and housing (about 200 dwellings). In addition, the Council had approved in 1998 a Planning Brief that specified the building possibilities (augmenting the number of dwellings to 400) and prescribed the obligations likely to be paid (see frame 6d).

Frame 6d

The obligations in the 1998 Planning Brief for Harbourside

The 1998 Planning Brief has its first version in 1994. The City Council of Bristol approved in that year a Development Framework, and in 1995 a Planning Brief Implementation Phase for the Harbourside regeneration that amended and integrated the contents of the 1994 document. The 1998 document reviewed and amended the 1995 version, and included for example the following contributions:

- The 1998 document reaffirmed the previous requirement, broadly and openly stated by the Council in a first planning brief in 1992, following which profits should 'cross-subsidise the achievement of the essential infrastructure and the Council's leisure (...) objectives...' (p. 13, see also p. 51). 'Leisure objectives' include in any case a financial contribution to the construction of a non-commercial leisure facility, situated nearby but outside the plan area in question;
- The 1998 document includes the requirement to comply with local policy documents on affordable housing, making clear that the scheme will have to include affordable housing, of which a part must be social rented (p. 21).
- The 1998 document makes clear that the developer must provide directly related infrastructure (the roads and public space within the plan area, p. 51). Further on, it specifies that e.g. the 'remediation of contaminated land' (Appendix I: i) will also be the responsibility of the developer. It also establishes which development sites will assume the costs of which infrastructure, and establishes a realization schedule (Appendix I: ii-viii).

Although the 1998 document did not set down quantities, it seems that it created enough clarity for the developer to assess, within a certain margin, the financial feasibility of the scheme. Asked whether this choice was related to capturing value increase, an involved planning officer insisted that the goal was indeed to create beforehand enough certainty about the development value and costs. By doing so, the officer said, the chance that developers buy the land for too high a price is reduced (see sections 2.3.3 and 2.4.2 for more details about the working of the residual land price mechanisms) So it seems that Bristol created some certainty, about both future building possibilities and contributions, with the goal of improving capturing value increase. Nevertheless, this certainty was flexible. As said, the Council could deviate from both documents, as actually happened several times. For example, during the negotiations, the Council first added the requirement of 30% of affordable housing and augmented the total number of dwellings from 400 to 700; afterwards it lowered the requirement of affordable housing.

In *Temple Quay* the Council chose not to detail the vague determinations of the 1997 Local Plan. No other site-specific supplementary planning guidance was enacted for this site at the time of the application procedure and negotiations (May 2001-May 2003). The 1997 Plan established a variety of uses for the site. More than the half of the site was designated as 'regeneration area', 'mixed commercial area', and on several plots as both 'new housing site' and new 'industrial and warehousing' at the same time. However, the rest of the site (something less than the half) was zoned as 'Primarily Industrial and warehousing', or had no designation. This means that something less than half of the site was not foreseen as being regenerated into residential and offices. Thus, the certainty about the building possibilities was very low, both because of the lack of detail in the 1997 Plan, and because this Plan foresaw regeneration for only half of the site. The same could be said about the certainty about obligations, because the 1997 Plan said nothing about future contributions. It could be that the collaboration between the Council and the developer in making a Masterplan (2000-2003) for the site had created some informal certainty beforehand. However, the local authority did not formally adopt this document.

There is an exception to the lack of certainty in *Temple Quay*. In 2007 the developer decided to apply for a modification of part of the planning permission, regarding blocks ND1-5 (about one third of the site). He applied for an increase in the office space and in the number of dwellings. Modification means that planning obligations will be renegotiated. The Council approved in 2005 the Supplementary Planning Document Number 4 (SPD4, see frame 6e). This document, that has the status of supplementary planning guidance, details the obligations to be paid/fulfilled in all schemes in the City of Bristol, most of the time in the form of standard charges. Thus, since 2005, the SPD4 forms an evaluation criterion for all planning applications in the city. Thanks to this document, when the developer decided in 2007 to apply for a modification of the planning permission in blocks ND1-5, he had certainty about the obligations likely to be required. Nevertheless, this certainty is flexible. As said, the Council can deviate from this document.

Frame 6e
Bristol's 2005 SPD4 document
The Supplementary Planning Document Number 4 of the City of Bristol ('Achieving Positive Planning through the use of Planning Obligations') establishes standard contributions of the following sorts: affordable housing, educational and recreational facilities, landscape schemes, travel plan initiatives, park and ride facilities, highway infrastructure works, site specific measures, economic contribution from new development, areas of public realm, public art, community forest initiative and library facilities. Examples of these standard contributions are:

- Affordable housing: this applies to residential developments of 25 or more dwellings or one hectare or more in size; the developer is required to provide on-site a percentage of the total number of units, according to local affordable housing policy (30% in 2007, red.), or exceptionally to pay a sum for off-site provision of affordable housing;
- Educational facilities: this applies to residential developments of 40 or more dwell

ings if they generate additional pupil numbers in excess of the capacity of local schools; the developer is usually required to pay a sum for the provision of off-site facilities, or exceptionally to provide on-site these facilities. Per additional pupil in excess of the local capacity, the developer has to pay a sum: £ 9,136 per school place in a Nursery or Primary School, £ 14,346 per school place in a Secondary School;
- Landscape schemes: this applies to any development sort; the developer is required to submit a Landscape Scheme to, and receive written approval from, a competent public body, before commencing development, and to implement it, pay the maintenance costs during a period of 12 months, and finally transfer the land to the municipality free of charge.

In *Megabowl* the uncertainty about the future building possibilities was very high, as the Council had never considered regeneration. The 1997 Bristol Local Plan and the 2003 Proposed Modifications did not foresee at all the regeneration of the site. This is called a 'windfall site'. This uncertainty was reinforced by site-specific circumstances: the site is isolated by a highway and was in principle not very suitable for residential use. However, regarding future contributions, the certainty was very high. This is thanks to the fact that at the time of the application procedure and negotiations (April 2006-April 2007), the SPD4 document already established the obligations to be fulfilled. Nevertheless, this certainty was flexible: for example, during the negotiations, the Council lowered the requirements for social/affordable housing from 30% to 25%.

The question is now, what have been the results of the level of certainty/uncertainty for the captured value increase. Here, a distinction is made between certainty about building possibilities, and certainty about contributions.

6.4.1.2 Effects for capturing value increase of Uncertainty about building possibilities

In general, it seems that uncertainty about the future building possibilities has improved the capturing of value increase (Claydon and Smith, 1997; Campbell *et* alii, 2001: 18-19; Whitaker, interview 207). The cases seem to confirm this general conclusion. Case *Megabowl* provides interesting conclusions. Here, the uncertainty about the building possibilities was the largest of the three cases, as regeneration of the site was not foreseen at all. The Council required and obtained what could be considered a high level of obligations (see section 6.5 for a comparison between the degree of captured value increase in the three cases). Almost all possible contributions stated in SPD4 that are relevant to this site, were achieved here. This case is considered within the Council's planning department as a good example of obtaining section 106 obligations.

There are two possible explanations for this effect of uncertainty about building possibilities. First, uncertainty may reinforce the negotiation position of LPAs. Both the involved planning officer and the developer's agent in *Megabowl* agree that this uncertainty gave much negotiation room to the Council. This case-based finding fits within a general idea, already formulated in variable D1.1 of the causal model of section 2.4.2: if certainty is high about future building possibilities, LPAs have less to offer in the negotiations.

Second, uncertainty about building possibilities might have improved capturing value increase for another reason too. For low building expectations might lower the land price (variable D1.1). In *Megabowl*, as a consequence of the uncertainty, the site had not been the subject of speculation: no developer had yet been seriously interested in buying the land. It was the former owner and user that negotiated the planning permission and the obligations. This might have been one of the stimuli to the owner-developer to consider initially a lower land price, that is the residual value of the land taking into account *only* the actual use as bowling alley - the minimum land cost, about 3-4.5 € million - but not including any expectation of urban use. Thanks to this, the Final profit of the developer was large, giving him much room to pay (in money and in kind) more contributions than usual. The total development costs (postings 1-7 in Annex 3), taking into account the minimum land cost, amounted to circa € 20 million, and the total estimated returns about €37m. After agreeing the contributions, the landowner sold his land to a developer for about € 11 million. In a scenario in which the expectations for the site are clear beforehand, developers would most probably have paid a high sum for the land, and this would have reduced the financial room available for contributions. Both in *Temple Quay* and *Harbourside,* developers bought land from the former owners for a price presumably higher than the existing market value of these sites. However, it has not been possible to say what the price of land there was, for developers were not willing to provide the needed information.

6.4.1.3 Effects for capturing value increase of Certainty about contributions

In general for England, there is evidence that those local authorities that have standard charges, known beforehand, are able to gain more obligations (in number and in terms of their economic value). This suggests that standard charges have a positive effect on the number and economic value of obligations (Department..., 2006: 19, 22, 27-28, 54). The findings in the cases agree with this general opinion. Capturing value increase was higher in those cases in which certainty was higher: thus higher in *Megabowl* and *Harbourside*, and lower in the former permission for *Temple Quay*. For *Temple Quay* it seems that the renegotiation in 2007, once the SPD4 document had been approved, of the planning permission for one third of the site will provide more obligations than the first permission.

There are two possibly explanations for this apparent positive effect of certainty about contributions: it may first reinforce the negotiating position of LPAs, and second lower the acquisition cost of the land. Regarding the negotiating position: making explicit policy for obligations means that obligations become material to the determination of planning permission. This allows local authorities to successfully refuse those applications that do not fulfil the required contributions, and allows them also to subject the applications to conditions and obligations (Campbell et al., 2000: 773; 2001). A representative of the English developers considered that local authorities create strong arguments for possible refusal, and that this provides them with a strong starting point in the negotiations (Whitaker, interview 2007). The cases seem to confirm this general conclusion: in all three cases, the public officers in charge considered that a strong policy base for requiring planning obligations was very important for capturing value increase. In *Temple Quay*, at the time of the negotiations there was no such strong policy base, and the planning officer considered this lack as a crucial factor that influenced negatively the obligations. During the renegotiation of part of the planning permission in August 2007, both the former planning officer and the developer considered that obligations would turn out higher due to the approval in 2005 of SPD4. For example, contributions for library services and for funding car clubs (intended to lower the need of parking places on street level) were not possible before the approval of SPD4. Also, affordable housing will benefit from SPD4. The findings in our cases agree with the findings of other studies. In a case study in Newbury, Berkshire, the lack of such an obligations policy seems to have influenced capturing value increase negatively (Campbell et al., 2001: 24). In another study of three projects in London, Weymouth and Liverpool, the researchers came to similar conclusions (Claydon & Smith, 1997: 2017).

Regarding helping to lower land prices: the cases seem to confirm the positive role of certainty about contributions. In *Megabowl*, certainty about a high degree of contributions might have been relevant for lowering the Accounted land costs in two ways. First in combination with the uncertainty about the building possibilities explained above: initially the first landowner accepted a low 'book value' for his land not only because developers where not interested in buying his land, but probably also because he was aware of the high level of contributions stated in the SPD4-document. Second, once at the end of 2006 the planning permission was provisionally approved, together with a list of contributions that had to be detailed in a Development Agreement, the first landowner sold his land to a developer. The Development Agreement was not yet sealed, so there still was, in theory, negotiation room. However, the developer knew he had no choice than to secure in a Development Agreement all these contributions. The certainty created with the provisional approval of a list of contributions, based on the SPD4 document, must have played a role here. It seems very plausible that the price paid for the land (€ 11m) has taken into account the contributions. The fact that this price left financial room for all the contributions seems to confirm this (see Annex 3). In *Harbourside*, certainty has probably also lowered the price that the developer had to pay for the land, as developer and landowners agreed that this price depended on the final profit margins. In *Temple Quay*, it seems plausible that the lack of certainty has inflated the land price. In general, it seems that once the price paid for land has internalized part of the future urban expectations, it is difficult to reduce those expectations. *Harbourside* provides an example: when the

Council added afterwards the requirement of 30% affordable housing, the developer argued that he had no more financial room to accommodate this contribution in his budget. The developer was not willing to provide information about the land price, information that is crucial to accurately evaluate his arguments. However, our own estimations about the development value and costs in *Harbourside* show a large difference between the estimated development costs (excluding land price) and returns (see Annex 3 for a comparison of development costs and profits in the English cases). This suggests that there may have been enough financial room to pay 30% affordable housing. The problem could have been that the 30%-requirement came too late, in the sense that the developer and the landowners had already incorporated the full development surplus in the land price. It was finally decided that the developer will build 9% of affordable housing.

6.4.2 Choosing the contents of the binding rules (the planning permission)

In England, planning law, planning guidance and the jurisprudence make it possible to include a wide range of determinations in planning permissions: not only physical zoning aspects, but also aspects related to the implementation. For more details about the possibly contents of planning conditions and obligations see section 6.2.

Summary of the findings

One of the possibilities is to include the obligation to contribute in kind or in money social/affordable housing and off-site public infrastructure and facilities. This seems to have a positive influence on capturing value increase, especially for the construction and implementation by the developer himself of social/affordable housing on-site, and of public infrastructure and facilities off-site, but not so much for the developer constructing or transferring land for social/affordable housing off-site. Another possibility is to include deadlines, but here there are differences in their effectiveness. It is only possible to include in Development Agreements deadlines for the *completion of contributions*, but these deadlines are only in force once development *commences*. Since it is not possible to include deadlines for the *commencement* of development in Development Agreements, when planning permissions include commencement deadlines, these seem not to be very effective. The consequence is that many planning permissions are never implemented. However, if development does start, deadlines for the completion of contributions come into force and seem to be effective in stable market circumstances. The consequence is that once commenced, and provided market circumstances remain stable, developments and the related contributions are usually implemented within deadlines. The difference in effectiveness of commencement and completion deadlines suggests that another sub-variable and a third variables might be influential here: the sub-variable is the possibility of conditioning planning consent to securing the deadlines and contributions (see next section 6.4.3), and the third variable are the market circumstances (variable A2, see causal model in section 2.4.2). Let us see in detail what are the possible contents of planning permissions, and what are the consequences for capturing value increase.

6.4.2.1 Including social/affordable housing

Planning permissions can include contributions for social/affordable housing, both on-site and off-site. Circular 06/98 prescribes thresholds for seeking contributions: usually 25 or more dwellings, or a site larger than one ha, above which there is in principle the obligation for the developer to provide affordable housing. In Inner London this is 15 dwellings/0.5 ha (Gurran et al., 2007: 40). It seems clear that in England, in general, planning obligations are increasingly being used to provide affordable housing. For example, in a survey in 1999 it was found that 78% of LPAs had specific affordable housing policies in development plans (Holmans et al, 2000; quoted in Crook & Whitehead, 2002: 1274). It is possible to conclude that this general trend is also present in Bristol, where the threshold is 25 dwellings, or a site larger than one hectare rules. Many of the interviewed public officers and developers considered this to be so, and the cases confirm this. The more recent the project is, the higher the proportion of affordable housing. In cases *Temple Quay* and *Harbourside* (planning permissions definitively valid in 2003), planning agreements stated the parcels where social/affordable housing has to be built and a minimum percentage of units: 14% respectively 9%, that are expected to result in about 71 respectively 63 units. In *Megabowl* (planning permission definitively valid in 2007), the planning agreement established the number of affordable units (25%, 46 units). It seems that other recent applications are negotiating similar requirements as in *Megabowl*. None of the studied cases included contributions in money or contributions to off-site affordable housing.

What have been the consequences of the fact that LPAs can include social/affordable housing in planning permissions? Presumably this statutory power, together with having created certainty about this sort of contribution (see previous section), is helping to strengthen the LPA's negotiation position. Also, it must influence the Accounted land costs because once such a contribution is included in a planning permission, developers know it cannot be avoided. The fact is that LPAs are increasingly including social/affordable housing in planning permissions and that the amount of social/affordable housing being built in England has been increasing since 2004. The studied cases show the positive effect in Bristol too, where the building rates of social/affordable housing are higher than in the rest of England (see for a comparison of the results in each case, and figures for Bristol and England, section 6.5). However, the minimal threshold (25 dwellings/larger than 1 ha in Bristol) seems to have disadvantages: according to many of the interviewed (public parties and developers) many developers remain under the threshold, although they could develop more than 25 dwellings. The City of Bristol is currently studying the possibility of lowering this threshold to about 4-6 dwellings.

6.4.2.2 Including off-site public infrastructure and facilities

Planning permissions can also include contributions for off-site public infrastructure and facilities. This might include contributions for off-site social/affordable housing (just handled above). Presumably this statutory power, together with having created certainty about this sort of contribution (see previous section), is helping to strengthen both the negotiation position of LPA's and to lower the accounted land costs.

Regarding contributions in land, it seems not to be very common to include such a requirement in planning permissions. The findings in the cases support this: in none of the three cases did the planning permission include the obligation or the condition to provide land outside the plan area. Regarding contributions for the construction and implementation of public facilities and infrastructure, it seems that in the last years LPAs are increasingly asking for this sort of obligation. This seems to have a positive effect in practice, and in the cases the results were varied. Contributions were larger in *Harbourside* than in *Megabowl* and *Temple Quay*. This seems to be the result of the decision of the Council in *Harbourside* to focus on a large monetary contribution for a leisure facility located outside the development site in question.

6.4.2.3 Including implementation schedules

Planning permissions can also include, as planning conditions or obligations, deadlines for the implementation of public infrastructure and facilities, or for the payment of contributions. Presumably this statutory power is helping, with differing success, to reinforce the negotiation position of LPA's and accelerate the realization of the contributions. There is a distinction between deadlines for the *commencement* of the development, and deadlines for the *completion* of development and contributions.

Deadlines for the *commencement of development* cannot be included in Planning Agreements. Since 1968, power has been given to LPAs to impose deadlines within which the development must start. However, these deadlines can be included only as planning condition, but not as planning obligations, which means that these deadlines cannot be included in the Planning Agreement. This is because Circular 05/2005 rules that obligations are only meant for mitigation of undesirable aspects of development. And if development has not commenced, there can be no undesirable aspects to mitigate. In cases *Temple Quay* and *Harbourside* (permissions granted in 2003), planning conditions included a deadline of five years, and in *Megabowl* (permission granted in 2007) three years. If the holder of the planning permission does not start the development within the deadline, the permission will expire (Moore, 2005: 304-305). What are the consequences of not being able to include commencement deadlines in the Planning Agreement? It seems that, in England, commencement deadlines are not always achieved. Many granted permissions are not used. It is estimated that in 2003/04, 80% of full planning permissions and 75% of outline planning permissions were actually implemented, and the rest not (Department..., 2006: 43). Asked about this, two experts considered that this happened more frequently some time ago, in the 90's, and less in recent years (Lyons and Henneberry, interviews in 2007). The case *Temple Quay* seems to support the general conclusion that commencement deadlines are not always fulfilled: during the 90's, various planning applications have been granted for redevelopment of the site. At least four of these permissions have expired without having been implemented. In cases *Temple Quay* and *Harbourside,* the commencement deadlines for the planning permissions were achieved. At the time of data gathering in June 2007, in *Megabowl* development has not yet commenced, but the deadline had not yet passed. Because not commencing on time would imply the expiration of the planning application only, there was at that time no certainty about whether the agreed contributions would finally be achieved or not.

Deadlines about when parts of the development and the contributions *must be completed* can be included in Planning Agreements. This is because LPAs can include these deadlines not only as planning conditions, but also as planning obligations. However, these deadlines become in force only *if and when development commences*. Thus, these deadlines are irrelevant until development begins. They were at the time of data gathering in June 2007 relevant in *Temple Quay* and *Harbourside,* but not in *Megabowl* (development commenced only later in 2007). It is uncertain whether, in general, those planning permissions that are commenced are also completed within the deadlines. There are no general figures to support whether these deadlines, once activated, are effective or not, but asked about this, two experts interviewed in 2007 considered that these deadlines are indeed effective. Their argument was that commencement of development involves investments, so once they are made developers cannot afford to delay (Lyons and Henneberry, interviews in 2007). Our cases however show a more nuanced picture. In two of them, *Temple Quay* and *Harbourside*, development has commenced indeed, and deadlines for the completion had been so far, in June 2007, achieved. However, the economic crisis in 2009 seems to affect seriously the building schedules. In at least *Megabowl* the completion of the building is having serious delays. The infrastructure provision stopped at the end of 2007 and in April 2010 the building was not yet completed. At the beginning of 2010 it is unknown to us whether the building in the other cases has been completed or not.

Thus, the effectiveness of the deadlines seems to depend not on the fact that they are included in planning permissions, but partially on the fact that they are secured in a Planning Agreement, and partially on market circumstances. This suggests that this sub-variable (possible contents planning permission) influences only partially the variable 'capturing value increase'. That is, there is some risk that the inferred causal relationship is, partly, spurious. The sub-variable 'conditioning permission to securing deadlines' (see next section) and market circumstances (variable A1, see causal model in section 2.4.2) seem to play the role of third variables because deadlines are effective only if they are secured and provided that market circumstances do not change dramatically.

6.4.3 Conditioning binding rules (the planning permission) on securing capturing value increase

The English planning permission can be made conditional on a contractual agreement (Planning Agreement) with the developer. Initially, the Council approves the permission provisionally, including the planning conditions and obligations that it expects from the developer. The definitive approval of the planning permission happens only after the planning obligations (but not the planning conditions) are secured in a Planning Agreement. What are the consequences of being allowed to make planning consent conditional on securing the planning obligations, but not on securing the planning conditions and thus commencement deadlines? The cases (see previous section) and some interviews suggest that because commencement deadlines cannot be secured, contributions are often implemented with delay, or not at all. In conclusion, not the fact of being able to include contributions in planning permissions seems to be effective, but the fact of being able to condition planning consent to securing contributions. With other words, *i)* being able to condition planning consent to securing the contributions reinforces *ii)* the positive effect of being able to include certain contributions in planning permissions on *iii)* the negotiation position of LPA's, on the Accounted land costs and on the speed of the implementation.

6.4.4 Modulating property rights

Summary of the findings
The right to develop (i.e. the exclusive right to develop land, once permission has been granted) belongs in England to the landowner. This, together with the distribution of the other necessary resources in urban regeneration (planning permissions and financial means), creates a strong interdependency between local authorities and landowners. This interdependency gives to the landowners the option to wait, which it is often used to contravene local authorities' requirements, and often leads to delaying the development.

6.4.4.1 Who owns development rights in England?

The nationalization of development rights might have had consequences for the legal limits to capturing value increase, as we saw in section 6.2.1. However, this has not altered the principle that landowners are the only ones that can develop their land. It is therefore clear that the right to develop belongs exclusively to the landowner. Planning permission attaches to the land, and not to the developer. Before being entitled to develop, developers have to acquire the land (Williams & Wood, 1994: 78, Ratcliffe, 2001: 152-153; Cullingworth & Nadin, 2006: 195-197). However, the landowner is limited in his right to develop, he has no right to any kind of 'minimum' and must apply for and obtain the needed permits. Other legislation (e.g. compulsory purchase) might even lead to removal of his right.

Infrastructure provision requires several transactions: 1) land purchase and assembling, 2) financing, and 3) land preparation and development. By analyzing who has the control over each of these transactions, it has been possible to discern the extent to which development rights belong to the landowners.

6.4.4.2 Mutual dependence of local authorities and landowners in England

To analyse the consequences for the power-relationship between municipalities and landowners of the practical possibilities for controlling transactions 1-3, this research developed and applied a model of dependence (see table 15; for more details of the model, see section 3.1.1). In England there is a strong mutual dependence between municipalities and developers/landowners, so the possibilities in practice for gathering the land (1), gathering the financial resources (2), and developing the land to produce serviced plots (3) depend heavily on the landowner's passive consent or active collaboration. This strong mutual dependence is caused by the fact that none of the actors control all the needed resources, and because the dependence is not easily avoidable. The landowner controls two important resources - land and investment capacity - and local authorities depend on the landowner because of this. As a rule, without agreement about the purchase and assembly of land and about the financing of the infrastructure provision, municipalities that want things to happen, have to compulsorily purchase the land. In other words, the only way of avoiding dependence on the landowner is public land development, or at least public infrastructure provision. But doing that is not easy: compulsory purchase and public land development mean a direct public involvement and the assumption of the corresponding financial costs and risks. Furthermore, compulsory purchase is a sensitive

Table 15. Dependence analysis England.

	Dependence because of land	**Dependence because of investment capacity**	**Dependence because of regulatory resources**
LPA depends on the landowner/ developer	**Dependence.** Developer/Landowner owns all the land. Dependence is only avoidable through compulsory purchase, but this is only used in exceptional circumstances. Expropriation is considered slow, expensive and risky.	**Dependence.** The developer was able to invest in buying the land and developing it. Dependence is thus avoidable only if Bristol has enough financial means. However, Bristol did not have the financial means.	
Landowner/ developer depends on LPA			**Dependence.** The LPA grants the required permissions. Dependence is not avoidable.

matter, politically. On the other hand, the landowner depends on the local authority because of its regulatory powers to grant the planning permission. This dependence can also be labelled as strong because it is not avoidable: public bodies are the only actors who can exercise these regulatory powers.

In all the studied cases, all or most of the land was in private hands. The City of Bristol could have avoided mutual dependence by applying compulsory purchase and developing the site itself. However, in practice, this instrument is used only in exceptional circumstances in Bristol; only when there is no agreement with a minority of the landowners and the majority of the landowners support the measure and are willing to pay the costs of it. An interviewed public officer considered compulsory purchase a slow instrument, expensive and fraught with risk. Besides, Bristol did not have the financial means to develop the sites.

The consequences in practice of this strong mutual dependency were significant. Landowners had the option of not agreeing with the contributions package or other requirements of the municipality. Since waiting can bear advantages, it was a favourable option to wait (see variable D2.2 in causal model section 2.4.2). As developers may not control all the land, and thus depend on various landowners, it might take some time to reach an agreement with all the landowners about the desired price of land. Success depends on the expectation that, by delaying negotiations, development profits could increase in the future. LPAs might be confronted with landowners/developers that are not willing to agree with the required financing and implementation schedules. This might affect the negotiating position of the local authorities, the accounted land costs and the profit margins of the developer, and thus capturing value increase. Authorities might be forced to lower the contributions package if they want to reach an agreement, allowing landowners to ask a higher price for their land and developers to enlarge their profit margins. And anyway, this affects the speed of implementation, as landowners/developers do not proceed quickly and development is delayed.

In at least the cases *Harbourside* and *Temple Quay,* the developers were not willing to agree to the requirements, arguing that they threatened the financial feasibility of the operations. For example, in *Harbourside* the developer was not willing to agree to the requirement of 30% social/affordable housing. Finally the developer included 9%. According to a representative of housing developers, in general about 50% of negotiations do not succeed because LPAs ask too large a contributions package (Whitaker, interview 2007). Several of the interviewed public officers in Bristol argued that contribution packages are determined taking into consideration the financial feasibility of schemes; in their view, the delay is caused by the price that the landowner expects the developer pay for his land, and whether it incorporates the development value or not. In other words, whether LPAs 'ask too much' or not, depends not only on the expected profit margins and the development costs, but also on the accounted land costs.

The cases offer some information that suggests that Bristol did not 'ask too much', thus confirming that resistance or acceptance of requirements might have been based more on the expected land price than on the true feasibility of the operation. In addition, the cases suggest that the expected profit margin (of the developer) might also have been relevant (see posting 8 in Annex 3 for a calculation of development costs and profits in the English cases). In *Megabowl,* the price of the land at the moment of the planning application was relatively low, about 3-4.5 € million[1]. This was thanks to uncertainty about the building possibilities, which had discouraged developers from buying the land previously. This gave the owner-applicant room to contribute much more than usual. The total development costs, which included this low land price and the contributions package, amounted circa € 20 million, and the expected returns circa € 37 million. In other words, thanks to a minimum land price, a large package of contributions has not threatened the financial feasibility of the scheme. These figures suggest that profit margins have been large and an even larger contribution package would have been financially feasible (37 – 20 = 17); at least, before the landowner sold his land to a developer for about € 11 million. In *Harbourside* and *Temple Quay,* developers were reluctant to provide information. Based on own estimations, it is possible to conclude that there was a significant margin between development costs (excluding the accounted land price, postings 2-7 in Annex 3: € 183m in *Harbourside* and € 133m in *Temple*) and the total returns (posting 8: € 404m respectively € 409m)[2]. For *Harbourside,* there is some more evidence that seems to confirm the idea that Bristol did actually not ask too much and that landowners and developers might have profited from it. Here the definitive land price was calculated once planning permission was secured, i.e. after negotiating the contributions. Both the interviewed developer and public officer confirmed that landowners have finally received a higher price for the land than the initially agreed basic price. This means that the developer was actually able to contribute more than he did, because he would have been able to pass the costs on to the landowners in the form of a lower land price. More recently, the City of Bristol has introduced several measures to improve the insights into the financial feasibility of operations; (1) the City is hiring specialist consultants; and (2) developers are required now to submit a viability appraisal to the Housing Department instead of the Planning Department: this avoids the duty of publication of such commercially sensitive information. The Housing Department estimates the suitable percentage of affordable housing.

1 This is about € 200-350 per m^2 of land, for in total 13.104 m^2 with a bowling alley on it.

2 A very approximate rough calculation is for *Harbourside* ca. € 2,800 per m^2 of land (€ 220 : 78,900 m^2); and for *Temple Quay* ca. € 4,180 per m^2 of land (€ 276m : 66,000 m^2).

6.4.5 Procedure for the preparation and approval of the binding rules (the planning permission)

Summary of the findings

It seems that procedural guarantees in England offer developers some valuable tools to reduce the discretion that LPAs have in determining planning permissions. The consequences for capturing value increase might have been negative, and the consequences for the speed of implementation are unclear. The relative flexibility to modify planning permissions seems to have positive effects for capturing value increase, while the possibility of approving first outline permissions and afterwards detailed ones does not. Finally, the flexibility in England to determine the size of the development area seems not to be relevant for capturing value increase.

6.4.5.1 Guarantees for those taking the initiative

In the English planning system there are several legal guarantees for the applicants of planning permissions. First, local authorities are obliged to decide about planning applications in a proper fashion. This implies the obligation of publicizing the application and starting the formal procedure. Second, there are strict deadlines within which local authorities have to determine the applications, deadlines that are moreover usually met in practice. And third, applicants can appeal against a non-determination, or against an unfavorable determination of the LPA, to the Planning Inspectorate, which evaluates the planning merits of LPA's decisions. Appeals regarding the legality of the procedures are decided by the courts of law (Williams & Wood, 1994: 67). The effects of these guarantees can be divided into consequences for capturing value increase, and side effects for the tempo of implementation.

Regarding the consequences for capturing value increase, these may be negative. A representative of the development industry considered that the right to a proper determination of planning applications, and the right to appeal, might have influenced negatively the negotiation position of local authorities because those authorities that require too many obligations are confronted with the risk of an appeal (Whitaker, interview 2007). The right to appeal seems to be an important way for developers to counter those local authorities that are requiring larger contributions. Asked about this, an expert supported partly this conclusion. Indeed, public officers seem to keep the right to appeal in mind when determining obligations and they seem to follow the obligations policy guidance strictly in order not to risk losing an appeal. It seems that the threat of appeals might come not only from the applicant. In competitive situations, especially in retail developments, developers might want to ensure that any obligation is perfectly respectable and legitimate in order to avoid appeal by other frustrated competitors. Other developers might seek to appeal against the legitimacy of the planning gains as a means of trying to frustrate the development (Claydon & Smith, 1997: 2018). In polemical applications, it may be other parties (civic society, neighbours,...) that use the argument of illegitimate obligations to impede development (Campbell *et alii*, 2001: 22-23). However, the expert put the weight of the right to appeal into perspective: appeals are expensive and time-consuming, which diminishes their usability for developers (Lyons, interview 2007).

The studied cases seem to support the above-mentioned generalization that the threat of appeal stimulates local authorities, and possibly developers also, to strictly follow policy guidance. Local authorities in the studied cases did not risk requiring more obligations than those strictly based on local policy. In *Harbourside* the application in question was the third one, after the Council had already rejected two other applications. An involved public officer considered that if this third application were refused, the applicant would have had a big chance to win an appeal. The developer confirmed that refusal would definitely have led to appeal, and that he probably would have won it. In *Temple Quay*, Bristol seemed to have already required much (the transfer of some land for a school), taking account of the poor policy guidance at the time of the negotiations. Both the public officer and the developer considered that an appeal against a refusal of the application would have had a good chance of success. In *Megabowl* the situation was different. Here, the specific features of this site (isolated, not foreseen in the 1997 Local Plan) seemingly gave good reasons for refusing the application, if Bristol had wished to do so. As a consequence, the Council seemed to have a good negotiation position, as it did not fear an appeal by the applicant. Also, the Council had a more generous planning guidance (the SPD4 document).

Regarding the consequences for the tempo of implementation, these are not clear. On the one hand, the representative of the development industry considered that the right to a proper determination of planning applications, and the right to appeal, have stimulated developers to submit applications, since they reduce the uncertainties (Whitaker, interview 2007). A consulted expert agreed with this conclusion (Henneberry, interview 2007). On the other hand, an increasing emphasis by local authorities on meeting the strict determination deadlines seems to have led since 2001 to an increase in refusals. Some local authorities seem not to be able to evaluate all applications properly within the deadlines. To achieve the legal deadlines, it appears that some authorities refuse applications that are difficult to evaluate and can thus lead to not achieving the deadlines. In turn, the increase of refusals seems to be one of the causes of the increase of appeals (Office of the Deputy Prime Minister, 2004a: 5-6, 50). The interviewed representative of the development industry was in favour of more flexible deadlines, especially for larger applications of more than 200 dwellings. Instead of the current deadlines, the local authority and the applicant should be obliged to agree an *ad hoc* schedule that allows a proper assessment of the application. The consulted expert considered that the current legislation already gives many possibilities for making deadlines more flexible. For example, developers and councils usually get involved in pre-application consultations that allow afterwards, once the application has been submitted, a smooth handling of the application.

6.4.5.2 Flexibility in modifying the granted planning permission

Modification

A modification of the planning permission, however minor it might be, requires a new application, and the full procedure has to be completed again. However, if the modification regards only planning conditions, there is no need to publicize the application. Further, if the modification regards only planning obligations, the LPA and the developer can agree to the modification, without extended procedure (Moore, 2005: §§ 11.33-35, 15.80; Circular 05/2005: §A15). The cases suggest that modification of the planning permission, conditions and obligations is a relatively flexible instrument, which can improve the negotiation position of LPAs and thus influence positively capturing value increase. In *Harbourside* the developer submitted in 2003 an application to modify, for several plots, the main aspects of the planning permission granted in that same year. The modifications followed the full procedure, which lasted for about one year. These modifications had positive consequences for capturing value increase, as the Council added some more contributions in money. In 2007 the developer of *Temple Quay* and the Council entered into negotiations to modify for one third of the site the planning permission granted in 2003. It seems that renegotiation will lead to some additional contributions.

Detailment

Developers can apply for Outline Planning Permission and detail it afterwards. An outline permission leaves several matters open (mostly design and external appearance) and reserves approval about them to a later moment. It seems that, up to recently, the subsequent approval of the full planning permission could have consequences for the negotiation position of LPAs and thus for capturing value increase: LPAs seemed to be able to add new contributions under certain circumstances. However, recent changes in legislation (2004 Act) and in policy guidance seem to have diminished the discretionary power of local authorities. Applications for outline permissions must now be more detailed than before (Moore, 2005: §10.11, §10.13). The studied cases seem to support the idea that reserved matters do not significantly effect anymore the negotiation position of LPAs. In *Temple Quay* and *Harbourside*, quite elaborated outline permissions were granted in 2003. Their detailing concerned only the external appearance of the buildings, landscaping (including detailed design and layout of public space) and detailed design of routes within the site. These detailed permissions did not entail any additional contribution.

6.4.5.3 Flexibility to determine the geographical scope (the plan area) of planning permission according to negotiations with landowners

There is in England much freedom for the applicant to delimit the plan area of planning permissions. In principle it is the applicant that proposes a certain delimitation of the development area. The applicant can follow, if he wishes, the property boundaries of his plot. In principle this means that the system allows scoping planning permissions according to the negotiations with each landowners. However, it is the applicant that has this freedom, and LPAs have not much freedom here. When considering the application, local authorities can ask applicants to modify the plan area, but if the applicant does not agree, it might be not easy to refuse the application. Authorities need then good arguments: e.g. a local zoning plan or planning guidance that includes a proposal to delimit, or at least enough arguments and criteria for the new delimitation; or when it is clear that the applicant is submitting small applications in order to develop his land bit by bit, for example to avoid reaching the legal threshold of 25 dwellings per scheme; or when the proposed plan area jeopardizes the use of an adjacent plot. Most of the interviewed public officers and one of the interviewed developers considered it difficult, in practice, to refuse planning applications on the ground that the plan area is not appropriately delimited.

Asked about this, an expert considered that, in general, on allocated sites (sites that are foreseen for regeneration in local planning guidance) local authorities usually delimit the development area beforehand, while on 'windfall' sites it is the developers who usually delimit the development area (Henneberry, interview 2007). The cases suggest that it is the developer that has in practice the most powers to delimit the plan area, both on allocated and on windfall sites. In *Harbourside* (7.9 ha) the 1998 Planning Brief had previously delimited two development areas, but it was the applicant who decided to submit an application for both areas together. In *Temple Quay* (7.4 ha) the applicant followed his own criteria to delimit the development areas, in which property boundaries played a central role. In *Megabowl* (1.3 ha) it was the applicant who delimited the plan area following his property boundaries.

It seems plausible that this flexibility has helped in the negotiation processes, in the sense that proposals included only those landowners who are willing to develop. However, since local authorities seem not to have much freedom to decide the boundaries of the development area, there is no evidence of positive effects for capturing value increase, nor does this seem likely.

6.5 The actual degree of captured value increase in England

This section is about whether the goals for capturing value increase have been achieved or not, and about the actual distribution of costs between the involved parties: who has paid which public infrastructure and facilities, and possibly some extras? We assess also whether the capturing value increase goals have been achieved on time. The main sources of information are the studied cases, complemented with other written sources and interviews with relevant experts. The conclusions are summarized in table 16.

Table 16. Comparison table results for capturing value increase in England.

	On-site land development costs		Land for on-site public infrastructure		Land for on-site public buildings		On-site public buildings		Affordable housing		Contributions off-site public infrastructure and facilities	Cream off betterment
	Developer/ landowner	**Public body**	**Developer/ landowner**	**Public body**	**Developer/ landowner**	**Public body**	**Developer/ landowner**	**Public body**	**Developer/ landowner**	**Public bodies**		
General knowledge England	(Almost) all the costs	Indirect through land/ cheap financing	Most of the land	Part of the land	Part of the land	Part of the land	Not very often	Almost always	Increasing number affordable/ social houses	Part of	Important contributions, which are increasing the last years.	In principle not.
Harbourside (total value real estate € 404 m)[3]	€ 28m (7% total value real estate)	Council paid share, Eng Partner issued cheap loan	30% total plan area	20% total plan area	-	0.3% total plan area	Developer builds small public building	-	4% rent, 5% shared ownership	-	€ 32.5m (8% total value real estate)	
Temple Quay (total value real estate € 409 m)	€ 13.2m (3% total value real estate)	Probably indirect subsidy SWRDA	27% total plan area	27% total plan area	3% total plan area	12% total plan area	-	School (already existing)	4% rent, 10% shared ownership	-	€ 5.9m (1.5% total value real estate)	
Megabowl (total value real estate € 37 m)	€ 1.2m (3% total value real estate)	-	65% total plan area	-	-	-	-	-	20% rent, 5% shared ownership	-	€ 1.6m (4% total value real estate)	

Grey: case in which the developer/landowner contributes the most of the three cases.
Light Grey: case in which the developer/landowner contributes the second of the three cases.
White: case in which the developer/landowner contributes the less of the three cases.

3 'Total value real estate' are the total returns accruing from the selling of the final real estate (thus includes the selling of the new buildings).

On-site infrastructure provision costs

It seems that, in general, all the costs of on-site infrastructure provision are paid by the developer/landowner. This includes, in principle, compensation costs that might be payable to existing users. Sometimes the developer does not transfer the legal ownership of the resulting infrastructure to the local authority, but keeps the legal ownership for himself. This infrastructure usually has however to remain accessible for the general public. The system of planning obligations has succeeded in general in financing the on-site infrastructure provision costs (Campbell *et alia*, 2000 and 2001; Department for Communities and Local Government, 2006). It seems that developers prefer payment in kind to payment in money, because this might be cheaper for them and because they have more certainty about the delivery of the public facilities. The studied cases support this conclusion: in the three cases, the developer paid all on-site infrastructure provision costs, almost all in kind.

However, in regeneration schemes, there might be exceptions to the general conclusion. In one of the studied cases, Harbourside, the local authority, which sold to the developer part of the land, had to pay part of the costs. Furthermore, the central government regeneration agency English Partnerships issued a cheap loan for the infrastructure works. In Temple Quay the SWRDA, a regional public development agency owning about 25% of the land, might have sold its land to the developer for a low price, a kind of indirect subsidy. Consulted about this, a relevant expert confirmed that it is not an exception that regeneration schemes encounter additional land development costs, and that many LPAs and other public bodies still have substantial properties on these sites. It is very common that public bodies use their land to facilitate development (Henneberry, interview 2007).

Land needed for on-site public infrastructure and facilities

Regarding the land needed for on-site infrastructure provision (excluding the land under the public buildings) the available literature supports the idea that, in general, the system of planning obligations has succeeded in providing this land free of charge (Campbell *et alia*, 2000 and 2001; Department for Communities and Local Government, 2006). However, the cases confirm this general statement only partly. Here the developer/landowner provides *most* of the land needed for on-site public infrastructure and facilities, but public bodies provide also *an important part* of it. Only in *Megabowl* did the developer provide all the land. Regarding the legal ownership of the land, sometimes the developer retains the legal ownership (all the public space in *Megabowl*, one fifth of the public space in *Harbourside*), and sometimes the local authority receives it free (four fifths of the public space in *Harbourside*, all the public space in *Temple Quay*). Consulted about this, an expert confirmed that it is common in urban regeneration schemes that public bodies provide part of the needed land (Henneberry, interview 2007).

Regarding the land needed for public buildings: in *Harbourside*, the only public building was a small pavilion occupying 0,3% of the total plan area, and situated on council land. In *Temple Quay*, there was just one public building: a school occupying about 15% of the plan area, of which 15% only one fifth has been ceded for free by the developer. In *Megabowl* there were no public buildings in the plan area. It seems therefore that, at least in the studied cases, developers usually do not contribute with land for public buildings. Two case studies in the 90's (Newbury, Berkshire, 50,000 m^2 office space, planning permission granted in 1999; and Shepton Mallet, Somerset, 360 dwellings, planning permission granted in 1994) show the same differentiated picture as in our cases: the office scheme did not include contributions in land for on-site public buildings, whereas the housing scheme included a contribution in land meant for a primary school within the site in question. However, these cases were of greenfield schemes, not regeneration (Campbell *et alii*, 2001: 21-33).

On-site public facilities (the buildings)

Only in *Harbourside* and *Temple Quay* were there some public buildings. In *Harbourside* the developer himself will build a small public building. The developer in *Temple Quay* has not contributed, either in kind (except some land, see above) or in money, to the re-building of the existing school. Asked about this, an expert considered that this finding could be generalized. Usually, neither the developer nor the respective public departments seem to favour giving to developers the responsibility for developing the public buildings. Developers usually concentrate on the products familiar to them. And the public departments responsible for the public buildings prefer to remain in charge of developing them (Lyons, interview 2007).

Land and money for on-site and off-site social/affordable housing

In 1999/2000, 9,244 affordable units were delivered through planning agreements in England. In 2000/01 this was 9,227 units, in 2001/02 10,303 units, in 2002/03 12,700 units, and in 2003/04 16,380 units. It is estimated that this would be 15,000/ year by 2005/2006 (ODPM, 2005: 9, 32; Department for Communities and Local Government, 2006: 33). The proportion of affordable units secured through planning agreement, in relation to the total new affordable units was in 1999/00 21%, in 2000/01 21%, in 2001/02 32% and in 2002/03 44% (Office of the Deputy Prime Minister, 2005: 9). In general, provision of social/affordable units through planning obligations seems to work better in greenfield than in regeneration sites, and also better in the south of the country than in the north. A source however suggests that affordable units obtained through planning agreements often profit from social housing grants (Crook et al., 2001: in Crook & Whitehead, 2002: 1274-5). The interviews with public officers and developers and the cases suggest that in Bristol in the last few years, the number of social/affordable housing obtained through planning agreement is increasing, which could explain the relatively good results in this city. The percentages of new affordable dwellings (whether obtained through planning agreement or not) of the total completed new units are in Bristol higher than the average in England: in 2003 15% in Bristol and 9% in England, in 2004 23% and 11%, in 2005 5.6% and 11%, and in 2006 22% and 13% (see table 17).

None of the studied cases included contributions in money for affordable housing; in all of them, the developer himself developed the affordable units within the site in question. The more recent the project, the higher the proportion of affordable housing. In cases *Temple Quay* and *Harbourside* (planning permissions definitively valid in 2003) the proportion was 14% respectively 9%. In *Megabowl* (2007) 25%. The following figures are meant to make clear that developing social/affordable housing actually involves a financial charge to the developers. In *Harbourside,* the development costs of the affordable units (the costs of serving the land and constructing the building, excluding the price of land and excluding the planning obligations) amount to about € 5.5m, and the agreed selling price (to the Registered Social Landlord) will be about € 4.7m. The developer thus bears not only the difference between the price for the social landlord and the free-market price of the houses, but also a shortage (returns less costs) of about € 800,000. In *Temple Quay* this shortage was about € 270,000, and in *Megabowl* about € 650,000. The developers must thus bear these costs, plus the corresponding accounted land costs and contributions.

Table 17. Completed affordable housing in England and the City of Bristol (all new affordable units, those obtained through planning agreement and through other ways).

	England		**City of Bristol**	
	Registered Social Landlord's units (% of total completed new units)	Local Authority's units (% of total completed new units)	Registered Social Landlord's units (% total completed new units)	Local Authority's units (% total completed new units)
1999	17,775 (12.6%)	54 (0.0%)		
2000	16,681 (12.3%)	87 (0.1%)		
2001	14,502 (11.2%)	160 (0.1%)		
2002	13,309 (9.7%)	177 (0.1%)		
2003	12,822 (8.9%)	177 (0.1%)	72 (14.8%)	0.0%
2004	16,604 (10.8%)	131 (0.1%)	140 (22.9%)	0.0%
2005	17,535 (11.0%)	182 (0.1%)	99 (5.6%)	0.0%
2006	20,752 (12.9%)	277 (0.2%)	143 (22.3%)	0.0%

Definitions:
- Affordable housing: those units that are provided to rent (or on shared ownership bases) by Local Authorities or Registered Social Landlords.

Sources:
- England: Own elaboration, based on P2m/P2Q returns from local authorities, National Housebuilding Council (NHBC), available on-line on http://www.communities.gov.uk/index.asp?id=1156032, live table 244 'Permanent dwellings completed, by tenure, England, historical calendar year series', visited on 15 Augustus 2007.
- City of Bristol: Own elaboration, based on P2m returns from local authorities, returns from National Housebuilding Council (NHBC), available on-line on http://www.communities.gov.uk/index.asp?id=1156032, live table 253 'Starts and completions by district', visited on 15 Augustus 2007. The available data refer to 2002-2003, 2003-2004, 2004-2005 and 2005-2006, and are referred in this table respectively as 2003, 2004, 2005 and 2006.

Land and money for off-site public infrastructure and facilities
It seems that developers do not usually contribute land for off-site infrastructure and facilities, i.e. they do not usually cede land situated outside the development in question (Department for Communities and Local Government, 2006: 9-10). The findings in the cases support this: in none of the three cases has the developer provided land outside the plan area. The situation is different with contributions, both in kind and in money, for the construction or implementation of off-site public infrastructure and facilities. These seem to have increased very much in the last years (Campbell et alia, 2000, 2001; Department for Communities and Local Government, 2006). At the end of the 90's, obligations regarding off-site infrastructure and facilities were already very common in England. There is a strong geographical differentiation depending on the economic prosperity of local authorities: the stronger the economy, the more the contributions. Thus more in London and the South East than in the North (Campbell et alia, 2000: 764-765, 772; Department..., 2006: 17-18). The cases confirm the general idea that obligations include nowadays contributions in money for off-site public infrastructure and facilities. In Harbourside the developer will pay in money a considerable contribution for a leisure facility, about 8% of the total value of the final real estate. In Temple Quay this will be about 1.5% (for off-site highways, pedestrian and cycle facilities, educational, social and community facilities and a labour initiative), and in Megabowl about 4% (for off-site pedestrian, cycle and public transport facilities, training/apprenticeship programme, education, recreational and library facilities).

Creaming off plus value
Insofar as the above mentioned payments for off-site public infrastructure and facilities are not related to the development in question, they might be considered as creaming off plus value. But, in principle, the English system of planning obligations is not meant for the local authorities to share the economic rent generated by the granting of planning permission.

Tempo of implementation of the capturing value increase goals
Sections 6.5 and 6.6 (so far) have analyzed the working of binding rules within the mechanisms for capturing value increase and the results in practice. Now, possible side effects are assessed, with special attention given to the tempo of implementation of the capturing value increase goals.

In section 6.4.2.3 it has been pointed out that planning permissions, in general for England, do not always succeed in being realised within deadlines. Many planning permissions are never built, not even commenced. However, until the moment of data gathering in June 2007, those planning permissions of which the implementation is commenced seem to be completed on time. Since then, probably fuelled by unstable market circumstances, it seems that building schedules are experiencing large delays, even if development already commenced. In other words, once and if development commences, and provided that market circumstances remain stable, developers seem to complete the public infrastructure and facilities, including possible payments in money, within time.

6.6 Causal relationships between formal rules relevant to zoning and capturing value increase in England

Section 6.4 gave an answer to Preparatory research question 3: it inferred the possible causal relations between the independent variable 'formal rules relevant to zoning' and the dependent variable 'capturing value increase'. This section summarizes first the inferred causalities and assesses then the effect of possible third variables.

6.6.1 The inferred causalities

The findings suggest that the following sub-variables can influence positively and/or negatively the degree of captured value increase (see also the causal model in section 2.4.2 and Figure 24):

- Sub-variable a, Uncertainty about the future building possibilities, together with Certainty about the future contributions
  This seems to have been positive for intermediary variables *negotiation position* (of the municipality) and *accounted land costs,* i.e. positive for capturing value increase;
- Sub-variable b, Contents planning permissions
  (1) Zoning and agreeing social/affordable housing; (2) Including contributions for off-site public infrastructure and facilities; (3) Including financing and implementation schedules; the first two seem to have been positive for capturing value increase, probably because they have been positive for intermediary variables *negotiation position* (of the municipality) and *Accounted land costs*. The third sub-variable (schedules) seem to be sometimes positive, but sometimes not so effective, for intermediary variables *negotiation position* (of the LPAs) and *delay;*
- Sub-variable c, Conditioning permission to agreement
  The possibility of making the approval of planning permission conditional on securing the public infrastructure and facilities and other possible contributions: this seems to have been positive for capturing value increase, plausibly through reinforcing the positive effects of sub-variables b on intermediary variables *accounted land costs, regular profit margins* (of the developer) the *negotiation position* (of the municipality) and *delay;*
- Sub-variable d, property rights
  The high interdependency between LPAs and landowners seems to have a negative effect on intermediary variables *negotiation position* (of the LPA's),

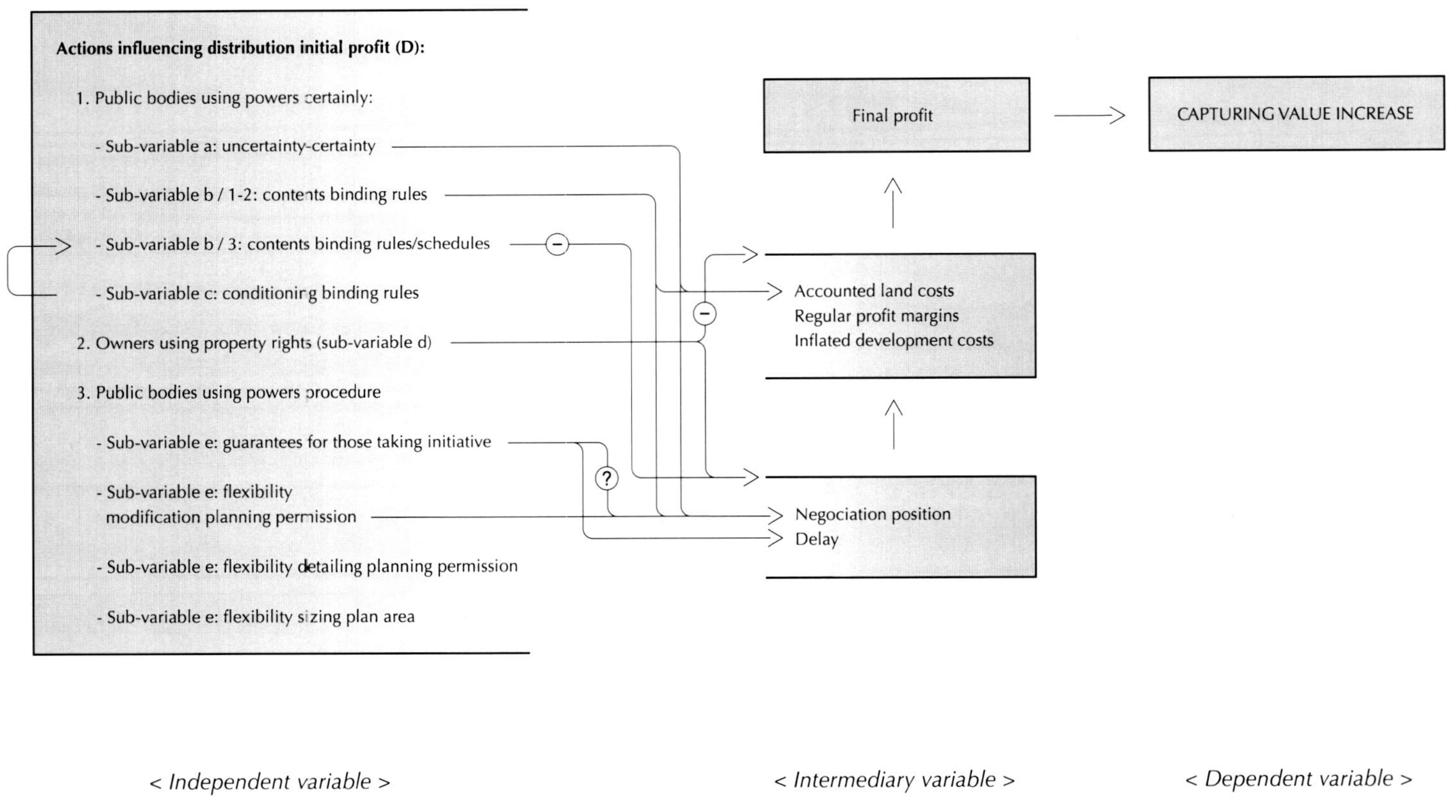

Figure 24. Scheme of the inferred causal relations in England between independent variable 'formal rules relevant to zoning', the intermediary variables and the dependent variable 'capturing value increase'.

accounted land costs, regular profit margins (of the developer) and *delay*, and thus a negative effect on capturing value increase;
- Sub-variable e, Guarantees for those taking initiative
  The right to appeal against the determination or non-determination of planning applications might be positive or negative for accelerating the tempo of implementation (thus for intermediary variable *delay*), but anyway negative for intermediary variable *negotiation position* (of the developer), and thus negative for capturing value increase;
- Sub-variable e, Flexibility in modifying granted planning permissions
  The relatively flexibility to modify planning permissions might be positive for intermediary variable *negotiation position* (of LPAs) and thus for capturing value increase.

The findings also suggest that the following sub-variables might have no effect on any intermediary variable and/or the degree of captured value increase:
- Sub-variable e, Flexibility in detailing 'a posteriori'
  This seems not to be relevant anymore;
- Sub-variable e, Flexibility to scope the size of the plan area of permissions according to negotiations with each landowner
  This seems not to be relevant.

Part of sub-variable b (those contents of permissions that can be secured through an agreement), and sub-variable c (conditioning permission to agreement) are causally related to each other, in an inverse order as expressed. Sub-variable c seems to be an important cause of the effectiveness of those contributions that can be secured in the agreement (part of sub-variable b).

6.6.2 Possible third variables

Here, possible third variables are assessed, related first to the specific circumstances in the studied cases (variables D4 and D5 of the causal model in section 2.4.2), and second to market circumstances (variable A1). The goal is to examine the possibility that the inferred causal relationships turn out to be spurious (see for more detail section 3.2.1.2).

Specific circumstances in the studied cases
In *Harbourside* and *Temple Quay* two specific circumstances might have favoured the capturing of value increase: the size and skills of the teams of public officers in charge, and the intervention of supra local public agencies. Regarding the first, in both cases the interviewed public officers were happy about the team of officers that had handled the applications. These were large applications, which allowed the constitution of larger teams with more resources. It seems plausible that this might have influenced positively capturing value increase, especially in *Temple Quay*, where there was no

good policy base for obligations. In *Harbourside*, the interviewed developer did not mention this factor, but another one: in his opinion, the lack of vigorous political leadership in the Council at that time delayed development. In *Megabowl* the public officer in charge complained about the lack of resources to handle the application.

Regarding the intervention of supra local public agencies, in *Harbourside* and *Temple Quay* it seems that this intervention has influenced capturing value increase, by helping to make both projects more profitable. In *Harbourside,* English Partnership, a central government regeneration agency, supported the regeneration of the site through a cheap loan for the infrastructure provision. In *Temple Quay,* the South West of England Regional Development Agency (SWRDA), a regional public body, took over the land from a Development Corporation in 1996, and since then has stimulated regeneration and might have given an indirect subsidy by selling the land for a low price.

Market circumstances

Another possibly third variable, housing prices, can also affect capturing value increase (variable A1, see causal model in section 2.4.2) and the speed of implementation (because more profits attract more investments, and remove obstacles). This research concludes that the influence of housing prices has been relevant, influencing capturing value increase in a positive way.

Since 1997 housing prices have risen very much (often above 10% each year) above the general monetary inflation. This increase took place in England in general, and also in the South-West of England and in the City of Bristol, and continued till 2005. In 2005 and 2006 prices grew more moderately (0% to 5%) above the general monetary inflation (see figure 25). This means that cases *Harbourside* (application procedure and negotiations: March 2001-February 2003) and *Temple Quay* (May 2001-May 2003) started in a time of splendid expectations about market prices in general, and specifically in Bristol: 13% increase above inflation in 2000, 17% in 2001, 20% in 2002 and 13% in 2003. In *Megabowl* (April 2006-April 2007) the expectations might have been different, although not necessarily pessimistic: 1,5% increase above inflation in 2005 and 6% in 2006[4].

4 In 2007 prices in Bristol for new apartments were between € 3,000 to 5,000 per m^2 floor space, or even more. Because of the unavailability of general statistics of housing prices per square meter floor space, we had to support on alternative sources:

- In case *Megabowl* the developer estimated roughly the total price of the 138 free-market apartments in about € 34 million. As these 138 units were about 10,000 m^2 floor space, the average is about € 3,400/m^2 floor space. The prices in *Megabowl* must be considered however as belonging to a cheaper segment, as this site is relatively isolated and located outside the City Centre of Bristol. Cases *Harbourside* and *Temple Quay* are located in top-locations near by the City Centre. Therefore, another sources are necessary to give an approximate idea of prices of new apartments in these two cases:
- In housing scheme *Crescent Harbourside Anchor Road,* located besides case *Harbourside/Cannon's Marsh*, prices of new apartments vary from € 5,000/ m^2 floor space to more than € 7,000/ m^2 floor space. Source: own elaboration, based on current selling prices, http://www.smartnewhomes.com/development/Harbourside/506690/11/gallery.aspx, visited on 22 augustus 2007.

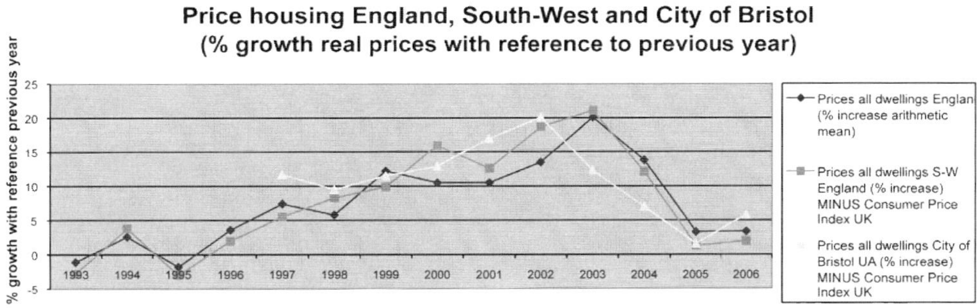

Sources:
- Prices all dwellings in England and South West England: Own elaboration, based on Department Communities and Local Government, 'Table 505 Housing market: simple average house prices, by new/other dwellings, type of buyer and standard statistical regions, from 1969 1, 2, 3', on-line, visited on 21 Augustus 2007, http://www.communities.gov.uk/pub/114/Table505_id1156114.xls.
- Prices new and all dwellings in City of Bristol: Own elaboration, based on Department Communities and Local Government, 'Table 585 Housing market: mean house prices based on Land Registry data, by district, from 1996', on-line, visited on 21 Augustus 2007, http://www.communities.gov.uk/pub/159/Table585_id1156159.xls.
- Consumer Price Index UK (CPI): National Statistics Online, visited on 21 Augustus 2007, http://www.statistics.gov.uk/STATBASE/tsdataset.asp?vlnk=7174.

Figure 25. Growth of real prices (minus general monetary inflation) dwellings in England, the South-West and the City of Bristol.

In general it seems clear that the increase in housing prices has played a very important role in all the cases. Almost all the involved persons who were interviewed considered that price rises in the last years have been of capital importance for the financial feasibility of both cases. In Harbourside high market prices seems to have created a large surplus between the land price of the previous use (former docks and industrial area, largely vacant, public parking) and of the future use (housing, office and some others). The developer did not provide information about the land price, but own estimations suggest that the difference between the development costs (excluding the accounted land price, postings 2-7 in Annex 3), and the returns are very large [5]. In Temple Quay the public officer considered that the poor market circumstances in the 90's were the reason that the four previously granted planning permissions expired without being used. Also, he assessed that the current high prices created a large surplus between the land price of the previous use (former railway sidings and industries, largely flattened and vacant) and of the future use (housing, office and some others). Here also, the developer did not provide information about the land price, but own estimations suggest that the difference between the development costs, and the returns is very large[6]. In *Megabowl* the surplus was also large between the land price of the previous use (the bowling alley) and of the future use (housing). Here the difference between the development costs and the returns is also very large.[7]

5 A very approximate and rough calculation is for *Harbourside* ca. € 2,800 per m² of land (€ 220m : 78,900 m²).

6 A very approximate rough calculation is for *Temple Quay* ca. € 4,180 per m² of land (€ 276m : 66,000 m²).

7 A very approximate rough calculation is for *Megabowl* ca. € 1,600 per m² of land (€ 21m : 13,104 m²)

These large surpluses suggest that the cases would have been feasible with lower housing prices also. The interviewed developer of *Harbourside* confirmed that *Harbourside* was already feasible ten years ago, and that the price rises have provided the landowners and the developer with profits additional to the initially calculated profits. The surplus might in any case have stimulated developers to contribute more generously. A public officer considered that the last years many other difficult regeneration sites in Bristol have come up, thanks to the favourable market circumstances. An interviewed expert also considered, in general terms for England, that price rises have been one important factor for the financial feasibility of many projects. According to this expert, expired planning permissions have diminished in the last years partly because of this (Henneberry, interview in 2007).

CHAPTER 7

The Netherlands

Chapters 5 and 6 have been about the working of the formal rules relevant to zoning and the results for capturing value increase in urban regeneration in the Spanish region of Valencia and in England. The findings are meant for some theoretical reflections in chapter 8 and especially for formulating recommendations for the Dutch practice in chapter 9. But before the reflections and recommendations can be made, it is necessary to examine the working of formal rules in the Netherlands also. After all, the main goal is to formulate recommendations inspired by the experience in other countries, but taking account of the Dutch planning system and legislation.

In the Netherlands, at the end of the 1980s important changes took place in land and housing policies, changes that have modified the mechanisms for capturing value increase. Besides the traditional forms of active land policy, public bodies are pursuing nowadays new forms of public-private partnerships to reduce the financial risks involved in urban regeneration. Also, local public bodies are looking for less active methods of land policy, in which private parties assume the responsibility for implementing the plans and for the corresponding risks. In general it can be said that public bodies nowadays aim for a larger private involvement in the financing of the unprofitable parts in urban regeneration. In 2008 the legislative framework that governs this private involvement was modified (for more details about these changes in the Netherlands, see sections 1.1 and 1.2).

Frame 7a

The institutional context: national government, provinces and municipalities

The Netherlands occupies an area of 33.929 km^2 and has more than 16 million inhabitants. It is a decentralized, unitary state, with a system of constitutional parliamentary monarchy. There are twelve provinces (*provincies*) and 431 municipalities (*gemeenten*).

The legislative powers on planning law lie primarily with the central government and parliament. They produce the 'formal legislation'. Formal legislation can, within certain limits, transfer authority to issue 'legislation in a material sense' (decrees and regulations) to the provinces and to the municipalities. Planning and property law and policies of each governmental body are subordinated to the law and policies of the higher governmental bodies (Needham et al., 1993: 3-7). In practice, however, the autonomy of provinces and municipalities is important. For a list of relevant legislation, relative to planning, see Annex 2.

Sections 7.1 and 7.2 introduce the context of how value increase is captured in urban regeneration. Section 7.3 introduces the studied cases, and section 7.4 the working of the formal rules relevant to zoning within the value capturing mechanisms. This is the answer to Preparatory research question 3: how can formal rules relevant to zoning influence capturing value increase? The question has been divided into several sub-questions that correspond to the sub-variables a-e (for more details about these sub-variables, see section 3.3.3). Each of the answers to these sub-questions consists of an assessment of whether the sub-variable can influence capturing value increase. There is therefore not one conclusion, but as many conclusions as sub-questions. All these conclusions, together with the findings in Valencia and England, have provided the ingredients for the final conclusions in chapters 8 and 9. Section 7.5 assesses the results of the actual degree of captured value increase, taking account of the side effects for the tempo of implementation. Finally, section 7.6 summarizes the inferred causalities between the formal rules relevant to zoning and capturing value increase, and assesses the role of third variables.

7.1 Urban Regeneration in the Netherlands

Urban regeneration in the Netherlands is an important topic in national and local planning policies. In general, there is preoccupation that the relative advantages of urban development on greenfield sites might threaten existing urban areas. Strengthening of existing cities and towns is therefore the goal (Kolpron, 2000: 1-2; Korthals Altes, 2007: 1498). This has translated into policies for the regeneration of urban areas and for the stimulation of new building within the boundaries of existing cities, making use of old deteriorated urban sites. The central government has the goal that 40% of the new housing should be built within the existing cities (Vrom, 2004; 2008). Recently this goal has been lowered to between 25 and 40%: between 20,000 and 40,000 dwellings per year (AZ, 2007: 35; Buitelaar et al., 2008: 12, 34-40).

There are different sorts of urban regeneration sites, each of them with different features and each of them being the subject of specific urban regeneration policies (Kolpron, 2000: 8-31): multifunctional central areas, monofunctional residential districts and old brownfield sites.

Multifunctional central areas

Multifunctional central areas consist of central areas and of sites around railway stations. Local urban regeneration policies for both sorts of sites usually focus on improving public and private facilities to better serve the local and regional population and to attract residential functions. In central areas, the dominant uses are retail, cafés and restaurants, offices, public facilities and housing. Property ownership is very fragmented, with many small owners and some institutional landlords, such as large retail businesses and stores, investors in real estate, and housing associations. However, municipalities are often the only substantial party. For the sites around railway stations, the dominant uses are more or less the same as in central areas, but related to the transport function of the railway station. Some of these sites - those that will accommodate the high speed railway - are intended and expected to develop into centers of stature. These are: Breda, Rotterdam, The Hague, Amsterdam, Utrecht and Arnhem. These sites are being regenerated nowadays, as the case *Stationskwartier* shows for the railway station of Breda. Property patterns are usually less fragmented than in central areas, with almost always two big landowners, the municipality and the Dutch Railways.

Frame 7b

Private parties in urban regeneration

In the Netherlands, public or commercial organisations usually control most of the land, more in urban regeneration than in greenfield development. These institutional agents are public (local governments), private non-profit (housing associations, *woningcorporaties*) and/or private commercial (property developers). Former landowners might be present at the beginning of the development, but if present they usually share neither risks nor do they participate in the operation. Most of the times their role is limited to that of providers of land. That is, urban redevelopment in the Netherlands is most of the time the task of institutional agents.

From the 1990s forward, commercial property developers have become important actors in urban regeneration, as the cases *De Funen* and *Kop van Oost* show. Commercial developers commission the development of offices and dwellings for sale to the final user or to a property investment company. When profit rates increase, developers tend to augment the proportion of offices and dwellings developed at their own risk, without having sold them before commencing the building, and *vice versa*. Churches, sport clubs and the like usually commission their own buildings, as do production firms (Segeren e.a., 2005: 124). There are very few people that commission their own house.

Most of the public facilities (hospitals, homes for the elderly, education, universities, social housing) are commissioned by non-profit companies with a religious, political or other kind of social background. These non-profit organizations, previously closely related to the public administration due to their dependence on public subsidies, have become the last years more autonomous. The most important non-profit agents in urban regeneration are the housing associations. These social landlords develop social housing either themselves or they commission property developers to build it for them. They are the most important property management companies in the country, owning approximately one third of the Dutch housing stock. Until the 90s, benefiting from strong public subsidies, housing associations were the leaders in housing building. From 1994 on, since public subsidies diminished, most of them have restructured and/or fused with others, and have begun to develop, besides social housing, commercial real estate (Priemus, 1996). This is the case in *Kruidenbuurt* (Eindhoven), where a social landlord is developing 45% of the total number of dwellings as social housing, and the rest as free market housing and some commercial space. In 2005 there were 492 housing associations (Vrom, 2007a: 156).

In the last few years, most of the former public utility companies (energy and water supply, telecommunication, railways) have become more autonomous or have even been privatized. Some of them owning land have become important partners in urban regeneration. Cases *De Funen* and *Stationskwartier* are an example of this: here the Dutch Railways owned most of the land and became the initiating developer.

Monofunctional residential districts

A second category of urban regeneration sites is districts with a predominantly residential use. Urban regeneration policies here aim to strengthen the residential use, and therefore provide housing, facilities and public space of good quality. Especially in pre-war districts, this might involve the removal of old factories that are no longer compatible with housing. In the last few years, the Ministry of Housing, Planning and Environment has been intensifying its efforts for the regeneration of 56 districts, and more recently a new selection has been made of 40 districts (the *prachtwijken*), most of them located in monofunctional residential areas. This research has made a brief survey of these 56 regeneration districts. Based on this, it is possible to conclude that regeneration takes place predominantly on land owned by municipalities or housing associations. Regeneration on privately owned land of any significance happens only in a minority of cases and concerns small sites: shopping centres and/or residential with about 50-100 dwellings (for more details of this survey, see Annex 5).

It is possible to distinguish between two sorts of monofunctional residential districts, pre-war and post-war. Pre-war districts are mostly located near or in the multifunctional central areas mentioned above. Many of them have been the subject of regeneration twice: first physical regeneration from the mid-1970s to 1990 (Korthals Altes, 2007: 1501), and second nowadays again, e.g. case *Kruidenbuurt*. Property ownership is usually fragmented, even though previous physical regeneration has concentrated property to some extent: municipalities and housing associations have become the most important landowners. The increased value of the land after re-development is usually lower than in multifunctional central areas.

After the 2nd WW and until 1970, municipalities and housing associations developed 1.6 million new houses around the existing cities, most of them social housing. The deterioration nowadays in these districts is evident and has led the central and local governments to initiate and stimulate large regeneration projects. These post-war districts were built in a systematic way by municipalities and housing associations, supported by central government subsidies. They incorporated many of the design principles of the *Congrès Internationaux d'Architecture Moderne* (CIAM). The main characteristics of these residential districts are monofunctionality, buildings of repeated morphology located in the middle of much green, low building density, much road infrastructure, many public facilities and a predominance of social housing. Property ownership is concentrated: municipalities own the public infrastructure and facilities, and sometimes also the land under the dwellings, which is given in leasehold (*erfpacht*) to housing associations. Corporations own the majority of the dwellings and sometimes also the land. In addition, some investors own some land and buildings (e.g. shopping centres) and there are also some owner-occupiers (both housing and factories). The increased value of the land after regeneration is lower than in multifunctional central areas. From 1970 to 1999, another 2.7 million dwellings were developed, not only around the existing cities, but also around small suburban towns, especially in the western part of the country. This time more attention was paid to the quality of housing. Generally speaking, the regeneration of these districts is not yet a policy issue.

Old brownfield sites

A third category of urban regeneration sites is old brownfield sites. It is possible to distinguish between the following: businesses and other sorts of economic-industrial activities (case *Kop van Oost*); gas and electricity factories; harbour areas; railway infrastructure (cases *De Funen* and *Stationskwartier*); and hospitals, government buildings and military sites. In the whole of the country there are about 23,000 ha of old business estates that might be the subject of regeneration in the next years (Buitelaar et al., 2008: 10-11; Gordijn et al., 2007: 5). Regeneration almost always involves replacing the existing uses with new ones. Property ownership varies but is in general characterized by the presence of large institutional public or private parties controlling the property: this is certainly the case in the three mentioned cases. The increased value of the land after regeneration is low when the existing uses are maintained and higher when replaced by housing and offices (Korthals Altes, 2007: 1502).

7.2 Capturing value increase and its legal limits in the Netherlands

In the Netherlands, the financing of public infrastructure and facilities, in urban regeneration on privately owned land, is based on contributions from both municipalities and developers. These contributions might be in kind or in money and are usually agreed in private law development agreements. This was the case in all the studied projects. These agreements are called here 'private law' because they are not regulated in planning law and because they are legally enforceable under private law. Since the 2008 Physical Planning Act (*Wet ruimtelijke ordening*) it has been possible, within certain limits, to impose a contribution without the need of a development agreement. Frame 7c gives an overview of the binding rules and other planning documents that are relevant for capturing value increase in the Netherlands.

Frame 7c
Indicative plans and the relevant binding rules
At the local level, Dutch municipalities have the competence to prepare and approve zoning plans, both of an indicative and of a binding character. Regarding the indicative plans, these have no legally binding force, neither for the citizen nor for municipal planning documents. They are often ***ad hoc* documents**, not defined in planning law: this was the case in all the studied projects. Planning law prescribes only one sort of indicative plan: **Structure Plans (*Structuurplan*)**, often used in practice, although not so much as the *ad hoc* documents. Two of the four studied schemes included, besides *ad hoc* documents, a Structure Plan. Structure Plans might cover the whole municipality or just a part of it (Klaassen, 2000: 85-88), and have been replaced in 2008 by **Structure Visions (*Structuurvisie*)**.

Municipalities have also the competence to make and adopt **Land-use Plans (*Bestemmingsplan*)**, which can cover the whole municipality (although this does not happen often) or a part of it (happens most frequently: for example, Rotterdam has over 400 Land-use plans, and Nijmegen over 800; Buitelaar et al, 2007: 54). Municipalities are obliged to cover the territory outside the built-up area with land-use plans, and since the 2008 Physical Planning Act the whole municipal territory. An important part of the land use plan has a legally binding character: this is the part that determines the use possibilities of land and real estate. A land use plan includes an Explanation (*Plantoelichting*), a Map (*Plankaart*), and the Land-use Regulations (*Planvoorschriften*). The Regulations contain at least a definition of the permitted land uses (*doeleindenomschrijving*), and possibly an Outline Definition (*Beschrijving in Hoofdlijnen*). The Map and the Regulations have a legally binding character, and the Explanation in principle has not. However, the Explanation might be relevant in those cases in which Map and Regulations leave room for interpretation (Van Zundert, 1996: 97-98)

A land use plan can be detailed or outline. Article 11.1 of the old Physical Planning Act, and 3.6 of the 2008 Act, give to the municipality the possibility of stating in the land-use plan the obligation to add details later. If the municipality states in the land-use plan that it has to be detailed later, it becomes an 'Outline Land-use plan with obligation of further elaboration' (*Globaal bestemmingsplan met uitwerkingsplicht*). In such a plan, a part or the whole plan area is given outline binding land-use regulations (*globale bestemmingen*). Also, such a plan has to include the rules that will regulate the detailing. Then, later, the municipality has the obligation to detail, following the rules given in the plan, the outline regulations up to the detailed level of a normal land-use plan. Data from 1987 until 1993 show that detailing Outline land-use plans is used frequently (Van Damme & Verdaas 1996: 79-80). In the cases *Stationskwartier* and *Kruidenbuurt,* the land use plan included outline regulations, covering one small plot respectively almost all the plan area.

Both the central and provincial governments might freeze or modify the land use plans of municipalities, and even replace them with their own documents: in practice, this does not happen often. The central government exercises this control through four Physical Planning Inspectorates (*Inspectie Ruimtelijke Ordening*), and the provinces also have inspectors. Until the 2008 Physical Planning Act, provincial governments had to approve all land use plans definitively. Since then, provinces no longer have to approve them, but they retain the power to intervene.

The Physical Planning Act states deadlines for the procedures for a land-use plan. Previous to the modification of the Act in 2008, if there were neither objections nor appeals against the plan, the definitive approval of the province had to take place within 8 months after publishing the draft land-use plan. If there were objections and/or appeals against the plan, the definitive approval could extend up to thirteen months. In general, procedures seem to fall within these terms. Cases *De Funen, Kop van Oost* (8 months each) and *Stationskwartier* (12 months) fell within these deadlines, case *Kruidenbuurt* took a little longer (14 months). The 2008 Act has shortened the deadline. Nowadays a land use plan must be definitively approved 12 weeks after the close of the consultation period.

In urban regeneration, it is possible to approve, instead of a normal land use plan, another similar document: an **Urban Renewal Plan (*Stadsvernieuwingsplan*)**. None of the studied cases used this. The 2008 Act gave to provinces and central government also the competence of making and approving a **Land use Plan (*Inpassingsplan*)**.

The 2008 Act introduced a new sort of plan, the **Development contributions Plan (*Exploitatieplan*)**. In case the implementation of a land use plan implies costs for public infrastructure and facilities, and these are not secured[1], the municipality must approve, together with the land use plan, a Development contributions plan. Both documents must be processed together. The Development contributions plan *must* include: a map with the delimitation of the development site, a description of the infrastructure provision works, and a calculation of the costs, revenues, implementation terms and the way the costs must be charged among the landowners (*exploitatieopzet*). In addition, it *can* include additional prescriptions related to the public infrastructure, social housing and parcels meant for owner-occupiers building their own house (Hijmans & Fokkema, 2008: 239-240). The prescriptions of the Development contributions plan are legally binding when planning applications are judged. All the studied cases fall under the planning law previous to the 2008 Act, and not one of them included a Development contributions plan, nor a provincial or national land use plan.

Land use plans of any sort can be departed from. **Major departures (*vrijstelling/projectbesluit*)** became a common alternative or complement to the land-use plan (Thomas et al., 1983, quoted in Faludi, 1987: 116, 185; Bosch & Hanemaayer, 1992, quoted in Bregman & Sievers, 2002 and Buitelaar et al., 2007: 54; Bröcking & Geest, 1982, quoted in Buitelaar et al., *ibidem*; Van der Ree, 2000: 20, 26). In cases *De Funen, Kruidenbuurt* and *Kop van Oost,* the municipality, together with making a new land use plan, approved during the procedure also major departures from the old existing plan for a part of the site, in order to be able to start the works some months before the completion of the procedure for the new land use plan.

7.2.1 Betterment belongs to the landowner

In the Netherlands, the value increase of land, caused by a change to the permitted land use in the binding rules (for example from industrial land to residential and offices), falls to the landowner (Needham, 2007a: 154-155). There is no legal principle in the Netherlands, as for example in the Spanish 1978 Constitution, which acknowledges the principle of a public share in the value increase generated by public policies or by changes of the binding rules (see section 5.3.1). The British 1947 Town and Country Planning Act, which nationalized the betterment that accrues from changes of the binding rules, might serve also as example but has nowadays no real consequences for capturing value increase (see chapter 6.2.1).

However, in general the legislator has the power to make rules about value capturing: there is no legal obstacle as long as the legislator stays within the boundaries of the

1 The definition in this research of 'public infrastructure and facilities' is broader than those costs that must be secured. It is difficult however to precisely define those costs that must be secured because the 2008 Physical Planning Act does not define them clearly. They comprise in any case physical interventions, actions and works and fall anyway within the definition of public infrastructure and facilities given in this research.

Dutch General Administrative Act (*Algemene wet bestuursrecht*) and international Treaties and Conventions, like the European Convention on Human Rights. However, only to a limited extent has the legislator used the power to make such legislation. The new 2008 Physical Planning Act can be considered as one of the few examples of legislation regulating capturing value increase. Another example is the modification in 2004 of the Physical Planning Act to allow municipalities to agree with developers that the developer pay the compensation for the decrease in economic value of surrounding properties that are consequence of the approval of a new land use plan (*planschade*). The actual legal possibilities for the government to capture the increased value in case of private development are mainly limited to cost recovery. 'Cost recovery' is the recovery, through contributions from private developers, of those costs that are directly related to the realization of public infrastructure and facilities that benefit the development. Developers might contribute either by realising this infrastructure and facilities directly, or paying public bodies to do so. This has not changed with the new 2008 Act. For more details about cost recovery and other forms of capturing value increase, see section 1.4.

7.2.2 Capturing value increase through private law agreements

In those cases in which municipalities make costs for providing infrastructure, there is the possibility of making a Development Agreement (*Exploitatieovereenkomst*) with the developer in order to recover (some of those) costs. This agreement does not fall under the mentioned category 'private law' because its contents are regulated in the Physical Planning Act and the Land Development Regulation (*Exploitatieverordening*). The agreement must be based on the local Land Development Regulation, which states the conditions and the costs that can be included. The Physical Planning Act previous to the 2008's modification stated in article 42 some limitations to the costs that could be included in the local Land Development Regulation (see frame 7d). If the local government negotiated a higher contribution, which exceeded the limits of the local Regulation, a judge could rescind the contract. In such a case, the local government had to refund the whole contribution (De Wolff & Muñoz, 2007: 533-534).

Frame 7d
Limitations to costs in local Land Development Regulation previous to 2008 Act

- The financial contribution had to be limited to a contribution to the costs of servicing the land. This includes the infrastructure provision directly related to the development in question. The costs of, for example, off-site infrastructure may not be recovered. Value capturing that exceeds the recovery of the named costs was not allowed;
- The developer's contributions in land had to be limited to that land that is needed for this on-site public infrastructure.

The situation is different in those cases in which the municipality is not directly involved in providing infrastructure, which is in those cases in which the municipality incurs no costs for the infrastructure provision. In these cases, municipalities and developers are free to make another sort of Development Agreement (*Overeenkomst*[2]), in which they agree that the developer provides public infrastructure, or affordable housing, etc. There are fewer limitations to these agreements than to the other sort, because they are not governed by the Physical Planning Act. In principle, municipality and developer can agree any contribution, also for off-site infrastructure, as long as the developer himself provides the public infrastructure. However, if contributions consist of a payment to the municipality for the costs made, the above mentioned system of the Land Development Regulations, including its limitations, applies.

An important difference with England and Valencia is that planning consent (the approval of the land use plan, or the departure from it, or granting the building permit) cannot formally be made conditional on a Development Agreement of any sort. With the first sort of agreement, the municipality can ask for contributions in exchange for providing the infrastructure, but not in exchange for granting a planning consent. The second sort of agreement must be voluntary. In neither case may the municipality, formally, condition the granting of planning consent on securing investments or implementation of public infrastructure and facilities.

7.2.3 The 2008's novelties

In 2008, a new Physical Planning Act, which included a new Land Development Act (*Grondexploitatiewet*), and a new Physical Planning Decree (*Besluit op de ruimtelijke ordening*) came into force. This act introduced important novelties for capturing value increase (see De Wolff, 2007): (1) they introduce the possibility of imposing on the landowners a contribution without the need of the municipality itself making the costs, and without the need for a Development Agreement; and (2) they give more detail about the sorts of costs that can be imposed to the landowners.

Cost recovery through public law (Development contributions plan)
In case the implementation of a land use plan implies costs for public infrastructure

2 This sort of Development Agreement receive different names, but its contents are not clearly regulated anywhere, so contracts with the same name can be very different in detailing and practical consequences. Usually, contracts with outline determinations might receive the name *Intentieovereenkomst, Samenwerkingsovereenkomst* or *Ontwikkelingsovereenkomst*. Contracts with more detailed determinations use to receive the name *Realisatieovereenkomst*.

and facilities, and these costs have not been secured[3], the municipality *must* approve a Development contributions plan together with the land use plan. A Development contributions plan calculates these costs, and the municipality can make granting the building permit conditional on a contribution. This is the first time that planning consent (in this case, only the granting of the building permit, not the approval of the land use plan or departure from it) can be formally made conditional on securing or paying a contribution. When a landowner submits a building application, the municipality can refuse the building permit if the contribution according to the Development contributions plan for the area has not been secured or paid (De Wolff & Muñoz, 2007: 535). The new 2008 Physical Planning Decree regulates the costs that can be included in a Development contributions plan (see frame 7e).

Frame 7e
List of possibly costs in a Development contributions plan
The new 2008 Physical Planning Decree prescribes in articles 6.2.3 to 6.2.6, and 6.2.11 the sorts of costs[4] that can be included in a Development contributions plan (Vrom, 2008: 109-123, 131-139; Klaassen, 2008: 354-362; Baardewijk, 2008: 758-759). It is expected that the central government will detail soon some of these articles (article 6.2.4.g-j, regarding fundamentally the preparation of plans). These are the costs that can be included in the Development contributions plan:

1a. Public infrastructure within or in the immediate surroundings of the development site: roads, sewerage, parks, public buildings, etc. Also, in case the new land use plan diminishes the economic value of surrounding properties, the compensation costs to the owners (*planschade*);
2a. Public infrastructure and facilities situated within the plan area, which serve this and at least another development scheme (*bovenwijkse voorzieningen*); it is however not clear whether if, when situated *outside* the plan area, these public infrastructure and facilities can also be considered as *bovenwijkse voorzieningen*, or instead as *bovenplanse kosten* (see under);
3a. Contributions to *i)* other schemes (*bovenplanse* ***verevening***) or to *ii)* investments somewhere else (*bovenplanse* ***kosten***): *i)* refers to contributions to unprofitable schemes run by public or private parties somewhere else within or outside the

3 Costs are 'secured' when there is certainty that there is, or will be, financial means available to pay them. This certainty can be created in different ways: *i)* When there is a development agreement or any other form of private law contract that commits any party to pay; *ii)* When any public body commits itself to subsidy the costs; *iii)* When the municipality has the land and has calculated that the profits of selling the land will cover the costs. In this third case, the municipal executive power (*Burgemeester en Wethouders*) or the Local Council (*Gemeenteraad*) must approve those calculations and include them in the municipal budget.

4 It might be that the Development contributions plan does not include the costs and contributions as such, i.e. as a sum of money or a contribution. Instead, it can include it as an obligatory prescription that in fact means that the developer must make a cost or contribution. E.g. the plan can zone land for social housing, which can cost the developer money.

municipality; *ii)* refers to contributions to public infrastructure and facilities situated outside the plan area. Neither *i* nor *ii* are necessarily directly related to the development in question. Both sorts of contributions can be a contribution in kind, (the developer himself might construct the infrastructure or facility), a payment in money meant for an specific unprofitable scheme or for a specific infrastructure or facility, or a payment in money to a fund[5] meant for more than one specific investment. This fund can be used to contribute to both *i* and *ii* (*confero* article 6.13.7 2008 Physical Planning Act; Zundert, 2008: 472; Baardewijk, 2008: 762-763);

4a. Social housing within the plan area: percentage and/or number, location, adscription to allocation rules for the tenants and buyers of social rented housing and social housing for sale, as long as these allocation rules derive their status from housing legislation and local regulations (Vrom e.a. 2008: 139; Klaasen, 2009-2010: chapter 11.3.4, consulted on 11/02/2010; Nijland, interview in 2010);

5a. The land that is needed for all these public infrastructure and facilities: the landowners must be compensated with the market value of their land, and this compensation can be included as a cost in the Development contributions plan.

6. Green and nature areas (parks, water, etc) that have been lost in the development site (*verloren gegane natuurwaarde, groenvoorzieningen en watervoorzieningen*), which must be compensated with new green areas in or outside the site.

However, not all the costs included in the Development contributions plan can be charged to the landowners. First, only the costs of *construction* of the infrastructure can be charged to the landowners, but not the costs of *maintenance* and *exploitation* of this infrastructure. With other words, it is not possible to charge a contribution meant for running a public infrastructure for a specific period of time after finishing its construction (Vrom et al, 2008: 111-112). Only maintenance costs of soil decontamination measures might be charged (Nijland, interview in 2010).

Second, during the consideration of the new Land Development Act, the parliament rejected the possibility of charging for the social facilities (*maatschappelijke voorzieningen*), using as examples of social facilities educational facilities and social welfare facilities (*welzijn*). This means that developers cannot be required to contribute neither to the *construction* of the buildings, nor to the *maintenance* and *exploitation* of these buildings (thus all costs except the land costs) of social facilities (Van den Brand, interview 2008).

Third, article 6.13.5 of the 2008 Physical Planning Act establishes the criteria that govern the degree to which the costs can be charged to the landowners: profit (*profijt*), attributability (*toerekenbaarheid*) and proportionality (*proportionaliteit*). This means that several costs cannot be charged to the landowners:

5 In Dutch, the correct term for 'fund' is 'reserve' because it is called so in the *Besluit Beheer en Verantwoording*. However, the popular term is 'fonds' (Baardewijk, 2008: 761).

- The costs of that part of infrastructure serving a wider area, including the land under the infrastructure, that do not fulfil these criteria;
- Now (Autumn 2009) there is no unanimity about how strict the three legal criteria should be interpreted when assessing whether the contributions to 3a (other schemes or public infrastructure and facilities -*bovenplanse verevening* respectively *bovenplanse kosten*) can be charged to the landowners. If the criteria are interpreted very strictly, it is questionable whether these contributions can be charged to the landowners, as the relation with the development in question is not direct. Especially the contributions to other schemes would hardly meet the criteria (*confero* Van den Brand, interview 2008; Vrom et al, 2008: 115; Baardewijk, 2008: 759-761; Groot, 2009: 465-466).
- It is questionable whether all the costs of refurbishing existing old infrastructure would meet these criteria. Municipalities might be obliged to assume part of the costs when the existing infrastructure is old and the respective municipal body already has reserved some means for its renewal (Vrom et al, 2008: 112; Klaassen, 2008: 358).
- Not all the costs of plan preparation (the making of plans and studies, and the preparation and control of the infrastructure provision) can be charged to the landowners. A circular (*ministeriële regeling*) of the central government will provide more details about which of these costs can and cannot be charged (Vrom et al., 2008: 116-118, 122, 161);

Fourth, regarding those costs that have been already made, these can only be charged in case the municipality, at the time that the costs were made, did made explicit in the municipal budget which part of the costs should be charged in the future to the development in question. If the municipality didn't, then these costs cannot be charged, even if they fulfil the three legal criteria (Vrom et al, 2008: 115-116).

Fifth, if the calculated profits do not cover the costs included in the Development contributions plan, the deficit (costs minus profits) cannot be charged to the landowners. If there is a deficit, this might be due to the method of assessment of the accounted value of the land. Land is included as cost in the Development contributions plan for a price equivalent to the price that should be established in case of expropriation. This expropriation price follows a residual method of calculation, which includes the value increase due to rezoning, actually the price of land has to be assessed taking into account all the profits that will accrue after development, i.e. all the increased value. This means that the accounted land costs in Development contributions plans will be much higher than the minimum land costs, so high that a deficit will be common. With other words, the method of calculation of the land costs in the Development contributions plans implies that an important part of the value increase leaks away to the owner. In regeneration sites this problem is worse, as land prices in previous transactions are usually inflated. As the price in previous transactions serve as complementary sources to the residual method of assessment, this finally contributes to inflating the accounted land costs large above the minimum land costs. In addition, in regeneration sites development costs are often higher due to the existence of previous installations and buildings, contaminated soil and the like (variable A2). In short, it is likely that deficits will be common, especially in urban regeneration (Dieperink, 2009: 9-10). In our opinion, the first signs after one year of application of the 2008 Planning Act confirm this conclusion. A recent evaluation of the first results in practice in the first year after the introduction of the 2008 Act confirms this conclusion too (Planbureau voor de Leefomgeving, 2010: 63-64)

Cost recovery through private law (anterior Development Agreement)

There is the possibility that the developer agrees to pay the costs *before* the approval of the Development contributions plan. This can be established in what is called an 'anterior Development Agreement' (*anterieure overeenkomst*). If the costs are in that way secured, the Development contributions plan does not need to be approved. An anterior agreement may include more contributions than those chargeable to landowners through a Development contributions plan. First, an agreement can secure the already mentioned costs that can be *included* in a plan, but not *charged* to the landowners. Second, an agreement may secure also some other costs that cannot be included in a plan. Frame 7f lists both sorts of additional contributions.

Frame 7f
Additional contributions

The following costs cannot be charged to landowners in a Development contributions plan, but may be secured through an anterior Development Agreement (Vrom et al, 2008: 21-22, 31, 33, 38, 41-42, 45-48, 50, 52, 160; Klaassen, 2008: 379-380; Baardewijk, 2008: 756-765; Groot, 2009: 464, 465; Nijland, interview in 2010):

1-5b. The costs that can be included in a Development contributions plan, but cannot be charged to landowners: maintenance and exploitation costs of infrastructure, those costs that do not meet the three criteria (profit, attributability, proportionality), those that are already made but are not chargeable because such is not made explicit in the municipal budget, or those costs that are not covered by the calculated profits. The *maintenance* and *exploitation* costs of *public buildings* cannot, in principle, be charged because they cannot be considered as belonging to land development (*grondexploitatie*). It is however not clear if, when the public buildings are prescribed as a 'spatial development' (see under), it is possible or not to agree not only a contribution for its *construction*, but also for its *maintenance* and *exploitation* (Klaassen, 2009-2010: chapter 11.3.8, consulted at 11-02-2010; Nijland, interview in 2010). Another open question is whether it is possible to agree contributions (of any kind: to the construction, maintenance or exploitation costs) for 'social facilities' (*Maatschappelijke voorzieningen*). At one side the above-mentioned parliamentary statement, against this possibility, was in principle meant for the Development contributions plan, but might also determine the possible contents of an anterior Development Agreement. At the other side, the 2008 Act and Decree allow municipalities and landowners to seal a development agreement and do not limit what a contribution for 'spatial developments' might include, so if social facilities are prescribed as 'spatial development' there could be the possibility of asking a contribution not only for their construction, but also for their maintenance and exploitation (*cfr.* Van den Brand, interview in 2008; Nijland, interview in 2010)[6].

4b. Additional requirements for social rented housing, additional to those that can be included in a Development contributions plan (4a). E.g. indications of maximal prices of the dwellings to be sold to the housing associations, allocation rules even if not derived from housing legislation or local regulation, etc. Also, additional requirements for social housing for sale, e.g. indications of the maximal selling prices to the buyers in case of no previous regional agreement on this matter, and allocation rules regarding the selection of the buyers even if not derived from housing legislation or local regulation.

7. Contributions to 'Spatial development' (*ruimtelijke ontwikkeling*) situated outside the scheme in question. It is not clear what exactly *ruimtelijke ontwikkeling* means. The concept is still vague and might include a large variety of public facilities: e.g. parks, green and recreational areas, water storage works, landscape works, industrial areas to be regenerated, infrastructure and possibly some sorts of public buildings (e.g. cultural facilities), and as long as they concern physical functions related to urban development. The contribution could maybe not only for the *construction* of the facility, but also for its *maintenance* and *exploitation*. As mentioned above, it is not clear whether the contributions might concern 'social facilities'. The contribution can be not only for specific public facilities, but also for an unprofitable scheme run by private parties.

---

6 More specifically, the legal question is as follows: in Dutch law, private law agreements cannot in principle include contributions that go further than what public law prescribes for a Development contributions plan. However, there are exceptions to this (Van Rossum, 2005: 1st to 7th page):

- In case public law makes explicit that municipality and landowners are allowed to agree contributions in a development agreement. This is the case here, as articles 6.12.2.a and 6.24.1 Physical Planning Act prescribe that municipalities and landowners can agree, in a development agreement, contributions for the 'land development' (*grondexploitatie*), this including also contributions for 'spatial developments'. This means that it should be possible to agree contributions for the construction, and maybe also for the maintenance and exploitation of 'social facilities' (*maatschappelijke voorzieningen*);
- However, Dutch law also recognizes that there might be an 'unacceptable contradiction' (*onaanvaardbare doorkruizing* in Dutch) with public law in case a development agreement includes a contribution that goes against the 'meaning' of the law (*strekking van de publiekrechtelijke regeling*). The 'meaning' of a law is for example the intention that the legislative power had when it approved the law. As in this case the Dutch Parliament explicitly rejected the possibility of charging landowners with any cost of 'social facilities' (except the costs of providing the land for the social facility), the question remains open whether contributions to social facilities (construction, maintenance or exploitation) would not imply an 'unacceptable contradiction' with public law.

8. Creaming off plus value: in case the municipality enter into agreement with the landowner to develop his land in such a way that the municipality bears financial risks (because it itself invests in public infrastructure, or buys the land or part of the land, etc), municipality and landowner can also agree that the municipality will share the profits. Such an agreement can have a variety of forms, depending of the nature of the municipal involvement (*bouwclaim-overeenkomst* and *publiek-private samenwerkingsovereenkomst*). This goes thus further than cost recovery (Nijland, interview in 2010). As this research aims only at cost recovery, this possibility of creaming off plus value will be not handled any more in the rest of the sections. However, as it is not precisely clear what it means that an infrastructure is 'related' to the site in question, in practice there might be ways of creaming off plus value by requiring contributions under 2, 3 and, specially, 7. The boundary between which infrastructure one could consider as 'related' and which not is not easily defined, nor is there agreement about it.

Actually, *bovenplanse verevening, bovenplanse kosten* (3a) and *ruimtelijke ontwikkelingen* (7) are meant for very similar sorts of investments. All three might consist of a contribution in kind, a payment for a specific investment, or a payment to a fund that can be used for several investments. The difference is that 3a might fulfil (or not) the three legal criteria set out above and thus be charged to the landowners through a Development contributions plan, while *ruimtelijke ontwikkelingen* will by definition never fulfil these criteria and thus can only be charged through an anterior Development Agreement.

In short, a municipality can recover more costs in an anterior Development Agreement than through a Development contributions plan. It is uncertain whether the approval of a Development contributions plan might affect the contents of an already existing anterior Development Agreement. In principle, the Agreement cannot contradict any of the prescriptions included in the Plan (Vrom et al, 2008: 34; Kluwer, 2008: 132). This means that some of the contributions agreed in the Agreement might be nullified in case a Plan becomes approved.

The costs that can be secured in an anterior Development Agreement are greater than those allowed under the old local Land Development Regulation. In other words, in those cases in which municipalities themselves provide public infrastructure and facilities, and they require landowners to contribute, an anterior agreement implies an enlargement of the possibilities for cost recovery. This might be different when a municipality does not require any payment in money, but does require that the developer realizes in kind the public infrastructure and facilities. These cases fell before 2008 under the old 'private law' Development Agreement (*Overeenkomst*). It is not clear whether the possible contributions in the new anterior Development Agreement are greater or not.

7.3 Introduction to the studied cases in the Netherlands

In most of the studied cases, indicative plans foresaw regeneration. However, before regeneration took place, two matters needed to be resolved. First, because in all the studied cases new public infrastructure and facilities were needed, the municipalities negotiated with the developers about their contribution and sealed one or more Development Agreements of the second sort mentioned above (*overeenkomst*)[7]. And second, the existing binding rules had to be modified because they did not foresee the regeneration of the site: a new land use plan had to be approved, and in some cases, for some plots, also one or more departures from the existing land use plan. Here follows a brief introduction to the cases (for an overview, see figure 26). The rest of the case-based information has been included in the rest of the chapter.

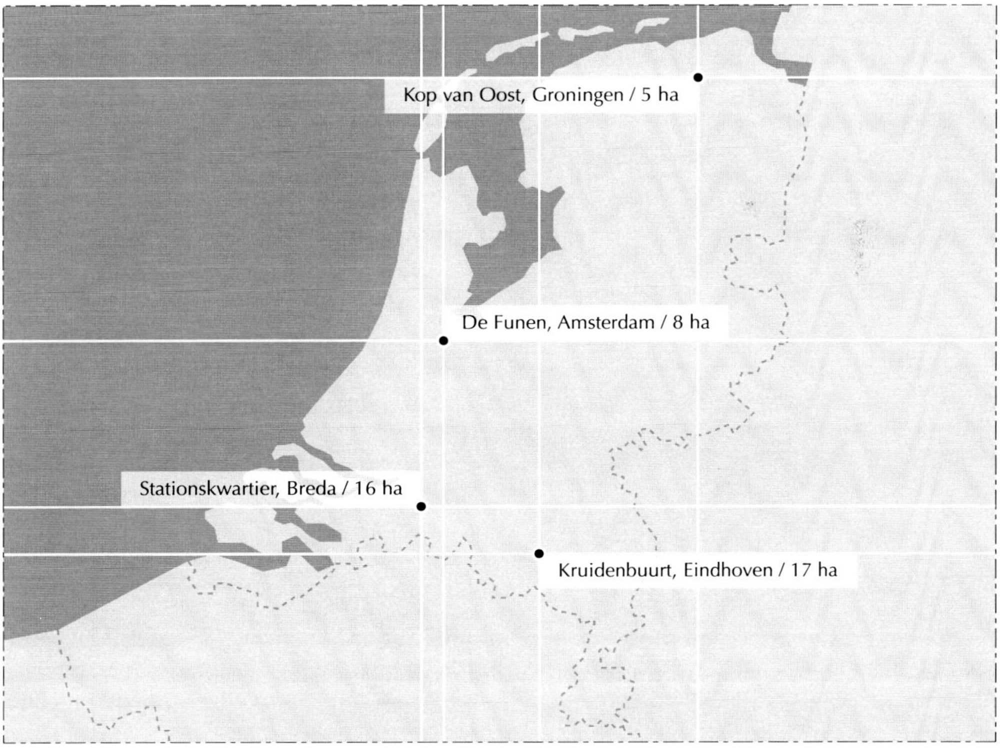

Figure 26. Location of the cases in the Netherlands.

7 Only in two cases was it possible to read the development agreement, and of them it was possible only in one to make a copy and keep this copy for later analysis. Based on the indirect evidence, we conclude however that all of them belong to the private law-sort *overeenkomst*.

7.3.1 *De Funen*, Amsterdam

Urban Regeneration project 'De Funen' (8 ha, 565 apartments, 70 units/ha, about 2,500 m² office space, see figure 27) is located to the east of the centre of Amsterdam. At the beginning of the 1980s, the site attracted the attention of the planning department of the Amsterdam Municipality. In 1991, the Structure Plan of Amsterdam, an indicative zoning plan, proposed the redevelopment of the whole site. At that time, the site had been abandoned and parts were leased to various tenants (*Van Gend & Loos* and others), who used the buildings for warehousing and storage. Initially Dutch Railways, owner of most of the land, was neither interested in developing the site nor in selling it to the municipality. This situation remained unchanged until IBC, a commercial developer, showed an interest. The first *ad hoc*, site-specific indicative plan on which the current development is based was approved in 1993 (*Nota van Uitgangspunten 'Czaar Peterbuurt-Oost'*). The existing binding rules did not foresee regeneration, thus a new Land-Use plan had to be approved, which occurred definitively in 2000.

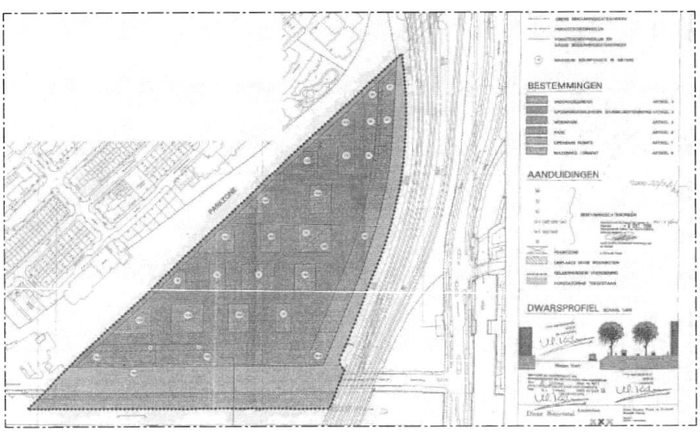

Figure 27. Map of 2000 Land use Plan.

The Dutch Railways owned most of the land, the municipality owned some plots and the existing public space, and some private individuals owned various other plots. In 1997, after signing a Development Agreement with the municipality, Dutch Railways sold most of its land to the property developer, IBC. In 1999 the municipality signed a second Development Agreement, this time with IBC. In 2002 Heijmans, another commercial developer, bought IBC, and in January 2008 Heijmans was still in charge of the development. At that time implementation was in course and more than the half of the dwellings were already inhabited.

7.3.2 *Kruidenbuurt Noord*, Eindhoven

Urban Regeneration project 'Kruidenbuurt Noord' (17 ha, 650 dwellings, single family and apartments, 45 units/ha, plus some offices, see figure 28) is located in the south-east of Eindhoven. The neighbourhood was built in the 1930s. At the end of the 1990s the first indicative *ad hoc,* site-specific plans were made for regeneration. Of some 850 existing houses, almost all of them social housing, 750 units have been or will be demolished, leaving some 100 units untouched. Of the 650 new dwellings, about 45% will be social housing.

In 1994 the Eindhoven Municipality sold the (freehold rights to the) land under the social housing to Trudo (*Trudo Stichting*), a housing association, and since then ownership has been divided. Trudo owns almost all the buildings and the land under them (50% of the plan area), while the municipality retains ownership of one public building and a playground (2%) and the public space (39%). The 100 houses that remain untouched (9% of plan area) are owned privately. Trudo and the municipality sealed a Development Agreement in 2004, and the new Land-Use Plan was approved definitively in 2005. By November 2007, 189 dwellings had been delivered and inhabited and 194 dwellings were under construction. Phase 3 is expected to start at the end of 2009, and phase 4 in 2011.

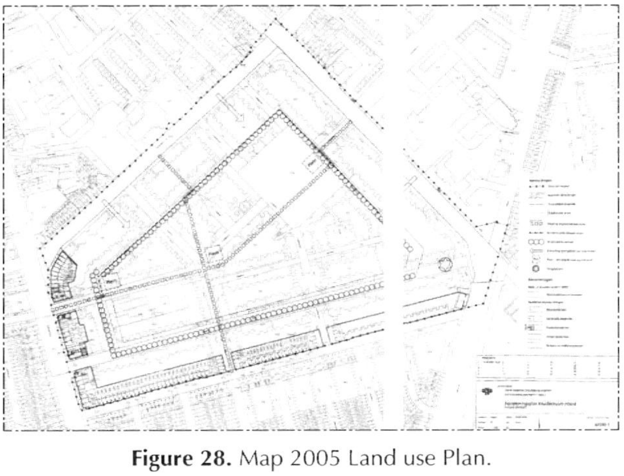

Figure 28. Map 2005 Land use Plan.

7.3.3 *Kop van Oost*, Groningen

Urban Regeneration project 'Kop van Oost' (5 ha, 430 dwellings, mainly apartments, about 85 units/ha, plus about 4,000 m² commercial space, see figure 29) is located to the east of the centre of Groningen. The site is situated alongside a main road (the *Sontweg*) that will become the main connection between the city centre and a future greenfield scheme, *Meerstad*. The site used to be occupied by a wood-processing company and a gas station, but at the time of the development initiative in 2000 the site was no longer in use. Only five dwellings were occupied, and these will not be demolished but will be accommodated in the regeneration. The *Sontweg* and a small road will be refurbished.

In its 1996 Structure Plan, the Groningen Municipality foresaw the redevelopment of this site as a mixed-use scheme mainly for housing and with some commercial facilities. Negotiations with the developer crystallized in the 2005 Development Agreement. The new land-use plan was definitively approved in 2006.

The initial property situation, before the development initiative took place, was as follows: Houtgroup-Pont Eecen owned 60% of the land, the municipality owned most of the public space (37%), and several private individuals owned the rest (4%). In 2000 Jaap Hollestelle, an intermediary/property developer, took the initiative to redevelop the site. He bought the land belonging to the wood-processing company. After general development terms had been negotiated with the municipality, the land was resold, first in 2001 to property developer IBC, and again in 2002 to Heijmans, another property developer that had bought IBC. In October 2007, Heijmans was providing the infrastructure.

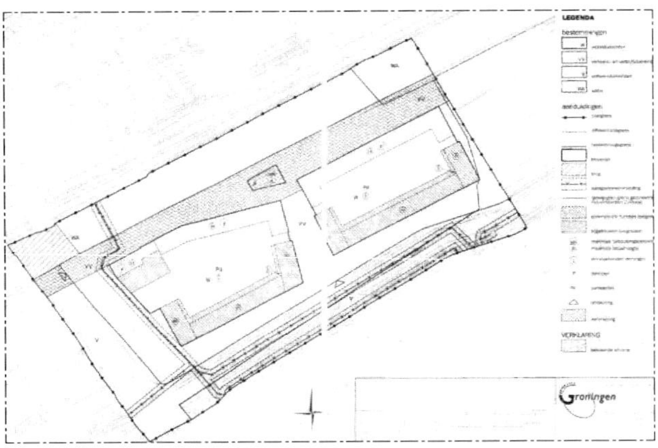

Figure 29. Map 2006 Land use Plan.

7.3.4 *Stationskwartier*, Breda

Urban Regeneration project 'Stationskwartier' (16 ha, about 80,000 m² apartments, 650 units, 45 units/ha, plus 140,000 m² office space, some shops, a new railway station and 50,000 m² parking, see figure 30) is located to the north of the centre of Breda. The plan area includes the existing Central railway station and its surroundings. The area that will effectively be redeveloped is 14 ha, because about 2.5 ha of railway land will remain untouched. The station will be completely rebuilt. The existing use is mainly related to the railways, but this function has ceased in most of the plan area. Nowadays there is, besides the railway station and rail tracks, some infrastructure for bus stops, parking places, abandoned land, a small green area and a hotel. There are some buildings (the hotel and station), but most of the area is not built.

Since the 1980s, Breda Municipality has developed indicative plans for the regeneration of the site into a mixed-use scheme for public transport (railways and bus), housing, offices and facilities. In 1998, the Dutch national government designated the site as one of the six 'New Key Projects' (*Nieuw Sleutelproject, NSP*). Key projects are railways stations to be connected to the high-speed railways network. Both national and provincial governments are involved in the regeneration of the site, for example, by giving substantial subsidies. Negotiations between the involved parties (municipality, national and provincial governments, and the main landowner Dutch Railways) have already crystallized into several development agreements.

The property is divided between Dutch Railways, specifically *NS Vastgoed* and *NS Railinfrastrust* (together 80% of the plan area), the municipality of Breda (the existing public space, 11%, and some plots, 5%: in total 16%) and a private developer and a supermarket (together 3%). The municipality approved the new Land-use plan in May 2007, and in December 2007 the provincial government approved it definitively. At the end of 2007, work on infrastructure provision had started on the northern side of the railway, and delivery of the last buildings is expected sometime in 2016 (*cfr.* Krabben & Needham, 2008).

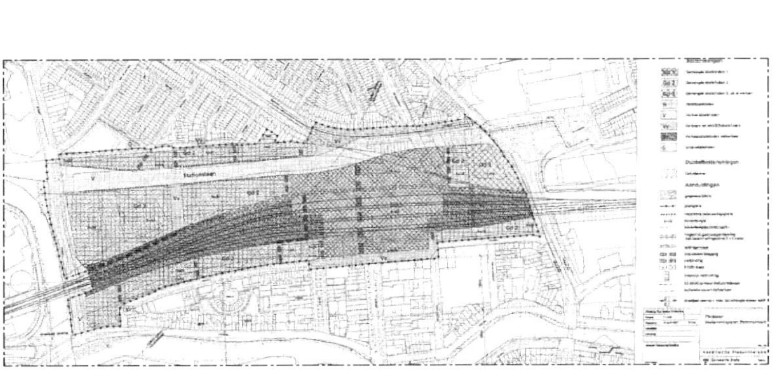

Figure 30. Map 2007 Land use Plan.

7.4 How formal rules relevant to zoning in the Netherlands can be used

This chapter describes the working in the Netherlands of the formal rules relevant to zoning within the value capturing mechanisms. There are different ways (or sub-variables) in which these rules can be used in an operational way to capture more of the value increase:

- Creating certainty or uncertainty beforehand about future building possibilities and contributions;
- Choosing the contents of the binding rules;
- Making the relevant binding rules conditional on securing capturing value increase;
- Modulating property rights;
- Using the procedure for the preparation and approval of the binding rules.

Here follows an assessment of whether each of these sub-variables can affect capturing value increase.

7.4.1 Certainty beforehand about future building possibilities and contributions

Summary of the findings

Dutch municipalities can and usually do approve in early stages indicative zoning plans that sketch the future development possibilities. This might be a Structure plan or an ad hoc document. Binding rules (land use plan or departures from it) are usually approved after the negotiations with developers have been successfully completed. In the studied cases, indicative plans created some certainty, or expectations, about the future building possibilities. However, they created almost no certainty about the future contributions. The exceptions were Kruidenbuurt and Stationskwartier: here there was some certainty beforehand about the costs and about who should pay them. This certainty arose during the plan process, not before, but in any case before negotiations had led to definitive development agreements. It seems that specific circumstances explain the exceptionality of both cases: in Kruidenbuurt the specific circumstance was the special relation between the municipality and the developer, a housing association; and in Stationskwartier the special nature of the project itself, a national infrastructure NSP-project. In both cases, municipalities created some certainty about the value capturing goals, namely to limit the public contributions to a 'lump sum' in Kruidenbuurt, and probably with more ambitious goals in Stationskwartier. It seems that in 'normal' private land schemes (e.g. De Funen and Kop van Oost), usually there is no certainty at all, beforehand, about the future obligations (Verdaas and Fokkema, interviews 2007). Table 18 summarizes the level of certainty in each case.

The findings suggest that certainty about the future building possibilities may be negative for capturing value increase because it weakens the negotiating position of municipalities and might have an inflationary effect on the price of land. In addition, the findings suggest a negative effect of uncertainty about future contributions, because of the same reasons. Let us see in detail whether public bodies create certainty or uncertainty about what, in which sort of documents, and what are the inferred consequences for capturing value increase.

Table 18. Level of certainty, before negotiations took place, about building possibilities and about obligations in the Dutch cases.

	Certainty about future building possibilities	Certainty about future contributions
De Funen, Amsterdam	Some	Very low
Kruidenbuurt, Eindhoven	Some	Some
Kop van Oost, Groningen	Some	None
Stationskwartier, Breda	Some	Some

7.4.1.1 Binding rules are approved after negotiations, so in early stages only indicative documents give some certainty

No legally binding rules before negotiations

The Dutch planning system is supposed to be 'plan-led', in the sense that the land use plan is supposed to be approved before negotiations take place. However, there is no legal obligation on municipalities to approve the land use plan beforehand, and a relatively flexible use is allowed (see frame 7g). In practice this has translated into the fact that Dutch municipalities, at least when confronted with comprehensive urban regeneration developments, usually wait until the negotiations with developers/ landowners are finished. When negotiations are finished and, mostly after a Development Agreement is sealed, municipalities modify the binding rules, that is, they process and approve a new land-use plan to replace the old one, or they approve a departure from the old one (interviews with Verdaas and Fokkema, 2007; Vrom et al, 2008: 67). This suggests that, in practice, the Dutch planning system works similarly to the British 'development-led' system, in the sense that binding rules are approved only after the development initiative has taken place and negotiations have ended successfully. For details about the distinction between plan-led and development-led planning systems, see section 2.3.1.

The studied cases support this general conclusion. The municipalities approved the new binding rules after the negotiations had been completed. They did so because of the consequences for capturing value increase. Municipalities saw the land use plan as the final phase of the planning process, because land or most of it was in private hands and municipalities could not steer the process through the ownership of land. Municipalities waited until some costs had been secured, before approving the land use plan or departures from it.

Frame 7g

Flexible legal rules regarding the place of the land use plan in development processes

First, a land use plan or a departure from it can be adapted to the boundaries of the development. Neither the law nor the jurisprudence establishes general limitations to the minimum geographical scope (plan area). This can cover a whole municipality (does not occur very often) or just a few plots ('postage stamp' plans –*postzegelplan*). Departures cover in practice usually just one or several plots, but also large developments (Bosch & Hanemaayer 1992: quoted in Bregman & Sievers 2002; Van Damme & Verdaas 1996: 73-78). In other words, municipalities can freely delimit the boundaries of the plan area. Second, there is no legal prescription that determines when the land use plan should be approved, in relation to the rest of the development process. There is no prescription whether it should be approved 5, 10 or X years/weeks before the development process takes place.

There might be exceptions to this general conclusion. Two experts point out that in some cases municipalities approve first, before the negotiations, an outline land-use plan with obligation of further detailing. Once the development agreement has been sealed, they detail the outline plan (De Wolff and Van Zundert, interviews in 2008). Cases *Kruidenbuurt* and *Stationskwartier* show indeed the use of outline land use plans. However, they were approved after the negotiations had ended successfully. Only in *Stationskwartier* did the approval of outline land use regulations for a small plot (3% of the total plan area) precede the negotiations.

Some certainty through indicative plans

Instead of approving binding rules in early stages, Dutch municipalities usually approve indicative zoning plans. They might be *ad hoc* for a specific site, or area, or they might cover the whole municipal territory or a large part of it. Planning law regulates one sort of indicative plan, the Structure Plan, which was replaced in 2008 by the Structure Vision. More common are indicative plans with a form, contents and approval procedure that are not regulated in planning law (e.g. *Nota van Uitgangspunten, Stedenbouwkundig Plan/visie, Ontwikkelingsprogramma, Programma van Eisen, Masterplan*¸ etc.). The level of certainty offered by these indicative plans, whether they are regulated in planning law or not, is limited. This is because (1) they are not usually very detailed, and (2) because binding plans can and usually do depart from their determinations.

In *De Funen* several indicative plans have preceded the signing of the first Development Agreement in 1997. In 1991 the Structure Plan of Amsterdam foresaw the redevelopment of the whole site, and in 1993 the municipality approved a site-specific document (*Nota van Uitgangspunten 'Czaar Peterbuurt-Oost'*) that established many aspects of the future programme (450-500 dwellings, of which 30% social housing, offices and work-places, the situation of most of the public space –including a park -, and a list of public facilities and buildings). This means that there was some certainty about the future building possibilities. Regarding the future obligations, the 1993 document determined to some extent the unprofitable parts: 30% social housing, a park and some public buildings. However, it did not say anything about who should pay them.

In *Kruidenbuurt* several indicative plans have preceded the signing of the Development Agreement in 2004. In 1999 the municipality approved a site-specific document (*Masterplan*), which established that 630 to 770 housing units could be built there. In 2001 the municipality approved another site-specific plan document (*Programma van Eisen*), which specified to some extent the programme: 650 housing units (of which 300 social houses and 175 'middle-expensive' units), a supermarket and possibly a public building. This document also vaguely described the public space. Altogether, this means that there was some certainty about the future building possibilities. In addition to these two documents, another document has been important: in 2000 the Municipality of Eindhoven and all the housing associations in the city agreed the financial contribution which the municipality would give for urban regeneration in the city, which included *Kruidenbuurt*. Following this agreement, the municipality would contribute € 9 million to the regeneration of *Kruidenbuurt*, and the housing association was responsible for the rest of development costs. Thanks to this document, it has been since 2000 clear what was going to be the municipal contribution, and that the housing association should pay the rest. Dutch housing associations and municipalities have in general a close relationship and are used to sealing such agreements.

In *Kop van Oost* several indicative plans have preceded the signing of the Development Agreement in 2005. In 1996 the Structure Plan of Groningen foresaw 'house and business' on this site (p. 64), and in 1999 and 2004 other documents confirmed this zoning, without specifying it very much. In 2004 a plan for a wider area than the development in question (*Eemskanaalzone – verbinding in Stad. Een visie op de ontwikkeling van de Eemskanaalzone*) made this outline zoning more specific: circa 400 units for the site (p. 40). This means that there was some certainty about the future building possibilities. Regarding the future obligations, there was no certainty at all, as the mentioned documents specified neither any specific unprofitable elements nor any cost allocation principle.

In *Stationskwartier* several indicative plans have preceded the signing of the Development Agreement in 2006. The municipality of Breda has prepared since the 1980s plans for the regeneration of the site into a mixed-use scheme for public transport (railways and bus), housing, office and facilities. These plans were revitalized when the central government designated the site as New Key Project (NSP), initially in 1998, and definitively in January 2000. This made clear the redevelopment possibilities of the site. In 2003 the municipality and the central government approved the Masterplan Central Breda (*Masterplan Centraal Breda*), a document that specified the building possibilities: 50,000 m^2 floor space for housing, between 400 and 650 units; 20,000 m^2 flexible, preferably for housing; 80,000 m^2 for office, enlargeable up to 120,000 m^2; and 8,000 m^2 for hotel and shops. It defined further the location of the new railway and bus stations, but it did not define the public roads and space. In 2005 another important document (*Structuurvisie Via Breda Spoorzone 2025*) ratified the figures of the 2003 Masterplan. All this together meant that there was some certainty about the future building possibilities. Regarding the future obligations, NSP-projects usually specify *a priori* development costs and their allocation, because of the financial involvement of the provincial and the central government. It seems that this was also the case in *Stationskwartier*: The 2003 Masterplan included a business case that might have played an important role but that was not available for this research. This document included, according to the interviewed developer and public officers, a rough calculation of the development costs and a proposal for their allocation. So this document gave some certainty about the future obligations, before the signing of a first agreement in 2003 (*Planontwikkelingsovereenkomst*) and a second Development Agreement in 2006 (*Samenwerkingsovereenkomst, SOK*).

The question is, what the results of this certainty have been for capturing value increase. Here, a distinction is made between certainty about building possibilities, and certainty about contributions.

7.4.1.2 Effects of the certainty about building possibilities: weakening or strengthening the negotiation position of municipalities

The fact that municipalities used the land use plan as the final phase in negotiations created uncertainty about the future building possibilities. It has not been possible to measure in our cases the effects of this, because all the cases had done the same and there was no example of the contrary. However, it seems reasonable to conclude that this, in general, has strengthened the negotiation positions of municipalities. This may have influenced positively capturing value increase. Municipalities had 'more to offer' in the negotiations. In *Stationskwartier* an interviewed public officer considered that using the land use plan as the final step had been important to achieve a good level of capturing value increase. A consulted expert and a representative of the Dutch developers consider that, in general, this operational use of the land use plan has improved capturing value increase (Verdaas and Fokkema, interviews 2007). The representative of the developers considered that, sometimes, this operational use of the land use plan has allowed public bodies to receive even part of the plus value, going further than cost recovery (Fokkema, interview 2007).

Despite this initial uncertainty, the cases show that indicative plans created some certainty about the future building possibilities. In other words, the uncertainty that follows the practice of approving the binding rules after the negotiations has been reduced by the certainty created by indicative plans. It has not been possible to measure the effects of this because all the cases had done the same and there was no example of the contrary. However, it seems reasonable to conclude that this diminishes somehow the negotiation position of municipalities. Municipalities cannot easily and credibly refuse to cooperate in the development of the site, so they have 'less to offer'. Developers might count on that. In addition, it might have stimulated the increase of the land price. An interviewed expert suggested that municipalities might be not aware of these negative effects of creating expectations in the early stages (Verdaas, interview 2007).

7.4.1.3 Effects of certainty about contributions: lowering land price

Regarding the certainty about future contributions, the studied cases show some differences between those without certainty (*De Funen* and *Kop van Oost*) and those with some certainty (*Kruidenbuurt* and *Stationskwartier*). The differences in value capturing between the four cases are not very large, but *Kruidenbuurt* and *Stationskwartier* stand out. Both cases included an important contribution from the developer to public goals: 45% units for social housing in *Kruidenbuurt*, the costs of which will be paid by the developer (a housing association), and a new railways and bus station in *Stationskwartier*, the costs of which will mainly be paid with public subsidies, but the developer (Dutch Railways) pays a minor part and will provide all the needed land. *De Funen* also includes social houses (30% of the units), but they seem to be subsidized by public bodies (for a comparison of the realized value capturing among the cases, see section 7.5). In general, the interviewed public officers and developers in *Kruidenbuurt* and *Stationskwartier*, explicitly or implicitly emphasized that certainty about contributions (the 2000 agreement respectively the 2003 Business case) has improved capturing value increase. In *Kop van Oost*, an interviewed developer suggested that uncertainty about the future obligations has allowed landowners to 'drain' most of the value increase by asking a high price for their property. Here land has been sold three times, and in the second transaction in 2001 the developer paid about € 12m, which is much higher that the estimated market value of the previous use (industrial land), about € 3.6m.

A possibly explanation for this apparently positive effect of certainty about future obligations on value capturing refers to land price mechanisms. Certainty beforehand about future contributions can help developers to pay the right price for land (for more details about this economic arguments, see section 2.3.3). This could explain the low captured value increase in *De Funen* and *Kop van Oost*, and the relatively higher value capturing in *Stationskwartier*. In these three cases, land has been transferred during the development process. In *De Funen* and *Kop van Oost* the price of land in the transactions was agreed before there was any certainty about future obligations, before the negotiations thus. This might have increased the price of land. In *Stationskwartier* the situation was the opposite: the price of land was agreed once there was some certainty about future obligations, which might have moderated land price increases. *Kruidenbuurt* seems however to be less suitable for this explanation, as here almost all the land was already in the ownership of the developer, and has not been transferred. Additionally, it seems plausible to conclude that the higher level of certainty about future contributions in *Stationskwartier* and *Kruidenbuurt* made these contributions a starting point in the negotiations, reinforcing thus the negotiation position of the municipality.

7.4.2 Choosing the contents of the relevant binding rules

Summary of the findings

The range of legally binding prescriptions that can be included in the land use plan and departures from it are remarkably small, when compared with Valencia and England. Planning law and the jurisprudence in the Netherlands have considerably limited the legally binding determinations that land use plans and departures can include: only physical zoning aspects, and no development-oriented aspects such as contributions and implementation schedules. It is also remarkable that, up to 2008, land use plans and departures could not require social housing. These limitations seem in the studied cases to have affected negatively capturing value increase. The 2008 Physical Planning Act has introduced a new sort of binding plan, the Development contributions plan, which can include development-oriented aspects. Let us see in detail what are the possibly contents of the land use plan, the departures from it, and the Development contributions plan, and what are the consequences for capturing value increase.

7.4.2.1 Possible contents of the land use plan, before the 2008 Physical Planning Act

Up to 2008, the Physical Planning Act (article 10.1) and the Physical Planning Decree (article 12.1.a), together with the judicial scrutiny, had defined the limits of the possible contents of the land-use plan and departures from it. The land-use regulations had to be directly related to the building and/or the use of the land and the building. This means that indirect relationships were not allowed, for example that it is allowed to build only when a road shown in the land-use plan had been constructed (Klaassen, 2000: 107-108). The regulations had also to be 'spatially relevant' (*ruimtelijk* or *planologisch relevant*) (Priemus and Louw, 2000: 58-59). These limitations meant that land use regulations might concern little more than the outline design of the infrastructure and the building (building line, height, width and depth of the building) and the general zoning (housing, shops, offices, industry, traffic roads, public parks, canal, parking place, etc). See frame 7h.

Frame 7h

Limitations to the contents of binding rules before the 2008 Physical Planning Act

Taking account of the mentioned limits, up to 2008, the legally binding parts (the Regulations and the Map) of land use plans and departures from it *could not contain* the following aspects (see, among others mentioned below: Needham, 2000):

- Social housing: it was not possible to include social housing (De Groot and Van der Veen, 2003: 660-661; Van der Ree, 2000: 605-607). Indeed, none of the four studied cases included social housing in the Regulations. In *Kruidenbuurt* the Explanation did this, but this is the non-legally binding part of the land use plan;
- Obligations: it was not possible to include any kind of financial return or contribution in kind, no matter whether they were intended for on-site or off-site infra-

structure (De Groot and Van der Veen, 2003: 655; De Jong, 1999: 537). For example it was not possible to require in the land use plan and departures from it that the developer has to pay and/or to construct himself the public infrastructure and facilities.

- Financing and implementation schedules: it was not possible to include temporal regulations, i.e. when to commence or to finish development. None of the four studied cases included deadlines in the Regulations. In *Kruidenbuurt* and *Stationskwartier* only the Explanation included some vague deadlines.

In the studied cases (all of which fall under the Physical Planning Act before 2008) these limitations might have had a negative influence on the negotiation position of the municipality, and thus on capturing value increase. In *De Funen* and *Stationskwartier,* the municipality included in development agreements requirements that could not be included in the binding rules: in *De Funen* implementation schedules, most of which have not been fulfilled, and in *Stationskwartier* requirements regarding social housing, which will probably not be fulfilled. According to public officers in charge of the legal affairs in both cases, these requirements might have been legally enforceable if they had been included not only in the agreements but also in the Regulations of the land use plan.

7.4.2.2 Possibly contents of the land use plan and Development contributions plan, since 2008

The 2008 Physical Planning Act has added the possibility of including in the land use plan itself and departures from it regulations regarding social housing, but the other limitations remain. Articles 3.1.1 and 3.10.3 of the Act allow including in a land use plan or departures from it land-use regulations regarding the 'performability' (*uitvoerbaarheid*) of their prescriptions[8]. Article 3.1.2, lid 1 of the 2008 Physical Planning Decree specifies what are 'performability'-regulations: regulations regarding the possibility of establishing *the percentage* (but not the location) of the total dwellings that must be used for affordable housing (for rent and for sale) and for self-build housing (Vrom, 2007b; Vrom, 2007c: 6-7)[9].

The 2008 Act introduced a new sort of legally binding plan, the Development contributions plan. This includes a calculation of development costs, and can include in any case the following aspects:

8 "(...) *Deze regels* (regels met het oog op de bestemming, red.) *kunnen tevens strekken ten behoeve van de* ***uitvoerbaarheid*** *van in het plan opgenomen bestemmingen* (...)." (article 3.1.1 2008 Physical Planning Act).
"*Aan het besluit* (een aan een BP voorafgaand projectbesluit, red.) *kunnen voorschriften en beperkingen worden verbonden, welke tevens kunnen strekken ten behoeve van de* ***uitvoerbaarheid*** *van het project,* (...)" (article 3.10.3 2008 Physical Planning Act).

9 "*Ten behoeve van de uitvoerbaarheid kan een bestemmingsplan eisen bevatten met betrekking tot sociale huurwoningen, sociale koopwoningen of particulier opdrachtgeverschap.*" (article 3.1.2, lid 1 Physical Planning Decree).

- Land for social housing and other contributions: it includes a calculation of the development costs, and rules for the allocation of these costs to each plot. It can also include a differentiation between social housing for rent, social housing for sale and free market housing, and can allocate these categories to each plot and prescribe the number of units. For details about the costs that can be included in the Development contributions plan, and those that cannot, see section 7.2.3;
- Financing and implementation schedules.

In sum, the 2008 Physical Planning Act partly repairs the limited contents of binding rules in the Netherlands. An interviewed expert said that the possibility of requiring a certain percentage of social housing in the land use plan will stimulate municipalities to enforce social housing requirements (Verdaas, interview 2007). It seems likely that a similar positive effect can be expected from the possibility of introducing other contributions and implementation schedules in the Development contributions plan.

7.4.3 Making binding rules conditional on securing capturing value increase

As we saw above in section 7.4.1.1, municipalities usually wait until some contributions have been secured before processing and approving the binding rules that make the intended development possible. It seems as if the approval of the binding rules was part of the game during the negotiations. Municipalities make clear to developers that some contributions must be secured before the land use plan or departures from it are approved. However, in the Netherlands the legal room for making the approval of binding rules conditional on securing capturing value increase is narrower than in Valencia and England. This practice of municipalities is disputable from a legal point of view because securing contributions from the developer, or fixing deadlines, cannot be considered as 'spatially relevant'. Therefore, it is not possible for the municipality to formally make the approval of the Land use Plan conditional on achievement of a Development Agreement in which the developer commits itself to fulfil investment and implementation schedules.

Summary of the findings

There is an alternative way of conditioning that can help to overcome this shortcoming of the Dutch planning system: conditioning through the economic feasibility or performability (*economische uitvoerbaarheid*) requirements of the land use plan. The side effects here is that, after agreement, the land use plan still must follow the complete procedure (which implies a risk of delay and modifications), that developers might easily appeal to the judges, and that this alternative makes it very difficult for the municipality to build up a clear public discourse. The new 2008 Act can be used to diminish to some extend the last two side effects by making a draft of Development contributions plan (but not *approving* it) to make clear that *only* an agreement can make the development economically feasible. This alternative way can help to overcome this shortcoming of the Dutch planning system, i.e. it can help to strengthen the negotiation position of the municipality, and thus to better the capturing of value increase. The other possibility for the municipality is to approve a Development contributions plan and condition the granting of the building permit (thus not the approval of the Land use plan) on payment of a contribution. However, this brings many disadvantages: the municipality might be obliged to advance investments without yet having received all the contributions, must assume a heavy administrative procedure, bear some cost-increasing risks, and also the risk of delay in case the landowners do not want to apply for building permit on time. In addition, approving a Development contributions plan involves that the municipality cannot recover all the costs. Let us see this in more detail.

7.4.3.1 Conditioning the land use plan and departures from it indirectly through the Explanation

The first alternative is indirect: contributions can be considered as essential for the economic feasibility or performability (*economische uitvoerbaarheid*) of the implementation. The Explanation of land use plans, that part of the document that does not have a legally binding character, can include considerations related to the feasibility of the plan: e.g. the conditions that are needed to implement the plan, necessary contributions, etc. Therefore, if the developer does not agree to make contributions, the municipality can refuse to initiate the administrative procedure of approval of the land use plan or departure from it, arguing that implementation is not feasible. The municipal decision can refer to this paragraph (De Wolff, Van Zundert, Hoekstra, Van den Brand, interviews 2008). It is very important that the municipality handles a coherent discourse, which is that negotiations are meant to make feasible the implementation of the land use plan. If as a result of no agreement the plan becomes unfeasible, the municipality *has no other choice* than to refuse to initiate the administrative procedure of modification of the binding rules.

However, this indirect conditioning through the Explanation might have some negative side effects:

1. Procedural risks: after the sealing of Development Agreement, the land use plan (or departure from it) must follow the complete procedure, which implies a risk of delay and modifications because of objections and appeals. Formally speaking, agreements cannot restrict the room of the Local Council to decide on the plan. As a consequence, municipalities seal the agreement but might not be able to avoid modifications to the land use plan, or to avoid delay. Thus, agreements are always subjected to the risk, not unthinkable, that the land use plan is later modified, or its approval delayed, which can nullify partly or totally the Development Agreement (Vrom et al, 2008: 51). In the studied cases this however did not seem to be a problem: the land use plans have been processed within the legal deadlines and without large modifications;
2. Appeal risks: should a municipality refuse to initiate the administrative procedure of approval of the land use plan or departure from it because the developer does not agree to contributions and schedules, there is always a risk of an ap-

peal to the courts (*cfr.* Gerritsen, 2010: 26). The reason is that this indirect way of conditioning through the economic feasibility paragraph is not the same as enumerating, openly, in a municipal decision, the contributions that the developer has to make. Dutch municipalities cannot behave so openly, and need to properly and carefully argue why implementation is not feasible and thus why approval is not possible. This is not always easy. If implementation seems feasible, municipalities cannot use this argument of economic feasibility to refuse to initiate the administrative procedure[10], even if developers have not agreed to all the required contributions[11]. The introduction of the 2008 Land Development Act makes a refusal on these grounds even more difficult: as the municipality is now entitled to make a Development contributions plan, in theory the feasibility can be guaranteed, so the municipality can no longer argue unfeasibility of the implementation (thus: lack of agreement with the developer) as a reason for refusing to initiate the administrative procedure;

3. Credibility of the municipality's public discourse: a too complex argumentation can threaten the credibility of the municipality's public discourse. Because direct and open conditioning is not allowed, the public discourse might in practice need to hide some of the 'real reasons' for the approval or refusal of land use plans.

7.4.3.2 Conditioning the Land use Plan and departure from it indirectly through the Development contributions Plan

The 2008 Act created another alternative way of indirect conditioning. If the developer does not voluntarily commit himself to contributions and schedules (e.g. in an anterior Development Agreement), the municipality can make a draft Development contributions plan of all needed investments in public infrastructure and facilities. If the draft makes clear that the municipality cannot recover all the costs through the Development contributions plan[12], municipalities can openly refuse to process and approve it, arguing that they cannot bear this deficit (Vrom, 2008: 106). The approval of the Development contributions plan is linked to the approval of the land use plan: if the approval of this plan implies costs, and these costs are not secured in advance

10 Or if they do, they will risk losing the case if the developer brings it to the courts of justice.

11 A recent sentence illustrates very well how difficult it can be for a Municipality to construct a coherent discourse: in De Lutte the Municipality achieved a development agreement with a developer who owned part of the plan area. However, several small landowners refused to pay to the developer their contribution to the costs. The Municipality refused then to modify the Land use plan for these specific landowners, arguing that paying that contribution was necessary to guarantee the economic feasibility of the Land use plan. However, the judge sentenced against the Municipality with the argument that the economic feasibility was already guaranteed with the development agreement that was agreed with the developer [Vz. ABRS 27 January 2010 (De Lutte), nr. 200808233/1/R1].

12 It is already said that Development contributions plans, especially in urban regeneration, have often a financial deficit. This is mainly because all the land is included as cost for a price that includes the increased value, see section 7.2.3. In other words, the legal rules for the elaboration of a Development contributions plan 'create' a deficit by accounting land for the highest possible price. While a Development contributions plan *must account* the land for it highest value, municipality and developer can freely agree, in an Anteriour Development Agreement, a lower value and thus make a project feasible that following a plan was not.

(in a Development Agreement or in any other way[13]), a Development contributions plan *must* be approved. By conditioning the approval of the Development contributions Plan to guarantees that the deficit will be covered, in fact the municipality can condition the approval of the land use plan to the developer covering this deficit. If the developer agrees in an anterior Agreement to secure the costs, the municipality can approve the land use plan *without* necessarily approving also the Development contributions plan (*cfr.* interviews with Van den Brand and Hoekstra, 2008).

This alternative might diminish two of the mentioned side effects. First, the chance of developers appealing successfully might diminish (side effect 2) because the municipality can better argue the non-feasibility. Second, municipalities can be open about their decision (side effect 3). However, this alternative might also create a new side effect: if the developer agrees in an Anterior Development Agreement to secure only the deficit of the Development contributions plan (i.e. those costs that *cannot* be charged to the landowners through this plan), but not those costs that *can* be charged to the landowners, municipalities cannot anymore argue economic feasibility to refuse. Namely, the costs that can be charged are theoretically guaranteed, i.e. landowners are supposed to pay them afterwards, when obtaining a building permit. Remember that in an Anterior Development Agreement municipality and developer can agree more contributions than allowed in a Development contributions plan. In any case, side effect 1 remains: after the sealing of an Anterior Agreement, the land use plan still has to be processed, which implies the risk of modifications and delay.

7.4.3.3 Conditioning the building permit directly and openly

The 2008 Act has introduced the possibility of conditioning the *building permit* in an open and direct way: if the municipality approves a Development contributions plan, it is possible now to condition the granting of the *building permit* on the payment of a contribution. This occurs as follows: the Development contributions plan calculates the costs that can be charged to the landowners and allocates those costs to each plot. The building permit is conditional on paying this contribution and on some requirements about the payment. If payment does not take place, and the developer has not secured the contribution in other ways, the municipality can require the money, stop the building, and finally cancel the building permit. However, approving a Development contributions plan has some side effects:

1. Risks:
   - The municipality might be obliged itself to finance investments in the public infrastructure in anticipation of collecting the costs later;

13 Costs are 'secured' when there is certainty that there is, or will be, financial means available to pay them. This certainty can be created in different ways: *i)* When there is a development agreement or any other form of private law contract that commits any party to pay; *ii)* When any public body commits to subsidy the costs; *iii)* When the municipality has the land and has calculated that the profits of selling the land will cover the costs. In this third case, the municipal executive power (*B&W*) or the Local Council (*Gemeenteraad*) must approve those calculations and include them in the municipal budget.

- The municipality has to prepare the plan following certain guarantees and checks: this is an important task and implies a risk for the municipality, such as the risk of appeals against the appraisal and assessment methods of profits and costs (Vrom, 2008: 33-34; Korthals Altes, 2008: 203). At the beginning of 2010 many municipalities still are struggling with the lack of knowledge and skills necessary to make these plans;
- Landowners have to pay only after applying for the building permit, so if no one applies to build, the costs will not be recouped, or recouped with delay. This too implies a financial risks for the municipality or any other party in charge of the public infrastructure and facilities (Vrom, 2008: 28);
- If the municipality wants to oblige landowners to apply for building permits following the schedules included in the Exploitation Plan, the only way of doing that is to use expropriation, which implies the obligation to pay compensation for the highest market value of the land, which includes the increased value due to the future use of the land;
- The approval of a Development contributions plan might nullify some prescriptions of an anterior Development Agreement, as the Agreement cannot contradict the prescriptions of such a plan (Vrom et al, 2008: 34; Kluwer, 2008: 132). So the Development contributions plan might nullify some contributions agreed in the Agreement.

2. Not all the costs can be charged to the landowners (for more details see chapter 7.2.3). These include:
   - Costs of maintenance and exploitation of the public infrastructure and facilities;
   - Costs for social facilities;
   - Costs that do not meet the three criteria of profit, attributability and proportionality, such as many costs of infrastructure serving wider areas, and/or located off-site;
   - A possible deficit (frequent in urban regeneration);
   - Additional costs for social housing, related to requirements that cannot be included in a Development contributions plan, such as not being able to prescribe the maximal selling price of social housing for sale in case there is no regional agreement on this;
   - Costs for 'Spatial development' (*ruimtelijke ontwikkelingen*) situated outside the scheme in question and not necessarily related to it.

7.4.4 Modulating property rights

Summary of the findings

The right to develop (i.e. the exclusive right to develop land, once permissions have been granted) belongs in the Netherlands to the landowner. This, together with the distribution of the other resources which are necessary for urban regeneration, creates a strong interdependency between municipalities and landowners: municipalities have the statutory powers over binding rules, and landowners have the financial means and the exclusive right to develop the land. This interdependency gives to the landowners the option to wait, which it is often used to oppose municipalities' requirements, and often leads to a delay in the development processes.

7.4.4.1 Who owns development rights in the Netherlands?

In the Netherlands, development rights belong, in principle, to the landowner. Although in practice municipalities usually feel responsibility for the infrastructure provision, this is not, as such, regulated by law. Dutch planning law does not explicitly refer to infrastructure provision as a public task, responsibility or right. The property rights of landowners are primarily defined in the Civil Code (which, in principle, gives the owner unlimited rights) and are afterwards limited by the law and the way that is worked out in binding rules. There is no kind of 'minimum building right' for the landowner. These rules, however, in no way affect the owner's right to be the only one entitled to develop whatever the binding rules and the laws foresee on his plot. This includes both the infrastructure provision and the building. Once the landowner applies for and obtains the needed permits, the landowner can exclude others from both providing the infrastructure and building on the land (Needham, 2007a: 152).

By analyzing who has the control over each of the transactions in infrastructure provision, it has been possible to discern the extent to which development rights belong to the landowners. The transactions are: 1) land purchase and assembling, 2) financing and 3) land preparation and development.

7.4.4.2 Mutual dependence of local authorities and landowners in the Netherlands

To analyse the consequences for the power relationship between municipalities and landowners of the practical possibilities for controlling transactions 1-3, this research developed a model of dependence (see table 19; for more details of the model, see section 3.1.1). There was in all the four Dutch cases studied a mutual dependence between the involved actors, and this dependence was very strong. It seems that the possibilities in practice for assembling the land (transaction 1), gathering the financial resources (transaction 2), and indirectly, developing the land to produce serviced plots (transaction 3) depend heavily on the landowner's passive consent or active collaboration. Transactions 1 and 2 are directly dependent on agreement between the municipality and the developers/landowners, and transaction 3 is also dependent, but indirectly because it cannot take place without transactions 1 and 2. This is because none of the actors controls all the needed resources and because the dependence is not avoidable.

The municipality depends on the landowners

On the one hand, the landowner/developer controls two important resources, land and investment capacity, which make the municipality dependent on him. In theory the municipality has some instruments to avoid this dependence: a public pre-emption right (*voorkeursrecht*) to acquire the land (step 1), the Profit Tax (*Baatbelasting*) to gather financial means (step 2), or expropriation to assembly the land (step 1). However, these instruments have limitations. The pre-emption implies a dependence of public bodies on the landowner: pre-emption requires that the landowner wants to sell his property. The Profit Tax can be applied both in built-up urban areas, whether the benefitted serviced building parcels are built or not, and also in greenfield developments (Klaassen, 2002: 264-268). This tax however plays a marginal role in value capturing in the Netherlands: it is rarely used (Groetelaers, 2004: 135; Vrom, 2008: 19). Regarding expropriation, it is only permitted if it is 'necessary' (*'noodzakelijk'*, former article 79 Compulsory purchase Act before modification 2010). If a landowner is willing to meet the specifications of the land use plan, and if he is capable of developing the land, the jurisprudence considers that there is no necessity to expropriate the land: the landowner can realise the new development himself. This scenario is called 'self realisation' (*zelfrealisatie*). However, the specifications of the land use plan are not always unambiguous (Priemus & Louw, 2003: 371), not in the last place because such plans can neither include contributions nor financing and implementation schedules. Normally, an agricultural landowner will not be able to fulfil the specifications. However, if he sells his land to a private developer or a building company, or if he decides to cooperate with such an organisation, the situation changes. In that case, the appropriate court will decide that there is no necessity for expropriation. Along other aspects that in practice might hamper expropriation (e.g. political sensitivities, or procedural risks), the legal criteria that expropriation has to fulfil, and specially the criterion that expropriation is not needed if the landowner can himself develop the land, has hampered an important number of expropriations. By declaring that he is capable of and willing to implement the binding rules, the landowner can avoid expropriation. Actually, it is not common to expropriate land in the Netherlands for the implementation of land-use plans. Expropriation is used only in exceptional circumstances, and then for just a few plots. For example, in Breda (case *Stationskwartier*), there has been no expropriation of land from developers in recent years. The new 2008 Physical Planning Act might increase the possibilities for municipalities to apply expropriation. The new Development contributions plan can include contributions and financing and implementation schedules. This can make less ambiguous the specifications under which self realisation can take place, so landowners who do not apply for building permits (and pay the corresponding contribution) within the schedules included in the Development contributions Plan can no longer argue that they are willing to implement the plan (Vrom, 2008: 206-207).

Summarizing, as a rule, municipalities that want development to take place but do not reach an agreement with the landowners (about the purchase and assembly of land and about the financing of the infrastructure provision) have the only alternative of trying to compulsorily purchase the land and pay for the works.

The landowners depend on the municipality

On the other hand, landowner/developers depend on the municipality because of its regulatory powers of approving the binding rules and granting the building permit. This dependence also can be labelled as strong because it is not avoidable; public bodies are the only actors who can exercise these regulatory powers.

Table 19. Dependence analysis in the Netherlands.

	Dependence because of land	Dependence because of investment capacity	Dependence because of regulatory resources
Municipality depends on the landowner/ developer	Developers own most of the land. Dependence is only avoidable through expropriation. However, expropriation is a rare instrument, and 'self realisation' gives preference to developer.	Municipalities do not have financial means to invest, so developers are only ones who could invest. Only in Breda was the municipality ready to assume some financial risks.	
Landowner/developer depends on Municipality			The municipality approves the land-use plan and departures from it, and grants the building permits. Dependence is not avoidable.

Consequences of the strong mutual dependency

The consequences in practice of this strong mutual dependency are significant. Landowners /developers have the option of not agreeing with the contributions package or other development requirements of the municipality. As developers do not always control all the land, and thus depend on various landowners, it might take some time to reach an agreement with all the landowners about the desirable (for the landowners) price of land. This stimulates the raising of the price of land. An agreement with all the landowners depends on the expectation that by delaying negotiations, profits for the developer and the price of land could increase in the future. Whether it is the developer who owns the land and decides to wait, or it is one or more landowners who decide not to sell to the developer: municipalities might be confronted with developers that are not willing, and maybe not able, to agree with the required contribution package. This might affect negatively the negotiation position of municipalities, as they might be forced to lower the contributions package if they want to reach an agreement. Also, this can delay development because negotiations are prolonged. Let us see in detail the findings in the cases.

Findings in De Funen (only apartments)

Dutch Railways, the former landowner, negotiated with the Municipality of Amsterdam from the beginning of the 90's till the signing of an outline Development Agreement in March 1997. It seems that this semi-autonomous public company had chosen several times to wait. During a period of several years, negotiations did not succeed: the municipality approved in 1994 and 1995 two site-specific indicative plans (*Stedenbouwkundige Programmas van Eisen*), but Dutch Railways rejected both plans, arguing that they were financially not feasible. From 1994 to 1997, the average national prices of new housing grew in line with or above the general inflation, with a peak of 12% above inflation in 1996 (see figure 31 for prices of new dwellings in the Netherlands, and for all dwellings in the province of North Holland, where Amsterdam lies). This means that delaying the development had no negative financial consequences for Dutch Railways, also because they had owned the land for more than 100 years, so there were no financial costs of waiting.

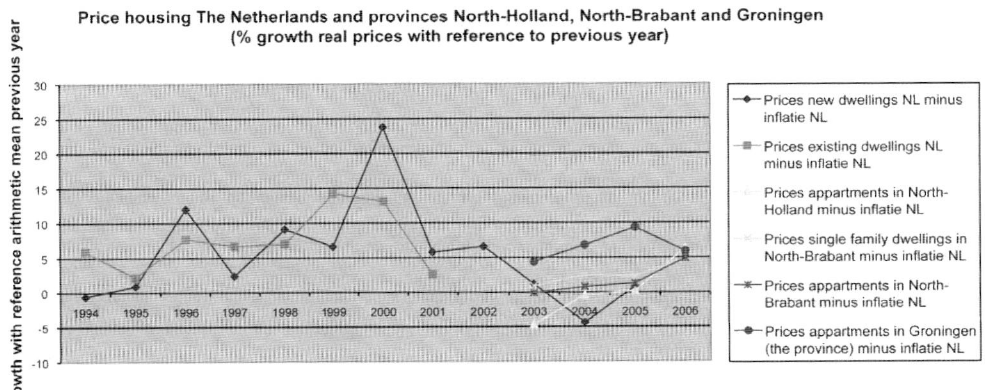

Sources:
- Prices new dwellings NL upto 2001: own elaboration, based on BNW (in Vrom 2002);
- Prices new dwellings NL from 2001: own elaboration, based on CBS Statline, Nieuwbouwwoningen outputindex 2000 = 100 (on-line consultation on 5 Februari 2008: www.cbs.nl).
- Prices existing dwellings NL upto 2001: own elaboration, based on NVM (in NVB 2001).
- Prices new and existing dwellings (single family and appartments) in North-Holland, North-Brabant and Groningen: own elaboration, based on Vrom 2007a.
- Inflatie NL: Centraal Bureau Statistiek (www.cbs.nl), Comsumentenprijzen; historie inflatie.

Figure 31. Growth of real prices (price increase minus general monetary inflation) of dwellings in the Netherlands and the provinces of North-Holland, North-Brabant and Groningen.

In 1997, after signing the first outline Development Agreement, the Dutch Railways sold most of the land to IBC, a property developer. During the following two years IBC and the municipality negotiated, and they sealed a second Development Agreement in September 1999. The average national prices of new housing grew spectacularly at that time: 2.4% above inflation in 1997, 9.1% in 1998 and 6.6% in 1999. According to a public officer, Dutch Railways and IBC agreed that IBC would pay the price and receive formally the land at the moment of starting the building, not before. This means that besides benefiting from general price rises, IBC did not have to pay interest charges until the start of the building works; so waiting was, from an economic point of view, an interesting option. During the negotiations, the developer seems to have been clear that he would not accept hard deadlines. The indicative plans and the agreements include schedules, but almost none of them has been fulfilled, and the chances to impose them through the courts seem to be low. Two involved public officers considered that if the municipality had had the choice to exclude the developer's option to wait, the development process might have been faster.

The fourth moment at which the developer clearly seems to have used his option to wait was the start of the building. Although the developer had building permits for all the buildings since June 2001, he only started with the first buildings in the summer of 2002, and he waited about five years before starting the buildings in the rest of the site. The negotiations between IBC and the actual developer, Heijmans, have played here a clear role. Heijmans bought IBC in the summer of 2002 and decided to submit new applications to modify the already granted building permits for the remainder of the buildings, arguing that they were financially not feasible. Building these dwellings started during 2005 and 2006, when average prices had begun to rise again.

Besides causing delay, it seems plausible that the option to wait has weakened the negotiation position of the municipality, and thus diminished value capturing. The Municipality of Amsterdam seemed worried about the tempo of the development. Many public goals established in the first indicative plan of 1993 have finally not been included in the Development Agreements of 1997 and 1999. The impression arises that the municipality has gradually reduced value-capturing requirements during the planning process in order to achieve an agreement with the developer.

Findings in Kruidenbuurt (single-family dwellings and apartments)

Trudo, a social landlord and owner of about the half of the land (the rest was public space, owned by the Municipality of Eindhoven), negotiated with the municipality from the second half of the 90's till 2004. In 1998, intense consultation with the neighbourhood led to a first site-specific indicative plan. In May 2004, negotiations ended with the signing of a Development Agreement. From 1997 till 2002, average prices of all new dwellings in the Netherlands grew spectacularly, with 2000 being the record year (24% increase above inflation). In 2003 and 2004 the increase above inflation in the Netherlands might have been negative, but in the province of North-Brabant, where Eindhoven lies, the increase was moderated (1% in the Netherlands and 2.5% in North-Brabant for single family houses, and 0% respectively 1% for apartments). Moreover, because Trudo had received the land for free in 1994 there were no interest charges in case of delay. In sum, it seems clear that waiting was, from an economic point of view, an interesting option. However, we did not find evidence of specific decisions of Trudo to use its option to wait and delay. Also, it is not clear whether the option to wait has affected value capturing significantly, as the lump-sum contribution from the municipality (about €10m) was already clear and agreed in 2000. Thus, since 2000 the room for negotiating contributions was quite narrow.

Findings in Kop van Oost (apartments)
In 2000, the property developer Mr. Hollestelle, who had agreed with the former landowner *Houtgroep-Pont Eecen* what seems to have been an option to buy the land, initiated negotiations with the Municipality of Groningen. After the selling of the land in 2001 (Hollestelle sold the land to IBC), and in 2002 (Heijmans bought IBC), negotiations ended with the signing of a Development Agreement in June 2005. In 2001 and 2002, the national average prices of new dwellings increased above inflation by about 6% each year. For apartments in the province of Groningen also, prices increased above inflation during 2003 (4.5%), 2004 (7%) and 2005 (9.5%). There is not much information available about the price of land, and whether IBC and Heijmans had to pay interest charges or not, but based on the large price increases during the negotiation process (2000-2005), it seems reasonable to conclude that waiting, from an economic point of view, was an interesting option.

The option to wait seems to have delayed the process. During the negotiations between Hollestelle and IBC (about 2000-2001) Hollestelle might have chosen to delay selling until these negotiations ended. The situation that rose after Heijmans bought IBC in 2002 is clearer. Heijmans decided to 'redefine' the plan, as this developer used other profit criteria than IBC. This led to the re-making the plans, something similar to what happened in *De Funen*. In other words, Heijmans used its option to wait in order to change the plans (Buitelaar et al., 2008: 58; Interview with Segeren, 2008).

It seems that the option to wait has not only delayed, but also weakened the negotiation position of the municipality and thus lowered capturing value increase. From the beginning of the negotiations, the developer argued that there was no much financial room in the project, making clear to the municipality that there were not many value capturing possibilities. The municipality, which has not had access to the financial calculations of the developer, seems to have assumed, in the early stages, that it could not ask much from the developer. Also, the municipality accepted several reductions in the costs for public space (Buitenlaar et al., 2008: 113-114). The municipality may have accepted because it was in a hurry: the site influences the image of the area, which is situated between the historic city and the new greenfield scheme *Meerstad*.

Findings in Stationskwartier (apartments and offices)
Stationskwartier in Breda is peculiar, compared with the other cases. Here, the Municipality of Breda bought the land from the developer (Dutch Railways), provides the infrastructure, and sells the land back. The municipality and Dutch Railways were since the 90's involved in getting this project accepted; together they lobbied by the Central Government to get Breda designated as a New Key Project. However, it seems that serious negotiations between the public bodies and the Dutch Railways only came after the municipality and the central government had reached an agreement about the public subsidies in February 2002. In 2003, the municipality approved the Masterplan Central Breda (*Masterplan Centraal Breda*), which included a business

case. Negotiations ended in May 2006 with a definitive Development Agreement with Dutch Railways. During the negotiations (2002?-2006), prices of apartments in North-Brabant, where Breda lies, increased moderately above inflation (0% in 2003, 1% in 2004, 1.5% in 2005 and 5% in 2006). There were no interest charges: Dutch Railways had owned the land for a long time, and the municipality had not yet bought the land from Dutch Railways. The municipality had bought at that time only a few small plots. Hence, it seems that waiting was, from the economic point of view, an interesting option for Dutch Railways. However, in this case it seems that this was an interesting option for the municipality also, which shares part of the financial risks of the operation and might also profit from higher market prices.

It is not possible to conclude, based on direct evidence, whether the option to wait has played a significant role in delaying the project. Nevertheless, it seems reasonable to think that this might have been the case: it seems that the municipality has aimed to get a share in the profits, and that Dutch Railways has offered some resistance to this. That is, either the developer, or the municipality, or both have used their option to wait. This could explain the relatively long negotiation process. Another study of this case includes similar conclusions (Krabben & Needham, 2008: 660). Besides delay, the option to wait might also have weakened the negotiation position of the municipality and lowered capturing value increase. It seems reasonable that the option to wait exercised by Dutch Railways has influenced the final negotiation results, i.e. that Dutch Railways has got a higher price for its land.

Conclusions

It seems plausible to conclude that the option to wait is exercised often. This was clear in *Kop van Oost*, and probable in *De Funen* and *Stationskwartier*. Asked about whether these findings might be exceptional within urban regeneration in the Netherlands, several experts considered that it is not unusual that landowners exercise their option to wait and delay development, although they also emphasized that this is not the only factor causing delay in Dutch urban regeneration (Van den Brand en Hoekstra, interviews in 2008). The cases suggest that the option to wait may have had important consequences for the price of the land, the profits of the developer, and the negotiation position of the municipality also. In *De Funen* and *Kop van Oost* this was clear.

Exercising the option to wait might have been financially advantageous for the landowners and/or the developers, as we have argued. However, there is a second possible explanation, namely a low economic feasibility of the operations: in at least *De Funen* and *Kop van Oost,* the developer objected to municipalities' requirements, arguing that they threatened the financial feasibility of the operation. According to this explanation, confronted with too high development costs, developers might have no other option than to delay (because inflated development costs influence the final profit of developers and thus their possibilities to contribute, see causal model in section 2.4.2). However, it was not so easy to assess in *De Funen* and *Kop van Oost* whether this was indeed the real reason for delay. To accurately assess the economic feasibility, accounted land costs, profit margins of the developer and development costs, together with the initial profit, should be known. However, information about this is a sensitive matter, and usually developers do not disclose such information. My own estimations provided interesting information (for an overview of development costs and profits in the Dutch cases, see Annex 4). In *Kruidenbuurt*, according to figures given by the developer (most of postings 1-7) and by own estimations (posting 8, total returns), it is not clear what the profit margin was. The developer's final profit might be about €24m, but this excludes a minimum land price (which the developer did not had to pay because he obtained the land for free in 1994). In *Kop van Oost*, according to figures given by the developer (Heijmans), his final profit is very narrow: €112m minus €110m = €2m. However, my own estimations suggest that there might be a larger final profit, about €29m. This suggests that the developers' financial objections to the municipality's requirements might not be strong. In *Stationskwartier*, according to my own estimations, there is a clear final profit for Dutch Railways: €480/520 minus 350/360m= €120/180m. In other words, this estimation suggests that the Municipality of Breda could have asked for more contributions for public infrastructure and facilities.

Both possible explanations of the findings in the studied cases seem to be generalizable. They largely match with several experts' view about the general situation in urban development in the Netherlands. In general, for those cases in which landowners exercise their option to wait, experts give the following possible reasons: (1) it is a way of counteracting the requirements of municipalities, such as those related to value capturing. Another source confirms that developers threatening to withdraw a plan if municipalities do not lower requirements is not exceptional in the Netherlands (Buitelaar et al., 2008: 17, 94-96, 108-110, 112-114); (2) developers expect higher selling prices if they wait; (3) they expect to sustain the market prices by rationing the delivery of new dwellings; and (4) it might be handy when confronted with many projects at the same time. Specifically for urban regeneration, two additional reasons are mentioned: (5) land is here owned by many landowners, just some of whom prefer to wait; (6) developers are confronted with higher development costs, so the financial feasibility is insecure (Van den Brand en Hoekstra, interviews in 2008). An interviewed representative of the developers argued similarly when he said that development was often delayed because municipalities require too much (Fokkema, interview 2007).

7.4.5 Procedure for the preparation and approval of binding rules

Summary of the findings

The 2008 Physical Planning Act has introduced changes in the guarantees given to initiators. From 2008 onwards, municipalities are obliged to determine within eight weeks an application for modification of the land use plan. This might affect capturing value increase. On the one hand, this measure could diminish the freedom of municipalities in the negotiations, and thus worsen the capturing of value increase. On the other hand, it could encourage developers to submit more applications, and accelerate thus the implementation. Regarding the possibilities to modify and detail the binding rules, and to adapt the geographical scope of the plan area in order to facilitate the negotiations: this flexibility seems not to affect the capturing of value increase significantly, but might be relevant for the tempo of implementation. Finally, regarding the possibility of detailing an outline land use plan, this might potentially offer, in some cases, some negotiation room for municipalities.

7.4.5.1 Guarantees for those taking the initiative

Under the 2008 Act municipalities, more than before, might be now obliged to take a formal decision about an application to modify the binding rules (*verzoek tot bestemmingswijziging*), and this must happen within eight weeks (article 3.9 for a modification of the land use plan and 3.12 for a departure). The municipality must argue its decision properly, which means that the decision must be in accordance with the policy stated in the land use plan and in the Structure Vision, if such document exists. The municipality can refuse the application within the period of eight weeks; afterwards he is supposed to have agreed with the application. If the municipality nevertheless refuses after this period the applicant can appeal to the courts. Of course, the applicant can anyway appeal against the decision of refusing, whether it has taken place within or after the period of eight weeks. Actually, this is new: before the 2008 Act appeal was not possible, and now it is. This means that a municipality cannot ignore such an application, that it is obliged to assess each application, and cannot reject without a proper argumentation (Tweede Kamer der Staten-Generaal (2003: 31; Vrom, 2007c: 31-32; Buuren et al, 2009: 116). It is not possible to empirically assess whether the novelty influenced capturing value increase in the studied cases, because the cases fell under the previous Physical Planning Act. However, it seems plausible to conclude that the novelty of the 2008 Act will have some consequences for value capturing. A consulted expert said the following (De Wolff, interview 2008): on the one hand, in some specific cases, the room to refuse applications could decrease, and this could weaken the negotiating position of the municipality. For example, it could be that no proper arguments could be found to refuse an application because the land use plan and/or the Structure Vision already foresee the development. On the other hand, the novelty might reduce the risks that developers have to bear, and therefore stimulate development initiatives, which might imply an acceleration of the development process. There is however no unanimity about whether this aspect might be relevant (Verdaas, interview in 2008).

7.4.5.2 Flexibility to modify and detail afterwards approved binding rules

There is in the Netherlands the possibility to modify (*wijziging*) and depart (*vrijstelling/projectbesluit*) from the land use plan following a shorter procedure than if a new land use plan must be approved, and there is also the possibility of detailing afterwards an outline land use plan (*uitwerking*).

Modification of the land use plan following a short procedure (wijziging)
There is the possibility of modifying the land use plan without having to make and approve a new one, following a much shorter procedure. This happens as follows: the land-use plan can prescribe that the municipality can modify it later (article 11.1 of the old Act, article 3.6 new Act). Data from 1987 until 1993 show that this way of modification was used very often (Van Damme & Verdaas 1996: 79-80). It seems that nowadays this form of modification is common too. Cases *Kop van Oost* and *Stationskwartier* included it in their land use plan. Public officers in the municipalities of Groningen and Rotterdam confirm that it is still a frequently used instrument (Interviews with Dollinga and Egberts, 2007).

The land-use plan must then prescribe the limits to the modification. Jurisprudence has developed the criterion that a land-use plan that includes the possibility of modification must include also an objective delimitation (*objectieve begrenzing*) of the modification. The jurisprudence has also defined how far a modification can go. Land uses can be replaced by new ones, or the allowed building volume can be increased, provided that the land-use plan states explicitly the alternative land uses and volume, and provided that the new land uses and volume do not change significantly the structure of the plan (Van der Ree 2000: 428, 435; Klaasen, 2002: 175, 179; interview with Porrey, 2007; Database Kluwer, 2006)[14].

In case *Kop van Oost* the 2006 land use plan foresees the possibility both of rezoning the land use (rezoning the given residential use into commercial facilities) and of modifying the building envelop (modifying the given building envelope, relocating the building sites, and even introducing new buildings, provided that noise nuisance remains under the legal limits). In case *Stationskwartier* the 2007 land use plan prescribes several possibilities for modification that imply a change of land use: any given use can be rezoned into constructions as masts, antenna's, etc, of no more than 50 meter height. It is possible to make such a construction upon the building, but also to substitute a building for such a construction. Another possibility, limited to a specific plot, is to rezone the given uses housing, office space and commercial facilities into hotel.

However, it seems clear that in the cases, this possibility of modification did not lead to more contributions. The development agreements were already sealed before the approval of the land use plan. Modifications of the plan have not led in the studied

---

14 Examples of this are:
- The municipality of Woensdrecht was able to change the existing land-use from business area to housing, after the present companies moved to other location [Vz. ABRS 29 May 1995 (Woensdrecht), nr. F01.94.0300];
- Small municipalities that are allowed to build only to accommodate their own population can use modification to re-zone later to housing, when the new housing is needed. This was the case in the municipalities of Zeevang and Leende [Vz. ABRS 3 April 1997 (Zeevang), nrs. E01.97.0046 and F01.97.0026; ABRS 6 July 1998 (Leende), nr. E01.96.0165].

cases to renegotiations of the contributions. However, this possibility of modification might facilitate implementation, as it creates flexibility to change the programme to adapt to changing circumstances. This can be important for developers when reacting to more favourable possibilities during the development process.

Departure from the land use plan following a shorter procedure (vrijstelling/ projectbesluit)

Major departures from the land use plan are possible (following articles 19 and 19a of the Physical Planning Act previous to 2008, and chapter 3.3 of the new Act), and are very common in practice. The departure can change substantially the permitted land uses and building volume. In cases *De Funen*, *Kruidenbuurt* and *Kop van Oost* the municipalities processed, together with the new land use plan, major departures from the old land use plan for part of the site: a small plot meant for offices in *De Funen*, and about one quarter of the plan area in *Kruidenbuurt* and *Kop van Oost*. However, the departures did not lead to more contributions, additional to those already agreed in the negotiations that preceded the approval of the new land use plan. Instead, in *Kruidenbuurt* and *Kop van Oost* the departures have accelerated the commencement of the works by about half a year or more. This allowed granting the first building permits without having to wait for the definitive approval of the new land use plan. In *De Funen* this was not clear: the departure was granted on November 2000, while the land use plan was definitively approved one month earlier. However, departures can be used in another way than in the studied cases. Instead of being processed parallel to a new land use plan to anticipate the granting of a building permit, it can be and is often used alone, as a way of allowing the regeneration of the site without having to approve a new land use plan. It seems reasonable to conclude that such a use of the legal possibility of departure has similar effects on capturing value increase as when processing a normal new land use plan (see sections 7.4.1 to 7.4.3).

Detailing the outline Land use Plan (uitwerking)

Land use plans can include outline land use regulations that can be detailed afterwards (*Globaal BP met uitwerkingsplicht*). The detailing follows a short procedure. The law[15] and the jurisprudence[16] delimit the 'minimum' contents of the outline land-use regulations and prescribe that the plan must state the objective delimitation (*objectieve begrenzing*) for the detailing. This means that the detailing must take place within established limits (Van Zundert 2004: 148; Van der Ree, 2000: 434). As a consequence of these limits, the detailing cannot introduce 'new' land-use possibilities,

15 Article 13.2 1985 Physical Planning Decree; Explanatory Memorandum of the 1985 Physical Planning Act (Tweede Kamer zitting 1955-56, no. 2, p.p. 14-15).

16 KB 19 February 1982 (Norg), in Bouwrecht 1982, p. 511; Afdeling rechtspraak 4 June 1985 (Amsterdam), in Bouwrecht 1985, p. 915; ABRS 9 june 1998 (Amsterdam), in AB 1998, 338, and in Gst. 1999, 7105/6; Afdeling rechtspraak 4 June 1985 (Amsterdam), in Bouwrecht 1985, p. 915; HR 23 September 1988 (Purmerend), in Bouwrecht 1989, p. 113; KB 1 September 1987 (Rozenburg), nr. 9, in Bouwrecht 1988, p. 31; ABRS 9 june 1998 (Amsterdam), in AB 1998, 338, and in Gst. 1999, 7105/6.

nor can it exclude any of the possible land-uses prescribed in the outline regulations. However, it can shift the use possibilities between different plots and is therefore potentially interesting in negotiations with the landowners.

In *Kruidenbuurt* the land use plan, approved in April 2005, prescribes outline land use regulations for most of the plan area. The detailing for the first half of the site was approved in January 2007, and affected significantly the building possibilities: the exact number of dwellings, for which the 2005 plan established a minimum number of 650; the building volume, for which the plan established some elements of the building envelope, without fixing a maximal number of m^2; and some other possibilities. However, detailing has not had consequences for capturing value increase because the development agreements were already sealed before the approval of the land use plan. In *Stationskwartier* the situation is different. Here only 3% of the plan area is covered by outline land use regulations, which have not been detailed at the moment of data gathering. The Development Agreement sealed before the approval of the land use plan did not include the landowners of this part of the plan area. It is unclear whether detailing will be preceded by negotiations and thus to additional capturing value increase, but potentially it could offer some negotiation room to the municipality to ask some contributions to the landowners.

7.4.5.3 Flexibility to adapt the geographical scope (the plan area) of the binding rules accordingly to negotiations with landowners

It seems that land use plans and departures from them can be quite flexibly adapted to the negotiation process. Neither the law nor the jurisprudence establishes general limitations to the minimum size of the plan area, which means that they can be as small as a specific plot (Bosch & Hanemaayer 1992: quoted in Bregman & Sievers 2002; Van Damme & Verdaas 1996: 73-78). Also, in principle there is no maximal number of plots, which means that, if necessary, a plan or departure can be made for each plot, no matter how many plots they are. The jurisprudence gives no general criterion for disapproving developments based on different small plans. On the contrary[17], the use of many small binding plans is very common. Data from 1987 until 1993 seem to confirm this. In that period, more than 50% of all the land-use plans in the province of Gelderland were small plans (Van Damme & Verdaas 1996: 76-78). After 1993 the use of small binding plans has remained very common in practice.

The studied cases refer to larger sites, of at least 5 ha (*Kop van Oost*). In all of them the municipality was free to delimitate the plan area. They did so very carefully, following most of the time considerations related to the property boundaries. In general it seems plausible that this flexibility has helped to facilitate the tempo of implementation, in the sense that proposals included only those landowners willing to develop.

17 Afdeling Rechtspraak Raad van State 21 March 1991 (Roosendaal en Nispen), in AB 1992 p. 353.

7.5 The actual degree of captured value increase in the Netherlands

This chapter focuses on whether the capturing value increase goals are achieved or not and on the distribution of costs between the involved parties: who has paid which public infrastructure and facilities, and possibly some extras? We look also at whether the goals have been achieved on time. The main sources of information are the four cases, complemented with other written sources and interviews with relevant experts. The conclusions are summarized in table 20.

On-site infrastructure provision costs

In all the studied cases, public bodies contributed heavily to on-site infrastructure provision costs. In *De Funen* the municipality assumed an important part: the refurbishing of an adjacent road (with a clear, but not exclusive, on-site character), and part of the public space (parking places and part of a park). The developer paid the costs of the public space with an exclusive on-site character and the other part of the park. In *Kruidenbuurt* the municipality paid about one third of the costs and some additional costs for public infrastructure situated within the plan area that serves a wider area. The developer (a housing association) contributed two thirds[18]. In *Kop van Oost* the municipality paid a small part of the public space, and the full costs of refurbishing a main road situated within the plan area but serving a wider area. The central government subsidized 25% of the soil decontamination costs, which were not very high. The developer paid the rest: constructing most of the on-site public space and possibly paying minor damage compensation to neighbours. In *Stationskwartier,* subsidies from the municipality, province and central government covered about two thirds of the costs: the public roads and space within the site, and part of other on-site infrastructure (soil decontamination, preparation of plans). The developer (Dutch Railways) paid about one third of the costs. The new railway and bus stations (situated within the plan area, but serving a much wider area) are considered below.

It seems that, in general, these findings cannot be considered an exception. Public bodies in the Netherlands usually contribute heavily, in urban regeneration, to on-site infrastructure. Both a study of the participation of housing associations in 31 regeneration sites (De Kam & Needham, 2001: 69), and a more recent study of eight cases of private land development in urban regeneration sites (Buitelaar et al., 2008; Segeren, interview 2008) include similar findings. Not only the municipality, but also other governmental levels, contribute heavily, with subsidy programmes (e.g. *Investeringsbudget Stedelijke Vernieuwing*). Interviewed experts confirm this (Verdaas and Van Wageningen, interviews 2008). These conclusions coincide with the recommendation made by the Ministry for Housing, Planning and the Environment

18 And in addition provided new accommodation for all the former inhabitants.

Table 20. Comparison table results on capturing value increase in the Netherlands.

	On-site land development costs		Land for on-site public infrastructure		Land for on-site public buildings		On-site public buildings		Affordable housing		Contributions off-site public infrastructure and facilities	Cream off betterment
	Developer	**Public body**	**Developer**	**Public body**	**Developer**	**Public body**	**Developer**	**Public body**	**Developer**	**Public bodies**		
General knowledge NL	Part of the costs	Heavy subsidizing	Important part of the land	Important part of the land	Commercial dev nothing, housing assoc possibly	Public body provides most of the land	Commercial dev nothing, housing assoc do contribute	Almost always	Commercial dev do not, housing association do	Sometimes	Almost no contributions of developers to public infra/fac situated outside plan area, and modest contribution to infra/fac situated within plan area but serving a wider area.	none
De Funen Amsterdam	Important part	Important part	Important part	Important part	none	none	none	none	30% units, less than 30% volume	Subsidy €23,000/unit	A small piece park at border plan area.	none
Kruidenbuurt Eindhoven (total value real estate € 150 m)[19]	€ 20 m (13% total value real estate)	E 10 m (7% total value real estate)	7% total plan area	25% total plan area, 36% incl adjacent roads	none	none	none	none	45% units (developer is housing association)	none	€ 0.5 for public facility outside plan area and small contribution to road within plan area.	none
Kop van Oost Groningen (total value real estate € 140 m)	€ 6 m (5% total value real estate) excl VAT	A minor part	23% total plan area	6% total plan area, 29% incl adjacent roads	none	none	none	none	none	none	none	none
Stationskwartier Breda (total value real estate € 500 m)	€ 20-30 m (4-6% total value real estate)	€ 42 m (8% total value real estate)	27% total plan area	14% total plan area	none	none	none	none	none	none	Minor part of costs, and most of the land needed for new Railways Station (developer is Dutch Railways)	Eventual share in profits.

Grey: case in which the developer/landowner contributes the most of the four cases.
White: case in which the developer/landowner contributes the less of the four cases.

19 Total value real estate' are the total returns accruing from the selling of the final real estate (thus includes the selling of the new buildings).

over the allocation of costs in urban regeneration between municipalities, housing associations, real estate investors, commercial developers and inhabitants owning their house in de regeneration areas. According to this recommendation, public bodies in urban regeneration should be financially responsible for the refurbishing of the public infrastructure, at least when the public space is old and needs refurbishing to bring it to current quality standards (Vrom, 2005: 22-23).

Land needed for on-site public infrastructure and facilities

Regarding the land needed for on-site infrastructure provision (excluding the land needed for public buildings), in the studied cases public bodies provided most, or an important part, of it (roads, public space). In *De Funen* the municipality provided a road at the border but within the plan area of the land use plan, and part of the park. The developer provided the land for the public space that has a clear on-site character, and for part of the park. In *Kruidenbuurt* the municipality provided most of the needed land, and the developer a minor part. In *Kop van Oost* the estimation depends on whether some adjacent roads (situated within but at the borders of the plan area) are included or not: the municipality provided more than the half of the needed land if the adjacent roads are included in the calculation, and a minor part if excluded. In *Stationskwartier* the municipality provided one third of the land for on-site infrastructure provision and the developer (Dutch Railways) the other two thirds. The new railway station is not included here, for this is considered below as off-site infrastructure. It seems that, in general, these case-based findings cannot be considered an exception. Public bodies in the Netherlands, in urban regeneration, usually provide most or at least an important part of the land that is needed for on-site public infrastructure. Municipalities usually own land in such areas. Most of the time this land is former public space, sometimes normal plots. A recent study supports this, and also that municipalities not only provide former public space, but often also building plots that were already public or have been bought for the purpose of regeneration (Buitelaar et al., 2008: 82, 100; Segeren, interview 2008). Several experts confirm this (Segeren, Verdaas and Van Wageningen, interviews 2008). Again, these conclusions coincide with the principles of allocation of costs recommended by the Ministry (Vrom, 2005: 21-23). Although that document refers explicitly only to the costs and not to the land, its general principle that public infrastructure and public space are the responsibility of public bodies includes the land under them.

In all studied cases the municipality received free the ownership rights over the public infrastructure and the land under it (the land that was not already its property). This also seems to be a generalizable conclusion, although there are exceptions. There are cases in which public infrastructure finally becomes shared ownership of the owners of the real estate, for example public space situated above parking garages (Segeren and Verdaas, interviews 2008).

Regarding the land needed for public facilities (the land under the public buildings): the studied cases do not include public buildings of any kind within the plan area of the land use plan. It seems that in *Stationskwartier* in Breda several public bodies will open an office in the new station (court of justice, post office). However, this cannot be considered as capturing value increase because those public bodies will have to pay the normal commercial price for the office space they are planning to use. The new railway station is considered below. Data from an own survey of 56 urban regeneration districts suggest that these case-based findings are not an exception when projects are led by commercial developers (of those districts a minority, see Annex 5). None of the studied regeneration schemes led by commercial developers on privately owned land include privately financed public buildings. It seems that, in general, in urban regeneration on privately owned land led by commercial developers in the Netherlands, this is normal. The land needed for public buildings, if they exist, is usually provided by the respective public body. Again, this matches with the mentioned recommendation of the Ministry. That document states that in urban regeneration, public bodies should be responsible for the public buildings. Although no explicit reference is made to the land under public buildings, it seems clear that the Ministry considers that public bodies are also responsible for acquiring the needed land (Vrom, 2005: 22, 24). On the other hand, it seems to be common that housing associations contribute to public facilities such as care facilities or other buildings with a public function, although specific figures are not available.

On-site public facilities (the buildings)

This has already been handled above together with the land that is needed for the public buildings.

Land and money for on-site and off-site social/affordable housing

Of the four studied cases, only *Kruidenbuurt* and *De Funen* included social/affordable housing. In *Kruidenbuurt* the developer, a housing association, will develop about the half of the total number of units as social dwellings. The developer bears thus the difference between the price of each unit (*bedrijfswaarde*) and the free market price. Besides the social rented units, the developer will sell about one quarter of the dwellings for a maximal selling price of € 240,000 final price (price of 1-1-2003, to be updated each year). However, it is not clear whether this could be considered as a cost to the developer, as we do not know whether this price (€240,000) is below the price in the free market. In *De Funen* the developer builds some social housing (less than one third of the units). However, here the developer receives an important public subsidy from the central government, thus it is not clear whether the developer actually subsidizes the social units, probably not.

The findings in the mentioned own survey of 56 regeneration districts seem to confirm the exceptionality of case *De Funen*. None of those schemes that were found to be located on privately owned land and implemented by commercial developers[20] included any social housing. It seems that, in general, in urban regeneration in the Netherlands, commercial developers neither develop social housing, nor do they pay the costs of it. Social housing seems to be a task almost exclusively for housing associations. A recent study of eight urban regeneration cases agrees (Buitelaar et al., 2008; Segeren, interview 2008). As a consequence, social housing most of the time is built only in those projects where housing associations or public bodies control (part of) the land, such as in *Kruidenbuurt*. This conclusion matches with the mentioned recommendation of the Ministry. This states that it is the housing association, in urban regeneration, which is financially responsible for the deficit that is implied in the development of social houses (Vrom, 2005: 23).

Land and money for off-site public infrastructure and facilities

Regarding public infrastructure and facilities situated outside the plan area: of the four studied cases, only in two of them did the developer contribute to this, and then only modestly. In *Kruidenbuurt* the developer contributed € 0.5m towards a public facility situated outside the plan area. In *De Funen* the developer provided about half of a park (land and costs of construction) situated outside the plan area of the land use plan, between the new building and the existing neighbourhood. However, the land use plan here was delimited very tightly, and actually this park serves clearly and mainly the new building in the plan area. In general it seems that the conclusion is generalizable that developers in urban regeneration on privately owned land do not contribute significantly to public infrastructure or facilities located outside the plan area. In the mentioned survey of 56 urban regeneration districts, none of those projects located on privately owned land and implemented by commercial developers included contributions for off-site infrastructure, whether this was situated outside or inside the plan area. Kolprom (2000: 31-53) and a recent study of eight cases (Buitelaar et al., 2008: 90; Segeren, interview 2008) agree with this. Also, this conclusion seems to fit with the mentioned recommendation of the Ministry. This does not even mention the possibility of charging the development in question with public infrastructure located elsewhere. Moreover, that document follows the principle that public infrastructure is the responsibility of public bodies (see above). However, it seems also that, sometimes, urban regeneration schemes do contribute to off-site public infrastructure and facilities with a monetary payment to a fund (*Fonds Bovenwijkse Voorzieningen*). Contributions, if they are made, could be between €4.5 and €10 for every square metre of serviced building plot (Van Wageningen, Stauttener, interviews 2008).

---

20 Hoograven, Vicona, Onixweg 1-3 (in the city of Utrecht); Kanaleneiland/Transwijk, Winkelcentrum (in Utrecht); Malburgen, Winkelcentrum Drieslag (in Arnhem); Zuilen/Ondiep, winkelcentrum Rokade (in Utrecht); Heuvel, WSST (in Breda); Presikhaaf, Weldamlaan (in Arnhem). On two others the situation was doubtful, for land was private owned but will be acquired by a Public-private Partnership (Berflo Es, in Engelo), or land was only partly private owned (Centrumgebied Kanaleneiland, in Utrecht)

Regarding public infrastructure and facilities situated within the plan area, but serving a wider area (that is why they are considered here off-site): schemes might include these in their plan area. In the studied cases this was sometimes clear, sometimes not, and in any case developers did not contribute much, except in *Stationskwartier*. In *De Funen* a street situated at the border but within the plan area has been refurbished. The developer will not contribute to this. In *Kruidenbuurt* several streets situated at the borders but within the plan area will be refurbished. The developer will not contribute significantly: the land was already public (the existing roads) and the municipality will pay most of the costs of refurbishing. In *Kop van Oost* a street situated at the border but within the plan area will be refurbished. The developer will not contribute; the municipality provides the land (the existing road) and pays the refurbishing costs. In *Stationskwartier* a new street and, especially, the new railway and bus station will clearly serve a wider area. Most of the costs (not the land) will be paid with public subsidies. The developer (Dutch Railways) will contribute with a relatively minor amount to the costs of the new railway station, but will provide all the land needed for this station and most of the land for the new public streets. In short, in the studied cases, developers pay, if they pay at all, only a small or marginal part of the costs of the public infrastructure and facilities situated within the plan area that serve a wider area. Also, public bodies provide most of the needed land, with the exception of *Stationskwartier*. The mentioned survey of 56 urban regeneration districts confirms these case-based findings: the surveyed schemes on privately owned land and implemented by commercial developers include, at the most, only a little public space directly related to the scheme. An expert confirmed that in urban regeneration on privately owned land the contribution of private parties to this is usually modest (Van Wageningen, interview in 2008). And, again, these conclusions seem to fit with the mentioned recommendation of the Ministry (Vrom, 2005): public infrastructure is a responsibility of public bodies.

Creaming off plus value

In the studied cases, public bodies, as such and not as landowners, receive no share of the profits. The exception might be *Stationskwartier*, where the municipality bears some risks in the infrastructure provision and might enjoy some profit. Also, the municipality will obtain the market value of the future use possibilities for its land, which is about 5-7% of the total plan area. But in general, in case of regeneration schemes on privately owned land, municipalities do not receive a share in the profits of operations (Segeren, Verdaas and Van Wageningen, interviews in 2008).

Tempo of implementation of the capturing value increase goals

Now we take into account possible side effects, of which special attention has been given to the tempo of implementation of the capturing value increase goals. In the studied cases, if land use plans include implementation schedules (*Kruidenbuurt* and *Stationskwartier*), these are very vague and are included in the Explanation, the part of the plan that is not legally binding. The legally binding parts of land use plans cannot include deadlines for the start or completion of development. In *De Funen, Krui-*

denbuurt and seemingly also in *Stationskwartier*, it was the development agreement (not the Land use plan) that included clear deadlines for the delivery of public infrastructure and facilities. Deadlines, if existing (whether in the not legally binding part of the land use plans and/or in the development contracts) were or will be sometimes fulfilled (phases 1 and 2 in *Kruidenbuurt*) and sometimes not (the deadlines for most of the scheme in *De Funen*, included in the development agreement). It seems that in all of the cases there were almost no deadlines that were very hard, in the sense that delay of start or delivery of development would lead to significant sanctions for the developer. For example, in *De Funen* the delay was very significant, without this bringing any disadvantages for the developer. An interviewed public officer considered in this case that the municipality would not have had much chance to win a legal suit on this point. In *Kruidenbuurt* the deadlines, included in the agreement, seem also not very hard. The exception could be *Stationskwartier*. Based on interviews, it seems that the deadlines included in the Development Agreement (which was not available to me) might have legal consequences: the developer will be obliged to sell his land for a low price if he delays more than two years the acquisition of the serviced building plots. In short, deadlines, if existing, were not very hard, with the exception of *Stationskwartier*.

These case-based findings seem not to be an exception in urban regeneration in the Netherlands. Deadlines, if they are made, are very soft, and delay is common. Schemes in which land use plans have been approved, but in which there are significant development delays, are not an exception at all. Also, there are cases known of development that has never started, or started only after many years of delay and only after development terms, and sometimes also the land use plan, have been substantially redefined (Segeren, interview 2008). It seems clear that delay is very common in urban regeneration in the Netherlands (Segeren, Van den Brand, Hoekstra, interviews in 2008).

7.6 Causal relationships between formal rules relevant to zoning and capturing value increase in the Netherlands

Section 7.4 gave an answer to Preparatory research question 3: it inferred the possible causal relations between the independent variable 'formal rules relevant to zoning' and the dependent variable 'capturing value increase'. This chapter summarizes first the inferred causalities and then assesses the effect of possible third variables.

7.6.1 The inferred causalities

The findings suggest that the following sub-variables can influence positively and/or negatively the degree of capturing value increase (see also the causal model in section 2.4.2 and figure 32):

- Sub-variable a, Some Certainty about the future building possibilities, together with Uncertainty about the future contributions: this might have been negative for intermediary variables *negotiation position* (of the municipality) and *accounted land costs*, and thus negative for capturing value increase;
- Sub-variable b, Contents of binding rules: not being able to include obligations and implementation schedules seems to have influenced negatively intermediary variable *negotiation position* (of the municipality);
- Sub-variable c, Making binding rules conditional on agreement: the indirect possibilities of conditioning the approval of binding rules to securing public infrastructure and facilities can be positive for intermediary variable *negotiation position* (of the municipality), and thus on capturing value increase. However, legal limitations to these indirect possibilities have some negative effects;
- Sub-variable d, Property rights: the interdependency between municipalities and landowners seems to have a negative effect on intermediary variables *accounted land costs* (higher costs), *regular profit margins* (negative for capturing value increase, but positive for the developer), *negotiation position* (of the municipality), and *delay*;
- Sub-variable e, Guarantees for those taking initiative: the obligation, introduced in 2008, to determine an application within eight weeks might be negative for intermediary variable *negotiation position* (of the municipality), but positive for intermediary variable *delay*;
- Sub-variable e, Flexibility in modification/departure binding rules: (1) the relative flexibility to modify the land use plan (*wijziging*) seems only to be positive for intermediary variable *delay*. (2) The possibility of departing from the existing land use plan (*vrijstelling/projectbesluit*), when used as complement to the new land use plan, can affect positively intermediary variable *delay*;
- Sub-variable e, Flexibility departing binding rules: the possibility of departing from the existing land use plan (*vrijstelling/projectbesluit*), but not as a complement to the new land use plan, can have, the same as sub-variables a, b and c, a positive effect on intermediary variables *accounted land costs* and *negotiation position* (of the municipality);
- Sub-variable e, Flexibility detailing 'a posteriori': it is not clear whether the possibility of approving outline land use regulations and detailing them afterwards (*globale bestemming met uitwerkingsplicht*) has consequences for capturing value increase, but in some cases it might potentially offer some negotiation room to municipalities. In other words, it might strengthen intermediary variable negotiation position (of the municipality);
- Sub-variable e, Flexibility to adapt the size of the plan area according to negotiations with each landowner: this might be relevant for intermediary variable *delay*.

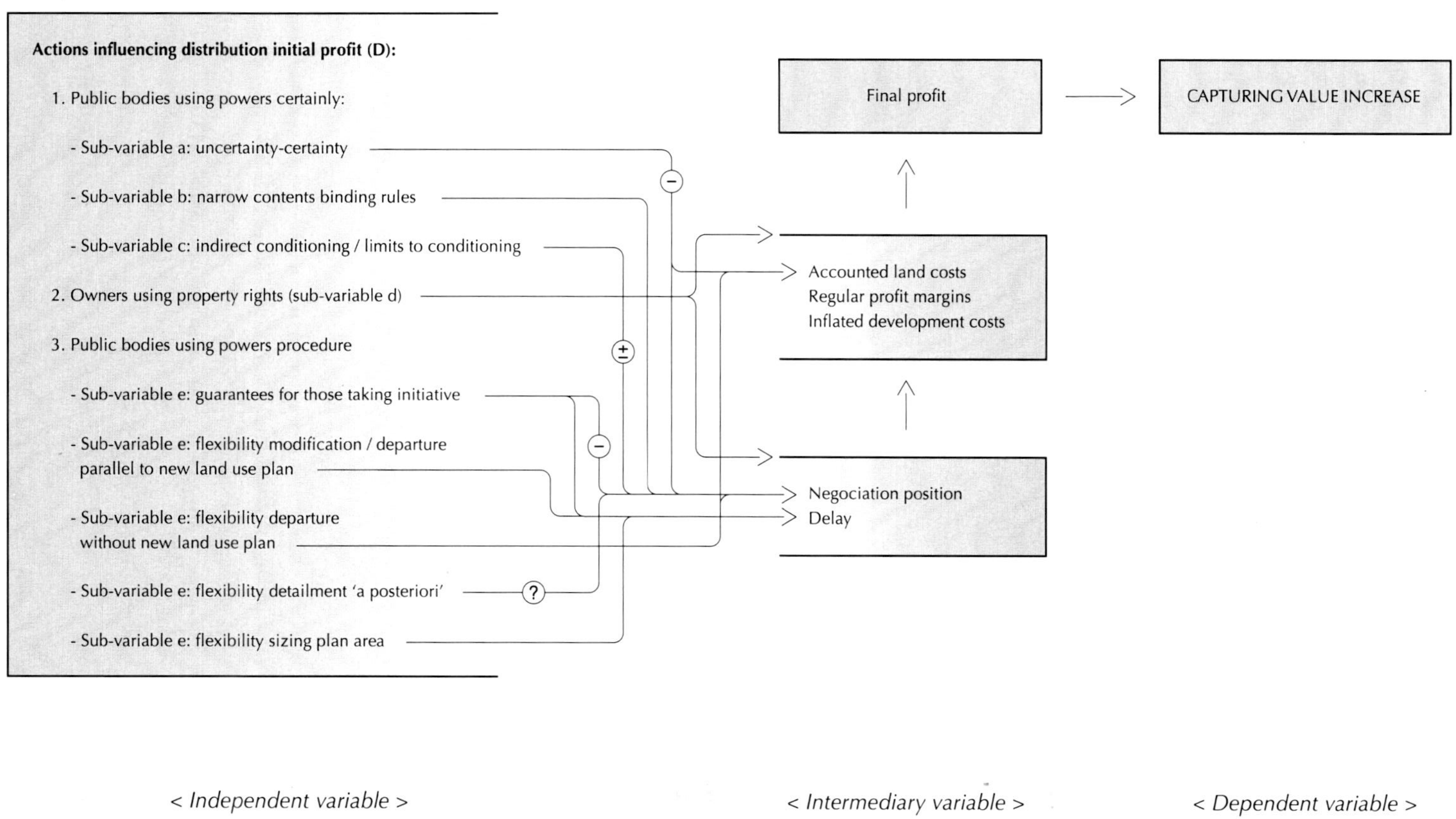

Figure 32. Scheme of the inferred causal relations in the Netherlands between independent variable 'formal rules relevant to zoning', the intermediary variables and the dependent variable 'capturing value increase'.

7.6.2 Possible third variables

Here the effect of other, possible third, variables is assessed, related first to the specific circumstances in the studied cases (variables D4 and D5 of the causal model in section 2.4.2), second to market circumstances (variable A1) and third to presumed high development costs (variables A2 and A3). The goal is to investigate the possibility that the inferred causal relationships turn out to be spurious (see section 3.2.1.2 for more detail about this methodological approach).

Specific circumstances in the studied cases

In Eindhoven, the municipality, at the time of the negotiations about the redevelopment of *Kruidenbuurt,* was used to implementing the public space itself. Both the interviewed developer and a public officer considered that it took some effort to reach an agreement about how the developer should be allowed to take over this task. This might have delayed the process.

In two cases, involved parties considered that internal organizational aspects might have been relevant. This is the case in *Kruidenbuurt,* where according to both the developer and a public officer, a lack of continuity in the municipal organization delayed the process. In *Stationskwartier* also the developer named this as a delaying factor. In *Stationskwartier* an involved public officer considered that the employment of skilled managers in both the central government and in the municipality influenced value capturing positively.

In two cases, involved parties considered that a good personal relationship between the developer and the municipality might have speeded the development process. In *Kruidenbuurt* both the developer and a public officer considered that the good relationship between both has been relevant. In *Kop van Oost,* the developer considered that a good relationship at managerial level might have been of importance.

In *Kop van Oost* the removal of a gas filling station was a relevant delaying factor (interview with Segeren, 2008).

Market circumstances

It has already been considered above that rising housing prices might have stimulated the use of the option to wait in most of the studied cases. For landowners, waiting was an interesting option from the economic point of view as the rising of housing prices translated into risings of the profits (in the form of higher accounted land prices and/or higher regular and final profit margins). Market circumstances, together with the property rights of landowners, which gave them the option to wait and delay development, have thus influenced largely the behaviour of the landowners and the results on the finally captured value increase (for more details see 7.4.4.2) [21].

Financial feasibility

It has already been considered that in urban regeneration schemes some involved parties perceive the financial feasibility as a problem, a problem that might have stimulated the use of the option to wait in several cases. Some of the involved developers had the wish or the need to undertake time-consuming negotiations to enlarge or ensure financial feasibility (see 7.4.4.2). This third variable is mentioned as a general problem in urban regeneration schemes. In other words, in the Netherlands in urban regeneration, high land development costs (which consist of the accounted land costs, the infrastructure provision costs, the plan preparation costs, the soil decontamination costs, the compensation costs and the contributions, see section 2.4.3 for an explanation of these sorts of costs), in combination with a low initial profit, might cause delay and the lowering of requirements because final profits might be insufficient.

---

21 In the studied cases, prices for new apartments (which are most of the new buildings) vary from about € 2,000 to 3,000 per m² floor space, depending on the location, and maybe even higher in Amsterdam:

- *Kop van Oost*, in Groningen: based on the selling brochure of the developer, it was possible to assess the prices of the apartments to be about € 2,500/m² floor space.
- *Stationskwartier*, in Breda: based on the total expected returns given by the developer, it was possible to assess that the prices of the new apartments could be about € 2,000/m² floor space. This estimation seems low when compared with prices in the centre of Breda, where *Stationskwartier* is located. Prices of new apartments in the centrum of Breda vary from € 2,393/m² in scheme WSST (arithmetic average of prices of 19 apartments, on-line site consulted on 9/1/08), to € 2,555/m² in 'Aan de kade' (price of the only apartment to sell when site consulted on 9/1/08), and € 2,600/m² in 'Vista Baluarte' (price of the two apartments to sell when site consulted on 9/1/08).
- *De Funen*, in Amsterdam: here prices must have been higher, as prices in Amsterdam are significantly higher than in Breda and Groningen.
- *Kruidenbuurt*: it was not possible to obtain prices per m² floor space.

TESSORI COLLEGE OOST

CHAPTER 8

Conclusions

The goals of this research are two fold. First we want to learn how to use those formal rules that are relevant to zoning to improve cost recovery in the Netherlands. 'Formal rules relevant to zoning' are all those formal rules for the exercise of both legally binding rules (e.g. a land use plan), including the implications for property rights in land, and non-legally binding policy documents. 'Cost recovery' refers to the recovery, through contributions from private developers, of those costs that are related to the realization of public infrastructure and facilities that benefit the development. Second we want to draw conclusions for the theoretical reflections set out in chapter 2, reflections that have laid the foundations, together with the definition of the problem in chapter 1, for the research questions and their operationalization in chapter 3. The first goal (improving cost recovery in the Netherlands) is achieved in chapter 9 in the form of recommendations to be applied in Dutch urban development practice and legislation. The second goal (theoretical reflections) is achieved in this chapter 8. Both chapters rest on the findings of chapters 5 to 7.

Chapter 2, based on policy network literature and current debates on property rights in land and flexibility in planning, developed two specific methods of 'Network management' for influencing the interactions within the policy networks in urban regeneration, and for influencing the outcomes for capturing value increase. These two methods have been included in a model that explains the various causalities of capturing value increase. The methods have also been formulated as two hypotheses, which have been tested empirically. The first speculates about the effects on capturing value increase of the definition of property rights in land and how this influences the power relationship between the involved public and private parties. The second speculates about the effects of the certainty created by binding rules and non-binding policy documents during development processes. In the causal model a third speculation came up that has also been empirically tested: the assumption that the flexibility in procedures could be relevant for capturing value increase.

Power in the policy networks

It seems that the first two hypotheses might indeed be valid. About the third assumption, it has not been possible to infer clear and generalizable relationships between flexibility and the results on capturing value increase. The findings in all countries suggest that the variables named in the first two hypotheses are indeed relevant for capturing value increase, because they can influence the interactions within the policy networks in urban regeneration. Public bodies in England and especially in Valencia seem, thanks to these tools, to play a role that fits better in the traditional interorganizational approach than in the policy network approach. In other words, public bodies manage to play a role which is more central hierarchical than that of a mere coordinating body.

Municipalities in England and especially in Valencia prescribe beforehand and unilaterally clear requirements and obligations to be fulfilled by property developers and landowners. That is, public bodies set the goals that developers and landowners must fulfil, without previously agreeing this with them. These requirements are the bottom-line during the negotiations. This results in a high level of captured value increase. In Valencia, municipalities go further than in England, as the Valencian municipalities not only set unilaterally the goals, but they have also, thanks to a compulsory land readjustment regulation, powers to select the developer they prefer, if necessary by-passing the landowners and without the need of buying or expropriating the land.

Criticisms of the policy network approach

These findings support a first conclusion regarding the advocated role of public bodies in the policy network approach. The dominant role of public bodies in urban regeneration, especially in Valencia, clearly does not fit within the role that the policy network literature gives them, and it undermines some of the basic assumptions of that literature: that actors are necessarily interdependent, that public bodies must assume a more modest role and cannot be dominant. The findings suggest that public bodies in Valencia and, to a lesser extent in England, are clearly not *primus inter pares*: on the contrary, they are able to unilaterally set out value capturing goals and impose their implementation. An important basis for this dominant role is the possibility in Valencia of avoiding mutual dependency between public bodies and developers/landowners. The policy network approach might have insufficiently worked out the basic idea that underlies the role that it advocates for public bodies. This basic idea is that the government always depends on private actors because these have a veto power on policy-making and implementation. In Valencia, public bodies can effectively avoid this veto power through compulsory land readjustment. This finding should stimulate a reconsideration of the basic assumptions in the advocated role of public bodies in urban development.

The rest of this chapter summarizes the findings for each country, compares them and enumerates the consequences for the theoretical reflections. Here we follow the narrative structure set out in section 3.3.3, which distinguished between the following sub-variables:

1. Certainty beforehand about future building possibilities and contributions;
2. Choosing the contents of the legally binding rules;
3. Making the legally binding rules conditional on the developer securing his contributions;
4. Modulating property rights.

8.1 Certainty beforehand about future building possibilities and contributions

Binding rules and also indicative policy documents can create certainty about future building possibilities and about the contributions that developers will have to make. Certainty can be created before, during, or after negotiations with developers. There are important differences between the studied countries. Spain and the region of Valencia belong to a group of 'plan-led countries', in which there is an important level of legally binding certainty in early stages of the development process. The Netherlands also belongs theoretically to this plan-led system. However, in practice there is flexibility, as a consequence of which the Dutch planning system shows similarities with the 'development-led' planning system. In this system, characteristic of the UK, binding rules are approved after negotiations finish, not before. This is the practice in the Netherlands, not only in recent years, but also from at least the early 1980's. This deviation of the Dutch system from the theoretical working of the plan-led model (a model which the Dutch legislation pre-supposes) seems not to be an exception internationally (for a comparison of the Netherlands with other eight Western European countries, see section 4.1). Let us look at the findings in Valencia, England and the Netherlands in more detail:

Certainty about future building possibilities

Municipalities usually create certainty in the early stages, in different degrees, about the future building possibilities, that is about what the landowner will be able to build. In Valencia this happens through the approval of general land use plans that must cover the whole municipal territory. These plans are highly detailed and legally binding. In the Netherlands and England, municipalities usually approve indicative, not legally binding plans, which create some certainty. Examples of these documents in the Netherlands are *Nota van Uitgangspunten*, *Stedenbouwkundig Plan/Visie*, *Ont-wikkelingsprogramma*, *Programma van Eisen*, *Masterplan*, *Structuurplan*, *Structuurvisie*, etc; and in England *Local Plans*, *Development Plans*, etc. These documents, besides being of an indicative character, include often much more vague and outline prescriptions that the Spanish general plans. Within these clear differences, there seems to be however a trend to increase certainty, at least in Valencia and England. This trend is visible in Valencia since the 1980s and, more recently, in England. Local public bodies tend to increase certainty in order to improve transparency and accountability in their planning decisions. Based on these findings, a first conclusion is that part of the literature on comparative planning systems in Europe may not have distinguished accurately enough the actual differences in this variable between national planning systems, at least with regard to the Spanish versus English and Dutch systems. This literature has tended to conclude a convergence in this that does not match our findings and fundamentally contradicts the literature in Spain, which has repeatedly claimed the singularity of the Spanish planning system because it offers in very early stages of development processes a much higher level of certainty about the development possibilities than any other European country (*confero* European Commission, 1997; Nadin & Stead, 2008: 40, 44-45; Comisión de Expertos sobre Urbanismo, 1996: 31-47; García-Bellido, 1999).

Another conclusion is that more certainty beforehand may result in less public value capturing. It seems that municipalities that prescribe building possibilities early in the development process might stimulate land price increases and might lose a valuable negotiation tool. This seems to lead to less capturing of value increase. However, this sub variable (certainty about future building possibilities) seems to interact closely with the following sub variable (certainty about future contributions, see under). Certainty about building possibilities might be negative for capturing value increase, but if accompanied by certainty about future contributions, it does not necessarily have to be negative.

Certainty about future contributions

The differences between Valencia, England and the Netherlands are larger when looking at the certainty beforehand about the future contributions, that is, the certainty about what the landowner will have to contribute to public infrastructure and facilities. In Valencia there is in the early stages much certainty about future contributions through (1) legal minimal standards for public infrastructure and facilities, (2) local policy and (3) the approval of legally binding General land use plans. This certainty has certainly enlarged the capturing of value increase compared to before the introduction of these measures. English municipalities usually create, increasingly in the last years, some certainty through the approval of (1) site-specific indicative plans that establish the contributions for the development in question, and (2) non site-specific indicative policy documents about generic public value capturing that establish standard contributions for the whole municipality. The approval of these generic documents has been stimulated in recent years by the central British government, and has influenced the capturing of value increase positively. In the Netherlands, most of the time there is no certainty at all, neither created through legally binding nor indicative documents. And if there is some certainty, it is limited. In two of the Dutch cases, the future contributions were clear neither before negotiations took place, nor before the price of land was established. In the other two Dutch cases there was some certainty, but this was due to exceptional circumstances. This uncertainty seems to lower the extent of captured value increase.

Table 21. Degree of certainty in Valencia, England and the Netherlands

	Certainty beforehand about building possibilities	Certainty beforehand about contributions
Valencia	Always, much certainty	Always, much certainty
England	Sometimes, some certainty	Sometimes, some certainty
The Netherlands	Always, some certainty	Almost never, and limited certainty

Table 22. Effects certainty on captured value increase.

	Certainty beforehand about contributions	No certainty about future contributions
Certainty beforehand about building possibilities	+ some capturing value increase	- less capturing value increase
No certainty about future building possibilities	++ more capturing value increase	+ some capturing value increase

++ : more capturing value increase
+ : some capturing value increase
- : less capturing value increase

The explanation for the positive effect which certainty has on contributions is three fold: (1) certainty may reduce the price of land, as developers do indeed take account of the future contributions when calculating the price to be paid to the landowner, and lower land prices augment the financial room for contributing to public infrastructure and facilities; (2) certainty might also influence the accounted land costs (that is, the price at which the land is entered into the accounts for the regeneration project) and the regular profit margin of the developer. The accounted land cost and the regular profit margins are often not set at the start of development processes. At that time, developers often have some room to set them higher or lower. A developer confronted with a high contributions package will tend to account the land for a lower price in the accounts, and accept that this development site will not contribute much to possible losses on other sites. Conversely, a developer confronted with a low contributions package will tend to account the land for a higher price. Regarding regular profit margins, developers can consider at the beginning of development process the size of the profit, which may vary from 5% to 20% or more. Once the price of land and the regular profit margin have been established, lowering them is usually complicated. (3) A third explanation for the positive effect of certainty on contributions is that certainty strengthens the policy base and the moral authority for the public officers to require contributions, so contributions do not need to be introduced as something new in the negotiations. Tables 21 and 22 summarize the findings.

Results of testing the 2nd hypothesis
Within the causal model explained in section 2.4.2, the second hypothesis is that a modification of one of the context variables (formal rules about certainty about development terms, variable B2) could modify the actions of the involved actors (how the local public bodies use their formal powers about certainty on development terms, variable D1). The second hypothesis speculates therefore that:

Creating uncertainty in early stages of development processes about future building possibilities, and certainty about future contributions, can influence capturing value increase in a positive way.

The findings seem to confirm this. In the studied cases, creating certainty or leaving uncertainty open seems to have had important consequences for the residual price mechanisms of the land and for the negotiation position of each party. This can be relevant in the debate in the planning profession about the need for flexibility. This debate often focuses on the consequences of socio-economic dynamics in planning practice, and tends to embrace flexibility as *the* solution for the unpredictability of these dynamics. Flexibility is advocated as the way of achieving a non-linear and multi-layered decision-making system. However, the findings underline the importance of the converse: namely the influence of planning practice on economic dynamics that are central to the outcome of planning processes. That is, too much flexibility, at least regarding the private contributions, can affect negatively the quality and quantity of private contributions to public infrastructure and facilities. In sum, the findings suggest that there must be a certain level of certainty about contributions, in order to strengthen the obligations on the private sector for the realization of public infrastructure.

8.2 Choosing the contents of legally binding rules

Binding plans might be useful in negotiations if the municipality can include in them not only the physical zoning, but also aspects related to the financing and implementation of public infrastructure and facilities. Do binding plans regulate only a desired final picture, without stating who is responsible for its implementation? Or also the obligations that must be fulfilled by the developer? The findings suggest that this sub-variable might be relevant for capturing value increase.

Both in Valencia and England, planning law makes it possible to include in binding plans a wide range of requirements:

- Social/affordable housing: both in Valencia and England it is possible to prescribe social/affordable housing in the binding plans;
- On-site and off-site public infrastructure and facilities: both in Valencia and England it is possible to prescribe the obligation to contribute to on-site and off-site public infrastructure and facilities. In England, municipalities can also prescribe contributions for the building, maintenance and exploitation costs of public buildings, including those of social facilities (for example education and social services).
- Investing and implementation schedules: in both countries, binding plans include schedules and deadlines within which contributions must be made.

All these possibilities are positive for capturing value increase. In the Netherlands, until the 2008 Physical Planning Act, none of these requirements could be prescribed in the binding plans[1]. After the exploratory research about the Netherlands and another eight Western European countries, we presumed that the fact that, in the Netherlands these requirements could not be prescribed in the binding plans, would be negative for capturing value increase. The findings confirm this.

The consequences for the 2nd hypothesis
This finding can be used to refine the 2nd hypothesis (in black letters the addition):

Creating uncertainty in early stages of development processes about future building possibilities, and certainty about future contributions ***(specially if it is possible to include all the contributions as obligatory in legally binding rules)*** *can influence capturing value increase in a positive way.*

8.3 Making binding rules conditional on the developer securing his contributions

The definition of relevant variables handled at the start of data gathering referred only to the possible contents of binding plans as a determinant sub-variable. However, the findings soon showed that it might be ineffective to do no more than prescribing contributions and temporal deadlines, because their effectiveness depends on another sub-variable: whether binding plans can be made conditional on sealing a Development Agreement.

1 The 2008 Act might have introduced some changes, but they came too late for the data gathering of this research. For an assessment of whether the 2008's novelties could improve the capturing of value increase, see section 9.2.

The approval of binding plans containing generous value capturing arrangements and strict deadlines, as such, does not automatically mean that the developers will indeed implement them. It is important to remember that non-fulfilment of arrangements and deadlines may lead to no or almost no sanctions. In order to secure the implementation, additionally the developer needs to be bound to do that. England and Valencia belong to a group of countries in which it is possible to condition, in a formal, open and direct way, the approval of the binding plans to a development agreement. This happens as follows: first the binding plans (Planning Permission in England, Joint Development Programme in Valencia), including the contributions and deadlines, are approved, but only provisionally, following extensive procedures. The municipality then openly conditions the definite approval of these binding plans to an agreement that secures these contributions and deadlines. When the agreement is sealed, the municipality, without the need of further procedures, approves the documents definitely. If such an agreement is not reached, the binding plans never come in force. Of the nine studied countries, only Italy seems to show similar features to Valencia and England (for an international comparison, see section 4.2.3). This clear and open conditioning seems to have improved the capturing of value increase, and specially the speed of plan implementation. In Valencia this was very clear: the generalization of this statutory power since 1994 has significantly accelerated urban development.

In practice, Dutch municipalities often condition the Land use plan and departures from it to securing contributions. However, there is no formal possibility of doing so in an open and straightforward way, which we think might have a negative influence: 1) because in the Netherlands, after an agreement has been reached, the Land use plan must follow an *extensive* procedure (including public participation), which means that there is the risk that the plan becomes annulled or seriously modified; 2) it implies the risk of the developer appealing to the courts because of an improper use of statutory powers; and 3) it makes it very difficult for the municipality to follow an open and transparent public discourse, because an open conditioning might be illegal (see section 7.4.3.1).

The consequences for the 2nd hypothesis

This finding can be used to refine the 2nd hypothesis (in black letters the addition):

Creating uncertainty in early stages of development processes about future building possibilities, and certainty about future contributions (specially if it is possible to include the contributions as obligatory in legally binding rules, ***and if it is possible openly and straightforwardly to make the approval of these rules conditional on a development agreement that secures the contributions****) can influence capturing value increase in a positive way.*

8.4 Modulating property rights

Section 2.2 handled the recent debate in the Netherlands and Spain about the possibility of splitting development rights from land ownership. An exploratory study in section 4.4 of these and another seven Western European countries (England, Germany, France, Italy, Flanders, Denmark and Sweden) showed that none of them could split property rights in that way, so there were no possibilities of doing empirical research on this. However, the exploratory study also showed the singularity of a modification in 1994 of the land readjustment regulation in the Spanish region of Valencia, which could be considered as a light form of splitting. Thanks to this modified land readjustment regulation, infrastructure provision there is separated from property rights. Actually, the Valencian 1994's novelty turned out to be the result of this very same debate about splitting development rights from land ownership.

Summary of the findings and the results of testing the 1st hypothesis

These preliminary findings inspired the first hypothesis in this research, which was about the effects of modifying the formal rules on property rights in land (such as the Valencian land readjustment does) on the capturing of value increase:

A specific form of splitting the property rights in land (separating infrastructure provision from property rights) can modify the power-relationships in the network of actors involved in urban regeneration, and this can improve capturing value increase.

The findings of the in-depth research in Valencia, England and the Netherlands confirm the hypothesis. The definition of property rights in England and the Netherlands, which do not have a land readjustment regulation for urban areas, seems to affect the capturing of value increase in a negative way. There is a strong interdependency of local authorities and landowners: authorities have the statutory powers over planning consent, but landowners have the financial means and the exclusive right to develop the land. This interdependency gives to the landowners the option to wait, which it is often used to combat local authorities' requirements, and leads frequently to delaying development processes. In addition, the findings suggest that interdependency leads to an inefficient and sluggish development process, in which costs are unnecessary high and different actors manage to appropriate part of the value increase, this all leading to higher land development costs such as the costs made in preparing plans and negotiating the terms of development. High land development costs seem to form an important obstacle for capturing value increase, especially in the Netherlands.

These findings suggest some interesting conclusions for the theoretical debate and reflections set out in section 2.2. First, however, let us look at the findings in more detail.

Who owns development rights?
We must here differentiate between the right to the *economic value* that arises from rezoning land, and the right to *develop* the rezoned land. The rightful owner of the *economic value* that arises from the new use possibilities after the binding zoning rules have been modified is different in the studied countries. In England, it is the public administration that has right to tax this economic value; in Valencia, most of the value belongs to the landowner, and public bodies have right to a part of it (but not all); and in the Netherlands, the landowner is the rightful owner of the entire value (see section 5.3.1 for Valencia, 6.2.1 for England and 7.2.1 for the Netherlands). However, what does not vary, not only in those three countries, but also in Germany, France, Italy, Flanders, Denmark and Sweden, is that the right to develop belongs to the landowner. The landowner is always the only one entitled to build on the land, subject to basic compliance with the zoning regulations and upon obtaining the necessary permits. However, in Spain, Germany, France and Sweden, planning law explicitly refers to the *infrastructure provision* as something differentiated from the rest of the development rights. In those countries, infrastructure provision is a ´responsibility´ or ´task´ of the public bodies, but not of the landowner or the developer. In England, the Netherlands, Flanders, Italy and Denmark, there is in the law neither an explicit mention of infrastructure provision as a differentiated component of development rights, nor of a public priority in this.

Differences in dependence between public and private actors
The answer to the question 'who owns the development rights' was however not specific enough for gathering the empirical data. To make it more specific, section 3.3.1 developed a model to analyse the power/dependency relationships between the involved actors (municipality, developer, landowners) in each transaction in development processes. These transactions are those needed for infrastructure provision namely: 1. land purchase and assembling; 2. financing and; 3. land preparation and development, and those needed for the building on the serviced plots namely: 4. land disposition; 5. construction and; 6. property transfer. Each of these steps implies transactions of some kind: land, money, property, planning consent, etc. Infrastructure provision can only take place after resolving at least the first three transactions, and the building after resolving the last three transactions. By analysing who has the control over each of these transactions, it has been possible to discern who has exactly which development right, and how this could affect the capturing of value increase.

For an exploratory analysis of the nine Western European countries see section 4.4.2. Regarding the in-depth research in England, Valencia and the Netherlands, there seem not to be important differences in the position of actors in the transactions involved in the building (transactions 4 to 6). However, regarding the infrastructure provision (transactions 1 to 3), there are clear differences in the position of public and private actors, and these differences lead to different degrees of interdependency. It is possible to distinguish between England and the Netherlands on the one side, and Valencia on the other. In England and the Netherlands, as a rule, the transactions that are needed to gather the land (transaction 1), find the money (transaction 2) and provide the infrastructure (transaction 3) are quite dependent on agreement with the landowners. This is because none of the actors controls all the needed resources. Municipalities have a monopoly on the regulatory powers for approving the binding rules, but the landowners/developers control the land and have the investment capacity. This mutual dependence is very strong: as a rule, in the absence of a voluntary agreement, municipalities have no other alternative than to expropriate/buy the land and construct the infrastructure, and maybe pay part of the costs with taxes imposed afterwards. The only way for the municipality to avoid dependence on the landowner is thus through direct organisational and financial public involvement (see Table 23).

Expropriation has not been applied in the studied cases. In Bristol, where the English cases come from, expropriation is rarely used, only in exceptional circumstances. For example, in cases where there is disagreement with a minority of the landowners and the majority of the landowners support a compulsory buy-out of the minority owners' share and are willing to pay the associated costs. In the Netherlands expropriation is also exceptional and only justified if it is 'necessary' (*noodzakelijk* in Dutch). As a consequence of this, it is often difficult, or even impossible, to expropriate the land for urban regeneration.

Table 23. Dependence analysis English, Dutch and Valencian (before 1994) cases.

	Dependence because of land	**Dependence because of investment capacity**	**Dependence because of regulatory resources**
Local public body depends on the landowner/developer	**Dependence.** Developer/Landowner owns the land. Dependence is only avoidable through compulsory purchase, but this is only used in exceptional circumstances. Expropriation is considered slow, expensive and risky. In the Netherlands the 'necessary' criterion gives preference to the landowners.	**Dependence.** The developers were able to invest in buying the land and developing it. Dependence was not avoidable because local public bodies were not willing to invest. Only in the Dutch case of Breda the municipality was ready to assume some financial risks.	
Landowner/developer depends on the local public body			**Dependence.** The public bodies grant the required permissions (and in the Netherlands and Valencia approve the Land use Plan). Dependence is not avoidable.

Table 24. Dependence analysis region of Valencia after 1994 Planning Act.

	Dependence because of land	Dependence because of investment and management capacity	Dependence because of regulatory resources
Municipality depends on the landowners	**Dependence, avoidable.** Landowners have most of the land. However, dependence is avoidable without much difficulty because of the possibility of applying compulsory land readjustment, if necessary.	**No dependence.** There is no municipal dependence on the landowners in this matter. The municipality can point out a third party, the urbanizing agent, as the one who invest and provides the infrastructure.	
Landowner depends on Municipality			**Dependence, not avoidable.** Landowners cannot develop without being selected as urbanizing agent or without the municipality selecting a third party as urb. agent. Also, the municipality approves the binding rules. Dependence is not avoidable.
Municipality depends on urbanizing agent		**No dependence.** There is no municipal dependence on the urbanizing agent in this matter. The municipality can point out in a public tender another party as urbanizing agent, or select right away a public company as urbanizing agent.	
Urbanizing agent depends on Municipality			**Dependence, not avoidable.** Urbanizing agents cannot provide the infrastructure without being selected as urbanizing agent. Also, the municipality approves the relevant binding rules. Dependence is not avoidable.
Landowner depends on Urbanizing agent		**Dependence, avoidable.** Landowners cannot invest without the urbanizing agent. Dependence is avoidable since landowners may submit an own plan to the public tender and became themselves urbanizing agent.	
Urbanizing agent depends on landowner	**Dependence, avoidable.** Landowners control the land. However, dependence is avoidable because of the possibility of applying compulsory land readjustment, if necessary.	**No dependence.** There is no dependence on the landowners in this matter. If the municipality selects him as urbanizing agent, he will be able to invest and provide the infrastructure, while the landowner is obliged to pay the costs. So actually it is not he who is investing, but the landowners.	

Before the 1994 Act, the situation in Valencian municipalities was very similar to that in England and the Netherlands. Even if there was a land readjustment regulation, this regulation relied on the support and active collaboration of a majority of the landowners, and the only way of forcing readjustment was through a direct public organisational involvement.

This changed in 1994. In that year the regional government introduced a new planning law, and since then there is no more mutual dependence (see Table 24). Valencian municipalities can now opt for compulsory land readjustment, without having to become directly involved. The municipality selects in a public tender the urbanising agent, who may be a public company, the landowners themselves joining in a company, but most of the time the agent is a commercial developer. Landowners can choose for voluntary expropriation or can participate in the development. If they choose expropriation, the urbanising agent pays the compensation and acquires the land. If they participate, the landowners have to deliver the land needed for public infrastructure and pay to the urbanising agent a proportional share of the land development costs (which consist mainly of the infrastructure provision costs). In exchange, landowners share the economic value increase: after providing the infrastructure, the urbanising agent delivers the serviced building parcels to the landowners and transfers the public infrastructure, free of charge, to the municipality. In sum, although landowners still control land, municipalities can now avoid being dependent on the landowners, as municipalities can appoint a third party (who does not need to own the land) as the urbanising agent, and as municipalities do not need to get directly financially involved. Also, the municipalities are not dependent on one particular urbanising agent, for this agent can be selected through a public tender.

Option to wait is negative for capturing the value increase

One important consequence of mutual dependence is the option to wait. On the one hand, in Valencia after 1994, because there is no mutual dependence, landowners do not have the option to wait. On the other hand, in the English and Dutch cases, due to the mutual dependence, landowners/developers had the option of waiting. Waiting might be a preferred behaviour as land also has an option value that can be profitable. When landowners are allowed to wait, it might take some time to reach an agreement with all the landowners about the price for the land, for the landowners expect that by delaying negotiations, their profits (the accounted land costs, see financial analysis in section 2.4.3) could increase in the future.

In the studied English and Dutch cases, public bodies were often confronted with landowners who were not willing to agree with the required contributions package. Often public bodies were forced to lower this package in order to reach agreement. Also, in several cases in both countries, development processes were delayed after developers refused to accept the requirements and plans of the municipality, and negotiations about these issues dragged on. In two Dutch cases, the developer decided to prepare the plans anew, although they were already very advanced, and this delayed significantly. It is no exception in the Netherlands and also in England, that urban regeneration is delayed due to landowners using their option to wait. For example, in the English case *Harbourside,* in the city of Bristol, the developer was against the requirement of constructing 30% social/affordable housing, finally accepting a 9% requirement. A Dutch example is *Kop van Oost,* in the city of Groningen. Here, from the beginning of negotiations, the developer argued that there was little financial room in the project, thus making it clear to the municipality that there were not many value-capturing possibilities. The municipality, which did not have access to the financial calculations of the developer, seems in the early stages to have accepted that it could not ask for large contributions. Also, the municipality accepted several cost saving changes in the quality of the public space constructed by the developer.

Similarly, Valencian municipalities were confronted before 1994 with landowners who were not willing to agree with municipal requirements. This affected the capturing of value increase, forcing municipalities to lower the contributions package in order to reach an agreement, this producing irregular, unsystematic and illogical (from an urban planning point of view) urban growth, distinguished by low quality and scarce public infrastructure. Development sites were too narrow and too small, just large enough to provide infrastructure for several plots. Building schemes included only the bare minimum of public infrastructure. Most of the time, readjustment followed very much the wish of landowners to receive serviced building plots on their former property. Instead of following a plan for the most suitable parcelling, readjustment followed the landowners' property boundaries and interests. The urban periphery in the City of Valencia at the end of the 1980's, which is still visible nowadays, is a good example. There were large buildings in the middle of deteriorated agricultural land and no adequate public infrastructure to support them.

The introduction of the 1994 Valencian Act has had large consequences in practice. Nowadays there is no mutual dependence and landowners do not have the option to wait. Although compulsory readjustment is not common, it does play an important role in dissuading landowners from taking actions that may delay development. According to available data, the 1994 Act had a positive effect on capturing the increased value. The regulation broke through the previous pattern of landowners dragging their feet, not agreeing to infrastructure provision and speculating on improved market conditions. When a developer submits a proposal and the municipality approves it, landowners must follow suit. The consequence was an extraordinary increase in public and in private initiatives that resulted in accelerated urban development. The improvement has been both in the quantity and the quality of public infrastructure.

The Valencian cases confirm this general conclusion. For example, in *Guillem de Anglesola,* in the city of Valencia, neither the initiating party nor the other three developers who in the public tender submitted alternative plans, were linked to the landownership in the area. The possibility of selecting a developer without land has been a crucial factor. As there were hundreds of owners (many of them residents or small landlords), it seems very unlikely that all these actors would have agreed on a voluntary land readjustment. Therefore, the option to 'by-pass' the landowners has been a crucial factor in redeveloping the site. The landowners and the developer had to accept the full contributions package, including additional compensation to the owners of the old deteriorated houses.

Financial feasibility as an explanation of the popularity of the option to wait

There might be at least two different possible motivations for landowners and developers in England and the Netherlands to choose the option to wait. First, there is the expectation that longer negotiations lead to higher profits (in the form of higher accounted land costs, or higher regular profit margins, or a higher Final profit, see financial analysis in section 2.4.3), due to housing prices increase over time and/or reduced contributions. Second, it is possible that municipal requirements endanger the financial feasibility of the operation. According to a representative of a British housing developers' umbrella organisation, about half of negotiations in the UK fail because Local Planning Authorities demand inappropriately large contribution packages (Whitacker, interview 2007). Public officers in the studied English cases argued the contrary and confirmed that contribution packages took into consideration the financial feasibility. An interviewed representative of the Dutch developers' umbrella organisation had a similar argument, when he claimed that development is often delayed because of unreasonably high municipal requirements (Fokkema, interview 2007).

We can discuss this in terms of several third variables in the causal model set out in section 2.4.2: the real estate markets and the plan and site features determine how much are the costs (variables A1 and A2), and also relevant is how much and how good are the public infrastructure and facilities which public bodies pursue, and how high are the contributions that public bodies expect from landowners and developers (variable C1). Indirectly the context variables are also relevant that influence the distribution of the initial profit (variables B): they are relevant because they influence the actions of those directly involved in the project (variables D). Table 25 summarizes which are de costs, returns and the final balance of regenerating a site. Section 2.4.3 provides more explanation, and Annexes 3, 4 and 6 give the data for the studied cases.

Third variables A, B1 and B2 and the actions of those involved in the project (variables D1.1, D2.1, and probably also D4 and D5), together with variable C1 influence the costs that must be made to redevelop a site: the accounted land costs, the infrastructure provision costs, the plan preparation costs, the soil decontamination costs, the compensation costs and the size of the contributions that must be paid/implemented (costs postings 1-6). In turn, these costs influence the distribution of the Initial profit, which in turn influences the size of the Final profit and thus whether the landowner/developer is able or not to contribute. It was difficult to empirically assess in the studied cases the size of the Final profit because of the lack of reliable sources.

Table 25. Costs, returns and balance of operations in urban regeneration.

1) **Land costs**	**1a. Minimum land costs:** the market value of the land in its current use; **1b. Accounted land costs:** the land price that the developer includes into the calculations.
2) **Infrastructure provision costs**	This includes not only the infrastructure provision works, but also reserved amounts for unexpected expenses, the overhead costs, eventual 'hidden' profit margins of the developer, etc. In the Netherlands, they comprise: *Slopen, bouw en woonrijp maken, risico en onvoorzien.* It should also include the financial costs.
3) **Plan preparation costs**	This includes the costs of the preparation of plans, studies, etc (*Plankosten*, or *Voorbereiding, toezicht en planontwikkeling*).
4) **Soil decontamination costs**	This includes the costs of decontaminating the land.
5) **Compensation costs**	This includes compensation to existing owners and inhabitants, for removal of activities and residence, demolition of constructions and buildings, etc.
6) **Additional contributions of the developer**	This includes the contributions, in cash or in kind (constructions, buildings) to public goals (payments, construction of public infrastructure or public buildings, etc) **additional** to his contributions to the on-site infrastructure provision costs (even if they might serve a wider area than the development in question), which are already included in (2).
7) **Real estate development costs**	This includes the whole development of the real estate, thus not only the building costs, but also the preparation of plans (not for providing the infrastructure but for the building), overhead costs, possible 'hidden' profit margins of the developer, etc.
8) **Total returns**	This includes the total returns accruing from the selling of the real estate (office, dwellings, etc).
INITIAL PROFIT	The value increase that accrued from the regeneration of the site and could have been initially available to pay public infrastructure and facilities: 8 – [$(1a + 2 + 3 + 4 + 5 + 6 + 7)^{\text{not-inflated}}$ – (those costs of 2-7 subsidised by public bodies)]. Here we assume costs 1 till 7 are not inflated.
DEVELOPER'S FINAL PROFIT	The profits of the final developer: 8 – [(1b + 2 + 3 + 4 + 5 + 6 + 7) – (those costs of 2-7 subsidised by public bodies)]. This profit must be added to a regular profit margin in case the final developer has included a regular profit in posting 7.

Information about development costs and profits is a sensitive matter, and developers were not willing to disclose it. In the Dutch cases, according to estimates based on information given by developers, the financial margins appear to be very narrow. However, according to my own estimates (posting 9 in Annex 4) there was room for higher contributions. For example, according to the developer, in *Kop van Oost* his Final profit was very narrow, €2m. However, my own estimates suggest that it may be much larger, around €29m (see section 2.4.3 for a detailed analysis of case *Kop van Oost*). If this was the case, then clearly the developer's objections to the municipality's requirements were not justifiable from a financial point of view. In sum, in the Dutch cases it is not clear if the Final profit of the last involved developer were so narrow that opposition against the municipal requirements was justified. The question is thus: did developers use the option to wait because land development costs were too high, or did they abuse this option in order to increase their profit margins? And: how does it comes that in the Valencian cases, despite the fact that contributions were very large, the financial feasibility of the operations was not a problem?

In the English cases, following our own estimates, the Final profit margins were bigger and allowed for greater contributions (see posting 9 in table in Annex 3). Resistance or acceptance of the requirements was based more on the *expected* land price (how much the initial landowner or the developer who bought the land expect to receive for his/her land, which translates into the accounted land costs of an operation, i.e. cost posting 1b of Table 25) and the *expected* profit (how much the developer expects to profit, i.e. a possible regular profit margin + Final profit) than on the objective financial feasibility of the project. For example, in *Megabowl*, in the city of Bristol, the initial price of the land was relatively low, about 3-4.5 € million[2], due to uncertainty regarding building possibilities, which had discouraged developers from purchasing the site in the previous years, and to a heavy competition from other bowling alleys in the city. This gave the owner-applicant leeway to contribute more than usual.

Differences in infrastructure provision and plan preparation costs

When analyzing the financial aspects of the cases, this research provided remarkable and unexpected findings that helped to answer the above question. We discovered large differences in the costs of infrastructure provision and plan preparation in the three studied countries (postings 2 and 3). These costs are the highest in the Dutch cases, when compared with those in the English and Valencian cases (for details see Annex 6, for summary see Table 26): both costs together are in *Kruidenbuurt* and *Kop van Oost* respectively €438 and €368 per m² for new public space, and respectively €158 and €148 per m² total redeveloped land[3]; in *Stationskwartier* these costs are much higher, €1,212/m² new public space and €570/m² total redeveloped land, which might be explained by the fact that this figure includes the accounted land costs, soil decontamination, compensation costs (postings 1, 4 and 5) and probably contains a hidden profit for the municipality. In the English cases the two costs of infrastructure provision and plan preparation together are €153/€99, €269/€111 and €332/€166 per m² new public space/total redeveloped land. In the Valencian cases, those two costs together are €94/€70, €693/€306, €103/€79 and €94/€74[4].

2 Calculated at an exchange rate of € 1.5 per £ 1.

3 In our opinion, the most appropriate way of measuring these costs and comparing them with other cases is relating costs to the 'new public space', which is the surface that becomes redeveloped and will be used for public uses. Most of these costs relate to the construction of public infrastructure above or under this surface. It can be expected that a case with more public space will have more of these costs than a case that includes less public space. By comparing costs per m² new public space the risk diminishes that a case with little public space scores similarly to a case that includes a larger area of public space.

4 The figure for the second case is not representative for the entire Valencian region, but the other three cases are (Fernández & Fernández, 2002: 68-74; Gascó, 2006: 72-76; Raga, interview in 2008).

Table 26. Comparison development costs in the Dutch, English and Valencian cases.

		Dutch cases			Three additional Dutch cases, expert opinion			English cases			Valencian cases			
		Kruid	*KvO*	*Stati*[5]	*1*	*2*	*3*	*Mega*[6]	*Temp*	*Harb*	*Guill*	*Period*	*Camin*	*Benal*
2. Infrastructure provision costs	€/m² new public space	438	368	1212	249	222	94	153	269	332	77	418	85	75
	€/m² total redeveloped land	158	148	570	164	107	67	99	111	166	57	187	65	59
3. Plan preparation costs	€/m² new public space	Plan preparation costs are included in Infrastructure provision costs			102	61	24	Plan preparation costs are included in Infrastructure provision costs			17	269	18	19
	€/m² total redeveloped land				67	29	17				13	119	14	15

5 Includes Accounted land, soil decontamination and compensation costs.

6 Includes Soil decontamination and compensation costs.

Two Dutch experts confirmed the generalisability of the figures from the Dutch cases to other Dutch regeneration projects, with nuances, by analysing three recent urban regeneration cases initiated by housing associations (projects 1, 2 and 3 in Table 26 and Annex 6)[7]. Infrastructure provision and plan preparation costs were together €352/€231 in Project 1 and €283/€136 in Project 2. Such figures are not at all exceptional in urban regeneration in the Netherlands. Project 3 (€118/€84) is an exception to the general conclusion that these costs are much higher in the Netherlands than in Valencia. Also, the figures of Projects 1 and 2 suggest that it is not clear whether these costs are, on average, higher in the Netherlands than in England (Stauttener and Van Bladel, interviews 2008).

Option to wait has inflationary effects on infrastructure provision and plan preparation costs

A possible explanation for the high cost of infrastructure provision and plan preparation costs in England and the Netherlands is that the option to wait has an inflationary effect on these costs:

- Delay results in additional studies, meetings, etc, increasing the plan preparation costs. In the Dutch Projects 1 and 2, plan preparation costs are €102/€67 and €61/29 respectively, in the Valencian cases they are about €18/€14. Unfortunately, it was not possible to specify these costs for the other Dutch and English cases;
- Delay and the corresponding uncertainties increase the risks, which translate into higher infrastructure provision costs, e.g. allocating higher reserves for unexpected expenses (*risico en onvoorzien* in Dutch), and generating higher financial costs.

---

7 A possible criticism to the validity of the data of the second-opinion projects is that they might be not representative of the total population of urban regeneration projects because of the fact that they are initiated by housing associations and not by commercial developers. The argument is that housing associations pursue more quality of the public infrastructure and facilities, thus the figures should not be compared with cases ruled by commercial developers. I reject this criticism with three arguments:

- The three second-opinion projects are used to measure the infrastructure provision and plan preparation costs (cost postings 2 and 3 in Table 25), but not to measure the final quantity and quality of public infrastructure and facilities;
- The available data of the three second-opinion projects (e.g. the percentage new public space of the total redeveloped land) do not induce me to think that they might include much more or less public infrastructure and facilities than cases initiated by commercial developers. Thus there is in my opinion no reason to think that in the second-opinion projects the infrastructure provision and plan preparation costs are higher because the housing associations might have built more public infrastructure and facilities. Case *Kruidenbuurt* (initiated by a a housing association) showed also no significant differences with the other three Dutch cases (initiated by commercial developers);
- There might indeed be in the second-opinion projects large differences regarding the building of social housing and buildings meant for public facilities. I.e. housing associations might indeed build more social housing and buildings for public facilities than commercial developers do, as the Dutch cases show. However, this does not invalidate my comparison of infrastructure provision and plan preparation costs because the costs of social housing and buildings for public facilities are not included there, but most probably in cost postings 6 or 7 of Table 25.

In short, it is possible not only that high costs explain why developers use their option to wait and cause delay, but also that delay can increase the costs. However, it does not seem reasonable to conclude that delay can explain *all* the differences between the infrastructure provision and plan preparation costs in the Dutch (between €118 and €438 per m² for new public space, and between €84 and €231 per m² total redeveloped land) and the Valencian cases (between €94 and €103 per m² for new public space, and between €70 and €79 per m² total redeveloped land). There might be many other variables that can explain *part* of the differences. The complexity of causalities has been set out in the causal model in section 2.4.2. For example differences in labour costs in the building sector (that might be about 30% higher in the Netherlands than in Valencia), in construction materials, in fiscal regime (variables belonging to sort A3 in causal model) and conditions of the soil (variable A2) (Stauttener en Van Bladel, interviews 2008). It is plausible to conclude that the option to wait can explain *part* of the differences in the infrastructure provision and plan preparation costs, but that there are other, third variables that can also be relevant.

Option to wait might have inflationary effects on the accounted land costs

In addition, the option to wait can also have an inflationary effect on land prices; since market parties owning the land can exercise the option to wait, and this puts them in a strong negotiation position, they would be more interested in acquiring land, which in turn increases the price of real and expected transactions in the land markets. This expectation of higher land prices can have the effect of rising the land price that the developer includes in the financial calculations of the operation, i.e. the accounted land costs. It seems plausible that the accounted land costs are based on the economic value of the new use possibilities of the land after regeneration, instead of the previous use possibilities. The findings in the Dutch cases seem to support this argument: land was often sold for higher prices than the market price in the former use. In *De Funen* the landowner sold his land to the developer in 1997 for a price certainly much higher that the value of the actual use possibilities at that time. In *Kop van Oost* the estimated market value of the previous use (industrial land) was about €3.6m. However, this land was then sold speculatively in 2000, 2001 and in 2002. We know that in 2001 it was sold for around €12m, so when it was sold again in 2002 the price must have been even higher. Higher accounted land costs influence the final profit of developers, diminishing their possibilities of contributing.

The option to wait reinforces the effects of the certainty about future building and contributions and vice versa

The effects of the option to wait might reinforce and be reinforced by another variable: the certainty about future building possibilities and future contributions (variables of the sort B2 and D1 in causal model explained in section 2.4.2, also explained above in section 8.1). This can happen in two ways:

- The first landowner, if he has the power to wait, if there is certainty in early stages about the building possibilities, and if there is no certainty about the contributions to be made, asks a higher price for his land;

- The developer, if he has the power to wait, and if there is no certainty in early stages about the contributions to be made, might choose the price of the land that he accounts in the financial calculation, and his regular profit margin, to appropriate as much value increase as possible. At the start of regeneration processes, developers often have some room to set them higher or lower. Once the accounted land cost and the regular profit margin have been established, lowering them is usually complicated.

Need of further research to land prices and development costs
The availability of reliable information in the studied cases was low, which did not allow us to collect important details about the land prices and development costs. For example, it was not possible to discern to which degree other sorts of costs such as labour costs in the building sector, in construction materials, in fiscal regime (variables belonging to sort A3 in causal model) and conditions of the soil (variable A2) contribute to the higher infrastructure provision costs in England and the Netherlands. Another example is that it was not possible to discern whether the developer has indeed inflated the price of the land, or whether he included in the infrastructure provision costs a 'hidden' profit margin. Further research should focus on the differences in land prices, infrastructure provision costs and plan preparation costs and provide more data that could be used to fine-tune the conclusions of this research.

Conclusions for the theoretical debate and reflections about property rights
This research sought empirical evidence relevant to the debate and the theoretical reflections about separating development rights from property rights in land. The findings support the assumption that a specific form of shaping property rights, the Valencian land readjustment regulation, which separates infrastructure provision from the control of landowners, can improve the capturing of value increase. In addition, the findings strongly suggest that in urban regeneration the regulation has a deflationary effect on the costs for providing infrastructure and preparing plans, and possibly also on the accounted land costs.

This supports the idea that property law in relation to the goal of producing urban space and housing is not only a matter of rights; it also involves obligations. The adoption of a combined approach to property rights and duties, through a land readjustment regulation, may help regulate the initiatives taken by landowners and commercial developers in such a way that they fulfil a greater role in the creation of public infrastructure. It can also help to overcome problems of stagnation in constructing new housing. Here I agree with the advocated role of land readjustment regulations as an alternative to problems with the traditional forms of land assembly (voluntary exchange or public intervention in the form of expropriation) in the UK and the United States of America (Hong & Needham, 2007: xv-xix), while at the same time the shortcomings of land readjustment regulations should not be forgotten, if they do not include enforcement mechanisms to avoid the speculative behaviour of landowners (Muñoz & Korthals Altes, 2007).

The findings are interesting for the Dutch debate. First, they coincide with the position taken by Priemus and Louw, who argue that the increase in private control of the land since the 1990s has led to inflation in accounted land costs and impoverishment of public infrastructure (2003). A second topic is the dilemma whether Dutch municipalities can or cannot satisfactorily achieve their public goals within the current legal framework. In this discussion, the concept 'satisfactorily' has not been clearly defined; therefore, it is not possible to say whether the definition of property rights in land in the Netherlands results in "satisfactorily accomplished" public goals. However, it is possible to conclude that shaping property rights using a land readjustment regulation can significantly improve the capturing of value increase and accelerate urban development. That is, it can help to better achieve public goals, because public goals usually concern either the finance of public infrastructure and facilities, or the implementation on time of building schemes, or both. Section 9.4 gives specific recommendations to Dutch public bodies of how to improve the capturing of value increase.

For the Spanish debate, the findings support the critical approach of García-Bellido and others in the 1990s. In a context of privately owned land and the absence of public subsidies and of direct public intervention in urban land markets, breaking the monopolistic/oligopolistic position of landowners is the only way to assure good quality and adequate quantity of public infrastructure and facilities.

FitnessFirst
FitnessFirst
Now
For all
PLAY TODAY
BAR & GRILL
OPENING 2007
Keep out

CHAPTER 9

Recommendations for the Netherlands

One of the goals of this research is to learn how to use formal rules relevant to zoning in order to improve cost recovery in the Netherlands. Chapters 5 to 7 made clear that formal rules relevant to zoning in the Spanish region of Valencia and in England differ significantly from those in the Netherlands. A comparison between how much value increase public bodies manage to capture also shows remarkable differences: in Valencia and England, private parties are more committed in urban regeneration on private owned land to financing and/or realizing unprofitable elements (i.e. the public infrastructure and facilities) than in the Netherlands. This affects not only the variety of sorts of contributions, but also the total economic value of the contributions.

More captured value increase in Valencia and England than in the Netherlands

The differences mainly involve (see Table 27; for details per country see section 5.6 for Valencia, 6.5 for England, and 7.5 for the Netherlands):

- **On-site infrastructure provision costs:** in England and Valencia these are mostly or fully paid by the developers, while in the Netherlands these are financed with large public subsidies;
- **Land for on-site public infrastructure:** in Valencia this is provided free of charge by the landowners, while in England and the Netherlands there are much larger public contributions for providing this land;
- **Social housing:** in England and Valencia, this is paid to a large extent or almost fully by the developers, while in the Netherlands this is covered primarily by municipalities and housing associations;
- **Off-site public infrastructure:** in England and Valencia, developers contribute significantly (in England primarily with financial means while in Valencia primarily with land). On the other hand, in the Netherlands these contributions are rare;

Table 27. Comparing captured value increase in the Spanish region of Valencia, England and the Netherlands

	On-site land development costs		Land for on-site public infrastructure		Land for on-site public buildings		On-site public buildings		Affordable housing		Contributions to off-site public infra-structure & facilities	Creaming of plus value
	Developer	Public body	Developer	Public body	Developer	Public body	Developer	Public body	Developer	Public bodies		
Spanish region of Valencia	All or almost all these costs	No (only if receiving building plots)	Almost all the land	Land that already was public infrastructure	Almost all the land	Land that already was public infrastructure	Sometimes	Almost always	Almost all	Some minor object subsidies	Landowners cede significant quantities of land, and sometimes pay for construction.	10% building volume in developable land; often money
England	Almost all the costs	Indirect through land/ cheap financing	Most of the land	Part of the land	Part of the land	Part of the land	Not often	Almost always	Increasing amount of affordable / social housing	Partly	Important contributions, that increase in the final years.	In principle, no.
The Netherlands	Part of the costs	Heavy subsidies	Important part of the land	Important part of the land	Commercial developer none; housing association possibly	Public body provides most of the land	Commercial developer none; housing association contributions	Almost always	Commercial developers do not build; housing associations do	Sometimes	Almost no contributions by developers to public infrastructure/ facilities outside plan area, and modest contribution to infra./fac. situated within but serving wider area.	none

Grey: Country in which the developer/landowner contributes the most out of the three countries.
Light Grey: Country in which the developer/landowner contributes the second out of the three countries.
White: Country in which the developer/landowner contributes the least out of the three countries.

– **Creaming off plus value:** local public bodies in Valencia cream off a significant share of the increase in economic value, even if they own no land. In England this does not officially take place, but because of the broad definition of *developers' contributions* one might conclude that it does take place; in the Netherlands this is the case only when the municipality owns the land and/or invests and shares the risk.

Correlation with formal rules relevant to zoning
We concluded in chapter 8 that, when comparing the three countries, there is a strong correlation between the captured value increase (the highest in Valencia, lower but also high in England, and lowest in the Netherlands) and the possibilities offered by the formal rules relevant to zoning: 1) In England and Valencia, the level of certainty about future contributions is higher than in the Netherlands (before negotiations start and developers buy the land); 2) In England and Valencia, binding rules can include more prescriptions than in the Netherlands; 3) In England and Valencia, it is formally possible to directly condition the approval of binding rules on the developer securing contributions, while the legal framework in the Netherlands does not provide this possibility; 4) In Valencia, municipalities can avoid dependency on developers and landowners thanks to a land readjustment regulation, while in England and the Netherlands there is no such possibility.

It is also apparent that this is not a perfect correlation: there are other variables that might also explain *part* of the differences in the captured value increase. One such relevant variable is the market price of real estate. This is a context variable of the sort A1 described in the causal model (see section 2.4.2). When the data was gathered, housing prices in the English cases were significantly higher (€ 3,000-5,000 per m^2 floor space and even more) than prices in the Valencian and Dutch cases (about € 2,000-3,000 per m^2). This could *partly* explain why English developers offered more generous contributions than their Dutch counterparts, but not why Valencian developers, despite similar market prices with the Netherlands, still contributed somewhat more than the English and much more than the Dutch. Other variables that can also explain *part* of the differences in captured value increase are the plan and site features (variable of the sort A1), the markets of workforce and building materials, and fiscal regimes (variable A3), the definition of the contents and geographical scope of the plan (variable C1), and specific circumstances of the involved interactions and persons (variables D4 and D5).

Recommendations for the Dutch urban regeneration practice
We saw when describing the research problem for this thesis (section 1.5) that Dutch municipalities usually have high ambitions for their public regeneration schemes, but, in those cases in which the land is not in public hands, the difficulties in financing the unprofitable parts (i.e. the public infrastructure and facilities) hamper the actual realization of these ambitions and lead to high public subsidies. The findings in this research strongly suggest that this is caused by the fact that in the Netherlands

the increased value that accrues from regenerating a site often 'leaks out'. It might be that developers profit from this, taking possession of an important part of the value increase, or it might be, optionally or additionally, that the profit margin leaks to landowners and to unreasonable development costs. Whatever the reason, it is a fact that Dutch developers do not contribute as much as their English and Valencian counterparts. It is also clear that this situation in the Netherlands can be explained, to a large extent, by the differences in the formal rules relevant to zoning.

I do not assert that urban regeneration in the Netherlands *always* generates enough value increase to pay *all* the unprofitable parts. Rather, the claim is that, whatever the value increase, often it is not available to pay the unprofitable parts. In order to assess the magnitude of the problem, and despite the lack of information, I estimated the financial structure of the cases and I concluded that an important part of the value increase has leaked out. For example, in case *Kop van Oost* the initial profit of the operation (i.e. the profit taking into account a non-speculative land price and reasonable, non-inflated infrastructure provision and plan preparation costs) could have been between € 16 and € 43 million. This money has leaked out into speculative land prices (at least € 8.4 million), probably also into inflated infrastructure provision and plan preparation costs (about € 5 million), and also into a possible large profit for the developer. These leakages left no room for contributions by the developer to the public infrastructure and facilities and thus created the need for public subsidisation. See Table 4 in section 2.4.3 for more details of case *Kop van Oost*, and Annexes 4 and 6 for details for the other Dutch cases.

It follows that, if it is desired to improve cost recovery in the Netherlands, this could be achieved by changing aspects of the formal rules relevant to planning. The rest of this chapter focuses on those rules that allow Valencian and English public bodies to improve the capturing of value increase, and investigates whether and how they could be introduced into Dutch practice.

The recommendations seek to answer the main research question, which is the same as solving the problem addressed by this research, namely: how to improve cost recovery in the Netherlands, by stimulating those parties that profit from development to finance the unprofitable parts. Some of these proposed recommendations do not require legal modifications of Dutch planning law while others do require. This is almost the same as distinguishing between recommendations implementable in the short and in the long term. In addition, a fictitious example of an urban regeneration scheme has been used to illustrate the recommendations: Urban Regeneration in *Sturingerland*. The example has been inspired by the example used in Vrom et al. (2008) to illustrate the workings of the new Physical Planning Act, introduced on the 1st of July 2008. My example is the regeneration of an old deteriorated urban area, which has buildings and streets and is divided into four parcels A-D (see Figure 33). In the example, the abstract recommendations are made more detailed, adapted to the specific circumstances. The example is meant to make the recommendations clearer.

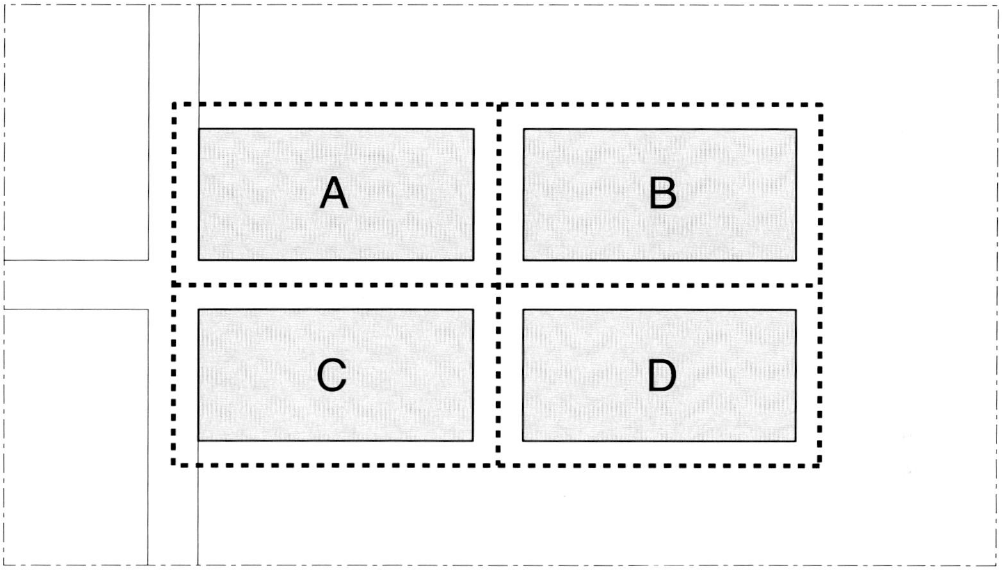

Figure 33. Urban regeneration scheme in *Sturingerland.*

Structure of this chapter

When enumerating the relevant rules and the subsequent recommendations for Dutch practice, I follow the narrative structure set out in section 3.3.3 and distinguish between the following sub-variables:

1. Creating Certainty beforehand about future building possibilities and contributions;
2. Choosing the contents of the legally binding rules;
3. Making the legally binding rules conditional on the developer securing his contribution;
4. Modulating property rights.

9.1 Creating certainty beforehand about future building possibilities and contributions

Summary of the findings

Here follows a summary of the findings that underpin the recommendations. See section 8.1 for more details.

Certainty about future building possibilities

Municipalities in all three countries, in order to improve transparency and accountability in their planning decisions, usually create certainty in early stages and in different degrees, about what the landowner will be allowed to build. In the Netherlands, municipalities usually approve indicative, not legally binding plans, and these indicative plans create some certainty, for example *Nota van Uitgangspunten, Stedenbouwkundig Plan/Visie, Ontwikkelingsprogramma, Programma van Eisen, Masterplan, Structuurplan, Structuurvisie* etc. In England something similar is done, also through indicative documents; in Valencia this is accomplished through the approval of legally binding General land use plans that must cover the entire territory of the municipality.

However, the findings suggest that more certainty beforehand may result in less value capturing. If municipalities prescribe early on in the development process building possibilities, it might stimulate land price increases, and municipalities could lose a valuable negotiation tool. However, certainty about building possibilities is not necessarily disadvantageous if accompanied by certainty about future contributions (see below).

Certainty about future contributions
There are large differences in the certainty beforehand about what the landowner will have to contribute to public infrastructure and facilities. In Valencia in the early stages there is high certainty about future contributions through (1) legally prescribed minimum standards, (2) local policy, and (3) the approval of legally binding General land use plans. English municipalities usually create some certainty through the approval of (1) site-specific indicative plans that establish the contributions for the development in question, and (2) non site-specific indicative generic policy documents that establish standard contributions. In the Netherlands, most of the time there is no certainty at all, neither through legally binding nor indicative documents, before negotiations take place, or before the price of the land is determined.

This certainty in Valencia and England has influenced the capturing of value increase in a positive way because: 1) it has lowered the price of the land, because if there is no certainty the developer pays too much for the land and has less financial room to contribute; 2) certainty lowers the price at which the developer accounts the land in the financial calculation of the operation, and the regular profit margin that the developer aims for; (3) certainty gives the public officers a strong policy base to require contributions, which do not need to be introduced as something new during the course of the negotiations.

9.1.1 Short-term recommendations: create Certainty in indicative documents

Although creating certainty about future building possibilities might have negative consequences for public value capturing, this research does not recommend increasing uncertainty. Such a recommendation would not fit within the trend in planning policy that pursues transparency and predictability about future development sites. Also, the findings show that the possible negative effects can be compensated by creating beforehand certainty about future contributions. Thus, the recommendation is that Dutch municipalities, before or together with the preparation of indicative plans, should create certainty about which contributions will be required from developers. The new Structure vision (*Structuurvisie*) can play a central role in achieving this goal. In general, it does not seem that this recommendation would encounter significant resistance. The adoption of cost recovery policy documents, of the sort set out here, fits well within the traditional autonomy of Dutch municipalities, and within the legal framework. The only objection could be that the preparation of such documents requires that municipalities better foresee their future needs for public infrastructure and facilities. Dutch planning is characterized by being vague, open and flexible in early stages of development processes. Municipalities usually specify and detail their requirements during the plan process, adapting to the specific circumstances and needs that arise close to the start of development activities. This is not compatible with specifying future contributions in the early stages. The following will provide more details regarding the recommendation.

9.1.1.1 Certainty about what

Section 7.2.3 shows the costs that can legally be included in a Development contributions plan (*Exploitatieplan*) and designates which portion can be charged to the landowners. It also shows the costs that can be secured in an anterior Development agreement (*anterieure overeenkomst*) and thus charged to the landowners.

The sorts of costs that can be included in the Development contributions plan are listed in the new 2008 Physical Planning Decree, and not all of them can be charged to the landowners. This regulatory base itself is, however, not enough for creating certainty, as developers need to be able to: 1) accurately calculate in an early stage of the process those costs that can be included in a Development contributions plan; and 2) which portion they will have to pay in case the municipality approves such a plan. Table 28 lists the aspects that municipalities should specify in order to make those calculations possible.

However, not all of these costs can be charged to the landowners. Probably only part of the costs of refurbishing old existing infrastructure within or in the immediate surroundings (1a) can be charged, the other part not, and anyway the maintenance/exploitation costs of this infrastructure, whether refurbished or new, cannot be charged at all. The construction *and* maintenance/exploitation costs of social facilities (*maatschappelijke voorzieningen*, 1a) cannot be charged; part of the costs of infrastructure serving a wider area (2a) cannot be charged; and probably contributions to other schemes (3a) too cannot be charged. The already incurred costs most likely cannot be charged. In addition, if the calculated profits do not cover the full costs, the deficit cannot be charged to the landowners, regardless whether the costs fulfil all the criteria making landowners liable. In regeneration sites this may be frequently the case,

Table 28. Certainty, to be created by Dutch municipalities about the costs that, in case they finally approve a Development contributions plan, would be included in this plan

Categories of costs that can be included in a Development contributions Plan	**Municipalities should create certainty by specifying the following...**
1a. Public infrastructure and facilities within or in the immediate surroundings of the development site, plus possible damage to surrounding property owners.	Outline characterization, location and dimensions of roads, sewerage, parks, public buildings, etc. This is needed in case the development site is big. In smaller sites, there is no need of much infrastructure and the infrastructure that is needed is easily predictable without the municipality having to prescribe it beforehand. Regarding damage to surrounding property owners, municipalities should make clear that the developer is liable to pay the compensation.
2a. Public infrastructure and facilities serving a wider area (*bovenwijkse voorzieningen*)	Because of the confusion regarding the differences between what the 2008 Act calls *bovenwijkse voorzieningen*, *bovenplanse verevening/kosten* and *ruimtelijke ontwikkelingen* (3 and 7, see under), it is recommended to include a similar argumentation as for 3a, and include that argumentation in a Structure vision.
3a. Contributions to (i) other schemes (*bovenplanse verevening*) or to (ii) public infrastructure and facilities (*bovenplanse kosten*), not necessarily related in a direct way to the development in question.	**Argumentation** The location and characterization of the needed investments, and at least an outline indication of the costs. It is also necessary to characterize the relation between the investments and the scheme that must contribute. The relationship between them must be argued, without necessarily having to prove a direct relationship in terms of the three legal criteria of profit (*profijt*), causality/attributability (*toerekenbaarheid*) and proportionality (*proportionaliteit*).[1] In Dutch terms, the *ruimtelijke en functionele samenhang* must be argued. It is enough if it is argued why both are related in 'planning' terms, i.e. with arguments related to traffic, economic, social issues, etc., but *it is not enough* just to prescribe that the scheme must contribute. In addition, it must be argued why the investments are in the public interest. Also an indication of all the schemes that must contribute should be given. Contributions can be in kind, a payment for a specific investment, or a payment to a fund. In case of payments to a fund,[2] the goals for the fund must be prescribed, i.e. where is the money going to be spent. This must be done as detailed as possible, but, in case investments are not yet well defined and decided, an outline of not detailed prescriptions might be enough. However, probably it will not be possible to include the contributions in a Development contributions plan if the investments: a) are not detailed enough to apply the three legal criteria, or b) have not yet been spent before the Development contributions plan becomes definitely closed. The contributions could then only be included in an anterior Development agreement (see below). Finally, the criteria must be set out following which the projects must contribute to the fund.

	In which document The 2008 Act prescribes that in order to be included in a Development contributions plan *and* charged to the landowners, this argumentation must be included in a Structure vision. If the contribution is to be agreed in an anterior agreement (see below), there is in theory no need to include this argumentation in a Structure vision. However, because of the confusion about the differences between *bovenwijkse voorzieningen* (2), *bovenplanse verevening/kosten* and *ruimtelijke ontwikkelingen* (7, see below), it is desirable to include the argumentation in a Structure vision. In case of contribution to a fund, the argumentation, no matter how detailed, should be included in the implementation paragraph (*uitvoeringsparagraaf*), to be added to the Vision. **Sources:** Vrom et al., 2008: 46-48, 85, 127-128, 153; Zundert, 2008: 472; Baardewijk, 2008: 756-757, 759, 762-763; Groot, 2009: 464-465.
4a. Social housing within the plan area	Minimum percentage and/or minimum number, and the location, of social rented housing and social housing for sale, both in the scheme in question and in a wider area (distribution of social housing between the scheme and all other schemes in the area) should be specified. Also, some additional requirements that might have consequences for the development costs: for social rented housing, allocation rules (as long as these rules derive their status from housing legislation and local regulations) and requirements about the minimum period of social function and maximal rent price (e.g. that the landowner must secure in a Development agreement that he/she will maintain the social function for at least the first 10 years); for social housing for sale, rules for the selection of buyers (as long as these rules derive their status from housing legislation and local regulations), anti-speculation rules, and, provided there is a previous regional agreement on the matter, the maximum price for sale to individual buyers.
5a. The land needed for all this infrastructure, also for social services	This is already clear from the above-mentioned.
6. Green/natural areas in the development site that will be lost (*verloren gegane natuurwaarde, groenvoorzieningen en watervoorzieningen*)	a) Location of the green areas that will disappear and qualification of these areas as green area (vegetation or water, but not for example agricultural land); b) the necessity and the obligation that the projects that are responsible for the loss must compensate it; and c) the location and outline indications of the costs of creating new areas that replace the areas lost, in or outside the development site. It is necessary that at least a) and b) are included in any plan of the central, provincial, regional or municipal governments (e.g. structure visions or land use plans, Vrom e.a, 2008: 47).

1 In section 1.5 it is said that the goal of this research is to improve cost recovery, not to make it easier for public bodies to cream off the added value. However, the definition of which costs fall under 'cost recovery' is not undisputed. The same public infrastructure can be considered as related to the development by one person, but at the same time as going too far by another person. The arguments are on both sizes largely of a normative/ideological character. Especially contributions of the sorts 2, 3 and 7 might be the subject of discussion.

partly because the method of calculation of the land costs include the highest possible price, i.e. a maximal accounted land costs (*inbrengwaarde* in Dutch) instead of the minimum land costs (see section 7.2.3 for more details).

Table 29. Certainty to be created by Dutch municipalities, in addition to the costs listed in Table 28, about the costs that they wish to include in an anterior Development agreement.

Categories of costs that can be included in anterior agreement	**Municipalities should create certainty by specifying the following...**
1-5b. Those costs that can be included in Development contributions plan but not charged to landowners (see section 7.2.3 for more details)	This is already clear if municipalities make clear that *all* the costs listed above in Table 28, also those that cannot be charged through a Development contributions plan, will be charged.
4b. Additional requirements for social housing	Requirements that might have consequences for the development costs: for rented units e.g. allocation rules even if not derived from housing legislation or local regulation, or indications of maximum price of the units to be sold to housing associations; for units for sale e.g. allocation rules regarding the selection of the buyers even if not derived from housing legislation or local regulation, and in case of no previous regional agreement on this matter, indications of maximum selling prices to buyers.
7. Contributions to 'Spatial developments' (*ruimtelijke ontwikkelingen*) situated outside the development in question. The contributions can be for *construction* costs, and maybe also for *maintenance* and *exploitation* costs.	The argumentation should be the same as for contributions to other schemes or to public infrastructure and facilities (3). The 2008 Act prescribes that the argumentation must be included in a Structure vision (Vrom et al., 2008: 46-48).

When instead of approving a Development contributions plan, the municipality and the developer achieve an anterior Development agreement, it is possible to recover more costs: 1) it is possible to include the not-covered costs mentioned in previous paragraph; 2) and in addition it is possible to include in the agreement some other costs that cannot be included in a Development contributions plan. Of course, finally there must be enough final profit (i.e. profit available to the developer to allow him to contribute more) to pay all the costs, but with an anterior Development agreement this is easier. The reason is that in this agreement parties have the freedom to agree a higher or lower accounted land price, while in a Development contributions plan the accounted land price *must be* the maximum possible (i.e. the price of the use of the land after regeneration). In other words, while in a Development contributions plan the accounted land costs *must be* the value of the land after regeneration, in a Development agreement it is possible to agree a value that falls more in the neighbourhood of the land use prior to regeneration.

The recommendation is that municipalities that want to recover more costs should focus their strategy on signing an anterior Development agreement with the developer. The first step is to create certainty about the costs that the municipality wishes to include in this agreement. This certainty is necessary to allow developers to accurately calculate the development costs and contributions they have to pay in an early stage of the development process. Table 29 lists which aspects municipalities should specify in order to make those calculations possible.

EXAMPLE OF URBAN REGENERATION IN STURINGERLAND, Part One
In our fictitious example, the Municipality of Sturingerland has created certainty about contributions to the costs. These costs cover both those that can be included in a Development contributions plan, and in a Development agreement:

1a. Public infrastructure and facilities within or in the immediate surroundings of the site (map 1a):

- Roads to be refurbished and a new road to connect to the general road network;
- The sewerage within the plan area, and connection to the general sewerage network;
- A park with a playground for children;
- An estimate of the maintenance/exploitation costs for all this infrastructure and facilities that should be charged to the developer.

2a: Public infrastructure and facilities serving a wider area (*bovenwijkse voorzieningen*) (map 2a):

- Road alongside the plan area, which must be refurbished and which serves three schemes, including the development in question;
- A new sewerage pipeline that connects the general network to this scheme and to five other schemes;
- A park that serves the entire district;
- An estimate of the maintenance/exploitation costs of all this infrastructure and facilities that should be charged to the developer.

3a: Contributions to a fund meant for paying investments in off-site schemes and public infrastructure and facilities not directly related to the development in question (*bovenplanse verevening/kosten*). These schemes and public infrastructure and facilities are those prescribed in categories 2 and 7. Also included is the estimate of the maintenance/exploitation costs of this infrastructure and facilities that should be charged to the developer.

4a: Social housing (map 4):

- A minimum percentage in this part of the city (20% for rent, 20% for sale);
- Indications about location of social housing (in plots along 30 km per hour-roads);

- Social housing for rent: housing association Z has the competence to select the tenants according to criteria to be agreed with the municipality and based on housing legislation and housing local regulations, the owner of the houses must maintain the social function for at least 25 years (15 years more than the legal minimum), rental price must be X% under the maximum price prescribed in national standard (in *Besluit op de huurtoeslag*);
- Social housing for sale: housing association Z has the competence to select the buyers according to criteria to be agreed with the municipality and based on housing legislation and housing local regulations, the buyer cannot sell the house on the free market for at least 10 years, and the selling price must be, following a regional agreement with other municipalities, Y% under the maximum price prescribed by a national standard (in *Besluit beheer sociale-huursector*) or in this regional agreement.

6: Four green areas will be lost (*verloren gegane natuurwaarde, groenvoorzieningen en watervoorzieningen*), one of which is situated within the development in question and will be lost, and three outside. Three green areas will be created or refurbished to compensate this loss (map 6-7). In addition, also included is the estimate of the maintenance/exploitation costs that should be charged to the developer.

4b: Additional requirements for social housing:
- Social housing for rent: housing association Z has the competence to select the tenants according to criteria to be agreed with the municipality but not based on housing legislation and housing local regulations. Further, in case housing association Z buys the units from the developer, the maximum selling price is to be set so that Z does not incur any loss (the *bedrijfswaarde*);
- Social housing for sale: housing association Z has the competence to select the buyers according to criteria to be agreed with the municipality but not based on housing legislation and housing local regulations. Further, in case a regional agreement fails, the selling price must be Y% under the maximum price prescribed by a national standard (in *Besluit beheer sociale-huursector*).

7: 'Spatial developments' (*ruimtelijke ontwikkelingen*) situated outside the development in question (map 6-7):
- A district of old social housing that must be regenerated;
- A new International Congress Center;
- Global calculation of the costs of both: € 5 and € 20 million respectively;
- An estimate of the maintenance/exploitation costs of this infrastructure and facilities that should be charged to the developer;
- The area within which all development schemes will have to contribute to those spatial developments: besides the development in question, also schemes A-M, € 100 per each m^2 of floor space.

Also, it includes 'spatial developments' situated within the development in question but which can only be charged if labelled as 'spatial developments' (map 1a):

- School, community centre (*buurthuis*), social welfare facility (*welzijn*) and the estimate of the associated maintenance/exploitation costs of this infrastructure and facilities that should be charged to the developer.

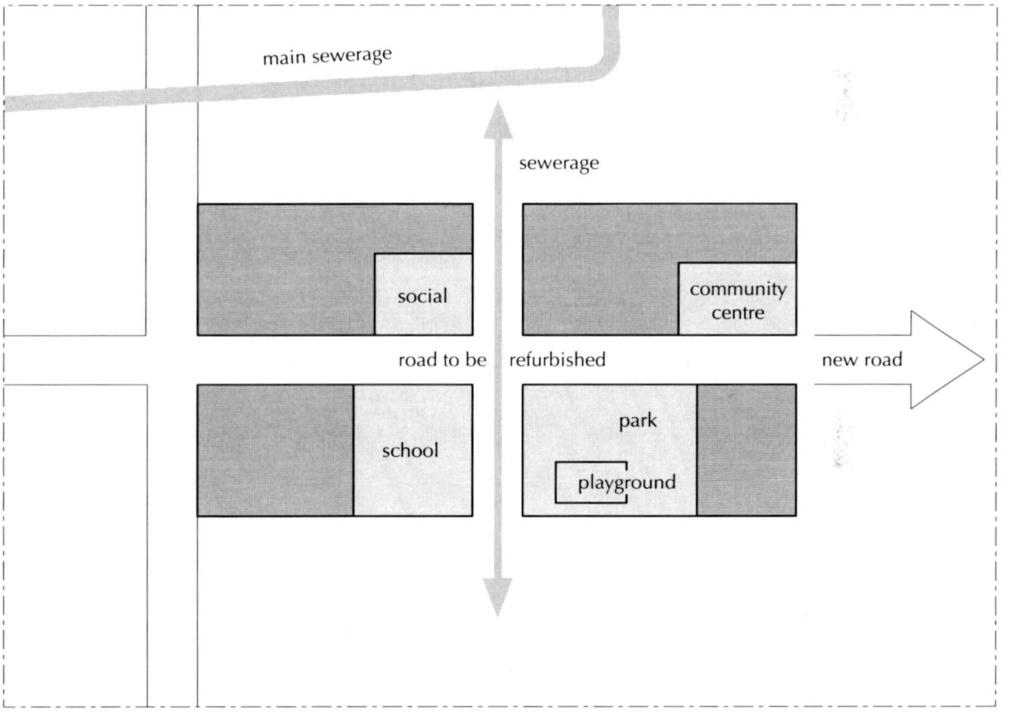

Map 1a. Public infrastructure and facilities within or in the immediate surroundings of the site in *Sturingerland*.

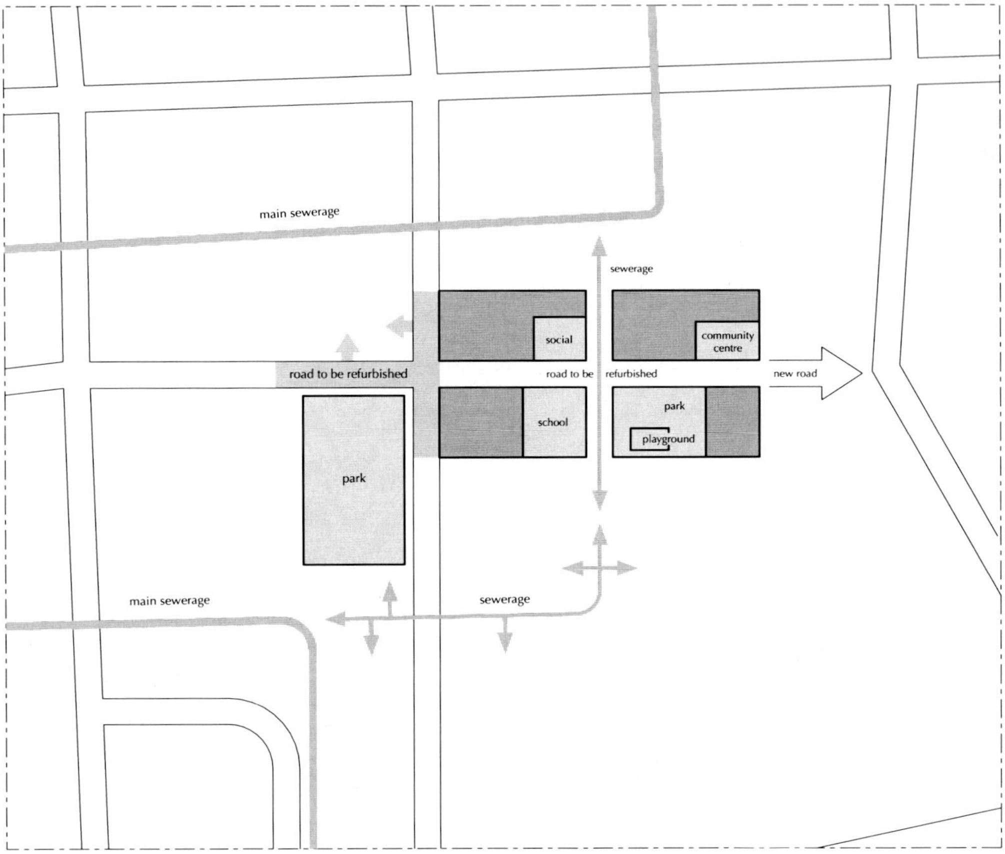

Map 2a. Public infrastructure and facilities serving a wider area in *Sturingerland* (*bovenwijkse voorzieningen*).

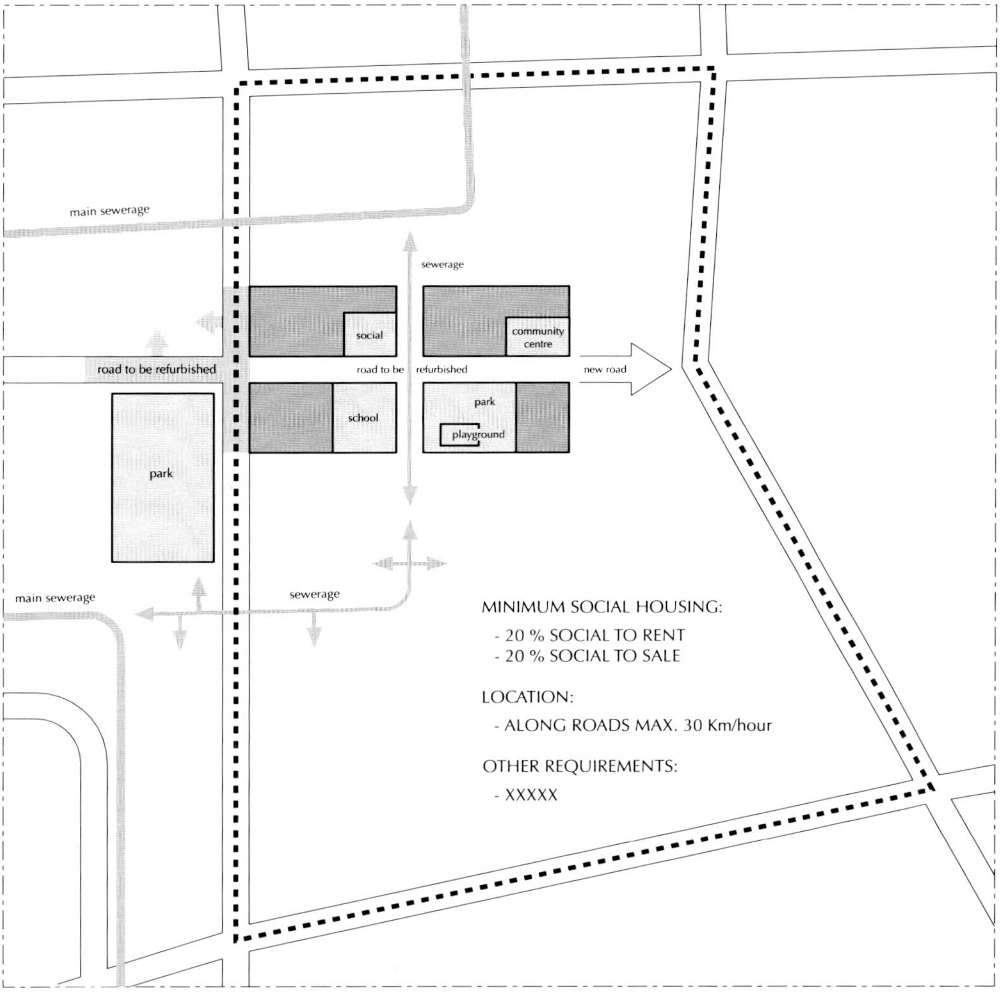

Map 4. Social housing in *Sturingerland*.

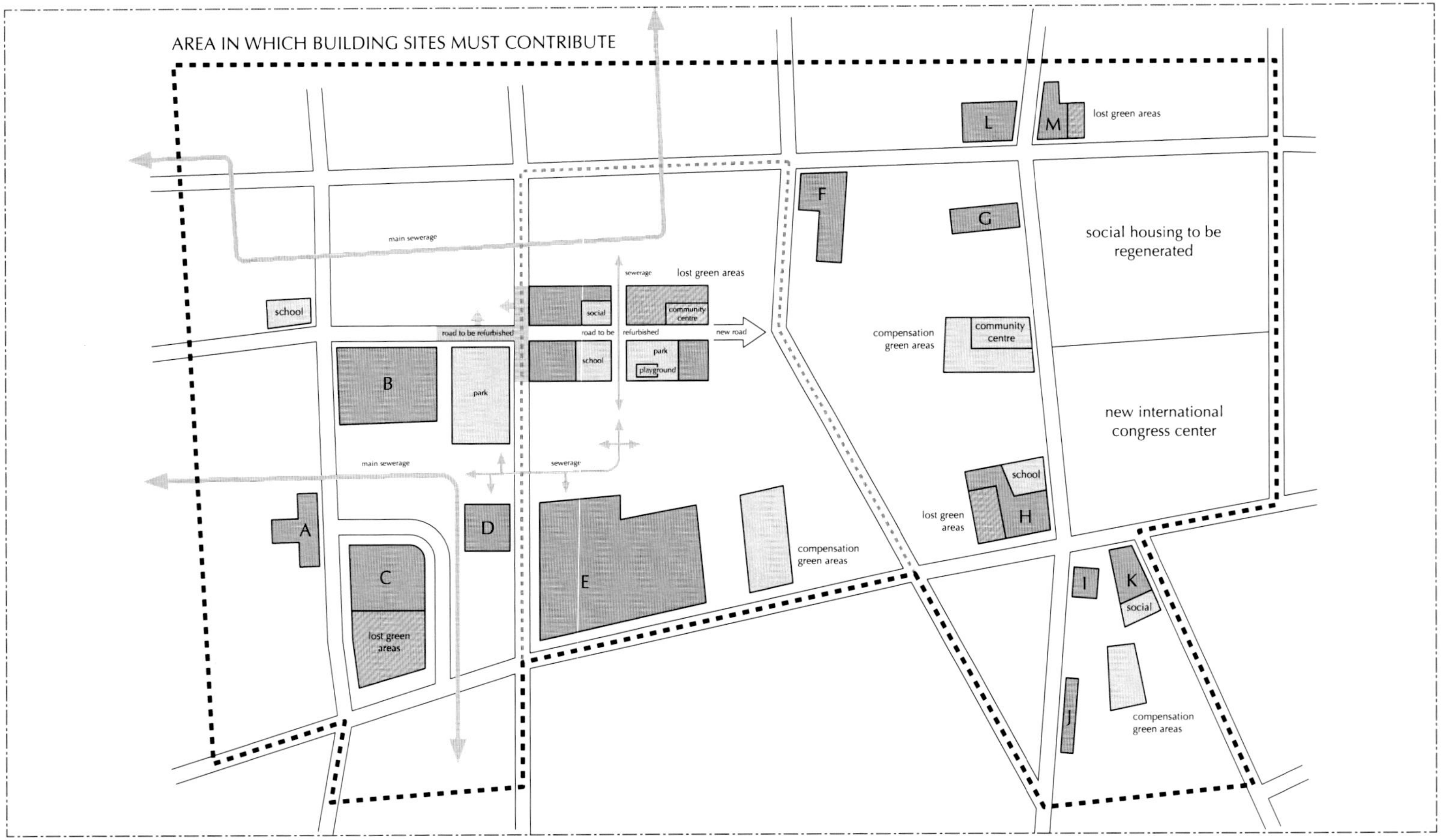

Map 6 and 7. Contributions to other schemes (*bovenplanse verevening/kosten*), to 'Spatial developments' (*ruimtelijke ontwikkelingen*), and green areas that will be lost (*verloren gegane natuurwaarden, groen- en watervoorzieningen*) in *Sturingerland*. A to M are the regeneration sites that, in addittion to the contributions by our site, must also contribute.

9.1.1.2 Sorts of documents to create certainty: site-specific document, generic documents and General zoning plan

Municipalities can create this certainty in different sorts of documents. They can choose one or several of them depending on the specific circumstances and many of the documents can complement each other. The following demonstrates four different possibilities:

Site-specific documents

It has already been said that Dutch municipalities usually work in early stages of the development processes towards indicative site-specific plans that create development expectations. At the same time, municipalities should also include the obligatory contributions in similar site-specific documents. These site-specific documents about contributions can include contribution categories 1 to 7 and should preferably be included within the site-specific plans (*in* the plans or *enclosed* as an appendix) to guarantee a simultaneous approval and publication. A possible example is the 1998 Planning Brief that preceded the negotiations in case *Harbourside*, England. This document prescribed a contribution for an off-site facility, the obligation to comply with local social housing policy and to pay the entire on-site infrastructure, including soil decontamination costs (for more details see frame 6d in chapter 6.4.1.1).

Generic document, integral character

Generic documents are valid for the territory of the entire municipality, a part of it or for a specific category of schemes. They include standard contributions (so they do not necessarily include a map) focussing on all policy fields (social housing, off-site infrastructure, social facilities, etc). The standard contributions are applicable to any development that takes place within the predefined boundaries or categories, for example, standard contributions for greenfield sites, and other standards for regeneration sites. This can be a policy document (*nota*), approved alone or together with the land policy document (*nota grondbeleid*), or just a decision (*besluit*) of the Local Council. An example from abroad is the decision of the Municipality of Valencia in 2004, in which the municipality specified the contributions that developers should pay/implement, in addition to the contributions already established in planning legislation, in the rezoning of former industrial or offices sites into housing (for more details see frame 5i in chapter 5.5.1.2). Another example is the 2005 SPD4 document from Bristol, which includes detailed standard contributions for all new developments within the city boundaries (for more details see frame 6e in chapter 6.4.1.1).

Generic document, sectoral character

An alternative to the generic integral document is a document that focuses on specific policy fields, like social housing. For example, local social housing policy documents can prescribe standard requirements for social housing (categories 4a and 4b). Other examples include a policy document for public facilities that serve wide areas (*nota bovenwijkse voorzieningen*, Vrom, 2008: 121, 128), which can prescribe categories 2a, 3a, 4a, 4b and 7; and a policy document for long-term investments in public infrastructure (*meerjarig investeringsplan infrastructuur*, op. cit.: 157), which can prescribe categories 2a, 3a and 7. The sectoral document should be seen as a second best option: the integral document is preferable because it guarantees that all contributions in all policy fields are clear. Relying on sectoral documents carries the inherent risk of fragmentation and lack of transparency. Both integral and sectoral generic documents can be complementary, for example an integral document can summarize and integrate prescriptions from several sectoral documents.

General zoning plans
General zoning plans cover the entire territory of the municipality or a part of it (without focusing on just one development site), and can include all cost categories. Possibly, they can also incorporate standard charges, meaning that they also become Generic documents. In Dutch practice there are already many indicative zoning plans covering the entire territory of the municipality or a large part of it (e.g. *Structuurplan/Structuurvisie*), but usually they include only vague prescriptions for categories 1a, 2a, 3a and 7, and say nothing about the others. Furthermore, these indicative plans do not usually prescribe who is going to pay/implement the contributions.

9.1.1.3 Indicative Structure vision
Should these sorts of documents (Site-specific document, Generic documents and General zoning plan) be of an indicative or a legally binding character? It seems that indicative plans fit better in the Dutch planning culture and practice: in early stages of development processes, municipalities usually work with indicative plans, but not with binding ones. The documents should be binding for the public body that approves them, but not for the use possibilities of the land. This means that the executive body or the Local Council must take into consideration the contents of the plan, but can also depart from it after proper argumentation. In other words, the documents should prescribe the development's basic requirements that must be taken into account as a hard starting point in the negotiations. During the negotiations, municipalities can consider modifications in order to adapt to specific circumstances. Another argument in favour of flexible indicative documents is that a stronger legally binding character would create the necessity of regulating by law both the contents of the documents and the approval/adoption procedure (Vrom, 2003: 13).

The 2008 Spatial Planning Act introduced a new sort of indicative document that may be the ideal document for including any of the mentioned categories of costs and sorts of documents: the Structure vision (*Structuurvisie*). The new Act does not prescribe procedural or formal requirements for this document. Structure visions can include a broad range of elements: besides the physical zoning, also determinations regarding the implementation of the development (article 2.1.1 2008 Act). They can have an outline character, but also contain detailed maps and determinations (Vrom, 2003: 11-13). This means that Site-specific documents and General zoning plans can be put in the form of a Structure vision. Also, a Structure vision can focus on one singular aspect of planning policy, or several aspects, and on how the developments prescribed in it can be implemented (article 2.1.2). This means that Generic documents can also be shaped as a Structure vision.

The 2008 Act prescribes several direct links between structure visions and cost recovery; for some sorts of costs, it is obligatory to use the Structure vision as a vehicle:

- First, anterior Development agreements can include contributions for 'spatial developments' (category 7, *ruimtelijke ontwikkelingen*) only if prescribed by the Structure vision (Vrom et al., 2008: 46-48, 85). Table 29 above shows exactly what the vision must prescribe;
- Second, a Development contributions plan can include the obligation for the landowners to contribute to other schemes or to funds meant for investments outside the site in question (category 3a, *bovenplanse verevening/kosten*) only if it is prescribed by a Vision (Vrom et al., 2008: 85). Table 28 gives more details about what the Vision must prescribe.
- Third, currently confusion exists regarding the differences between *ruimtelijke ontwikkelingen*, *bovenplanse verevening/kosten* and *bovenwijkse voorzieningen*. Because this confusion will not be resolved until jurisprudence has developed clear criteria, which will take several years, it is highly recommended to also include the *bovenwijkse voorzieningen* in a Structure vision, with a similar argumentation as for *ruimtelijke ontwikkelingen* and *bovenplanse verevening/kosten* (*confero* Baardewijk, 2008: 759). This will prevent possible surprises in the courts.
- Fourth, compensation costs for green and nature areas (category 6, *verloren gegane natuurwaarde, groen- en watervoorzieningen*) can be included in a Development contributions plan only if they are already mentioned as such in a policy document, such as a Structure vision. Furthermore, this document should prescribe the necessity of compensation (Vrom et al., 2008: 115).

In short, the Structure vision seems not only to be a logical and handy document. Also, the new 2008 Physical Planning Act and Decree create the obligation to use it for capturing value increase, at least for cost categories 3a, 6 and 7 (op. cit.: 84-85, 115). The documents can be reviewed each year, together with the yearly municipal budget, in order to provide up-to-date calculations of the contributions.

EXAMPLE URBAN REGENERATION IN STURINGERLAND, Part Two

The Municipality of Sturingerland has specified the future contributions through a set of documents. Thanks to all these documents, when the Municipality of Sturingerland initiated the negotiations with the developers, the required contributions were the starting point. Also, the developers who bought parcels B, C and D (see Figure 33) took into consideration these contributions in the price they agreed with the former landowners. The documents are:

Structure vision Sturingerland 2020
A Structure vision covering all regeneration schemes in the city. This document corresponds with the sort General zoning plan and includes cost categories 1a, 2a, 6 and 7, already detailed in the Part One of the example.

Housing Policy Sturingerland 2020
Together with the Vision 2020, the municipality approved a Housing Policy note for the entire territory of the municipality. This document corresponds to the Generic sectoral document type and has been added to the 2020 Vision as an appendix. It includes cost categories 4a and 4b, already detailed in Part One of the example.

Standard charges in implementation paragraph Structure vision Sturingerland 2020
Together with the Vision 2020, the municipality approved some standard charges, which apply for all developments in the city. This document corresponds with the Generic document type and has been added to the 2020 Vision as part of its implementation paragraph (*uitvoeringsparagraaf*). It includes several additional prescriptions about cost category 7, already detailed in Part One of the example: a global calculation of the costs of all *ruimtelijke ontwikkelingen*, estimated at € 25 million. When this is divided by the estimated m^2 of dwellings and office space to be built in the scheme in question and in schemes A-M, the standard contribution is €100 per m^2 of floor space.

9.1.1.4 The central government stimulates municipalities to prepare Generic documents

There is the risk that expectations of future building possibilities arise quickly and catch the municipality unprepared or (or even unwilling to prepare) any of the abovementioned sorts of documents. The English experience shows that municipalities do not always make the necessary efforts. Only after the British central government began to actively stimulate the approval of Generic integral documents, has the number of municipalities that draft these documents grown significantly. The 2005 SPD4 document in Bristol is an example of such an intervention. The Dutch central government should follow the British example, and stimulate municipalities to do their homework. For example, the central government can stimulate municipalities by preparing model documents. It is preferable that the central government's efforts focus on stimulating Generic integral documents, which can be but do not necessarily have to be integrated in General zoning plans. The advantage of Generic integral documents is that they guarantee that all developments in the municipality, from very early stages, start with a reasonable level of certainty about future contributions. Afterwards, once the development possibilities and the desired contributions are clearer, municipalities can also prepare Site-specific documents to further specify the contributions. In this task, the central government should work together with the Association of Netherlands Municipalities (*Vereniging Nederlandse Gemeenten*), which often produces model documents for daily use by municipalities.

9.1.2 Long-term recommendations: legal modifications

For the longer term, legal modifications might be necessary to guarantee that in all municipalities there is a minimum level of certainty about future contributions. Legal modifications must be seen as a second best option, should the above-mentioned voluntary measures not be widely applied in practice. The legal modification can be accomplished in two ways: first by obliging municipalities to prepare Generic integral documents, and second by introducing minimum standard charges in planning law. These measures may encounter some political resistance. Dutch municipalities are used to acting very autonomously in determining their planning policy and may see these measures as interference in their competences.

Stimulating and obliging municipalities to introduce Generic integral documents

As we have seen, the first recommendation was to elaborate a model document and to offer it to municipalities, which can use it freely and do not need to 'rediscover the wheel' on their own. But a model voluntary document is not enough. Article 2.1.2 Physical Planning Act should add the obligation that municipalities approve a Structure vision specifically including a Generic integral document, or to include this document in the implementation paragraph of a broader Structure vision. These Structure visions must be based on a flexible but also obligatory list of contents, a sort of index, to be specified in the Physical Planning Decree in addition to the actual list of sorts of costs (articles 6.2.3 to 6.2.6). This obligatory index guarantees a certain level of uniformity among municipalities, and eliminates the danger of municipalities approving documents that are too vague. This gives to landowners and developers the certainty that they can expect the same contributions everywhere in the country.

EXAMPLE URBAN REGENERATION IN STURINGERLAND, Part Three

The central government in The Hague is not happy with the progress made by municipalities in elaborating an adequate policy base for cost recovery. Sturingerland, with its Structure vision 2020 and complementary documents (see example Part Two), is a positive exception.

Model document

To stimulate municipalities, the central government and the Association of Netherlands Municipalities (*VNG*) elaborated a model document, based on the experience in Sturingerland. It is not obligatory to follow this model, but it can help municipalities to elaborate their own documents.

Obligatory Structure vision about cost recovery, and obligatory national list of contents

The Hague decides to go further. The Parliament introduces in the Physical Planning Act the obligation for municipalities to approve Structure visions (as a separate document or in its implementation paragraph) focusing on cost recovery. Also, the Parliament

introduces in the Physical Planning Decree the minimum topics that such a document must include, inspired by the documents from Sturingerland. These minimum topics, which municipalities must fill in, are an elaboration based on these main categories:
- Social Housing (cost categories 4a and 4b);
- Public infrastructure and facilities serving wider areas (cost category 2a);
- Green/natural areas that will be lost (cost category 6);
- Spatial developments (cost category 7).

Introducing legal minimum standard charges and prescriptions

If, despite this legal obligation, there are still many municipalities that have no or have insufficiently elaborated cost recovery documents, the Dutch central government could consider a second measure: a modification in the Physical Planning Decree to introduce legal minimum standard charges for the entire country. The legal standard charges could differentiate between different categories of development sites (e.g. residential, offices, industrial, urban regeneration, greenfield development). Minimum standard charges prescribed in law have the side effect that they do not leave much flexibility for adaptation to specific circumstances. Therefore, legal minimum standard charges could sometimes refer to outline instead of detailed standards, and could prescribe the requirement that the municipality must further hammer them out in detail. Actually, this means a combination of legal minimum standard charges and the above mentioned obligation for municipalities to fill in an obligatory list of contents. The Valencian legal standard charges are an example of such a combination. First, they include minimum standard charges, more or less detailed, such as minimum public space, minimum public buildings and parking places depending on the land use (residential, industrial, etc). But they also prescribe the obligation for municipalities to prepare local planning documents that further detail/complement a predefined set of topics (for more details about Valencian legal standard charges, see frame 5h in chapter 5.5.1.1).

EXAMPLE URBAN REGENERATION IN STURINGERLAND, Part Four

Despite the measures, there are still many municipalities that have no, or have insufficiently elaborated, cost recovery documents. Usually, large cities have good documents, but smaller municipalities do not. An evaluation show that municipalities with good documents generally obtain good results in practice, while the others show results that are worse and very varied (sometimes adequate, sometimes very bad) depending on specific circumstances (negotiations skills of involved public officers, local market circumstances, quality and commitment of local politicians, etc.).

National detailed standard charges and prescriptions for cost recovery

The central government in The Hague decides to introduce in the Physical Planning Decree detailed standard charges and prescriptive determinations:

Standard charges (inspired often by the documents of Sturingerland, see Parts One and Two of the example):

- Spatial developments (*ruimtelijke ontwikkelingen*, cost category 7): € 100 per each new m² of floor space;
- Lost green/natural areas (*verloren gegane natuurwaarde, groenvoorzieningen en watervoorzieningen*, cost category 6): applies to all developments, the developer is required to submit a compensation plan (if there is no document already specifying the compensation locations), to implement compensation green and finally to transfer it to the municipality;
- Social housing (cost category 4a): a minimum of 20% rent units and 20% selling units, taking account of the total m² of floor space, not the number of units, to prevent developers from constructing social houses that are too small.

Prescriptive determinations, to be detailed by municipalities:

- Public infrastructure and facilities serving wider areas (*bovenwijkse voorzieningen*, cost category 2): municipalities must characterize them, prescribe the locations, calculate the global costs, argue the relationship between the infrastructure and facilities and the schemes, and prescribe the schemes that benefit and the schemes that must contribute;
- Spatial developments (cost category 7): municipalities must review the national standard charge of €100 per m², that serves as a minimum, and prescribe the schemes that must contribute;
- Green/natural areas to be lost (cost category 6): municipalities must prescribe the compensation locations, and calculate the global costs.

Thanks to these legal standard charges and prescriptions, the required minimum future contributions are clear in the Netherlands. These measures have been useful especially in those small municipalities that had not prepared any, or prepared insufficient, cost recovery documents.

9.2 Choosing the contents of binding rules

As section 8.2 already showed, being able to include aspects related to the financing and implementation of public infrastructure and facilities in binding plans can have a positive effect on capturing value increase. In Valencia and England, planning law makes it possible to prescribe in binding rules a wide range of requirements: contributions to social/affordable housing, contributions to on-site and off-site public infrastructure and facilities, contributions to social facilities (*maatschappelijke voorzieningen*), and also the possibility of prescribing investment and implementation schedules for these contributions.

In the Netherlands, until the 2008 Physical Planning Act, none of these requirements could be prescribed in the binding rules, and this had a negative effect on capturing value increase. The 2008 Physical Planning Act made it possible for the first time to include almost all these requirements. Nowadays, it is possibly to include social/affordable housing both in the Land use plan and the departures from it (a percentage) and in the Development contributions plan (allocation to the plots and number of units). It is also possible to introduce implementation schedules and contributions for most of the on-site infrastructure and for some sorts of off-site infrastructure in the Development contributions plan. However, two limitations remain:

1. It is still uncertain whether it is possible to prescribe contributions for maintenance/exploitation costs in general, and for construction and maintenance/exploitation costs of social facilities (*maatschappelijke voorzieningen*) in particular. The Dutch parliament decided during the deliberation on the 2008 Land Development Act to exclude the possibility of charging social facilities through a Development contributions plan. Thus, also after the adoption of the 2008 Act, Development contributions plans cannot include these contributions, i.e. these cannot be charged to the landowners. Besides this, it is not clear whether this parliamentary decision has consequences not only for the Development contributions plan, but also for the contents of anterior Development agreements. If plans cannot include contributions for social facilities, can agreements? Could such contributions be required from the developer, or can they result from a unilateral undertaking by the developer (see frame 7f in section 7.2.3)? If developer and municipality agree to such a contribution in an agreement, this might afterwards be the subject of a legal intervention, in case there is an appeal (Van den Brand, interview 2008). To make it possible to charge such contributions without the risk of facing appeals, a section should be added to the list of sorts of costs in article 6.2.5 of the Physical Planning Decree: *"i. Social facilities"*.[2]
2. Many of the costs included in a Development contributions plan cannot be charged to the landowner (see sections 7.2.3 and 9.1.1.1): parts of the on-site infrastructure, the entire maintenance/exploitation costs, a larger part of the off-site infrastructure, the entire costs of off-site public investments not directly related to the development in question, and probably also not the costs that have been already incurred on the site. To make it possible to charge these costs through a Development contributions plan, the list of sorts of recoverable costs (articles 6.2.3 up to 6.2.6 2008 of the Physical Planning Decree) should be enlarged. In addition, nowadays landowners must receive the highest value for their land, which increases the accounted land costs and thus the probability of a deficit, a deficit that must be paid by the municipality. To diminish the possibility of a deficit and lower the accounted land costs, article 6.13.5 of the 2008 Physical Planning Act, which prescribes that assessment of the value of land must follow expropriation law, should be modified. Instead of following expropriation law, assessment should follow the market value based on the land use prior to regeneration.

2 In Dutch: *"i. maatschappelijke voorzieningen."*

These are not recommendations that could be introduced in the short term, as this shortcoming of the Dutch planning system can only be addressed with legislative modification. Relatively speaking, the first one is easier to introduce than the second.

EXAMPLE URBAN REGENERATION IN STURINGERLAND, Part Five
A majority in Parliament supports the modification of article 6.2.5 of the Physical Planning Decree to make it possible to charge the costs of the building of social facilities to landowners through a Development contributions plan. As a consequence of this support, anterior Development agreements can now also include contributions to these costs.

Addition to Structure vision Sturingerland 2020
Thanks to the first legal modification, the Municipality of Sturingerland is now free to require a contribution for social facilities. The municipality labels all the social facilities as 'spatial developments' in the Vision 2020, and also prescribes in this document that our scheme and schemes A-M must contribute to all these social facilities. In total, these encompass 3 schools (one in our scheme), 2 community centres (one in our scheme) and 2 social welfare facilities (one in our scheme) (see map 6-7). Now the municipality can motivate and determine properly which part of the costs must be charged to our scheme.

Addition to Standard Charges in implementation paragraph Structure vision Sturingerland 2020
The municipality includes to the standard charges in the implementation paragraph of the Structure vision 2020 (see Part Two of the example) another standard charge regarding social facilities. The costs of all social facilities in the district (the 3 schools, 2 community centres and 2 social welfare facilities) are calculated (€ 20m) and divided by the estimated number of dwellings and m^2 of office space to be built in our scheme and in schemes A-M. The resulting standard contributions are set at €1.000 per dwelling and €80 per m^2 of floor space for offices.

The second recommendation (enlarging the list of sorts of recoverable costs and modifying the assessment method of the value of land) seems more difficult to introduce, as it requires a more profound legal modification and is politically sensitive (value of land). Therefore, it will take more time to harness the necessary support in Parliament, and to carefully design the best way of modifying the law. Its effects will be illustrated in Part Ten of this example.

EXAMPLE URBAN REGENERATION IN STURINGERLAND, Part Six
The situation in our scheme in Sturingerland is as follows:

Costs that can be included in a Development contributions plan, *and* charged to the landowners:

- The on-site public infrastructure and facilities, including part of the costs of the social facilities (the land and the building): the school, community centre and social welfare facility (here we do as if the first legal modification illustrated in the 5th part of the example has taken place), and excluding some of the costs of refurbishing the old roads situated within the plan area, and excluding the entire maintenance and exploitation costs of any infrastructure or facility (see map 1a).
- That part of the public infrastructure and facilities and of the social facilities that serve a wider area (see maps 1a and 2a) and satisfy the three legal criteria (profit, attributability and proportionality): the municipality, thanks to the Structure vision Sturingerland 2020 (see Part Two of the example) can motivate properly which of these infrastructure and facilities serve a wider area, and thus which part of the costs corresponds to our scheme and can thus be charged to the landowners.
- Social housing (20% rented, 20% for sale, see map 4a): the municipality, thanks to the Housing Policy note Sturingerland 2020 (see Part Two of the example) can motivate properly this requirement.

The followings costs probably cannot be included in the Development contributions plan, or can be included but probably cannot be charged to the landowners/developers:

- Some costs of refurbishing the old roads and all the costs of maintaining and exploiting both the public infrastructure and the social facilities (see map 1a);
- The parts of the public infrastructure and facilities (including the social facilities) that serve a wider area but do not satisfy the three legal criteria (see maps 1a and 2a);
- Part of the costs made by the municipality for the preparation of plans;
- Spatial developments not directly related to this scheme (see map 6-7);
- A deficit in the Development contributions plan: the calculated profits do not cover the costs, which are very high in this site due to high infrastructure provision costs and soil decontamination costs, but also due to expensive land (high accounted land costs). This deficit cannot be charged to the landowners.

The Municipality of Sturingerland has the ambition of lowering the accounted land costs to achieve a cost-neutral operation, i.e. that the profits pay all the involved costs, also those that cannot be charged to the developers/landowners in a Development contributions plan. Therefore, the Municipality has a strong preference for agreeing the contributions in an anterior Development agreement, instead of approving a Development contributions plan. In a Development agreement, the Municipality and the landowners/developers are free to agree a lower price for the land than in a Development contributions plan. The Municipality has already calculated that if land is assessed on its value prior to regeneration, there will be enough final profit for the landowner/developer to pay all the costs.

Additional consideration for preferring an anterior agreement
Besides this economic consideration, there is another reason for the Municipality to prefer an anterior agreement: the Municipality is facing many development schemes at the same time, and has no internal capacity to make, approve and implement a Development contributions plan for each scheme.

9.3 Making binding rules conditional on the developer securing his contributions

Summary of the findings

As section 8.3 demonstrated earlier, it is necessary to commit the developer to secure the value capturing arrangements and to the strict deadlines that might have been included in the binding rules. In England and Valencia it is possible to make, in a formal, open and direct way, the approval of the relevant binding rules conditional on a Development agreement. This happens as follows: first, the binding rules (Planning Permission in England, Joint Development Program in Valencia), including the contributions and deadlines, become provisionally approved following an extensive procedure. The municipality openly conditions the definite approval to an agreement that secures these contributions and deadlines. When the agreement is sealed, the municipality, without the need of further extensive procedures, approves the binding rules definitely. If such an agreement is not reached, the binding rules never come into force. This clear and open conditioning seems to have improved public value capturing, and specially the speed of plan implementation.

Actual practice in the Netherlands: informal conditioning

In practice, Dutch municipalities also often condition the Land use plan and departures from it on securing contributions; however, they do not have the formal possibility of doing so in an open and straightforward way, as in Valencia and England. This can have negative side-effects: 1) in the Netherlands municipalities hold back the approval of the Land use plan until an agreement has been achieved, so after achieving the agreement the plan must follow an *extensive* procedure (including public participation), which means that there is the risk that the Land use plan becomes annulled or seriously modified; 2) there is the possibility that the developer appeals to the courts against an improper use of statutory powers; and 3) it makes an open and transparent public discourse of the municipality very difficult, because an open conditioning is illegal (see section 7.4.3.1).

Consequences 2008 Physical Planning Act

Since the 2008 Physical Planning Act, Dutch municipalities, provided they approve a Development contributions plan, can make granting the building permit conditional on the payment of contributions. Once the Land use plan and the Development contributions plan have been approved, the developer/landowner can submit an application for a building permit. The novelty is that the municipality can now condition the building permit on the applicant securing his/her contributions; before 2008 this was not possible. However, approving a Development contributions plan has some side effects: municipalities assume some financial risks because they are responsible for the calculations and may need to advance investments; they must put resources into making the plan and up-dating it yearly; and they must bear the consequences of delay in case developers/landowners do not apply for the building permit. In addition, not all the costs can be charged to the developers/landowners (for more details about these side effects see section 7.4.3.3).

Best option: anterior Development agreement

Thus in principle the best option for municipalities, especially in urban regeneration where the deficit in the Development contributions plan may be large, is to seal an anterior Development agreement before the approval of the Land use plan, which assures that contributions and deadlines are secured and no Development contributions plan is needed. Municipalities can thus informally request that developers sign such an agreement (Vrom et al., 2008: 197). However, the actual practice of informal conditioning may become more difficult after the 2008 Act. The Act reinforced the obligation for the municipality to take a formal decision (in Dutch terms *besluit*) about an application to modify or depart from the Land use plan (article 3.9 for modification and 3.12 for departure). If the municipality wishes to refuse the application, this decision must be taken within eight weeks. It is not necessarily so that the municipality *wants* to refuse, but the possibility of refusing has a strategic importance: the power to refuse increases the negotiation powers of the municipality. If the municipality does not refuse within these eight weeks, it is assumed to have agreed with the application, i.e. to agree to start the formal modification/departure procedure. This means that municipalities have eight weeks to decide whether to refuse the application. Following the Explanatory Memorandum of the 2008 Act, when making the decision to refuse, municipalities have to justify their decision by referring to the contents of the Land use plan, and, if existing, of the Structure vision (Tweede Kamer der Staten-Generaal, 2003: 31). The enforcement-mechanism is that the applicant has now the possibility to appeal (*beroep*) against a refusal or a non-determination. This means that the municipality may be confronted with the following situation: a) a developer submits an application that involves the need for investments in public infrastructure and facilities; b) the municipality prefers to secure these investments through an anterior agreement, so it wants to refuse the application in case the applicant does not want to sign the agreement; c) however, formally speaking, the municipality cannot openly and directly condition the approval of the Land use plan or departure from it on such an agreement. In other words, the municipality cannot openly and directly refuse the application with the argument that the applicant does not want to seal an agreement, but must find other arguments in the existing Land use plan, the Structure vision or other policy documents. If the municipality has already discussed the application with the developer, and already concluded that its physical and functional characteristics are acceptable, there is actually little room left to refuse (Gerritsen, 2010: 26). Thus the municipality should decide within eight weeks and, if for example the application fits within the Structure vision, or if the municipality has publicly already agreed to the physical and functional characteristics of the applications, it may be obliged to say "yes" and approve a Development contributions plan.

9.3.1 Short-term recommendation: alternative ways of conditioning

Although open and straightforward conditioning is not allowed, there are some alternative ways, and the new 2008 Act has added additional possibilities. Here follow some recommendations for acting on these alternative possibilities, which do not require any legal modification. In general, implementation of these recommendations should not encounter significant resistance, because they are a continuation and refinement of local practice. Nevertheless, these alternative possibilities have some negative side effects. For this reason I provide in the following section a second group of recommendations that do require some legal modifications.

Conditioning through the Explanation of the Land use plan

The first alternative is to include in the Explanation (*Toelichting*) of the draft Land use plan considerations related to the economic 'performability' of the plan (*economische uitvoerbaarheid* in Dutch): these are the conditions that are needed to implement the plan, the necessary contributions, whether there are enough financial sources, subsidies, etc. Based on this paragraph, the municipality can argue that contributions are necessary for the economic feasibility of the plan. If the contributions are not secured, the plan is not feasible, and can thus not be approved. This alternative has some negative side effects, very similar to the above mentioned negative side effects of the practice of informal conditioning:

1. *Procedural risks:* after the sealing of Development agreement, the Land use plan (or departure from it) must follow the complete procedure, which implies a risk of delay and modifications because of objections and appeals. Formally speaking, agreements cannot restrict the decision-making power of the Local Council. In Valencia and England,.the procedure of approval of the binding plan *precedes* the sealing of the agreement, after which there is only a short definite approval (see Figure 34). This means that in Valencia and England, parties can seal the agreement with a high certainty that the zoning plan is not going to be modified, and that there will be no delay. In the Netherlands, agreements are always subjected to the possibility that afterwards the Land use plan will be modified or its approval will be delayed (Vrom et al.: 51);
2. *Appeal risks:* if a municipality refuses to approve a Land use plan because the developer does not secure contributions, there is always a risk of an appeal to the courts. Indirect conditioning through the Explanation is not the same as enu-

merating, openly, in a municipal decision, the contributions that the developer has to secure in exchange for definite approval of the binding rules. Municipalities in the Netherlands need to properly and carefully argue why implementation is not feasible and thus why approval is not possible. This is not always easy: if implementation seems feasible, municipalities cannot refuse, even if developers have not secured all the contributions (to 'look like being feasible' is different than to 'be secured'). The introduction of the 2008 Land Development Act added an additional disadvantage: a Development contributions plan secures in theory part of the needed contributions, so the municipality might not be able to use the argument of performability. As demonstrated above, a Development contributions plan is less secure than one may think. In England and Valencia, there is no need for complex argumentation: planning law establishes that the developer has to secure the contributions stated in the provisionally approved document, as a condition for definitive approval;

3. *Incongruent municipal public discourse:* indirect conditioning through the Explanation poses a threat to the credibility of the municipality's public discourse, which in practice may need to hide some of the 'real reasons' for the approval or refusal of Land use plans. In England and Valencia, the 'real reasons' are publicly approved by the Local Council, and form the open and transparent criteria for assessing whether or not to formally approve the binding rules.

Conditioning through the Development contributions plan and proper cost recovery policy documents

The 2008 Act has introduced a second alternative. After a planning application has been submitted, which requires the modification or departure from the Land use plan, the municipality can calculate what would be the costs and which part could be charged to the landowners/developers through a Development contributions plan. Such a calculation (*exploitatieopzet* in Dutch) is part of the plan. The municipality may ask the applicant to perform the calculation, instead of doing it itself. If municipalities apply the recommendations in chapter 9.1 to make and adopt cost recovery policy documents (site-specific, generic documents or general zoning plans), they can properly justify all the related costs for providing public infrastructure and facilities (and, in case the applicant provides the calculations, municipalities can argue why all the costs must be included). This is especially important for public infrastructure and facilities that go beyond the absolutely necessary on-site infrastructure provision. That is, the municipalities can adequately defend the statement that the application involves costs that surpass minimum on-site infrastructure provision, and also include wider contributions to other public infrastructure and facilities within and outside the development site in question.

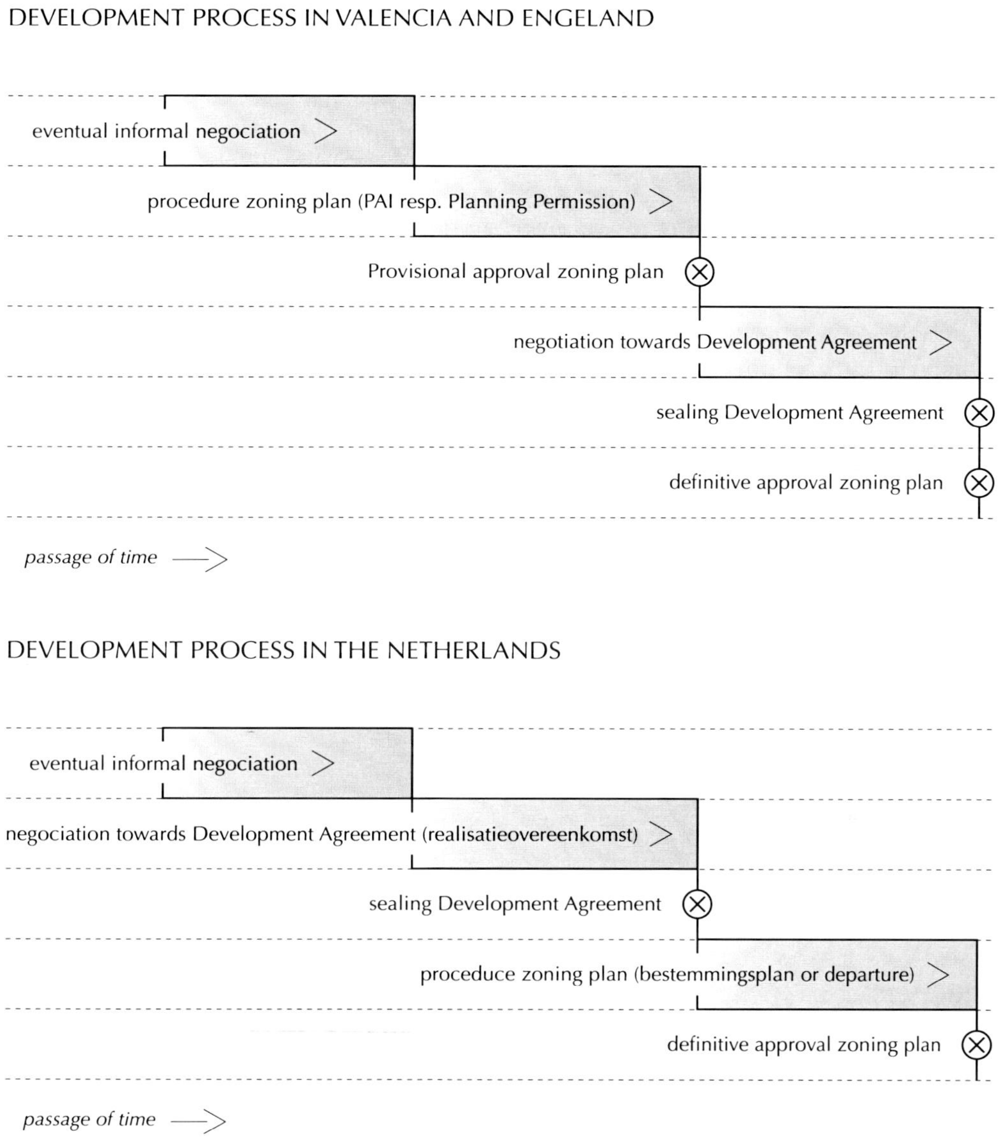

Figure 34. Negotiations, sealing of Development Agreement and approval of legally binding zoning plan in development processes in Valencia, England and the Netherlands.

These cost recovery policy documents are very important. Without them, the municipality would most probably not be able to calculate and properly argue the costs, certainly not within the stipulated eight weeks period for responding to applications. And, in case it is the applicant that must make the calculations, the municipality would also not be able to properly argue why the applicant should include all those costs that are not strictly needed for on-site infrastructure provision. It is likely that the applicant will consider them as 'extra' costs and will not be willing to include them as part of the costs that must be charged to his plan. In case the calculation makes clear that the municipality cannot recover all the costs through the Development contributions plan (which is not unthinkable, especially in urban regeneration, and especially if the costs involve not only minimum infrastructure provision but also wider contributions), municipalities can openly refuse to process and to approve the Development contributions plan, arguing that they cannot bear this deficit (Vrom et al., 2008: 106). This is equivalent to refusing to approve the Land use plan.

This conditioning through the Development contributions plan has some advantages compared with conditioning through the Explanation in the Land use plan. First, it reduces the possibility of success of the developers appeal (side effect 2) because the municipality can better argue the non-feasibility of the project. Second, municipalities can be open about their decision (side effect 3). However, if the developer wants to secure only the additional costs (but not those costs that can be charged through a Development contributions plan) municipalities cannot use the argument of economic feasibility to refuse the application. The reason is that the costs that can be charged are theoretically guaranteed, even if the developer does not want to seal the agreement: the municipality is expected to approve the Development contributions plan and landowners/developers are expected to pay these costs when obtaining a building permit. The municipality must therefore approve a Development contributions plan, which was exactly what it wanted to avoid because of the mentioned disadvantages, risks and costs of having to approve it. In any scenario, side effect 1 remains: after the sealing of an anterior Agreement, the Land use plan still has to be processed, which carries with it the risk of modifications and delay.

EXAMPLE URBAN REGENERATION IN STURINGERLAND, Part Seven
The Municipality of Sturingerland owns parcel A, Developer B owns parcel B, Developer C owns parcel C and Developer D owns parcel D (see Figure 33).

Conditioning the Land use plan through Development contributions plan and proper cost recovery policy documents
Developer B submitted at moment 0 an application for modification of the Land use plan. The initiative is in line with the urban regeneration policy of Sturingerland, which is prescribed in the Structure vision 2020 (see Part Two of the example). The municipality decided to stimulate the initiative, but adopting a 'facilitating' role, i.e. leaving the implementation to the developer. The municipality calculated (in an *exploitatieopzet*) the costs that can be attributed to the plan through a Development contributions plan. Thanks to the Structure vision 2020 and its implementation paragraph, the municipality calculated right away the total costs, and motivated them properly. Without these documents the municipality would not have been able to motivate either the contribution for the public infrastructure and facilities that serve a wider area (the road

to be refurbished, the sewerage and park), or the contributions for the 'spatial developments' (the regeneration of the social housing neighbourhood, the International Congress Center and the social facilities), or the compensation green areas provided as a compensation for the lost green areas (four areas, to be compensated with three new/refurbished ones). It turned out that not all of these costs could be charged to the landowners through a Development contributions plan (see Part Six of the example). Further, the profits from selling the real estate would not cover all the chargeable costs (the costs that can be charged to the landowners) if the land were to be appraised at the market value with the future use possibilities. In addition to this deficit, there were significant costs that were not secured: the other schemes that were supposed to pay the facilities serving a wider area and the 'spatial developments' had not yet been developed, so their contribution was still uncertain. As the municipality had no financial resources to pay these costs, the municipality was able to properly motivate that the investments were not secured and thus the Land use plan could not be modified. In other words, the municipality was able to properly argue why the application of developer B had to be refused.

The calculations made clear that the profits were large enough to cover all the costs, as long as the land is not appraised at the full market price with the future use possibilities. The municipality made clear to Developer B that he had to pay all the costs, i.e. to accept a lower price for the land. Both entered negotiations that ended in Developer B agreeing with the municipal requirements. Below, this example is worked out in three alternative scenarios: Ia, Ib and II:

- Scenario Ia: Developer B succeeds in buying all the land for a low price;
- Scenario Ib: Developer B succeeds in buying all the land for a low price *and* direct conditioning of the Land use plan is made possible through a legal modification;
- Scenario II: Developer B is not successful in buying all the land for a low price (see section 9.4).

Below, scenario Ia is worked out, while the other scenarios are expanded in subsequent portion.

Scenario Ia: Developer B succeeds in buying all the land for a low price

Developer B succeeded in buying all the land from the Municipality and from Developer C and Developer D for a price that allowed him to pay all the costs, i.e. for a price lower than the full market price with the future use possibilities. He signed an anterior Development agreement with the Municipality securing the costs that could not be charged through a Development contributions plan. However, Developer B refused to secure the costs that were supposed to be recovered through the Development contributions plan. According to planning law, the Municipality can recover these costs when granting the building permits. As a consequence, the Municipality could not refuse the application because these costs were in theory already secured. The Municipality had to approve the Development contributions plan, together with the Land use plan, which was displeasing for the local politicians. The Municipality had to advance the investment for refurbishing the road, the purchase of the land needed for the school, community centre, park and sport field, and also some investments for an infrastructure that serves a wider area (e.g. refurbishing the adjacent road, and contributions to other facilities in the district). Also, the municipality had to face more risks: first, other parties submitted appeals against the Land use plan, which had to be modified and suffered delay (side effect 1); and second, Developer B delayed his application for a building permit (because of market circumstances), so finally the municipality had to deal with the financial costs of the delay.

On the positive side, the Municipality had initially a strong argumentation to refuse the application, so the risks of appeals against its request to seal an anterior agreement were lower (side effect 2). That is why developer B agreed to secure at least part of the costs. Furthermore, the municipality could be open about the real reasons behind accepting or refusing the application (side effect 3).

9.3.2 Long-term recommendation: direct conditioning through legal modification

As shown, short-term recommendations leave some negative side effects unresolved: even if the municipality successfully seals an anterior Development agreement, the Land use plan still has to be processed. This carries the risk of modification and delay (side effect 1). Possibly, if the developer is not willing to secure the costs that theoretically can be charged through a Development contributions plan, municipalities might be obliged to approve the Development contributions plan in any case. It is already said that this implies some side effects: municipalities might need to assume risks and part of the costs. To remove these disadvantages, it is recommended to allow in planning law for direct conditioning, similar to how this happens in Valencia and England. The central government should introduce several legislative modifications. First, it is necessary to allow contributions to be prescribed in the Land use plan, instead of only in a Development contributions plan. One paragraph could be added to article 3.1.2 of the 2008 Physical Planning Decree or to the Physical Planning Act itself:

> *With regard to economic feasibility, a Land use plan/departure from it can include requirements related to the implementation of public infrastructure and facilities, and, if necessary, schedules for the realization*

> *of the works, activities, measures and buildings, and if needed phasing them in relation to each other.*[3]

Second, to make it possible to make the approval to an agreement conditional, a sentence should be added to chapter 3.2 of the 2008 Physical Planning Act (for the procedure of the Land use plan) and to chapter 3.3 (for the departure from it):

> *When and if the Land use plan or departure from it prescribes requirements related to the performability* (requirements about social housing to rent and to sell, owner-occupied building, sorts of shopping, selling prices of social dwellings, the realisation of public infrastructure and facilities, and implementation schedules, red.)*, the realization of these requirements must be secured in a development agreement before the Land use plan or departure are formally approved.*[4]

It is to be expected that these modifications would encounter some political resistance. Criticisms would be made that municipalities are 'selling' planning consent. The argument might be made that the planning activity of public bodies must take account only of spatially relevant considerations, and that securing contributions does not fall under this competence. However, this is misplaced criticism, as the introduction of the Development contributions plan and the possibility of conditioning granting of building permit to a financial contribution has already weakened the legal argument that only spatially relevant considerations are relevant for assessing building applications.

URBAN REGENERATION IN STURINGERLAND, Example Part Eight

Scenario Ib: direct conditioning Land use plan through legal modification, and Developer B manages to buy all the land for a low price

The Dutch central government, after receiving a lot of complains from municipalities like Sturingerland, decides to make it legally possible to make the Land use plan conditional on securing contributions.

---

3 In Dutch: *"Ten behoeve van de uitvoerbaarheid kan een bestemmingsplan/projectbesluit eisen bevatten met betrekking tot de uitvoering van openbare infrastructuur en voorzieningen, en voor zover nodig een fasering van de uitvoering van werken, werkzaamheden, maatregelen en bouwplannen, en zo nodig koppelingen hiertussen"*.

4 In Dutch: *"Wanneer het bestemmingsplan of projectbesluit eisen bevatten met betrekking tot de uitvoerbaarheid* [eisen m.b.t. sociale huurwoningen, sociale koopwoningen, particulier opdrachtgeverschap, branches van detailhandel, geldende koopprijsgrenzen voor sociale koopwoningen, de uitvoering van openbare infrastructuur en voorzieningen, en tijdschema's waarin dat moet gebeuren, red.]*, definitieve vaststelling zal kunnen plaatsvinden pas nadat uitvoering van deze eisen binnen de gestelde termijnen verzekerd is in een privaatrechtelijke overeenkomst"*.

After Developer B submitted at moment 0 an application for modification of the Land use plan, the Municipality of Sturingerland motivated properly within the period of 8 weeks the contributions that the developer had to face. The municipality enumerated the requirements, without having to calculate the costs that can be charged through a Development contributions plan (i.e. without having to make a *exploitatieopzet*), which saved much time and effort for the municipality. Initial contacts with Developer B revealed that he was willing to accept a lower land price and to assume the requirements, which resulted from the fact that developer B managed to agree with the other landowners a low price for their land (low enough to allow paying the contributions). The Municipality initiated the procedure for modifying the Land use plan. During the procedure, the municipality and Developer B negotiated and discussed the requirements, and the Local Executive decided finally to accept some modifications to the original list of requirements because it became clear during the negotiations that this was necessary in order to make the operation feasible. The Local Council provisionally approved the modification of the Land use plan. This provisionally approved Land use plan included a list of all the contributions, including the agreed changes. The Land use plan stated that all these contributions must be secured within one year, otherwise the plan cannot be definitely approved. Public consultation had already taken place, and all parties had already had the chance to make objections and appeals. The Municipality and Developer B negotiated a Development agreement that secured all the contributions, conscious of the fact there would be no further possibility to object or appeal against the plan. After the sealing of the Agreement, the Local Council approved the plan definitely in a shortened procedure.

9.4 Modulating property rights

Summary of the findings

Section 8.4 has already explained how the definition of property rights in England and the Netherlands (where, contrary to Valencia, there is no land readjustment regulation that modulates the right to provide the infrastructure) seems to hinder the capturing of value increase. In short, these are the conclusions:

- There is in England and the Netherlands a strong interdependency between local public bodies and landowners and developers: as a rule, the transactions that are needed to provide the infrastructure are highly dependent on agreement with the landowners/developers. This is because none of the actors control all the needed resources: public bodies have the statutory powers for planning consent, but landowners/developers have the financial means and the exclusive right to develop the land. This interdependency cannot be resolved using expropriation or the pre-emption right (*voorkeursrecht* in Dutch), because these instruments have severe limitations in practice, and they imply a direct organisational and financial involvement of public bodies;

- The situation in Valencia has changed radically after the regional government introduced a new planning law in 1994: since then there is, to provide the infrastructure, no longer any unavoidable mutual dependence between public bodies and landowners. Valencian municipalities can now opt for compulsory land readjustment, without having to become directly involved. The municipality selects in a public tender the urbanising agent, who may be a public company or the landowners themselves joining in a company but most of the time is a commercial developer. Landowners can choose for voluntary expropriation or can participate in the development. If they choose expropriation, the urbanising agent pays the compensation and acquires the land. But if they decide to participate, they have to deliver the land needed for public infrastructure and facilities and pay to the urbanising agent a proportional share of the infrastructure provision, plan preparation, soil decontamination, compensation costs and additional contributions (costs postings 2-6, see financial analysis in section 2.4.3). In exchange, landowners share the economic betterment: after providing the infrastructure, the urbanising agent delivers the serviced building parcels to the landowners and transfers the public infrastructure, free of charge, to the municipality. In sum, although landowners still control the land, the mutual dependence is now easily avoidable as municipalities have the possibility to appoint a third party (who does not necessarily need to own the land) as the urbanising agent, and do not need to become directly financially involved. Also, the municipalities are not dependent on one particular urbanising agent, for he/she can be selected through a public tender.
- The interdependency between public bodies and landowners in England and the Netherlands gives to the landowners the option to wait, which it is often used to oppose the requirements set by local public bodies. Specially in the Netherlands, public bodies conclude that they cannot ask too much, which leads to low capturing of the value increase;
- This interdependency frequently leads to delays in the development processes. Often development is delayed because developers refuse the requirements and plans of the municipality, and the negotiations about these issues are prolonged. Also, sometimes the developers do not succeed in buying the land for a reasonable price. Success of the negotiations depends on the developers' and landowners' expectations that, by delaying negotiations, their profits (regular profit margin, included in posting 2, and final profit for the developer, posting 9, and accounted land costs for the landowner, posting 1) would increase.
- This interdependency leads to higher accounted land costs (posting 1); market parties are more interested in acquiring land, as control of the land puts them in a strong negotiating position, and they are thus ready to pay more for it, which in turn inflates the real and expected market value of land.
- In addition, the findings suggest that interdependency leads to an inefficient and sluggish development process, in which costs are unnecessarily high and different actors each manage to appropriate part of the value increase. This leads to higher costs for infrastructure provision (posting 2) and plan preparation (posting

3); in England and the Netherlands they are very often between 1.5 and 4 times higher than in Valencia. This can partly explain why Valencian developers, although able to sell the real estate for market prices similar to those in the Netherlands, can contribute much more than the Dutch developers. This can also partly explain why Valencian developers, although not selling the real estate for market prices as high as those in England, can contribute similarly or even more than the English developers. In other words, in England and the Netherlands, inflated infrastructure provision and plan preparation costs seem to form an important obstacle to capturing value increase.

EXAMPLE URBAN REGENERATION IN STURINGERLAND, Part Ten

Scenario II: Developer B does not manage to buy all the land

After the Municipality of Sturingerland and Developer B agreed that all the costs should be paid out of profits, (see Part Seven of the example), Developer B started, with the support of the Municipality, contacts and negotiations with Developers C and D. However, Developers C and D had other goals. Developer C was also positive about the initiative, but he was neither willing to sell his land (he wants to implement the plan), nor to be so 'generous' as Developer B. He only wants to contribute to the costs that, according to planning law, can be included in a Development contributions plan and charged to the landowners. Developer D is truly a 'free rider'. He wants to implement the plan, but expects to be able to do so without having to contribute his fair share.

During the contacts and negotiations, the landowners have exercised the option to wait several times:

- Developer D was from the very beginning not willing to negotiate;
- Developer C was positive about the initiative, but the negotiations were blocked since he did not accept having to sell his land, nor to pay a full contribution;
- Developer B also exercised the option to wait, first, during his negotiations with the former landowner of parcel B, one year after moment 0. At that time, the Developer B decided to freeze the negotiations with the municipality (when Developer B took the initiative at moment 0, he did not own the land). Second, two years later, when another developer bought Developer B, the new developer B, who paid a very high price for the land, needed higher profit margins and decided to reconsider the plan.

It is clear that there is a strong mutual dependence between de municipality and landowners B, C and D. The municipality does not even consider the possibility of buying or expropriating parcels C and D. First, the owners say that they are willing to develop their land and this hampers expropriation. Second, the Municipality of Sturingerland does not have the financial means to do so. Buying or expropriating land in Sturingerland is something that only happens in very special circumstances, and, if it occurs, just for few plots.

The consequences for value capturing are important. The municipality is considering lowering the requirements (to recover only the costs that can be included in the Development contributions plan and charged to the landowners, but not the additional costs). In the meantime, the process has suffered delays; five years after moment 0 (when Developer B, not yet the owner of parcel B, took the initiative) still nothing has happened, only a lot of deliberation and plan preparation. The price of land has risen, and Developer C has sold his land to another developer, for a much higher price than the price in the former use. Also, the costs are growing, costs made by the municipality (negotiations with Developers B, C and D, some research, negotiations with province about possible subsidies to cover the deficit) and costs made by Developer B (negotiations with the Municipality and Developers C and D, some research and financial costs derived from the money he had to borrow at year 1 to buy parcel B).

9.4.1 Short-term recommendation: assessment of financial feasibility

It has already been said that it is often not clear whether the final profit of the developers could have allowed for higher contributions. In the studied Dutch cases, there was little available information, and the developers did not provide much additional information. In *Kop van Oost* and *Stationskwartier* my own estimates suggest that more contributions would have been feasible. Indirect evidence that there might have been more financial room than argued by the developers is that in *De Funen* and *Kop van Oost*, during or after the negotiations, land was sold several times for higher prices than the price in the former use.

Municipalities could conduct more research into the profit margins in the early stages of development processes, and use this information as a clear and transparent starting point in the negotiations with developers. This research should be made together with the first document that creates development expectations, for example in the recommended site-specific cost recovery documents mentioned in section 9.1.1.2. *Stationskwartier* could serve as an example. Here the municipality calculated the development costs and profits in a business case attached to the 2003 *Masterplan Centraal Breda*, and these calculations served as a starting point in the negotiations, in which the municipality might have succeed in getting part of the increased value. Municipalities can fine-tune the calculations as negotiations come nearer. This recommendation is in line with some relevant recent conclusions (Vrom et al., 2008: 41; Vrom-raad, 2009: 5). Another complementary possibility is that developers are required to submit a calculation of the costs and profits (*exploitatieopzet*) to the municipality.

9.4.2 Short-term recommendation: land readjustment through private law agreements, supported by expropriation and pre-emption

To avoid the negative consequences of the dependency of municipalities on landowners/developers, it is recommended to work with a specific contractual formula, inspired by the Valencian land readjustment model. Commercial developers, acting as a sort of Valencian urbanizing agent, can agree with landowners that, in exchange for sharing development profits, they do not use their option to wait. This recommendation is based not only on the Valencian model, but also on the experience with the preparation for the redevelopment of an industrial site of about 16 ha in the Municipality of Zevenhuizen-Moerkapelle (Zuidplaspolder, Province of South Holland). During 2007 and 2008, I was asked to advise how the owners of the firms and the land could themselves regenerate their land by involving a commercial developer to play the role of an urbanizing agent. Although this experiment failed, the experience has served to fine-tune this recommendation (see Annex 7). One of the conclusions is that Dutch developers are not always comfortable with the role of urbanizing agent, i.e. of a developer that in principle only profits from land development, but not from the development of the real estate. This experience has led us to refine the recommendation: to carefully select a property developer who is familiar with less conservative ways of developing land. A possibility to be seriously taken into account is to involve a Valencian urbanizing agent, possibly in partnership with a Dutch developer.

The recommendation is to involve landowners in urban development, thus to involve them in sharing the land development costs (postings 1 to 7) and the final profits (posting 9). This should provide several advantages: (a) it annuls the need to buy the land, or at least to buy *all* the land, as landowners themselves participate in the operation (in Zevenhuizen this could have led to a reduction in the amount of money that must be borrowed, by at least € 45.5 million); (b) it reduces the risks of delay resulting from landowners, instead of supporting the operation, behaving in an strategic way (i.e. waiting) to obtain the highest possible price for their land; (c) *a* and *b* should considerably reduce the costs of the operation: there should be no need to buy land in advance (posting 1), and it should reduce the amounts reserved for unexpected expenses (posting 2, in Zevenhuizen this could have led to a reduction of about € 1.15 million) and the plan preparation costs (posting 3); (d) *c* should considerably reduce the financial costs (in Zevenhuizen this could have led to a reduction of at least € 14.3 million), as there is need of less external financing. But, how does one convince landowners to share the risks and the profits?

Plan documents

First, two plan documents must be prepared, which will form the basis for anterior Development agreements I and II (see under):

Land use plan (Bestemmingsplan)
The municipality and/or the urbanizing agent must prepare a draft of a Map (*Plankaart*) of the Land use plan, detailing the following aspects:
- The zoning of land uses, building alignments and building envelopes;
- The volume of the building, per land use.

If detailed prescriptions are not possible, the draft must at least prescribe the minimum building volume and the approximate location of serviced building parcels[5]. The goal of these documents is to sufficiently support the negotiations around Agreement I (see below): at that time, it must be possible to provide details to the landowner about the serviced building plots and the building volume which he/she can expect if he/she signs the agreement.

Draft plan infrastructure provision works
This is similar to the Valencian Infrastructure Provision Project (*Anteproyecto de Urbanización*), and includes: (a) a scheme of the infrastructure, with a description of those elements that determine the total costs, such as the quality of the public space; (b) a scheme of the sewerage network; (c) a scheme of the road network and the other facilities; (d) a description of existing infrastructure networks, and the feasibility and the costs of connection to the new development. In principle, it is the urbanizing agent who should prepare this document, as it requires his/her expertise in cost calculations and full commitment to the calculations.

Anterior Development agreement I: urbanizing agent-landowners
The urbanizing agent proposes Agreement I to the landowners. This can be done individually, whereby the developer separately proposes Agreement I to each landowner. Alternatively, or complementarily, landowners might join an *ad hoc* organization, similar to the Valencian Association of Urban Interest (*Asociación de Interés Urbanístico*), which would deal with the urbanizing agent. In the experiment in Zevenhuizen, landowners have joined in a cooperative (see Annex 7). A combination of both is possible: the urbanizing agent could deal with both an organization of the majority of landowners and with individual landowners who opt not to join the *ad hoc* organization.

---

5 Before deciding for a detailed or for an Outline Land use plan, one important aspect should be considered: the degree of detail in a Land use plan can have consequences for the calculation of the compensation that landowners should receive in case of expropriation of their land. In an Outline Land use plan, the compensation is an average of the whole plan area (the so-called *complexwaarde*), which means that the owner of the land for the profitable construction receives less than in case of a Detailed Land use plan. In a Detailed Land use plan, the compensation is calculated based on smaller areas, which means that the owner of the land for the profitable construction receives an average of the values of similar plots of land, e.g. land zoned for profitable housing, but not land zoned for a park (Needham & Geuting, 2006: 4). In case municipalities want to use expropriation to stimulate landowners to collaborate, an Outline Land use plan could be more useful than a Detailed Land use plan.

In Agreement I, the urbanizing agent agrees with the landowners/cooperative, to provide himself the infrastructure and produce serviced building parcels for a given price and within a given deadline. This requires the following ingredients to be included in the Agreement: (*i*) a **calculation of the total land development costs**, i.e. the infrastructure provision costs, the costs of preparing plans, compensation costs, eventual soil decontamination costs, possible additional contributions to public infrastructure and facilities (postings of the sort 2-6, see financial analysis in section 2.4.3); (*ii*) the circumstances under which these costs can be reviewed and how this review should take place; (*iii*) the regular profit margin of the urbanizing agent (included in posting 2); (*iv*) a calculation of the share each landowner will have to pay; (*v*) the method of payment (in money or in kind –in serviced building parcels); and (*vi*) the implementation schedules. The experience in Zevenhuizen, where it took more than one year before there was certainty about which contributions the landowners should pay (see Annex 7), leads me to ascertain the importance of the recommendation given in section 9.1.1: it is important that, before the elaboration of the plan documents and the negotiations, there is already certainty about at least the contributions that should be made. In other words, before the urbanizing agent starts elaborating the plan documents and negotiating, the municipality must clearly define and publicly announce the required contributions.

Also, the agreement must include a set of **rules for the land readjustment**. These rules must be specific enough to make clear to the landowner the main features of the serviced building parcels he can expect to receive under the Agreement. Possibly, the Agreement can include a provisional proposal for readjustment that specifies the number, location and dimensions of the new parcels, and which landowner is going to receive them.

In exchange, the landowners agree with the urbanizing agent to provide their land and pay their share of the costs within a given deadline, for example to pay in instalments while the infrastructure provision works are being carried out. A variant of this is to agree payment in kind, i.e. the landowners transfer to the urbanizing agent part of the final serviced building parcels as payment. For this purpose, the urbanizing agent should make explicit in Agreement I the price of the serviced parcels, and/or negotiate a price separately with each landowner or group of landowners.

Anterior Development agreement II: urbanizing agent-municipality

The urbanizing agent agrees with the municipality the following: (a) possibly, in case of an outline Land use plan, to prepare afterwards a detailed plan and submit it to the municipality; (b) possibly, in case there are some landowners not willing to participate, to prepare the expropriation dossier and to pay the compensation; (c) to provide the infrastructure according to the Draft plan infrastructure provision; (d) to maintain the public infrastructure until it is transferred to the municipality; (e) implementation schedules; (f) the circumstances under which the agreement ceases to be in force; and (g) a scheme of monetary and non-monetary penalties for the case of not fulfilling the agreement.

In exchange, the municipality agrees with the urbanizing agent the following: (a) to exert all reasonable efforts to process and approve the Land use plan and possibly a detailed plan and a Development contributions plan; (b) to apply pre-emption rights (*voorkeursrecht*) on the industrial site, which means that the municipality can block the selling of land, and make the selling of land conditional on sealing anterior Development agreement I; (c) possibly and if necessary, to use all reasonable efforts to expropriate the property of non-collaborating landowners; (d) possibly and if necessary, to use all reasonable efforts to facilitate the relationship between the urbanizing agent and the public utilities companies; (e) to accept the public infrastructure once it is finished and to assume thereafter responsibility for maintenance (an option, in case costs of maintenance could be agreed in an anterior Agreement, is also to agree here and in Agreement I a contribution by the landowners/developer to future maintenance costs, posting 6); and (f) the circumstances under which the agreement ceases to be in force.

Stimulating and enforcing agreement

The feasibility of this recommendation depends on agreement, because the landowners, the urbanizing agent and the municipality must all agree. Dutch municipalities should use some instruments to stimulate landowners to cooperate:

1. Municipalities can make the processing and approval of the Land use plan (or possibly the outline Land use plan) conditional on the landowners' and the urbanizing agent's signing of the agreements (see section 9.3.1 for details of how to do that);
2. Municipalities can settle pre-emption rights on the development area and make the selling of land and removal of pre-emption conditional on agreeing with the anterior Development agreement I;
3. In case a minority of landowners oppose, municipalities can use the Development contributions plan as an enforcement instrument. The Development contributions plan can reinforce the possibility of municipalities to expropriate those landowners who oppose implementation. Municipalities can include in the Development contributions plan a clear scheme of implementation and the moment at which the landowner has to apply for a building permit and pay his/her contribution. Once the opposing landowner pays his/her contribution to the municipality, the municipality gives the money to the other landowners who have to assume all the costs. If an opposing landowner does not apply for a building permit on time, municipalities could consider expropriation. Municipalities can even announce publicly in the early stages that they intend to apply expropriation in case of delay, which might have a dissuasive effect. In a possible expropriation procedure, the landowner can declare that he/she is willing to implement. However, if he/she does not apply for a building permit (and pay the corresponding contribution) within the deadlines included in the Development contributions plan, municipalities have good arguments for executing expropriation (Verdaas, interview in 2007; Van Gelder, interview in 2008; Vrom et al., 2008: 207). There is even the possibility of accelerating the expropriation pro-

cedure, provided that no appeals against the Development contributions plan have been submitted concerning the plot to be expropriated (Vrom et al., 2008: 206-207);

Side effects

This recommendation has some side effects, mainly because the enforcement instrument implies the possible approval of a Development contributions plan and expropriation:

- Approving a Development contributions plan, as demonstrated in section 9.3.1, involves financial risks, direct organizational involvement of the public bodies and allows less public value capturing than in case of an anterior Development agreement;
- In principle, the Agreement cannot contradict any of the prescriptions included in the Development contributions plan (Vrom et al., 2008: 34; Kluwer, 2008: 132). This means that some of the contributions agreed in the Agreement might be nullified after the approval of the plan;
- Expropriation increases the financial risks because compensation follows market values after regeneration, i.e. the value takes account of an important part of the future building possibilities. Expropriation takes place once the Land use plan is already approved, and hence when future building possibilities are already certain and land prices inflated. This problem can be partly resolved if the second recommendation in section 9.2 (introducing legal modification that allow for assessment of land value according to the market value of land use prior to rezoning) is introduced. A lower compensation would diminish the financial risks; however, as compensations must be paid in advance, there are still associated financial risks.
- Even with lower compensations, expropriation may be an unpopular instrument politically. In the studied Dutch cases, municipalities considered it only in very exceptional circumstances, such as to expropriate some marginal land in case landowners clearly opposed and delayed development. Expropriation of a substantial part of the land seems not to be an option in Dutch practice. In none of the examined cases in which developers exercised their option to wait (i.e. *De Funen, Kop van Oost* and probably *Stationskwartier*), was the municipality able to bear the financial responsibility of expropriating the land, especially because the developers owned most of the land (most of it in *De Funen*, 60% in *Kop van Oost* and 80% in *Stationskwartier*). In all the three cases, expropriation was not an alternative in the first place because the landowners themselves expressed willingness to develop.

Considerations about the feasibility of the recommendation

In principle, this recommendation fits within existing planning law because it is primarily based on private law agreements. However, it involves a new approach in Dutch practice and this encounters some difficulties. The experience in Zevenhuizen illustrates these very well. In Zevenhuizen, the plan documents described above have been elaborated, but they were not detailed enough in their contents because the developer did not spend enough money on elaborating them. The consequence was that the involved parties never reached the recommended agreements. It is important to remember that in the Netherlands, unlike in Valencia, planning law does not regulate the prescribed content of these documents, so it is free for developers to decide. Without detailed documents and without the agreements, there was too much uncertainty for landowners to decide. Also, the municipality needed a long time to decide on the needed contributions, and then hesitated to proceed further. As a consequence, the experiment in Zevenhuizen failed. See Annex 7 for a more detailed explanation of the specific mismatches with the above recommendation that can explain the failure of this experiment.

EXAMPLE URBAN REGENERATION IN STURINGERLAND, Part Ten

Continuation of Scenario II, in which Developer B did not succeed in buying all the land for a low price (see Part Nine of the example): there is enough support for land readjustment through private law agreements

The Municipality of Sturingerland and Developer B conclude that, if nothing changes, regeneration will last for years. They decide to apply land readjustment through private law agreements. Developer B makes a draft Land use plan and calculates the costs of land development. He offers, in anterior Agreement I, to Developers C and D that they will each pay, proportionally to the area of their land, the costs of developing the land (postings 2-6, see financial analysis in section 2.4.3) and Developer B will provide the land that is needed for public infrastructure and facilities. Developer B also proposes a schedule for the payments and transfer of land. As compensation, developers C and D will receive serviced building parcels. To compensate for differences in the economic value of the resulting building parcels (half of parcel C is zoned for a school, and most of parcel D is zoned for a park, see map 1a), Agreement I includes land readjustment rules: each developer will receive building parcels with an economic value proportional to their share. This means that developers C and D will each receive a building plot on parcels A and B.

In addition, developer B and the municipality agree in anterior Agreement II the mutual obligations: the developer will prepare the draft Land use plan and the municipality will process the plan. In addition, they agree an option that Developer B will buy parcel A, which is municipal property.

Initially, Developer C rejects the proposal because he is not willing to pay all the costs. Without the support of at least Developer C there is no hope. The municipality settles a pre-emption right on the whole plan area, and makes clear that this right will be revoked, and the Land use plan will be modified, *only when and if* Agreement I is signed. It is also helpful that the Parliament has recently decided to enlarge the lists of recoverable costs through a Development contributions plan (see the first part of the second recommendation in section 9.2). Developer C realizes that there are not longer differences between paying through a Development contributions plan and through an anterior Agreement. Municipality and Developers B and C negotiate and finally Developer C signs Agreement I.

Developer D is more difficult to persuade. He is not willing to pay any contribution, and does not give in to the pressure. The municipality decides to approve, together with the Land use plan, a Development contributions plan including detailed schedules for the payments. The municipality announces expropriation in case developer D does not apply for the building permit and pay his contribution on time.

Developer B constructs the public infrastructure on parcels A, B and C, and developer C contributes with money and with land. Because the approval of the Development contributions plan has invalidated part of Agreement II in parcel D, the municipality has to assume part of the costs. Fortunately, thanks to the recent legislative changes about the costs that can be charged through a Development contributions plan, the municipality has to assume lower costs than without those legislative changes. Nevertheless, the municipality must assume some costs. In addition, the following happens: Developer D refuses to apply for a building permit on time. Now, the municipality can argue that Developer D is not willing to implement, and expropriates his parcel. Following Agreement II Developer B receives parcel D and pays the compensation. This increases his risks: he already bought parcels A and B, the process has lasted for years, and now he also has to pay expensive compensation for parcel D. Compensation is expensive because the Expropriation Act prescribes that it must follow the market value of the land use after regeneration. In case Parliament agrees with the second part of the second recommendation in section 9.2, expropriation will be cheaper, but Developer B must still advance more investments and assume higher risks and financial costs. As a consequence, Developer B must renegotiate the quality of the public infrastructure and diminish his contributions. The Municipality, which realizes that the financial feasibility is under strong pressure, accepts reluctantly these modifications. It will have to either subsidize more costs, or just accept a lower quality of the public infrastructure and facilities. Developer B constructs the park and the basketball playfield on parcel D. Finally Developer B transfers the public infrastructure to the municipality.

9.4.3 Long-term recommendation: land readjustment regulation

As illustrated above, there are not many possibilities for the municipality to avoid dependency on the landowners, and the only ultimate enforcement mechanism is expensive expropriation. In order to have an alternative to expropriation, the Dutch central government can introduce a land readjustment regulation in planning law. The idea is that, in addition to the possibility of expropriation, municipalities have also the alternative of land readjustment. Complementary to the possibility of expropriating the land and paying compensation in money, municipalities should then be able to oblige those landowners who want to share development profits, to provide land and contribute to the costs, in exchange for serviced building parcels. The proposed regulation, inspired by the Valencian land readjustment, includes the following features:

- The one who provides the infrastructure and organizes the land readjustment is a third party, not necessarily one of the landowners. This third party can be a public or a private body playing the role of urbanizing agent;
- The municipality selects the urbanizing agent based on the qualities and the costs of the submitted plan for the infrastructure provision. Possibly, in case the urbanizing agent also prepares the Land use plan, the municipality will also evaluate this plan;
- Landowners must provide the land necessary for public infrastructure and facilities, and pay, in instalments during the works, the costs (postings 2-6, see financial analysis section 2.4.3). In exchange they receive serviced building parcels.
- The regulation includes the possibility of applying compulsory land readjustment.

Considerations about the feasibility of introducing a public law land readjustment regulation

The current level of protection of property rights in the Netherlands implies strong legal and procedural guarantees in the expropriation procedure. The land readjustment procedure in Valencia also requires extensive procedural and legal guarantees. However, introducing a land readjustment regulation in the Netherlands could encounter political resistance because landowners are accustomed to enjoying a stronger position.

EXAMPLE URBAN REGENERATION IN STURINGERLAND, Part Eleven

Continuation of Scenario II, in which Developer B did not succeed in buying all the land for a low price (see Parts Nine and Ten): there is not enough support for land readjustment through private law agreements, so the central government introduces a public law land readjustment regulation.

Developers C and D do not agree with Agreement I, despite the pressures. The only choice for the Municipality of Sturingerland is to approve the Development contributions plan and assume the corresponding risks and deficit, and possibly to expropriate parcels C and D. However, this means assuming a large part of the costs and expropriating half of the plan area. The Municipality decides to halt the efforts to redevelop the site.

The Dutch central government, based on this and other experiences of frustrated urban regeneration, decides to introduce a land readjustment regulation in planning law. Now the Municipality of Sturingerland can apply land readjustment. Developer B submits his proposal (Land use plan & infrastructure provision costs & proposals of Agreements I and II). The Municipality, after considering the proposal, decides to organize a public tender. Any party is eligible to submit an alternative plan. Developer C submits an own proposal. Developer X, who has no land, also submits a proposal. The Municipality evaluates the three proposals and draws the conclusion that Developer X has the best plan, followed by Developer B. Developer C has the worst plan, because it offers less contributions than the others. The Municipality finally decides to select the proposal of Developer B, because one of the selection criteria gives preference to landowners.

Once Developer B has been selected as urbanizing agent, developer C finally agrees with Agreement I. Developer D still does not want to collaborate. Developer B submits a Land Readjustment plan to the Municipality, a plan that includes the contributions and the land that developer D has to deliver. The Municipality approves it, after which Developer D decides to collaborate. He provides part of his land (the land needed for the park and basketball playfield) and pays his contribution. Finally he receives the same reimbursement as Developers B and C: building parcels with an economic value that corresponds to his proportional share in the development. This means that he receives a building parcel in parcel D, and another one in either parcels A or parcel B.

9.5 Epilogue

The way planning policy is implemented in the Netherlands has changed dramatically in the last decades. Until the end of the 80's and the start of the 90s, there was a predominance of public parties in land development. Today, private parties are taking over the lead, also implying a transition from public to private ownership of development land. This change has been fuelled by the diminishing of public subsidization and the need for public parties get rid of the financial risks involved in land development. However, practice in urban regeneration shows that this privatization has not reduced the need for public subsidization and has not produced new neighbourhoods with public infrastructure and facilities of high quality. Instead, due to a lack of good regulation, the change has resulted in an increase in land speculation, high development costs and the leaking away of the increased value. Both public and private parties are at a disadvantage: public bodies still must subsidize, and private parties are confronted with high costs and risks. The general public is also at a disadvantage: there is a general dissatisfaction with the public infrastructure and facilities in new neighbourhoods.

The Dutch central government has made efforts to solve this problem, the most relevant effort being the 2008 Land Development Act (*Grondexploitatiewet*). This act consists of a timid step that, if developed and brought to its ultimate consequences, might help in some cases to regulate the private implementation of planning policy in a more effective way. However, this act, in its present form, will not resolve all the problems by far. Probably it was very hard for the legislator to introduce all the necessary changes. After all, the Dutch planning system, as in any other country, consists of close interrelated sets of rules, customs and interests. In addition, there is in the Netherlands no long experience of public regulation when there is private predominance in land development. However, instead of looking abroad to other countries with more experience in this, the Dutch legislator, consciously or not, inherited and assumed several Dutch paradigms without a fundamental, critical view of them. First, the predominant normative paradigm in the Netherlands that the landowner is the only legitimate owner of the value increase. Here the legislator overlooked, for reasons obvious in the Dutch context, another possibility that is popular in other European countries: that public bodies also have right to a share of the value increase. Second, the Dutch legislator assumed, with the Dutch experience in public land policy in mind, the paradigm that the only way of enforcing an adequate private involvement must be a direct and financial involvement of public bodies. The translation of both paradigms in the 2008 Land Development Act has resulted in an unnecessarily complex set of legal instruments that charges municipalities with too many tasks and risks - too many in the light of their capacities. The experience in England and Spain shows that when private parties control the land, public regulation must be based on simple and clear roles: public bodies regulate beforehand, private bodies implement and assume all the corresponding risks. Public bodies *must* clarify the rules under which private parties operate, leaving less room for discretion during the negotiations with landowners and property developers. Instead, the Dutch legislator chose the most difficult path: *obliging* public bodies to assume direct responsibility, costs and risks in land development. In addition, the 2008 Act does not answer the most fundamental challenge: how to dissuade land speculation and divert part of the value increase to finance public infrastructure and facilities.

The international financial and economic crisis is exasperating the shortcoming of not being able to finance the public infrastructure and facilities with the economic value increase that arises when land is rezoned. The size of the public expenditure meant to fight the economic crisis has no precedent. Also the Netherlands has introduced massive investment programs to postpone budgetary cuts, save banks and industries and pump money in the economy. However, that large public expenditure will lead to a long period of cuts in public budgets. In the Netherlands, from 2011 onwards, public bodies will severely cut their expenditure, and since 2009 many municipalities are already suffering serious cuts. Most probably, theses cuts will adversely affect the subsidization of urban planning and, especially, of urban regeneration. This reduction in public funds takes place at the same time as the Dutch governments are pursuing the ambitious goal to give priority to the regeneration of old and deteriorated urban areas instead of greenfield developments. This is additionally problematic because urban regeneration is easier to say than to do, as it usually involves more costs than greenfield development, at least in the short term. The concurrence of these two factors (public budgetary cuts and renewed focus on urban regeneration) is placing urban development and its quality under serious pressure. The risk is that, due to absence of adequate funds, the development and quality of the new urban areas will suffer. This makes it necessary to improve the capturing of value increase in order to finance public infrastructure and facilities.

This research seeks to provide an answer to this need. As the examples of England and Spain show, it is possible to improve the situation. It is true that the economic crisis can delay improvement: it shall take indeed some time until landowners, developers and investors accept that their land is over-assessed. But finally they will assume (and some of them are already assuming) that land must be entered for lower prices in the accounts of urban projects. It is important that public bodies introduce soon the recommendations in this chapter 9 in order to a) divert part of the released value increase towards the public goals; b) to lower land development costs; c) and to prevent landowners, developers and investors from again over-assessing their land once market prices recover in the future!

The recommendations in chapter 9 follow a gradual approach, from voluntary measures that fit within the 2008 Land Development Act, to more profound, legal modifications for the longer term. The recommendations focus first on helping public bodies, especially municipalities, to fully take advantage of the opportunities offered in the 2008 Land Development Act. If municipalities act appropriately, they can significantly improve the capturing of value increases. At the same time, there are serious limitations of the Act and it is not likely that all municipalities will be able to fulfil all the requirements that are needed to fully take advantage of the Act. Therefore, I have also provided recommendations that aim to address the legal limitations. In this, I have tried to propose changes of the law only where this was strictly necessary, and to stay as much as possible within the existing legal framework. Finally, conscious of the fact that there are limitations that cannot be resolved with timid modifications, also more fundamental long-term legislative changes are offered.

COSTA

Annexes

Annex I: Check lists

Check-list Preparatory Research Question I

These are the sub-variables of the independent variable 'formal rules relevant to zoning', and the check-lists that were handled to gather the data for Preparatory Research Question 1:

Where (in which planning documents) are the relevant binding rules brought into force?
First, all sorts of planning documents have been studied that might bear legally binding rules for the use of land. Here this research operated with the methodological principle of comparative law, 'functionality', which states that in law the only things that are comparable are those that fulfill the same function (Zweigert & Kötz, 1998: 34-35). In this case the common function was that of bearing binding rules.

Second, those sorts of planning documents have been selected that might be relevant for this research project: (1) they might be operationally used by the local authorities, from which follows that the competences of making and/or approving them have to be in the hands of those local public authorities. It also follows that local public authorities need room for a certain amount of discretion when deciding whether or not to approve them; (2) the planning documents can imply a substantial modification of the land use possibilities, as to have a clear effect on the value of the property.

When (in relation to the negotiations) are the relevant binding rules approved?
The following aspects have been studied: First the procedure of approval: which steps form the procedure? How long does it take to make and approve the relevant binding rules? Second the moment of formal approval, with regard to: the negotiations between the local authority and the developers/ landowners and the start of the works. Third the legal constraints regarding the moment of approval: do land use plans have obligatorily to cover the whole municipal territory? And does planning law conceive

land use plans as a procedural chain among other planning instruments, and fix the moment in which they must be approved?

What are the possibly contents of the relevant binding rules?
Not all possible contents of binding rules are important. Only those aspects are studied that could be relevant for public value capturing: land-use classes (housing, office, industry, public space, open space: are they fixed in the law?); building envelope (length, width, and height); price category of housing (social or free market housing); distinction between rented and owner occupied housing; temporal regulations (when to start and/or to finish the infrastructure provision and the building); financial contributions or other kind of contributions (contributions in kind such as infrastructure provision, construction of public facilities, etc, contributions in money, in land, damage compensation); development agreements that secure the contributions?

Who has the right to implement the relevant binding rules?
To whom belong the development rights? To the landowner, to the developer, to the municipality or to a combination of them? To make the question more specific, the sub-variable has focussed on five different questions:

1. *Who has the control on each of the six transactions in development processes?*
2. *Which are the resources (material and regulatory resources) needed for each of the transactions?*
3. *How are these resources distributed between the involved parties?*
4. *What are the dependence patterns that result from the allocation of resources?*
5. *Are these dependence patterns avoidable?*

These questions might have a different answer depending on the specific formula of development. E.g. it is different if land is owned by commercial developers that if it is owned by the municipality. Three scenarios have been considered:

- Fully private development: private actors develop the location, also the public infrastructure. The land, or a majority of it, is in their hands;
- Private development with public infrastructure provision: land, or a majority of it, is in private hands, and the developer produces serviced plots and develops the building. However, a public authority plays an active role by providing part or all the public infrastructure;
- Public development: a public authority develops the location. It acquires the land, invests in infrastructure provision and, finally, sells the serviced building plots.

How flexible are the relevant binding rules?
Related to the procedural guarantees, these aspects have been studied:
(1) Have initiative takers right to a proper municipal decision?
(2) Have initiative takers right to appeal against the municipal decision?

Related to the flexibility of modification, three aspects have been researched:
(1) What are the procedural requirements of modifying (*wijziging* in Dutch);
(2) Departing from (*vrijstelling*) and
(3) Detailing (*uitwerking*) the existing binding rules?

Related to the flexibility to approve binding rules gradually, three aspects have been researched:
(1) The rules for the delimitation of the geographical scope of the plan areas;
(2) Whether there is a maximum allowed number of different binding rules documents per area;
(3) Whether municipalities were free to approve the detailing of global plans.

Check-list Preparatory Research Question 2

These are the sub-variables of the dependent variable 'capturing of value increase' and the check-lists that were handled to gather the data for Preparatory Research Question 2:

Who pays the following value capturing goals?
These are: on-site land development costs; land needed for on-site public infrastructure and facilities; on-site public facilities (public buildings); on-site and off-site social/affordable housing; off-site public infrastructure and facilities; and creaming off betterment.

Are the value capturing topics implemented on time?
More specifically: have the deadlines for the implementation of the value capturing goals been achieved or not? This regards both the deadlines included in development agreements and in the binding rules.

Annex 2: Planning legislation

Planning legislation in the Spanish region of Valencia

This is the most important body of legislation directly related to urban development (Parejo & Blanc, 1999: 25):

1. National legislation: 1954 Expropriation Act (*Ley de Expropiación Forzosa*); 1956 Land Act (*Ley del Suelo*); 1976 Refunded Act (*Texto Refundido de la Ley del Suelo 1976*) of the 1975 Land use and Urban Planning Act (*Ley sobre el Régimen del Suelo y Ordenación Urbana*); 1978 Planning Regulation (*Reglamento de Planeamiento*); 1992 Refunded Act (*Texto Refundido de la Ley del Suelo 1992*) of the 1990 Land use and Urban Planning Act (*Ley sobre el Régimen del Suelo y Ordenación Urbana*); 1998 Land Use Planning and Appraisal Act (*Ley sobre Régimen del Suelo y Valoraciones*); 1999 Building Act (*Ley de Ordenación de la Edificación*); 2003 Urgent Liberalisation Measures on Real Estate and Transport Sectors Act (*Ley de medidas urgentes de liberalización en el sector inmobiliario y transportes*); 2007 Land Act (*Ley de suelo*); Some environmental and sectorial legislation, that might also rule the land-use: Water Act (*Ley de Aguas*); Coasts Act (*Ley de Costas*); Natural Espaces, and Wild Flora and Fauna Conservation Act (*Ley de Conservación de los Espacios Naturales y de la Flora y Fauna Silvestres*).
2. Valencian legislation: 1990 Nomenclator of Nuisance Activities Decree (*Nomenclátor de actividades molestas, insalubres, nocivas y peligrosas*); 1994 Planning Act (*Ley Reguladora de la Actividad Urbanística*, LRAU), substituted in 2006 by the 2005 Planning Act (*Ley Urbanística Valenciana*, LUV); 1998 Planning Regulation (*Reglamento de Planeamiento*), substituted in 2006 by a new Planning Regulation (*Reglamento de Ordenación y Gestión Territorial y Urbanística*); 1999 Standard Building Regulation Order (*Reglamento de Zonas de Ordenación Urbanística*); 2004 Territory and Landscape Act (*Ley del Territorio y el Paisaje*); 2006 Landscape Regulation (*Reglamento del Paisaje*); 2006 Golf Courses Act (*Ley de los Campos de Golf*).

Planning legislation in England

This is the most important body of legislation directly related to urban development in England (Williams & Wood, 1994: 68; Evans & Davoudi, 2005: 25; Cullingworth & Nadin, 2006: 533-535):

1. Basic legislation, issued by the UK Parliament: Town and Country Planning Act 1990 (TCP); Listed Building and Conservation Act 1990 (LBCA); Planning and Compensation Act 1991; Planning and Compulsory Purchase Act 2004;
2. Statutory Instruments, issued through delegated legislative powers:
   a) Regulations: Town and Country Planning (Modification And Discharge Of Planning Obligations) Regulations 1992; Town and Country Planning (Environmental Impact Assessment) (England and Wales) Regulations 1999;
   b) Orders: Town and Country Planning (Use Classes) Order 1987; Town and Country Planning (General Development Procedure) Order 1995;
3. 'Circulars' or 'Policy Guidance notes': Circular 15/92, 'Publicity for Planning Applications'; Circular 11/95, 'Use of conditions in planning permission'; ODPM Circular 05/2005, 'Planning obligations', which substituted the previous Circular 1/97;
4. Planning policy guidance notes (PPGs), Minerals policy guidance notes (MPGs) and Planning Policy

Statements (PPS): there are many of them. In 2005, there were 25 PPGs and 17 MPGs. PPG's are nowaday being gradually replaced by the PPSs. Important PPG's and PPSs are: PPG3 "Housing", published in 2000; PPS11 "Regional Spatial Strategies', published in 2004; PPS12 "Local Development Frameworks", published in 2004.

Planning legislation in the Netherlands

This is the most relevant body of legislation on planning that might be involved in urban development (Needham et al., 1993: 23 and 48-54; Hijmans and Gerzon, 1995: 30-32; Klaassen, 2000: 28 and 487): Physical Planning Act (*Wet op de Ruimtelijke Ordening*), approved in 1962, substantially modified in 1985 and the last time on 1 July 2008; 2008 Land Development Act (*Grondexploitatiewet*), included in articles 6.12-6.24 of the 2008 Physical Planning Act; Physical Planning Decree (*Besluit op de Ruimtelijke Ordening*), approved in 1985 and modified significantly in 2008; 2001 Building Decree (*Bouwbesluit*); Housing Act (*Woningwet*), approved in 1901 and substantially modified in 1992; Town and Village Regeneration Act (*Wet op de Stads- en Dorpsvernieuwing*) and the Town and Village Regeneration Decree (*Besluit op de Stads- en Dorpsvernieuwing*), introduced both in 1985; 2000 Urban Regeneration Act (*Wet Stedelijke vernieuwing*); Monuments Act (*Monumentenwet*), approved in 1961 and modified substantially in 1988; Act General Administrative Law (*Algemene wet bestuursrecht, Awb*); Civil Code (*Burgelijk Wetboek*); Expropriation Act (*Onteigeningswet*).

Some environmental legislation and other sectorial legislation also regulate the use of land: Noise Nuisance Act (*Wet Geluidhinder*), Soil Protection Act (*Wet Bodembescherming*), Superficial Water Contamination Act (*Wet Verontreiniging Oppervlaktewateren*), Atmospheric Contamination Act (*Wet Inzake de Luchtverontreiniging*), Underground Water Act (*Grondwaterwet*), Environment Management Act (*Wet Milieubeheer*), Railway Act (*Spoorwegwet*), Roads Act (*Wegenwet*) and Traffic Act (*Wegenverkeerswet*).

Annex 3: Development costs and returns in the English cases

	Megabowl		Temple Quay		Harbourside	
	Paid by developer	**Paid by public bodies**	**Paid by developer**	**Paid by public bodies**	**Paid by developer**	**Paid by public bodies**
1) Land costs	€11m [1]		No data available	No data available	Not available	
2-3) Infra prov and plan preparation costs (€/m^2 new public space; total redeveloped land)	€1.2m [2]	€0.1m	Estimation: €8m[3]	€0.2m	€12.5[4]	€0.6m [5]
	(€153/m^2; €99/m^2)		(€269/m^2; €111/m^2)		(€332/m^2; €166/m^2)	
4) Soil decontamination costs			Estimation: €5m		€15m	
5) Compensation costs			Estimation: probably no/low		Estimation: probably no/low	
6) Additional contributions of developer	€1.7m[6]		About €6m[7]		€33m[8]	
7) Real Estate development costs Average costs (€/m^2 floor space)[9]	€13.2m (€985/m^2)[10]		Estimation: €114m (€1,000/m^2)[11]		Estimation: €123m (€1,000/m^2)[12]	
8) Total returns	€37.1m[13]		€409m[14]		€404m[15]	
9) Developer's Final Profit (incl/excl the price paid for the land)	€10m (incl land price)		€276m (excl. land price)		€220m (excl. land price)	

1. The price paid for the possible purchase of land;
2-3. Infrastructure provision and plan preparation costs: this includes the whole development up to the delivery of serviced building plots, thus not only the infrastructure provision works, but also the preparation of plans, reserved amounts for unexpected expenses, the overhead costs, possible 'hidden' profit margins of the developer, etc. It is not known whether the figures include or exclude the financial costs.
4. Soil decontamination costs.
5. Compensation costs: this includes compensation to existing owners and inhabitants, for removal of activities and residence, demolition of constructions and buildings, etc.
6. Additional contributions of the developer: contributions, in cash or in kind (constructions, buildings) to public goals (payments, construction of public infrastructure or public buildings, etc) **additional** to his contributions to the on-site infrastructure provision costs (even if they might serve a wider area than the development in question), which are already included in (2).
7. Real Estate development costs: this includes the whole development of the real estate, thus not only the building costs, but also the preparation of plans, overhead costs, possible 'hidden' profit margins of the developer, etc;
8. Total returns: the total returns accruing from the selling of the real estate (office, dwellings, etc).
9. Developer's Final Profits: 8 - [1dev + 2-3dev + 4dev + 5dev + 6dev + 7dev]. This regards the profits of the developer, i.e. it excludes the possibility of costs paid by public bodies.

1 € 11m is the price paid by a developer to the landowner after agreement was achieved about the contributions. The minimum land cost (the value of the land taking into account only the use of the site as bowling alley) was € 3-4.5m. Change rate € 1.5 per £ 1.

2 Megabowl: This information is based on an assessment given by the consultancy that assesses the developer. Own assessment of compensation costs is that they are not significant, as there are no contracts that must be cancelled and the existing building belonged to the developer. Also, soil decontamination costs are probably nothing or very low. Calculation average costs, with possible but improbable compensation and soil decontamination costs: €1.3m : 8,500 m^2 new public space (65% total plan area Planning Permission) = €153/m^2 public space; Or €1.3m : 13,104 m^2 total redeveloped land (100% total plan area Planning Permission) = €99/m^2 total redeveloped land.

3 Temple Quay: figures were not available, this is an own estimation, based on these assumptions: (1) probably there are no compensation costs (as most of the former industrial buildings and premises were already demolished); (2) Infrastructure provision costs are an own estimation based on costs in Megabowl and Harbourside. Calculation average costs, excl. soil decontamination costs, incl. possible but improbable compensation costs: €8.2m : 30,400 m2 new public space (55% plan area, minus an existing school, which will remain untouched) = €269/m^2; Or €8.2m : 74,000 m^2 total redeveloped land (100% total plan area, includes existing school) = €111/m^2. About 66,000 of the 74,000 m^2 of the total plan area has been effectively redeveloped. The other ca. 8,000 m^2 correspond to an existing school of which only part has been refurbished. Possible explanation for relatively high costs: figures are an estimation based on figures of Megabowl, plus better quality for the public space.

4 Harbourside: probably there are no compensation costs (as most of the area was not anymore in use); Figures are based on information given by the developer and the public officer. Calculation average costs, with possible but improbable compensation costs: €13.1m : 39,500 m^2 new public space (50% total plan area) = €332/m^2 new public space; Or €13.1m : 78,900 m^2 total redeveloped land (100% total plan area) = €166/m^2 total redeveloped land.

5 Harbourside: these costs are stated in the Planning Agreement.

6 Megabowl: This information is based on the Planning Agreement, which was available for this research.

7 Temple Quay: €3.1m are stipulated as payment in Planning Agreement, the other €3m concern off-site high way works and are an own rough estimation.

8 Harbourside: €30.5m in payments to LPA (stipulated in Planning Agreement), about €2m in kind in construction works off-site high ways, €0.6 payment to LPA that invest them in on-site infra.

9 Real Estate Development costs are similar probably because there is only one empirical source, the costs in Megabowl. Therefore, these averages are not much valid.

10 Megabowl: The developer estimates real estate development costs of social dwellings (10.050 m^2 floor space) and open market dwellings (3,350 m^2 floor space) in €985/m^2 floor space: 13,400 m^2 floor space x €985/m^2 floor space = €13.2m.

11 Temple Quay: figures were not available, this is an own estimation, based on costs Megabowl (about €1,000/m^2 floor space); 114,000 m^2 floor space x €1,000 = €114m.

12 Harbourside: figures were not available, this is an own estimation, based on costs Megabowl (about €1,000/m^2 floor space); 122,740 m^2 floor space x €1,000 = €123m.

13 Megabowl: estimation affordable units, based on Planning Agreement and information given by developer, is €3.1m; estimation for free market units, based on market prices and estimation developer, is €34m (about €3,380/m^2 floor space).

14 Temple Quay: estimation for affordable units (€5.3m) is based on Planning Agreement; estimation commercial part (dwellings, office and commercial, in total €404m) is own assessment based on prices Megabowl and on actual market prices in the area. Prices dwellings are about €4,000-4,500/m^2 floor space.

15 Harbourside: estimation for affordable units (€4.7m) is based on Planning Agreement; estimation commercial part (dwellings, office and commercial, in total €399m) is own assessment based on prices Megabowl and on actual market prices in the area. Prices dwellings are about €4,000-4,500/m^2 floor space.

Annex 4: Development costs and returns in the Dutch cases

	Kruidenbuurt		*Kop van Oost*		*Stationskwartier*	
	Paid by developer	Paid by public bodies	Paid by developer	Paid by public bodies	Paid by developer	Paid by public bodies
1) Land costs	Developer bought only some plots for €1.4m		Developer bought in 2001 land for €12m[16]		€30-40m + small amount for new Station[17]	€65-€15m= €50m[18]
2-3) Infra prov and plan preparation costs (€/m² new public space; total redeveloped land)	€12.6m[19]	€11.5m + costs roads and sewer pipelines	€7m (€368/m²; €148/m²)[20] + Refurbishing road and some public space			
	(€438/m²; €158/m²)				(With soil decontamination costs and possible compensation costs: €1,212/m² new public space; €570/m² total redeveloped land)[21]	
4) Soil decontamination costs	-		€0.37m	€0.12m		
5) Compensation costs	€5.4m		€0.16m			
6) Additional contributions of developer	€0.5m[22]					About €15m
7) Real Estate development costs	€106 m[23]		€90m[24]		€ 320 m[25]	
Average costs (€/dwelling and/or m² floor space)	€144,000/dwelling, about €1,200/m²		€210,000/dwelling, about €1,600/m²		About €1,300/m²	
8) Total returns	€150 m[26]		€112 or €139m[27]		€480-520m[28]	
9) Developer's Final Profit (incl/excl the price paid for the land)	€24 m (excl. 'boek-waarde' most of land)		€2m (112-110), or €29m (139-110) (incl. land price)		€120-180m (incl. land price)	

1 = The price paid for a possible purchase of land;
2-3 = Infrastructure provision and plan preparation costs: this includes the whole development up to the delivery of serviced building plots, thus not only the infrastructure provision works, but also the preparation of plans,, reserved amounts for unexpected expenses, the overhead costs, possible 'hidden' profit margins of the developer, etc. It is not known whether the figures include or exclude the financial costs.
4 = Soil decontamination costs.
5 = Compensation costs: this includes compensation to existing owners and inhabitants, for removal of activities and residence, demolition of constructions and buildings, etc.
6 = Additional contributions of the developer: contributions, in cash or in kind (constructions, buildings) to public goals (payments, construction of public infrastructure or public buildings, etc) **additional** to his contributions to the on-site infrastructure provision costs (even if they might serve a wider area than the development in question), which are already included in (2).
7= Real Estate development costs: this includes the whole development of the real estate, thus not only the building costs, but also the preparation of plans, overhead costs, possible 'hidden' profit margins of the developer, etc.
8= Total returns: the total returns accruing from the selling of the real estate (office, dwellings, etc).
9= Developer's Final Profits: 8 - [1dev + 2-3dev + 4dev + 5dev + 6dev + 7dev]. This regards the profits of the developer, i.e. it excludes the possibility of costs paid by public bodies.

16 This is the price paid by IBC to Hollestelle in 2001. Because Heijmans bought the land in 2002 (as part of IBC), the price paid by Heijmans, the actual developer, could be higher.

17 Stationskwartier: there are probably no or few compensation costs, as most of the area was empty before development takes place. There are significant soil decontamination costs.

18 Stationskwartier: this €65m include the subsidies for both the land development and for the new Railways and bus Station. A rough own estimation of the costs of 3 km off-site roads are between €10-20m, for the sake of calculation €15m. These €15m are considered as a contribution.

19 Kruidenbuurt: this information is based on the 'Grondexploitatie', which was available for this research. Calculation average costs, which excludes costs roads and pipelines: €24.1m : 55,000 m^2 new public space (32% total plan area Land use Plan, it excludes refurbished Heezerweg and Korianderstraat) = €438/m^2 new public space; Or €24.1m : 153,000 m^2 total redeveloped land (89% total plan area Land use Plan, it excludes the Heezerweg and Korianderstraat) = €158/m^2 total redeveloped land.

20 Kop van Oost: this information is based on interviews with developer and public officers. Calculation average costs: €7m : 19,000 m^2 new public space (24% total plan area Land use Plan, it excludes Sontweg, Europa weg, the canal, about 4,000 m^2 new public space and the building) = €368/m^2 new public space; Or €7m : 47,200 m^2 total redeveloped land (59% total plan area Land use Plan, excludes Sontweg, Europaweg and the canal) = €148/m^2 total redeveloped land.

21 Stationskwartier: Calculation average costs, which include possible but improbable compensation costs, and soil decontamination costs: €80m : 66,000 m^2 new public space (41% total plan area land use Plan, includes the new Station, excludes the Belcrumweg and the 3 km off-site roads that will be refurbished) = €1,212/m^2 new public space; Or €80m : 140,000 m2 total redeveloped land (88% total plan area Land use Plan, includes the land occupied by the commercial buildings, the rest, about 10%, will remain untouched) = €570/m2 total redeveloped land. Possible explanation for relatively high costs: it includes the land for new road and new station, land that has been 'bought' to NS, a possible profit for the municipality and the soil decontamination costs.

22 Kruidenbuurt: This information is based on the 'Grondexploitatie', which was available for this research.

23 Kruidenbuurt: The developer estimates real estate dev costs of dwellings (650 units) in €144,000/unit. Own estimation is that costs commercial space (about 10,000 m^2) are about €1,240/m^2 gross floor. Calculation average costs: €106m : (650 dwellings + 10,000 m^2 commercial space), about €1,200/m^2 gross floor.

24 Kop van Oost: €90m is an estimation of the developer. Calculation average costs: an own estimation of total m^2 gross floor is 56,000 m^2 (44,000 m^2 apartments + 8,000 m^2 single family houses + 4,000 m^2 commercial space); Thus, €90m : 56,000 m^2 = €1,600/m^2 gross floor.

25 Stationskwartier: € 320 m is an estimation based on information given by a former developer, and regards only the development costs of the commercial real estate (i.e. housing, office, shops and parking, whether this is in the normal plots or in the building of the new Station), but not the transport function of the new Station. Calculation average costs: an own estimation is that the total building volume is 240,000 m^2 gross floor (including all the commercial space, i.e. housing, office, shops and parking; and excluding the transport function of the new Station); Thus €320m : 240,000 m^2 gross floor = €1,300/m^2 gross floor space.

26 Kruidenbuurt: This is an own estimation, based on actual selling prices of the real estate; the developer gave no estimation.

27 Kop van Oost: The developer estimates the total revenues for the selling of the real estate in € 112m, inclusive BTW. Own estimations, based on the actual selling prices of real estate, produce higher figures, € 139m and € 189m. Consulted about this, experts assessed the first estimation (€ 139m) as more realistic (Stauttener & Van Bladel, interview 2008).

28 Stationskwartier: two estimations, both based on selling price of 150,000m2 in 'Gemengde doeleinden 2'; one based on information given by former developer is €480m; own estimation, based on general market prices in the area, is €510-520m.

Annex 5: Survey of Monofunctional residential districts

On behalf of this research, a brief survey has been made of a significant part of 56 urban regeneration districts (*56 wijken* in Dutch). This list of 56 districts is made by the Ministry of Housing, Planning and Environment. This survey focused on development schemes on privately owned land situated within these districts. The survey consisted of:

- Based on an overview of 56 Urban Regeneration areas of the Ministry of Housing, Planning and Environment (http://www.vrom.nl/pagina.html?id=11136, consulted on September 2007), 15 districts were selected that showed some indications of development on privately owned land: Heuvel (Breda), Berflo Es (Hengelo), Rustenburg/Oostbroek (The Hague), Q4 (Venlo), Crooswijk Noord and Hoogvliet (Rotterdam), GMS (Heerlen), Bartjes/Eikendonk/Hofstad (Den Bosch), Binnenstad (Helmond), Nieuw Noord (Tilburg), Presikhaaf and Malburgen (Arnhem), and Zuilen/Ondiep, Hoograven/Tolsteeg and Kanaleneiland/Transwijk (Utrecht);
- Public officers responsible for and/or familiar with these 15 districts were interviewed telephonically during September 2007;
- Of the 15 districts, only 7 districts (8 schemes) seemed indeed to have development on privately owned land. They are all small sites (50-100 dwellings): Hoograven, Vicona, Onixweg 1-3 (in the city of Utrecht); Kanaleneiland/Transwijk, Winkelcentrum (in Utrecht); Malburgen, Winkelcentrum Drieslag (in Arnhem); Zuilen/Ondiep, winkelcentrum Rokade (in Utrecht); Heuvel, WSST (in Breda); Presikhaaf, Weldamlaan (in Arnhem). On two others the situation was doubtful, for land was privately owned but will be acquired by a Public-private Partnership (Berflo Es, in Engelo), or land was only partly privately owned (Centrumgebied Kanaleneiland, in Utrecht). So in total 7 clear private schemes, and 2 doubtful. 4 schemes regard shopping centers;
- In the mentioned 8 private schemes, private regeneration includes hardly any private financing of public infrastructure and facilities. Developers do not finance social housing in any of these 8 schemes, and, at the most, they construct themselves some public space, which is directly related to the scheme, or within the scheme itself. Only in one case (Winkelcentrum Rokade) is was not possible to discover whether the developer had paid or not a contribution to the municipality.

Annex 6: Comparison development costs and returns in the Valencian, English and Dutch cases

	Valencian cases				English cases			Dutch cases			Dutch cases (second opinion)		
	Guillem	*Periodista*	*Camino*	*Benalúa*	*Megabowl*	*Temple*	*Harbourside*	*Kruidenbuurt*	*KopvOost*	*Stations-kwartier*	*Project 1*[29]	*Project 2*[30]	*Project 3*[31]
1. Land costs	Not available				€11m	Not available	Not available	€1.4m + 'boekwaarde'[32]	at least €12m	€80m (€1,212/m^2; €570)[33]	€ 14.6m	€0.9m	€31.3m
2. Infras prov costs (€/m^2 new public space; total redeveloped land)	€0.66m (€77/m^2; €57/m^2)[34]	€1.1m (€418/m^2; (€187/m^2)[35]	€3.3m (€85/m^2; €65/m^2)[36]	€5.5m (€75/m^2; €59/m^2)[37]	€1.3m (€153/m^2; €99/m^2)[38]	Estimation: €8.2m (€269/m^2; €111/m^2)[39]	€13.1m (€332/m^2; €166/m^2)[40]	€24.1m (€438/m^2; €158/m^2)[41]	€7m (€368/m^2; €148/m^2)[42]		€ 9.8m (€249/m^2; €164/m^2)	€6.2m (€222/m^2; €107/m^2)	€12.2m (€94/m^2; €67/m^2)
3. Plan prep costs (€/m^2 new public space; total redeveloped land)	€0.15 (€17/m^2; €13/m^2)[43]	€0.7 (€269/m^2; (€119/m^2)[44]	€0.7 (€18/m^2; €14/m^2)[45]	Ca. €1.1m (€19/m^2; €15/m^2)[46]							€4m (€102/m^2; €67/m^2)	€ 1.7 (€61/m^2; €29/m^2)	€3.1m (€24/m^2; €17/m^2)
4. Soil decontamination costs	-	-	Evt costs are included in 2)	Evt costs are included in 2)		€5m	€15m	-	€0.5m		-	-	-
5. Compensation costs	€1.9m	€2.2m	€7.8m	€1.9m		No/low	No/low	€5.4m	€0.16m		-	€2.6m	€2.4m
6. Additonal contributions of developer	-	€1.6m	€14.2m	2.683 m^2 floor space [47]	€1.7m	About €6m	€33m	€0.5m		About €15m	-	-	€1m?
7. Real estate dev costs (€/m^2 floor space)	No data	No data	€86.5m (€1,150/m^2)	No data	€13.2m (€985/m^2)	Estimation: €114m (€1,000/m^2) [48]	Estimation: €123m (€1,000/m^2) [49]	Estimation: €106 m (about €1,200/m^2)	€90m (about €1,600/m^2)	€ 320 m (about €1,300/m^2)[50]	No data	No data	No data
8. Total returns (average €/m^2 floor space)	No data	No data	€432m (€5,750/m^2)	No data	€37.1m (€3,380/m^2)	€409m (€4,000-4,500/m^2)	€404m (€4,000-4,500/m^2)	€150m	€112 m, €139m[51]	€480-520m[52]	No data	No data	No data

1. The price that the developer paid for the land;
2. Infrastructure provision costs: this includes not only the infrastructure provision works, but also reserved amounts for unexpected expenses, the overhead costs, possible 'hidden' profit margins of the developer, etc. In The Netherlands, they comprise: *Slopen, bouw en woonrijp maken, risico en onvoorzien.* The Valencian cases do exclude financial costs, second opinion Dutch cases too. It is not known whether the figures for the Dutch and English cases include or exclude the financial costs.
3. Plan preparation costs: the costs of the preparation of plans, studies, etc (*Plankosten*, or *Voorbereiding, toezicht en planontwikkeling*).
Soil decontamination costs.
4. Compensation costs: this includes compensation to existing owners and inhabitants, for removal of activities and residence, demolition of constructions and buildings, etc.
5. Additional contributions of the developer: contributions, in cash or in kind (constructions, buildings) to public goals (payments, construction of public infrastructure or public buildings, etc) additional to his contributions to the on-site infrastructure provision costs (even if they might serve a wider area than the development in question), which are already included in (2).
6. Real Estate development costs: this includes the whole development of the real estate, thus not only the building costs, but also the preparation of plans, overhead costs, possible 'hidden' profit margins of the developer, etc;
7. Total returns: the total returns accruing from the selling of the real estate (office, dwellings, etc).

29 Project 1: demolition of social facility (zorginstelling) in a large city, developer is foundation that owned all the land, plan area 59,900 m^2, 39,300 m^2 public space (66% plan area), 80 single family dwellings, 180 apartments, 1,500 m2 commercial facilities, 13,000 m2 public facilities, 800 underground parking places.

30 Project 2: demolition of social housing in a small town, developer is the housing association owning the land, plan area 57,700 m^2, 27,900 m^2 public space (51% plan area), 160 single family dwellings, 60 apartments.

31 Project 3: demolition of social housing in a medium city, developer is the housing association owning the land, plan area 182,000 m^2, 129,900 m^2 public space (71% plan area), 180 single family dwellings, 280 new apartments, 500 renewed apartments, 650 parking places in buildings.

32 NL, Kruidenbuurt: developer bought only some plots. The value of the rest of the land ('boekwaarde') is not known.

33 NL, Stationskwartier, with possible but improbable compensation costs, and incl. soil contamination costs and the price of land: €80m : 66,000 m^2 new public space (41% total plan area land use Plan, includes the new Station, excludes the Belcrumweg and the 3 km off-site roads that will be refurbished) = €1,212/m^2 new public space. Possibly explanation high costs: it includes the land for new road and new station, and that has been 'bought' to Dutch Railways, soil decontamination costs, and an possible profit for the Municipality.

34 Valencia, Guillem de Anglesola: €0.66m : 8,552 m^2 new public space (74% total plan area Land use Plan) = €94/m^2 new public space. €0.66m : 11.489 m^2 total redeveloped land = €57/m^2 total redeveloped land.

35 Valencia, Periodista Gil Sumbiela, incl. possible soil decontamination costs: €1.1m : 2,597 m^2 new public space (44% total plan area Land use Plan) = €418/m^2 new public space. €1.1m : 5.867 m^2 total redeveloped land = €187/m^2 total redeveloped land.

36 Valencia, Camino Hondo del Grao, included possible some decontamination costs: €3.3m : 38,720 m^2 new public space (76% total plan area Land use Plan) = €85/m^2 new public space. €3.3m : 50.716 m^2 total redeveloped land = €65/m^2 total redeveloped land.

37 Valencia, Benalúa Sur, included possible some decontamination costs: €4.4m : 58,701m^2 new public space (79% total plan area development unit-1 Land use Plan) = €75/m^2 new public space. €4.4m : 74.168 m^2 total redeveloped land development unit-1 = €59/m^2 total redeveloped land.

38 England, Megabowl, with possible but improbable compensation and decontamination costs: €1.3m : 8,500 m^2 new public space (65% total plan area Planning Permission) = €153/m^2 new public space.

39 England, Temple Quay: figures were not available, this is an own estimation, based on these assumptions: (1) probably there are no compensation costs (as most of the former industrial buildings and premises were already demolished); (2) Infrastructure provision costs are an own estimation based on costs in Megabowl and Harbourside, plus scenario of better quality public space. The average costs, included possible but improbably compensation costs, are: €8.2m : 30,400 m^2 new public space (55% plan area, minus an existing school, which will remain untouched) = €269/m^2. Possible explanation for higher costs: figures are estimation based on scenario of public space probably of higher quality in this part of the city than in Megabowl.

40 England, Harbourside, with possible but improbable compensation costs: €13.1m : 39,500 m2 new public space (50% total plan area) = €332/m2 new public space. Possibly explanation higher costs: figures are estimation based on scenario of public space probably of higher quality in this part of the city than in Megabowl.

41 NL, Kruidenbuurt: this €24.1m excludes some costs for roads and sewer pipelines. €24.1m : 55,000 new public space (32% total plan area Land use Plan, it excludes refurbished Heezerweg and Korianderstraat) = €438/m2 new public space.

42 NL, Kop van Oost: this €7m excludes the costs of refurbishing some public space within the plan area and a main road alongside the plan area. €7m : 19,000 m2 new public space (24% total plan area Land use Plan, it excludes Sontweg, Europaweg, the canal, about 4,000 m2 new public space and the building) = €368/m2.

43 Valencia, Guillem de Anglesola: €0.15m : 8,552 m^2 new public space (74% total plan area Land use Plan) = €18/m^2 new public space. €0.15m : 11.489 m^2 total redeveloped land = €13/m^2 total redeveloped land.

44 Valencia, Periodista Gil Sumbiela, incl. possible soil decontamination costs: €0.7m : 2,597 m^2 new public space (44% total plan area Land use Plan) = €269/m^2 new public space. €0.7m : 5.867 m^2 total redeveloped land = €119/m^2 total redeveloped land.

45 Valencia, Camino Hondo del Grao, included possible some decontamination costs: €0.7m : 38,720 m^2 new public space (76% total plan area Land use Plan) = €18/m^2 new public space. €0.7m : 50.716 m^2 total redeveloped land = €14/m^2 total redeveloped land.

46 Valencia, Benalúa Sur, included possible some decontamination costs: €1.1m : 58,701m^2 new public space (79% total plan area development unit-1 Land use Plan) = €19/m^2 new public space. €1.1m : 74.168 m^2 total redeveloped land development unit-1 = €15/m^2 total redeveloped land.

47 Valencia, Benalúa Sur: Municipality receives 2.683 m^2 floor space as building rights;

48 England, Temple Quay: figures were not available, this is an own estimation, based on costs Megabowl (about €1,000/m2 floor space): 114,000 m^2 floor space x €1,000 = €114m.

49 England, Harbourside: figures were not available, this is an own estimation, based on costs Megabowl (about €1,000/m2 floor space); 122,740 m2 floor space x €1,000 = €123m.

50 Stationskwartier: development costs of the commercial real estate (i.e. housing, office, shops and parking, whether this is in the normal plots or in the building of the new Station), but excludes the transfer function of the new Station.

51 NL, Kop van Oost: The developer estimates the total revenues for the selling of the real estate in €112m, inclusive BTW. Own estimations, based on the actual selling prices of real estate, produce higher figures, €139m and €189m. Consulted to this, experts assessed the first stimation (€ 139m) as more realistic (Stauttener & Van Bladel, interview 2008).

52 NL, Stationskwartier: estimation former developer is €480m; own estimation, based on general market prices in the area, is €510-520m.

Annex 7: Experiment in Zevenhuizen, South-Holland

Introduction to the experiment

The Valencian urban development model became an inspiration for a group of 17 companies, all of them located in the industrial area ´Nijverheidscentrum´ (16 ha) in the municipality of Zevenhuizen-Moerkapelle, located inbetween the cities of The Hague, Gouda and Rotterdam. Three of the companies own 85% of the land, and most of them have a strong commitment to Zevenhuizen, as they are or were originally local companies. Most of the companies joined together in a cooperative, Coöperatie ´De Viergang' U.A. The goal of the cooperative was to move the industrial area to a new location, situated not far away and called 'De Viergang' (64 ha, see Figure). The companies were concerned about the continuation and modernization of their industrial activities, which are threatened by new plans that foresee the construction of 1,200 houses around the industrial

Figure Annex 7. In grey colour, business area 'Nijverheidscentrum' (16 ha); in light grey, the town of Zevenhuizen; circumscribed in black, the new location for the business and horticulture area, called 'De Viergang' (64 ha).

area 'Nijverheidscentrum'. 'De Viergang' is located besides the A12, one of the most important highways in Holland. Besides new sites for the firms, it was also planned to accommodate in-door horticulture (greenhouses) that must be relocated from other places. 35% of the area should be industry, 45% greenhouses and 20% double use. *Rabobank Vastgoed,* the property development department of a cooperative bank, supported initially the initiative by assuming the costs of plan preparation. Later, once *Rabobank Vastgoed* fused with developer *Bouwfonds*, a new management took over the operation.

The costs of the operation are: the costs of preparing the plans (posting 3, see financial analysis in section 2.4.3), of transferring the firms to the new location (posting 5), of buying the land in the new location (posting 1), of demolishing the old plants and providing the infrastructure in both the former and the new location (posting 2), and of developing 611 new houses in the former industrial area (posting 7). Table Annex 7 specifies most of these costs in Zevenhuizen. The idea was that the companies participate in the operation to move their industries to the new location and finance the costs by: (1) selling the 611 new houses in the former industrial area; (2) selling plots to the horticulture farmers in the 'De Viergang'; and (3) paying for the increase in value of their property (land and industrial buildings) that accrue from the removal to a first-class site and the renewal of the installations. The basic principle was that the operation would be 'value neutral' for the companies: that the value of their existing property (plant plus land) plus their investment would be the same as the value of their new properties. In other words: that the value increase that accrues from rezoning the former and new business area serves to pay all the necessary costs. The operation was planned to be finished in 2015.

Conclusions about the experience in Zevenhuizen

The plan documents recommended in section 9.4.2 have been elaborated in Zevenhuizen, but they were not detailed enough in their contents, as a result of which the involved parties never reached the recommended agreements. Without detailed documents and without the agreements, there was too much uncertainty: landowners did not want to decide until they knew exactly how much they would have to contribute and which building parcels they would receive. Also, the municipality needed a long time to decide which contributions were needed, and then hesitated to proceed further until all the costs of public infrastructure and facilities had been secured. As a consequence, the experiment in Zevenhuizen failed. In our opinion, the following mismatches with the recommendations in section 9.4.2 can explain the failure (*cfr.* HD Projectrealisatie, 2009; Lamot, Vriend, Penning and Hunen, interviews in 2010):

- Financial calculations not detailed enough: the initiating developer (*Rabobank Vastgoed*) had spent a limited amount of money for the elaboration of a draft plan for the infrastructure provision works, for calculating the costs of implementing these works, for calculating the costs of removal of the firms, and for properly assessing the costs of acquiring the 64 ha land for the new business area. Initially the developer had planned to elaborate more detailed studies and calculations. However, after it fused with one of the largest Dutch developers (*Bouwfonds*), a new project leader took over the operation and decided not to spend more on it. Lack of certainty about the real costs influenced negotiations in a negative way, making it difficult for the landowners to achieve an agreement with each other and with the developer and the municipality. This was very clear for the removal costs of the firms, which were calculated on the basis only of the figures provided by the companies instead of on detailed research. This was also very clear for the fiscal consequences of the operations (which were not researched), for the costs of acquiring the 64 ha land in the new business area (the municipality initially estimated them at € 24 per m² of land, based on the estimated compensation for the possible expropriation of the land, but changed afterwards the assessment to € 50), and for the reserved amount for unexpected expenses (€ 2.3 million, part of posting 2 in Table Annex 7, which was higher than usual because the lack of detail of the plans increased the uncertainties, this leading to reserving 20% of the infrastructure provision costs, instead of a more normal rate of 10%).

- Unclear land readjustment: another consequence of a limited budget for plan preparation is that during the negotiations there was no proposal concerning the rules for the land readjustment, so it was not possible to make clear to the firms/landowners how the serviced building plots in the new industrial location would be distributed between the different owners. In other words, the firms/landowners had not a final, clear picture of their future location.
- Unclear public contributions: it took too long to clarify which contributions to public infrastructure and facilities were obligatory. After the above mentioned plan documents had been submitted to the municipality in March 2007, it took more than one year (till June 2008) until the local and provincial public bodies clarified which contributions should be made to social housing (30%) and to off-site public infrastructure (a contribution of € 10m). The fact that the certainty about the contributions came very late hampered the negotiations, and in October 2008 it became clear that the contributions would lead to a large deficit. This leads us to ascertain the importance of the recommendation given in section 9.1.1: it is important that, before the elaboration of the plan documents and the negotiations, there is already certainty about at least the contributions that should be made. In other words, before market parties start elaborating the plan documents and negotiating, public bodies must have made clear what the contributions must be.
- Unprofessional attitude of the firms/landowners: the data that were necessary for elaborating the plan documents were gathered during 2006 and 2007. Important data, obtained from the firms/landowners, were: a) how much does it cost to move the firms to the new location, and to maintain production during the transition from the old to the new location; and b) the fiscal consequences of the increase in value of the properties (*vennootschapsbelasting* in Dutch). Both were important for calculating the financial feasibility of the operation, and the possibilities for the firms to borrow the necessary money. Regarding the costs of moving the firms (a), afterwards it appears that the firms did not provide accurate information, or at least that they did not make the necessary efforts to elaborate and provide accurate information. It is also possible that the delay in the negotiations made it increasingly difficult for them to maintain their initial assessment, which reinforces the analysis that their assessment was not professional enough. Another possible explanation is that the companies became more pessimistic due to the financial crisis that arose the end of 2008 and consciously decided to inflate the costs to hamper the project.

Additional factors can explain why the experiment in Zevenhuizen failed:

- Economic crisis: at the end of 2008, when negotiations entered the vital phase, an international credit crisis broke out, and soon it became clear that it would have large effects on the market price of real estate. For example, in the calculations made by the developer at the end of 2007 that served as basis for the negotiations, the selling price of the houses was expected to increase yearly by 3%, while after one year the reality was that prices lowered by 5%. This is a very relevant context variable that influences the size of the initial profit in urban development (see section 2.4.2 - variable sort A1). In general, the sentiment among the firms worsened significantly. It is important to remember that this sort of project, in which landowners become actively involved in regeneration, sharing costs and profits, are a novelty in the Netherlands. In those times of uncertainty, the landowners became more conservative and pessimistic. For example, they changed their mind about the initial estimation of the above mentioned costs of moving the firms and the fiscal consequences;

- High demolition costs (posting 2): the costs for demolishing the industrial buildings and cleaning the land (€ 43 per m² for new public space[1], plus the financial costs and the actualization costs -i.e. the costs of bringing the costs up to date) were higher than normal because in business areas like this there is more asphalt that has to be removed than in housing areas;
- Land costs: the price of the land in business area Nijverheidscentrum was high, as the firms to be removed are active and have a high economic value. This is also a context variable that influences the size of the initial profit (variable sort A2). Although the firms were ready to deliver their property (land + plant on it) for a very low price[2], renouncing any increase in value that would accrue from the rezoning into housing, the fact is that the minimum land costs (the value of the properties in their former use) was still very high, about € 45.5 million (€ 330-360 per m² of land).
- Land costs: the experiment was based upon a novelty in the Netherlands, namely that landowners themselves participate in urban regeneration, sharing costs and profits. Following this there was no need to acquire the land in the business area Nijverheidscentrum. Although the final evaluation of the operation (redevelopment Nijverheidcentrum + building new business area in De Viergang) accounted the value of the land (€ 45.5m) as a cost, the fact is that it was not necessary to account this value as a cost in the calculations of the redevelopment of Nijverheidcentrum. The reason is that, there was no need to advance this investment of € 45.5m because there was no need to buy this land. However, this changed with the new management in charge after the fusion of *Rabobank Vastgoed* with *Bouwfonds*. The new management wanted to buy the land in advance to become the developer of the 611 houses. As a consequence of this fundamental change of the financial structure of the operation, the land costs increased considerably. First, the € 45.5m and an actualization of the costs with another € 4.2m had to be accounted as a cost of redeveloping Nijverheidcentrum (posting 1 in Table Annex 7). In addition, this led to more financial costs (about € 14.3m). The total accounted land costs became the largest part of the land development costs (€ 64m of in total €93.5m). In other words, redeveloping Nijverheidscentrum became more expensive when the developer decided to buy the companies out instead of collaborating with them.
- Fundamental disagreement between developer and landowners: although the Cooperative (i.e. the landowners) was not in principle reluctant to allow a commercial developer to acquire the land and develop the real estate on it, they wanted to be independent and they considered this move of the developer as a transgression of the starting point of the experiment: active participation of landowners, facilitated by an urbanizing agent, to diminish land development costs and accelerate the development. The claim of the new management of *Rabobank Vastgoed/Bouwfonds* was actually an attempt to organize things as usual. After several meetings with the Cooperative, during the autumn of 2008 *Rabobank/Bouwfonds* decided to withdraw from the operation. It seems clear that Dutch

1 New public space is the surface that is redeveloped and will be used for public uses. Most of infrastructure provision and plan preparation costs relate to the construction of public infrastructure above or under this surface.

2 Only the cadastral value for property taxes purposes (*WOZ waarde* in Dutch), plus 20%. The cadastral value for property taxes purposes is based on the land use 'industry', but not on the future, more profitable land use 'housing'.

developers are not comfortable with the role of urbanizing agent, i.e. of being a developer that in principle only profits from land development, but not from the development of the real estate.

- Infrastructure and plan preparation costs: the infrastructure provision and plan preparation costs for transforming the current industrial site Nijverheidscentrum into serviced land for housing were calculated at ca. € 297/m² new public space. This is similar to usual realized costs in urban regeneration in the Netherlands (from € 300 to 500), and much higher than in Valencia (from € 90 to 110). The actual definition of property rights in the Netherlands, that give to the landowners the option to wait, might explain why the costs were so large: (a) the reserved amount for unexpected expenses (€ 2.3 m, € 23/ m² new public space, plus actualization and financial costs) was twice as high due to the uncertainties about the calculations and about whether it is possible to achieve an agreement with landowners; (b) it might be that the calculations in Zevenhuizen included hidden costs for compensating losses in other schemes, and/or high regular profit margins. It is however important to remember that differences with Valencia can *also* be caused by other third variables such as labour costs in the building sector, in construction materials, in fiscal regime (variables belonging to sort A3 in causal model in section 2.4.2) and conditions of the soil (variable A2). A final remark: although being high compared with Valencia, infrastructure and plan preparation costs in Nevenhuizen are not among the highest in the Netherlands. This could be explained by the fact that the calculations implicitly have presupposed that the landowners were going to be supportive and thus that the development process would be smooth and would not suffer delay. This might have avoided the need, frequent in the Netherlands, of making additional studies, negotiations (plan preparation costs), of extra financial costs, etc.

Doing things as usual is expensive

The experience in Zevenhuizen shows how the actual definition of property rights in the Netherlands, which gives to landowners the option to wait, and the uncertainties and strategies that result from it, lead to the initial profit margin leaking away into high accounted land costs (at least € 14.3m more than necessary), and into high infrastructure provision and plan preparation costs (both together about € 297/m² new public space). In addition, they lead to the need of advancing large investments to buy the land (€ 45.5m). This clearly shows that only a fundamental change in the development strategy towards formulas that incorporate landowners into the operation will lead to lower costs.

Table Annex 7. Comparison land development costs for the regeneration of the existing industrial site 'Nijverheidscentrum' (not the new business area, and taking into account the acquisition of the land) in Zevenhuizen, the Netherlands and Valencia (see also section 9.4 and Annex 6).

	Valencia	*Nederland*	*Nijverheidscentrum Zevenhuizen*	
1. Accounted land cost			€45.5m; plus €4.2m bringing costs up to date (actualization costs); plus €14.3m financial costs; in total €64m	
2. Infras prov costs (€/m^2 new public space)	(Between 70 and 90 €/ m^2)	(Most of the time between 250 and 400 €/m^2, some times even higher)	€ 18m (179€/m^2)	Bringing costs up to date: € 5.6m; Financial costs: € 2.7m. In total thus €29.6m (297 €/m^2)
3. Plan prep costs (€/m^2 new public space)	(Circa 20 €/ m^2)	(Most of the time between 50 and 100 €/m^2)	€ 3.3m (33€/m^2)	

Accounted land cost: The price that the developer (expects to) pay for the land and includes in the accounts as cost.

Infrastructure provision costs: this includes not only the infrastructure provision works, but also reserved amounts for unexpected expenses, the overhead costs, possible regular profit margins of the developer, etc. In The Netherlands, they comprise: *Slopen, bouw en woonrijp maken, risico en onvoorzien*.

Plan preparation costs: the costs of the preparation of plans, studies, etc. In Dutch: *plankosten*, or *Voorbereiding, toezicht en planontwikkeling*.

Actualization costs: all costs are presupposed to increase yearly by 2% the accounted land costs and by 3% the rest of the cots.

Financial costs: the financial costs that accrue from having to anticipate investments, with other words, form having to spend money before the final products (real estate) are sold.

Land decontamination costs and compensation costs are excluded.

New public space is the surface that is redeveloped and will be used for public uses. Most of infrastructure provision and plan preparation costs relate to the construction of public infrastructure above or under this surface.

Lists of terms

List of terms English-Spanish

Association of Urbanistic Interest	*Agrupación de Interés Urbanístico*
Autonomous Community (region)	*Comunidad Autónoma*
1978 Constitution	*Constitución Española*
Compulsory land readjustment	*Sistema de Cooperación*
Definitive Infrastructure Provision Project	*Proyecto de Urbanización*
Detailed binding rules	*ordenación pormenorizada*
Detailed Planning	*Planeamiento de desarrollo*
Development Agreement	*Convenio Urbanístico*
Development unit	*Unidad de Ejecución*
Economical-financial Proposal	*Proposición Económico-Financiera*
Equitable redistribution of betterment, costs and duties	*redistribución equitativa de beneficios y cargas*
Expropriation	*Expropiación*
General Municipal Planning	*Planeamiento General Municipal*
General Land-use Plan	*Plan General de Ordenación Urbana, PGOU*
Housing cooperative	*Cooperativa de viviendas*
Joint Development Program	*Programa para el desarrollo de una Actuación Urbanística, PAI*
Joint development organisation	*Junta de Compensación*
Juridical-economical Proposal	*Proposición Jurídico-Económica*
Land Readjustment	*Reparcelación*
Land Readjustment Project	*Proyecto de Reparcelación*
Land to be developed	*Suelo urbanizable*
Legal standards public infrastructure and facilities	*Estándares Urbanísticos*
Local Council	*Pleno del Ayuntamiento*
Municipal Patrimony of Land	*Patrimonio Municipal de Suelo*
Municipality	*Ayuntamiento*
Partial Plan	*Plan Parcial*
Physical zoning	*Planeamiento físico*
Pre-emption right (right of first refusal)	*derecho de tanteo y retracto*
Property register	*Registro de la Propiedad*
Provincial government	*Diputación Provincial*
Provisional Infrastructure Provision Project	*Anteproyecto de Urbanización*
Redistribution Area	*Área de reparto*

Reference Development Allowance	*Aprovechamiento tipo*
Rezoning one urban use to other	*recalificación*
Rezoning a non urban use to an urban one	*reclasificación*
Sector	*sector*
Social-affordable housing	*Vivienda con Protección pública/ Vivienda protegida*
Special Plan	*Plan Especial*
Structural binding rules	*ordenación structural*
Technical Alternative	*Alternativa técnica*
Unit of modal use	*unidad de aprovechamiento*
Urban Land	*Suelo urbano*
Urban Renewal Plan	*Plan de Reforma Interior*
Urbanization	*Urbanización*
Urbanizing agent	*agente urbanizador*
Urbanization charges	*Cargas de urbanización*
Urbanization canon	*Canon de urbanización*
Urbanization costs	*Costes de urbanización*
Voluntary land readjustment	*Sistema de Compensación*
Zoning land into urban and non-urban	*clasificación*
Zoning land into different urban uses	*calificación*

List of terms English-Dutch

Accountability	*Toerekenbaarheid*
Anterior Development Agreement	*Anterieure overeenkomst*
Contributions for other schemes	*Bovenplanse kosten*
Definition of land uses	*Doeleindenomschrijving*
Departure from the Land-use Plan	*Vrijstelling/Projectbesluit*
Detailing of Land-use Plan	*Uitwerking*
Development Agreement	*Exploitatieovereenkomst/ Realisatieovereenkomst*
Development Regulation	*Exploitatieverordening*
Economic performability/feasibility	*Economisch uitvoerbaarheid*
Explanation	*Plantoelichting*
Housing association	*Woningcorporatie*
Development contributions Plan	*Exploitatieplan*
Land development contributions Act	*Grondexploitatiewet*
Land-use plan	*Bestemmingsplan*
Land-use regulations	*Planvoorschriften*
Leasehold	*Erfpacht*
Lost green areas	*Verloren gegane groenvoorzieningen*
Map	*Plankaart*
Modification Land-use Plan	*Wijziging*

Municipality	*Gemeente*
New Key Project	*Nieuw Sleutelproject, NSP*
Objective delimitation	*Objectieve begrenzing*
Outline binding land-use regulation	*Globale bestemming*
Outline Definition	*Beschrijving in Hoofdlijnen*
Outline Land-use plan with obligation of further elaboration	*Globaal bestemmingsplan met uitwerkingsplicht*
Performability/feasibility	*Uitvoerbaarheid*
Physical Planning Decree	*Besluit op de ruimtelijke ordening*
Physical Planning Inspectorate	*Inspectie Ruimtelijke Ordening*
Pre-emption	*Voorkeursrecht*
Profit	*Profijt*
Profit tax	*Baatbelasting*
Proportionality	*Proportionaliteit*
Province	*Provincie*
Public facilities and interventions	*Ruimtelijke ontwikkelingen*
Public infrastructure and facilities serving a wider area	*Bovenwijkse voorzieningen*
(Provincial) Land-use Plan	*Inpassingsplan*
Self realisation	*Zelfrealisatie*
Social facilities	*Maatschappelijke voorzieningen*
Spatially relevant	*Ruimtelijk/planologisch relevant*
Stamp plan	*Postzegelplan*
Structural Plan	*Structuurplan*
Structural Vision	*Structuurvisie*
Urban Renewal Plan	*Stadsvernieuwingsplan*

Literature

ABF-research (2008), *Overheidsbeleid en ruimtelijke investeringen. Onderzoek naar aanleiding van de motie Van Heugten, Vermeij, Wiegman-van Meppelen Schepping*, Delft.

Acosta, Rodrigo & Renard, Vincent (1993), *Urban land and property markets in France*, UCL Press Limited, London.

Adams, David; Disberry, Alan; Hutchison, Norman; Munjoma, Thomas (2001), 'Ownership constraints to brownfield redevelopment', in *Environment and Planning A*, vol 33, p.p. 453-477.

Advocate General of the European Union (2010), *Opinion of Advocate General Jääskinen*, delivered on 16 September 2010, Case C-306/08, European Commission v Kingdom of Spain, available in http://eur-lex.europa.eu/LexUriServ/LexUriServ.do?uri=CELEX:62008C0306:EN:HTML

Aldrich, H.A. (1979), *Organisations and Environments*, Englewood Cliffs, NJ, Prentice-Hall.

Alexander, E.R. (2001a) 'A transaction-cost theory of land use planning and development control', in *Town Planning Review*, 72, 45-75.

- (2001b) 'Governance and transaction costs in planning systems: a conceptual framework for institutional analysis of land-use planning and development control – the case of Israel', in *Environment and Planning B: Planning and Design*, 28, 755-76.

Allison, G.T. (1971), *The Essence of Decision*, Little Boston, MA: Brown & Company.

Alterman, Rachelle (2009), *Can the "unearned increment" in land values be harnessed to supply affordable housing?*, paper in Conference 'Financing affordable housing and infrastructure in cities: towards innovative land and property taxation system', UN Habitat GLTN, Warsaw 15 and 16 October 2009.

Askew, Janet (1996), 'Case Study: Canon's Marsh', in Greed (1996, ed.), p.p. 181-191.

Ave, Gastone (1996), *Urban land and property markets in Italy*, UCL Press Limited, London.

AZ (Ministerie van Algemene Zaken, 2007), *Samen werken, samen wonen. Beleidsprogramma Kabinet Balkenende IV 2007-2011*, Den Haag: Ministerie van Algemene Zaken.

Baardewijk, E.J. van (2008), 'Bovenplanse verevening via het exploitatieplan?', in *Bouwrecht*, nr. 11 November 2008, p.p. 753-766.

Ball, M. (1983), *Housing Policy and Economic Power (The Political Economy of Owner Occupation)*, Methuen, London, p.p. 112-113 and 148.

- (2003), 'Markets and the Structure of the Housebuilding Industry: An International Perspective', in *Urban Studies*, Vol. 40: 5, p.p. 897-916.

Barker, Kate (2004), *Review of Housing Supply. Delivering Stability: Securing our Future Housing Needs*, Barker Review, London, March 2004, p.p. 149.

Bassols Coma, Martín (1985a), *Constitución y sistema económico*, 1st edition, Tecnos, Madrid 1985.

- (1985b), [idem], 2nd edition, Tecnos, Madrid 1988.
- (1996a), "Los inicios del derecho urbanístico en el período del liberalismo moderado y en el sexenio revolucionario (1846-1876): el Ensanche de la ciudad como modelo urbanístico y sistema jurídico", in *Ciudad y Territorio-Estudios Territoriales*, number 107-108, spring-summer, p.p. 19-52;
- (1996b), "El derecho urbanístico de la Restauración a al II República (1876-1936): crisis de los Ensanches y las dificultades para alumbrar un nuevo modelo jurídico-urbanístico", in *Ciudad y Territorio-Estudios Territoriales*, number 107-108, spring-summer, p.p. 53-90.
- (2002), "Urbanismos Comparados/Francia: Estudio de las líneas básicas de su legislación urbanística", in *Ciudad y Territorio-Estudios Territoriales*, Vol. XXXIV, n. 131, p.p. 85-127.

Benson, J,K, (1982), 'A framework for policy analysis', in D.L. Rogers and D.A. Whetten (eds, 1982), 'Interorganizational Coordination: Theory, Research, and Implementation', Iowa State University Press, Ames, pp. 137-176.

Bentley, A.F. (1967), *The Process of Government: A Study of Social Pressure*, Cambridge, MA.: Harvard UP (Chicago 1908).

Betancor Rodríguez, Andrés & García-Bellido, Javier (2001), "Síntesis general de los estudios comparados de las legislaciones urbanísticas en algunos países occidentales", in *Ciudad y Territorio-Estudios Territoriales*, vol. XXXIII, n. 127, p.p. 87-144.

BCR (1999), 'Grondbeleid tussen particuliere beschikkingsmacht en overheissturing', Bestuurlijke Commissie Randstad, working document, not published, BCR secretariaat, Utrecht.

Bidagor Lasarte, Pedro (1996), "Circunstancias históricas en al gestación de la Ley sobre Régimen del Suelo y Ordenación Urbana de 12 de mayo de 1956", in *Ciudad y Territorio-Estudios Territoriales*, number 107-108, spring-summer, p.p. 91-100.

Blanc Clavero, F. (1997) 'Los efectos de la LRAU sobre la actividad urbanizadora: causas y consecuencias de una transformación', *Ciudad y Territorio-Estudios Territoriales*, **29**, 257-94.

- (2003) 'The new legal planning system in Valencia', not published, available through d.munozgielen@tudelft.nl

Booth, Philip (2003), *Planning by Consent. The origins and nature of British development control*, Routledge, London, 213 p.p.

- (2005), 'Partnerships and networks: The governance of urban regeneration in Britain', in *Journal of Housing and the Built Environment*, 20: 257-269.

Borja et al. (1990, eds.), *Las Grandes Ciudades en la década de los noventa*, Ed. Sistema, Madrid, 736 p.p.

Bosch, N. & Hanemaayer, D. (1992), *Artikel 19 WRO: planafwijking of anticipatie*, Ministerie Vrom, Den Haag, 20 November 1992.

Braakensiek, M; Grotenhuis, R. te; Hendriksen, E.M.; Meeuwissen, A.J.; Perenboom, G.R.J.; and Woudstra, P.J. (2009), *Grondexploitatie en het bestemmingsplan. Concept-Supplement 2009-2. Leergang Op dezelfde leest*, Nirov, Den Haag, Oktober 2009.

Bregman, A.G. & Sievers, I.P. (2002), 'Ruimtelijke samenhang en de fundamentele herziening van de WRO', in *Bouwrecht* nr. 4 april 2002, p. 291-296.

Bröcking, B. & Geest, H. Van (1982), *Anticiperen en ruimtelijk beleid*, Tjeenk Willink, 1982.

Bryman, Alan (2004), *Social Research Methods*, first edition in 2001, Oxford University Press.

Buitelaar, E. (2007), *The Costs of Land Use Decisions. Applying transaction costs economics to planning & development*, RICS Research, Blackwell Publishing, 199 p.p.

Buitelaar, E.; Cobussen, T; Needham, B. (2007), 'Sturen met bestemmingsplannen: ruimtelijke ordening tussen uitzondering en regel', in *Stedebouw & Ruimtelijke Ordening* (6), pp. 53-55.

Buitelaar, E.; Segeren, A.; & Kronberger, P. (2008). *Stedelijke transformatie en grondeigendom*, Den Haag/Rotterdam: Ruimtelijk Planbureau/Nai uitgevers, pp. 61.

Burón Cuadrado, Javier (2006), 'Las reservas de suelo para vivienda protegida: lecciones del caso de Vitoria-Gasteiz', in *ACE Architecture, City and Environment*, vol. 1, number 2, October 2006, Barcelona, 85-103 p.p.

Burriel de Orueta, Eugenio (2008), *La "Década prodigiosa" del Urbanismo Español (1997-2006)*, paper in X Coloquio Internacional de Geocrítica, Barcelona, 26 - 30 de mayo de 2008 Universidad de Barcelona, available in http://www.ub.es/geocrit/-xcol/383.htm#_edn28.

- (2009), 'The European Union and urban policy in the Comunidad Valenciana: a legal or political conflict?', in *Boletín de la A.G.E.*, nr. 49, 337-341.

Buuren, P.J.J. van; Gier, A.A.J. de; Nijmeijer, A.G.A.; Robbe, J. (2009), *Hoofdlijnen ruimtelijk bestuursrecht*, Kluwer, Deventer.

Campbell, D.T. & Stanley, J.C. (1963), *Experimental and quasi-experimental designs for research,* Rand McNally, Chicago.

Campbell, Heather; Ellis, Hugh; Henneberry, John; Gladwell, Caroline (2000), "Planning obligations, planning practice, and land-use outcomes", in *Environmental and Planning B: Planning and Design,* volume 27 (5), p.p. 759-775.

Campbell, Heather; Ellis, Hugh; Gladwell, Caroline; Henneberry, John; Poxon, J.; Rowley, S. (2001), *Planning Obligations and the Mediation of Development,* RICS Foundation Research Papers, 4(3), p. 44, London.

Canoy M, Van Ewijk C (1999), 'De Grondwolf bijt niet', in *Economisch Statistische Berichten* 84 (4233), D24-D30.

Capozza, D.R., and Li, Y. (2002) 'Optimal Land Development Decisions', in *Journal of Urban Economics,* 51, 123-42.

Centraal Planbureau, CPB (1999), *De grondmarkt. Een gebrekkige markt en een onvolmaakte overheid,* Netherlands Bureau for Economic Policy Analysis (Sdu Uitgevers, Den Haag).

Christensen, K.S. (1985), 'Coping with uncertainty in planning', in *Journal of the American Planning Association,* 51(1), pp. 63-73.

Christman, John (1994), *The Myth of Property: Toward an Egalitarian Theory of Ownership,* New York: Oxford University Press, 219 p.p.

Claydon, Jim, and Smith, Bryan (1997), 'Negotiating Planning Gains through the British Development Control System', in *Urban Studies,* Vol. 34, No. 12, p.p. 2003-2022.

Clusa, Joaquim & Mur, Sara (2007), 'La experiencia británica 1973-2006 de JGB y el pago de una deuda pendiente´, in *ACE Architecture, City and Environment,* nr. 3, February 2007, p.p. 122-149, Barcelona.

Cohen, M.D., March, J.G. and Olsen, J.P. (1972), 'A Garbage Can Model of Organisational Choice', in *Administrative Science Quarterly,* 17:1, p.p. 1-25.

Colegio Oficial de Arquitectos de la Comunidad Valenciana, Deleg. Alicante (1991, ed.), *Ley de reforma del regimen urbanístico y valoraciones del suelo,* Alicante: COACV.

Comisión de Expertos sobre Urbanismo (1996), *Informe sobre suelo y urbanismo en España,* Ministerio de Obras Públicas, Transportes y Medio Ambiente, Madrid, 295 p.p.

Corkindale, J. (2004), *The Land Use Planning System: Evaluating Options for Reform,* Hobart Paper 148, Institute of Economic Affairs, London, 113 p.p.

Crook, A.D.H.; Curry, J; Jackson, A; Monk, S; Smith, K; Whitehead, C.M.E. (2001), *The provision of affordable housing through the planning system,* discussion paper, Department of Town and Regional Economy, University of Cambridge, Cambridge.

Crook, Anthony & Whitehead, Christine (2002), 'Social housing and planning gain: is this an appropriate way of providing affordable housing?', in *Environmental and Planning A,* volume 34, p.p. 1259-1279.

Cullingworth, J. Barry & Nadin, Vincent (2006), *Town & Country Planning in the UK,* Fourteenth edition, Routledge, London, 624 p.p.

De Bruijn, J.A. & Ringeling, A.B. (1997), 'Normative Notes Perspectives on Networks', in Kickert e.a. (eds. 1997), 152-165 p.p..

De Groot, Egbert and Van der Veen, Gerrit (2003), "Contracteren over ruimtegebrik en publiekrechtelijke bevoegdheden; wat kan en wat niet kan", in *Bouwrecht,* nr. 8, augustus 2003, p.p. 649-662.

De Jong, Jitske (1999), "'Acts of God', overmacht en onvoorziene omstandigheden in het bouwrecht. Verslag Jaavergadering 1998 Vereniging voor Bouwrecht", in *Bouwrecht,* nr. 7, juli 1999.

De Kam, George & Needham, Barrie (2001), *Met beide benen... een onderzoek naar de strategie van corporaties op de grondmarkt,* Aedes vereniging van woningcorporaties.

De Wolff, Herman (2000), "Vlaams decreet op de ruimtelijke ordening", in *Bouwrecht,* nr. 8, August 2000.

- (2007), "The new Dutch Land development Act as a tool for value capturing", paper 2007 ENHR International Conference on Sustainable Urban Areas.

De Wolff, Herman & Muñoz Gielen, Demetrio (2007), 'Algunos aspectos del rescate de plusvalías en el Urbanismo: el caso de los Países Bajos', in *Ciudad y Territorio-Estudios Territoriales,* XXIX (152-153): 532-536.

Department for Communities and Local Government (2006), *Valuing Planning Obligations in England,* London, DCLG Publications, May 2006.

Dieperink, M.A.M. (2009), 'Bovenplanse verevening', in *Vastgoedrecht,* 1, p.p. 7-14.

Dieterich, Hartmut; Dransfeld, Egbert; and Voss, Winrich (1993), *Urban land and property markets in Germany,* UCL Press Limited, London.

DoE (1992), *The Use of Planning Agreements,* London: Department of the Environment/HMSO.

Elias, N. (1971), *Wat is sociologie?,* Utrecht: Het Spectrum.

Emans (2002), *Interviewen. Theorie, techniek en training*, Stenfert kroese, Groningen, The Netherlands.

Enemark, Stig (2002), *The Danish Way: Spatial Planning System in Denmark*, The Danish Association of Chartered Surveyors.

Ennis, Frank (1997), 'Infrastructure Provision, the Negotiating Process and the Planner's Role', in *Urban Studies*, Vol. 34, No. 12, pp.: 1935-1954.

- (ed, 2003), *Infrastructure Provision and the Negotiating Process*, Ashgate, 234 p.p.
- (2003), 'Infrastructure provision and the Urban Environment', in Ennis (ed, 2003), p.p. 1-18.

European Commission (1997), *The EU compendium of spatial planning systems and policies*, Regional development studies 28, Luxembourg: Office for Official Publications of the European Communities, 191 p.p.

- (1999), *The EU compendium of spatial planning systems and policies. Denmark*, Regional development studies, 28C, Luxembourg: Office for Official Publications of the European Communities, 121 p.p.

Evans, Neil & Davoudi, Simin (February 2005), *Governance of Territorial and Urban Policies from EU to Local Level (2004-2006). Draft UK National Overview*, ESPON Project 2.3.2, working paper.

Faludi, Andreas (1973, ed.), *A Reader in Planning Theory*, Oxford: Pergamon Press.

- (1986) *Critical rationalism and planning methodology*, London: Pion.
- (1987), *A Decision-centred View of Environmental Planning*, Pergamon Press, Oxford.

Fernández Fernández, Gerardo Roger & Fernández Monedero, Pablo (2002), 'Balance actual del modelo urbanístico valenciano. Apuntes para un análisis propositivo', in *Revista de derecho urbanístico y medio ambiente*, Year nº 36, Nº 193, 2002 , p.p. 59-82.

Fernández Fernández, Gerardo Roger & Marín Ferreiro, Blanca & Fernández Monedero, Pablo (2003), *Guía básica para el análisis de viabilidad económica de las actuaciones urbanísticas*, Colección Manuales de Urbanismo, Icaro, Colegio Territorial de Arquitectos de Valencia, Valencia, Spain.

Friedmann. J. (1973), 'A Conceptual Model for the Analysis of Planning Behavior', in Faludi, Andreas (1973, ed.), p.p. 344–370.

- (2003) 'Why do planning theory?', in *Planning Theory*, 2(1), p.p. 7-10.

Friend J.K., Power, J.M., and Yewlett, C.J.L. (1974), *Public Planning: The Inter-Corporate Dimension*, London, Travistock Publications.

Gallent, Nick & Tewdwr-Jone, Mark (2007), *Decent home for all*, Routledge, Abingdon, UK, 300 p.p.

Gascó Verdier, Carles (2006), 'El modelo valenciano para la gestión a través de la experiencia aplicativa de la LRAU en Alicante (1995-2005)", in *ACE: architecture, city and environment* (on-line), vol.1, nr. 2, p.p. 56-84.

García-Bellido, Javier (1975), 'Gran Bretaña: *Community Land Act 1975*. ¿Hacia una socialización del suelo', in *Ciudad y Territorio*, 4/75, p.p. 81-94, Madrid.

- (1989), "Hacia una renovación de la racionalidad urbanística", in *Ciudad y Territorio-Estudios Territoriales*, number 81-82, pp. 167-222, Madrid.
- (1991a), "A (r)evolutionary framework for Spanish town planning", European Viewpoint, in *Town Planning Review*, vol. 62, nr. 4, pages v-viii.
- (1991b), "Perspectiva ilustrada sobre el contenido urbanístico de la propiedad ante la Ley 8/90 de Reforma de la del Suelo", in Colegio Oficial de Arquitectos de la Comunidad Valenciana, Deleg. Alicante (1991, ed.), p.p. 67-127.
- (1993), "La liberalización efectiva del mercado del suelo", in *Ciudad y Territorio-Estudios Territoriales*, number 95-96, p.p. 175-198, Madrid.
- (1994), "Configuración de la 'propiedad desagregada': dualidad de derechos en la propiedad inmobiliaria", in *Revista de Derecho Urbanístico,* (1st part) number 138, may-june, p.p. 547-634, and (2nd part) number 139, july-september, p.p. 793-884, Madrid.
- (1996), "Editorial: Siglo y medio de singularidades en el urbanismo español", in *Ciudad y Territorio-Estudios Territoriales*, number 107-108, spring-summer, p.p. 5-13.
- (1999), ´La excepcional estructura del Urbanismo español en el contexto europeo´, in *Documentación Administrativa*, nr. 252/253, p.p. 11-83.

George, Henry (1879), *Progress and Poverty*, 2006 edited and abridged edition, Robert Schalkenbach Foundation, New York, 210 p.p.

Gerritsen, W.H.F. (2010), 'De Anterieure exploitatie: Wanneer en met wie?', in *Grondzaken in de praktijk*, Februari 2010, p.p. 26-27.

Greed, Clara (1996, ed.), *Implementing Town Planning: The Role of Town Planning in the Development Process*, Longman, Essex.

Giddens, Anthony (1984), *The Constitution of Society. Outline of the Theory of Structuration.* Cambridge: Polity.

Gordijn, Hugo; Renes, Gusta; Traa, Michel (2007), *Naar een optimaler ruimtegebruik voor bedrijventerreinen*, Ruimtelijk Planbureau, Den Haag, p.p. 32.

Greef, Johan de (1997), *Het gevecht om het residu. Gemeente versus marktpartijen op grond van de residuele waardemethode*, not published, Thesis at the University of Amsterdam, April 1997, available through J.H.de.Greef@minlnv.nl.

Groot, E.W.J. de (2009), 'Groenfondsen, Blauwfondsen, Landschapsontwikkelingsfondsen, Natuurontwikkelingsfondsen én de (on)mogelijkheden om deze op grond van de Wro te financieren', in *Bouwrecht*, nr. 6, June 2009, p.p. 463-471.

Groetelaers, D.A. (2004), "Instrumentarium locatieontwikkeling: Sturingsmogelijkheden voor gemeenten in een veranderde marktsituatie", Dissertation, DUP Science.

Gurran, N; Milligan, V; Baker, D; Bugg, L.B. (2007), *International practice in planning for affordable housing: lessons for Australia*, positioning paper, AHURI, September 2007.

Hanf, K.I. and Scharpf, F.W. (eds, 1978), *Interorganizational Policy Making: Limits to Coordination and Central Control*, Sage, London, 373 p.p.

HD Projectrealisatie B.V. (2009), *Haalbaarheidsstudie verplaatsing Nijverheidscentrum Zevenhuizen naar de Viergang. Second opinion*, 26 November 2009, not published.

Healey, P. (1992), 'An institutional model of the development process', in *Journal of Property Research*, nr. 9, pp. 33-44.

Healey, P. & Williams, R. (1993), 'European urban planning systems: Diversity and convergence', in *Urban Studies*, 30(4/5), pp. 701-720.

Hijmans, E.R. & Fokkema, M. (ed. 2008), *Recht rond Grondtransacties*, Tauw bv, Deventer.

Hjern, B. & Porter, D.O. (1981), 'Implementation Structures: A New Unit for Administrative Analysis', in *Organisational Studies*, 3, p.p. 211-237.

Hoesel, P.H.M. van (1985), *Het programmeren van sociaal beleidsonderzoek: analyse en receptuur*, dissertation R.U.L., z.uitg., p.p. 131-161.

Holmans A., Kleinman N., Royce C., Whitehea C.M.E. (2000), *How Many Homes Will We Need?*, Technical Volume Shelter, 88 Old Street, London EC1V 9HU.

Hong, Yu-Hung & Needham, Barrie (eds. 2007), *Analyzing Land Readjustment. Economics, Law, and Collective Action*, Lincoln Institute of Land Policy.

Jacobs, Harvey M. (2008), 'The Future of the Regulatory Takings Issue in the United States and Europe: Divergence or Convergence?', in *The Urban Lawyer*, Vol. 40, No. 1, p.p. 51-72.

Jordan, G. (1990), 'Sub-Governments, Policy Communities, and Networks: Refilling the Old Boots', in *Journal of Theoretical Politics*, 2: 319-338.

Kalbro, Thomas & Mattsson, Hans (1995), *Urban land and property martkets in Sweden*, UCL Press Limited, London.

Kalbro, Thomas (2002), "Land Readjustment: The Swedisch Experience", conference paper, Lincoln Institute of Land Policy, code: CP02C07.

Karki, T.K. (2003), 'Implementation experiences of land pooling projects in Katmandu Valley', in *Habitat International* 28 (1): 67-88.

Kaufmann, F.X; Majone, G. and Ostrom, V. (1986, eds.), *Guidance, Control and Evaluation in the Public Sector: The Bielefeld Interdisciplinary Project*, Walter de Gruyter, Berlin

Kenis, Patrick & Schneider, Volker (1991), 'Policy Networks and Policy Analysis: Scrutinizing a New Analytical Toolbox', in Marin & Mayntz (eds. 1991), p.p. 25-62.

Kickert, Walter J.M. & Klijn, Erik-Hans & Koppenjan, Joop F.M. (eds. 1997), *Managing Complex Networks*, London: SAGE Publications.

Klaassen, A.W. (2000), *Ruimtelijk beleid in theorie en praktijk*, sixth revised edition, Elsevier bedrijfsinformatie bv, The Hague.

- (2002), *De Woningwet weer gewijzigd*, Praktijkreeks ruimtelijke ordening, Kluwer b.v., 236 p.p.
- (2008), "Handboek Ruimtelijke Ordening & Bouw", 3th edition, Berghauser Pont Publishing, Amsterdam, 706 p.p.
- (2009-10), digital and regularly actualized version of Klaasen (2008).

Klijn, Erik-Hans (1996), *Regels en sturing in netwerken; De invloed van netwerkregels op de herstructurering van naoorlogse wijken*, Dissertation, Eburon, Delft.

Klijn, Erik-Hans (1997), *Policy Networks: An Overview*, in Kickert *et alii* (eds. 1997), p.p. 14-34.

Klijn, Erik-Hans & Koppenjan, J.F.M. (2000), 'Public management and policy networks: Foundations of a network approach to governance', in *Public Management Review*, vol. 2, Issue 2, Routledge, 135-158.

Kluwer Database (2006), *artikelsgewijscommentaar op artikel 11 en 15 WRO, raadpleging gedaan op 20 juni 2006: 'Reikwijdte wijzigingsbevoegdheid in relatie tot vrijstellingsbevoegdheid'*, on-line database, Kluwer.

Kluwer (2008), Memo Bestemmingsplan en bouwvergunning onder de nieuwe Wro 2008/2009, Kluwer (Wolters Kluwer business), Alphen aan den Rijn, p.p. 407.

Koffijberg, Jos (2005), *Getijden van beleid: omslagpunten in de volkshuisvesting. Over de rol van hiërarchie en netwerken bij grote veranderingen*, Dissertation, Delft University Press.

Kolpron Consultants (2000), *Grondbeleid en stedelijke herstructurering*, 17 October 2000, Kolprom, Rotterdam, 76 p.p.

Koppenjan, J.F.M., De Bruijn, J.A. and Kickert, W.J.M. (1993, eds.), *Netwerkmanagement in het openbaar bestuur: over de mogelijkheden van overheidssturing in beleidsnetwerken*, Vuga, 's-Gravenhage (The Hague).

Korthals Altes, W.K. (1995), *De Nederlandse planningdoctrine in het fin de siècle*, Dissertation, Van Gorcum.

- (2006), 'Stagnation in housing production: another success in the Dutch 'planner's paradise'?', in *Environment and Planning B: Planning and Design*, 2006, volume 33, p.p. 97-114.
- (2007), 'The impact of abolishing social-housing grants on the compact-city policy of Dutch municipalities', in *Environment and Planning A*, volume 39, p.p. 1497-1512.
- (2008), 'Grondexploitatiewet als vorm van comprehensive development zoning', in *Rooilijn*, Jg. 41, Nr. 3, p.p.: 198-203.

Korthals Altes, Willem and Groetelaers, Danielle (2000), 'De ontwikkeling van uitbreidingslocaties: context en praktijk', in *Acthergrondinformatie mededelingenblad van de Vereniging van Grondbedrijven*, 18(1), pp. 35-45.

Krabben, Erwin v/d & Needham, Barrie (2008), 'Land readjustment for value capturing: A new planning tool for urban redevelopment', in *Town Planning Review*, 79 (6), 651-672.

Kreukels, A.M.J. & Spit, T.J.M. (1990), 'Public-private partnership in the Netherlands', in *Tijdschrift voor Economie en Sociale Geografie*, 81, nr. 5, p.p.: 388-392.

Krueckeberg, D.A. (1995), 'The Difficult Character of Property: To Whom Do Things Belong?', in *Journal of the American Planning Association*, Vol. 61, nr. 3, p.p. 301-309.

Kruijt, B. & Needham, B. (1980), *Grondprijsvorming en grondprijspolitiek, Theorie en praktijk,* Stenfert Kroese, Leiden/Antwerpen, 181 p.p.

Kruijt, B., Needham, B. and Spit, T. (1990), *Economische grondslagen van grondbeleid*, SBV, Amsterdam, 192 p.p.

Larsson, Gerhard (1997), 'Land readjustment: A tool for urban development', in *Habitat International* 21 (2): 141-52.

- (2006), *Spatial Planning Systems in Western Europe, an overview*, IOS Press.

León, Orfelio G & Montero, Ignacio (1997), *Diseño de investigaciones. Introducción a la lógica de la investigación en Psicología y Educación*, Segunda edición, MacGraw-Hill, Madrid.

Levine, S. and White, P.E. (1961), 'Exchange as a Conceptual Framework for the Study of Interorganisational Relationships', in *Administration Science Quarterly*, 5 p.p. 583-601.

Lindblom, C.E. (1965), *The Intelligence of Democracy: Decision Making through Mutual Adjustment*, London, Free Press.

Lindblom, C.E. and Cohen, D.K. (1979), *Usable Knowledge: Social Science and Social Problem Solving*, New Haven, CT/London: Yale University Press.

Louw, Erik (2008), 'Land assembly for urban transformation – The case of 's-Hertogenbosch in The Netherlands', in *Land Use Policy*, 25, issue 1, p.p. 69-80.

Lowi, T.J. (1969), *The End of Liberalism*, New York, Norton.

MacIntyre, Alasdair (1984), *After Virtue: A Study in Moral Theory*, 1st edition 1981, 2nd edition 1984, Notre Dame, University of Notre Dame Press.

Mangada, Eduardo (1990), "Las políticas del suelo: control de la especulación y dinamismo económico", in Borja et al. (1990, eds.), p.p. 175-200.

Marsh, D. and Rhodes, R.A.W. (eds. 1992), *Policy networks in British Government*, Oxford, Clarendon Press, p.p. 309.

- (1992), 'Policy Communities and Issue Networks, Beyond Typology', in Marsh & Rhodes (eds. 1992), p.p. 249-268.

Marin, B. and Mayntz, R. (eds. 1991), *Policy Networks: Empirical Evidence and Theoretical Considerations*, New York, Free Press.

Martín Mateo, Ramón (1980), "La plusvalía. Estudio de derecho comparado", in *Revista de Derecho Urbanístico y Medio Ambiente*, 68, pp. 13-67.

Mazzoni, Pierandrea (1990), *Diritto urbanistico*, Giuffrè editore, Milano.

Menéndez Rexach, Ángel (1996), "Constitución y democracia: 1976-1996. La segunda reforma de la Ley del Suelo, in *Ciudad y Territorio-Estudios Territoriales*, number 107-108, spring-summer, p.p. 127-148.

Merlo Fuertes, José Luis & Ribes Andreu, Juan (2004), *Guía básica para la redacción de programas para el desarrollo de actuaciones integradas*, Fifth edition, Colección Manuales de Urbanismo, Icaro, Colegio Territorial de Arquitectos de Valencia, Valencia, Spain.

Miles, Matthew B. & Huberman, A. Michael (1994), *Qualitative Data Analysis*, SAGE Publications.

MiljØministeriet (2002), *Spatial planning in Denmark*, Ministry of the Environment Denmark.

Mill, J. Stuart (1846), *A System of Logic, ratiocinative and inductive, being a connective view of the principles of evidence and the methods of scientific investigation*, 2nd ed., Londen: Parker.

Mitroff, I.I. (1983), *Stakeholders of the Organizational Mind. Toward a New View of Organizational Policy Making*, Jossey-Bass Publishers, San Francisco, 178 p.p.

Modrego Caballero, F. (2000) 'Cuarenta meses de aplicación de la Ley Reguladora de la Actividad Urbanística de la Comunicad Valenciana', in *Ciudad y Territorio-Estudios Territoriales*, 32, 11-28.

Moore, Victor (2005), *A Practical Approach to Planning Law*, Ninth edition, Oxford University Press, 666 p.p.

Moroni, S. (2007), 'Planning, liberty and the rule of the law', in *Planning Theory*, 6, 2, pp. 146-163, London.

Moya, Luis (2008, ed.), *La Vivienda Social en Europa. Alemania, Francia y Países Bajos desde 1945*, Mairea Libros, Madrid, p.p. 225.

Muñoz Gielen, D., Brouwer, P., and Winsemius, J (2004) 'De Valenciaanse ontwikkelingsplanologie', in *Tijdschrift voor de Volkshuisvesting*, volnr, 17-21.

Muñoz Gielen, Demetrio & Korthals Altes, Willem (2007), 'Lessons from Valencia: Separating Infrastructure Provision from Land Ownership', in *Town Planning Review*, 78 (1), p.p. 61-79.

Muñoz Gielen, Demetrio & Hoekstra, Joris (2008), 'De la política de Vivienda Social en los Países Bajos', in Moya, Luis (2008, ed.), p.p. 201-209.

Myers, D. & Banerjee, T. (2005), 'Toward greater heights for planning', in *Journal of American Planning Association*, 71(2), pp. 121-129.

Myers, Margaret (2000), 'Qualitative Research and the Generalizability Question: Standing Firm with Proteus', in *The Qualitative Report*, online journal (http://www.nova.edu/ssss/QR/QR4-3/meyers.html), Volume 4, Numbers 3/4, March 2000.

Nadin, V. & Stead, D. (2008), 'European Spatial Planning Systems, Social Models and Learning', in *DISP*, Vol. 172, Nr.1, pp. 35-47

NVB (2001): *NVB Thermometer Koopwoningen Najaar 2001*, Nederlandse Vereniging van Projectontwikkelaars en Bouwondernemers.

Needham, Barrie; Kruijt, B. y Koenders, P. (1993), *Urban land and property markets in the Netherlands*, University College London (UCL) Press, London, pp. 243.

Needham, Barrie & De Kam, George (2004), 'Understanding How Land is Exchanged: Co-ordination Mechanisms and Transaction Costs', in *Urban Studies*, Vol. 41, Nr. 10, p.p. 2061-2076, September 2004.

Needham, Barrie & Geuting, Esther (2006), *Afschaffing van het zelfrealisatierecht, economische effecten*, not published, commissioned by Ministry of Housing, Planning and the Environment (Vrom).

Needham, B. (2000), *Aspecten van 'de ruimtelijke inrichting' die een gemeente (c.q. provincie c.q. rijksoverheid) zou willen realiseren, die d.m.v. actief grondbleid wél kan (via de gronduitgifte), en d.m.v. een bestemmingspaln niet kan, noch met andere publiekstrechtelijke bevoegdheden*, working paper, SER-werkgroep Grondpolitiek, Nijmegen 25 february 2000.

- (2006), *Planning, Law and Economics. The rules we make for using land*, London: Routledge, 178 p.p.

- (2007a), *Dutch land-use planning: planning and managing land-use in the Netherlands, the principles and the practice,* Den Haag: Sdu Uitgevers, 299 p.p.
- (2007b), 'Final comment: Land-use planning and the law', in *Planning Theory*, 6,2, p.p. 183-189, London.

Negandhi, A.R. (ed. 1975), *Interorganisation Theory*, Kansas City, Kansas University Press.

Nelissen, N.J.M. (1993), 'Over "net" werken in netwerken', in Koppenjan e.a. (1993, eds.), p.p. 169-75.

NEPROM (2007), *Investeren in ruimtelijke kwaliteit*, Vereniging van Nederlandse Projectontwikkeling Maatschappijen, Voorburg.

Niederkofler, M. (1991), 'The influence of strategic alliances: opportunities for managerial influence', in *Journal of Business Venturing*, 6, p.p. 237-257.

Office of the Deputy Prime Minister (2004a), Investigating the Increasing Volume of Planning Appeals in England, London, February 2004.
- (2004b), *Reforming Planning Obligations: the Use of Standard Charges*, London, November 2004. Document available online via www.odpm.gov.uk
- (2005), *The Value for Money of Delivering Affordable Housing through Section 106*, London, July 2005.

Oliva, Federico (2006), 'De nuevo un aplazamiento (en la sombra)', in *Ciudad y Territorio-Estudios Territoriales*, Vol. XXXVIII, nr. 147, p.p. 195-203.

Ostrom, E. (1986), 'A method for institutional analysis', in Kaufmann e.a. (1986, eds.), p.p. 459-479.

O'Toole, L.J. (1988), 'Strategies for intergovernmental management: implementing programs in interorganizational networks', in *Journal of Public Administration*, 11(4), p.p. 417-441.

Overwater, P.S.A. (1999), *Naar een sturend (gemeentelijk) grondbeleid*, commisioned by VNO-NCW, AVBB, and NEPROM, Den Haag.

Oxley, Michael (2006), 'The Gain from the Planning-Gain Supplement: A Consideration of the Proposal for a New Tax to Boost Housing Supply in the UK', in *European Journal of Housing Policy*, Vol. 6, No. 1, p.p. 101–113, April 2006.

Parejo Alfonso, Luciano (1991), *Suelo y urbanismo: el nuevo sistema legal*, Tecnos, Madrid.
- (1993), "Reflexiones sobre la situación actual y las posibles líneas de reforma del ordenamiento urbanístico", in *Ciudad y Territorio-Estudios Territoriales*, I (95-96), spring-summer, p.p. 231-243.
- (1996), "Apuntes para una interpretación del sistema legal urbanístico español en clave histórica", in *Ciudad y Territorio-Estudios Territoriales*, number 107-108, spring-summer, p.p. 149-166.

Parejo Alfonso, Luciano & Blanc Clavero, Francisco (1999), *Derecho urbanístico valenciano. (Análisis de la ley reguladora de la actividad urbanística)*, 2nd edition, Tirant lo blanch, Valencia, Spain, 598 p.p.

Perales Madueño, Francisco (1996), "La primera reforma de la Ley del Suelo: 1956-1975", in *Ciudad y Territorio-Estudios Territoriales*, number 107-108, spring-summer, p.p. 101-126.

Pierre, Jon (2005), 'Comparative Urban Governance: Uncovering Complex Causalities', in *Urban Affairs Review*, Vol. 40, No. 4, March 2005, p.p. 446-462.

Planbureau voor de Leefomgeving (2010), *Ex-durante evaluatie Wet ruimtelijke ordening*, PBL, Den Haag/Bilthoven.

Polit, Denise F.; Beck, Cheryl Tatano; Hungler, Bernadette P. (2001), *Nursing research. Methods, Appraisal, and Utilization*, Fifth Edition, Lippincott, Philadelphia, New YOrk, Baltimore.

Prest, A.R. (1981), *The taxation of urban land*, Manchester University Press, p.p. 190.

Priemus, Hugo (1996), 'Recent changes in the social rented sector in the Netherlands', in *Urban Studies*, Vol. 33, Nº 10, blz. 1891-1908.

Priemus, Hugo & Louw, Erik (2000), *Gemeentelijk grondbeleid. Regiefunctie bij de realisatie van ruimtelijk beleid*, Delft University Press, Delft.

- (2003), 'Changes in Dutch land policy: from monopoly towards competition in the building market', in *Environment and Planning B: Planning and Design*, volume 30, pp. 369-378.

Quigg, L. (1993) 'Empirical Testing of Real Option-Pricing Models', in *Journal of Finance*, 48, 621-40.

Ratcliffe, John; Stubbs, Michael; and Shepherd, Mark (2002), *Urban Planning and Real Estate Development*, Second Edition, Spon Press, London and New York.

Rhodes, R.A.W. (1997), *Understanding Governance*, Open University Press, Buckingham.

Rhodes, R.A.W. & Marsh, D. (1992), 'Policy Networks in British Politics', in Marsh & Rhodes (eds. 1992), p.p. 1-26.

Ricardo, D. (1817), *On the principals of political economy and taxation*, 3rd edition in 1821, John Murray, London.

RIGO (2008) *Kosten en opbrengsten bij projecten voor verstedelijking tot 2020; Bijlage bij de beantwoording van de motie Van Heugten*, commissioned by Ministry VROM, Amsterdam.

Ripley, R.B. and Franklin, G. (1987), *Congress, the Bureaucracy and Public Policy*, Dorsey, Homewood, IL. First published 1976.

Roca Cladera, Josep (1992), "Valor de reposición versus valor de mercado: Análisis del concepto 'coeficiente de mercado'", in *Catastro*, 13, pp. 9-16.

- (2007), 'García-Bellido y la renovación del paradigma urbano. Post-escriptum a la Propiedad Desagregada', in *ACE Architecture, City and Environment*, nr. 3, February 2007, p.p. 160-169, Barcelona.

Roca Cladera, Josep; and Burns, M.C. (2000) 'The Liberalization of the Land Market in Spain: The 1998 Reform of Urban Planning Legislation', in *European Planning Studies*, 8, 547-64

Rodríguez de Santiago, José María (2001), "Urbanismos Comparados/Alemania: líneas básicas de la legislación urbanística en la República Federal Alemana", in *Ciudad y Territorio-Estudios Territoriales*, Vol. XXXIII, n. 128, p.p. 301-320.

Rossum, A.A. van (2005), 'Contracteren met de overheid: wanneer mag de overheid gebruik maken van het privaatrecht en welke normen zijn op privaatrechtelijk handelen van de overheid van toepassing?', in *Contracteren. Tijdschrift voor de contractspraktijk*, 2005/04, p.p. 85-93.

Romero Aloy, Maria Jesús (2002), *Los planes municipals en el Derecho Urbanístico Valenciano*, Tirant lo blanch, Valencia, Spain.

Rotterdam, Dienstenstructuur Ruimtelijke Ordening en Stadsvernieuwing (1985), *Standsvernieuwing Rotterdam 1974-1984*, Uitgeverij 010, Rotterdam.

Rowan-Robinson, Jeremy & Lloyd, Greg (1988), *Land development and the infrastructure lottery*, T&T Clark Ltd, Edinburgh, 160 pages.

Ruiz de Lobera y Pérez-Mínguez, Cecilia (1996), *Estudio de la estructura urbanística italiana*, not published, available through d.munozgielen@tudelft.nl

Scharpf, F.W. (1978), 'Interorganizational policy studies: issues, concepts and perspectives', in Hanf, K.I. and Scharpf, F.W. (eds, 1978), p.p. 345-370.

Scharpf, F.W., Reissert, B. and Schabel, F. (1978), 'Policy Effectiveness and Conflict Avoidance in Intergovernmental Policy Formation', in Hanf, K.I. and Scharpf, F.W. (eds, 1978), 57-114.

Segeren, A., Needham, B. and Groen J. (2005), *De markt doorgrond: een institutionele analyse van grondmarkten in Nederland*, Den Haag, NAi Uitgevers / Ruimtelijk Planbureau.

Smith, J. J., & Gihring, T. A. (2006), 'Financing Transit Systems through Value Capture', in *American Journal of Economics and Sociology*, Vol. 65, No. 3, July, pp. 751-786.

Spaans, Marjolein; Golland, Andrew & Carter, Norma (1996), 'Land Supply and Housing Development: A Comparative Analysis of Britain and The Netherlands 1970-1995', in *International Planning Studies*, Vol. 1, No. 3., pp: 291-310.

Spaans, M. (2002), *The implementation of urban revitalization projects: An international comparison*, Delft, DUP Science.

Swanborn, P.G. (1987), *Sociaal wetenschappelijk onderzoek*, Boom, Meppel.

- (1994), *Methoden van sociaal-wetenschappelijk onderzoek*, Boom, Amsterdam/Meppel.
- (1996), *Case-study's. Wat, wanneer en hoe?*, Boom, Amsterdam/Meppel.

Tasan-Kok, T. (2008), 'Changing interpretations of 'flexibility' in the planning literature: from opportunism to creativity?', in *International Planning Studies*, Vol. 13, No. 4, pp. 183 - 195.

Taskforce (her)ontwikkeling Bedrijventerreinen (2008), *Kansen voor kwaliteit. Een ontwikkelingsstrategie voor bedrijventerreinen*, Ministerie Economische Zaken and Ministerie Vrom.

Thomas, H,D.; Minett, J.M.; Hopkins, S.; Hamnett, S.L.; Faludi, A. and Barrell, D. (1983), *Flexibility and Commitment in Planning*, Martinus Nijhof, The Hague, Boston and London.

Truman, D. (1971), *The Governmental Process. Political Interests and Public Opinion*, New York: Knopf.

Turk, Sevkiye Sence (2008), 'An examination for efficient applicability of the land readjustment method at the international context', in *Journal of Planning Literature* 22 (3): 229-242.

Turnbull, G. K. (2005), 'The investment incentive effects of land use regulations', in *Journal of Real Estate Finance and Economics*, 31, 357–95.

Tweede Kamer der Staten-Generaal (2003), *Nieuwe regels omtrent de ruimtelijke ordening (Wet ruimtelijke ordening). Memorie van Toelichting*, Vergaderjaar 2002-2003, 28 916, Sdu Uitgevers, 's-Gravenhage (The Hague).

Van Damme, Lennard & Verdaas, Co (1996), *Plannen laten zich niet plannen*, Dissertation, NOW.

Van der Putten, E., De Lint, R. and De Wolff, H. (2004), *Onderzoek naar de mogelijkheden van een regeling voor stedelijke herverkaveling*, Den Haag/Delft: Akro Consult/OTB Delft.

Van der Ree, P. (2000), *Met woord en kaart. Over detaillering en reikweidte van bestemmingsplanregeling*, Bouwrecht Monografieën, Stichting Instituut voor Bouwrecht, Kluwer, Deventer.

Van der Schaar, J. & Hereijgers, A. (1991), *Volkshuisvesting: een zaak van beleid*, Spectrum, Utrecht.

Van Gunsteren, H.R. (1976), *The Quest for Control: A critique of the rational-central-rule approach in public affairs*, London: Wiley.

Verhage, Roelof (2002), *Local Policy for Housing Development, European experiences*, Ashgate, Hampshire.

- (2005), 'Renewing urban renewal in France, the UK and The Netherlands: Introduction', in *Journal of Housing and the Built Environment*, 20: 215-227.

Verhage, R. & Sluis, R. (2003), *Samenwerking bij stedelijke vernieuwing*, DUP Science, Amsterdam.

Verhage, R. & Needham, B. (2003), 'Financing Public Facilities in Housing Projects: a Method for Understanding Negotiating Processes', in Ennis (ed, 2003), p.p. 19-38.

Vrom (Ministry for Housing, Planning and the Environment, 2002), *Cijfers over Wonen 2002. Feiten over mensen, wensen, wonen*, march 2002, The Hague..

- (2004), *Nota Ruimte. Ruimte voor ontwikkeling*, The Hague.
- (2005), *De kosten in beeld, de kosten verdeeld*, The Hague.
- (2006), *Brief minister Vrom aan Tweede Kamer*, 16 June 2006, Vergaderjaar 2005-2006, 27581, nr. 26.
- (2007a), *Cijfers over Wonen 2006*, April 2007.
- (2007b), *De Grondexploitatiewet: nieuwe regeles voor de ontwikkeling van bouwlocaties*, also available in English version, The Hague, April 2007.
- (2007c), *Nota van Toelichting bij Ontwerp Besluit ruimtelijke ordening* (which is published in *Staatscourant* on 3 May 2007, red.).
- (2008), *Structuurvisie Randstad 2040. Naar een duurzame en concurrerende Europese Topregio*, The Hague.

Vrom, Vereniging Nederlandse Gemeenten, Vereniging van Grondbedrijven (2008), *Handreiking Grondexploitatiewet*, Sdu Uitgevers bv, The Hague, 279 p.p.

Vrom-raad (2000), *Het instrumetn geslepen. Voorstellen voor een herziene WRO en voor een betere kostenverdeling bij grondexploitatie*, The Hague.

- (2009), *Grond voor kwaliteit. Voorstellen voor verbetering van overheidsregie on (binnen)stedelijke ontwikkeling*, Advise 070, February 2009, The Hague.

Waldron, J. (1990), *The Law*, London: Routledge.

White, Paul (1986), 'Land availability, land banking and the price of land for housing: a review of recent debates', in *Land Development Studies*, 3 (2), p.p. 101-111.

Williams, Richard H. & Wood, Barry (1994), *Urban Land and Property Markets in the UK*, serial 'European Urban Land & Property Markets 4', UCL Press, London.

Yin, Robert K. (1989), *Case Study Research, Design and Methods*, SAGE publications, Thousand Oaks, CA, USA.

Zundert, J.W. van (1996), *Het bestemmingsplan, een juridisch bestuurlijke inleiding in de ruimtelijke ordening*, 8th edition, Samsom HD Tjeenk Willink, Alphen aan den Rijn, p.p. 313.

- (2004), [idem], 11th edition, Kluwer, Alphen aan den , p.p. 335.
- (2008), 'De structuurvisie in de Wro', in *Bouwrecht*, nr. 7 july 2008, p.p. 470-478.

Zweigert, Konrad & Kötz, Hein (1977), *Introduction to Comparative Law*, 3rd edition 1998, Oxford University Press and J.C.B. Mohr (Paul Siebeck).

Interviews

Specific interviews

Meant to collect specific knowledge to fill in the gaps in literature and cases. Interviews were structured following the specific questions, each interview being therefore specific and different from the others. For the list of specific interviews of persons involved in the cases, see section 'Cases'. Here follows a list of this sort of interviews made to experts. The interviews took from 15 minutes to 3 hours:

- Spain/Valencia:
  - García-Bellido García de Diego, Javier; long talks during 29 and 30 August 2005, Madrid.
  - Blanc Clavero, Francisco; live interviews on 24 February 2007, 21:45-23:00 (telephone interview); 9 June 2008, 23:00-23:40 (telephone interview), and e-mails 12 June, 2, 3 and 17 July 2008.
  - Sanchís Cuesta, José Alberto; telephone interview 27 May 2008, 16-16.30.
  - Raga, Francisco; telephone interview 15 October 2008; short interview by email on 27 January 2010.
- England:
  - Stephen Crow, Cardiff School of City and Regional Planning, telephone interview on 11 April 2006, 14:00-15:00.
  - Vincent Nadin, University of the West of England; live interviews on 22 March 2007, 13.00-15.15, and on 5 April 2007, 13:30-16:00.
  - Chris A. Lyons, London School of Economics; telephone interview on 24 Augustus 2007, 10:30-11:35.
  - John Henneberry, University of Sheffield; telephone interview on 29 Augustus 2007, 17:00-18:00.
- The Netherlands:
  - J.J. van Dollinga, Municipality of Groningen, Planning and Economy Department, division Legal Affairs; telephone interview on 11 September 2007, 15:30-16:20; 13 September 16:45-17:00.
  - K. Porrey, Municipality of Rotterdam, Legal Affairs Department of Planning and Housing; telephone interview on 12 September 2007, 15:30-16:20.
  - W.A. Egberts, Municipality of Rotterdam, Legal Affairs Department of Planning and Housing, telephone interview on 13 September 2007, 16:00-16:30.
  - Arno Segeren, Ruimtelijk Planbureau, written comments to written interview, 28 January 2008. Written comments on 11 February 2008.
  - Co Verdaas, Gedeputeerde Gelderland; written answer to questionnaire on 12 February 2008.
  - Herman de Wolff, Delft University of Technology, live interviews, 11 February 2008, 16:50-17:00; 12 March 2008, 15:00-15:15.
  - J.W. van Zundert, telephone interview, 14 March 2008, 14:30-15:10.
  - Ernst van Gelder, Municipality of Rotterdam, telephone interviews, 12 March 2008, 14:45-15:10; 1 April 2008, 17:00-17:45.
  - J.A.M. van den Brand, telephone interviews, 28 March 2008, 11:30-12:00; 4 April 2008, 10:30-11:30; 11 April, 11:00-11:20.

- Jaap Hoekstra, telephone interviews, 3 April 2008, 10:00-10:50; 16 April 2008, 16:35-16:50.
- Kim van Wageningen, Van Keulen & van Zutphen, email-interview in June 2008.
- Theo Stauttener and Robin van Bladel, City Beautiful, live interviews, 9 May 2008, 15.30-17.30; 27 June 2008, 15:00-17:30.
- Arno Lamot, Zuidplas Advies, live interview, 12 February 2010, 11.00-13.00.
- Arend Vriend, Van Keulen & van Zutphen, telephone-interview, 3 March 2010, 13-13:20.
- Harry Nijland, Municipality of Apeldoorn, telephone-interview, 3 March 2010, 14:45-15:25; email-interview 5 March 2010.
- Martien Penning, Hillenraad, telephone interview, 3 March 2010, 15:45-16:10.
- Hunen, Dennis van, e-mail interviews, Bouwfonds Ontwikkeling, 10 and 29 March 2010.

- Germany: Benjamin Davy, University Dortmund, telephone interview on 22 may 2006, 15:00-16:00.
- France: Vincent Renard, École Polytechnique, CNRS, telephone interview on 17 march 2006, written comments on 9 June 2006, telephone interview on 4 January 2007, 17:00-17:15, and 11 January 2007, 11.15-11.45.
- Italy: Federico Oliva, Professor urban planning at the Polytechnic University of Milano, telephone interview on 5 January 2007 (16:30-17:30) and on 6 January (11-11:45).
- Sweden: Thomas Kalbro, Royal Institute of Technology, telephone interview on 11 mei 2006, 13.00-15.00; and live interview on 12 oktober 2006, 13.00-15.30.
- Flanders: Herman de Wolff, TU Delft, Studiegroep Omgeving, live interview on 3 April 2006; Elisabeth Wouters, OMGEVING, telephone interview and written comments on 8 January 2008, 17-18:45.
- Denmark: Stig Enemark (University Aalborg), telephone interviews on 24 may 2006, 13.30-14.30, and 30 may 2006, 11-12.15.

Generic interviews

Meant for obtaining knowledge about the possible causal relationship between variables 'formal rules relevant to zoning' and 'public value capturing', i.e. meant for answering Preparatory Research Question 3. All these interviews followed also a semi-structured form: all possibly relevant sub-variables of 'formal rules relevant to zoning' were listed that might have had influence on sub-variables of 'public value capturing'. The construction of the questionnaire has followed a meticulous method (Emans, 2002: 114-160). A transcription of the generic interviews was sent to the interviewed, which had the opportunity to comment on their contents. Two different groups of persons have been interviewed here.

(1) Persons involved in the studied cases: per case at least an involved public officer and the developer. The questionnaire differed a little depending on the position of the person in the case and country in question, as each case and each country show different relevant sub-variables of 'formal rules relevant to zoning'. Also, the questionnaire differed depending on the available time (minimal 45 minutes, maximal ca. 2 hours). A list of the interviewed persons can be found in section 'Cases'.

(2) Experts and representative of interest groups: relevant experts at national level, and the representatives of the developers, also at national level. The questionnaires here differed a little depending on the country in question, as each country shows different relevant sub-variables of 'formal rules relevant to zoning'. These interviews used to last longer, about 1.5 till 3 hours. The interviewed experts were:

- Spain/Valencia:
  - Baño León, Jose María; Universitat de Valencia, live interview on 22 December 2006, 12:05-14:00.
  - Blanc Clavero, Francisco; live interviews on 1 November 2006, 18:30-21:30; on 27 November 2006, 11.00-15.00 (visit to building sites) and 18.30-21.30 (interview);
  - Escribano, Alejandro, live interview 20 December 2006, 18:30-19:45, and telephone interviews some days later, about 1 hour.
  - Fernández, Gerardo Roger; live interview 26 oktober 2006, 12.30-15.00 uur.
  - Montiel, Antonio, significative member of Salvem, civil organization for the defence of natural environment and historic and cultural urban patrimony. 21 November 2006, 20:30-22:30.
  - Muñoz Solsona, Benjamín, chairman Asociación Procincial de Promotores Inmobiliarios y Agentes Urbanizadores de Valencia [Provincial Association of Developers and Urbanizing Agents of Valencia], and Cañellas Sierra, Carlos, legal adviser same association. 20 December 2006, 11.35-13.15.
  - Rubio, Rafael chairman of local representatives social democratic party (PSPV) in Local Council of Valencia. 23 November 2006, 9:45-11:15.

- England:
  - Hellen Holland, leader of Labour in the Local Council of Bristol; telephone semi-structured interview on 26 July 2007, 14:30-14:00.
  - Andrew Whitaker, Head of Planning of the Home Building Federation; live semi-structured interview on 2 July 2007 9.30-11.45.

- The Netherlands:
  - Co Verdaas, Gedeputeerde Gelderland, telephone interview, 14 November 2007, 8:00-9:00; and 19 November 2007, 8:30-9:00; written comment to the transcription on 21 November 2007.
  - Jan Fokkema, voorzitter Neprom, live interview on 27 November 2007, 15:15-16:30; schriftelijk commentaar van Jan Fokkema ontvangen op 29 Nov, en verwerkt op 30 Nov.

Cases

The *in situ* data gathering for the cases took place in the following periods:

- Region of Valencia: November and December 2006;
- England: June 2007;
- The Netherlands: beginning of 2005 for case *De Funen* and Winter of 2007-2008 for rest of cases.

Live interviews took place in these periods. Interviews made by telephone took place afterwards. The interviews were both above-mentioned sorts 'specific' and 'generic' interviews:

- Valencian cases:
  - Case *Guillem de Anglesola:*
    - Francisco Raga, chief of the Department PAI of the Municipality of Valencia, interviews on Wednesday 25 October (13:00-14:00) and Monday 6 November 2006 (9:30-10:30);
    - Tomas Garcia Robles, chief of the Department Land Readjustment of the Municipality of

Valencia, interview on 9 November 2006 (13:00-13:20).
    - Jorge Anglada Such, lawyer, and Ana Cantos, lawyer, Consulting Cantos Anglada, commissioned by the urbanizing agent, Proara; interview on Wednesday 29 November 2006, 16:00-17:45.
  - *Case Periodista Gil Sumbiela*
    - Francisco Raga, chief of the Department PAI of the Municipality of Valencia, interviews on Wednesday 25 October (13:00-14:00) and Monday 27 November 2006 (13.30-14.45);
    - Jose Antonio Berzosa Lamata, Architect-planner; Guillermo Berzosa, lawer; and Miguel Angel Sanjose Calabuig, Developer, GRUPO INMOBILIARIO DAEMI; interview on Tuesday 28 November 2006, 17.00-18.45.
  - *Case Camino Hondo del Grao*
    - Francisco Raga, chief of the Department PAI of the Municipality of Valencia, interviews on Wednesday 25 October (13:00-14:00) and Monday 27 November 2006 (13.30-14.45);
    - Raúl Peñalver Cabanero, developer, Vallehermoso Valencia; interview on Thursday 30 November 2006 (16:30-17:45).
  - *Benalúa Sur*
    - José Manuel Santamaría Vidal, director of *TERRA Recursos Inmobiliarios*, leading party in NUEVO SECTOR, the urbanizing agent, upto July 2002; Interview on 21 December 2006, 9:00-10:30.
    - Rosa Rocamora, lawer of *Perez Segura & Asociados*, commissioned by the urbanizing agent, Grupo P.R.A.S.A. since 2002. Interview on 21 December 2006, 10:45-11:45; telephone interview on 3 January 2007, 10:50-11.40.
    - Manuel Beltra, Municipality of Alicante, Chief Planning Department (*Servicio Planeamiento y Gestion, Departamento Tecnico de Planeamiento*); Telephone interview on Thursday 26 October (12:00-13:00), and live interview on 21 December 2006 (12:15-15:15);
    - Miguel Garulo, Municipality of Alicante, Management Department; Telephone interview on Friday 12 January 2007 (18:05-19:00).

- English cases:
  - *Case Megabowl*:
    - Jim Cliffe, Planning Obligations Project Manager of the Strategic and Citywide Policy Team of the Bristol City Council, the person that monitors the fulfilment of planning obligations: live not structured interview on Thursday 7 June 2007 (10-11.10); written answers to written questions on 18 June 2007;
    - John Douglas, Planning Officer of the Bristol City Council, the person who was in charge of this planning application; live semi-structured interview on 26 June 2007 (14-15.00); written comments to the transcription of the interview on 2 July; written answer to written questions on 22 June.
    - Jonathan Jarman, Angus Meek Partnership Ltd (the agent of Applicant Tenpin Limited, the applicant), the person in charge of this planning application: live semi-structured interview on Thursday 21 June 2007, 10:00-11:30; written and live answers to written questions on the same day, 9:30-10:00; other telephone comments on 24 July 2007, 17:50-17:55.
  - *Case Temple Quay:*
    - Jim Cliffe, Planning Obligations Project Manager of the Strategic and Citywide Policy Team of

the Bristol City Council, the person that monitors the fulfilment of planning obligations: live not structured interview on Thursday 7 June 2007 (10-11.10); written structured interview answered on 6 Augustus 2007;

- Ian Collinson, planning officer of the City of Bristol in charge of this project at the time of the granting of Planning Permission; live semi-structured interview on Thursday 28 June 2007, 14.00 -15.00, and written comments by e-mail on 2 July 2007;
- Erik Hall, Planning Director Castlemore Securities Ltd, the developer of Temple Quay; telephone semi-structured interview on 8 Augustus 2007, 15:00-15:50.

- *Case Harbourside*:
  i. Jim Cliffe, Planning Obligations Project Manager of the Strategic and Citywide Policy Team of the Bristol City Council, the person that monitors the fulfilment of planning obligations: live not structured interview on Thursday 7 June 2007 (10-11.10); written answers to written interview on 6 Augustus 2007;
  ii. Richard Holden, Planning Officer Bristol City Council: live semi-structured interview on 3 July 2007 (11.00-12.30); written answers to written interview on 6 Augustus 2007; several comments per E-mail along Augustus 2007.
  iii. Ian Cawley, developer Crest Nicholson: telephone semi-structured interview on 28 Augustus 2007, 11:00-12:10.

- Dutch cases:
  - *Case De Funen*
    - Dries Jense, projectmanager Municipality of Amsterdam in this project from 1995 to 2000. Interview January 2005 the 20th, 11-12:30.
    - Arthur van Gemmert, developer Heijmans IBC Real Estate Development. Interview January 2005 the 25th, 13-14:00.
    - Jenny Brummelman, housing association De Key. Interview February 2005 the 3th, 16-17:15.
    - David Holtes, legal expert in the Centre Borough of the Municipality of Amsterdam, author of the Development obligations contract of 1997. Interview April 2005 the 29th, 11:30-14:00.
    - Hilda de Boer, chief Department of Planning Policy, and Conny van Rijk, legal expert, maker of the Local Land-use plan 'Quarter Czaar Peter-East', both from the Central District of the Municipality of Amsterdam. Interview July 2005 the 11th, 10-12:00.
  - *Case Kruidenbuurt*
    - Rob Thijssen (developer, Trudo) live interview on 13 November 2007, 14:00-16:00; written answers to written questions on 28 November 2007;
    - Cees Zeeuwen (Land Development Company Municipality of Eindhoven), live interview 13 November 2007, 14:00-16:00.
  - *Case Kop van Oost*
    - Richard Crebs, jurist Real Estate development of the Municipality of Groningen: live interview on 29 November 2007, 11:20-12:20; written answers to written questionnaire on 6 December 2007;
    - Jaap Dallinga, jurist Planning and Economy Department, division Legal Affairs of the Municipality of Groningen: written answers to written questionnaire on 6 December 2007;
    - Gerrit Liefering, Municipality of Groningen: written answers to written questionnaire on 6 December 2007;

- Lonneke Zuijdwijk, developer Heijmans: live interview on 10 December 2007, 16:30-17:30;
- Vincent Tuiten, developer Heijmans: written answers to written questionnaire on 18 December 2007.

◦ *Case Stationskwartier*

- J.M. Vollaard, planner, Department Juridical Plans, Municipality of Breda. Mr. Vollaard was the author of the 2007 Land use Plan; live interview on 8 November 2007, 11:30-13:15.
- J. Bosma, *Stichting Stationskwartier* (civic organization), written questionnaire, answered on 26 November 2007.Gerard van Veggel, project leader, and Van Berkel, plan economist, both of the Municipality of Breda; live interview on 7 January 2008, 14:00-15:15.
- Bram Loggers, ex project leader of NS Real Estate; live interview on 21 January 2008, 14:10-15:00.

Summary

Chapter 1 - Introduction: problems in the financing of public goals in urban regeneration in the Netherlands

Traditionally Dutch public bodies used to follow an 'active' land policy: they bought the land to be developed or regenerated, provided the infrastructure, and sold the serviced building plots to housing associations and commercial developers. At the end of the 80's, several policy changes caused a gradual shift to more passive or facilitating formulas. Increasingly, it is the housing associations and the market parties that buy the land, or most of it, and develop sites. Urban development in general (both greenfield development and the regeneration of urban sites) usually implies an economic value increase of the land, but also the need to invest in new roads and public space, drainage, public buildings and social housing, compensations, etc (from now on: "public infrastructure and facilities"). If municipalities follow an active land policy, they can pay those costs by selling the serviced building plots. However, since Dutch municipalities decreasingly have disposal over the land, they encounter problems with covering those costs, while the landowners are not willing to contribute. This has led to lowering public targets, for example in the regeneration of deteriorated Dutch neighbourhoods, and to the need for public subsidization.

This research asks the question whether, when land is in private hands, the economic value increase caused by regeneration could be used (all or at least part of it) to pay the public infrastructure and facilities. This research investigates whether a particular set of legal instruments, the 'formal rules relevant to zoning', could be useful to stimulate landowners to contribute, i.e. to improve the capturing of value increase.

Formal rules relevant to zoning are: binding rules regulating the use of land and real estate, and the administrative approval procedure for these binding rules; property rights in land; and not-legally binding policy documents. Value increase in urban regeneration can be of different sorts: caused by investments in infrastructure, by re-zoning the site, or just by the general increase in the demand for land. This research distinguishes three different meanings attached to 'capturing value increase': 'cost recovery' (recovery, through contributions from landowners, of the costs of public infrastructure and facilities), 'value capturing' (capturing by public bodies that have invested in, for instance, infrastructure, of the increased property values) and 'creaming off plus value' (public body capturing all sorts of value increase). All three types of capturing are considered in this research.

A fundamental question is, who should receive the value increase. Following a conservative liberal tradition, any value increase belongs to the landowner, while an alternative tradition advocates that it belongs to the community. A common topic in the neo-classical theory of economic rent is the idea of taxing it. These ideological differences have led to different instruments for capturing value increase, some of them seeking to capture all of the value increase and others seeking only to internalize the negative impacts of urban development (that is, cost recovery). Because in the Netherlands only the latter is allowed, this research makes recommendations for cost recovery and not for creaming off the plus value. Some recommendations fit within the existing Dutch legal framework, including the new Physical Planning Act (*Wet ruimtelijk ordening*) and Land Development Act (*Grondexploitatiewet*). Other recommendations imply a modification of this legal framework. So the problem to which this research wants to find a solution is formulated as follows:

How could formal rules relevant to zoning be used in the development phase of comprehensive urban regeneration developments on privately owned land in the Netherlands in order that the profitable parts finance the unprofitable parts?

In order to answer it, the following research questions need first to be answered:

- Preparatory research question 1: *How can those formal rules relevant to zoning be used in comprehensive urban regeneration developments on privately owned land?*
- Preparatory research question 2: *What is the extent of capturing value increase in comprehensive urban regeneration developments on privately owned land?*
- Preparatory research question 3: *How does the way in which formal rules relevant to zoning are used influence capturing value increase?*
- Main research question: *How could formal rules relevant to zoning be used in the Netherlands in order that the profitable parts finance as much as possible the unprofitable parts?*

Chapter 2 - Theoretical framework: capturing value increase within policy networks

An urban regeneration project can be analyzed as a policy network in which public bodies try to improve the capturing of value increase by interacting with other parties. The 'policy network approach' results from the academic debate about the changing role of public bodies and market parties in the last decennia. The foundations can be found in policy science in the early 1970s. While in the traditional intra-organizational approach, public management is a top-down authoritarian activity, in the policy network approach, the power relation between actors is less hierarchical. Resource dependence is a method to discover the structural factors that can explain this relation. A first structural factor is that policy networks consist of different actors each of them pursuing its own goals. This carries the potentiality of a conflict. At the same time, the actors are mutually dependent because none of them controls all the resources that are needed to pursue its goals. The strength of this dependence depends on the importance and 'substitutability' of the resource. Both the distribution of resources and the power relations of actors are regulated and shaped by formal rules (laws). In turn, the power relations often shape, consolidating or altering, the formal rules. A second structural factor is that governments always depend on the resources of others and are thus not anymore the dominant actor but a *primus inter pares*. Critics say that the policy network approach devalues the status of the public sector, and that a close involvement of public bodies in interactions and partnerships is undesirable because networks are non-transparent and uncontrolled.

My research can be seen as criticism of the basic assumption that public bodies in land development projects *always* have to depend on other actors. I provide two measures to modify the interactions within the policy networks, and thereby to modify the outcomes in capturing value increase: first modifying property rights in land, and second modifying certainty and flexibility in planning.

Property rights in land

One might think that property rights give the owner total freedom to decide how to use his land. However, the reality is that formal rules restrict this. Formal rules can come from private law and are meant to regulate the normal traffic of property rights between persons. But formal rules can also come from public law and are meant to regulate how public bodies can impose restrictions on property rights. Especially after the introduction in the 19th Century of the *social function* of property and of sanitary considerations, public law has significantly limited property rights in land. Nowadays the owner can enjoy his property only if he/she does so within the legal rules and prescriptions, and after receiving a public authorization or concession. In Great Britain, the Netherlands and Spain there is much debate about this. In 1947 a British law introduced and operationalized what was called the nationalization of development rights. As a consequence, the value increase became the subject of a charge, a charge that however does not exist anymore. This nationalization did not go further, and the principle remained that landowners are the only ones who can develop their land.

The mentioned problems in the Netherlands with the financing of the public infrastructure and facilities have been the subject of controversy and debate. The question has been discussed whether public law offers public bodies enough instruments to influence urban development. Some authors are more optimistic about this, while others are sceptical. Some consider that property rights in land create a sort of oligopoly of landowners and advocate a modification of property rights in order to stimulate free competition.

Since the 19th Century, the difficulties faced in Spain by public bodies in financing public infrastructure and facilities inspired proposals and measures that affected property rights. In 1956 a land readjustment regulation was introduced that made profiting from the value increase conditional on taking responsibility for infrastructure provision. Landowners are, since then, obliged to provide the infrastructure. As compensation, they share the serviced building plots. Municipalities are obliged to approve a General Land use Plan covering the entire municipal territory to give certainty to the landowners about the building possibilities. The detailed character of this plan, and its strong legal binding status has made Spain a singular case in the international context. The land readjustment regulation failed however to assure good and enough public infrastructure and facilities. Since the 1980s, critics (singularly García-Bellido) advocated breaking the oligopoly of landowners by giving the development rights to the public bodies. Inspired by this proposal, in 1994 the region of Valencia introduced a new law to tackle land speculation and to improve capturing value increase. In fact this law separated infrastructure provision from land ownership.

Certainty and flexibility in planning

There is a lively debate about the desirable degree of flexibility in planning: must planning create certainty at early stages of development processes (so that public bodies can control urban development) or be flexible (to adapt to circumstances)? If zoning plans are approved early, and include detailed prescriptions, and it is not possible to modify them, then there will be less flexibility and more certainty. While flexibility was seen as a negative feature in the 1960s, nowadays the perception has changed. As we will see later, the degree of certainty has important consequences for capturing value increase.

There are two traditions related to the degree of flexibility and certainty in urban planning. The 'plan-led' traditions (like the Dutch planning system) are supposed to provide at early stages certainty about the future development possibilities through the approval of legally binding land use plans. The 'development-led' tradition (like the British planning system), although there might be some indicative zoning plans in early stages, is assumed to give less certainty and leave more room for negotiations with developers and landowners. These differences are the consequence of historic differences: the plan-led system rests on the centrality of the rule of law and the development-led system on judge-made law and procedural fairness.

Causal model: which variables influence the capturing of value increase in urban regeneration?

Different actors are involved in urban regeneration: public and private, with regulatory powers or not, with or without land, with a direct or indirect interest. All of them interact with each other within a complex set of variables to finally shape the degree of captured value increase. If the economic value of the site clearly increases due to the regeneration, there is an initial profit. But this initial profit should be distributed in such a way that contributions for public infrastructure and facilities are paid for. If the final profit is large enough, it is possible to subtract those contributions. The size of the initial profit, and whether it translates into a final profit depends on several variables:

A. Context variables influencing size initial profit: real estate markets, plan and site features, markets of workforce and building materials, and fiscal regimes.
B. Context variables influencing distribution initial profit, **i.e. the formal rules relevant to zoning**.
C. Actions of those directly involved in the project, **including those with formal powers**, which influence the size of the initial profit: definition of the contents and geographical scope of the plan.
D. Actions of those directly involved in the project, **including those with formal powers,** which influence the distribution of the initial profit: how the local public bodies and the owners use the formal rules relevant to zoning, how local public and private bodies interact informally, and specific circumstances.

This research focuses on how the variables in bold print can be manipulated, but must also take into account all the other variables, for all of them together influence the size and the distribution of the initial profit, i.e. capturing value increase. There are many ways in which the initial profit 'leaks out' so it is no longer available to pay the public infrastructure and facilities. One way is that the accounted cost of the land (*inbrengwaarde* in Dutch) can be much higher than the minimum land cost, i.e. higher than the value of the possibilities in the previous use. For example, in the studied Dutch case *Kop van Oost*, the minimum land cost was about € 3.6 million, while the accounted cost was at least € 12 million. Another sort of 'leak' is the regular profit margin that the developer charges as a kind of normal fee. Both the accounted land cost and the regular profit are often not defined at the start of development processes, and landowners and developers can at that time set them higher or lower: higher if there is certainty about the *building possibilities* (how much and what the landowner will be able to build), and lower is there is certainty about the *future contributions* (how much the landowner will have to contribute, in kind or in money). Also relevant is the negotiation position of the public bodies. If there is certainty about building possibilities, the negotiation position of a municipality weakens because it cannot negotiate more contributions in exchange for allowing building possibilities. If there is certainty about the future contributions, its negotiation position will be better as these contributions become the starting point of negotiation. Finally, its negotiation position will also be better if the public body openly makes the approval of the zoning plan conditional on the developer securing his contributions. Landowners are in a good negotiating position because their ownership of land allows them to ask the maximum possible price for their land. Besides, they might delay the development processes, and in turn delay implies higher development costs in e.g. financial costs, longer plan preparation, etc. Higher development costs jeopardize also the initial profit. For example, in the Dutch case *Kop van Oost* de land development costs were about € 7 million, while they could have been much lower, about € 2 million. Delay can be the result of difficult negotiations with a multitude of landowners, and/or a deliberate strategy of landowners if they expect that the price of land could increase in the future. As a consequence of all these interactions, the initial profit disappears. In case *Kop van Oost* the municipality had to subsidize the public infrastructure and facilities while an initial profit of about € 18.5 million seems to have leaked out.

Two measures to improve capturing value increase: two hypotheses
The above mentioned measures to improve capturing value increase (modifying property rights in land and certainty and flexibility in planning) are formulated as two hypotheses:

1. *A specific form of splitting the property rights on land (separating infrastructure provision from property rights) can modify the power-relationships in the network of actors involved in urban regeneration, and this can improve capturing value increase.*

2. *Creating uncertainty in early stages of development processes about future building possibilities, and certainty about future contributions, can influence capturing value increase in a positive way.*

Chapter 3 - Method

This research studies a 'phenomenon': the interaction between municipalities, when making use of the formal rules relevant to zoning, and the developers/landowners regenerating a site. I focus on two variables: whether the application of formal rules relevant to zoning (the independent variable) could contribute to a more effective capturing of value increase (the dependent variable). The final goal is to produce knowledge that supports the formulation of recommendations for how Dutch practice could improve capturing value increase, but at the same time not delay urban regeneration.

I made several choices. First, mainly to base the research on a limited number of cases: four in Valencia, three in England, and four in the Netherlands. It was possible neither to gather data from a large enough sample of cases that would allow a representative statistical analysis, nor to perfectly isolate from possible intervening variables the relationship between the independent and the dependent variables. Besides, case research offers more information about the phenomenon and its interaction with the context than a one moment-survey. The data gathering took place before the start of the international financial and economic crisis in the Summer/Autumn of 2008, and specifically for Spain before the start of the crisis in the Spanish real estate markets at the end of 2007. For important data, I made a last round of data gathering at the end of 2009 and during 2010.

My second choice was to produce findings with a high validity and to avoid the risk, inherent to case-based research, of producing knowledge, so specific that it could not lead to general conclusions and recommendations for the Netherlands. This meant introducing three groups of provisions to increase both the internal and the external validity of the findings:

1. Using the hypothetical-deductive method to empirically test the two hypotheses;
2. Using variants of the method of difference to avoid the risk of third variables and of spurious correlations between the independent and dependent variables: elaboration of a list of possible third variables to assess their role in each country and case; limiting the total population of the cases and selecting countries with a similar political, economical and social background in order to maintain the context as constant as possible; selecting for in-depth research those countries with contrasting planning models in order to maximize the variance in the independent variable, which led to choosing an international comparison of planning systems; selecting cases that might include innovative practices; finally, when possible I studied the phenomenon before and after a modification of the independent variable (a modification of a law);
3. Using some techniques specifically to strengthen the external validity or generalizability of the findings: selecting representative cases, and using data sources additional to the cases.

This research was not interested in studying the whole phenomenon, i.e. in a description of *all* the characteristics of the phenomenon, but in identifying the relevant variables from the rest of the infinite number of other variables that could characterize the phenomenon. Therefore this research focused on several sub-variables of the independent and dependent variables. To distinguish them, this research developed a dependence model, and used the theoretical framework (included the two hypotheses) and the causal model. The independent variable (formal rules relevant to zoning) was subdivided into five sub-variables to analyse how public bodies use the formal rules relevant to zoning (preparatory research question 1):

a) Certainty beforehand about future building possibilities and contributions;
b) Choosing the contents of binding rules;

c) Making binding rules conditional on the developer securing his contributions;
d) Modulating property rights in land;
e) Procedure for the preparation and approval of relevant binding rules: guarantees to the initiative-holders; flexibility to modify existing binding rules; flexibility to determine the geographical scope of the binding rules accordingly to negotiations with landowners.

The dependent variable (capturing value increase) too was subdivided into several sub-variables: all possible forms of contributions from developers/landowners and also possible side effects, especially the tempo of implementation. This allowed evaluating the degree of finally captured value increase (preparatory research question 2). Preparatory research question 3 has been answered by inferring the sort of causal relationship between the independent and the dependent variables. The answers are in fact the tested hypotheses, for example: "if municipalities establish in early stages of development processes which contributions developers will have to pay/realize, capturing value increase will improve".

After answering each preparatory research question for each country in chapters 5 to 7, chapter 8 draw conclusions for the academic debate based on the tested hypotheses. All those answers and tested hypotheses, but incorporating also specific knowledge of the Dutch situation (legislation, political and cultural considerations), are used to give in chapter 9 an answer to the main research question, i.e. to make recommendations for the Dutch practice.

Chapter 4 - Quick scan: formal rules relevant to zoning in Western European countries

The first step in international comparative research is exploratory research into the independent variable 'formal rules relevant to zoning' in the Netherlands and another eight Western European countries: Germany, England (part of the UK), Flanders (part of Belgium), France, Sweden, Denmark, Italy, and Spain (region of Valencia). By studying countries with a similar context, as these have, reduces the influence of third variables. The second step is to select the Spanish region of Valencia and England because they show the broadest variation in the independent variable (they stand for contrasting models of planning systems). The reason is that this increases the possibilities of producing significant findings. These two countries and the Netherlands are the subject of in-depth research in chapters 5-7.

The differences found in the exploratory research in the nine countries were remarkable. Regarding the place of binding rules in the negotiation processes, England represents the 'development-led' planning system model, and Spain/Valencia (together, although to a lesser extend, with France, Italy and Flanders) the 'plan-led'. The Netherlands, the same as Germany, Sweden, and Denmark, follows in practice the development-led approach because the binding rules that make new developments possible are approved only after intending developers have negotiated the content with the municipality. Regarding the contents of binding rules, the Netherlands (up to 2008), together with Denmark, has almost no development-oriented binding rules (these are documents that prescribe the practical development of an area: temporal and financial regulations, or other kind of regulations intended for the implementation), while England and Valencia do. Further, the Dutch binding rules (except the new Development contributions plan after 2008), together with the Danish, have the narrowest contents (i.e. they can include not much more than the physical zoning), while England has the broadest. Finally, in the Netherlands, Germany, France, Sweden, Denmark and Flanders the approval of the binding rules (planning consent) cannot be made, formally and openly, conditional on the developer securing the implementation (the developer committing in a contract to provide the infrastructure, to cede land for free, to contribute to the costs, etc), while in England, Valencia and Italy this is possible and is the standard procedure.

Regarding the property rights in land, in all the studied countries, ownership rights include the right to build. There is no case where property rights are fully separated from the right to develop the land. That is, landowners are the only ones entitled to build on their land, and they can exclude others from doing so. However, in Valencia, Germany, France and Sweden the infrastructure provision is in the planning law explicitly identified as a public task, while in the Netherlands, England and the other countries it is not. Further, in Valencia and, to a lesser extent also in Germany and Sweden, infrastructure provision can be implemented without need of agreement with the landowner, as there is the possibility of compulsory land readjustment. On the contrary, in the Netherlands, England, France, Italy, Sweden, Flanders and Denmark, infrastructure provision is dependent on agreement with the landowners, and this dependence can only be avoided through major public involvement in financial and organizational terms (buying land and applying pre-emption, expropriation or *a posteriori* special tax formulae). Regarding the procedure for approval of the binding rules, in England certain major modifications are possible with a very simple procedure, while in the Netherlands and Valencia a heavy procedure is needed.

Chapter 5 - Valencia

The Spanish region of Valencia has almost full competence to make and implement planning law, and it subsidizes, together with the central government of Madrid and many municipalities, several policies oriented to the revitalization of historic areas and some other deteriorated neighbourhoods. But most urban regeneration has been undertaken in the last decennia by private initiatives to rezone into new residential, retail and office schemes old industrial and offices sites located within the existing urban areas. This research focuses on these sorts of regeneration projects, where there is no public subsidization. To rezone the land, public bodies must first modify the previous binding rules, which are of two sorts: 'General Land use Plan' and 'Detailed Plans'. General Plans cover the entire municipal territory and have a legally binding character. In extension areas, they zone the land into urban and not urban, prescribe the possible building typologies, the main public infrastructure and facilities and the exact extent of the building rights that belong to each landowner (the 'Reference Development Allowance', a sort of floor space index). This allowance gives a very high certainty about the future building possibilities. In addition, in extension areas to be developed soon and in regeneration areas, General Plans include also very detailed prescriptions: alignment, height and volumes of the buildings and the minor public infrastructure and facilities. Detailed Plans are meant for specific sites, and can modify and must anyway detail, if they are not detailed already, the General Plans.

Traditionally, Spanish public bodies have aimed to finance the unprofitable parts in urban regeneration with the profitable parts. This aim has led to the introduction of the already mentioned land readjustment in 1956. The readjustment of the property boundaries and the infrastructure provision had to be organised by all the landowners themselves. If landowners did not cooperate, the municipality could overrule them applying compulsory land readjustment or expropriation. In 1978 the central government introduced a set of legal minimal standards of public infrastructure and facilities that, together with the General Plans, created certainty about the future contributions to be paid/realized by the landowners. However, the 1956 land readjustment regulation stimulated land speculation (which led to high accounted land costs), suffered from great difficulties in organizing landowners and in addition delayed the development processes (which both led to inflated development costs). This resulted in poorly serviced building sites, with inferior public infrastructure and facilities and huge building volumes. In 1994 the Valencian regional government introduced important novelties in the land readjustment regulation. First, it introduced a third party, in addition to the municipality and the landowner/developer: the urbanising agent (*agente urbanizador*). This third party is not required to own land and can be directly appointed by the municipality (public land development company) or be chosen in a public tender (commercial builder or developer). After being assigned, the urbanising agent assumes responsibility for the infrastructure provision and for the land readjustment. Second, the 1994 law gave guarantees to the commercial parties if they wanted to participate in the public tender. Third, Detailed Plans had to be complemented with a document including all the development-oriented aspects and a Development Agreement. Anyone can participate in the public tender by submitting a proposal to the municipality, as landownership is not required, and anyone can submit objections or alternative proposals. After evaluation, the Local Council decides on a definitive proposal and selects the urbanising agent. The urbanising agent makes and submits to the municipality a detailed proposal for the public infrastructure and for the land readjustment. After readjusting the property boundaries (compulsorily if necessary), the municipality receives the public infrastructure and facilities and often also some serviced building plots, and the landowners the remaining plots. Finally, the owners of the plots submit building applications and the municipality issues building permits. The Valencian novelty has been introduced in most of the other seventeen Spanish regions.

How far can the contributions of landowners and developers go? In Spain, municipalities capture part of the value increase in urban extension areas, and they to this by requiring landowners to cede between 5 and 15% of the serviced building plots to the municipality. In addition, landowners must pay the infrastructure provision costs and provide the land needed for that, and pay to the urbanizing agent his overhead costs and a profit margin. In principle, the public buildings (schools, hospitals etc) must be paid by the respective public body, except social housing, which must be built and paid by the landowners. Additionally, it is also possible to oblige landowners to cede land situated elsewhere that is needed for off-site infrastructure. Municipalities are free to agree additional obligations with the urbanizing agent, which must pay them from his own resources and cannot charge them to the landowners.

Three cases are located in the City of Valencia: *Camino Hondo del Grao* (5.7 ha, 465 apartments plus considerable amount of offices and retail); *Guillem de Anglesola* (1.2 ha, 125 apartments, plus some retail); and *Periodista Gil Sumbiela* (0.6 ha, 100 apartments, plus some retail). One case is located in the City of Alicante: *Benalúa Sur* (8 ha, 600 apartments, plus considerable amount offices and retail). In all four cases, there was a General Plan that prescribed in detail the future development possibilities, but a Detailed Plan had anyway to be approved before being allowed to redevelop the site. In cases *Camino* and *Benalúa,* the Detailed Plan modified major aspects of the General Plan. In *Guillem* and in *Periodista,* the Detailed Plan detailed and modified only minor aspects. In all the cases, the urbanizing agent is a private party selected in a public tender, sometimes a professional developer, as in *Guillem* and *Periodista,* sometimes the landowners themselves joining together as urbanizing agent, as in *Camino* and *Benalúa*. Most of the time, urbanizing agents not only provide the infrastructure, but also buy some land and become developer of the buildings. In *Periodista* most landowners sold their property relatively quickly to the urbanizing agent. In *Guillem* they waited and most of them sold at the time of the land readjustment procedure. In *Camino* and *Benalúa* the land was already the property of the urbanizing agent (as landowners themselves became the urbanizing agent).

Chapter 6 - England

The central UK government and the regional and local public bodies have produced two main urban regeneration policies: policies meant for inadequate housing (which have a long tradition), and policies for the regeneration of the inner cities (which started in the 1970s). In the last decennia, as the studied cases show, public bodies have been seeking a larger involvement from commercial developers in financing public infrastructure and facilities for urban regeneration. To rezone the land, the Local Planning Authorities (LPAs) must first modify the previous binding rules. In England, zoning plans covering wider areas might play an important role, but they are of an indicative character, i.e. they have no direct statutory consequences for the use of land and real estate. The only legally binding land use plan is the 'Planning Permission', which focuses on a specific site. Once a developer submits an application for a planning permission, the LPA can impose planning conditions on the permission, or can negotiate contributions in a Planning Agreement ('106-agreement').

In England public bodies have in principle the right to tax the increase in value caused by the rezoning of land. In the past, several types of tax have been introduced, but all have been rescinded. Capturing value increase in practice takes place through requiring developers to contribute towards mitigating the impact of development. Contributions have become generalized since the 1970s, evolving from physical infrastructure provision on the specific site (on-site), towards also environmental, community and social infrastructure often located outside the specific site (off-site). This includes developers being asked to provide affordable housing. Controversy in the last years about the scope of contributions has led to a more tight regulation of the contributions that can be asked from developers, but this has not reduced the contributions.

The three studied cases are located in the City of Bristol: *Harbourside/Canon's Marsh* (7.8 ha, 700 apartments, 44,000 m^2 office, 30,000 m^2 leisure and facilities); *Temple Quay* (7.4 ha, 495 apartments, 61,000 m^2 office, and 7,000 m^2 leisure and facilities); and *Megabowl* (1.3 ha, 184 apartments). The 1997 Bristol Local Plan (a zoning plan of an indicative character covering the entire city) gave, for all the three cases, non-legally binding and outline prescriptions. Before redevelopment was allowed, one or more planning permissions had to be granted, and these permissions included requirements about contributions that had been negotiated with the developers and finally secured in Development Agreements.

Chapter 7 - The Netherlands

The Dutch national and local public bodies pursue urban regeneration and stimulate new building within the boundaries of existing cities. There are specific policies for: multifunctional central areas, including railway stations (case *Stationskwartier*, 16 ha, 650 apartments, plus much office space, some shops, a new railway station and much parking); monofunctional pre- and postwar residential districts (case *Kruidenbuurt*, 17 ha, 650 dwellings, plus some offices); and old brownfield sites (cases *De Funen* -8 ha, 565 apartments, some offices- and *Kop van Oost* -5 ha, 430 apartments, plus some commercial space). Urban regeneration usually involves the making of indicative zoning plans, many of which are not regulated in planning law. However, before regeneration takes place, first the financial means must be found to pay the public infrastructure and facilities, and second a new land use plan (*bestemmings-plan*) or departures from it must be approved.

In the Netherlands, the value increase of land falls to the landowner. The actual legal possibilities for capturing the increased value are limited to cost recovery, i.e. to asking developers to pay those costs of public infrastructure and facilities that benefit the development. This has not changed with the new 2008 Physical Planning Act and Physical Planning Decree. In general, contributions of developers are a result of negotiation. Since the 2008 Act it is possible to require from the landowners a contribution without the need of negotiation. The municipality must then approve a Development contributions plan, and can then formally condition the building permit (not the approval of the land use plan or departure from it) on the landowner contributing to the costs. The 2008 Decree regulates the sorts of costs that can be imposed on the landowners through a Development contributions plan: costs of on-site infrastructure and social housing, and of off-site infrastructure directly related to the development site. This excludes the costs of maintenance and exploitation, of social facilities (*maatschappelijke voorzieningen*) and part of the costs of refurbishing old infrastructure and of plan preparation. Moreover, as landowners cannot be required to contribute part of the increased value of their land towards those costs, making a Development contributions plan in urban regeneration sites often implies the municipality having to pay an additional deficit. Instead of approving a Development contributions plan, municipalities and developers/landowners are, since 2008, free to agree contributions in a Development agreement, called an 'anterior Development agreement' (*anterieure overeenkomst*). An anterior Agreement may include more contributions than a Development contributions plan.

Chapters 8 and 9 - Conclusions and recommendations for the Dutch practice

More captured value increase in Valencia and England than in the Netherlands

The findings make clear that formal rules relevant to zoning in the Spanish region of Valencia and in England differ significantly from those in the Netherlands (see following sections). A comparison of how much value increase public bodies manage to capture shows also remarkable differences: in Valencia and England, private parties are committed in urban regeneration on private owned land to contribute more than in the Netherlands. The differences mainly involve:

- On-site infrastructure provision costs: in England and Valencia these are mostly or fully paid by the developers, while the Netherlands finances these with large public subsidies;

- Land for on-site public infrastructure: in Valencia this is provided free of charge by the landowners, while England and the Netherlands there are much larger public contributions for providing this land;
- Social housing: in England and Valencia, this is paid to a large extent or almost fully by the developers, while in the Netherlands this is covered primarily by municipalities and housing associations;
- Off-site public infrastructure: in England and Valencia, developers contribute significantly (in England primarily with financial means while in Valencia primarily with land), while in the Netherlands these contributions are rare;
- Creaming off plus value: local public bodies in Valencia cream off a significant share of the economic value increase, even if they own no land. In England this does not happen officially, but because of the broad definition of developers' contributions one can conclude that it does happen. In the Netherlands this is the case only when the municipality owns the land and/or invests and shares the risk.

I conclude that there is a strong correlation between the captured value increase (the highest in Valencia, lower but also high in England, and the lowest in the Netherlands) and the different possibilities offered by the formal rules relevant to zoning. However, the correlation is not perfect. There are other variables that might also explain *part* of the differences in the captured value increase. A relevant one is the market price of real estate. When the data were gathered, housing prices in the English cases were significantly higher than prices in the Valencian and Dutch cases. This could *partly* explain why English developers offered more generous contributions than their Dutch counterparts, but not why Valencian developers, despite similar market prices to those in the Netherlands, still contributed somewhat more than the English, and much more than the Dutch. Other variables that can also explain *part* of the differences are the plan and site features, the markets for labour and for building materials, fiscal regimes, the definition of the contents and geographical scope of the plan, and specific circumstances of the involved interactions and persons.

General conclusions for the academic debate

Chapter 2 developed two specific measures, formulated as hypotheses, for influencing the interactions within the policy networks in urban regeneration and the resulting captured value increase. These two hypotheses have been tested empirically. The first speculates about the effects on capturing value increase of the definition of property rights in land and how this influences the power relationship between the involved public and private parties. The second speculates about the effects of the certainty created by binding rules and non-binding policy documents during development processes. In the causal model in chapter 2, a third speculation came up that has also been empirically tested: the assumption that the flexibility in procedures could be relevant for capturing value increase.

About the third assumption, it has not been possible to infer clear and generalizable relationships between flexibility and the results for capturing value increase.

However, it seems that the first two hypotheses might indeed be valid. The formal rules regarding property rights and certainty are indeed relevant because they can influence the interactions within the policy networks. Public bodies in England and especially in Valencia seem, thanks to these formal rules, to play a more powerful role than in the Netherlands. Municipalities in England and especially in Valencia prescribe beforehand and unilaterally clear requirements and obligations, which result in a high level of captured value increase. In Valencia, municipalities go further than in England, as the Valencian municipalities have also, thanks to a compulsory land readjustment regulation, powers to select the developer they prefer, if necessary by-passing the landowners and without the need of buying or expropriating the land. The dominant role of public bodies, especially in Valencia, clearly does not fit within the role that the policy network approach gives them, and it undermines some of the basic assumptions of that approach: that actors are necessarily interdependent, that public bodies must assume a more modest role and cannot be dominant.

The next paragraphs explain the different ways (or sub-variables) in which formal rules are used to influence capturing value increase. Per sub-variable, some further conclusions for the academic debate and the recommendations for the Dutch practice are given. The recommendations follow a gradual approach, from voluntary measures that fit within the 2008 Land Development Act, to more profound, legal modifications for the longer term.

Creating certainty beforehand about future building possibilities and contributions.

Summary of the findings

Municipalities in all three countries usually create certainty in early stages (before the negotiations with developers) and in different degrees, about what the landowner will be allowed to build. In the Netherlands, municipalities usually approve indicative, not legally binding plans, which create some certainty, for example *nota van uitgangspunten*, *stedenbouwkundig plan/visie*, *structuurvisie*, etc. In England something similar is done, also in indicative documents, and in Valencia through the approval of the legally binding General Land use Plans. The findings suggest that more certainty beforehand may result in less value capturing because it might stimulate land price increases, and municipalities lose a valuable negotiation tool. However, certainty about building possibilities, if accompanied by certainty about future contributions (see below), is not necessarily negative.

There are large differences in the certainty beforehand about future contributions. In Valencia, in early stages there is much certainty through (1) legal minimal standards, (2) local policy and (3) the approval of the General Plans. English municipalities usually create some certainty through the approval of (1) site-specific indicative plans that establish the contributions for the development in question, and (2) non site-specific, indicative generic policy documents that establish standard contributions. In the Netherlands, most of the time there is no certainty at all, neither created through legally binding nor indicative documents, before negotiations take place, or before the price of land is established. This certainty in Valencia and England has influenced the capturing of value increase in a positive way because: 1) it lowers the price of the land, because if there is no certainty, the developer pays too much for the land and has less financial room to contribute; 2) certainty lowers the price for which the developer accounts the land in the financial calculation of the operation, and the regular profit margin which the developer aims for; 3) certainty gives the public officers a strong policy base for requiring contributions during the negotiations.

Conclusions for the academic debate

The findings seem to confirm the second hypothesis:

Creating uncertainty in early stages of development processes about future building possibilities, and certainty about future contributions, can influence capturing value increase in a positive way.

Part of the literature on comparative planning systems in Europe may have wrongly concluded, at least with regard to the Spanish versus English and Dutch systems, that planning systems are tending to converge in their level of certainty. The findings might also be relevant to the debate in the planning profession, a debate in which flexibility is often advocated as a positive asset: for the findings underline that there should be a certain level of certainty about contributions, in order to better capturing value increase.

Recommendations for the Dutch practice

Dutch municipalities, before or together with the preparation of indicative plans that precede development, should create certainty about which contributions will be required from developers. The list of sorts of contributions included in the 2008 Decree is not enough for creating certainty, because that list is too general and in an early stage of the process does not allow developers to accurately calculate exactly which costs they have to contribute. Therefore, municipalities should create certainty about those costs that will be charged through a Development contributions plan. However, because this plan does not allow all the costs to be recovered, municipalities should not approve a Development contributions plan, but try to negotiate with the developer more contributions in an anterior Development agreement. Therefore, municipalities should create certainty about those costs that they wish to recover through anterior agreements, in addition to those that can be recovered through a Development contributions plan.

The recommended certainty can be created in different sorts of documents, many of which can complement each other: (1) site-specific documents accompanying the commonly used indicative site-specific plans; (2) generic documents including standard charges of an integral (covering all policy fields) or sectoral (covering just one policy field) character; and (3) general zoning plans including the obligatory contributions, possibly in standard form. Any of these sorts of documents should be preferably of an indicative character, because this fits better within the Dutch planning tradition. The recently introduced Structure vision (*Structuurvisie*) can be the ideal sort of document, not only because it is a flexible document, but also because it is obligatory for charging some sorts of contributions. The Dutch central government should also help and stimulate municipalities to create certainty, for example by making, together with the Association of Netherlands Municipalities, model documents. Should the voluntary measures not be widely applied in practice, then the central government should introduce some legal modifications: first obliging municipalities to prepare generic integral documents to be included in Structure visions, and second introducing minimal legal standard charges and prescriptions for the entire country.

Choosing the contents of binding rules

Summary of the findings and recommendations for the Dutch practice
Binding plans might be useful in negotiations if the municipality can include in them not only the physical zoning, but also aspects related to the financing and implementation of public infrastructure and facilities. Do binding plans regulate only a desired final picture, without stating who is responsible for its implementation? Or also the contributions that must be provided by the developer? Both in Valencia and England, planning law makes it possible to include in binding plans a wide range of requirements:

- Social/affordable housing: both in Valencia and England it is possible to prescribe social/affordable housing in the binding plans;
- On-site and off-site public infrastructure and facilities: both in Valencia and England it is possible to prescribe the obligation to contribute to on-site and off-site public infrastructure and facilities. In England, municipalities can also prescribe contributions towards the building, maintenance and exploitation costs of public buildings, including those of social facilities (for example education and social services).
- Investing and implementation schedules: in both countries, binding plans include schedules and deadlines within which contributions must be made.

All these possibilities are positive for capturing value increase. In the Netherlands, until the 2008 Act, none of these requirements could be prescribed in the binding rules, and this had a negative effect on capturing value increase. The 2008 Act made it possible for the first time to include almost all these requirements. Nowadays, it is possible to include social/affordable housing both in the Land use plan and the departures from it (a percentage of such housing) and in the Development contributions plan (allocation to the plots and number of units). It is also possible to introduce implementation schedules and contributions for most of the on-site infrastructure and for some sorts of off-site infrastructure in the Development contributions plan.

However, three limitations remain:

1. It is not possible to include in Development contributions plans contributions towards construction and maintenance/exploitation costs of social facilities (*maatschappelijke voorzieningen*), and it is uncertain whether such contributions can be agreed in anterior Development agreements. To make it possible to charge such contributions, article 6.2.5 of the 2008 Decree should be modified.
2. As already explained, many costs cannot be charged to the landowners through a Development contributions. Therefore the list of sorts of recoverable costs (articles 6.2.3 up to 6.2.6 of the 2008 Decree) should be enlarged.
3. In a Development contributions plan, landowners has right to the highest value for their land, which increases the accounted land costs and thus the probability of a deficit, a deficit that must be paid by the municipality. Therefore, article 6.13.5 of the 2008 Act, which prescribes that assessment of the value of land must follow expropriation law, should be modified.

Conclusions for the academic debate

This finding can be used to refine the 2nd hypothesis (in black letters the addition):

Creating Uncertainty in early stages of development processes about future building possibilities, and Certainty about future contributions ***(specially if it is possible to include all the contributions as obligatory in legally binding rules)*** *can influence capturing value increase in a positive way.*

Making binding rules conditional on the developer securing his contributions

Summary of the findings

The approval of binding plans containing generous value capturing arrangements and strict deadlines, as such, does not automatically mean that the developers will indeed implement them. In order to secure the implementation, additionally the developer needs to be bound to do that. In practice, Dutch municipalities often do condition the Land use plan and departures from it on a Development agreement in which the developer secures the contributions; however, they do not have the formal possibility of doing so in an open and straightforward way. This has negative side effects:

1. *Procedural risks:* after the sealing of the Development agreement, the Land use plan (or departure from it) must follow the complete procedure, which implies a risk of delay and modifications because of objections and appeals. In Valencia and England, the procedure of provisional approval of the binding plan *precedes* the sealing of the agreement, after which there is only a short definite approval. This means that in Valencia and England, parties can seal the agreement with a high certainty that the zoning plan is not going to be modified, and that there will be no delay;
2. *Appeal risks:* if a municipality refuses to approve a Land use plan because the developer does not secure contributions, there is always a risk of an appeal to the courts. In England and Valencia, planning law establishes that the developer

has to secure the contributions stated in the provisionally approved Land use plan, as a condition for definitive approval;
3. *Incongruent municipal public discourse:* in practice the municipality may need to hide the 'real reason' for the approval or refusal of Land use plans, i.e. whether the developer agrees to sign a Development agreement. In England and Valencia, the 'real reason' is publicly approved by the Local Council, and forms the open and transparent criteria for assessing whether or not to formally approve the plan.

In the Netherlands, once the Land use plan and the Development contributions plan have been approved, the developer/landowner can submit an application for a building permit. The novelty is that the municipality can now condition the building permit on the applicant securing his/her contributions; before the 2008 Act this was not possible. However, approving a Development contributions plan has some side effects: municipalities assume some financial risks because they are responsible for the calculations and may need to advance investments; they must put resources into making the plan and up-dating it yearly; and they must bear the consequences of delay in case developers/landowners do not apply for the building permit. In addition, as we saw above, not all the costs can be charged to the landowners. Thus in principle the best option for Dutch municipalities is to seal an anterior Development agreement before approving the Land use plan: this assures that contributions and deadlines are secured and no Development contributions plan is needed. Municipalities can informally request that developers seal such an agreement. However, the actual practice of informal conditioning may become more difficult after the 2008 Act. The Act has reinforced the obligation on the municipality to take a formal decision about an application to modify or depart from the Land use plan. If the municipality wishes to refuse the application (the possibility to refuse increases the negotiation powers of the municipality), this decision must be taken within eight weeks. Municipalities must justify their decision by referring to approved policy and zoning plans, and the applicant has now the possibility to appeal against a refusal or a non-determination. In other words, the municipality cannot openly and directly refuse the application with the argument that the applicant does not want to seal an agreement, but must find other arguments in the existing Land use plan, the Structure vision or other policy documents. If the municipality has already concluded that the physical and functional characteristics of the application are acceptable, there is actually little room left to refuse and thus to negotiate.

Conclusions for the academic debate

The findings can be used to refine the 2nd hypothesis (in black letters the addition):

Creating Uncertainty in early stages of development processes about future building possibilities, and Certainty about future contributions (specially if it is possible to include the contributions as obligatory in legally binding rules, ***and if it is possible openly and straightforwardly to make the approval of these rules conditional on***

a development agreement that secures the contributions*) can influence capturing value increase in a positive way.*

Recommendations for the Dutch practice
Although open and straightforward conditioning is not allowed, there are some alternative ways, and the new 2008 Act has added additional possibilities:

- To argue that contributions are necessary for the economic feasibility of the Land use plan: if the contributions are not secured and/or there is a deficit, the municipality should pay these costs. But because the municipality has no financial means to do so, it can refuse the plan, arguing that it is economically not feasible. This alternative has the same three side effects mentioned above: (1) procedural risks, (2) appeal risks (indirect conditioning through the economic feasibility of the plan is not the same as openly enumerating the contributions that the developer has to secure), and (3) incongruence of the municipality's public discourse.
- To condition through the Development contributions plan and proper cost recovery policy documents. After a planning application has been submitted, a calculation of the costs (*exploitatieopzet*) can make clear which part could be charged to the landowners through a Development contributions plan. If municipalities apply the recommendations made above to make and adopt cost recovery policy documents, it is possible to adequately defend that the application involves costs that surpass minimal on-site infrastructure provision, and also to include wider contributions towards other public infrastructure and facilities within and outside the development site in question. These cost recovery policy documents are very important: without them, it would most probably not be possible to calculate and properly argue *all* the costs. In case the calculation makes clear that the municipality cannot recover all the costs, municipalities can openly refuse the application, arguing that they cannot bear the deficit. This alternative for conditioning still has the 1st side effect mentioned above (procedural risks), and an additional side effect: if the developer agrees to secure in an anterior Development agreement the additional costs (but not those costs that can be charged through a Development contributions plan) municipalities cannot use the argument of economic feasibility to refuse the application.

To remove the disadvantages of both alternatives, it is recommended that the central Dutch government should allow in the planning law direct conditioning, similar to how this happens in Valencia and England. Therefore two specific modifications should be added to the 2008 Act and possible also to the Decree.

Modulating property rights in land

Summary of the findings
There is in England and the Netherlands a strong interdependency between local public bodies and landowners and developers. As a rule, the transactions that are needed to provide the infrastructure are quite dependent on agreements between

public bodies and the landowners and developers because none of the actors control all the needed resources: public bodies have the statutory powers for planning consent, but landowners/developers have the financial means and the exclusive right to develop the land. This interdependency cannot be resolved by using expropriation or the pre-emption right, because these instruments have severe limitations in practice, and they imply a direct organisational and financial involvement of public bodies. The situation in Valencia has changed radically after the regional government introduced the new planning law in 1994: since then there is, to provide the infrastructure, no longer any unavoidable dependence between public bodies and landowners. Valencian municipalities can now opt for compulsory land readjustment, without having to become directly involved. The municipality selects in a public tender the urbanising agent, and landowners can choose voluntary expropriation or participation in the development. If they choose expropriation, the urbanising agent pays the compensation and acquires the land. But if they decide to participate, they have to deliver the land needed for public infrastructure and facilities and pay to the urbanising agent a proportional share of the land development costs. In exchange, landowners share the value increase: after providing the infrastructure, the urbanising agent delivers the serviced building parcels to the landowners and transfers the public infrastructure, free of charge, to the municipality. In sum, although landowners still control the land, the mutual dependence in now easily avoidable as municipalities have the possibility to appoint a third party (who does not necessarily need to own the land) as the urbanising agent, and municipalities do not need to become directly financially involved. Also, the municipalities are not dependent on one particular urbanising agent, for they can point out a public land development company as urbanising agent or select the agent through a public tender.

The interdependency between public bodies and landowners in England and the Netherlands gives to the landowners the option to wait, which it is often used to oppose the requirements set by local public bodies. Especially in the Netherlands, public bodies often conclude that they cannot ask too much, which leads to low captured value increase. This interdependency frequently leads also to delays in the development processes, because landowners/developers refuse the requirements of the municipality, or because developers do not succeed in buying the land for a reasonable price. The outcome of the negotiations depends on the developers' and landowners' expectations that, by delaying negotiations, their profits would increase. Another consequence is higher accounted land costs: market parties are more interested in acquiring land, as control of the land puts them in a strong negotiating position, which in turn inflates the real and expected market value of land.

In addition, the findings suggest that interdependency leads to an inefficient and sluggish development process, in which costs are unnecessary high and different actors manage to appropriate part of the value increase. This leads to higher costs for infrastructure provision and plan preparation; in England and the Netherlands they are very often between 1.5 and 4 times higher than in Valencia. This leaves more financial room for the Valencian developers to contribute than for the Dutch and English developers.

Conclusions for the academic debate
The findings confirm the first hypothesis:

A specific form of splitting the property rights in land (separating infrastructure provision from property rights) can modify the power-relationships in the network of actors involved in urban regeneration, and this can improve capturing value increase.

This research sought empirical evidence relevant to the debate about separating development rights from property rights in land. The findings support the assumption that separating infrastructure provision from the control of landowners through a land readjustment regulation can improve the capturing of value increase. In addition, the findings suggest that the land readjustment regulation can have a deflationary effect on the costs for providing infrastructure and preparing plans, and possibly also on the accounted land costs. The regulation can also help to overcome problems of stagnation in constructing new housing. The findings are interesting for the Dutch debate. They coincide with the position taken by those who argue that the increase in private control of development land since the 1990s has been disadvantageous for the public goals and public finances. They also support the conclusion that shaping property rights can help to better achieve public goals in urban planning. For the Spanish debate, the findings support the critical approach of those who, in the 1990s, argued that breaking the monopolistic/oligopolistic position of landowners is the only way to assure good quality and adequate quantity of public infrastructure and facilities. More research is needed into an international comparison of land prices and development costs. Further research should focus on the differences in land prices, infrastructure provision costs and plan preparation costs, and should provide more data that could be used to fine-tune the conclusions.

Recommendations for the Dutch practice
First of all, municipalities could conduct more research into the profit margins in the early stages of development processes, and use this information in the negotiations with landowners and developers. This research should be made together with the first documents that create development expectations.

Second, to avoid the negative consequences of the dependency of municipalities on landowners/developers, it is recommended to work with a specific land readjustment contractual formula based on two different anterior Development agreements. A commercial developer, acting as a sort of Valencian urbanizing agent, can agree with landowners that, in exchange for sharing development profits, they participate in the development. The municipality should support this by conditioning the binding rules on the landowners achieving an agreement with the developer-urbanizing agent, by if necessary making use of the expropriation and pre-emption powers, and by approving a Development contributions plan. The recommendation, if applied, should provide several advantages: (a) it annuls the need to buy the land, or at least to buy *all* the land, as landowners themselves participate in the operation; (b) it reduces the risks of delay resulting from landowners, instead of supporting the operation, behaving in an strategic way (i.e. waiting) to obtain the highest possible price for their land; (c) *a* and *b* should considerably reduce the costs of the operation: there should be no need to buy land in advance, and it should reduce the amounts reserved for unexpected expenses and the plan preparation costs; (d) *c* should considerably reduce the financial costs, as there is need of less external financing.

However, the approval of a Development contributions plan, which in the recommendation might be necessary to force some landowners to cooperate, has some disadvantages, as mentioned before. Also, expropriating land is very expensive and involves a direct financial involvement of the municipality, and in addition is a politically sensitive measure that cannot be exercised if landowners express willingness to carry out the development themselves. To remove these disadvantages, the Dutch central government, inspired by the Valencian land readjustment regulation, should introduce a land readjustment regulation in planning law.

Epilogue

At the end of the 80's and begin of the 90's, the Dutch government introduced relevant changes to diminish public subsidization and reduce the financial risks of public bodies in urban development. However, practice shows that this has not reduced the need for public subsidization and has not produced new neighbourhoods with good public infrastructure and facilities. The 2008 Land Development Act is an effort to solve this problem. Although the Act might, under certain circumstances, be helpful, it suffers from two fundamental shortcomings. First, it assumes that the landowner is the only legitimate owner of the value increase that arises from rezoning the land. Here the Dutch legislator refused to introduce another possibility that is popular in other European countries: that public bodies also have right to a share of the value increase. Second, it assumes that the only way of enforcing public goals must be a direct and financial involvement of public bodies. This resulted in an unnecessarily complex set of legal instruments that charges municipalities with too many tasks and risks - too many considering their capacities. The experience in England and Spain shows that public leadership in urban development must be based on simple and clear roles: public bodies regulate beforehand, private bodies implement and assume all the corresponding risks.

A final remark: the international financial and economic crisis is leading already to less public expenditure. If no measures are taken to deviate part of the value increase to pay public infrastructure and facilities, public budgetary cuts will place urban development and its quality under serious pressure, especially in the regeneration of urban sites.

PARKING

Samenvatting

Hoofdstuk 1 - Introductie: problemen met de financiering van publieke doelen in stedelijke herstructurering in Nederland

Het is nog niet zo lang geleden dat Nederlandse overheden vaak een actief grondbeleid voerden: ze kochten de grond, maakten die bouw- en woonrijp en verkochten de bouwkavels aan woningcorporaties of commerciële ontwikkelaars. Eind jaren '80 werd een aantal beleidsveranderingen doorgevoerd die tot een geleidelijke overgang naar meer passieve of faciliterende vormen van grondbeleid leidde. Het zijn tegenwoordig steeds vaker de woningcorporaties en marktpartijen die grond kopen en locaties ontwikkelen.

Zowel stadsuitbreiding als herstructurering van binnenstedelijke locaties brengen meestal een stijging van de economische waarde van grond met zich mee, maar ook de noodzaak aan investeringen, zoals in openbare faciliteiten, wegen, kabels en leidingen, maatschappelijke voorzieningen en sociale woningbouw, schadevergoedingen, en dergelijke (hierna kortweg: 'openbare infrastructuur en faciliteiten'). Wanneer gemeenten een actief grondbeleid voeren, kunnen ze deze kosten betalen dankzij de uitgifte van bouwkavels. Echter, sinds gemeenten steeds minder vaak over de grond beschikken lukt dat steeds minder goed, terwijl grondeigenaren niet geneigd blijken te zijn om bij te dragen aan de kosten. Dit heeft geleid tot een versobering van de openbare infrastructuur en faciliteiten en tot de noodzaak van publieke subsidiëring.

In dit onderzoek wordt de vraag gesteld of, in die gevallen waarbij de grond in binnenstedelijke locaties in private handen is, de economische waardestijging die het gevolg is van bestemmingswijziging (geheel of gedeeltelijk) zou kunnen worden gebruikt om de openbare infrastructuur en faciliteiten te betalen. In dit onderzoek wordt nagegaan of een aantal wettelijke instrumenten, de 'formele regels relevant voor ruimtelijke ordening', gebruikt zou kunnen worden om grondeigenaren te verleiden om mee te betalen. Met andere woorden: om overheden beter van waardestijging van de grond te laten profiteren om de nodige infrastructuur en faciliteiten te betalen (kortweg: 'publiek waardestijgingsverhaal').

Formele regels die relevant zijn voor ruimtelijke ordening zijn: bindende voorschriften over het gebruik van grond en vastgoed, en over de administratieve procedure van deze voorschriften; grondeigendomsrechten; en niet bindende ruimtelijke beleidsdocumenten. Er zijn verschillende soorten waardestijging: veroorzaakt door investeringen in infrastructuur, door herbestemming van de grond, of gewoon door de algemene toename van de vraag naar grond. Dit onderzoek onderscheidt drie subbegrippen onder 'publiek verhaal van waardestijging': 'kostenverhaal' (het verhalen, via de bijdragen van grondeigenaren, van de kosten van openbare infrastructuur en faciliteiten), 'waardevangst' (vangst door overheden die bijvoorbeeld in infrastructuur geïnvesteerd hebben in de omgeving van het in waarde gestegen vastgoed), en 'baatafroming' (waarbij een overheidsinstantie alle soorten waardestijging vangen).

Een fundamentele vraag is wie de waardestijging zou moeten kunnen vangen. Volgens een conservatief-liberale traditie hoort alle waardestijging toe aan de grondeigenaar, terwijl een alternatieve traditie bepleit dat ze aan de gemeenschap toebehoort. Een vaak voorkomend onderwerp in de neoklassieke economische theorie is het belasten van de waardestijging. Deze ideologische verschillen hebben geleid tot verschillende instrumenten voor het verhalen van waardestijging, waarvan sommige een volledige baatafroming nastreven en andere alleen het internaliseren van de negatieve gevolgen van bouwplannen. Omdat in Nederland alleen deze tweede vorm van waardestijgingvangst is toegestaan, maakt dit onderzoek beleidsaanbevelingen voor kostenverhaal en niet voor baatafroming. Sommige aanbevelingen passen binnen het huidige wettelijke kader, inclusief de nieuwe Wet ruimtelijke ordening en de in afdeling 6.4 van deze wet inbegrepen Grondexploitatiewet. Andere aanbevelingen impliceren een wijziging van dit wettelijke kader. Dit is dus het probleem dat dit onderzoek probeert op te lossen:

Hoe zouden de formele regels relevant voor ruimtelijke ordening gebruikt kunnen worden in de ontwikkeling van omvangrijke herstructurering- en functieveranderingsplannen op private grond in Nederland, opdat de rendabele delen de onrendabele delen betalen?

Om hier een antwoord op te geven, dienen eerst de volgende onderzoeksvragen te worden beantwoord:

Voorbereidende onderzoeksvraag 1: *Hoe kunnen de formele regels relevant voor ruimtelijke ordening gebruikt worden in omvangrijke herstructurering- en functieveranderingsplannen op private grond?*

- Voorbereidende onderzoeksvraag 2: *Hoeveel waardestijging in omvangrijke herstructurering- en functieveranderingsplannen op private grond wordt verhaald om de openbare infrastructuur en faciliteiten te betalen?*
- Voorbereidende onderzoeksvraag 3: *Hoe wordt de mate van publieke waardestijgingsverhaal beïnvloed door de manier waarop de formele regels relevant voor ruimtelijk ordening worden gebruikt?*
- Hoofdonderzoeksvraag: *Hoe zouden de formele regels relevant voor ruimtelijke ordening gebruikt kunnen worden in Nederland om ervoor te zorgen dat de rendabele onderdelen de onrendabele onderdelen zo veel mogelijk betalen?*

Hoofdstuk 2 – Theoretisch kader: publiek verhaal van waardestijging binnen beleidsnetwerken

De herstructurering van een binnenstedelijke locatie kan worden bestudeerd als ware het een beleidsnetwerk waarin publieke partijen proberen meer waardestijging te verhalen door met andere partijen de interactie aan te gaan. De 'beleidsnetwerkbenadering' is het resultaat van academisch debat omtrent de veranderde rol van publieke en private partijen in de laatste decennia. De oorsprong van deze benadering ligt in de politieke wetenschap in de vroege jaren '70. Terwijl publieke sturing in de traditionele intra-organisaties benadering een autoritaire activiteit is, zijn in de beleidsnetwerkbenadering de machtsverhoudingen tussen partijen minder hiërarchisch. Door de beschikbaarheid van middelen en de resulterende onderlinge afhankelijkheden te bestuderen, is het mogelijk om de structurele factoren bloot te leggen die machtsverhoudingen verklaren.

1. Een eerste structurele factor is dat beleidsnetwerken uit verschillende actoren bestaan die elk hun eigen doelen nastreven, wat in potentie conflicten met zich mee kan brengen. Tegelijkertijd zijn partijen afhankelijk van elkaar omdat niemand alle middelen controleert die nodig zijn om ieders doel te bereiken. De sterkte van deze afhankelijkheid ligt aan het belang en de 'vervangbaarheid' van de middelen. Zowel de verdeling van middelen als de machtsverhoudingen tussen actoren zijn gereguleerd door formele regels (wetgeving). Aan de andere kant geven de verdeling van middelen en de machtsverhoudingen vaak juist vorm aan formele regels. Een tweede structurele factor is dat overheden altijd afhankelijk zijn van de middelen van anderen. Volgens de netwerkbenadering zijn overheden daarom niet meer dé dominante partij, maar meer een *primus inter pares*. Critici voeren aan dat de netwerkbenadering de status van de overheid devalueert. In deze kritische visie is de betrokkenheid van overheden in sa-

menwerkingsvormen met andere partijen - wat typerend voor beleidsnetwerken is - negatief omdat netwerken transparant noch controleerbaar zijn.

Dit onderzoek kan worden gezien als een kritiek op de veronderstelling dat overheden in stedelijke herstructurering *altijd* afhankelijk zijn van andere partijen. Overheden hoeven niet altijd de rol van *primus inter pares* te accepteren: zijn kunnen effectief en met recht boven de andere partijen staan en die sturen. Het onderzoek biedt twee maatregelen aan om interacties binnen beleidsnetwerken te veranderen en zodoende overheden meer waardestijging te laten verhalen: eerst door grondeigendomsrechten aan te passen en vervolgens door de mate van zekerheid en flexibiliteit in planvorming te veranderen.

Grondeigendomsrechten

Men zou kunnen denken dat eigendomsrechten aan de grondeigenaar een totale vrijheid bieden om zijn grond te gebruiken. Echter, de realiteit is dat formele regels deze rechten beperken. Privaatrechtelijke regels zijn bedoeld om het normale verkeer van eigendomsrechten tussen individuen te organiseren. Publiekrechtelijke regels reguleren hoe overheden beperkingen kunnen opleggen aan eigendomsrechten van derden. Het publiekrecht heeft, sinds in de 19^e eeuw de *sociale functie* van eigendom en volksgezondheid aan belang wonnen, aanzienlijke beperkingen opgelegd aan grondeigendomsrechten. Tegenwoordig kan de eigenaar zijn grond alleen gebruiken binnen de grenzen van wettelijke voorschriften, en waar nodig slechts nadat hij hier toestemming voor heeft gekregen.

In Groot-Brittannië, Nederland en Spanje bestaat al langere tijd debat over beperkingen van eigendomsrechten. In 1947 introduceerde een Britse wet de zogenaamde 'nationalisatie van eigendomsrechten', wat tot gevolg had dat waardestijging werd belast. Tegenwoordig bestaat deze belasting echter niet meer. De nationalisatie van eigendomsrechten is niet verder doorgevoerd, in die zin dat het principe dat grondeigenaren de enigen zijn die op hun grond kunnen bouwen, onaangetast bleef.

In Nederland zijn bovengenoemde problemen met de financiering van openbare infrastructuur en faciliteiten onderwerp van controversie en debat geweest. Zo is de vraag bediscussieerd of het publiekrecht aan overheden voldoende instrumenten biedt om regie te voeren op ruimtelijke ontwikkeling. Sommige auteurs zijn hier optimistisch over, anderen nogal sceptisch. De sceptici vinden dat eigendomsrechten een soort oligopolie van grondeigenaren creëert. Zij bepleiten een aanpassing van eigendomsrechten om vrije concurrentie te bevorderen.

In Spanje hebben overheden vanaf de 19^e eeuw moeilijkheden ondervonden om de openbare infrastructuur en faciliteiten te betalen. Dat heeft geleid tot meerdere voorstellen en maatregelen die betrekking hebben op eigendomsrechten. In 1956 werd een stedelijke herverkavelingregeling geïntroduceerd die het profiteren van de waardestijging voorwaardelijk stelde aan het nemen van verantwoordelijkheid over de grondexploitatie. Grondeigenaren zijn sindsdien verplicht om de openbare infrastructuur en faciliteiten te realiseren en te betalen. Ter compensatie delen ze de bouwkavels. Gemeenten zijn verplicht om een Algemeen Bestemmingsplan voor het gehele gemeentelijke grondgebied vast te stellen om hiermee grondeigenaren zekerheid te bieden over de bouwmogelijkheden. De gedetailleerdheid van dit plan en zijn sterk juridisch bindend karakter geven Spanje internationaal een bijzondere plek. De herverkavelingregeling resulteerde echter niet in voldoende en goede openbare infrastructuur en faciliteiten. Vanaf de jaren '80 bepleitten critici (in het bijzonder García-Bellido) om een einde te maken aan de oligopolie van grondeigenaren en de ontwikkelingsrechten aan de overheid te geven. Geïnspireerd door dit voorstel introduceerde de regio Valencia in 1994 een wet om de grondspeculatie te bestrijden en het publieke verhaal van waardestijging te verbeteren. In feite betekent deze wet een splitsing van de grondexploitatie van grondeigendomsrechten.

Zekerheid en flexibiliteit in ruimtelijke planvorming

In de academische wereld en in de ruimtelijke ordeningspraktijk wordt een levendig debat gevoerd over de noodzakelijke maat van flexibiliteit in ruimtelijke planvorming: moet planvorming in een vroeg stadium zekerheid creëren over het plan (opdat overheden het resultaat kunnen controleren) of juist flexibiliteit bieden (om aanpassing aan de omstandigheden mogelijk te maken)? Wanneer ruimtelijke plannen in een vroeg stadium vastgesteld worden, gedetailleerde voorschriften bevatten, en het niet mogelijk is om ze achteraf te wijzigen, dan is er minder flexibiliteit en meer zekerheid dan *vice versa*. In de jaren '60 had 'flexibiliteit' vaak een negatieve bijklank, tegenwoordig wordt daar vaak positiever naar gekeken. Later zullen we zien dat de mate van flexibiliteit belangrijke gevolgen heeft voor het publieke waardestijgingsverhaal.

Wat flexibiliteit en zekerheid in planvorming betreft, zijn er twee tradities. In de 'plangeleide' traditie (zoals het Nederlandse planologische stelsel) wordt uitgegaan van het bieden van een grote mate van zekerheid over de toekomstige ontwikkelingsmogelijkheden in een vroeg stadium met behulp van juridisch bindende ruimtelijke plannen (zoals het bestemmingsplan). In de 'ontwikkelingsgeleide' traditie (zoals het Britse stelsel) wordt uitgegaan van minder zekerheid en meer ruimte voor onderhandelingen met ontwikkelaars en grondeigenaren, ook al kunnen in een vroeg stadium indicatieve ruimtelijke plannen bestaan. Deze verschillen zijn het gevolg van historische verschillen in het rechtsstelsel: plangeleide tradities leunen op de centrale rol van wetgeving in de rechtsstaat, en ontwikkelingsgeleide tradities op de centrale rol van jurisprudentie en het principe van procedurele billijkheid.

Causaal model: welke variabelen beïnvloeden het publieke waardestijgingsverhaal in stedelijke herstructurering?

Verschillende actoren zijn betrokken bij stedelijke herstructurering: publieke en private, met regulerende bevoegdheden of niet, met of zonder grond, met een direct of indirect belang. Allen interacteren met elkaar binnen een complex van variabelen en een van de uitkomsten is een bepaalde mate van waardestijgingsverhaal. Wanneer herstructurering tot waardestijging leidt is er een initiële winst. Deze initiële winst dient echter zodanig te worden verdeeld zodat uiteindelijk een finale winst overblijft waarmee de openbare infrastructuur en faciliteiten betaald kunnen worden. De initiële winst, en of die zich laat vertalen in een finale winst, is afhankelijk van verscheidene variabelen:

A. Context variabelen die de hoogte van de initiële winst beïnvloeden: vastgoedmarkten, plan- en locatie-eigenschappen, arbeids- en bouwmaterialenmarkten, en belastingregime.
B. Context variabelen die de verdeling van de initiële winst beïnvloeden, dat wil zeggen: **de formele regels die relevant zijn voor ruimtelijke ordening**.
C. Acties van direct in het project betrokken actoren, **inclusief die actoren met formele regulatorische bevoegdheden**, welke de hoogte van de initiële winst beïnvloeden: hoe overheden de inhoud en fysieke begrenzing van plannen bepalen.
D. Acties van direct in het project betrokken actoren, **inclusief die actoren met formele regulatorische bevoegdheden**, welke de verdeling van de initiële winst beïnvloeden: hoe overheden gebruik maken van formele regels relevant voor ruimtelijke ordening, hoe publieke en private partijen interacteren, en specifieke omstandigheden.

Dit onderzoek focust op de manier waarop de vet gekleurde variabelen gemanipuleerd kunnen worden. Bovendien wordt rekening gehouden met alle andere variabelen omdat ze allemaal gezamenlijk de hoogte en de verdeling van de initiële winst (de publieke waardestijgingsvangst) beïnvloeden. Er zijn vele manieren waarop de initiële winst kan weglekken zodat die niet meer beschikbaar is om openbare infrastructuur en faciliteiten te betalen. Een manier is dat de inbrengwaarde van grond veel hoger kan zijn dan de minimale grondwaarde. Met andere woorden: hoger dan de waarde van de bestaande bestemming. Bijvoorbeeld, in het bestudeerde project *Kop van Oost* in Groningen, was de minimale grondwaarde circa € 3.6 miljoen, terwijl de inbrengwaarde tenminste € 12 miljoen was. Een andere manier waarop de initiële winst kan weglekken is door het reguliere winstpercentage dat ontwikkelaars als verdienste in rekening brengen.

Aan het begin van planprocessen zijn zowel de inbrengwaarde als het reguliere winstpercentage nog niet vastgelegd. Beide kunnen in een later stadium hoog vast komen te staan, bijvoorbeeld omdat er veel zekerheid is over de toekomstige *bouwmogelijkheden* (hoeveel en wat zal de grondeigenaar kunnen bouwen) terwijl de zekerheid over toekomstige *bijdragen* (hoeveel de grondeigenaar zal moeten bijdragen, *in natura* of *in pecunia*) laag is.

Daarbij is de onderhandelingspositie van overheden ook relevant. Wanneer ontwikkelaars of grondeigenaren al zekerheid hebben over bouwmogelijkheden, dan kan de gemeente minder gemakkelijk bijdragen van private partijen vragen. Wanneer er wel zekerheid is over de verplichte bijdragen, dan is de onderhandelingspositie van de gemeente juist sterker omdat deze bijdragen dan het uitgangspunt in de onderhandelingen zijn. De gemeentelijke onderhandelaars hebben in dat geval een sterke beleidsbasis voor hun eisen. Tenslotte, de onderhandelingspositie van de gemeente zal ook beter zijn wanneer de gemeente de vaststelling van het bestemmingsplan openlijk voorwaardelijk kan stellen aan een overeenkomst waarin de ontwikkelaar zijn bijdragen zekert. Grondeigenaren hebben een goede onderhandelingspositie omdat ze over de grond beschikken, wat hen in staat stelt om de maximale prijs te vragen voor hun grond. Tegelijkertijd kunnen grondeigenaren planprocessen vertragen, en vertraging brengt hogere grondexploitatiekosten met zich mee die ten koste gaan van de initiële winst. Bijvoorbeeld, in *Kop van Oost* waren de grondexploitatiekosten circa € 7 miljoen, terwijl ze veel lager hadden kunnen zijn, namelijk ongeveer € 2 miljoen. Vertraging kan het gevolg zijn van moeizame onderhandelingen met een veelheid aan grondeigenaren, maar ook een bewuste strategie van grondeigenaren wanneer ze verwachten dat de grondprijs kan stijgen in de toekomst. Het gevolg van deze interacties kan zijn dat er weinig overblijft van de initiële winst. In *Kop van Oost* moest de gemeente de openbare infrastructuur en faciliteiten subsidiëren terwijl een initiële winst van mogelijk € 18,5 miljoen was weggelekt.

Twee maatregelen om publiek waardestijgingsverhaal te verbeteren = twee hypotheses

De twee bovengenoemde maatregelen ter verbetering van publieke waardestijgingvangst worden geformuleerd als hypotheses:

1. Een specifieke vorm van scheiding van grondeigendomsrechten (grondexploitatie scheiden van eigendomsrechten) kan de machtsverhoudingen in het actorennetwerk in stedelijke herstructurering veranderen, en dit kan het publieke waardestijgingsverhaal verbeteren.

2. Onzekerheid creëren in een vroeg stadium van planprocessen over toekomstige bouwmogelijkheden, en zekerheid over toekomstige bijdragen, kan het publieke waardestijgingsverhaal positief beïnvloeden.

Hoofdstuk 3 – Methode

Dit onderzoek bestudeert een 'fenomeen', namelijk de interactie tussen gemeenten die gebruik maken van formele regels relevant voor ruimtelijke ordening en de ontwikkelaars en grondeigenaren die een locatie herstructureren. De focus ligt op een aantal variabelen, namelijk het gebruik van formele regels relevant voor ruimtelijke ordening (de onafhankelijke variabele) en het door overheden verhalen van de waardestijging (de afhankelijke variabele). Het einddoel is om kennis te produceren die als basis kan dienen voor het formuleren van beleidsaanbevelingen ten einde het waardestijgingsverhaal in de Nederlandse praktijk van herstructurering te verbeteren, en tegelijkertijd planprocessen niet te vertragen.

In dit onderzoek worden een aantal keuzes gemaakt. De eerste is dat deze studie op een beperkt aantal cases leunt: vier in Valencia, drie in Engeland en vier in Nederland. Het was niet haalbaar om voldoende cases te bestuderen waarmee een representatieve statistische analyse mogelijk was, noch om de relatie tussen de onafhankelijke en afhankelijke variabelen perfect te isoleren. Daarnaast biedt case-onderzoek meer informatie over het fenomeen en diens interacties met de context dan een eenmalig enquête. In Engeland en Nederland vond de dataverzameling plaats voor de aanvang van de internationale financiële en economische crisis in de zomer van 2008. In Spanje vond ze voor de aanvang van de vastgoedcrisis, aan het eind van 2007, plaats. Voor belangrijke aspecten is er een laatste dataverzamelingsronde uitgevoerd, aan het einde van 2009 en gedurende 2010.

De tweede keuze was om de validiteit van de bevindingen te optimaliseren en hiermee een risico dat inherent aan case onderzoek is, te vermijden, namelijk dat zodanige specifieke kennis wordt geproduceerd dat het niet kan leiden tot generaliseerbare conclusies en beleidsaanbevelingen. Dit leidde ertoe dat drie groepen maatregelen geïntroduceerd zijn om zowel de interne als de externe validiteit te versterken:

1. De hypothetisch-deductieve methode te hanteren om de twee hypotheses empirisch te falsificeren;
2. Varianten van de 'method of difference' te hanteren om het risico te vermijden van derde variabelen en van spurieuze correlaties tussen de onafhankelijke en afhankelijke variabelen: vervaardiging van een lijst met mogelijke derde variabelen om te evalueren wat hun rol is in elk land en case; beperking van de totale populatie van cases, en tevens die landen te selecteren met een vergelijkbare politieke, economische en sociale achtergrond om met beide maatregelen de context zo constant mogelijk te houden; voor uitvoeriger onderzoek landen te selecteren met tegenovergestelde planologische stelsels om hiermee de variantie in de onafhankelijke variabele te maximaliseren, wat geleid heeft tot een internationale vergelijking; die cases selecteren die innovatieve praktijken in zich meedragen, en tenslotte, als dat mogelijk was, het fenomeen bestuderen voor en na een verandering in de onafhankelijke variabele (een wettelijke wijziging);
3. Verscheidene technieken te hanteren waarmee de externe validiteit (of generaliseerbaarheid) kon worden versterkt: representatieve cases te selecteren en alternatieve, complementaire bronnen te gebruiken naast de cases.

Dit onderzoek is niet gericht op het bestuderen van het gehele fenomeen, dat wil zeggen op een omschrijving van *alle* eigenschappen van het fenomeen. In dit onderzoek gaat het om het identificeren van de relevante variabelen in het totaal van variabelen die het fenomeen kunnen karakteriseren. Daarom focust dit onderzoek op een aantal subvariabelen van de onafhankelijke en afhankelijke variabelen. Om die te identificeren werd een afhankelijkheidsmodel ontwikkeld en tevens gebruik gemaakt van het theoretische kader en het causaal model, inclusief de twee hypotheses. De onafhankelijke variabele (formele regels relevant voor ruimtelijke ordening) werd zodoende verdeeld in vijf subvariabelen om preciezer te kunnen analyseren hoe overheden de formele regels gebruiken (voorbereidende onderzoeksvraag 1):

a) Zekerheid voorafgaand over toekomstige bouwmogelijkheden en bijdragen;
b) Inhoud van bindende voorschriften;
c) Bindende voorschriften voorwaardelijk stellen aan zekering door ontwikkelaar van zijn bijdragen;
d) Grondeigendomsrechten wijzigen;
e) Procedure voor voorbereiding en vaststelling van relevante bindende voorschriften: garanties voor initiatiefnemers; flexibiliteit om bestaande bindende voorschriften te wijzigen; flexibiliteit om plangrenzen van bindende voorschriften af the stemmen op onderhandelingsproces met grondeigenaren.

De afhankelijke variabele (het publiek waardestijgingsverhaal) werd ook onderverdeeld in een aantal subvariabelen: alle mogelijke soorten bijdragen van ontwikkelaars en grondeigenaren, en tevens mogelijke neveneffecten, in het bijzonder het tempo van het planproces. Hiermee werd het mogelijk om de mate van publiek waardestijgingsverhaal te evalueren (voorbereidende onderzoeksvraag 2). Voorbereidende onderzoeksvraag 3 is beantwoord door het soort causale relatie tussen de onafhankelijke en afhankelijke variabelen af te leiden. Het antwoord is in feite een geteste hypothese, bijvoorbeeld: "wanneer gemeenten in een vroeg stadium van planprocessen vastleggen welke bijdragen ontwikkelaars moeten betalen, dan zal het publieke waardestijgingsverhaal verbeteren".

Nadat in hoofdstukken 5 tot en met 7 elke voorbereidende onderzoeksvraag is beantwoord voor alle drie landen, worden in hoofdstuk 8 op basis van de geteste hypotheses conclusies getrokken voor het academische debat. Al deze antwoorden en geteste hypotheses, met daarbij eveneens specifieke kennis over de Nederlandse situatie (wetgeving, politieke en culturele overwegingen) zijn nodig om in hoofdstuk 9 een antwoord te geven op de hoofdonderzoeksvraag, namelijk om beleidsaanbevelingen te formuleren voor de Nederlandse praktijk.

Hoofdstuk 4 – Quick scan: formele regels relevant voor ruimtelijke ordening in West-Europese landen

De eerste stap in het internationaal vergelijkende onderzoek is verkennend onderzoek naar de onafhankelijke variabele in Nederland en in acht andere West-Europese landen geweest: Duitsland, Engeland (onderdeel van Groot-Brittannië), Vlaanderen (onderdeel van België), Frankrijk, Zweden, Denemarken, Italië en Spanje (regio Valencia). Door deze landen, die een vergelijkbare context kennen, te bestuderen, is de invloed van mogelijke derde variabelen verminderd. De tweede stap is het besluit om de regio Valencia en Engeland te selecteren omdat zij de breedste variantie toonden in de onafhankelijke variabele (zij staan voor tegenovergestelde modellen van planologische stelsels). Hiermee zijn de kansen vergroot dat betekenisvolle bevindingen worden geproduceerd. Deze twee landen, samen met Nederland, zijn dan ook het onderwerp van diepgaand onderzoek in hoofdstukken 5 t/m 7.

Uit het verkennende onderzoek kwamen belangrijke verschillen tussen de landen naar boven. Wat betreft de plaats van bindende voorschriften in het onderhandelingsproces staat Engeland voor het 'ontwikkelingsgeleide' planologische stelsel, en Spanje/Valencia (samen, maar in mindere mate, met Frankrijk, Italië en Vlaanderen) voor het 'plangeleide' stelsel. Nederland, net zoals Duitsland, Zweden en Denemarken, volgt in de praktijk de ontwikkelingsgeleide aanpak omdat de bindende voorschriften die nieuwe ontwikkeling mogelijk maken pas vastgesteld worden nadat geïnteresseerde ontwikkelaars over de inhoud onderhandeld hebben met de gemeente. Wat betreft de inhoud van bindende voorschriften, heeft Nederland (tot 2008), samen met Denemarken, bijna geen uitvoeringsgerichte bindende voorschriften. Dat wilt zeggen: voorschriften gericht op de planuitvoering (dit zijn documenten die de praktische uitvoering van een plan voorschrijven: fasering- en financiële voorschriften, of andere soorten regels bedoeld voor de planuitvoering). Engeland en Valencia hebben dit soort voorschriften wel. De Nederlandse bindende voorschriften (geen rekening houdend met het nieuwe exploitatieplan) hebben samen met de Deense, de meest beperkte inhoud (zij kunnen niet veel meer voorschrijven dan ruimtelijk relevante aspecten), terwijl Engeland de breedste heeft. Tenslotte, in Nederland, Duitsland, Frankrijk, Zweden, Denemarken en Vlaanderen kan de vaststelling van bindende voorschriften (planologische inpassing) niet, formeel en openlijk, voorwaardelijk worden gesteld aan de bereidheid van de ontwikkelaar om de uitvoering te zekeren (dat de ontwikkelaar in een contract de verplichting op zich neemt om de openbare infrastructuur te realiseren, grond vrij van kosten over te dragen aan de gemeente, bij te dragen aan de kosten, en dergelijke). In Engeland, Valencia en Italië is dit wel mogelijk en is daar zelfs de standaardprocedure.

In alle landen is het recht om te bouwen onderdeel van de eigendomsrechten. Er is geen land waar eigendomsrechten volledig gescheiden zijn van het recht om de grond te ontwikkelen. Met andere woorden: grondeigenaren zijn de enigen die geautoriseerd zijn om op hun grond te bouwen, en zij kunnen anderen belemmeren om dit te doen. Echter, in Valencia, Duitsland, Frankrijk en Zweden wordt de aanleg van openbare infrastructuur en faciliteiten in de ruimtelijke ordeningswetgeving expliciet geïdentificeerd als een publieke taak, terwijl in Nederland, Engeland en de andere landen dat niet zo is. In Valencia en, in mindere mate ook in Duitsland en Zweden, kunnen de openbare infrastructuur en faciliteiten, dankzij de mogelijkheid van gedwongen herverkaveling, worden aangelegd zonder overeenstemming te hebben bereikt met de grondeigenaren. Daar tegenover staat dat in Nederland, Engeland, Frankrijk, Italië, Zweden, Vlaanderen en Denemarken, de aanleg van openbare infrastructuur en faciliteiten wel afhankelijk is van overeenstemming met de grondeigenaren. Deze afhankelijkheid kan alleen worden vermeden als de overheid directe verantwoordelijkheid draagt, in zowel financiële als organisatorische zin (de grond kopen, en/of voorkeursrecht, onteigening of baatbelasting toepassen). Wat de procedure voor de vaststelling van bindende voorschriften betreft, is het in Engeland soms mogelijk om reeds vastgestelde bindende voorschriften ingrijpend te wijzigingen door middel van een simpele en korte procedure, terwijl daar in Nederland en Valencia een zware procedure voor nodig is.

Hoofdstuk 5 – Valencia

De Spaanse regio Valencia heeft bijna alle bevoegdheden in ruimtelijke ordeningswetgeving en subsidieert, samen met de centrale regering in Madrid en een groot aantal gemeenten, een aantal programma's gericht op de herstructurering en revitalisering van historische gebieden en verpauperde buurten. Echter, het leeuwendeel van herstructurering dat in de laatste decennia heeft plaatsgevonden, is het initiatief geweest van private partijen, die zonder publieke subsidies verouderde binnenstedelijke bedrijfs- en kantoorlocaties hebben getransformeerd tot woningen, winkelruimte en kantoren. Dit onderzoek focust op dit soort herstructureringsprojecten.

Om een locatie te transformeren moeten eerst de bestaande bindende voorschriften worden gewijzigd. Er zijn twee soorten bindende voorschriften: het 'Algemeen bestemmingsplan' en het 'Gedetailleerde plan'. Algemene plannen dekken het hele gemeentelijk grondgebied en hebben een juridisch bindend karakter. In uitbreidingsgebieden bestemmen ze de grond in bebouwbaar en niet-bebouwbaar, schrijven ze de mogelijke typologieën voor, de openbare hoofdinfrastructuur en hoofdfaciliteiten, en het exacte aantal bouwrechten waar elke eigenaar recht op heeft (in de vorm van een *floor space index*). De bouwrechten geven een hoge mate van zekerheid over de toekomstige bouwmogelijkheden. Tevens, in uitbreidingsgebieden die binnen afzienbare tijd dienen te worden ontwikkeld, en in binnenstedelijke locaties, houden Algemene plannen ook zeer gedetailleerde voorschriften in. Die voorschriften hebben betrekking op de rooilijn, de hoogte en het volume van de gebouwen en de kleine openbare infrastructuur en faciliteiten. Gedetailleerde plannen zijn bedoeld voor specifieke locaties. Als het Algemene plan niet reeds gedetailleerd is, wordt dat in een Gedetailleerd plan gedaan.

Traditioneel hebben Spaanse overheden altijd getracht om de onrendabele onderdelen van stedelijke herstructurering te betalen met de rendabele onderdelen. Dit streven leidde in 1956 tot de introductie van de reeds genoemde stedelijke herverkavelingregeling. Grondeigenaren werden verplicht om de herverkaveling van eigendomsgrenzen en de grondexploitatie zelf te organiseren en te betalen. Wanneer grondeigenaren hier niet aan meewerkten kon de gemeente de eigenaren terzijde schuiven door gedwongen herverkaveling of onteigening toe te passen. In 1978 introduceerde de centrale regering een reeks wettelijke minimale standaarden van openbare infrastructuur en faciliteiten welke, samen met het Algemene plan, zekerheid schiep over de toekomstige verplichte bijdragen. Echter, de herverkavelingregeling uit 1956 stimuleerde grondspeculatie (wat leidde tot hoge inbrengwaardes voor de grond), ontmoette veel verzet van de grondeigenaren en leidde tot vertraging van planprocessen (beide leidden tot onnodige meerkosten in de grondexploitatie). Deze tekortkomingen leidden tot bouwplannen met onvoldoende openbare infrastructuur en te massieve, opgeblazen bebouwing. In 1994 introduceerde de regionale regering van Valencia belangrijke wijzigingen in de herverkavelingregeling. Eerst werd een derde partij geïntroduceerd, naast de gemeente en de grondeigenaar of ontwikkelaar: de urbaniseerder (*agente urbanizador*). Deze partij hoeft geen grond te bezitten en kan rechtstreeks worden geselecteerd door de gemeente (het gaat dan om een publiek grondbedrijf) of geselecteerd worden in een publieke tender (commerciële ontwikkelaar). Eenmaal geselecteerd neemt de urbaniseerder de verantwoordelijkheid voor de grondexploitatie en de herverkaveling. Ten tweede gaf de wet uit 1994 garanties aan de commerciële partijen wanneer ze mee wilden doen met de publieke tender. Ten derde werden Gedetailleerde plannen voortaan vergezeld met een document met daarin alle uitvoeringsgerichte bindende voorschriften en een realisatieovereenkomst. Een ieder (het is niet nodig om grond te bezitten) kan meedoen aan de publieke tender door een plan in te dienen bij de gemeente, en een ieder is vrij om bezwaren of alternatieve plannen in te dienen. Na evaluatie beslist de gemeenteraad over het definitieve plan en selecteert zij de urbaniseerder. Deze partij maakt en dient bij de gemeente in een gedetailleerd voorstel voor de openbare infrastructuur en faciliteiten en voor de herverkaveling. Nadat de eigendomsrechten zijn gewijzigd (dit kan desnoods worden afgedwongen) ontvangt de gemeente de openbare infrastructuur en faciliteiten en de grondeigenaren de resterende bouwkavels. Tenslotte dienen de eigenaren van de bouwkavels bouwaanvragen in bij de gemeente, die vervolgens bouwvergunningen gunt. De Valenciaanse noviteit is inmiddels in bijna alle Spaanse regio's geïntroduceerd.

Hoe ver kunnen de bijdragen van grondeigenaren en ontwikkelaars gaan? In Spanje hebben gemeenten in uitbreidingslocaties recht op de afroming van een deel van de waardestijging: grondeigenaren dienen tussen de 5% en 15% van de bouwkavels over te dragen aan de gemeente. Daarnaast dienen de grondeigenaren de grondexploitatiekosten te betalen (de aanleg van infrastructuur en faciliteiten, de plankosten en het winstpercentage van de urbaniseerder) en de nodige grond ter beschikking te stellen. In principe dienen de gebouwen met een openbare functie (scholen, ziekenhuizen en dergelijke) te worden betaald door de bevoegde overheid, maar dat geldt niet voor de bouw van sociale woningen, die betaald en gerealiseerd dienen te worden door de grondeigenaren. Tevens is het ook mogelijk om van grondeigenaren te eisen dat ze elders gelegen grond overdragen ten behoeve van bovenwijkse faciliteiten. Gemeenten zijn vrij om over aanvullende eisen te onderhandelen met urbaniseerders. Indien de urbaniseerder daarin toestemt, moet hij die extra kosten uit eigen middelen betalen en kan hij die niet in rekening brengen aan de grondeigenaren.

In de stad Valencia zijn er drie cases onderzocht: *Camino Hondo del Grao* (5,7 hectare, 465 appartementen plus aanzienlijk bouwvolume kantoor en detailhandel);

Guillem de Anglesola (1,2 hectare, 125 appartementen, plus een beetje detailhandel); en *Periodista Gil Sumbiela* (0,6 hectare, 100 appartementen, plus een beetje detailhandel). Een case is gelegen in de stad Alicante: *Benalúa Sur* (8 hectare, 600 appartementen, plus aanzienlijk bouwvolume kantoor en detailhandel). In alle vier cases is in een vroeg stadium een Algemeen plan opgesteld dat gedetailleerde voorschriften inhield, maar toch moest er een Gedetailleerd plan worden vastgesteld alvorens de locatie herontwikkeld mocht worden. In de cases *Camino* en *Benalúa* wijzigde het Gedetailleerde plan majeure voorschriften van het Algemeen plan; in *Guillem* en *Periodista* mineure voorschriften. In alle cases was de urbaniseerder een commerciële partij die geselecteerd werd in een publieke tender. Soms waren dat professionele ontwikkelaars (*Guillem* and *Periodista*), soms de grondeigenaren zelf die gezamenlijk urbaniseerder zijn geworden (*Camino* en *Benalúa*). In alle gevallen is vastgelegd dat de urbaniseerders de openbare infrastructuur en faciliteiten aanleggen. Omdat zij meestal ook een groot deel van de grond gekocht hebben, zullen zij ook de ontwikkelaars van het vastgoed worden. In *Periodista* verkochten bijna alle eigenaren de grond vrij snel aan de urbaniseerder. In *Guillem* wachtten ze. De meesten verkochten de grond pas ten tijde van de herverkavelingprocedure. In *Camino* en *Benalúa* was de grond reeds het eigendom van de urbaniseerder (aangezien de grondeigenaren zelf als urbaniseerder werden geselecteerd).

Hoofdstuk 6 – Engeland

De centrale Britse regering en de regionale en lokale overheden in Engeland hebben twee belangrijke vormen van herstructureringsbeleid ontwikkeld: beleid bedoeld voor verpauperde woningen (dit beleid heeft een lange traditie), en beleid bedoeld voor de stadsvernieuwing (ingezet vanaf de jaren '70). De bestudeerde cases laten zien dat overheden in de laatste decennia geprobeerd hebben een ruimere betrokkenheid van commerciële ontwikkelaars in de financiering van openbare infrastructuur en faciliteiten te verwezenlijken. Om een locatie te kunnen herontwikkelen dienen gemeenten (*Local Planning Authorities*) eerst de bestaande bindende voorschriften te wijzigen. Ruimtelijke plannen en visies kunnen in Engeland een belangrijke rol spelen, maar ze zijn indicatief. Met andere woorden: ze hebben geen rechtstreekse consequenties voor de gebruiksmogelijkheden van grond en opstallen. Het enige plandocument met een juridisch bindend karakter is de *Planning Permission*. Nadat een ontwikkelaar voor een concrete locatie een aanvraag heeft ingediend voor een *Planning Permission*, kan de gemeente ervoor kiezen om alleen voorwaarden te stellen, of verder te gaan en bijdragen te onderhandelen in een realisatieovereenkomst (*Planning Agreement*, oftewel *106-agreement*).

In Engeland heeft de overheid in principe recht om de waardestijging die dankzij herbestemming ontstaat, te ontvangen. In het verleden was hier een specifieke belasting voor, maar die bestaat niet meer. Publiek waardestijgingsverhaal vindt in de praktijk plaats door aan ontwikkelaars bijdragen te vragen om de negatieve externaliteiten van bouwplannen te repareren. Deze praktijk werd vanaf de jaren '70 gemeengoed. De soorten bijdragen evolueerden van aanvankelijk vooral het bouw- en woonrijp maken van de locatie zelf (*on-site*), richting bijdragen bedoeld om milieu- en maatschappelijke faciliteiten te bekostigen, vaak gesitueerd buiten de specifieke locatie (*off-site*). Ontwikkelaars worden tegenwoordig ook gevraagd om sociale woningbouw te realiseren. In de laatste jaren ontstond controversie over de vraag hoever gemeenten mogen gaan in hun eisen. Dat heeft geleid tot een strakkere regulering van het soort bijdragen dat men mag vragen, maar dat heeft niet tot een vermindering van bijdragen geleid.

De drie bestudeerde cases zijn gelegen in de stad Bristol: *Harbourside/Canon's Marsh* (7,8 hectare, 700 appartementen, 44.000 m^2 kantoor, 30.000 m^2 commerciële ruimte), *Temple Quay* (7,4 hectare, 495 appartementen, 61.000 m^2 kantoor, en 7.000 m^2 commerciële faciliteiten) en *Megabowl* (1,3 hectare, 184 appartementen). Het *Bristol Local Plan* uit 1997 (een ruimtelijk plan met een indicatief karakter dat de hele stad dekt) gaf, voor alle drie cases, niet juridisch bindende, globale voorschriften. Alvorens de herontwikkeling mocht aanvangen, moest de gemeente een of meerdere *Planning Permissions* verlenen, en deze *permissions* hielden eisen in over bijdragen die onderhandeld waren met de ontwikkelaars en uiteindelijk leidden tot realisatieovereenkomsten.

Hoofdstuk 7 – Nederland

De Nederlandse overheden streven stedelijke herstructurering na en stimuleren nieuwbouw binnen de grenzen van bestaande steden. Er is specifiek beleid voor: multifunctionele centrale locaties, inclusief spoorstations (case *Stationskwartier*, 16 hectare, 650 appartementen, plus veel kantoren, een beetje detailhandel, een nieuw station en veel parkeergebouwen); monofunctionele voor- en naoorlogse wijken (case *Kruidenbuurt*, 17 hectare, 650 woningen, plus een beetje kantoren) en oude bedrijventerreinen (cases *De Funen* -8 hectare, 565 appartementen, beetje kantoren en *Kop van Oost* -5 hectare, 430 appartementen, plus een beetje commerciële ruimte). Bij stedelijke herstructurering worden vaak indicatieve ruimtelijke plannen vastgesteld, waarvan de meerderheid niet is gereguleerd in wetgeving. Voorafgaand aan de herontwikkeling van de genoemde locaties moesten eerst de financiële middelen worden gevonden om de openbare infrastructuur en faciliteiten te betalen, en bovendien bestond er behoefte aan de wijziging van de bestaande bestemming.

In Nederland behoort de waardestijging van grond aan de eigenaar. De huidige wettelijke mogelijkheden om waardestijging te verhalen zijn beperkt tot kostenverhaal, met andere woorden: tot bijdragen om die openbare infrastructuur en faciliteiten te betalen waarvan de betreffende locatie baat heeft. Dit is niet veranderd met de nieuwe Wet ruimtelijke ordening (Wro) en Besluit ruimtelijke ordening (Bro) uit 2008. In het algemeen zijn bijdragen van ontwikkelaars het resultaat van onderhandelingen. De nieuwe Wro maakt het voor het eerst mogelijk om grondeigenaren een bijdrage te vragen zonder dat daar onderhandelingen noodzakelijk voor zijn. Hiervoor dient de gemeente een exploitatieplan vast te stellen, wat haar in staat stelt om formeel en openlijk de bouwvergunning (maar niet de vaststelling van het bestemmingsplan of vrijstelling/projectbesluit) voorwaardelijk te stellen aan een bijdrage. De Bro reguleert de soorten kosten die gemeenten kunnen doorberekenen aan grondeigenaren middels een exploitatieplan. Het gaat dan om kosten voor de openbare infrastructuur en faciliteiten en van sociale woningen binnen het plangebied, en van planoverschrijdende faciliteiten die rechtstreeks gerelateerd zijn aan de desbetreffende locatie. Niet inbegrepen zijn een deel van de planoverschrijdende faciliteiten, de kosten van onderhoud en exploitatie, van maatschappelijke voorzieningen, en een deel van de kosten van planvoorbereiding en van de herinrichting van oude infrastructuur. Daarnaast, omdat het niet aan grondeigenaren mag worden gevraagd om (een deel van) de waardestijging van hun grond af te staan, impliceert het maken van een exploitatieplan in stedelijke herstructureringsprojecten vaak een deficit in de grondexploitatie, die voor rekening van de gemeente komt. In plaats van het vaststellen van een exploitatieplan, zijn gemeenten en ontwikkelaars of grondeigenaren sinds 2008 vrij om bijdragen af te spreken in een overeenkomst. Een dergelijke overeenkomst wordt 'anterieur' genoemd. Een anterieure overeenkomst mag meer bijdragen inhouden dan een exploitatieplan.

Hoofdstukken 8 en 9 – Conclusies en beleids-aanbevelingen voor de Nederlandse praktijk

Publieke partijen verhalen meer waardestijging in Valencia en Engeland dan in Nederland

De bevindingen maken duidelijk dat formele regels relevant voor ruimtelijke ordening in Valencia en Engeland aanzienlijk anders zijn dan in Nederland (zie volgende secties). Een vergelijking tussen hoeveel waardestijging overheden kunnen verhalen toont ook opmerkelijke verschillen. In stedelijke herstructureringslocaties op private grond in Valencia en Engeland dragen private partijen meer bij dan in Nederland. De verschillen betreffen de volgende soorten bijdragen:

- Bouw- en woonrijp maken op locatie: in Engeland en Valencia worden deze kosten grotendeels of geheel betaald door de ontwikkelaars, terwijl ze in Nederland vaak betaald worden met publieke subsidies;
- Grond voor de openbare infrastructuur en faciliteiten op locatie: in Valencia dragen grondeigenaren deze grond gratis en vrij van kosten, terwijl in Engeland en Nederland er veel grotere publieke bijdragen zijn om deze grond te verkrijgen;
- Sociale woningen: in Engeland en Valencia worden sociale woningen (het hierbij behorend tekort) grotendeels of bijna geheel betaald door de ontwikkelaars,

terwijl in Nederland dit tekort voornamelijk betaald wordt door gemeenten en woningcorporaties;

- Bovenwijkse faciliteiten die buiten de locatie liggen: in Engeland en Valencia dragen ontwikkelaars hier substantieel aan bij (in Engeland voornamelijk met geldelijke bijdragen, in Valencia primair met grond), terwijl in Nederland dit soort bijdragen nauwelijks voorkomt;
- Baatafroming: gemeenten in Valencia romen een substantieel deel van de economische waardestijging van grond af, ook als ze geen grond bezitten. In Engeland is formeel gezien geen sprake van baatafroming, maar omdat de mogelijke soorten bijdragen van ontwikkelaars ruim zijn gedefinieerd zou het mogelijk zijn om te concluderen dat daar wel sprake van is. In Nederland is dit alleen het geval wanneer de gemeente de grond bezit en/of zelf investeert en risico's draagt.

Er is een sterke correlatie tussen de verhaalde waardestijging (het hoogste in Valencia, lager maar nog steeds hoog in Engeland, en het laagst in Nederland) en de verschillende mogelijkheden die de formele regels relevant voor ruimtelijke ordening bieden. Echter, deze correlatie is niet perfect. Er zijn andere variabelen die mogelijk ook *een deel* van de verschillen in verhaalde waardestijging verklaren. Toen de data werden vergaard, waren de woningprijzen in de Engelse cases aanzienlijk hoger dan de prijzen in de Valenciaanse en Nederlandse cases. Dit zou *gedeeltelijk* kunnen verklaren waarom Engelse ontwikkelaars meer genereuze bijdragen leveren dan hun Nederlandse collega's, maar geheel niet waarom Valenciaanse ontwikkelaars, ondanks vergelijkbare marktprijzen met Nederland, toch iets meer dan de Engelse en veel meer dan de Nederlandse ontwikkelaars bijdragen. Andere variabelen die ook *een deel* van de verschillen kunnen verklaren zijn de plan- en locatie-eigenschappen, arbeids- en bouwmateriaalmarkten, belastingregime, inhoud en fysieke begrenzing van plannen, en specifieke omstandigheden van de betrokken interacties en personen.

Algemene conclusies voor het academische debat

Hoofdstuk 2 zette twee specifieke maatregelen neer, geformuleerd als hypotheses, bedoeld om de interacties te beïnvloeden binnen de beleidsnetwerken in stedelijke herstructurering en het resulterende waardestijgingsverhaal. Deze twee hypotheses zijn empirisch getest. De eerste speculeert over de effecten op waardestijgingsverhaal van de definitie van grondeigendomsrechten en hoe dit de machtsverhouding beïnvloedt tussen de betrokken publieke en private partijen. De tweede speculeert over de effecten van de zekerheid die in de loop van planprocessen wordt gecreëerd, dankzij bindende en niet bindende voorschriften. In het causale model in hoofdstuk 2 ontstond een derde veronderstelling die ook empirisch is getest: de veronderstelling dat de flexibiliteit in planprocessen relevant zou kunnen zijn voor waardestijgingsverhaal.

Over deze derde veronderstelling was het niet mogelijk om een duidelijke en generaliseerbare relatie te concluderen tussen flexibiliteit en waardestijgingsverhaal.

Echter, het blijkt dat de twee eerste hypothesen wel valide zijn. De formele regels betreffende eigendomsrechten en zekerheid zijn inderdaad relevant omdat ze de interacties in beleidsnetwerken kunnen beïnvloeden. Overheden in Engeland en in het bijzonder in Valencia blijken, dankzij deze formele regels, een meer krachtige rol te spelen dan in Nederland. Gemeenten in Engeland en in het bijzonder in Valencia schrijven voorafgaand en zonder overleg met ontwikkelaars en grondeigenaren heldere eisen en verplichtingen voor, wat resulteert in een hoge mate van verhaalde waardestijging. In Valencia gaan gemeenten verder dan in Engeland omdat de Valenciaanse gemeenten, dankzij een afdwingbare stedelijke herverkavelingregeling, de bevoegdheid hebben om de ontwikkelaar te selecteren die zij prefereren, desnoods de grondeigenaren te omzeilen en hoeven zij geen grond te kopen of te onteigenen. Deze dominante rol van overheden, in het bijzonder in Valencia, past duidelijk niet binnen de rol die de beleidsnetwerkbenadering hen toekent, en ondergraaft sommige van de veronderstellingen die aan de basis van deze benadering ten grondslag liggen: dat actoren noodzakelijkerwijs onderling afhankelijk van elkaar zijn, dat publieke actoren een meer bescheiden rol moeten accepteren en niet krachtig kunnen zijn.

De volgende paragrafen verklaren de verschillende manieren (of subvariabelen) waarmee formele regels gebruikt worden om waardestijging te verhalen. Per subvariabele worden conclusies getrokken voor het academische debat en voor de beleidsaanbevelingen. Deze aanbevelingen volgen een graduele aanpak, van vrijwillige maatregelen die binnen de Grondexploitatiewet vallen en meteen kunnen worden toegepast, naar meer diepgaande, wettelijke wijzigingen voor de middellange termijn.

Zekerheid creëren voorafgaand over de toekomstige bouwmogelijkheden en bijdragen

Samenvatting van de bevindingen

Gemeenten in alle drie landen creëren vaak, in een vroeg stadium (voordat de onderhandelingen tussen gemeenten en ontwikkelaars plaatsvinden) en in verschillende mate, zekerheid over wat de grondeigenaar in de toekomst zal mogen bouwen. In Nederland stellen gemeenten vaak indicatieve, niet juridisch bindende plannen vast, plannen die een bepaalde mate van zekerheid creëren. Het gaat dan bijvoorbeeld om nota's van uitgangspunten, stedenbouwkundige plannen en visies, structuurvisies en dergelijke. In Engeland gebeurt iets vergelijkbaars, ook middels indicatieve plandocumenten, en in Valencia gebeurt dit middels de vaststelling van juridisch bindende Algemene bestemmingsplannen. De bevindingen suggereren dat meer zekerheid vooraf kan resulteren in minder publiek waardestijgingsverhaal omdat zekerheid de stijging van grondprijzen stimuleert, en omdat gemeenten een waardevol onderhandelingsinstrument kwijtraken. Echter, zekerheid over de bouwmogelijkheden, als die vergezeld wordt door zekerheid over toekomstige bijdragen (zie onder), hoeft niet negatief te zijn.

Er zijn grote verschillen wat betreft de zekerheid die voorafgaand aan het planproces over toekomstige bijdragen bestaat. In Valencia is er in een vroeg stadium veel zekerheid middels (1) wettelijke minimale standaarden, (2) gemeentelijk beleid en (3) de Algemene bestemmingsplannen. Engelse gemeenten creëren vaak enige zekerheid middels (1) locatiespecifieke indicatieve plannen die de bijdragen vastleggen voor de specifieke locatie, en (2) niet op specifieke locaties gefocust, indicatieve generieke beleidsdocumenten die standaard bijdragen vastleggen.

In Nederland is er meestal helemaal geen zekerheid, noch middels juridisch bindende, noch middels indicatieve documenten, voordat onderhandelingen plaats hebben, of voordat de grondprijs wordt bepaald. Deze zekerheid in Valencia en Engeland is positief geweest voor waardestijgingvangst omdat: 1) het verlaagt de grondprijs, omdat wanneer er geen zekerheid bestaat, de ontwikkelaar geneigd is te veel voor de grond te betalen waardoor hij minder financiële ruimte overhoudt om bij te dragen; 2) zekerheid dwingt de ontwikkelaar zijn reguliere winstpercentage en de prijs waarvoor hij de grond inbrengt in zijn exploitatieberekening te verlagen; 3) zekerheid geeft de onderhandelende gemeentelijke ambtenaren een sterke beleidsbasis om bijdragen te eisen.

Conclusies voor het academische debat

De bevindingen blijken aldus de tweede hypothese te bevestigen:

Onzekerheid creëren in een vroeg stadium van planprocessen over toekomstige bouwmogelijkheden, en zekerheid over toekomstige bijdragen, kan het publieke waardestijgingsverhaal positief beïnvloeden.

Wat de vergelijking tussen de Spaanse *versus* de Engelse en Nederlandse stelsels betreft, blijkt een deel van de literatuur over planologische stelsels in Europa verkeerde conclusies te hebben getrokken. Gesteld wordt namelijk dat steeds meer planologische stelsels vergelijkbare niveaus van zekerheid bieden (de zogenaamde 'convergentie'), wat door de bevindingen over Spanje, Engeland en Nederland in dit onderzoek wordt tegengesproken. De bevindingen van dit onderzoek zijn ook relevant voor het debat in de planologie, een debat waarin flexibiliteit vaak wordt nagestreefd als iets positiefs: de bevindingen benadrukken dat er juist behoefte is aan een bepaalde mate van zekerheid over bijdragen wanneer men het publieke waardestijgingsverhaal wil verbeteren.

Beleidsaanbevelingen voor de Nederlandse praktijk

Nederlandse gemeenten zouden zekerheid moeten creëren over de bijdragen die zij willen vragen aan ontwikkelaars. Dat kan voorafgaand of tegelijkertijd met de voorbereiding in een vroeg stadium van planprocessen van indicatieve plannen. De kostensoortenlijst uit de Bro is niet voldoende gedetailleerd om zekerheid te creëren omdat deze lijst het niet mogelijk maakt voor ontwikkelaars om in een vroeg stadium accuraat te berekenen welke kosten en bijdragen zij precies zullen moeten dragen.

Daarom zouden gemeenten zekerheid moeten creëren over de kosten die eventueel doorberekend zouden worden middels een exploitatieplan. Verder, omdat dit plan het niet mogelijk maakt om alle kosten te verhalen, zouden gemeenten eerst moeten proberen om met de ontwikkelaar meer bijdragen af te spreken in een anterieure overeenkomst. Daarom zouden gemeenten ook zekerheid moeten creëren over die kosten die ze middels anterieure overeenkomsten willen verhalen, aanvullend op de kosten die ze middels exploitatieplannen willen verhalen.

De aanbevolen zekerheid kan worden gecreëerd in verschillende soorten documenten, waarvan velen elkaar kunnen aanvullen: (1) locatiespecifieke documenten die de gebruikelijke locatiespecifieke indicatieve plannen vergezellen; (2) generieke documenten inclusief standaard bijdragen van een integraal (alle beleidsvelden dekkend) of sectoraal (betreffende alleen een beleidsveld) karakter; en (3) algemene ruimtelijke plannen met daarin de verplichte bijdragen, eventueel in standaard vorm. Al deze soorten documenten zouden bij voorkeur een indicatief karakter moeten hebben omdat dit beter past in de Nederlandse planologische traditie. De recent geïntroduceerde structuurvisie kan het ideale soort document zijn, niet alleen omdat het een flexibel plandocument is, maar ook omdat het verplicht is om een aantal soorten bijdragen te mogen verhalen. Het Rijk zou gemeenten moeten helpen en stimuleren om zekerheid te creëren, bijvoorbeeld door samen met de Vereniging Nederlandse Gemeenten model documenten te maken. Wanneer deze vrijwillige aanbevelingen niet breed zouden worden overgenomen door de gemeenten, dan zou het Rijk een aantal wetwijzigingen moeten introduceren: eerst door gemeenten te verplichten om generieke integrale documenten op te nemen in structuurvisies, en vervolgens door wettelijke minimale standaard bijdragen en voorschriften te introduceren voor het hele land.

De inhoud van bindende voorschriften bepalen

Samenvatting van de bevindingen

Bindende plannen kunnen bruikbaar zijn in de onderhandelingen wanneer de gemeente daarin niet alleen de ruimtelijke relevante aspecten kunnen opnemen, maar ook aspecten gericht op de praktische planuitvoering. Schrijven bindende plannen alleen het gewenst fysieke eindbeeld voor, zonder aan te geven wie verantwoordelijk is voor de implementatie van dit eindbeeld? Of ook de bijdragen die de ontwikkelaar moet leveren? Zowel in Valencia als Engeland maakt ruimtelijke ordeningswetgeving het mogelijk om in bindende plannen een breed assortiment aan bijdragen op te nemen:

a) Sociale woningbouw: zowel in Valencia als Engeland is het mogelijk om sociale woningbouw voor te schrijven in bindende plannen;
b) *On-site* en *off-site* openbare infrastructuur en faciliteiten: zowel in Valencia als Engeland is het mogelijk om de verplichting voor te schrijven van bijdragen aan *on-site* en *off-site* openbare infrastructuur en faciliteiten. In Engeland kunnen gemeenten ook bijdragen voorschrijven voor de bouw, onderhoud en exploi-

tatiekosten van openbare gebouwen en faciliteiten, ook van maatschappelijke voorzieningen (bijvoorbeeld onderwijs en sociale voorzieningen);

c) Termijnen en fasering van investeringen en de planuitvoering: in beide landen kunnen gemeenten in bindende plannen voorschrijven binnen welke termijn en fasering de bijdragen gerealiseerd/betaald moeten worden.

Al deze mogelijkheden zijn positief voor het publieke waardestijgingsverhaal. In Nederland kon, voordat de nieuwe Wro in werking trad, geen van deze bijdragen worden voorgeschreven in bindende voorschriften en dit had negatieve effecten voor het waardestijgingsverhaal.

Beleidsaanbevelingen voor de Nederlandse praktijk

De nieuwe Wro maakt het voor het eerst mogelijk om bijna al deze bijdragen op te nemen. Tegenwoordig is het mogelijk om sociale woningbouw in zowel het Bestemmingsplan als in de vrijstellingen daarvan op te nemen (een percentage), als in het exploitatieplan (concrete locatie en aantal eenheden). Het is ook mogelijk om in het exploitatieplan termijnen voor de planuitvoering op te nemen, en tevens bijdragen voor de meeste *on-site*, en voor een deel van de *off-site* openbare infrastructuur en faciliteiten. Echter, de volgende beperkingen zijn nog steeds van kracht:

1. Het niet mogelijk om in exploitatieplannen bijdragen op te nemen voor de bouw, het onderhoud en de exploitatiekosten van maatschappelijke voorzieningen. Bovendien is het onzeker of deze bijdragen afgesproken kunnen worden in anterieure overeenkomsten. Om deze bijdragen mogelijk te maken, zou artikel 6.2.5 Bro gewijzigd moeten worden.
2. Zoals reeds uiteengezet, kunnen veel kosten niet doorberekend worden aan de grondeigenaren middels een exploitatieplan. Daarom zou de kostensoortenlijst (artikelen 6.2.3 tot 6.2.6 Bro) moeten worden uitgebreid.
3. In een exploitatieplan hebben grondeigenaren recht op de hoogste waarde van hun grond, wat zich vertaalt in hoge inbrengwaardes en dat doet de waarschijnlijkheid van een tekort toenemen, een tekort dat door de gemeente dient te worden gedekt. Daarom zou artikel 6.13.5 Wro, dat voorschrijft dat de waardebepaling van grond de onteigeningswet moet volgen, gewijzigd moeten worden.

Conclusies voor het academische debat

Deze bevinding leidt tot een uitwerking van de 2e variabele (in vette lettergrepen de toevoeging):

Onzekerheid creëren in een vroeg stadium van planprocessen over toekomstige bouwmogelijkheden, en zekerheid over toekomstige bijdragen ***(vooral wanneer het mogelijk is om alle bijdragen als verplicht op te nemen in juridisch bindende voorschriften)****, kan het publieke waardestijgingsverhaal positief beïnvloeden.*

Bindende voorschriften voorwaardelijk stellen aan zekering door ontwikkelaar van zijn bijdragen

Samenvatting van de bevindingen

De vaststelling van bindende plannen met daarin genereuze bijdragen en strikte termijnen, als zodanig, betekent niet automatisch dat de ontwikkelaars die inderdaad gaan uitvoeren. Ten einde de implementatie te verzekeren dient de ontwikkelaar zich hier tevens aan te verbinden. In de praktijk stellen Nederlandse gemeenten vaak het bestemmingsplan en/of de vrijstellingen daarvan voorwaardelijk aan een overeenkomst waarin de ontwikkelaar zijn bijdragen verzekert. Echter, formeel is het niet mogelijk om dit op een directe en open manier te doen. Dit heeft negatieve neveneffecten:

1. *Procedurele risico's:* na de ondertekening van de overeenkomst, dient alsnog de hele administratieve procedure tot vaststelling van de nieuwe bestemming doorlopen te worden, wat het risico van vertraging en wijzigingen met zich meebrengt wegens eventuele zienswijzen en beroepsprocedures. In Valencia en Engeland, gaat de procedure van voorlopige vaststelling *vooraf* aan de ondertekening van de overeenkomst, en daarna is er alleen nog een korte definitieve vaststelling nodig. Dit betekent dat in Valencia en Engeland partijen een overeenkomst kunnen sluiten met een hoge mate van zekerheid dat het nieuwe Bestemmingsplan succesvol zal worden vastgesteld, en dat er ook geen vertraging gaat optreden;
2. *Beroepsrisico's*: wanneer een gemeente weigert een nieuw bestemmingsplan vast te stellen omdat de ontwikkelaar de bijdragen niet wil verzekeren, dan bestaat altijd het risico dat de ontwikkelaar een beroep indient bij de rechter. In Engeland en Valencia schrijft r.o.-wetgeving juist voor dat de ontwikkelaar de bijdragen die opgenomen zijn in het voorlopig vastgestelde bestemmingsplan *moet* verzekeren *alvorens* de definitieve vaststelling mag plaatsvinden;
3. *Inconsistentie van het gemeentelijk publieke betoog*: in de praktijk kunnen gemeenten gedwongen worden om de 'echte redenen' voor de vaststelling of weigering van het nieuwe bestemmingsplan te verbergen. De echte reden kan namelijk zijn dat de ontwikkelaar wel of niet bereid was om een overeenkomst te tekenen. In Engeland en Valencia worden de echte redenen publiekelijk vastgesteld door de gemeenteraad. De gemeenteraad stelt namelijk de open en transparante eisen vast waaraan de ontwikkelaar zal moeten voldoen en welke opgenomen dienen te worden in een overeenkomst. Pas nadat de ontwikkelaar aan deze eisen heeft voldaan, mag het bestemmingsplan definitief worden vastgesteld.

In Nederland kan de ontwikkelaar of grondeigenaar een bouwaanvraag indienen, nadat het bestemmingsplan en het exploitatieplan zijn vastgesteld. De noviteit met de nieuwe Wro is dat de gemeente nu de bouwvergunning voorwaardelijk kan stellen aan de zekering van de bijdragen; voor de nieuwe Wro was dat niet mogelijk. Echter, een exploitatieplan vaststellen heeft ook neveneffecten: gemeenten moeten financiële risico's dragen omdat ze verantwoordelijk zijn voor de exploitatieopzet en wellicht voorinvesteringen moeten plegen. Zij moeten investeren in het maken en het jaarlijks herzien van het plan en ze moeten de gevolgen dragen van vertraging wanneer de ontwikkelaars of grondeigenaren hun bouwaanvraag zouden uitstellen. Daarnaast, zoals hierboven vermeld, kunnen niet alle kosten worden doorberekend aan de grondeigenaren. Dus in principe is de beste optie voor Nederlandse gemeenten om een anterieure overeenkomst te sluiten alvorens het bestemmingsplan wordt vastgesteld. Hiermee zijn de bijdragen en de termijnen verzekerd en is er geen noodzaak voor een exploitatieplan. Gemeenten kunnen ontwikkelaars informeel vragen om een anterieure overeenkomst te sluiten. Echter, de huidige praktijk van informele voorwaardelijkstelling kan moeilijker worden met de nieuwe Wro. De Wro heeft namelijk de verplichting versterkt voor gemeenten om een formeel besluit te nemen wanneer een partij de gemeente verzoekt om de bestemming te wijzigen. Wanneer de gemeente het verzoek wenst te weigeren (deze mogelijkheid versterkt de onderhandelingspositie van de gemeente), dient dit besluit binnen een periode van acht weken na het verzoek te worden genomen. Gemeenten dienen hun besluit te verantwoorden door te verwijzen naar vastgesteld beleid en ruimtelijke plannen, en de verzoeker heeft nu de mogelijkheid om beroep in te dienen tegen een weigeringsbesluit. Met andere woorden, de gemeente kan niet openlijk en rechtstreeks het verzoek weigeren met het argument dat de verzoeker een overeenkomst niet wenst te sluiten, maar moet andere argumenten vinden in het bestaande bestemmingsplan, de structuurvisie of andere vastgestelde beleidsdocumenten. Wanneer de gemeente reeds bekend heeft gemaakt (bijvoorbeeld in gesprekken met de verzoeker welke genotuleerd zijn) dat er geen bezwaren zijn tegen de ruimtelijke relevante aspecten van het bouwplan, is er in feite weinig ruimte over om te weigeren en dus om te onderhandelen.

Conclusies voor het academische debat

De bevindingen worden gebruikt om de tweede hypothese verder uit te werken (in vette lettergrepen de toevoeging):

Onzekerheid creëren in een vroeg stadium van planprocessen over toekomstige bouwmogelijkheden, en zekerheid over toekomstige bijdragen (vooral wanneer het mogelijk is om alle bijdragen als verplicht op te nemen in juridisch bindende voorschriften, ***en wanneer het mogelijk is om openlijk en rechtstreeks de vaststelling van de bindende voorschriften voorwaardelijk te stellen aan de ondertekening van een anterieure overeenkomst die de bijdragen verzekert****), kan het publieke waardestijgingsverhaal positief beïnvloeden.*

Beleidsaanbevelingen voor de Nederlandse praktijk

Alhoewel een open en directe voorwaardelijkstelling niet toegestaan is, zijn er sommige alternatieve wegen om dit toch indirect te doen, en de nieuwe Wro heeft daar een aantal mogelijkheden aan toegevoegd:

- Beargumenteren dat de bijdragen noodzakelijk zijn voor de economische uitvoerbaarheid van het bestemmingsplan: wanneer de bijdragen niet zijn verzekerd en/of er is sprake van een tekort, dan zou de gemeente deze kosten moeten dragen. Maar wanneer de gemeente aanvoert geen financiële middelen te hebben om het tekort te dekken, dan kan zij het plan weigeren met het argument dat het economisch niet uitvoerbaar is. Deze alternatieve manier van voorwaardelijkstelling heeft dezelfde bovengenoemde negatieve neveneffecten: (1) procedurele risico's, (2) beroepsrisico's (indirecte voorwaardelijkstelling via de economische uitvoerbaarheidseisen van het bestemmingsplan is niet hetzelfde als openlijk opsommen welke bijdragen de ontwikkelaar dient te verzekeren), en (3) inconsistentie van het gemeentelijke publieke betoog.

- Bindende voorschriften voorwaardelijk stellen via het exploitatieplan en via goed onderbouwde kostenverhaalbeleidsdocumenten. Nadat een ontwikkelaar de gemeente benadert met een verzoek tot bestemmingswijziging/bouwaanvraag kan de gemeente middels een exploitatieopzet (onderdeel van het Exploitatieplan) duidelijkheid creëren over welke deel van de kosten voor rekening komen van de grondeigenaren wanneer de gemeente een exploitatieplan zou vaststellen. Wanneer gemeenten de eerder genoemde beleidsaanbevelingen introduceren en kostenverhaal-beleidsdocumenten vaststellen, is het mogelijk om deugdelijk te motiveren dat een bestemmingswijziging kosten met zich meebrengt die verder gaan dan een minimaal pakket aan *on-site* infrastructuur, maar ook bredere bijdragen vereisen voor andere openbare infrastructuur en faciliteiten binnen en buiten het plangebied. Deze kostenverhaal-beleidsdocumenten zijn van wezenlijk belang: zonder die documenten zou het zeer waarschijnlijk niet lukken om *alle* kosten te berekenen en deugdelijk te motiveren. Wanneer uit de exploitatieopzet blijkt dat de gemeente niet alle kosten kan verhalen, dan kan ze het verzoek openlijk weigeren met het argument dat ze dat deficit niet zelf kan dekken. Dit alternatief van voorwaardelijkstelling brengt nog steeds het eerste van bovengenoemde neveneffecten (procedurele risico's) met zich mee, en voegt er een nieuw negatief neveneffect aan toe. Wanneer de ontwikkelaar zou instemmen om in een anterieure overeenkomst het tekort te zekeren (maar niet de kosten die middels een exploitatieplan zouden kunnen worden verhaald) dan zouden gemeenten niet meer het argument van economische uitvoerbaarheid kunnen aanvoeren om het verzoek te weigeren.

Om alle negatieve neveneffecten van beide alternatieven weg te nemen wordt hier aan het Rijk aanbevolen om middels een wetswijziging directe voorwaardelijkstelling, op een vergelijkbare wijze als in Valencia en Engeland, mogelijk te maken. Hiervoor worden twee specifieke wijzigingen voorgesteld voor de Wro en wellicht ook voor de Bro.

Grondeigendomsrechten wijzigen

Samenvatting van de bevindingen

Zowel in Engeland als Nederland bestaat een sterke onderlinge afhankelijkheid tussen gemeenten, grondeigenaren en ontwikkelaars. In de regel zijn de transacties die nodig zijn om op een locatie de grondexploitatie te voeren, behoorlijk afhankelijk van overeenstemming tussen alle partijen omdat geen van hen over alle nodige middelen beschikt: gemeenten hebben de wettelijke bevoegdheid over planologische inpassing, maar grondeigenaren en ontwikkelaars hebben de financiële middelen en het exclusieve recht om de grond te ontwikkelen. Deze onderlinge afhankelijkheid kan lang niet altijd worden omzeild door gebruik te maken van onteigening of het voorkeursrecht. Dat is het geval omdat de toepassing van deze instrumenten aan beperkingen onderhevig is, en omdat zij met zich meebrengen dat de overheid direct, organisatorisch en financieel, betrokken raakt. De situatie in Valencia veranderde radicaal nadat de regionale overheid in 1994 een nieuwe wet introduceerde. Vanaf dat moment is er geen onvermijdbare onderlinge afhankelijkheid meer tussen gemeenten en grondeigenaren om de grondexploitatie te voeren. Valenciaanse gemeenten kunnen nu kiezen voor gedwongen herverkaveling zonder de behoefte om direct organisatorisch en financieel betrokken te raken. De gemeente selecteert in een publieke tender de urbaniseerder. Grondeigenaren kunnen kiezen tussen vrijwillige onteigening of deelname aan de grondexploitatie. Wanneer zij voor onteigening kiezen, betaalt de urbaniseerder de schadevergoeding en ontvangt hij de grond. Wanneer grondeigenaren kiezen om mee te doen, zijn zij verplicht om de grond te leveren die nodig is voor de openbare infrastructuur en faciliteiten, en aan de urbaniseerder een proportioneel deel van de grondexploitatiekosten te betalen. In ruil hiervoor delen de grondeigenaren de waardestijging. Nadat de urbaniseerder de grondexploitatie heeft gevoerd, levert hij de bouwkavels aan de grondeigenaren en draagt hij de openbare infrastructuur en faciliteiten, vrij van kosten, over aan de gemeente. Samengevat: alhoewel grondeigenaren nog steeds de grond controleren, is de onderlinge afhankelijkheid nu gemakkelijk vermijdbaar omdat gemeenten de mogelijkheid hebben om een derde partij (die geen grond hoeft te hebben) als urbaniseerder aan te wijzen. Hierbij hoeven gemeenten financieel noch organisatorisch direct betrokken te raken. Gemeenten zijn ook niet afhankelijk van een urbaniseerder omdat zij een publiek grondbedrijf kunnen aanwijzen als urbaniseerder of daarvoor via een publieke tender een commerciële partij kunnen uitkiezen.

De onderlinge afhankelijkheid tussen overheden en grondeigenaren in Engeland en Nederland geeft grondeigenaren de optie om te wachten. Die optie wordt door grondeigenaren ook vaak gebruikt om zich tegen eisen van gemeenten te verzetten. In het bijzonder in Nederland trekken gemeenten dan vaak de conclusie dat ze niet veel kunnen vragen, wat leidt tot laag waardestijgingsverhaal. Deze afhankelijkheid leidt vaak ook tot vertraging van het planproces omdat grondeigenaren of ontwikkelaars gemeentelijke eisen afwijzen, of omdat ontwikkelaars niet succesvol zijn in het verwerven van alle gronden voor een redelijke prijs. Het resultaat van de onderhandelingen is afhankelijk van de verwachtingen van ontwikkelaars en grondeigenaren dat, door de onderhandelingen te vertragen, hun winst zal toenemen. Hogere inbrengwaardes voor de grond zijn een ander gevolg: marktpartijen zijn meer geïnteresseerd in het verwerven van grondposities omdat die hun een sterke onderhandelingspositie geven, wat vervolgens de grondprijzen doet stijgen.

In aanvulling hierop, suggereren de bevindingen dat onderlinge afhankelijkheid tot een inefficiënt en stroperig planproces leidt waarin kosten onnodig hoog zijn en waarin verschillende actoren de waardestijging naar zich toetrekken. Dit leidt tot hogere grondexploitatiekosten (waaronder bouw- en woonrijp maken en de plankosten). In Engeland en Nederland zijn deze kosten vaak tussen 1,5 en 4 keer hoger dan in Valencia. Dit leidt ertoe dat Valenciaanse ontwikkelaars meer financiële ruimte hebben om bijdragen te leveren dan de Nederlandse en Engelse ontwikkelaars.

Conclusies voor het academische debat
De bevindingen bevestigen de eerste hypothese:

Een specifieke vorm van scheiding van grondeigendomsrechten (grondexploitatie scheiden van eigendomsrechten) kan de machtsverhoudingen in het actorennetwerk in stedelijke herstructurering veranderen, en dit kan het publieke waardestijgingsverhaal verbeteren.

Dit onderzoek zocht empirische evidentie die relevant is voor het debat over de splitsing van ontwikkelingsrechten en grondeigendomsrechten. De bevindingen ondersteunen de assumptie dat de grondexploitatie middels een herverkavelingregeling uit de controle van de grondeigenaren weggenomen kan worden en dat het publieke waardestijgingsverhaal daardoor kan verbeteren. Tevens suggereren de bevindingen dat de herverkavelingregeling een deflationair effect kan hebben op de grondexploitatiekosten, en mogelijk ook op de inbrengwaarde van grond. De regeling kan ook helpen om problemen met bouwstagnatie op te lossen. De bevindingen zijn interessant voor het debat in Nederland omdat ze overeenkomen met de positie van diegenen die beargumenteren dat de toename van private controle op ontwikkelingsgrond vanaf de jaren '90 onvoordelig heeft uitgewerkt op de publieke doelen en uitgaven. De bevindingen ondersteunen ook de conclusie dat het hervormen van grondeigendomsrechten kan helpen om publieke doelen in ruimtelijke ontwikkeling beter te verwezenlijken. In het Spaanse debat ondersteunen de bevindingen de kritische benadering van diegenen die, in de jaren '90, beargumenteerden dat het doorbreken van de monopolistische/oligopolistische positie van grondeigenaren, de enige weg is om voldoende en kwalitatief adequate openbare infrastructuur en faciliteiten te garanderen. Tenslotte is er meer onderzoek nodig naar een internationale vergelijking van grondprijzen en ontwikkelingskosten. Dit onderzoek zou moeten focussen op de verschillen tussen landen en hiermee meer data genereren die gebruikt kunnen worden om deze conclusies aan te scherpen.

Beleidsaanbevelingen voor de Nederlandse praktijk
In de eerste plaats zouden gemeenten in een vroeg stadium van planprocessen meer onderzoek moeten doen naar de winstmarges, en deze informatie vervolgens in de onderhandelingen met grondeigenaren en ontwikkelaars gebruiken . Dit onderzoek zou gelijktijdig moeten plaatsvinden met het opstellen van de eerste plandocumenten die ontwikkelingsverwachtingen wekken.

In de tweede plaats, om de negatieve gevolgen van de onderlinge afhankelijkheid tussen gemeenten en grondeigenaren of ontwikkelaars te vermijden, wordt hier een specifieke contractuele formule van herverkaveling aanbevolen die gebaseerd is op een tweetal anterieure overeenkomsten. Een commerciële ontwikkelaar, in de rol van een soort Valenciaanse urbaniseerder, kan met de grondeigenaren overeenkomen dat, in ruil voor de waardestijging, zij zullen participeren in de grondexploitatie. De gemeente zou dit moeten ondersteunen door bestemmingswijziging voorwaardelijk te stellen aan een overeenkomst tussen de grondeigenaren en de urbaniseerder. Desnoods zou de gemeente daarbij gebruik moeten maken van onteigening, voorkeursrecht of een of meerdere exploitatieplannen. Wanneer deze aanbeveling toegepast zou worden, zou dat een aantal voordelen met zich meebrengen: (a) het neemt de noodzaak weg om de grond te verwerven, of tenminste *alle* grond, aangezien de grondeigenaren zelf meedoen aan de grondexploitatie; (b) het verkleint het risico van vertraging dat zou plaatshebben wanneer de grondeigenaren, in plaats van meewerken, zich strategisch zouden gedragen om de hoogst mogelijke prijs af te dwingen; (c) *a* en *b* zouden de kosten aanzienlijk verminderen: er zou geen behoefte zijn om de grond vooraf te kopen. De gereserveerde bedragen voor onverwachte kosten en plankosten zouden hierdoor verminderen; (d) *c* zou de financiële kosten aanzienlijk doen verminderen omdat er dan minder of geen behoefte zou zijn aan externe financiering.

Echter, de vaststelling van een exploitatieplan, wat nodig zou kunnen zijn om sommige grondeigenaren te dwingen mee te werken, heeft zoals reeds gemeld nadelen. Tevens is het heel duur om grond te onteigenen en brengt dit een directe financiële betrokkenheid van de gemeente met zich mee. Dit is ook nog een politiek gevoelige maatregel die sowieso niet toegepast kan worden als grondeigenaren de bestemming zelf zouden willen realiseren. Om deze nadelige effecten weg te nemen zou het Rijk, geïnspireerd door de Valenciaanse herverkavelingregeling, een wettelijke stedelijke herverkavelingregeling moeten introduceren.

Slotwoord

Aan het einde van de jaren '80 en '90 introduceerde de Nederlandse overheid belangrijke beleidsveranderingen om de publieke uitgaven en financiële risico's te verminderen. Echter, de praktijk heeft sindsdien laten zien dat deze veranderingen noch geleid hebben tot minder subsidies, noch tot nieuwe wijken met voldoende en goede openbare infrastructuur en faciliteiten. De grondexploitatiewet is een poging om dit probleem op te lossen. Alhoewel deze wet onder bepaalde omstandigheden nuttig kan zijn, lijdt die aan twee fundamentele tekortkomingen. Ten eerste gaat de wet ervan uit dat de grondeigenaar de enige is die gelegitimeerd is om de economische waardestijging die door herbestemming is ontstaan, naar zich toe te trekken. Hier ontkende de wetgever een andere mogelijkheid die populair is in andere Europese landen: dat overheden ook recht hebben op een deel van de waardestijging. Ten tweede gaat de wet ervan uit dat de enige manier om publieke doelen te verwezenlijken een directe en financiële betrokkenheid van de overheid is. Dit resulteerde in een te complexe reeks van wettelijke instrumenten die gemeenten overlaadt met te veel taken en risico's. De ervaring in Engeland en Spanje laat zien dat publieke regie in ruimtelijke ontwikkeling gebaseerd moet zijn op simpele en duidelijke rollen: overheden reguleren vooraf, private partijen implementeren en dragen alle risico's.

Een laatste woord: de internationale financiële en economische crisis leidt er reeds toe dat overheden moeten bezuinigen om minder uit te geven. Wanneer geen maatregelen worden genomen om een deel van de economische waardestijging te gebruiken om de openbare infrastructuur en faciliteiten te betalen, zullen de bezuinigingen er toe leiden dat ruimtelijke ontwikkeling en diens kwaliteit onder druk komt te staan, in het bijzonder in stedelijke herstructureringslocaties.

Resumen

Capítulo 1 – Introducción: problemas con la financiación de los objetivos públicos en proyectos de reestructuración urbana en Holanda

Tradicionalmente la Administración Pública holandesa solía aplicar una política 'activa' de suelo: compraba el suelo, lo urbanizaba y vendía los solares a cooperativas de vivienda y a promotores inmobiliarios. A finales de los años 80 diversos cambios en las políticas de vivienda y suelo llevaron a una transición gradual hacia fórmulas más pasivas. Desde entonces, cada vez más son las cooperativas de viviendas y los agentes de mercado los que compran el suelo y lo desarrollan. Los desarrollos urbanos en general (tanto en ensanches como en reestructuración urbana) implican generalmente un incremento en el valor económico del suelo (a partir de ahora: "plusvalía urbanística"), pero también la necesidad de invertir en nuevas calles y espacio público, alcantarillado, edificios públicos y vivienda social y protegida, indemnizaciones, etc. (a partir de ahora: "infraestructura y dotaciones públicas"). Si un Ayuntamiento aplica una política activa de suelo puede recuperar estos costes al vender los solares. Sin embargo, como los Ayuntamientos holandeses tienen cada vez menos suelo están teniendo problemas para pagar los costes porque los propietarios del suelo no están dispuestos a contribuir. Esto ha llevado a que los Ayuntamientos hayan rebajado los objetivos de calidad urbanística, por ejemplo en reestructuración urbana, y a la necesidad de subsidios públicos.

Esta investigación se cuestiona si, cuando el suelo está en manos privadas, la plusvalía urbanística podría ser utilizada (toda o al menos una parte) para pagar las infraestructuras y dotaciones públicas. Se investiga si ciertos instrumentos legales, comprendidos dentro de la normativa urbanística, serían útiles para estimular a los propietarios del suelo a contribuir, es decir, a mejorar la recuperación de plusvalías urbanísticas. Esta investigación se centra en la siguiente normativa urbanística: el ordenamiento jurídicamente vinculante que regula el uso del suelo y su procedimiento administrativo de aprobación; derechos de la propiedad del suelo; y ordenamiento no vinculante. Las plusvalías urbanísticas pueden ser de diferentes tipos: las generadas por inversiones en infraestructura, por cambiar el uso del suelo, o por un aumento de la demanda de suelo causado por otros factores de carácter más general. Esta investigación distingue tres diferentes sub-conceptos dentro de 'recuperación de plusvalías': 'recuperación de costes' (recuperación, gracias a las contribuciones de los propietarios, de las inversiones en infraestructuras y dotaciones públicas), 'captura pública de plusvalía' (cuando las Administraciones Públicas que han invertido en, por ejemplo, infraestructuras, capturan la plusvalía generada por esa inversión) y 'recuperación pública de plusvalías' propiamente dicha (cuando las Administraciones Públicas recogen todos los tipos de plusvalías urbanísticas).

Una cuestión fundamental es quién debería recibir la plusvalía urbanística. Según una tradición liberal conservadora, toda plusvalía pertenece al propietario del suelo, mientras que una tradición alternativa defiende que pertenece a la comunidad. Un tema recurrente en la teoría económica neo-clásica es la idea de fiscalizar (recuperar mediante impuestos) la plusvalía urbanística. De estas diferencias ideológicas han resultado diferentes instrumentos para la recuperación de plusvalías, algunos de ellos destinados a recuperar todos los tipos de plusvalías y otros sólo a internalizar los impactos negativos del desarrollo urbano (es decir, recuperación de costes). Debido a que en Holanda la recuperación de plusvalías no puede ir más allá de la recuperación de las inversiones en infraestructuras y dotaciones públicas (es decir, recuperación de costes), esta investigación no hace recomendaciones para recuperar más allá de estas inversiones. Algunas de las recomendaciones encajan dentro del actual marco legal holandés, incluidas las nuevas Ley de Urbanismo y Ordenación Territorial (*Wet ruimtelijke ordening*) y Ley de la Urbanización del Suelo (*Grondexploitatiewet*). Otras recomendaciones implican modificaciones legales. Así pues, el problema que esta investigación pretende resolver es el siguiente:

¿Cómo se podría utilizar la normativa urbanística en Holanda con el fin de que en reestructuración urbana sobre suelo privado la plusvalía urbanística pagase las infraestructuras y dotaciones públicas?

Para poder responder esta pregunta hay que resolver primero las siguientes cuestiones:

- Cuestión previa 1: *¿Cómo se puede utilizar la normativa urbanística en reestructuración urbana sobre suelo privado?*
- Cuestión previa 2: *¿Cuánta plusvalía urbanística se recupera actualmente en reestructuración urbana sobre suelo privado?*

- Cuestión previa 3: *¿Cómo influye la forma en que se usa la normativa urbanística en la recuperación de plusvalías urbanísticas?*
- Cuestión principal: *¿Cómo podría usarse la normativa urbanística en Holanda para que la plusvalía urbanística pagase las infraestructuras y dotaciones públicas?*

Capítulo 2 – Marco teórico: recuperación de plusvalías urbanísticas en las redes de gestión de políticas

Es posible analizar un proyecto de reestructuración urbana como si fuese una red de gestión de políticas, red en la cual distintas Administraciones Públicas tratan, cuando interactúan con otros agentes, de mejorar la recuperación de plusvalías urbanísticas. El enfoque conocido como ' redes de gestión de políticas' (*Policy network approach*) es resultado del debate académico sobre los cambios habidos durante los últimos decenios en los roles desempeñados por la Administración Pública y por los agentes de mercado. Los fundamentos de este enfoque se pueden encontrar en la ciencia política de los primeros años 70. Mientras que en el enfoque tradicional 'intra-organizaciones' la gestión de políticas públicas es una actividad jerárquica, en el enfoque de redes las relaciones de poder público-privadas son menos jerárquicas. Para descubrir los factores estructurales que pueden explicar estas relaciones se puede utilizar el método de dependencia por recursos. Un primer factor estructural es que las redes de gestión de políticas consisten en diversos actores, cada uno de los cuales persiguiendo sus propios objetivos. Esto conlleva un potencial conflicto. Al mismo tiempo, los actores son recíprocamente dependientes porque ninguno de ellos controla todos los recursos necesarios para lograr sus objetivos. La fuerza de esta dependencia es proporcional a la importancia y a la 'sustituibilidad' del recurso. Tanto la distribución de recursos como las relaciones de poder están reguladas y moldeadas por la normativa legal. Por su parte, las relaciones de poder, con el tiempo, a menudo moldean, consolidándola o alterándola, la normativa legal. Un segundo factor estructural es que la Administración Pública depende siempre de los recursos de otros y no es, pues, el actor dominante sino un *primus inter pares*. Voces críticas argumentan que el enfoque de redes devalúa el estatus del sector público, y que la Administración Pública no debería involucrarse demasiado en interacciones y alianzas porque las redes no son transparentes ni democráticamente controlables.

Esta investigación critica la presunción básica de que la Administración Pública, en proyectos de desarrollo urbanístico, depende *siempre* de otros actores, y propone dos medidas para modificar las interacciones en las redes y de esta forma mejorar la recuperación de plusvalías: primero modificar los derechos de propiedad del suelo, y segundo modificar el grado de flexibilidad y seguridad en el Planeamiento urbano.

Derechos de propiedad del suelo

Se podría pensar que los derechos de propiedad dan al propietario del suelo una libertad total para decidir cómo usarlo. Sin embargo, la realidad es que la normativa legal restringe estos derechos. El Derecho Privado regula el tráfico normal de derechos de propiedad entre personas. El Derecho Público regula si la Administración Pública puede o no, y cómo, imponer restricciones a los derechos de propiedad. El Derecho Público ha restringido muy significativamente los derechos de propiedad del suelo, fundamentalmente a partir de la introducción en el siglo XIX de la función social de la propiedad y de consideraciones de carácter sanitario. En la actualidad el propietario puede disfrutar de su propiedad sólo si lo hace dentro de la normativa y de las prescripciones legales, y después de recibir una autorización o concesión pública. En Gran Bretaña, Holanda y España se debate sobre este tema. En 1947 una ley introdujo y llevó a cabo en Gran Bretaña lo que se vino a denominar la 'nacionalización del derecho a desarrollar urbanísticamente' (*nationalization of development rights*). Esta ley creó un impuesto que sin embargo ya no existe hoy en día. En realidad esta nacionalización no llegó más allá de este impuesto, ya que no alteró el principio legal de que sólo el propietario del suelo está autorizado a desarrollar (urbanizar y/o edificar) su suelo.

Los mencionados problemas en Holanda con la financiación de las infraestructuras y dotaciones públicas han sido objeto de controversia y debate. La discusión versa sobre si el Derecho Público ofrece a la Administración Pública instrumentos suficientes para influir en el desarrollo urbanístico. Algunos autores son más optimistas, otros más escépticos. Éstos últimos consideran que los derechos de propiedad del suelo crean una especie de oligopolio de propietarios y proponen una modificación de los derechos de propiedad para estimular la libre competencia.

Las dificultades que la Administración Pública española encontró desde el siglo XIX para financiar las infraestructuras y dotaciones públicas han inspirado propuestas y medidas que afectaban a los derechos de propiedad. En 1956 se introdujo la Reparcelación en el Derecho Administrativo para condicionar el disfrute de la plusvalía urbanística a la obligación de asumir la responsabilidad de urbanizar. Desde entonces los propietarios de suelo están obligados a urbanizar el suelo y como compensación comparten la plusvalía. Los Ayuntamientos están obligados a aprobar un Planeamiento General para todo el término municipal y de este modo dar seguridad al propietario sobre las posibilidades de edificación. El carácter detallado de este Planeamiento General y su carácter jurídico vinculante han convertido a España en una singularidad en el contexto internacional. La Reparcelación no logró sin embargo garantizar unas infraestructuras y dotaciones públicas de calidad. Desde los años 80, algunos críticos (especialmente García-Bellido) plantearon dar a la Administración Pública el derecho a desarrollar el suelo y así romper el oligopolio del propietario. Inspirada en esta propuesta, en 1994 la Comunidad Autónoma de Valencia (en adelante, CAV) introdujo una ley para combatir la especulación del suelo y mejorar la recuperación de plusvalías. En la práctica esta ley separó la urbanización de la propiedad del suelo.

Flexibilidad y seguridad en el Planeamiento urbano
Actualmente existe un vivo debate acerca de qué grado de flexibilidad debería tener el Planeamiento urbano: ¿debe crear seguridad en momentos tempranos de los procesos de urbanización (de forma que la Administración Pública pueda controlarlos) o ser flexible (y así poder adaptarse a las circunstancias)? Si el Planeamiento es aprobado tempranamente e incluye una ordenación detallada, y además no es posible modificarlo, entonces habrá menos flexibilidad y más seguridad. Mientras que en los años 60 la flexibilidad estaba considerada como algo negativo, en la actualidad esta percepción ha cambiado. Como veremos más adelante, el grado de seguridad tiene consecuencias importantes para la recuperación de plusvalías urbanísticas.

Hay dos tradiciones relacionadas con el grado de flexibilidad y seguridad en el Planeamiento. La tradición *plan-led*, es decir, 'guiada por el plan' (como por ejemplo los Urbanismos holandés y español) presuntamente ofrece seguridad en momentos tempranos sobre las posibilidades de desarrollo urbanístico gracias a la aprobación de una ordenación vinculante de los usos del suelo. La tradición *development-led*, o 'guiada por la dinámica del desarrollo urbanístico' (como el Urbanismo británico), aunque en momentos tempranos suele elaborar ordenación indicativa, no vinculante, supuestamente ofrece menos seguridad y deja un margen más amplio para las negociaciones con promotores y propietarios. Estas diferencias son la consecuencia de diferencias históricas: el Urbanismo *plan-led* se apoya en la centralidad de la ley escrita y el *development-led* en el sistema de *judge-made law* (derecho jurisprudencial) y el principio legal de *procedural fairness* (equidad).

Modelo de causalidad: ¿qué variables influyen en la recuperación de plusvalías en reestructuración urbana?
En reestructuración urbana están involucrados distintos actores: públicos y privados, con competencias reguladoras o no, con o sin suelo, con un interés directo o indirecto. Todos ellos interactúan dentro de un complejo de múltiples variables hasta moldear el grado final de plusvalía que cada uno de ellos logra recuperar. Si el valor económico de un suelo crece gracias a la reestructuración y a los cambio de usos, entonces se produce un beneficio inicial. Pero este beneficio inicial debe distribuirse de una forma tal que acabe resultando en un beneficio final que sirva para pagar las infraestructuras y dotaciones públicas. Si el beneficio final es suficientemente grande, será posible substraer esas contribuciones. El tamaño del beneficio inicial, y si acaba o no resultando en un beneficio final, depende de diversas variables:

A. Variables de contexto que influyen en el tamaño del beneficio inicial: mercados inmobiliarios, las medidas y características del suelo, mercados laborales y de materiales de construcción, y regímenes fiscales.
B. Variables de contexto que influyen en la distribución del beneficio inicial, esto es **la normativa urbanística**.
C. Actos de aquellos sujetos directamente involucrados en el plan, **incluyendo aquellos con competencias para regular**, que influyen en el tamaño del beneficio inicial: definición de los contenidos y delimitación del plan.

D. Actos de aquellos sujetos directamente involucrados en el plan, **incluyendo aquellos con competencias para regular**, que influyen en la distribución del beneficio inicial: cómo los Ayuntamientos y los propietarios usan la normativa urbanística, cómo actores públicos y privados interactúan informalmente, y circunstancias específicas.

Esta investigación se centra en cómo se pueden manipular las variables impresas en negrita, pero tiene además en cuenta las otras variables porque todas ellas influyen juntas en el tamaño y la distribución del beneficio inicial, es decir en la recuperación de plusvalías urbanísticas. Existen muchas maneras a través de las cuales el beneficio inicial puede acabar 'esfumándose' de tal forma que, al final, no esté disponible para pagar las infraestructuras y dotaciones públicas. Una de ellas es estimar el coste contable que se atribuye al suelo en los cálculos de la operación por un valor muy por encima del valor inicial del suelo, es decir, por encima del valor del uso preexistente del suelo. Por ejemplo, en el proyecto holandés *Kop van Oost*, el valor inicial del suelo era sobre € 3,6 millones, pero se incluyó en los cálculos por al menos € 12 millones. Otra forma de 'fuga' de la plusvalía es el márgen regular de beneficio que el promotor carga como compensación normal por la labor y riesgos que asume. A menudo, en etapas tempranas de un proyecto, tanto el valor contable del suelo como el márgen regular de beneficio no están definidos, y propietarios del suelo y promotores tienen cierto márgen para subirlos o bajarlos: los suben si existe seguridad acerca del *aprovechamiento urbanístico futuro* (cuánto y qué se podrá edificar), y los bajan si existe seguridad acerca de las *contribuciones obligatorias o estándares urbanísticos mínimos* (cuánto se tendrá que contribuir, en *pecunia* y/o en *natura*). También es relevante la posición negociadora de la Administración Pública. Si existe seguridad acerca de la futura edificabilidad se debilita la posición negociadora del Ayuntamiento porque no puede negociar contribuciones adicionales a cambio de más edificabilidad. Si existe seguridad acerca de las contribuciones y estándares, su posición negociadora mejora porque éstos pasan a formar el punto de partida en las negociaciones. Finalmente, su posición negociadora también mejorará si puede condicionar abierta y públicamente la aprobación de la ordenación vinculante a que el promotor garantice sus contribuciones mediante la firma de un Convenio Urbanístico. Los propietarios del suelo tienen una buena posición negociadora porque sus derechos de propiedad les permiten pedir el máximo precio por su suelo. También pueden retrasar el proceso de urbanización, lo que a su vez implica mayores costes, por ejemplo financieros o la necesidad de hacer más estudios y planes, etcétera, que acaban consumiendo el beneficio inicial. Por ejemplo, en el proyecto *Kop van Oost* los costes que implica la urbanización fueron de en torno a 7 millones de euros, mientras que podrían haber sido más bajos, en torno a 2 millones de euros. El retraso puede ser debido a negociaciones difíciles con una multitud de propietarios, y/o a una estrategia deliberada de los propietarios si esperan que el precio del suelo puede aumentar con el tiempo. Como consecuencia de todas estas interacciones, el beneficio inicial acaba desapareciendo. En el proyecto *Kop van Oost* el Ayuntamiento tuvo que subsidiar las infraestructuras y dotaciones públicas mientras que un beneficio inicial de en torno a € 18,5 millones parece haberse fugado.

Dos medidas para mejorar la recuperación de plusvalías: dos hipótesis
Podemos reformular las mencionadas medidas (modificar los derechos de propiedad y la seguridad & flexibilidad en el planeamiento urbanístico) como hipótesis:

1. *Una forma específica de separación de los derechos de propiedad del suelo (separar la urbanización del derecho de propiedad) puede modificar las relaciones de poder en las redes de actores involucrados en reestructuración urbana de tal forma que ello puede mejorar la recuperación de plusvalías urbanísticas.*
2. *En etapas tempranas de los procesos de urbanización, evitar la seguridad acerca de la edificabilidad futura, y crear seguridad sobre futuras contribuciones y estándares urbanísticos, puede mejorar la recuperación de plusvalías urbanísticas.*

Capítulo 3 – Metodología

Esta investigación estudia un 'fenómeno': la interacción entre Ayuntamientos, haciendo uso de la normativa urbanística, y promotores/propietarios a cargo de proyectos de reestructuración urbana. Dos variables son centrales aquí: si el uso de la normativa urbanística (la variable independiente) podría mejorar la recuperación de plusvalías urbanísticas (la variable dependiente). El objetivo final es producir conocimiento que apoye la formulación de recomendaciones acerca de cómo en la práctica urbanística holandesa se podría mejorar la recuperación de plusvalías sin por ello retrasar los procesos de urbanización.

Con este objetivo he tomado diversas decisiones. En primer lugar, basar la investigación en un número limitado de proyectos: cuatro en la CAV, tres en Inglaterra y cuatro en Holanda. No era posible ni recoger suficientes datos de una muestra suficientemente representativa que permitiese un análisis estadístico, ni tampoco aislar a la perfección de terceras variables la relación entre las variables independiente y dependiente. Además, el estudio de proyectos ofrece más información sobre el fenómeno y su interacción con el contexto que un estudio extensivo tipo encuesta. La recogida de datos tuvo lugar antes del comienzo de la crisis financiera y económica internacional durante el verano y otoño del año 2008, y para España antes del comienzo de la crisis inmobiliaria a finales del 2007. Para determinados aspectos relevantes, se llevó a cabo una última ronda de recogida de datos a finales del 2009 y durante el 2010.

Mi segunda decisión fue asegurar un alto grado de validez de las conclusiones para eludir el riesgo, inherente a estudios basados en un número limitado de proyectos, de producir conocimiento tan específico que no sería útil para producir conclusiones generales y recomendaciones para Holanda. Con este objetivo tomé tres grupos de medidas destinadas a incrementar tanto la validez interna como la externa:

1. Usar el método hipotético-deductivo para testear empíricamente las dos hipótesis;
2. Usar variantes del método de diferencia para eludir el riesgo de terceras variables y de correlaciones espurias entre las variables independiente y dependiente: elaboración de una lista de posibles terceras variables para asesorar su papel en cada país y proyecto; limitar la población total de proyectos y elegir países con un sustrato político, económico y social parecido, en ambos casos con el objeto de mantener el contexto lo más estable posible; para el estudio en profundidad seleccionar aquellos modelos urbanísticos contrarios con el objeto de maximizar la varianza de la variable independiente, lo que llevó a la decisión de hacer un estudio internacional comparativo de sistemas urbanísticos; seleccionar proyectos que pudiesen incluir prácticas innovadoras; finalmente, cuando fue posible, estudiar el fenómeno antes y después de una modificación de la variable independiente (una modificación legal y una modificación de política);
3. Usar algunas técnicas pensadas para reforzar la validez externa o posibilidad de extrapolar las conclusiones: seleccionar proyectos representativos y usar fuentes adicionales y complementarias a los proyectos.

Esta investigación no estudia la totalidad del fenómeno, es decir, no analiza *todas* las características del fenómeno, sino que separa las variables relevantes del resto del infinito número de otras variables que podrían caracterizar el fenómeno. Por ello, esta investigación se centra en varias sub-variables de las variables independiente y dependiente. Para distinguirlas, esta investigación desarrolla y aplica un modelo de dependencia y usa además el modelo teórico (incluidas las dos hipótesis) y el modelo de causalidad expuestos arriba. La variable independiente (normativa urbanística) ha sido dividida en cinco sub-variables para analizar cómo la Administración Pública usa esta normativa (cuestión previa 1):

a) Seguridad previa sobre la futura edificabilidad y sobre las contribuciones;
b) Contenido de la ordenación vinculante;
c) Condicionar la ordenación vinculante a que el promotor garantice sus contribuciones;
d) Moldear los derechos de propiedad del suelo;
e) Procedimiento administrativo para la preparación y aprobación de la ordenación vinculante: garantías para el que presenta propuestas; flexibilidad para modificar la ordenación vinculante existente; flexibilidad para delimitar el ámbito físico de la ordenación vinculante en sintonía con las negociaciones con propietarios.

La variable dependiente (recuperación de plusvalías) también ha sido subdividida en varias sub-variables: todas las posibles formas de contribuciones de promotores/propietarios y también posibles efectos colaterales sobre los ritmos de ejecución del Planeamiento. Esto hizo posible evaluar el grado de plusvalía finalmente recuperada (cuestión previa 2). La cuestión previa 3 ha sido resuelta deduciendo el tipo de relación causal entre las variables independiente y dependiente. Las respuestas son de hecho hipótesis confirmadas, por ejemplo: "si los Ayuntamientos establecen en etapas tempranas qué contribuciones tendrán que pagar/ejecutar los promotores, mejorará la recuperación de plusvalías".

Después de responder en los capítulos 5 a 7 cada cuestión previa para cada país, el capítulo 8 presenta las conclusiones, basadas en las hipótesis confirmadas, que pueden ser de interés para el debate académico. Todas estas respuestas e hipótesis confirmadas, incorporando además conocimiento específico de la situación holandesa (legislación y consideraciones políticas y culturales), sirven de base para responder en el capítulo 9 la cuestión principal, es decir, para hacer recomendaciones para la práctica urbanística holandesa.

Capítulo 4 – Estudio explorativo: normativa urbanística en Europa Occidental

El primer paso en un estudio internacional comparativo es un estudio explorativo sobre la variable independiente 'normativa urbanística' en Holanda y en otros ocho países de la Europa Occidental: Alemania, Inglaterra (parte del Reino Unido), Flandes (región belga), Francia, Suecia, Dinamarca, Italia y España (la Comunidad Autónoma de Valencia, CAV). Estudiar países con un sustrato similar como éstos reduce la influencia de terceras variables. El segundo paso fue seleccionar la CAV e Inglaterra porque estos muestran la mayor variación en la variable independiente (representan modelos contrarios de Urbanismo). De este modo se incrementan las posibilidades de producir conclusiones significativas. Estos dos países y Holanda son el objeto de una investigación en profundidad en los capítulos 5 a 7.

Las diferencias entre estos nueve países son remarcables. En lo que se refiere al lugar de la ordenación vinculante dentro de los procesos de urbanización, Inglaterra representa el modelo urbanístico *development-led*, y España/CAV (junto a Francia, Italia y Flandes, aunque éstos países en menor medida) el modelo *plan-led*. Holanda, al igual que Alemania, Suecia y Dinamarca, sigue en la práctica el modelo *development-led* porque la ordenación vinculante suele ser aprobada sólo después de que los Ayuntamientos han negociado con éxito el contenido de esta ordenación con los promotores inmobiliarios. En cuanto a los contendidos de la ordenación vinculante, en Holanda (hasta el año 2008), junto con Dinamarca, ésta no contiene casi ninguna prescripción programática (prescripciones temporales y financieras o cualquier otra prescripción que tenga como objetivo la ejecución del Planeamiento), mientras que la ordenación vinculante en Inglaterra y la CAV sí que contiene prescripciones programáticas. Además, la ordenación vinculante en Holanda (excepto el Plan de Urbanización, *Exploitatieplan*, introducido en el 2008), junto la Danesa, tiene los contenidos más reducidos (es decir, no puede incluir mucho más que prescripciones de ordenación física), mientras que la ordenación vinculante en Inglaterra tiene los contenidos más diversos. Finalmente, en Holanda, Alemania, Francia, Suecia, Dinamarca y Flandes la aprobación de la ordenación vinculante no puede condicionarse, formal, pública y abiertamente, a que el promotor garantice sus contribuciones (es decir, a que se comprometa en un Convenio Urbanístico a urbanizar, ceder suelo, contribuir a los costes, etc), mientras que en Inglaterra, la CAV e Italia esto sí es posible y constituye además el procedimiento estándar.

En cuanto a los derechos de propiedad del suelo, en todos los países estudiados el derecho de propiedad incluye el derecho a edificar. No se ha constatado ningún caso en el que los derechos de propiedad estén completamente separados del derecho a desarrollar urbanísticamente el suelo. Esto es, el propietario del suelo es el único autorizado a edificar sobre su suelo, y puede excluir a otros de hacerlo. Sin embargo, en la CAV, Alemania, Francia y Suecia la legislación urbanística identifica explícitamente la urbanización como una tarea pública, mientras que en Holanda, Inglaterra y los otros países no. Además, en la CAV y, en menor medida en Alemania y Suecia, la urbanización puede ser ejecutada sin necesidad de acuerdo voluntario con el propietario gracias a la posibilidad de aplicar reparcelación forzosa. Por el contrario, en Holanda, Inglaterra, Francia, Italia, Suecia, Flandes y Dinamarca, urbanizar depende de un acuerdo con los propietarios, y esta dependencia sólo puede ser eludida si la Administración Pública se implica significativamente, en términos financieros y de organización (comprando el suelo y aplicando el derecho de tanteo y retracto, expropiando o aplicando fórmulas fiscales *a posteriori*). En cuanto al procedimiento administrativo de aprobación de la ordenación vinculante, en Inglaterra es posible modificar algunas prescripciones estructurales por medio de un procedimiento muy sencillo, mientras que en Holanda y la CAV es necesario un procedimiento largo y complejo.

Capítulo 5 – La Comunidad Autónoma de Valencia (CAV)

La CAV tiene casi todas las competencias de elaboración y ejecución en materia de legislación urbanística, y además subsidia, junto al Estado Central y muchos Ayuntamientos, diversas políticas orientadas a la reestructuración y revitalización de áreas urbanas históricas y otras áreas urbanas en deterioro. Sin embargo, una gran parte de la reestructuración urbana en los últimos decenios ha sido el resultado de iniciativas privadas de recalificación a usos primordialmente residenciales de viejas áreas industriales situadas dentro del suelo urbano. El presente trabajo se centra en estos tipos de proyectos de reestructuración, donde no existen subsidios públicos. Para dar un nuevo uso al suelo, la Administración Pública tiene primero que modificar la ordenación vinculante previa, que es de dos tipos: Planeamiento general y de desarrollo. El Planeamiento general (Planes Generales) cubren todo el territorio municipal y tienen un carácter jurídico vinculante. En suelo urbanizable incluyen la ordenación estructural, es decir clasifican el suelo entre urbano, urbanizable y no urbanizable, prescriben las posibles tipologías edificativas, la red primaria de dotaciones públicas y los derechos de edificación de cada propietario (el aprovechamiento tipo, una especie de índice de edificabilidad por metro cuadrado de suelo). Todo esto da un alto grado de seguridad sobre las futuras posibilidades edificatorias. En el suelo urbanizable programado y en el suelo urbano, el Plan General incluye además la ordenación pormenorizada, es decir la calificación del suelo en usos urbanos específicos (vivienda, industrial, oficinas, etc.), alineación, altura y volúmenes de los edificios, y la red secundaria de dotaciones públicas. Los Planes de desarrollo (Planes Especiales, Parciales y de Reforma Interior) cubren áreas específicas y pueden modificar los Planes Generales, a los que han de detallar si que es que éstos no contienen aún la ordenación pormenorizada.

Las Administraciones Públicas españolas han perseguido tradicionalmente que la plusvalía urbanística pague las infraestructuras y dotaciones públicas. Este objetivo llevó a la introducción en 1956 de la mencionada Reparcelación. Los propietarios mismos habían de reparcelar sus propiedades y urbanizar el suelo. Si los propietarios no colaboraban, el Ayuntamiento podía aplicar reparcelación forzosa o expropiar los terrenos y ejecutar directamente la urbanización. En 1978 el Estado Central introdujo una serie de estándares mínimos de dotaciones públicas (los 'estándares urbanísticos') que, junto con los Planes Generales, crean seguridad acerca de las futuras contribuciones que habrán de ser satisfechas por los promotores y propietarios. Sin embargo, la aplicación de la Reparcelación de 1956 estimuló en la práctica la especulación del suelo (lo que llevó a elevados costes contables del suelo), conllevó tremendas dificultades para organizar a los propietarios y retrasó los procesos de urbanización (lo que comportó una inflación de los costes que implica la urbanización). Todo esto resultó en solares mal urbanizados, infraestructuras y dotaciones públicas de calidad inferior y una edificación masiva y físicamente inflada. En el año 1994 el gobierno regional de la CAV introdujo por medio de la Ley de Regulación de la Actividad Urbanística (LRAU) importantes novedades en la Reparcelación. En primer lugar, introdujo a un tercer actor junto al Ayuntamiento y al propietario/promotor: el agente urbanizador. Este agente no necesita poseer suelo y el Ayuntamiento puede seleccionarlo directamente (agente urbanizador público) o a través de un concurso público (agente urbanizador privado: los propietarios, o una promotora, o una constructora, etc). Una vez seleccionado, el agente urbanizador asume la responsabilidad de urbanizar y reparcelar los terrenos. En segundo lugar, la LRAU le dio garantías a los actores de mercado si éstos tomaban la iniciativa de presentar una propuesta de urbanización. En tercer lugar, los Planes de desarrollo habían de ser acompañados de ordenación programática (prescripciones temporales y financieras o cualquier otra prescripción que tenga como objetivo la ejecución del Planeamiento) y de un Convenio Urbanístico. Cualquier empresa o persona puede participar en el concurso público si presenta una propuesta al Ayuntamiento, ya que no es necesario ser propietario del suelo, y cualquier otra empresa o persona puede presentar alegaciones y/o una propuesta alternativa. Después de evaluar las propuestas, el Pleno Municipal selecciona una de ellas y selecciona al agente urbanizador. El agente urbanizador elabora y presenta al Ayuntamiento una propuesta detallada de urbanización y de reparcelación. Después de reparcelar las propiedades (aplicando reparcelación forzosa si fuese necesario), el Ayuntamiento recibe las infraestructuras, el suelo para dotaciones públicas (equipamientos y zonas verdes) y, a menudo, también algunos solares, y los propietarios del suelo reciben los restantes solares. Finalmente, los propietarios de los solares solicitan los permisos de edificación al Ayuntamiento. Esta novedad valenciana ha sido introducida en casi todas las otras 17 Comunidades Autónomas españolas.

¿Hasta dónde pueden llegar las contribuciones de propietarios y promotores? En España, los Ayuntamientos capturan parte de la plusvalía urbanística en suelo urbanizable, y lo hacen requiriendo entre un 5 y un 15% de los solares. Además, los propietarios han de pagar los costes de la urbanización, ceder el suelo necesario para esta urbanización y todas las dotaciones públicas y pagar al agente urbanizador sus gastos de gestión y un porcentaje de beneficio. En principio, los edificios y dotaciones públicos (escuelas, hospitales, etc) han de ser pagados por la respectiva Administración Pública, excepto en el caso de las viviendas protegidas, que han de ser construidas y pagadas por los propietarios. Adicionalmente, también es posible obligar a los propietarios a ceder suelo situado fuera del sector para destinarlo a sistemas generales de infraestructura, parques y dotaciones públicas. Los Ayuntamientos son libres de acordar contribuciones adicionales con el agente urbanizador, pero éste habrá de pagarlas con sus propios recursos y no puede cargarlas a los propietarios.

De los proyectos que son objeto de este estudio, tres están localizados en la ciudad de Valencia: *Camino Hondo del Grao* (5,7 ha, 465 apartamentos y una considerable cantidad de oficinas y terciario); *Guillem de Anglesola* (1,2 ha, 125 apartamentos y algo de terciario); y *Periodista Gil Sumbiela* (0,6 ha, 100 apartamentos y algo de terciario). Además, un proyecto está localizado en la ciudad de Alicante: *Benalúa Sur* (8 ha, 600 apartamentos y una considerable cantidad de oficinas y terciario). En los cuatro proyectos, existía previamente un Plan General que prescribía la ordenación estructural y, en los casos de *Guillem* y de *Periodista*, también fijaba la ordenación pormenorizada. También fue necesario aprobar un Plan de desarrollo. En los proyectos *Camino* y *Benalúa* el Plan de desarrollo modificó aspectos de la ordenación estructural del Plan General. En *Guillem* y en *Periodista*, el Plan de desarrollo detalló y modificó sólo elementos de la ordenación pormenorizada. En todos los proyectos, el agente urbanizador es un agente privado seleccionado en un concurso público, a veces un promotor profesional, como en *Guillem* y *Periodista*, a veces los mismos propietarios del suelo organizados en una Agrupación de Interés Urbanístico, como en *Camino* y *Benalúa*. Casi siempre los agentes urbanizadores no sólo urbanizan y reparcelan los terrenos, sino que además compran suelo y se convierten también en los promotores de la edificación, o al menos de parte de ella. En *Periodista* la mayoría de los propietarios vendieron su suelo relativamente rápido al urbanizador. En

Guillem esperaron y la mayoría vendió durante el procedimiento administrativo de aprobación de la reparcelación. En *Camino* y *Benalúa* el suelo ya era la propiedad del agente urbanizador (debido a que los propietarios mismos se convirtieron en agente urbanizador).

Capítulo 6 – Inglaterra

El gobierno central del Reino Unido, junto con las Administraciones Públicas regionales y locales, han producido principalmente dos políticas de regeneración urbana: las destinadas a mejorar las condiciones de vivienda (que tienen una larga tradición), y las destinadas a regenerar los centros urbanos (que se iniciaron en los años 70). En los últimos decenios, tal y como muestran los proyectos estudiados, la Administración Pública ha buscado que los promotores inmobiliarios paguen más infraestructuras y dotaciones públicas. Antes de dar un nuevo uso a los suelos, las Administraciones Públicas locales (*Local Planning Authorities, LPAs*) han de modificar la ordenación vinculante vigente. En Inglaterra, existen planes de usos del suelo que cubren amplias áreas, y estos planes pueden jugar un papel importante, pero son de un carácter jurídico indicativo, es decir, no vinculan directamente el uso del suelo. El único plan que contiene ordenación vinculante es el *Planning Permission*, que cubre una localización concreta. Una vez que un promotor presenta una solicitud de *Planning Permission* para un proyecto concreto, la LPA puede imponerle condiciones (*conditions*), o ir más allá y negociar en un Convenio Urbanístico (*Planning Agreement*, o *106-agreement*) que el promotor realice o pague contribuciones (*obligations*).

En principio la Administración Pública en Inglaterra tiene el derecho a fiscalizar la plusvalía urbanística causada por la decisión administrativa de cambio de uso del suelo. En el pasado se aplicaron distintos tipos de impuestos, pero en la actualidad ya no existen. En la práctica, la recuperación de plusvalías tiene lugar exigiendo a los promotores que contribuyan para mitigar las externalidades negativas de proyectos urbanísticos. Estas contribuciones se generalizaron en los años 70, evolucionando desde la urbanización física dentro de los límites físicos del proyecto, hasta incluir también infraestructura medioambiental, comunitaria y social localizada dentro y fuera de los límites del proyecto. Esto incluye por ejemplo exigir a los promotores que edifiquen vivienda social y protegida. En los últimos años ha habido controversia acerca de la envergadura y variedad de estas contribuciones, controversia que ha resultado en una regulación más detallada de qué contribuciones son exigibles y cuáles no, lo cual sin embargo no ha reducido ni la envergadura ni la variedad de las contribuciones.

Los tres proyectos estudiados están localizados en la ciudad de Bristol: *Harbourside/Canon's Marsh* (7,8 ha, 700 apartamentos, 44,000 m^2 de oficinas, 30,000 m^2 de terciario y comercial); *Temple Quay* (7,4 ha, 495 apartamentos, 61,000 m² de oficinas, y 7,000 m² de terciario y comercial); y *Megabowl* (1,3 ha, 184 apartamentos). El *Bristol Local Plan* de 1997 (un plan de usos del suelo de carácter indicativo, no vinculante, que cubre toda la ciudad de Bristol) prescribía la ordenación indicativa para estos tres proyectos. Antes de proceder a reurbanizar los terrenos hubieron de concederse uno o varios *planning permissions* que incluían las contribuciones que habían de ser negociadas con los promotores y que fueron finalmente incluidas en Convenios Urbanísticos.

Capítulo 7 – Holanda

Las Administraciones Públicas central y local holandesas fomentan activamente la reestructuración y revitalización de zonas urbanas y la construcción en ellas de nuevas viviendas y oficinas. Existen políticas específicas para: áreas centrales multifuncionales, incluyendo estaciones de ferrocarriles (proyecto *Stationskwartier*, 16 ha, 650 apartamentos más bastantes oficinas, algo de terciario, una nueva estación de ferrocarriles y bastantes edificios de aparcamientos); distritos monofuncionales de antes y después de la Segunda Guerra Mundial (proyecto *Kruidenbuurt*, 17 ha, 650 viviendas más algunas oficinas); y viejas áreas industriales (proyectos *De Funen* -8 ha, 565 apartamentos, algo de oficinas- y *Kop van Oost* -5 ha, 430 apartamentos, más algo de terciario). Todo proyecto de reestructuración urbana suele implicar la elaboración de planes de uso del suelo de carácter indicativo, muchos de los cuales no están regulados en la legislación urbanística. Ahora bien, antes de que la reestructuración pueda tener lugar efectivamente es necesario encontrar en primer lugar los medios que permitan la obtención de las infraestructuras y dotaciones públicas, y en segundo lugar aprobar la ordenación vinculante (el plan de usos del suelo vinculante – *Bestemmingsplan* – o modificaciones del mismo).

En Holanda la plusvalía urbanística pertenece al propietario del suelo. El actual marco legal de recuperación de plusvalías se limita a la recuperación de costes, es decir, a poder exigir a los promotores que paguen aquellos costes de infraestructura pública que les benefician. Este principio no ha sido modificado ni por la nueva Ley de Urbanismo y Ordenación Territorial (*Wet ruimtelijke ordening*) ni por el Reglamento de Urbanismo y Ordenación Territorial (*Besluit ruimtelijke ordening*), introducidos ambos en el año 2008. En general, las contribuciones de los promotores son el resultado de negociaciones. A partir del 2008 es posible, por primera vez, exigir al propietario una contribución sin necesidad de negociarla. Para ello el Ayuntamiento ha de aprobar junto con el *Bestemmingsplan* un Plan de Urbanización (*Exploitatieplan*), lo que le permite condicionar la *licencia de edificación* (pero no la aprobación de la *ordenación vinculante*, es decir, del *Bestemmingsplan*) al pago de una contribución. El Reglamento del 2008 regula qué tipos de costes se pueden cargar sobre el propietario a través de un Plan de Urbanización: la urbanización y la vivienda social/

protegida localizados dentro de los límites físicos del proyecto, y contribuciones a sistemas generales que beneficien directamente al proyecto. Esto excluye los costes de mantenimiento y explotación de equipamientos sociales, y parte de los costes de reurbanización de la infraestructura ya existente y de elaboración del planeamiento. Además, como no se puede exigir a los propietarios a emplear la plusvalía urbanística para pagar estos costes, la elaboración de un Plan de Urbanización suele implicar, sobre todo en proyectos de reestructuración urbana, que el Ayuntamiento ha de hacerse cargo de un déficit añadido a los costes no recuperables mencionados arriba. En lugar de aprobar un Plan de Urbanización, los Ayuntamientos y los promotores/propietarios son libres, desde el 2008, de negociar, previamente a la aprobación de la ordenación vinculante, contribuciones en un llamado Convenio Urbanístico 'anterior'. Un Convenio anterior puede incluir más contribuciones que un Plan de Urbanización.

Capítulos 8 y 9 – Conclusiones para el debate académico y recomendaciones para la práctica urbanística holandesa

Más recuperación de plusvalías urbanísticas en la CAV e Inglaterra que en Holanda

Los datos recogidos dejan claro que la normativa urbanística en la CAV y en Inglaterra se diferencia sustancialmente de la holandesa (ver las siguientes secciones). Una comparación entre el nivel de recuperación de plusvalías muestra también diferencias sustanciales: en la CAV y en Inglaterra, los promotores y propietarios del suelo contribuyen en reestructuración urbana significativamente más que en Holanda. Las diferencias se refieren fundamentalmente a:

- Los costes de infraestructuras y dotaciones públicas localizados dentro de los límites físicos del proyecto: en Inglaterra y la CAV los promotores/propietarios pagan casi todos estos costes, mientras que en Holanda la Administración Pública ha de subvencionarlos significativamente;
- Suelo para estas infraestructuras: en Valencia son los propietarios los que ceden este suelo, mientras que en Inglaterra y Holanda son necesarias contribuciones públicas para obtener este suelo;
- Vivienda social y protegida: en Inglaterra y la CAV son los promotores/propietarios los que pagan buena parte o casi todos estos costes, mientras que en Holanda son las Administraciones Públicas y las cooperativas de vivienda las que asumen esta carga;
- Infraestructuras públicas de sistemas generales: en Inglaterra y la CAV los promotores/propietarios contribuyen significativamente (en Inglaterra fundamentalmente *in pecunia*, en la CAV fundamentalmente con suelo), mientras que en Holanda estas contribuciones son muy excepcionales;

- Recuperación pública de plusvalías urbanísticas: los Ayuntamientos valencianos recuperan una parte significativa de la plusvalía, incluso si no son propietarios previos del suelo. En Inglaterra no existe formalmente recuperación pública de plusvalías, pero debido a la definición tan amplia de las contribuciones que pueden negociarse con los promotores, se podría concluir que en la práctica sí hay de algún modo recuperación pública de plusvalías. En Holanda los Ayuntamientos sólo pueden beneficiarse de la plusvalía urbanística en el caso de que fuesen previamente propietarios del suelo.

Mi conclusión es que existe una fuerte correlación entre la plusvalía recuperada (que es la más alta en la CAV, menor pero también significativa en Inglaterra, y la más baja en Holanda) y las posibilidades que ofrece la normativa urbanística. Dicho esto, es importante recalcar que esta correlación no es perfecta. Existen otras variables que podrían explicar también *parte* de las diferencias en plusvalía recuperada. Una variable relevante es el precio de mercado de los bienes inmobiliarios. Cuando los datos fueron recogidos, los precios de la vivienda en los proyectos ingleses eran significativamente mayores que los precios en los proyectos valencianos y holandeses. Esto podría explicar *parcialmente* por qué los promotores ingleses contribuyeron más generosamente que sus colegas holandeses, pero en absoluto por qué los promotores valencianos, a pesar de contar con precios de mercado parecidos a los holandeses y menores a los ingleses, contribuyen algo más que los promotores ingleses, y mucho más que los holandeses. Otras variables que podrían también explicar *parte* de las diferencias son las características específicas del proyecto, los mercados laborales y de materiales de construcción, los regímenes fiscales, los contenidos y límites físicos del proyecto, y otras circunstancias específicas de las interacciones y personas involucradas.

Conclusiones para el debate académico

El capítulo 2 presentó dos medidas concretas, formuladas como hipótesis, destinadas a influir en las interacciones que tienen lugar dentro las redes de gestión en reestructuración urbana y en el grado de plusvalía finalmente recuperado. Estas dos hipótesis han sido chequeadas empíricamente. La primera especula sobre los efectos en la recuperación de plusvalías de la definición de los derechos de propiedad del suelo y cómo esta definición influye en las relaciones de poder entre los agentes públicos y privados. La segunda especula sobre los efectos de la seguridad creada por la ordenación vinculante y no vinculante durante los procesos de desarrollo urbanístico. En el modelo de causalidad expuesto en el capítulo 2, descubrimos una tercera especulación que también ha sido testada empíricamente: la presunción de que la flexibilidad en los procedimientos administrativos podría ser relevante para recuperar plusvalías.

En lo que se refiere a esta tercera presunción, no ha sido posible deducir relaciones claras y generalizables entre la flexibilidad administrativa y la plusvalía recuperada. Sin embargo, parece que las dos primeras hipótesis sí son válidas. La normativa sobre derechos de propiedad y flexibilidad de la ordenación es ciertamente relevante porque puede influir las interacciones dentro de las redes de gestión de políticas. La Administración Pública en Inglaterra y, especialmente, en la CAV, parece tener, gracias a esta normativa, un papel más determinante que en Holanda. Los Ayuntamientos ingleses y sobre todo los Valencianos prescriben *a priori* y unilateralmente unos claros requisitos y unas contribuciones concretas, lo que resulta en un alto grado de plusvalía recuperada. Los Ayuntamientos valencianos van más allá que los ingleses, ya que tienen, gracias a la Reparcelación forzosa, el poder de elegir al urbanizador, si es necesario eludiendo a los propietarios del suelo y sin necesidad de comprar o expropiar el suelo. Este papel dominante de la Administración Pública, especialmente en la CAV, no encaja dentro del papel que le da el llamado enfoque de 'redes de gestión de políticas', y además desbarata algunas de las asunciones básicas de este enfoque: que los actores en las redes, tanto públicos como privados, son necesariamente interdependientes, y que la Administración Pública ha de asumir forzosamente un papel modesto y no puede ser dominante.

Los siguientes párrafos explican las diferentes maneras (o sub-variables) mediante las cuales la normativa urbanística puede ser utilizada para influir la recuperación de plusvalías. Para cada sub-variable se presentan algunas conclusiones para el debate académico que se añaden a las arriba presentadas, y se presentan además las recomendaciones para la práctica urbanística holandesa. En cuanto a estas recomendaciones, se trata primero de medidas voluntarias que encajan dentro de la Ley de Urbanización de 2008, y segundo de propuestas de modificación legislativa más profundas e introducibles en un plazo de tiempo más largo.

Crear seguridad temprana sobre las posibilidades edificatorias y sobre las contribuciones

Resumen de los hallazgos

Los Ayuntamientos en los tres países suelen crear seguridad en etapas tempranas (antes de las negociaciones con los promotores/propietarios) y en diferente medida, acerca de lo que el propietario podrá edificar en el futuro. En Holanda, los ayuntamientos suelen aprobar planes indicativos, no vinculantes, los cuales crean cierta seguridad. En Inglaterra ocurre algo similar, también en documentos indicativos, y en la CAV la seguridad se crea por medio de ordenación vinculante, del Planeamiento general. Los datos sugieren que una mayor seguridad temprana puede resultar en menor plusvalía recuperada porque puede estimular el incremento de los precios del suelo, y además los Ayuntamientos pierden un valioso instrumento de negociación. Sin embargo, la seguridad sobre posibilidades edificatorias, si está acompañada de seguridad sobre las futuras contribuciones (ver abajo), no es necesariamente negativa.

Existen grandes diferencias sobre el grado de seguridad temprana acerca de las contribuciones. En la CAV, en etapas tempranas hay mucha seguridad gracias a (1) estándares urbanísticos legales, (2) políticas locales y (3) el Planeamiento general.

Los Ayuntamientos ingleses suelen crear cierta seguridad a través de la aprobación de (1) planes indicativos para localizaciones concretas que prescriben las contribuciones para el proyecto de que se trate, y (2) documentos indicativos, no específicamente hechos para una localización concreta, que prescriben contribuciones estándar. En Holanda, antes de que se inicien las negociaciones o de que se fije el precio del suelo, casi nunca existe seguridad, ni creada por ordenación vinculante ni por documentos y planes indicativos. Esta seguridad en la CAV e Inglaterra ha influido positivamente en la recuperación de plusvalías porque: 1) reduce el precio del suelo, ya que si no existe seguridad, el promotor paga demasiado por el suelo y no tiene luego margen para contribuir; 2) reduce el precio por el cual el promotor estima el coste contable del suelo y su margen regular de beneficio; 3) da a los funcionarios públicos a cargo de las negociaciones una fuerte base legitimadora para sus exigencias.

Conclusiones para el debate académico
Los datos parecen confirmar la segunda hipótesis:

En etapas tempranas de los procesos de urbanización, evitar la seguridad acerca de la edificabilidad futura, y crear seguridad sobre futuras contribuciones y estándares urbanísticos, puede mejorar la recuperación de plusvalías urbanísticas.

Parte de la literatura comparativa de sistemas urbanísticos en Europa parece haber concluido erróneamente, al menos en lo que respecta a España *versus* Inglaterra y Holanda, que los sistemas urbanísticos tienden a convergir en lo que se refiere a su nivel de seguridad. Los datos recogidos también pueden ser interesantes para el debate en la profesión urbanística, un debate en el que se presenta la flexibilidad como algo positivo: los datos destacan que debe de haber cierto nivel de seguridad sobre las contribuciones si se quiere mejorar la recuperación de plusvalías urbanísticas.

Recomendaciones para la práctica urbanística holandesa
Los Ayuntamientos holandeses deberían, antes o junto a la aprobación de los planes indicativos que preceden a los desarrollos urbanísticos, crear cierta seguridad acerca de qué contribuciones exigirán a los promotores. La lista de tipos de contribuciones incluida en el Reglamento del 2008 no es suficiente porque es demasiado genérica y no le permite al promotor, en etapas tempranas, calcular exactamente qué le van a costar las contribuciones. Es por ello que los Ayuntamientos deberían crear seguridad acerca de los costes que serán cargados a través de un Plan de Urbanización. Sin embargo, como este plan no permite recuperar todos los costes, los Ayuntamientos no deberían aprobarlo, sino tratar de negociar con el promotor más contribuciones en un Convenio Urbanístico previo. Es por ello que los Ayuntamientos deberían crear seguridad acerca de los costes que desean recuperar mediante un Convenio previo, complementariamente a los costes que podría recuperar en caso de verse forzado a aprobar un Plan de Urbanización.

La seguridad aquí recomendada puede ser creada por medio de la aprobación de diferentes tipos de documentos, muchos de los cuales pueden complementarse los unos a los otros: (1) documentos cubriendo una localización concreta para acompañar los tan frecuentes planes indicativos; (2) documentos genéricos que incluyan contribuciones estándares de carácter integral (cubriendo todos los tipos de contribuciones) o sectorial (cubriendo un tipo específico, por ejemplo vivienda social, o zonas verdes, etc); (3) planes generales de usos del suelo que incluyan las contribuciones, estándares o no. Es preferible que los documentos, de cualquier tipo, sean de carácter indicativo porque esto encaja mejor en la tradición urbanística holandesa. Un documento ideal podría ser el recientemente introducido Visión Estructural (*Structuurvisie*), no sólo porque sus contenidos son de libre definición, sino porque además la Ley de la Urbanización del Suelo (*Grondexploitatiewet*) prescribe que es un documento necesario para poder cargar cierto tipo de costes. El gobierno central holandés debería además de ayudar y estimular a los Ayuntamientos a crear seguridad, por ejemplo elaborando, junto con la Federación de Municipios Holandeses (*Vereniging Nederlandse Gemeenten*), documentos modelos. En caso de que finalmente los Ayuntamientos no se decidiesen a aplicar estas medidas, el gobierno central debería introducir algunas modificaciones legales: en primer lugar obligar a los Ayuntamientos a elaborar documentos genéricos de carácter integral a incluir en Visiones Estructurales, y en segundo lugar introducir estándares y prescripciones urbanísticas legales válidos en todo el país.

Definir el contenido de la ordenación vinculante

Resumen de los hallazgos y recomendaciones para la práctica urbanística holandesa

El uso de planes vinculantes puede ser útil si el Ayuntamiento puede incluir en ellos no sólo la ordenación física, sino también la programática (prescripciones temporales y financieras o cualquier otra prescripción que tenga como objetivo la ejecución del Planeamiento). Tanto en la CAV como en Inglaterra la legislación urbanística permite incluir en planes vinculantes una amplia variedad de prescripciones:

- Vivienda social/protegida: tanto en la CAV como en Inglaterra es posible prescribirla en los planes vinculantes;
- Infraestructuras y dotaciones públicas dentro y fuera de los límites físicos del proyecto: tanto en la CAV como en Inglaterra es posible prescribir la obligación de contribuir a estos costes. En Inglaterra los Ayuntamientos también pueden prescribir contribuciones para la construcción, mantenimiento y explotación de edificios públicos, incluyendo equipamientos sociales (por ejemplo escuelas y servicios sociales);
- Esquemas de pago y ejecución: en ambos países los planes vinculantes pueden incluir el momento y límites temporales dentro de los cuales las contribuciones han de ser ejecutadas.

Todas estas posibilidades influyen positivamente en la recuperación de plusvalías. En Holanda, hasta la Ley del 2008, no era posible incluir ninguna prescripción programática en la ordenación vinculante, lo que ha tenido un efecto negativo en la recuperación de plusvalías. La Ley del 2008 hizo por primera vez posible incluir la mayoría de estas prescripciones. En la actualidad es posible incluir vivienda social/protegida tanto en el Plan de usos del suelo vinculante (un porcentaje de este tipo de vivienda) como en el Plan de Urbanización (localización y número de este tipo de vivienda). También es posible incluir en el Plan de Urbanización esquemas de pago y ejecución, además de contribuciones para buena parte de la urbanización interna y para una parte de los sistemas generales. Sin embargo, se mantienen una serie de limitaciones:

1. No es posible de incluir en el Plan de Urbanización contribuciones para la construcción, mantenimiento y explotación de equipamientos sociales, y es dudoso de que se pueda acordar este tipo de contribuciones en Convenios Urbanísticos. Para hacer posible el cargo de estas contribuciones habría que modificar el artículo 6.2.5 del Reglamento de 2008.
2. Ya se ha mencionado que mediante un Plan de Urbanización no se pueden cargar muchos de los costes. Es por ello que debería de ampliarse la lista de tipos de costes que se pueden cargar a los propietarios (artículos 6.2.3 hasta 6.2.6 del Reglamento del 2008).
3. En un Plan de Urbanización los propietarios tienen derecho a incluir sus suelos por el valor de su uso futuro, no por su valor inicial, lo que incrementa el coste contable del suelo y por lo tanto la probabilidad de un déficit, déficit del que tiene que hacerse cargo el Ayuntamiento. Es por ello que habría que modificar el artículo 6.13.5 de la Ley del 2008, que prescribe que la valoración del suelo ha de seguir la Ley de Expropiación (*Onteigeningswet*).

Conclusiones para el debate académico

Estos hallazgos han sido utilizados para refinar la segunda hipótesis (en letras negrita lo añadido):

En etapas tempranas de los procesos de urbanización, evitar sla seguridad acerca de la edificabilidad futura, y crear seguridad sobre futuras contribuciones y estándares urbanísticos ***(especialmente si es posible incluir todas estas contribuciones y estándares como obligatorios en la ordenación vinculante)****, puede mejorar la recuperación de plusvalías urbanísticas.*

Condicionar la ordenación vinculante a que el promotor garantice sus contribuciones

Resumen de los hallazgos

La aprobación de ordenación vinculante que incluya una generosa recuperación de plusvalías y términos estrictos para hacerla realidad no implica, automáticamente, que el promotor vaya efectivamente a ejecutarlos. Con el objetivo de asegurar su ejecución el promotor ha de comprometerse a ello. En la práctica los Ayuntamientos holandeses a menudo condicionan la ordenación vinculante a la firma de un Convenio Urbanístico que asegure las contribuciones; sin embargo, no tienen la posibilidad formal de hacerlo de un modo directo y abierto, lo cual conlleva una serie de desventajas:

1. *Riesgos de procedimiento administrativo*: después de cerrar el Convenio Urbanístico, la ordenación vinculante ha de someterse al entero procedimiento de aprobación, lo que implica riesgos de retraso y de modificaciones fruto del procedimiento de consulta pública y aprobación en el Pleno municipal. En la CAV y en Inglaterra, el procedimiento de aprobación provisional de la ordenación vinculante *precede* la negociación y firma del Convenio, después del cual sólo resta una corta aprobación final. Esto significa que en la CAV e Inglaterra, los agentes públicos y privados pueden cerrar un Convenio con un alto grado de seguridad de que el plan no va a ser modificado sustancialmente, y de que no ha de haber un retraso significativo;
2. *Riesgos de recursos contra el plan*: si un Ayuntamiento holandés se niega a aprobar la ordenación vinculante porque el promotor se niega a firmar un Convenio, siempre existe el riesgo de que alguien (por ejemplo el promotor) recurra la decisión. En Inglaterra y la CAV la legislación urbanística prescribe que el promotor está obligado a asegurar en un Convenio las contribuciones y obligaciones incluidas en la versión provisionalmente aprobada de la ordenación vinculante, y que este Convenio es un requisito *sine qua non* para aprobarla definitivamente;
3. *Incongruente discurso público del Ayuntamiento*: en la práctica urbanística holandesa los Ayuntamientos se pueden ver obligados a ocultar las 'razones verdaderas' por las cuales deciden modificar o no la ordenación vinculante, es decir, a ocular por ejemplo que la razón de negarse a aprobar un plan es que el promotor se niega a cerrar un Convenio. En Inglaterra y en la CAV, la 'razón verdadera' es aprobada en público por el Pleno Municipal y forma el marco abierto y transparente para evaluar la aprobación definitiva de la ordenación vinculante.

En Holanda, una vez que se aprueban el Plan de usos del suelo vinculante y el Plan de Urbanización, el propietario puede solicitar la licencia de edificación. La novedad tras la Ley del 2008 es que el Ayuntamiento, si aprueba un Plan de Urbanización, puede condicionar la licencia de edificación al pago de una contribución; antes del 2008 esto no era posible. Sin embargo, aprobar un Plan de Urbanización tiene serias desventajas: el Ayuntamiento ha de asumir algunos riesgos financieros porque es responsable de los cálculos del Plan y puede verse obligado a avanzar inversiones; tiene que emplear sus recursos en elaborar este documento y actualizarlo cada año; y tiene que cargar con las consecuencias (posiblemente financieras) en caso de que uno o varios propietarios decidan retrasar su solicitud de licencia de edificación. Además, tal como vimos más arriba, no todos los costes pueden ser cargados sobre los propietarios. Es por todas estas razones que en principio la mejor opción para los Ayuntamientos holandeses es negociar un Convenio Urbanístico y cerrarlo antes de aprobar la ordenación vinculante: de este modo se aseguran las contribuciones y no hay ya necesidad de aprobar un Plan de Urbanización. Los Ayuntamientos pueden requerir informalmente al promotor que negocie un Convenio. Sin embargo, como consecuencia de la Ley del 2008, este condicionamiento informal puede ser más dificultoso que antes. La Ley ha reforzado la obligación del Ayuntamiento de que tome una decisión formal sobre una propuesta de modificación del Planeamiento. Si el Ayuntamiento desea negarse (y poder negarse es un importante instrumento de negociación), debe tomar una decisión formal dentro de un periodo de ocho semanas. El Ayuntamiento debe justificar su decisión basándose en documentos y planes aprobados, y el solicitante puede ahora recurrir la decisión municipal (o la ausencia de decisión) a los tribunales. En otras palabras, el Ayuntamiento no puede, directa y abiertamente, negarse a modificar el Planeamiento porque el solicitante se niegue a cerrar un Convenio, y debe basarse en argumentos incluidos en la ordenación vinculante, una Visión Estructural u otro documento aprobado públicamente. Si el Ayuntamiento ya ha expresado (por ejemplo en un documento público, o en una reunión formal con el promotor del que conste el contenido de la conversación) que la propuesta de ordenación física es aceptable, en realidad ya no queda mucho margen legal para negarse, y por lo tanto, para negociar.

Conclusiones para el debate académico
Los datos han sido utilizados para refinar la segunda hipótesis (en letras negrita lo añadido):

*En etapas tempranas de los procesos de urbanización, evitar la seguridad acerca de la edificabilidad futura, y crear seguridad sobre futuras contribuciones y estándares urbanísticos (especialmente si es posible incluir todas estas contribuciones y estándares como obligatorios en la ordenación vinculante****, y si es posible de condicionar abierta y directamente la aprobación de esta ordenación a un Convenio Urbanístico que garantice las contribuciones y estándares****), puede mejorar la recuperación de plusvalías urbanísticas.*

Recomendaciones para la práctica urbanística holandesa
Aunque un condicionamiento abierto y directo de la ordenación a un Convenio es en realidad ilegal, existen algunas alternativas, y la Ley del 2008 ha añadido algunas posibilidades:

- Argumentar que las contribuciones son necesarias para que el Plan vinculante de usos del suelo sea viable desde el punto de vista económico: si las contribuciones no están aseguradas y/o hay un déficit, el Ayuntamiento habría de pagar estos costes. Pero si el Ayuntamiento no ha destinado recursos para ello puede negarse a aprobar el plan argumentando que su ejecución no es viable. Esta alternativa tiene las mismas desventajas mencionadas arriba: (1) riesgos de procedimiento administrativo, (2) riesgos de recursos contra el plan (condicionar indirectamente a través de la viabilidad económica del plan no es lo mismo que enumerar abiertamente las contribuciones que el promotor habría de asegurar), y (3) incongruente discurso público del Ayuntamiento.
- Condicionar la ordenación a un Convenio a través de un boceto del Plan de

Urbanización y sobre la base de documentos públicos sobre contribuciones obligatorias. Después de que un promotor solicita una modificación del Planeamiento, el Ayuntamiento debe hacer un cálculo de los costes y beneficios del proyecto siguiendo los requisitos que la ley establece para el Plan de Urbanización. Este cálculo dejaría claro, en caso de que el Ayuntamiento aprobase el Plan de Urbanización, qué parte de los costes podrían ser cargados a los propietarios. Si el Ayuntamiento ha aplicado las recomendaciones hechas arriba de crear seguridad sobre contribuciones por medio de diversos tipos de documentos, le será posible argumentar adecuadamente que la modificación del Planeamiento implica costes que sobrepasan el paquete mínimo de urbanización e incluye también contribuciones más amplias para infraestructuras y dotaciones dentro y fuera de los límites físicos del plan. Estos documentos públicos que crean seguridad son de vital importancia: sin ellos es improbable que fuese posible calcular y argumentar adecuadamente *todos* los costes. En caso de que los cálculos dejen claro que el Ayuntamiento no puede recuperar todos los costes, el Ayuntamiento puede negarse a modificar el Planeamiento argumentando que no puede hacerse cargo del déficit. Esta alternativa sigue teniendo el primer inconveniente mencionado arriba (riesgos de procedimiento administrativo), y un inconveniente añadido: si el promotor accede a garantizar en un Convenio los costes adicionales (pero no los costes que se podrían cargar a través de un Plan de Urbanización), el Ayuntamiento no podría ya utilizar el argumento de la viabilidad económica para rechazar la solicitud ya que en teoría el Plan de Urbanización ya lo asegura.

Para eludir las desventajas de ambas alternativas, se recomienda al gobierno central holandés que modifique la legislación urbanística para permitir un condicionamiento directo y abierto de modo similar a como ocurre en la CAV e Inglaterra. Con tal objeto habrían de introducirse dos modificaciones específicas en la Ley del 2008 y posiblemente también en el Reglamento del mismo año.

Moldear los derechos de propiedad del suelo

Resumen de los hallazgos

En Inglaterra y en Holanda existe una fuerte interdependencia entre la Administración Pública local y los propietarios y promotores. Por lo general, las transacciones que son necesarias para urbanizar un terreno dependen mucho de acuerdos voluntarios entre Ayuntamiento, propietarios y promotores porque ninguno de ellos controla todos los recursos necesarios: los ayuntamientos tienen las facultades legales de modificación del Planeamiento, pero los propietarios/promotores tienen los recursos financieros y el derecho exclusivo de desarrollar el suelo. Esta interdependencia no puede resolverse haciendo uso de la expropiación o del derecho de tanteo y retracto porque estos instrumentos legales sufren en la práctica de limitaciones e implican además una implicación directa y financiera de la Administración Pública. La situación en la CAV cambió radicalmente después de que el gobierno regional introdujo en 1994 la LRAU: desde entonces ya no existe, para urbanizar, una interdependencia entre Administración y propietarios que no pueda eludirse con relativa facilidad. En la actualidad, los Ayuntamientos valencianos pueden aplicar la reparcelación forzosa sin tener por ello que implicarse directamente ni asumir riesgos. El Ayuntamiento selecciona en concurso público al agente urbanizador, y los propietarios pueden elegir entre expropiación voluntaria o participar en la operación. Si eligen la expropiación, el agente urbanizador paga la compensación y se queda con el suelo. Pero si deciden participar están obligados a ceder el suelo necesario para las infraestructuras y dotaciones públicas y a pagar al agente urbanizador una parte proporcional de los costes que conlleve la urbanización. A cambio los propietarios comparten la plusvalía urbanística restante: después de urbanizar los terrenos el agente urbanizador entrega los solares a los propietarios y cede la infraestructura pública, junto con los solares destinados a dotaciones, al Ayuntamiento. En resumidas cuentas, aunque los propietarios aún controlan el suelo, la dependencia mutua es ahora fácilmente eludible porque los Ayuntamientos pueden seleccionar a un tercer actor (que no tiene necesariamente que poseer suelo) como agente urbanizador y no necesitan involucrarse ni en la gestión ni en la financiación. Los Ayuntamientos tampoco dependen de un agente urbanizador concreto, ya que pueden seleccionar a una empresa pública o a otro promotor como agente urbanizador.

Esta interdependencia entre Administración Pública y propietarios en Inglaterra y Holanda le da a los propietarios la opción de esperar, opción de la que hacen uso con frecuencia para oponerse a los requisitos del Ayuntamiento. La Administración Pública, especialmente en Holanda, suele concluir que no puede pedir demasiado, lo que deriva en unos niveles bajos de recuperación de plusvalías. Esta interdependencia también conlleva con frecuencia un retraso en la urbanización porque los propietarios rechazan las exigencias municipales o porque los promotores no consiguen comprar suficiente suelo por un precio razonable. El resultado de las negociaciones depende de las expectativas que puedan tener promotores y propietarios de aumentar sus beneficios retrasando dichas negociaciones. Otra consecuencia negativa es un aumento del valor contable del suelo: las promotoras están más interesadas en adquirir suelo porque poseerlo les da una firme posición negociadora, lo que resulta en un aumento de los precios reales y esperados del suelo.

Adicionalmente los datos sugieren que la interdependencia lleva a un proceso de urbanización ineficaz y tedioso en el que los costes son innecesariamente altos y diversos actores se apropian con éxito de la plusvalía urbanística. Esto conlleva un aumento de los costes que implica la urbanización; en Inglaterra y en Holanda estos costes son con mucha frecuencia entre 1,5 y hasta 4 veces superiores a estos costes en la CAV. Esto dota a los promotores valencianos de un mayor margen financiero para contribuir que en el caso de los promotores holandeses e ingleses.

Conclusiones para el debate académico

Los datos confirman la primera hipótesis:

Una forma específica de separación de los derechos de propiedad del suelo (separar la urbanización del derecho de propiedad) puede modificar las relaciones de poder en las redes de actores involucrados en reestructuración urbana de tal forma que ello puede mejorar la recuperación de plusvalías urbanísticas.

Esta investigación buscaba evidencias empíricas relevantes para el debate sobre la separación del derecho a desarrollar el uso urbano del de la propiedad del suelo. Los hallazgos apoyan la presunción de que separar la urbanización del control de los propietarios a través de una fórmula específica de reparcelación puede mejorar la recuperación de plusvalías. Además, los datos sugieren que la reparcelación puede tener un efecto deflacionario en los costes que implica la urbanización, y posiblemente también en el valor contable del suelo. La reparcelación también puede ayudar a resolver los problemas de estancamiento en la construcción de viviendas. Los hallazgos son interesantes para el debate en Holanda, ya que coinciden con la posición de aquellos que defienden que el aumento del control privado de los procesos de urbanización desde los años 90 ha sido desventajoso para los objetivos y finanzas públicas. Los hallazgos también apoyan la conclusión de que moldear los derechos de propiedad del suelo puede ayudar a mejorar la consecución de objetivos públicos en Urbanismo. En cuanto al debate en España, los datos apoyan la visión crítica de aquellos que, en los años 90, defendieron que la única forma de asegurar infraestructuras y dotaciones públicas de calidad es romper la posición monopólica/oligopólica de los propietarios. Para refinar estas conclusiones es necesario investigar en un futuro con más profundidad las diferencias entre países en los precios del suelo y en los costes que conlleva la urbanización.

Recomendaciones para la práctica urbanística holandesa

En primer lugar, los Ayuntamientos habrían de investigar los márgenes de beneficio reales en etapas tempranas de los procesos de urbanización, y utilizar esta información en las negociaciones con los propietarios y promotores. Esta investigación debería hacerse al mismo tiempo en que se elabora la ordenación indicativa que crea expectativas de edificabilidad.

En segundo lugar se recomienda aplicar una fórmula específica de reparcelación por medio de dos Convenios Urbanísticos anteriores para así evitar las consecuencias negativas de la dependencia entre Ayuntamientos y propietarios/promotores. Una promotora comercial, actuando como lo haría un agente urbanizador valenciano, puede acordar con los propietarios que participen en la operación a cambio de la plusvalía urbanística. El Ayuntamiento habría de apoyar al promotor-agente urbanizador condicionando la aprobación de la ordenación vinculante a que los propietarios lleguen a un acuerdo con él, si es necesario haciendo uso de la expropiación y el derecho de tanteo y retracto y aprobando un Plan de Urbanización. Esta recomendación, si se aplica, tendría las siguientes ventajas: (a) hace innecesario comprar el suelo, o al menos comprar *todo* el suelo, ya que los propietarios pasan a participar en la operación; (b) reduce el riesgo de retraso que resultaría si los propietarios, en vez de apoyar la operación, decidiesen obstaculizar la operación con el fin de obtener un precio más alto por el suelo; (c) *a* y *b* reducirían considerablemente los costes de la operación: no habría necesidad de comprar el suelo de antemano, y reducirían los costes de gastos inesperados y los gastos de gestión; (d) *c* reduciría considerablemente los costes financieros, ya que no se necesitaría tanta financiación externa.

La recomendación implica la aprobación de un Plan de Urbanización, y la amenaza expropiación para forzar a cooperar a algunos propietarios. Como ya se ha mencionado, aprobar un Plan de Urbanización tiene algunas desventajas. Junto a esto, expropiar suelo es muy caro, implica un enrolamiento directo del Ayuntamiento y es una medida impopular, no aplicable además si el propietario se muestra dispuesto a ejecutar él mismo el Planeamiento. Para eliminar estas desventajas, el gobierno central holandés debería introducir una regulación de reparcelación inspirada en el modelo valenciano.

Epílogo

A finales de los años 80 y comienzos de los 90 el gobierno holandés introdujo reformas significativas con el objeto de disminuir las ayudas públicas y de reducir los riesgos financieros que corrían habitualmente los Ayuntamientos cuando practicaban una política activa de suelo. Sin embargo, en la práctica ni se ha reducido la necesidad de ayudas públicas ni se están construyendo barrios con buenas infraestructuras y dotaciones públicas. La Ley de Urbanización del 2008 representa un esfuerzo para resolver este problema. Aunque bajo determinadas circunstancias esta ley podría ayudar, lo cierto es que adolece de dos carencias fundamentales. En primer lugar asume que el propietario del suelo es el único propietario legítimo de la plusvalía urbanística. Aquí el legislador holandés rehusó otra posibilidad, popular en otros países europeos: que la Administración Pública también puede tener derecho a compartir la plusvalía urbanística. En segundo lugar, la Ley del 2008 asume que la única forma de forzar la consecución de objetivos públicos es que la Administración Pública se implique y se comprometa directa y financieramente. Esto ha derivado en un aparato legal innecesariamente complicado (entre ellos el Plan de Urbanización) que carga a los Ayuntamientos con demasiadas tareas y riesgos. La experiencia en Inglaterra y España muestra que un liderazgo público en desarrollos urbanos, cuando la Administración Pública no posee el suelo, ha de estar basado en reglas simples y claras: la Administración Pública regula *ex ante*, los agentes de mercado ejecutan y asumen todos los riesgos correspondientes.

Una última observación: la crisis financiera y económica internacional está forzando un recorte generalizado de gasto público. Si no se toman medidas para capturar parte de la plusvalía urbanística al objeto de pagar las infraestructuras y dotaciones públicas, los recortes presupuestarios van a comprometer los desarrollos urbanos y su calidad, especialmente en reestructuración urbana.

Curriculum vitae

Demetrio (given name) Muñoz Gielen (family name) was born in Málaga, Spain, in 1970. After obtaining his Masters degree in Geography and History at the University of Málaga, he moved to Madrid to obtain a Master in Planning at the University Carlos III. In Madrid he became fascinated by the role that urban land markets play in the effectiveness of public policies in urban planning, and decided to learn more about the international differences in this important, although often forgotten aspect of urban planning. Thanks to a generous scholarship from the Dutch government, he moved in 1997 to the Netherlands to do research on public-private partnerships at the University of Amsterdam and since then he has been living in this city. From 1998 till 2004 he worked first at the consultancy DHV and second at the Municipality of Amsterdam, and began publishing articles about land policy instruments in Spain and in the Netherlands. In 2004 he started his PhD research at the OTB Research Institute for the Built Environment (Delft University of Technology), which he has finished at the Nijmegen School of Management (Radboud University Nijmegen). Since 2008 he has been active on several fronts. As freelance consultant he is specialized in land policies of public bodies and in private partnerships in urban development. In addition, he is university lecturer (till 2010 at the Amsterdam School of Real Estate, University of Amsterdam; from 2010 onwards at the Radboud University Nijmegen) and public official at the Municipality of Purmerend. In Purmerend he is developing policy instruments to improve the capturing of value increase to finance necessary public infrastructure and facilities. In addition he is directly involved in the application and refinement of this policy in the practice of urban development. He regularly participates in expert-panels of universities and public bodies, both in the Netherlands and in Spain. He publishes regularly in professional reviews and newspapers in the Netherlands, Belgium and Spain, and in international peer-reviewed scientific reviews.

Announcement of the Municipality of Purmerend (the Netherlands), sponsor of this book:

De gemeente Purmerend streeft in haar ruimtelijk beleid naar een samenhangende en kwalitatief hoogstaande ruimtelijke ontwikkeling van de stad, waarbij de herstructurering van locaties binnen de bebouwde kom een prominente rol moet gaan nemen. De stad heeft een aantal jaren geleden besloten om niet meer uit te breiden, maar te focussen op een verbetering en uitbreiding van het voorzieningenpakket binnen de bebouwde kom.

Deze ambitie plaatst Purmerend voor een belangrijke uitdaging. De gemeente heeft niet veel grondposities in binnenstedelijke locaties, waardoor een actief grondbeleid minder voor de hand ligt. Tevens ligt de komende jaren de gemeentelijke financiële situatie onder druk. Kortom, de gemeente koestert hoge ambities voor de kwalitatieve en programmatische invulling van ruimtelijke projecten, maar beschikt noch over de grond, noch over de financiële middelen om deze wensen in haar eentje uit te voeren. De uitdaging is om grondeigenaren en marktpartijen meer verantwoordelijkheid te geven in de realisering van ruimtelijke projecten en de financiering van openbare infrastructuur en faciliteiten. Dit vergt een andere rol van de gemeente: van allesbepalend tot kaderstellend. De in 2008 geïntroduceerde Grondexploitatiewet vormt een belangrijke basis voor de gemeentelijke strategie.

De toevoeging in 2009 van Demetrio Muñoz Gielen aan de gemeentelijke organisatie, levert een beslissende bijdrage aan het aangaan van deze uitdaging. Conclusies en beleidsaanbevelingen die in zijn proefschrift zijn opgenomen, zijn binnen de gemeentelijke organisatie belangrijke bouwstenen geworden in de gedachtevorming en totstandkoming van het gemeentelijke beleid en strategie. Wij wensen Demetrio veel succes in zijn verdere wetenschappelijke carrière en hopen hem lang als collega te behouden.

PURMEREND